Studies in
Louisiana Culture

ROBERT R.
MACDONALD
SERIES EDITOR

VOLUME III

THE SUN KING
LOUIS XIV AND THE NEW WORLD

An Exhibition Organized By
The Louisiana State Museum
Robert R. Macdonald, Director

Vaughn L. Glasgow
American Commmissioner for the Exhibition
Associate Director for Special Projects
Louisiana State Museum

Pierre Lemoine
French Commissioner for the Exhibition
Inspecteur Général des Musées
Conservateur en Chef
Musée National du Château de Versailles

Steven G. Reinhardt
Editor and Translator
Curator of French Manuscripts
Louisiana State Museum

The Louisiana Museum Foundation
New Orleans, Louisiana

THE SUN KING: LOUIS XIV AND THE NEW WORLD

EXHIBITION DATES

LOUISIANA
STATE MUSEUM
April 29-November 18, 1984

THE CORCORAN
GALLERY OF ART
December 15, 1984-April 7, 1985

Designer: Bob Coleman
Typeface: Goudy Old Style
Typography: Richard T. Devlin
Catalogue Layout: Emily Neiswender
Printer: E. S. Upton Printing Co., New Orleans, Louisiana
Binder: Nicholstone Book Bindery, Inc., Nashville, Tennessee

Library of Congress Cataloging in Publication Data

Main entry under title:

The Sun King.
    (Studies in Louisiana Culture; v. 3)
    Exhibition dates: Louisiana State Museum, New Orleans, La., April 29-Nov. 18, 1984; the
Corcoran Gallery of Art, Washington, D.C., Dec. 15, 1984-April 7, 1985
    Includes index.
    1. Louis XIV, King of France, 1638-1715 — Exhibitions. 2. France — History — Louis XIV,
1643-1715 — Exhibitions. 3. Louisiana — History — To 1803 — Exhibitions. 4. French —
Louisiana — History — Exhibitions. I. Reinhardt, Steven G., 1949-   . II. Louisiana State
Museum. III. Corcoran Gallery of Art. IV. Series.

DC126.S86   1984   944'.033   84-3907
                        ISBN 0-916137-00-7 (cloth)
                        ISBN 0-916137-01-5 (paper)

The Sun King: Louis XIV and the New World
has been organized by the Louisiana State Museum with the support of the Réunion des Musées Nationaux and
l'Association Française d'Action Artistique.
The exhibition is sponsored by Shell Oil Company and its subsidiaries through the
Shell Companies Foundation, Incorporated.

Additional funding has been provided by the following:
The Aetna Life and Casualty Foundation
New Orleans, Louisiana

The Louisiana Commmittee for the Humanities
the state-based affiliate of the National Endowment for the Humanities

The National Endowment for the Humanities
Washington, D.C., a Federal Agency

The Physicians New Orleans Foundation Fund
New Orleans, Louisiana

The Whitney National Bank
New Orleans, Louisiana

The Wisner Fund for the City of New Orleans
New Orleans, Louisiana

The publication of this catalogue has been made possible
by grants from the following sources:

The National Endowment for the Humanities
Washington, D.C., a Federal Agency

The Louisiana Committee for the Humanities
the state-based affiliate of the National Endowment for the Humanities
New Orleans, Louisiana

TABLE OF CONTENTS

Preface ———————————————————————————— 13
    Pierre Quoniam and Hubert Landais

Foreword ——————————————————————————— 14
    Robert R. Macdonald

Acknowledgements———————————————————————— 16

PART I: THE ESSAYS ——————————————————————— 20

Louis XIV in History, An Introduction to the Essays ——————————— 22
    Steven G. Reinhardt

LOUIS XIV: THE MAN AND THE KING ———————————————— 26

    Louis XIV, The Man Who Was King ————————————————— 28
        John B. Wolf

    Court, Capital, and Councils in the Reign of Louis XIV ———————— 38
        John C. Rule

    Louis XIV and Religious Absolutism ———————————————— 50
        Julius R. Ruff

    Louis XIV and Europe: War and Diplomacy in the Seventeenth Century ——— 58
        John T. O'Connor

LOUIS XIV AND THE COLONIES ————————————————— 70

    The Colonial Policy of the Sun King ———————————————— 72
        Philippe Jacquin

    From New France to Louisiana: Politics and Geography ———————— 84
        Monique Pelletier

    La Délaissée: Louisiana During the Reign of Louis XIV, 1699-1715 ——— 96
        Carl A. Brasseaux

LOUIS XIV: PATRON OF THE ARTS AND SCIENCES ———————— 104

    Louis XIV and the Mirror of Antiquity ——————————————— 106
        Robert Wyman Hartle

    From Politics to Collecting: Louis XIV and Painting ———————— 118
        Antoine Schnapper

    Monumental Art, or The Politics of Enchantment ——————————— 126
        Daniel Rabreau

    The Politics of Royal Opera in the Reign of Louis XIV ———————— 136
        Robert M. Isherwood

    Belles-Lettres Under the Sun King: An Age of Classicism ——————— 146
        Marcel Gutwirth

    Louis XIV: Patron of Science and Technology ——————————— 154
        E. Stewart Saunders

    Notes on Contributors ————————————————————— 168

PART II: THE EXHIBITION ————————————————————— 170

The Sun King: Louis XIV and the New World, An Introduction to the Exhibition ——— 172
    Vaughn L. Glasgow and Pierre Lemoine

Lenders to the Exhibition ——————————————————— 178

A Note on Gallery Changes and Object Conservation ——————————— 179

TABLE OF CONTENTS

THE ROYAL ICONOGRAPHY ____ 181

1. Apollo Mask ____ 181
2. Monogram of Interlaced L's ____ 182
3. Portière de Mars (The Royal Arms) ____ 182
4. Equestrian Statue of Louis XIV ____ 182
5. Apollo Tapestry ____ 183
6. Apollo Crowned by Minerva ____ 184

YOUTH, 1638-59 ____ 184

7. Louis XIV and His First Nurse, Lady ____ 184
   Marie Longuet de la Giraudière
8. Adoration of the Shepherds ____ 185
9. Louis XIV Enfant ____ 185
10. Anne d'Autriche and Louis XIV (and) ____ 186
    Church of the Val-de-Grâce
11. Louis XIII Between "France" and "Navarre" ____ 186
12. Anne d'Autriche, Queen of France and Navarre 186
13. The Château of St. Germain-en-Laye ____ 187
    with Louis XIV and Turenne in the Foreground
14. Armand Jean du Plessis, Duke ____ 187
    and Cardinal of Richelieu
15. Maxims of State or Political Testament ____ 188
    of the Emminent Armand, Cardinal Duke of Riche-
    lieu
16. Louis XIII, Louis XIV Enfant, ____ 189
    Anne d'Autriche, and Monsieur
17. Louis XIV Enfant ____ 189
18. Augustus Before the Tomb of Alexander ____ 189
19. Cardinal Mazarin ____ 190
20. Louis XIV, Vanquisher of the Fronde (painting) 191
21. Louis XIV, Adolescent, Trampling the ____ 191
    Fronde (bronze)

PEACE OF THE PYRENEES/MARRIAGE OF THE KING, 1659-60 ____ 192

22. Round Platters (Nevers) ____ 192
23. The Swearing of the Peace by the Two Kings ____ 192
    of France and Spain and The Entry of the King and
    Queen into Their Good City of Paris, August 26,
    1660
24. Bust of Louis XIV ____ 193
25. Nuptial Chant for the Marriage of the King ____ 193
    and Treaty of Peace Between the Crowns of France
    and Spain with the Marriage Contract of the King
26. Marie-Thérèse d'Autriche, Queen of ____ 194
    France and of Navarre
27. Office for Holy Week ____ 194

THE KING AT WORK ____ 194

28. Louis XIV, King of France and Navarre ____ 195
29. The Château of Fontainebleau ____ 196
30. Toussaint Rose, Secretary to the King ____ 197
31. Letter on the Affairs of Europe, Annotated ____ 197
    by Louis XIV
32. Fragment of a Letter Annotated by Louis XIV ____ 198
33. Manner of Showing the Gardens of Versailles ____ 198
34. Topographic Journal of the King in Flanders ____ 199
    During the Year 1680
35. Project for a Painted Fan Annotated by Louis XIV 199
36. Order of Louis XIV to Gédéon de Metz ____ 200
    to Pay 162,000 Livres to Bearer
37. Order of Louis XIV to Gédéon de Metz ____ 200
    to Pay 12,000 Livres to Boileau and to Racine
38. Jean-Baptiste Colbert ____ 201
39. Mémoire Addressed to Louis XIV ____ 202
40. Letter to the Marquis de Nointel ____ 202

THE KING AT WORK: WAR AND DIPLOMACY ____ 203

41. Chancellor Séguier ____ 203
42. The Great Book for Precious Stones ____ 204
43. Coded Dispatch from Constantinople ____ 205
44. Coded Dispatch from Adrianople ____ 205
45. Letter to Louis XIV ____ 206
46. Letter to Louis XIV ____ 206
47. The Royal and Magnificent Audience ____ 207
    Given to the Very Illustrious Ambassadors of the
    Magnificent King of Siam
48. Infantry Helmet ____ 208
49. Matchlock Musket ____ 208
50. Design of Fireworks Given by the Duc de Chaulnes 209
51. Crossing the Rhine ____ 209
52. Fortifications (by Vauban) ____ 210
53. The Peace of Nymegen (Treaty with Holland) ____ 210
54. The Peace of Nymegen (Treaty with Spain) ____ 210

THE KING AT WORK: ORDERS AND HONORS ____ 211

55. The Royal Recompenses of Louis the Great ____ 211
56. Cross of the Order of the Holy Spirit ____ 212
57. Badge of the Order of the Holy Spirit ____ 212
58. Cross of a Knight of the Order of Saint Louis ____ 212
59. Great Cross of the Order of Saint Louis ____ 212
60. Badge of the Great Cross of the Order ____ 212
    of Saint Louis
61. Cross of the Order of Saint Lazarus and ____ 212
    Our Lady of Mount Carmel
62. Cross of the Order of Saint Michael ____ 212

THE SUN KING: LOUIS XIV AND THE NEW WORLD

RELIGION: THE KING AND THE CHURCH _____ 214

63. The Pompous and Magnificent Entrance _____ 215
of Flavio, Cardinal Chigi, Lateran Legate in France
64. Unigenitus _____ 215
65. Jacqueline-Marie, Mère Angélique Arnauld ____ 216
66. Religion Trampling Heresy _____ 217

67. Letter to the Provost of Merchants and _____ 217
the Sheriffs of Paris
68. Edict of the King Establishing the General Hospital 218
69. The Colbert de Villacerf *Chapelle* _____ 218

THE KING AND PARIS: ACADEMIES AND EDUCATION _____ 219

70. The Establishment of the Academy of _____ 219
Sciences and the Observatory
71. View of the Observatory and Its Surroundings __ 220
72. The Terrestrial Globe Represented in Two _____ 220
Hemisphere Plans
73. Model of Coronelli's Celestial Globe _____ 221
74. Instrument for Calibrating Sundials _____ 222
75. Bracket Clock (of the "Religious" Type) _____ 222
76. Watch _____ 223
77. Watch _____ 224
78. René Descartes _____ 225
79. Blaise Pascal _____ 225
80. The College of the Four Nations _____ 226
81. Formalities to Be Observed on the Part of ____ 227
Pensioners for Admission to the Collège Mazarin

82. State of the Young Orientals Supported _____ 227
at the Collège Louis le Grand by the Liberality of the
King
83. Declaration of the King to Have the _____ 228
Experiments in the Royal Botanical Gardens Continued
84. Pharmaceutical Urn _____ 229
85. Jephté _____ 229
86. Draft of "Statutes and Rules That the King ____ 230
Wishes and Orders to be Observed in the Academy
. . . That His Majesty Has Resolved to Establish in
the City of Rome"
87. Establishment of the Royal Academy of _____ 230
Painting and Sculpture
88. Self-Portrait _____ 231

THE KING AND PARIS: THE URBAN ENVIRONMENT _____ 232

89. Plan (of Paris) Taken by Order of the King ____ 232
90. Map of Paris Taken at the Order of the King __ 232
91. The Pont-Neuf, the Louvre, and the _____ 233
College of the Four Nations
92. The Bread and Poultry Market on the _____ 234
Quai of the Grands Augustins (Painted Fan)
93. Left Foot of Louis XIV (Fragment of _____ 234
an Equestrian Statue)
94. Elevation of the Principal Façade of the _____ 235
Louvre on the Side of Saint-Germain l'Auxerrois,
Built Under the Reign of Louis XIV and the Ministry
of Jean-Baptiste Colbert, on the Designs of Claude
Perrault of the Royal Academy of Sciences
95. Elevation of the Entrance of the Tuileries _____ 236
Side, Design by Cavalier Bernini

96. Representation of the Machines That _____ 237
Served to Lift the Two Large Stones That Cover the
Pediment of the Principal Entrance of the Louvre
(Etching)
97. Representation of the Machines That _____ 237
Served to Lift the Two Large Stones That Cover the
Pediment of the Principal Entrance of the Louvre
(Engraved Copper Plate)
98. Bust of Louis XIV _____ 237
99. The King Accompanied by His Court Visits ____ 238
the Hôtel of the Invalides and Its New Church
100. View of the Church of the Royal Hôtel _____ 239
of the Invalides at the Time of the Visit of Louis XIV

THE KING AS BUILDER: VAUX-LE-VICOMTE _____ 240

101. Nicolas Fouquet _____ 240
102. View of the Château of Vaux-le-Vicomte, ____ 241
Seen from the Garden Side

103. Charles Le Brun _____ 241
104. Louis Le Vau _____ 242
105. André Le Nôtre _____ 243

THE KING AS BUILDER: VERSAILLES _____ 244

106. View of the Château of Versailles from the ____ 244
Avenue de Paris
107. View of the Orangerie of Versailles _____ 245
108. View of the Château of Versailles and _____ 245
Its Two Wings Seen from the Garden Side
109. View of the Château of Versailles Seen _____ 246
from the Large Square
110. The Magnificent Buildings of Versailles _____ 246
111. General Plan of the Château and Gardens ____ 247
of Versailles

112. Section Through the Vestibule of the Chapel __ 248
and the Salon d'Hercule (of the Château of
Versailles)
113. Elevation of the Government Wing _____ 248
and Section Through the Royal Apartments and the
Hall of Mirrors (of the Château of Versailles)
114. Project for the King's Bedroom: The _____ 249
Royal Alcove (at the Château of Versailles)

TABLE OF CONTENTS

115. Plan of the King's Apartment of the Château ___ 250
     of Versailles
116. The Hall of Mirrors (of the Château of Versailles) 250
117. The Hall of Mirrors (of the Château of Versailles) 251
118. Drawing for Louis XIV's Mirrored Cabinet, ___ 252
     Château of Versailles
119. Project for the Paving of the Chapel ___ 252
     (of the Château of Versailles)
120. Panel from the Royal Apartments of the ___ 253
     Château of Versailles

121. Panel from the Royal Apartments of the ___ 253
     Château of Versailles
122. Hercules (The Emperor Commodus as Hercules) 254
123. The Basin of Latona ___ 255
124. The Fountain of Fame ___ 255
125. Trophée in the Form of a Helmet ___ 256
126. Trophée in the Form of An Allegory of America 256

THE KING AND THE COURT: FAMILY AND FRIENDS ___ 257

127. Louise de La Baume Le Blanc, ___ 257
     Duchesse de La Vallière
128. Françoise Athénaïs de Mortemart, ___ 258
     Marquise de Montespan
129. Mademoiselle de Blois and Mademoiselle ___ 258
     de Nantes
130. Françoise d'Aubigné, Marquise de Maintenon ___ 259
131. Louis, Dauphin de France ___ 259
132. Proclamation of the Public Crier ___ 260
     Announcing the Deaths of the Dauphin and of the
     Dauphine

133. Edict According the Crown of France to ___ 261
     the Royal Bastards
134. Philippe de France, Duc d'Orléans ___ 261
135. Elizabeth-Charlotte de Bavière, ___ 262
     Princesse Palatine, Duchesse d'Orléans
136. Anne-Marie-Louse d'Orléans, ___ 262
     Duchesse de Montpensier
137. Anne-Louise Bénédicte de Bourbon-Condé, ___ 263
     Duchesse du Maine
138. Marie-Adélaïde de Savoie, Duchesse de ___ 263
     Bourgogne

THE KING AND THE COURT: PASTIMES ___ 264

139. The Triumph of Bacchus ___ 264
140. A Playing Card Factory (Painted Fan) ___ 265
141. Playing Cards ___ 265
142. Order of Payment of Louis XIV to Cover the ___ 266
     Gambling Debts of the Queen Marie-Thérèse d'Aut-
     riche
143. Note from the Queen Requesting 200 ___ 266
     Golden Louis to Pay a Gambling Debt
144. Blunderbuss ___ 267

145. Powder Flask ___ 267
146. "Tane" Pointing Partridge ___ 268
147. Still Life of Partridge and Pheasant ___ 269
148. Pheasants ___ 269
149. Courses de Testes et de Bague Faittes par le Roy 270
     et par les Princes et Seigneurs de Sa Cour en l'Année
     1662
150-151. Parade Helmet and Shield ___ 271
152. Fireworks on the Grand Canal at Versailles ___ 271

THE KING AND THE COURT: PERFORMING ARTS ___ 272

153. Poetry and Music with the Bust of Louis XIV ___ 272
154. Charles Couperin and the Daughter of the Painter 273
155. Charles Mouton, Lute Player ___ 273
156. Costume for "War" ___ 274
157. Costume for a "Fury" ___ 274
158. Jean Racine ___ 275
159. Jean-Baptiste Poquelin, Called Molière ___ 276

160. The Royal Troupe of Italian Comedians ___ 277
161. Scene of Glory or Transfiguration ___ 277
162. Festival on Water ___ 278
163. Theater Scene ___ 279
164. Theater Scene ___ 278
165. Theater Perspective ___ 280
166. Theater Perspective ___ 280

THE DECORATIVE ARTS ___ 281

167. Visit of Louis XIV to the Gobelins ___ 281
     (October 15, 1667)
168. Armchair ___ 283
169. Stool ___ 283
170. Platter ___ 284
171. Plate ___ 284
172. Ewer ___ 285
173. Sugar Caster (faïence) ___ 285
174. Sugar Caster (silver) ___ 286
175. Ewer in the Form of a Helmet ___ 286
176. Ewer (silver) ___ 287
177. Ewer (glass) ___ 288
178. Shop Sign for a Potter ___ 289

179. Bottle (Gourd) with Four Twisted Loops ___ 289
180. Pilgrim Bottle ___ 290
181. Gadrooned Cup and Saucer ___ 291
182. Pharmaceutical Vase ___ 292
183. Pair of Candlesticks ___ 293
184. Dish ___ 293
185. Grill ___ 294
186. Grill from an Imposte ___ 294
187. Kitchen Grill ___ 295
188. Lock and Key for a Porte-Cochère ___ 296
189. Coffer Lock and Key ___ 297
190. Gate Knocker ___ 297

THE SUN KING: LOUIS XIV AND THE NEW WORLD

THE ROYAL COLLECTIONS: THE CABINET DU ROI _____ 298

191. The Apotheosis of Germanicus _____ 298
192. Footed Bowl with Shaped Rim _____ 299
193. Henri IV and Marie de' Medici _____ 299
194. Septimius Severus and His Family _____ 300
195. The Dispute of Athena and Poseidon _____ 300
    for the Foundation of Athens
196. The Holy Virgin (and) Jesus Christ _____ 301
197. Louis XIII _____ 301
198. Standing Cup _____ 302

199. Vase _____ 303
200. Jupiter and Juno _____ 304
201. Jupiter _____ 304
202. Milo of Crotona _____ 304
203. Jesus Carrying His Cross _____ 305
204. Saint John Baptizing _____ 306
205. The Young Pyrrhus Saved _____ 307
206. Orpheus Before Pluto and Proserpina _____ 307

THE KING IN RETREAT _____ 308

207. The Château de Marly _____ 308
208. Louis XIV Crowned by Glory Between Abundance and
    Peace _____ 309
209. Louis XIV, King of France and of Navarre _____ 310

210. Proclamation of the Public Crier Announcing the Burial
    Service of King Louis XIV _____ 311
211. Letter to Louis XV _____ 311
212. Last Words of King Louis XIV (Spoken) to King Louis
    XV, His Great-Grandson _____ 312

THE KING AND THE COLONIES: LOUISIANA — DISCOVERY _____ 313

213. Bust of Louis XIV _____ 313
214. Map of the New Discoveries That the _____ 313
    Reverend Jesuit Fathers Made in 1672 and (That
    Were) Continued by Reverend Father Jacques Mar-
    quette of the Same Company, Accompanied by
    Some French in the Year 1673
215A. Description of Louisiana Newly Discovered _____ 314
    to the Southwest of New France
215B. New Discovery of a Very Large Land _____ 314
    Situated in America
216. Permission to the Sieur de La Salle to _____ 315
    Discover the Western Part of New France
217. Act of Possession of Louisiana at the _____ 316
    Mouth (of the Mississippi River at) the Gulf of
    Mexico

218. Map of North America and Part of South _____ 317
    America from the Mouth of the St. Lawrence River
    to the Isle of Cayenne with the New Discoveries of
    the Mississippi
219. Map of Louisiana in North America from _____ 317
    New France to the Gulf of Mexico, Upon Which
    Are Described the Lands Which the Sieur de La
    Salle Discovered in a Large Continent Comprised
    from 50° Elevation from the Pole to 25° in the Years
    1679-80-81-82
220. America Settentrionale (North America) _____ 318
221. "France" Personified as "Minerva" _____ 319

THE KING AND THE COLONIES: LOUISIANA - THE WAR OF THE LEAGUE OF _____ 319
AUGSBURG - THE PEACE OF RYSWICK (1697)

222. The Peace of Ryswick (Treaty with England) _____ 319
223. The Peace of Ryswick (Treaty with the Empire) _____ 320

THE KING AND THE COLONIES: LOUISIANA — EXPLORATION _____ 321

224. Pierre Le Moyne, Sieur d'Iberville _____ 321
225. Ship's Journal on Board the Badine _____ 321
226. Ship's Journal on Board the Renommée _____ 322
227. Cross of the Order of Saint Louis _____ 322
228. Jean-Baptiste Le Moyne, Sieur de Bienville _____ 322
229. Chalice and Paten _____ 323
230. Traveling Crucifix _____ 324
231. Lidded Box from a Toiletry Set _____ 324

232. Town and Fort of Mobile in 1702 _____ 325
233. Plan of the Town and Fort of Mobile, _____ 325
    Established by the French
234. Louis Phélypeaux, Comte de Pontchartrain _____ 326
235. Map of the Mississippi River (Based) on the _____ 327
    Mémoires of Monsieur Le Sueur
236. Environs of the Mississippi (River) _____ 328

THE KING AND THE COLONIES: THE WAR OF THE SPANISH SUCCESSION — _____ 328
THE PEACE OF UTRECHT (1713)

237. Philippe de France, Duc d'Anjou _____ 329
238. Maps and General and Specific Descriptions _____ 330
    Regarding Knowledge of Events of the Times on the
    Subject of the Succession of the Crown of Spain in
    Europe, in Asia, Africa and America, Addressed and
    Dedicated to His Catholic Majesty Philip V
239. The Peace of Utrecht (Treaty with England) _____ 330

240. The Peace of Utrecht (Treaty with Prussia) _____ 331
241. Layette or Treaty Box for England _____ 331
242. Antoine Crozat, Marquis de Chatel _____ 332
243. Letters Patent for the Commerce of Louisiana _____ 333
    in Favor of Sieur Crozat
244. Letter to Nicolas Desmarets _____ 333

Catalogue Contributors _____ 334
Illustration Credits _____ 335
Index of Authors, Artists and Makers _____ 340

PREFACE

HUBERT LANDAIS, DIRECTOR OF THE MUSEUMS OF FRANCE
PIERRE QUONIAM, INSPECTOR GENERAL OF THE MUSEUMS OF FRANCE

ere are reunited, and for the first time in the land which bears his name, the artifacts — art objects and historical documents — destined to evoke the Sun King, his Age, and the ties which united France with the New World during his reign. Since we have been granted the privilege, we would like to emphasize here, with the simplicity that old ties of friendship permit, the good will with which this exhibition was greeted in our country when its originators came to propose it, as well as the profound satisfaction we experienced in doing our best to support their undertaking.

Above all else, how could anyone remain insensitive to the fidelity to which it testifies? Who could believe that in New Orleans, on the occasion of a great international exposition in which the weight and dynamism of the present direct all eyes towards the future, one would not only recall the epoque of Cavelier de la Salle, Le Moyne d'Iberville, and Bienville, but also brilliantly depict the ruler who set them in motion — his motives, resources and lifestyle? Who in France could remain indifferent to such a project?

The project proved all the more attractive from a conceptual point of view because, as the present catalogue so aptly demonstrates, every effort was made to depict accurately and vividly Louis XIV's personality, iconography, private life, apprenticeship, and theory and practice of power. The catalogue also examines the king's European policies and colonial designs, the economic and religious problems of his time, the prestigious setting he created for royal power at Versailles, and the instrumental role he played in the development of the sciences, literature and art. Moreover, it explains with lucidity and objectivity how Absolutism and Classicism came to act as godparents at the baptism of Louisiana. Our thanks therefore go to the academics and curators, American and French, who added the brushstrokes to this vast canvas, lending their erudition and discernment to such a thorough analysis.

Finally, how could the planning and execution of the exhibition have failed to gain the support of the directors of our archives, libraries, and museums when such excellent care and effective support were promised? To all of the administrators, curators, technicians, and volunteers who showed so much devotion, our warmest thanks and congratulations, with our special gratitude and compliments reserved for Robert R. Macdonald, Director, and Vaughn L. Glasgow, Associate Director, both of the Louisiana State Museum — the highly valued partner of our Réunion des Musées Nationaux.

The accomplishment of such a project required, to be sure, considerable competence, perseverence and faith, all of which clearly exist on the banks of the Mississippi in sufficient quantity to rekindle the brilliance of the Sun King of Versailles. ∎

Detail of Catalogue 100

FOREWORD
ROBERT R. MACDONALD, DIRECTOR
LOUISIANA STATE MUSEUM

istory is marked by individuals whose accomplishments and personalities radiate beyond their time and place. Louis XIV of France, the Sun King, is one of those historic figures who stand at center stage in the drama of our common heritage. The Louisiana State Museum has gathered more than two hundred pieces from public and private collections in France and the United States to form an exhibition that provides a special opportunity to experience Louis XIV and his legacy. *The Sun King: Louis XIV and the New World* presents paintings, sculptures, prints, tapestries, decorative arts, maps, and manuscripts, many of which are appearing in the United States and together for the first time. Each item in the exhibition has singular historical and visual significance. As an aesthetic and intellectual composition, the exhibition is a multifaceted jewel reflecting both the glorious reign and human dimension of Louis XIV.

The Sun King: Louis XIV and the New World also represents a special moment in the seventy-eight-year history of the Louisiana State Museum. Established in 1906 to collect, preserve, and present the history of the land named for Louis XIV, the Louisiana State Museum is proud to have organized this exhibition and catalogue as learning resources for Louisianians and all Americans in search of an understanding and appreciation of the past. It is appropriate that this humanistic exhibition, the largest ever presented on Louis XIV, is premiering at the Cabildo in New Orleans. It was in this National Historic Landmark, one of the ten properties of the Louisiana State Museum, that the vast Louisiana Territory was transferred from France to the United States in 1803. The appearance of the exhibition at the Corcoran

Gallery of Art in Washington, D.C., following the New Orleans showing, provides an important occasion in the expanding cooperation between historical and art museums. The beauty and substance of this catalogue are witness to the commitment of the Louisiana State Museum and its colleagues to the pursuit of excellence.

The Louisiana State Museum has been fortunate in having the enthusiastic support of its French and American colleagues in the development of this exhibition. The inspired professionalism of Vaughn L. Glasgow, the museum's Associate Director for Special Projects and American Commissioner of the exhibition, and the generous participation of Pierre Lemoine, Inspector General of the Museums of France, Director of the National Museum of the Château of Versailles, and the exhibition's French Commissioner, have been the intellectual springs that have nourished this presentation from concept to reality. The encouragement and assistance of Hubert Landais, Director of the Museums of France, and Pierre Quoniam, Inspector General, have been invaluable. The Louisiana State Museum gratefully acknowledges the participation of Michael Botwinick, Director of the Corcoran Gallery of Art, and Edward J. Nygren, the gallery's Curator of Collections. The interest of S. Dillon Ripley, Secretary of the Smithsonian Institution, and Paul N. Perrott, Assistant Secretary for Museum Programs, has been invaluable. Colleagues such as André Chabaud, Director of the Musée du Louvre; Bernard de Montgolfier, Director of the Musée Carnavalet; Alain Gourdon, Administrator General of the Bibliothèque Nationale; Jean Favier, Director General of the Archives de France; Martial de la Fournière, immediate past director of the Archives of the Ministère des Relations

Extérieures, and others too numerous to mention in this space, have been munificent in sharing their ideas and collections.

A project as complex as *The Sun King: Louis XIV and the New World,* requires the commitment of governmental officials and private citizens to expend their time and energies to assure that the effort succeeds. Of particular note has been the support of David C. Treen, former Governor of Louisiana, and his Secretary of the Department of Culture, Recreation and Tourism, Mrs. Lawrence H. Fox, and her staff. The museum also recognizes the continuing support of Edwin W. Edwards, Governor of Louisiana, and his administration. The Honorable Mrs. Hale (Lindy) Boggs, representing Louisiana's Second Congressional District, has given freely of her wisdom and good will. Mrs. Robert H. Bolton, chairman of the Louisiana State Museum Board, and the members of the board have enthusiastically supported every aspect of the exhibition. The presidents of the museum's associate support organizations, Dr. Jack Holden of the Louisiana Museum Foundation, Stephen Moses of the Friends of the Cabildo, Mrs. Joan Samuel of the Old State Capitol Associates, and Mrs. Virginia Shehee of the Friends of the Louisiana State Exhibit Museum have generated the community involvement that is a measure of the exhibition's success.

The Sun King Steering Committee chaired by Mrs. Isidore Cohn, her subcommittees, and the hundreds of volunteers who worked tirelessly on all aspects of the exhibition are due a special debt of gratitude. In France, the exhibition has had remarkable assistance in development and logistics from various administrative offices of the Ministries of Culture and of External Relations. The Association Française d'Action Artistique has lent its technical expertise in organization and has coordinated international shipment and customs. The exhibition would not have been possible without the interest and support of Louis Vorms, Consul General for France in New Orleans, and the consulate's cultural attaché, Jack Batho.

Finally, a museum is measured by its collections and its staff. The Louisiana State Museum is fortunate in having a staff marked by excellence and dedication. I particularly want to note the work of Mrs. Frieda Morford, the museum's Deputy Director; Timothy Chester, Chief Curator; Mrs. Betty McDermott, the Sun King Program Coordinator; and the historical scholarship of the catalogue's editor, Dr. Steven G. Reinhardt, Curator of French Manuscripts.

Concepts require financial support to become reality. The Louisiana State Museum expresses its appreciation to the Louisiana State Legislature for its continuing support. The significant funding provided by Shell Oil Company and its subsidiaries through Shell Companies Foundation, Incorporated, the exhibition's National Corporate Sponsor, exemplifies the developing partnership between public and private sectors, cultural programming and America's corporations. *The Sun King: Louis XIV and the New World* as an exhibition and learning resource has been made possible in part through grants from the National Endowment for the Humanities, the Whitney National Bank of New Orleans, Aetna Life and Casualty Foundation, the Physicians New Orleans Foundation Fund, the Wisner Fund for the City of New Orleans, the Louisiana Committee for the Humanities, the Louisiana Museum Foundation, and the Department of Culture, Recreation and Tourism.

The most important reward for the many individuals and organizations that have made *The Sun King: Louis XIV and the New World* possible will be the appreciation of the students, scholars, and visitors who will tour the exhibition and study this catalogue. ∎

ACKNOWLEDGEMENTS

 he organizers of the exhibition would like to express their gratitude to the many individuals and institutions who have made *The Sun King: Louis XIV and the New World* a reality. To the following officials in Paris, the deepest thanks are offered: Monsieur François Mitterand, President of the Republic of France; and Monsieur Bernard Vernier-Palliez, Ambassador of the Republic of France to the United States.

The project has been favored by the unreserved cooperation, valuable assistance, and support of many offices of the French government:

The Ministry of External Relations, Monsieur Claude Cheysson, Minister; Monsieur Louis Vorms, former Consul General of France in New Orleans; and Monsieur Philippe Grégoire, Consul General of France in New Orleans. The Association Française d'Action Artistique, Monsieur André Gadaud, Director (retired); Madame Catherine Clément, Director; Monsieur Yves Mabin; and Madame Dominique Blondy.

The Ministry of Culture, Monsieur Jack Lang, Minister. The French National Museum Administration, Monsieur Hubert Landais, Director of the Museums of France; Monsieur Jacques Vistel, former associate director; and Monsieur Pierre Quoniam, Inspector General. The Administration of National Patrimony, Monsieur Christian Prévost-Marchilhacy, Principal Inspector of National Monuments; the Administration of Movable Patrimony, Monsieur Jack Meurisse and Madame Isabelle Vearn.

In the United States, the French Ministry of External Relations has been of great help. Our thanks to the North American offices of the French Cultural Services, particularly to Monsieur Jean-Marie Guéhenno and Monsieur Xavier North in New York. Very special thanks are due to Monsieur Jack Batho, former cultural attaché in New Orleans, whose tireless efforts facilitated the project, and to Monsieur Jean Charpantier, present cultural attaché.

In Paris, the U.S. Department of State has been of constant support. Heartfelt appreciation is extended to the Honorable Evan Galbraith, United States Ambassador to France; to Frazar Draper, director of the Cultural Office of the United States Embassy in Paris; and to Madame Hélène Baltrusaitis, Fine Arts Counselor, who gave so generously of her expertise and practical knowledge.

A very special *remerciement* is due to Monsieur Alain Parent, Director of the Musée du Nouveau Monde in La Rochelle, France, for his efforts to bring people together in meaningful ways and his useful suggestions and guidance.

The officials of the State of Louisiana have supported and helped the project since its inception. In particular, recognition is due to the Honorable David Treen, Governor; the Honorable Mrs. Hale (Lindy) Boggs, Congresswoman; the Honorable Russell Long, U.S. Senator; and the Honorable J. Bennett Johnston, U.S. Senator.

Institutional lenders to the exhibition have generously loaned from the collections in their care and have shared their technical expertise, research files, and interpretive materials. Thanks are expressed to the following public collections in France and their administrative and curatorial representatives:

The National Archives, Monsieur Jean Favier, General Director of the Archives of France; Mademoiselle Antoinette Menier, Chief Curator of

ACKNOWLEDGEMENTS

the Overseas Section; Madame Felkay, Curator of Maps and Drawings; Monsieur Jean Babelon, Chief Curator of Ancient Holdings; Monsieur Mahieu, Chief Curator; and Curators Villet and Guérout.

The Historic Library of the City of Paris, Madame Hélène Verlet, Director.

The Municipal Library of the Town of Versailles, Mademoiselle Alice Garrigoux, Director; and Monsieur J.-M. Roidot, Curator.

The National Library, Monsieur Alain Gourdan, General Administrator; Madame Thérèse Varlamoff, Department of Internal Exhibitions; Madame Marie-Odile Germain, External Exhibition Service; Mademoiselle Monique Pelletier, Director, Department of Maps and Plans, and Curator Jean Boutier; Monsieur Michel Melot, Director, Department of Prints; and Madame Jacqueline Sampson, Curator; Monsieur Michel Pastoureau, Curator in the Department of Medals and Antiquities; Mademoiselle Boussuat, Director of the Department of Printed Works; and Madame Veyrin-Forrer, Curator of the Rare Books Section.

The National Manufactory of Sèvres, Monsieur Jean Mathieu, Director.

The Ministry of External Relations, Monsieur Martial de la Fournière, Director of Archives (retired); Monsieur Guy de Commines de Marsilly, Director of Archives; Mademoiselle Monique Constant, Curator of Archives; and Curators Monsieur Martin de Framond, Madame Paul Pequin and Madame Maurice Hamon.

The National Furnishings Office, Monsieur Jean Coural, General Administrator; and Mademoiselle Denis, Technical Advisor.

The Museum of the Army, Monsieur le Général Lediberder, Director; and Curators Colonel Willing and Monsieur Reverseau.

The Museum of Decorative Arts, Monsieur François Mathey, Director; and Monsieur Gérard Mabille, Curator.

The Carnavalet Museum, Monsieur Bernard de Montgolfier, Director; and Mademoiselle Roslyne Hurel, Curator.

The Museums of the City of Rouen, Monsieur François Bergot, Director; and Madame Catherine Vaudour, Curator in charge of Ceramics and Metals.

The National Museum of Ceramics, Madame Hallé, Director; and Mademoiselle Elizabeth Fontan, Curator.

The National Museum of the Legion of Honor and Orders of Chivalry, Madame Claude du Courtial, Director; and Madame du Pasquier, Associate Director.

The Museum of the Louvre, Monsieur André Chabaud, Director; Madame Bellanger, Monsieur Gentil, and Madame Irène Bizot; in the Department of Paintings, Monsieur Pierre Rosenberg, Director; in the Department of Sculpture, Monsieur Jean-René Gaborit, Director, and Madame Geneviève Bresc, Curator; in the Chalcographie, Monsieur Jean-François Méjanès, Curator; in the Department of Decorative Arts, Monsieur Daniel Alcouffe, Director, and Monsieur Amaury LeFebure, Curator.

The Maritime Museum, Monsieur le Capitaine de Vaisseau Bellecq, Director; Commandant Roland, Curator in charge of External Exhibitions.

The National Museum of the Château of Versailles, Monsieur Pierre Lemoine, Inspector General and Director; Mademoiselle Claire Constans, Curator.

The Historic Service of the Navy, Monsieur le Contre-Amiral Chatelle, Director, and Monsieur J. P. Busson, Chief Curator.

Numerous private individuals and organizations in France have participated in the exhibition through loans from their collections and the sharing of expertise. Special recognition is tendered to the following:

Monsieur le Baron Georges de Grandmaison and Madame la Baronne.

Monsieur le Comte Jacques-Pierre Le Moyne de Martigny and Madame la Comtesse.

Monsieur and Madame Christian Prévost-Marchilhacy.

The Château of Vaux-le-Vicomte, Monsieur le Comte Patrice de Vogüé and Madame la Comtesse.

The Bricard Museum, the Bricard family, and Madame Catherine Prade, Curator.

The Museum of the Hunt and Nature, Monsieur le Marquis de Lastic, Director, Madame la Marquise, and Madame Chantal de Quiqueran Beaujeu, Associate Director.

In the United States, the Metropolitan Museum of Art has most generously made its rich collections available to the exhibition. Gratitude is particularly expressed to Philippe de Montebello, Director; Ashton Hawkins, Vice-President, Secretary, and Counsel; Olga Raggio, Chairman of the Department of European Sculpture and Decorative Arts; Curators Clare Vincent, Clare Le Corbeiller, and Jessie McNab; and Helmut Nickel, Chief Curator of the Department of Arms and Armor.

At the Louisiana State Museum in New Orleans, invaluable assistance has been rendered by faithful and determined volunteers in the curatorial offices, most particularly Mrs. Helen Perry and Ms. Judy Miller.

Presentation of *The Sun King: Louis XIV and the New World* has depended on the multifaceted involvement, dedication, and skills of the staff of the Louisiana State Museum. The organizers of the exhibition extend their appreciation to the entire staff and special recognition to Mrs. Freida Morford, Deputy Director; Mrs. Marie Grather, Administrative Assistant; Mr. Charles Wegmann, former Chief of Security; Mr. Terrence McGough, Personnel Officer; Mr. Walter Grather, Chief of Building Services; Mr. Manuel Weber, Engineering Supervisor; Mr. James Bourne, Maintenance Supervisor; Mr. Timothy Chester, Chief Curator of the Museum; Mr. J. Burton Harter, Curator of Paintings and Graphic Arts; Ms. Maud Lyon, Curator of Costumes and Textiles; Mrs. Mary Louise Tucker, former Curator of Photography; Mr. Donald Marquis, Curator of Jazz and Louisiana Music; Ms. Debbie de la Houssaye, Sun King Project Assistant; Dr. Edward F. Haas, Chief Curator of the Louisiana Historical Center; Mr. Joseph D. Castle, Curator of Cartography; Miss Rose Lambert, Chief Librarian; the late Miss Julie Barrois, Assistant Librarian; Mr. Penfield Cowan, Chief Technician; Mr. Gary Plum, Museum Technician; Mr. O. L. Bates, Museum Technician; Mr. Norbert Raacke, Jr., Registrar; and Mr. Charles de la Guéronnière, Photographer. ■

Catalogue 13

THE SUN KING

PART I
THE ESSAYS

LOUIS XIV AND THE NEW WORLD

LOUIS XIV IN HISTORY
AN INTRODUCTION TO THE ESSAYS
STEVEN G. REINHARDT

he goal of history is to understand, not to condemn or to praise. Whoever judges Louis XIV, warns the noted French historian Pierre Goubert, judges chiefly himself. With this admonition in mind, we must proceed to the assessment of Louis XIV, his impact on the world in which he lived, and his importance for our own. For the modern American, understanding Louis XIV is no easy task. Though vaguely familiar to many people, Louis is still basically unknown. When the average person hears the name Louis XIV, he or she may think of Versailles and perhaps of the Rigaud portrait of the king in full regalia, the epitome of royalty. But that is usually as far as their knowledge (or interest) extends. To be sure, Louis XIV epitomizes kingship, for he established the final form or culmination of monarchial government in France before the Revolution. At the same time, his reign was in many respects anachronistic: within his own lifetime, France was superseded by Great Britain, with its representative form of government, diversified capitalist economy, and ascendant middle class. Nonetheless, Louis XIV's France prefigured the modern state in significant ways, as will be seen in the essays that follow.

The purpose of the exhibition *The Sun King: Louis XIV and the New World* is to make Louis XIV comprehensible to Americans by placing him within the context of his own age and by showing how his reign was not only critical for the discovery and development of Louisiana but was also a critical stage in the development of the modern world. The France of Louis XIV was the first and best example of systematic state building that Europe had seen. Although the extension of

royal power occurred mainly in the fields of finance and justice, royal efforts at centralization also extended to the arts, architecture, science, religion, and intellectual life. In these and other areas, royal pressure for uniformity and control was beginning to moderate differences and promote the fusion of Frenchmen into a single nation, initiating the transformation of France into a modern state.

Although an exhibition is an ideal vehicle for conveying these concepts, the medium of an exhibition catalogue is a necessary adjunct to such an undertaking because it combines the illustrative and interpretive materials needed not only for a deeper appreciation of the exhibition itself but also for a more profound understanding of Louis XIV and his world. *The Sun King: Louis XIV and the New World* contains thirteen essays written or adapted expressly with the exhibition in mind. The first four essays consider Louis XIV as a personality and as a ruler, warrior, and Most Christian King. There is an almost inevitable mythologizing in all history, because historians tend to stress the elements of the record that agree with their personal perspectives. In the case of Louis XIV, this tendency is accentuated. Self-conscious of the picture of himself that he wished to bequeath to posterity, Louis cultivated his own mythology during his lifetime, and, to make matters worse, before his death ordered that his personal papers be destroyed. Because Louis was a consummate performer who was always on stage, even on his deathbed, one loses sight of the private individual behind the public figure, the man behind the myth. Therefore, it seem appropriate to begin with John B. Wolf's examination of Louis le Dieudonné, the man who was king. Next, John C. Rule discusses the emergence of court life under the Sun

King and the creation of Versailles to accommodate his burgeoning household and bureaucracy. The Sun King's drive to attain the ideal of "absolutism," which arose in response to the endemic disorder and nearly perpetual unrest inherent in seventeenth-century French social organization, convinced him of the necessity for religious uniformity among his subjects. Therefore, as Julius R. Ruff shows, Louis embarked on a policy of religious absolutism which, although applauded by the overwheming majority of his subjects, proved ruinous and futile in the long run. The seventeenth-century king who came to the throne when there were no battles to be fought or wars to be won considered himself most unfortunate. John T. O'Connor demonstrates how Louis XIV's quest for personal and dynastic fulfillment via military and diplomatic triumphs gained him the hatred, fear, and united opposition of other European countries. All four essays stress that Louis XIV acted in accordance with the spirit of his times; in these respects, as in others, the Sun King was limited not only by the material resources of his kingdom but also by his own mental preconceptions.

The essays in the second part focus on French colonial policies and practices, especially as they related to Louisiana. Philippe Jacquin describes the reasons behind France's delayed entry into colonialism and the factors that finally prompted the Sun King to commit French resources to the development of an overseas empire. As a result, by the time Louis died in 1715, France was stronger and better respected in America that it was ever to be again. Monique Pelletier examines the stages of French expansion in New France and Louisiana and illustrates the degrees of discovery and settlement of the latter region via the use of comtemporary maps and plans. But royal commitment often wavered, and financial aid dwindled due to Louis XIV's military involvement in Europe; consequently, the fledgling colony of Louisiana struggled to survive. In fact, Carl A. Brasseaux concludes that this legacy of neglect and stagnation continued to cripple the colony throughout the entire period of French rule (1699-1769).

A dedicated king, Louis, XIV held a concept of political greatness that expressed itself in the quest

A DEDICATED KING, LOUIS XIV HELD A CONCEPT OF POLITICAL GREATNESS THAT EXPRESSED ITSELF IN THE QUEST FOR OBEDIENCE AND MAGNIFICENCE

for obedience and magnificence. He left behind him an image of the monarchy which, although considered old-fashioned by contemporaries at the time of his death, continues to dazzle and intrigue. Part three of the essays examines the Sun King's promotion and political use of the arts and sciences for the glorification of the throne and the good of the state. In his biography of the king, John B. Wolf emphasizes that Louis XIV consciously created the cult of royalty necessary to justify the very real extension of royal power into all aspects of life in his kingdom. Therefore, to regard the ceremonial life of the court, royal patronage of the arts and sciences, adulation by artists and men of letters, and monumental royal architecture as merely emanations or reflections of the Sun King's megalomania ignores the fact that these policies were intended to promote the mystique needed to sanction the king's drive for absolutism. Louis XIV shrewdly realized that the reorganization of his bureaucracy, courts, and army had to be accompanied by the increased use of symbols and ceremonies that would convey to the populace a visual appreciation of the new political order. As a result, Wolf argues, Louis XIV constantly cultivated his own image in the popular mind. He was a master propagandist who utilized festivals, fireworks, statues, fountains, palaces, books, pamphlets, engravings, paintings, music, and even religious services to remove himself from the ranks of ordinary humans, even other nobles, and to associate himself more closely with divine power. All of the above methods were used to instill in the minds of his subjects the mystique that justified the reality of royal power. Royal servants like Jean-Baptiste Colbert and the marquis de Louvois did not organize the ritualized adulation of the king in order to flatter his royal ego, but to involve the people of France in the cult of the king so they would more freely submit to the extension of his power. By raising the throne above rival sources of power in the kingdom (particularly other great noble families and Parisian magistrates who had led the rebellion known as the Fronde), the Sun King and his men were, in effect, laying the groundwork for the modern state that would be able to exercise even greater control over the lives of its people.

The third part opens with Robert W. Hartle's examination of royal iconography, in which he reminds us that the age of Louis XIV sought its own reflection in the mirror of antiquity. Accordingly, in order to appreciate the secular cathedral of Versailles, one must recognize that its decorations have an allegorical meaning drawn from the idiom of antiquity. Antoine Schnapper demonstrates how the Sun King's personal taste eventually changed from the ponderous allegorical paintings typical of Versailles to landscapes and paintings of flowers, often of Dutch or Flemish inspiration, which he collected and displayed at the Grand Trianon. Daniel Rabreau's essay illuminates how Louis XIV and Colbert especially glorified the person of the king and the power of the state by structuring space and creating monumental open-air chapels dedicated to the worship of the divine-right monarchy. Louis XIV considered opera an excellent means of image building, Robert M. Isherwood argues, because it combined music and poetry with the very same rhetorical devices employed by artists and architects in the service of the king; it was as if all the allegorical creatures of Le Brun's paintings and decorations, all the imagery of Coysevox's sculptures came to life on the stage.

But, warns Marcel Gutwirth in his study of classicism, royal sponsorship of the arts is the *least* adequate explanation for the efflorescence of genius in seventeenth-century France; at best, patronage could have kept genius alive, but could not have brought it into being. Finally, E. Stewart Saunders identifies the various factors that motivated Louis XIV and his ministers to create the institutional foundations that set French science and technology on the road to excellence in the eighteenth century. The unifying theme of all the essays remains the Sun King's concern to harness the abundant artistic and intellectual energy of his age in the interest of the state.

The editor would like to thank the contributors for their help and cooperation in making their work available for publication. He is also grateful to Cornell University Press for permission to publish Robert M. Isherwood's essay, adapted from *Music in the Service of the King: France in the Seventeenth Century* (Ithaca, N.Y., 1973). Finally, he wishes to thank Margaret Fisher Dalrymple of Louisiana State University Press, John T. O'Connor, and Edward F. Haas for their aid and advice in the preparation of this volume. ■

Detail of Catalogue 24

LOUIS XIV:
THE MAN AND THE KING

THE MAN WHO WAS KING
JOHN B. WOLF

 ouis XIV is often portrayed by historians, journalists, and others as a man enormously conceited, pompously exhibitionistic, arrogantly proud, always seeking an undefined something called *gloire*. Louis himself and the men around him were partly responsible for this picture: the visitor to this exhibition will see the king bragging about his victories, identifying himself with Roman heroes, blatantly displaying the grandeur of his châteaus and the beauty of his art collections, all of which seem to show exaggerated ego. If this were all we knew about Louis XIV, it would make a sorry portrait of the man as a human being. But we must remember that Louis' magnificent châteaus, the displays of fireworks and papier-mâché tableaux, the art glorifying his person and achievements, the etiquette in his court and the near-deification of his person were all part of a plan. Mazarin taught Louis what many rulers both before and after him knew — that if he is to be successful in ruling his kingdom, a king has to impress his subjects with his grandeur and authority, and his potential enemies with his power. The strict etiquette that seems so ridiculous to many when, for example, it limited the wearing of certain clothes to a select few, was in fact a means of straitjacketing potential rebels in the king's entourage. Noblemen whose grandfathers had taken up arms against former kings could somehow be controlled by court functions and honors: a special costume, a footstool for a wife in the presence of the queen — such were often the outer trappings of political control. Louis' mother never forgot that her father ruled the Court of Spain with a strict and formal etiquette as a matter of policy, not because of an exalted ego. Thus

Louis very early learned that he must impress the world around him with his authority and power, and in an era when the king epitomized the kingdom this meant that the king must appear in grandeur, and his life-style must evidence the power and splendor of his kingdom.

In writing for his son, Louis insisted that the king must show respect for God who had made the king respected, that the king must be proud *for* his office and the position that God had given him, but not *of* himself. If we accept this belief that it is God who rules the world as fundamental to Louis' philosophy, we must revise our judgment of this king's behavior.

However, it is not an easy task to find the "real" Louis XIV. He wanted to be remembered as an institution rather than as a man, as the king who gave form to the emerging bureaucratic police state with an army able to impose order on the anarchy that had been just below the surface in the France of the preceding reigns, but not as a person living with family and friends. To be sure that this picture would prevail, he destroyed most of his personal papers; even the *Mémoires* were saved from the fire only by fortuitous chance. This leaves us with political and military documents often developed by others and only a fragment of his personal correspondence. Nonetheless, a blurred picture can be developed both from the letters that have survived and from the ongoing events of the reign as seen through the eyes of contemporaries.

Once, in the question period following a lecture on Louis XIV, a perceptive man asked me: "When do you think that a man's character is more or less permanently formed?" It is not easy to answer; even the psychologists do not agree. Obviously at twenty years many, perhaps most, of the characteristic patterns of behavior are firmly in place, and yet we all know that life experiences can modify and even change these patterns significantly. At twenty, Louis showed most of the patterns of behavior that were to be characteristic of him throughout his life, but we must remember that his life extended from 1638 to 1715 and that he was severely "punished" by the events that crowded in on the last two or three decades. There can be no doubt about it — if these patterns were not altered, the emphasis and direction that his behavior developed certainly were often reoriented.

Undoubtedly the most important people in the formation of the life patterns of the young Louis were his mother and Cardinal Mazarin. Queen Anne, a Spanish princess, doted on her firstborn son who had arrived fortuitously and rather late in her married life. Unlike most princes, Louis XIV was not left solely to the care of nursemaids. Anne gave him attention and love and carefully supervised his development. Shortly before his death, Louis XIII made Mazarin responsible for the education of his son, and the subsequent cooperation, affection, and love that developed between the cardinal and the queen regent soon gave Mazarin the status of substitute father of the young king. The letters that passed among these three leave no question about the love and respect that the members of this trio held for each other. The Italian cardinal and the Spanish queen gave the young king their values and taught him to accept responsibility for his own personality as well as his obligations as a man and a king. Many times in his life, his impulses and inclinations came in conflict with their precepts, and yet, so far as we can discover, Louis was uncomfortable and anxious even though he was often unable to resist his impetuous desires.

What were these precepts? Anne wanted her son to be a good man and a great king, and, like many a Catholic mother, for her the former was the more important. It was she who gave him his religious ideals and ideas rather than the priests who taught him the catechism and preached to him about his duty to God. Louis all his life was a "superstitious" Catholic: canticles, novenas, pilgrimages, prayers to the Virgin or to this or that saint, Spanish mysticism — these were the religious elements that

THE ITALIAN CARDINAL AND THE SPANISH QUEEN GAVE THE YOUNG KING THEIR VALUES

filled his consciousness. Boussuet once remarked that the king did not love God, he merely feared the Devil. This may have been true, yet later in his life, when reverses on the battlefield and tragic deaths in his family seemed to him to be God's punishment, we find Louis begging forgiveness. He obviously believed that he had offended God and hoped that he could make amends. However, even to his last years, Louis was practically innocent of the theology of St. Thomas or, indeed, of that of his own court preachers. He had little understanding of the basic teachings of his church.

While his mother tried to teach him that he should listen to his clergymen in framing his life values, Mazarin taught him that priests should never be allowed to interfere in politics. Mazarin was a protégé of Cardinal Richelieu and himself a prince (cardinal) of the church, but not a priest. His career included service in several princely Italian houses as well as in the Papal Curia; it may have shaped many of his attitudes. In any case, he was suspicious of clergymen who "knew" the will of God, and he passed that suspicion on to his own protégé. As king, Louis always respected the clergy's role in the formation of religious services, he listened to their sermons, but he would not give them political power. It is not out of place to note that the same was true for the women of his life. He enjoyed the favors of his mistresses, he loaded them with jewels, titles, and lands, but he would not allow them any place in his political life. He promised to banish any mistress who, in the opinion of his ministers, achieved power over his political decisions.

Whereas Anne's greatest desire was that her son should be a good man who would love God and obey his commandments, Mazarin believed that Louis had the qualities necessary to become the greatest king of the age, perhaps of the era. His emphasis was upon the obligation that God's gifts imposed upon his protégé for the grandeur and splendor of the kingdom and the *gloire* of the king. *Gloire* cannot be translated as "glory." It is rather the fulfillment of the potentials, the fullest development of the personal and professional capacities, the fullest exploitation of the gifts with which God has endowed a man — intellectual powers as well as social and political status.

Mazarin believed that Louis would become an exceptional king, and he imposed upon him the ideals and ambitions and sense of obligation needed to achieve that status in the world.

Both Mazarin and Queen Anne many times impressed upon the young king that God had given him talents and thus had imposed upon him the obligation that he be as good and as great a king as possible; they added that God would hold him responsible for doing his duty. At the most critical point in his relations with Mazarin, the crisis over his marriage to the Spanish Infanta, the cardinal thundered that God would punish the king, his kingdom, and his subjects if Louis should fail in his tasks as ruler. These two, mother and surrogate father, were the most important, although of course not the only determining forces in Louis' character.

Louis became the fourteenth king of France to bear that name when he was still a child. He was a handsome, pliable boy, reasonably intelligent, physically well developed, and easily persuaded to do the bidding of his mother, his preceptors, and his confessor. There were but few disciplinary problems with this prince; the punishment that he incurred for using language learned in the stables may account for the fact that as king his language was always guarded and "clean."

There were, however, many things that a prince had to learn beyond the use of decent language. From the time that he left the close custody of women — mother, nursemaids, ladies surrounding the queen — to become the charge of a governor who was a distinguished soldier, the young Louis was under the care of all sorts of teachers who were supposed to "educate" him. Saint-Simon and others insist, however, that Louis XIV was never educated, indeed that he was ignorant and intellectually unformed. These critics are correct if we are to judge the king's training by the standards of humanistic education common to the "educated" people of the era. Louis had but very little Latin and no Greek; he did not read the classics of antiquity nor, for that matter, the best writings of his contemporaries; he was not a scholar. He did have instruction in Spanish and Italian, and he learned to write and speak moderately elegant French. He had instruction in history (some of it rather dull) that taught him first of all that he did not want to be a "do-nothing" king, and secondly, gave him some insight into political problems as well as the methods of their solution by studying

the life of his grandfather Henri IV. He also became a crack shot with both musket and fowling piece, a good dancer, an experienced horseman, a competent fencer. These were achievements needed by a king of France.

Louis very early decided that he would not be a "do-nothing" king, and Mazarin continually assured him that he could be a "great king." But how does a prince learn to be a king? Louis had the good fortune to have a teacher who not only did not need to fear his pupil but also was able very early to introduce him to the paperwork of government. Mazarin gave Louis dispatches to read, admitted him to the council chamber that discussed state business, and carefully explained to him many of the secrets of government. In this way Louis learned to understand the map of Europe as well as that of France and became acquainted with men and affairs that could be important to his kingdom. Thus he came to understand the necessity of securing as correct and complete information as possible, and all his life he commanded his diplomats, his political officers, and his police scattered over the kingdom to give him complete news about "the place where you [the official] find yourself." This may have been Mazarin's most important advice, for in the seventeenth century there were no good sources of news beyond the *mémoires* and letters presented for government action or information. Louis' curiosity brought him to seek all sorts of information: he wanted to know the secrets of his own courtiers as well as those of foreign rulers and statesmen. His desire "to know" had no bounds.

Almost equal in importance for shaping of the royal policy was his insistence upon finding the best men possible for his advisors. "Possible," of course, meant men who were known to him or to his advisors. One could speculate that Louis' experience with Mazarin, who was a political genius, and the group of men who were the cardinal's "creatures" could have given the young king a feeling of inferiority that might have brought him to a point where he would prefer to have mediocre men around him rather than very able ones. In his *Mémoires*, Louis denies any feelings of inferiority in the presence of men like Colbert or Le Tellier; his own obvious ability and Mazarin's insistence upon his talents were enough to reassure him that he could preside at a council table staffed by strong and able men.

Mazarin did not limit his teaching to the council

chamber and the documents that he gave Louis to read; he also introduced him into the secrets of his statecraft and the principles of kingship with special attention to the writings of the great Florentine philosopher Machiavelli. Indeed, much of Louis' advice to his son could have been lifted from *The Prince.*

A royal court is a curious place to rear a child. At first sight, he will think that the whole world loves him, his mother, and everything about his family. Everyone bows or kneels before him; everyone praises him whether he deserves it or not. It is a child-centered world par excellence. But the Court of France after the death of Louis XIII was more complicated that this picture. The kingdom was engaged in a great war with enemies on all frontiers, a war that was costly and clearly difficult to win. The war was almost a decade old when the little boy ascended the throne. It had already imposed taxes on the kingdom that were hard to bear and, if there were to be a victory, those taxes must be increased. There were also other problems: the "reforms" — some called them the "revolution" — of Cardinal Richelieu had invaded the prestige, privileges, and position of both the military and the judicial nobility so deeply that revolt was just below the surface. During the later childhood years of the young king, revolt did occur in the form of the Frondes. These were civil rebellions led by the judges of the highest courts of the land and even a prince of the blood, the king's own cousin, as well as by some of the most important and richest noblemen of the realm.

The young king had to hear speeches that insulted his mother; he was taken from his bed and spirited out of Paris to avoid being taken captive by the rebels; he watched loyal soldiers attempt to recapture Paris and learned every day for two years or so of battles that saw French princes allied with Spanish soldiers fighting troops loyal to him and his mother. To make the lesson even more poignant, his aunt — who happened to be the queen of England — read letters to the family in the Palais-Royal from her husband about the civil war in his kingdom. Finally came a letter detailing his execution. No one had to tell Louis XIV after these experiences that the head of a king is never completely safe. Small wonder that he learned to

be suspicious, to dislike the city of Paris, to fear the possibility of rebellion.

It is highly possible that these childhood experiences were at the root of one of Louis' most characteristic behavior patterns: his secrecy and his suspicious distrust. No one could be depended on, not even his harmless brother, not his uncle who had revolted against Louis XIII, and surely not his cousin Condé, who had allied against him with the Spaniards. Even less trustworthy, perhaps, were the noblemen in his court whose fathers had joined rebellions in the past, and surely one could not trust the city of Paris with its Parlement and its fickle history of riot and revolt. Louis' letters to all and sundry in his service are filled with protestations of his belief that the recipient loved the king and desired to serve his state, but these were the letters of a politician who knew a bit of psychology and used it to try to persuade men to do their duty. The king himself never forgot that he was surrounded by self-seeking, egotistical men and that he must be sparing with his trust.

LOUIS TRIED TO SECURE THE ASSISTANCE OF WISE AND EXPERT MEN TO HELP HIM GOVERN HIS STATE

This does not mean that Louis tried to govern alone. He told his son that ordinary people seek counsel of wise men in the management of their affairs and, even more so, a king must seek the aid of competent people in the management of the kingdom. Throughout his reign, Louis tried to secure the assistance of wise and expert men to help him govern his state. Sometimes it would seem that he would have been pleased with the technocratic developments of our era that have produced so many "experts." This dependence on advice did not force him to depend upon a majority of his council, as did his cousin Emperor Leopold, yet it did at times lead to inaction. For example, at Hurtebise the king's armies were in a position to impose a catastrophic defeat on the Prince of Orange, but Louis listened to the advice of his military advisors who probably feared the possibility that the king could be killed if a battle should be engaged. Saint-Simon called it cowardice; it ought to be seen either as good judgment or as ambivalence in a confusing situation.

The king of France was a soldier, a statesman, a politician, a judge, and a ceremonial figure. Louis played all these roles with more competence than the vast majority of his predecessors or successors.

The king was the first nobleman in a company of soldier-nobles; he was expected to lead them to war. Louis was the last French king to do this, but he did not lead them, sword in hand, in a wild charge; he was a man of plans, foresight, pen and ink. He managed his armies and directed their actions with the aid of counselors who were either experts or supposed to be so. However, unlike his great grandfather Philip II of Spain, who directed all policy from his bedroom or study in the palace, Louis often took to the field, shared the hardships of mud, rain, cold, and camp life with his troops. Nonetheless, as his letter to his grandson on the "use of Vauban" indicates, he turned over the actual conduct of maneuvers and battles to men with competence whenever he could find them. We should also note here that in several cases when disaster overtook an officer in whom he had placed trust, Louis understood enough of the hazards of war not to place heavy blame on the unfortunate soldier who lost a battle. The unhappy general was usually replaced and then simply assured that things did not always go as men hoped.

Louis understood enough about war to know that the presence of the king or, when he became old, of a prince of the blood, gave a boost to the morale of the entire army. He also knew that as long as he had to use great noblemen with both family names and some military reputation, the presence of the king was essential if an officer like Vauban, a man of relatively humble origins, was to be obeyed by "the great ones." Both for the morale of his soldiers and for the support of effective officers, Louis was willing to put up with the discomforts of the field. He did have one characteristic that might provoke a smile: at the opening of any campaign Louis was always optimistic for success, but especially in the latter years, when his armies were defeated and his fortifications captured, his inevitable response was that he could not understand how these things could have happened! By the next spring and a new campaign, his optimism would return.

Undoubtedly the most important single military act of the reign was the establishment of the table of ranks that regulated the right to command and eventually broke the power of great noblemen who believed that command was theirs by right of their birth. It was difficult to force men with a marshal's baton to obey a chain of command, but there was no other way to establish the power of the war

office, representing the king's will, to direct the flow of troops and the course of strategy. It took courage and determination to do this, and Louis XIV ably demonstrated that he was the man to do it. He was not merely a soldier of pen and ink; he was also responsible for seeing that serious military decisions were actually carried out by his troops in the field. This was the only way that the old neo-feudal anarchy could have been curbed.

While Louis showed courage in some areas, there is good reason to believe that he also sometimes felt insecure. We have already mentioned Hurtebise. His decision there could have resulted from insecurity rather than good judgment or cowardice, but the manuscript history of the Dutch War in the Bibliothéque Nationale, undoubtedly written by someone close to the king, seems evidence that at least its author was sure that he should try to build up the self-esteem of the king. Also the fact that Louis' brother never again had a command after the victory at Cassel (the *Gazette* history of the battle reported at the time suggests that the victory was due to Louis' judgment rather than to Philippe's valor) may also support the insecurity theory. However, it must also be pointed out that Louis hated and feared the impetuous commander who, sword in hand, calls for "victory or death!" He liked Turenne's method of fighting rather than Condé's — and with good reason.

While the young noblemen regarded war as the important work for a king, a French ruler had other obligations as well. He was a politician with hundreds of offices, pensions, and sinecures to distribute, most of which were funded by land long since committed for that purpose. But who deserved these favors? An American president probably does not have to deal with more such personalities than did the French king three hundred years ago. Small wonder that Louis' pat answer was, "We shall see," whenever anyone asked a favor of him. The politician king also had to write hundreds of letters trying to persuade this one or that of his officers or clergymen that he must do his duty to the king and the state. An afternoon with these letters will convince anyone that the writer was a clever politician.

The politician also had to be a statesman. Fortunately for him, Louis was usually able to find capable men to fill his council, but he could not govern the kingdom in the mode of Richelieu or Mazarin because he could not use his relatives or friends as his "creatures," and were he to entrust the power to a first minister, he could not fulfill Mazarin's instructions that he should govern the kingdom himself. Thus his council was composed of several ministers equal in status and in competition with each other for royal favor. To manage men of the intellectual stature of a Colbert and a Le Tellier required skill, patience and a great deal of understanding. Louis XIV had to be a strong personality even to survive in that company. It is to his credit that he picked such strong men to help him govern the kingdom and was able to manage the direction of their political thrusts.

The king was also supposed to be a judge. He left most judicial matters to the chancellor and the law courts, but he did take an active interest in many of the family and other problems that came to him as "father" of his people. In this area Louis very seldom acted out the role of tyrant; most of his decisions were reasonably humane in light of the customs of the era. Even his much-condemned assault on the Huguenots (the Bolsheviks of the seventeenth century) must be seen in several lights to understand its meaning, and Louis was not the prime mover in forcing the direction of the religious laws. This is not to say that a Huguenot in the galleys could not justifiably regard his king as a tyrant; yet a considerable majority of the king's subjects agreed wholeheartedly with his program to force religious unity on the kingdom.

Lastly, Louis needed to be a statesman to operate on the great stage of Europe. In this role we find him seeking the "facts" about all sorts of situations, although his policy was always caught by the twin pressures of dynastic politics and advantage and/or state's interest. Fortunately for him, the religious pressures of the preceding reigns were much abated and only marginally affected policy. It was in this international arena that Louis XIV made most of his mistakes. They can be credited to inadequate information, personal ambition that so often lured princes into trouble, and the bad advice of his most vigorous war minister, Louvois, whose brutality rubbed over into high politics, giving Louis XIV an unhappy reputation quite undesired but nonetheless deserved (see essay by John O'Connor).

Voltaire in a perceptive passage compares Louis XIV with William of Orange, his contemporary and principal foe. The French king was a patron of

> IF A KING IS SUSCEPTIBLE TO WOMEN'S CHARMS, THE COURT IS NO PLACE TO TEACH HIM ABSTINENCE

the arts, literature, and science; his rival hardly gave recognition to any of these things. Indeed, Louis' government was a veritable prototype of the Guggenheim and Rockefeller foundations — perhaps even more generous than either of these in "seed money" for scholars, artists, and scientists. It was Mazarin who set the example for him, but Louis' own love of the beautiful, as he saw it, and his recognition of the importance of linguists, historians, scientists of all kinds, as well as musicians, painters, and architects was an important part of his makeup as a man. He probably never read many, perhaps any, of the important books produced through his generosity, but he did use and enjoy the works of the landscape gardeners, sculptors, architects, and painters.

How did the king live as a man? His health is the subject of a long account for every illness that he suffered. He lived to be seventy-seven years old — almost two lives for most people of his time — which is evidence of his sturdy construction. He loved to be out-of-doors, to hunt, to join the army in its campaigns, to wander in the gardens of Versailles and elsewhere, and, indeed, he gave his contemporaries every evidence of good health during most of his life. He did have two serious illnesses: a very high fever at Mardyck when he was a young man, and an operation for the removal of an anal fistula much later in his life. Both threatened him with death. However, if we believe the accounts of his doctors, he was beset with poor health all of his life. They gave him enemas and physic until he bled; they gave him pills and potions, often vile in nature and almost as a daily regime. Each bout with illness became a struggle between the doctor and the disease, surprisingly with victory to the former! We must conclude that Louis XIV was either a hypochondriac or that he was largely attended by quacks. We do know that he changed his wine choice from red to white after he got a new doctor who had extensive holdings of land in the white wine country. He was probably served by his doctors as well as could be expected for his day.

Louis' grandfather, Henri IV, and his great-grandfather, Philip II, were both notoriously weak in sexual restraint, and his great-grandson, Louis XV, was, if possible, even less able to resist feminine lures. On the other hand, his father and his own son avoided the temptations of the flesh. If a king is susceptible to women's charms, the court is no place to teach him abstinence, for many women who inhabited the royal courts well knew that their own and their husbands' promotions and prosperity could be dependent upon the favor of the monarch. Moreover, many of them believed that adultery with a king was no sin. Louis' mother and Mazarin both understood that their charge, when he reached maturity or at least fourteen years of age, would be confronted with the problem of illicit sex. Even before Louis reached that critical age, Mazarin quietly exiled a family from the court when a thirteen-year-old daughter showed too much maturity and eagerness. Both the minister and particularly the queen mother counseled Louis against "disorder" in the court and in the family. Anne did not want her son to be another Romeo king. Nonetheless, it does seem that she was also worried that her son might become "like his father": Louis XIII did not care for women, enjoyed the company of young men, and probably was a latent homosexual like Louis' own brother. One member of Anne's entourage, a woman in her late twenties, apparently took seriously this fear and, lightly clad, waylaid the teenage king; it would have been strange if "nature did not take its course." This lady enjoyed a modest pension all her life.

We really do not know much about the young king's problems with women. After the Fronde, the court became a place where there was gaiety and pleasure for the young people. Mazarin brought his nieces from Italy and attracted the young men and women of high noble families to the Palais-Royal and the other châteaus. They enjoyed much dancing, many amateur theater parties, boating on the lagoons with music of the king's violins, riding hard in the hunts of the stag or the wolf — it was all great fun for young people. Louis, it appears, did have several cases of "puppy love"; he may well have had sexual contact with one or more members of the court or at least with girls who found their ways somehow crossing his, but his first attack of "love" that seems to have filled his whole being came after he was twenty. Mazarin's niece, Marie Mancini, was the young woman.

It is worth some space to explain the importance of this young lady to the future life of the king. She was a beauty, both in figure and face; she had intelligence and sensitive charm. She knew Italian and French poetry (filling in Louis' ignorance in this area); she could sing, play musical instruments, and had a fine sense of humor. It is not important where or when he fell in love with Marie, only that he did and that he was hard smitten. He wanted to marry her, and his desire provided one rationalization after another to prove that he should marry her. He even tried to tell Mazarin that since the Bourbons owed so much to him for saving the throne during the Fronde, it was only proper that the Bourbon king should marry Mazarin's niece! There is no more dramatic correspondence in the letters of the reign than those concerned with this proposed marriage. Mazarin would have nothing of it. The duty of the king of France was to bring security, happiness, and good government to his kingdom; it was not to follow his personal urges. Whatever Louis may have thought about marriage, his fate was tied up with war between France and Spain and his mother's desire to marry him to her brother's daughter, a princess of Spain. Mazarin's diplomacy and Anne's family balked Louis' desire to marry Marie Mancini.

Yet that is only the first part of the story: he was married to Marie-Thérèse, the eldest daughter of Philip IV, a lady with delicate skin and fear of the sun (Louis loved to live out-of-doors), and a lady of very limited intelligence. In place of the brilliant Marie Mancini, he had to accept as bride a woman with little sense of humor and even less ability to understand the things that went on around her. She could talk publicly of the king's favors in bed, and she could lose huge sums of money at the gaming table; she knew how to pray in the Spanish fashion, but she could not carry on a sophisticated conversation or comprehend the wit that occasionally played about her. It was a bad deal for the young king.

Louis' response was to look elsewhere for female companionship and more satisfying sex. Even here, however, his mother's teachings as well as her presence interfered. Louis' first serious extramarital engagement had to be kept secret from Queen Anne, and he chose a girl who was willing to accept a "back-stage" role as his mistress. Mademoiselle Louise de La Vallière was something of a violet — willing, even eager to stay in the shade, yet she made many demands on the king for favors for her relatives. That she was not taken to the public gaming table until one day when Queen

Anne was ill speaks volumes about the young king's attitude toward his mother. He obviously did not trust himself to stand up to her objections. The fact that he picked such a simple young woman for companion may also mean that, at that moment, he did not trust himself to make good with a more spirited one. French historians have usually been kind to Mademoiselle de La Vallière, the "good mistress" who contrasted so nicely with the brazen behavior of the next one, but Mademoiselle de La Vallière was as self-seeking for family and as demanding of the king's attention as her more flamboyant successor.

Madame de Montespan attracted the attention and captured the affection of the king by being a good friend of Mademoiselle de La Vallière. She managed to be present often when Louis visited his mistress, and her wit soon became the center of the king's attention. However, she was a married woman with a husband who could claim as his own any issue that might result from the clandestine relationship. It is a nice commentary on the "power of an absolute monarch" that it took Louis years to persuade the Parlement of Paris to separate Madame de Montespan from her husband, and until that was accomplished the king's bastard children had to be hidden. While this new affair was not easy for the king, it was especially hard on poor Louise de La Vallière, who was really brutally treated by Louis and his new love. It was also important that his confessor and the court preacher, Bishop Bossuet, and other religious moralists verbally objected to the sinful liaison. In response, Louis tried several times to break with Madame de Montespan, only to find that she was important in his life. He showered on her titles, estates, jewels, and pensions; she gave him children who were his favorites. Toward the end of the affair, however, the flaming beauty began to fade in rolls of fat and Louis' eyes wandered again.

We must not imply that only the mistresses who enjoyed a measure of recognition received Louis' favors in bed. The court was crowded with women who were anxious to wrest the crown from the current favorite, and there is much evidence that Louis sampled rather widely even when he was "madly in love" with the favorite. In this period of his life he also continued to perform his duty as husband of the queen; the grandson of Henri IV could not be tethered by either wife or mistress if green pastures enticed experiment.

Madame de Montespan was followed by a young woman, Mademoiselle de Fontages, who had been brought to the court because her "backers" believed that her striking beauty would harness the king — she was as "beautiful as an angel, had an excellent heart, but was a stupid little fool." She did become the king's mistress, but Louis must have been ashamed of her every time she talked. She had a miscarriage, was fatally injured in the process, and died a painful death. Louis was shaken by the whole affair, and indeed it could have been an important factor in ending his era of gallantry.

Even before Mademoiselle de Fontages' arrival, another woman had appeared on the royal scene: Madame de Maintenon, the governess for the king's children by Madame de Montespan. She was the widow of a minor poet, Paul Scarron. Although she was born in a prison where her father was incarcerated for debt, she was a gentlewoman with language, manners, and culture that made her suitable as guardian of the king's bastard children. Madame de Montespan was delighted when she found her. It mattered not that she had been a Huguenot for a short time, since reconversion to Catholicism insured her orthodoxy. The king met her when he visited his children. At first he was put off by her distance and austerity; even though she loved the children, she agreed with the court moralists that adultery was a sin and the king's adultery a bad example. Louis, however, found himself visiting his children more and more as he came to enjoy conversations with this intelligent woman. La Fontages may have excited his sexual desires; Madame de Maintenon, two years his senior, appealed to his mind and emotions. There is good evidence that he tried to entice her to his bed: instead, she persuaded him to return to that of his wife, the queen. It was 1683; Louis was forty-five years old. He visited Madame de Maintenon every day in the company of others. He had given up gallantry and lived with his wife. Then Marie-Thérèse died and there was "a place open." Would the king marry a foreign princess and try to produce another son (for he had only one legitimate heir)?

Louis did not give France a new queen. He married Madame de Maintenon in secret — a

> ## WE CANNOT SEPARATE LOUIS THE KING FROM LOUIS THE MAN

secret that was kept since the lady was never introduced as his wife even though she played an important part in all subsequent family affairs. Louis also remained faithful to her, at least so far as we have any records of his behavior. Both memoirists and historians have tried to give interpretations of the king's action, but it is hard to produce a sound psychological explanation for the acts of a man so long dead.

We cannot separate Louis the king from Louis the man. His public reign almost coincided entirely with his life. During the first two decades of his reign, when Mazarin ruled the kingdom, Louis appears to us as a promising young prince, handsome, athletic, above average in intelligence — the cardinal's faith in him seemed well placed. In the next two decades, much of this promise seemed about to become political and economic reality, and Louis, still handsome, was capable of playing out the role of king, indeed seemed to become the "Sun King" who had been promised earlier. His personal life was somewhat clouded by sexual irregularity, but he stalked the stage as Louis the Great. However, while his courtiers were giving him this title, the political structure of Europe was changing so that even "victory" in the Dutch War had a slightly bitter taste by the time the treaty of peace was written. Nonetheless, the best seemed yet to come: Versailles emerged out of the cocoon of his father's hunting lodge, and the main structures of the developing bureaucratic military state that was to be the prototype for the Western world were already showing firm contours.

The next two decades, however, saw the gradual erosion of French power vis-à-vis Europe. Louis' France was too aggressive, its visage too brutal, while victory over the Turks gave impetus toward the formation of the Danubian Hapsburg monarchy, and revolution in England created an even more dangerous foe for France. Louis was growing older, his queen was dead, and his disorderly sexual conduct ended; the court became less frivolous, more conservative, more solemn to match the moods of the king. A picture of Louis at about sixty-two years of age is one of a serious man, a worried man, more so than the pictures painted when he was thirty. His last decades were a severe trial. Defeat stalked his armies and his political ambitions; his own illness (among other things, he lost his teeth) and the deaths in his family gave a grey tone to life at Versailles, even though the king continued to play out his role as

the first monarch of Europe. By his last years, Louis often presents a picture of a man concerned that God was punishing him for his sins, perhaps his arrogance — a man whose tears might be known to his intimates, while those who saw him stride defiantly in his court had to realize that he could proudly reduce defeats to unfortunate but insignificant events. When his foes' demands overreached reason, he rallied his subjects to his cause by stirring eloquence, and finally when fate threatened to unite the German and the Spanish empires under one crown, he was able to save much from the disastrous war that seemed never to end.

Louis XIV died as he lived — with dignity and style worthy of a great king. ∎

Catalogue 213

LA ROYALLE & MAGNIFIQVE AVDIENCE, Donneé Par le Greshaut Tres Puissant, Tres Auguste
Monarque LOVIS LE GRAND, Roy de France et de Navarre, Aux tres Illustres Ambassadeurs du Magnifique Roy de SIAM,
Dans le Superbe et Royal Chasteau de Versailles le 1er Sour de 7bre 1686. Ou Ses trois Seigneurs ont esté receus avec tout l'honneur
Qu'ils ont pù desirer, & Conduits en la grande Galerie du Palais ou sa Majesté les attendoit sur Son trosne Accompagné de Mgr le Dauphin et de
Messieurs les Princes, Ducs et Pairs, Prelats et des grands Officiers à Ses Illustres Ambassadeurs aprés avoir profondement Incliné en leurs Manieres ont
fait la harangue qui fut expliqué par Mr l'Abbé de Lyonne Presenta à Sa Majesté une grande Requeste Escritte au Roi faisant le Recit sur une feuille
Lettres Roullé dans un boëtte d'or &c, qui fut Reçeu par le Grand Roy avec toutes les Marques de Son Affection & ostime dont ils Cultez Charmez

ALMANACH POUR L'AN DE GRACE M. DC: LXXXVII.

A PARIS, Chez la Veuve BERTRAND, ruë S. Jacque, à la Pomme d'or.

COURT, CAPITAL, AND COUNCILS IN THE REIGN OF LOUIS XIV

JOHN C. RULE

In discussing European "courts" in the Age of Louis XIV, a useful definition of the function of a court may be drawn from the phrase *faire une cour:* to make one's court.[1] An appellant became a courtier through the performance of homage, by an appeal for grace and favor, or an entreaty for justice. The appellant made his court to a *principe*, a prince, individual or corporate, who embodied the principles of justice and legitimacy and who served as patron, arbiter, and judge. The appellant-as-courtier made his court within a well-defined geographical area, be that, in France, the vast presence chamber at Fontainebleau, a cramped council room at the Louvre, or the mirrored halls of Versailles. The appellant-as-courtier made his court before a gathering of witnesses: the entourage of the prince. These witnesses might be friendly, or hostile, or neutral, but that was of little concern to those assembled. Their chief function was to add legitimacy to the act of making court by serving as a link between the act and creation of the memory of the act.

Yet a witness's memory was fragile: it was difficult to find two obsevors who were not deceived or self-deceiving. Witnesses might be mad, or worse, knaves. They might sicken and die, causing the memory of making one's court to fade. Thus the act of making court had to be preserved in graphic fashion for the prince and his successors. A French king such as Louis XIV was surrounded by memorabilia linking him to the past: a Rubens panel apothesizing his grandmother Marie de' Medici's coronation, Gobelin tapestries memorializing an audience of a papal nuncio with Louis XIV or the reception of the doge of Genoa

by the king and his court.[2] Memory might be preserved in music such as André Campra's opera-ballet *The Venetian Festivals*, composed for the visit of the Venetian ambassador to the court, or in André Raison's offertory "Long Live the King of the Parisians," written to commemorate the recovery of Louis XIV from the operation of the fistula.[3] Memory might be enshrined in poetry, as in the "Let Us Rejoice in Peace," dedicated to the king and his foreign minister Colbert de Torcy at the time of the signing of the Peace of Utrecht:

> Divine Peace, object of our dearest desires
> You alone can reestablish confidence
> You alone can assure us abundance
> Let the arts flourish and the pleasures reign. . . .[4]

Poetic tributes might be sung, as in de la Coste's ballet *Aricie,* in which Apollo urges the Muses and the Parisians to celebrate "new conquests of the greatest king of the Universe."[5] Memory might be preserved in descriptive prose, as in Charles Perrault's vivid portrait of the provincial *président* who, in his first visit to the palace of Versailles, marveled at the state apartments, the menagerie for exotic birds and animals, the elaborate watercourses, the carefully tended gardens — all poignant reminders of the presence of a powerful prince. Perrault assured the president that Louis XIV is "as worthy of admiration as Augustus and Maecenas."[6]

Early modern Europe witnessed both a renewal and a transmutation of the idea of a court. In the fifteenth and early sixteenth centuries, as the West reached out to explore unknown continents, the kings of Portugal established a permanent residence for their government in the city of Lisbon, where

Vénerie, or the Hunt, provided hounds, falcons, and carriages for the king's hunting parties, while the grand marshal of lodgings and buildings dispersed the largest budget of any of the departments: over 40,000,000 livres in the later eighteenth century. The department of Ceremonies, smallest of the seven in size and budget, was perhaps the most important for understanding the ritual of kingship. The Grand Master of Ceremonies, along with two Masters and two Introducers of Ambassadors, interpreted the code of conduct for all those who sought audience with the king. The ritual of making one's court, like painting, gardening, sculpting, had been raised to a fine art.[19]

The duties of the seven departments of the civil *Maison du Roi* overlapped those of the departments of the controller general of finances and the secretaries of state. The several thousand clerks of the ministerial bureaus lived and functioned alongside the chamberlains, gentlemen of the chamber, almoners, scribes, and treasurers of the civil household. As the French king became increasingly a symbol and center of a unified state, so conciliar government gave continuity to the exercise of power.

Conciliar government underwent rapid and fundamental changes after Mazarin's death. One historian has termed these reforms "the ministerial revolution of 1661."[20] Actually, the so-called revolution took a long generation from the 1660s to the 1690s to effect. Immediately after the cardinal's death in 1661, as we have seen, Louis XIV ordered all petitioners "to make their court" directly to him. By a simple order the prince became his own prime minister. Over the years, Louis restricted his policy-making council, the *Conseil d'en haut*, to a small group of close advisers whom he summoned simply by a royal command. He excluded from his high council his own family, even his more distant relatives, the princes of the blood; members of the clergy; great administrative officials such as the chancellor; members of the greater nobility; and representatives of the armed forces. When in the 1670s and 1680s the chancellor, a great nobleman, and the dauphin sat on the council, they did so at the pleasure of the

> ## THE RITUAL OF MAKING ONE'S COURT, LIKE PAINTING, GARDENING, SCULPTING, HAD BEEN RAISED TO A FINE ART

king, not by right. Louis suppressed the office of superintendent of finances, appointing only a controller general whose authority had formerly been subordinated to the superintendent. To aid the controller general both in policy making and in routine matters, Louis established a Royal Council of Finances. By the end of the 1660s, the secretaryship of the marine (and colonies) was separated from the office of foreign minister and the secretaryship of foreign affairs was joined to the post of minister for foreign affairs. By the year 1690 there were five offices of secretary of state: those of foreign affairs, war, marine (and colonies), the royal household, and that for administration of the Reformed Religion (newly converted Catholics). Since the marine and the royal household were invariably joined, only four secretaries served at one time. The press of war and economic crises caused the tiny corps of clerks and secretaries who were responsible for the daily work of the ministries to grow to nearly two thousand in the year 1715. The age of the bureaucrat had indeed arrived.

Over the years the Councils of Dispatches, Pleas, Finances, and State were refurbished and the times of meeting set by the king with the exactness of a watchmaker. The Council of Dispatches, grown powerful during the Frondes in the 1650s, met weekly and was attended by the king, the four secretaries of state, the chancellor, the king's brother Philippe d'Orléans, and after the late 1680s by the dauphin. The secretary of state in charge of the administrative affairs of a certain province would discuss such concerns as the appointment of provincial officials, the administration of justice, municipal elections, regulations of religious orders, jurisdictional disputes, and the founding of schools or hospitals. Every two or three months the Council of Dispatches met to consider questions of ecclesiastical patronage: the appointment of church officials, the awarding of clerical benefices, the appeals to the king's justice. Once a month, the king sat with the secretary of state on duty to consider the listing (*rolle*) of personal pleas that touched on the inherent right of the king to dispense *les grâces* — gifts, pardons, exemptions — or his right as supreme seigneur to grant concessions in his own domain, or over waterways and royal forests. At the time of the month that these petitions were to be read, appellants often journeyed to Versailles to attend a minister's public audience or the king's *lever*, hoping by this act "of making court" to gain a favorable decision from the king or secretary.

More than any of the other councils, that governing finances was made up of experts. The duc de Saint-Simon has left us a precise account of its activities:

"The Council of Finances was composed [in 1710] of the Chancellor [Louis Pontchartrain] because he was once controller-general, the Duc de Beauvilliers [as president], and Desmaretz, the then controller-general, as well as two other counsellors. . . . Almost the entire time was spent by the King in signing bonds and documents, judging private quarrels . . . hearing appeals regarding prize-money for captured ships." The controller general, meeting with his intendants of finance and his chief clerk, decided weightier affairs — "everything in the nature of finance, tariffs, statutes, the levying of new taxes, and the increasing of those already levied."[21]

Although subordinate to the *Conseil d'en haut*, the *Conseil d'Etat* was the center of bureaucratic activity. To this council were assigned appeals to the king's justice and the task of drafting and promulgating royal laws. Presided over by the chancellor or his deputy, the council met every Monday and Tuesday, attended by a select group of councilors of state and masters of request. (Louis XIV reduced the number of councilors to thirty-six and increased the masters of request to ninety.) This group of dedicated royal judges and lawyers transformed into law the will of the king and his ministers.

Great officials of the crown led harried lives. Letters from two appellants, Abbé Renaudot and Colonel Nathanial Hooke, vividly illustrate this point. Abbé Renaudot, writing to a Scottish friend in an archaic and delightful English relates his encounter with Louis de Pontchartrain in the early 1690s: "At Versailles I found Mylord Pontchartrain so embarrassed with many businesses, and two Councils in the same day, that his Lordship after a very short but Substantial account of our last conference, told me that at his coming at Paris he will give me further audience." Later Renaudot confided that he had presented "Mylord Sec[ry] of

Catalogue 107

State Pontchartrain, with [your] exact and large memorial . . . and because it was not possible to insert too many material things in a paper I gave him a fuller account viva voce. . . . His Lordship will in all reasonable things make you know his gentleness and meekness . . . which he will send suddenly."[22]

A few years later another Scotsman, Lieutenant Colonel John Murray, urgently required the aid of the officialdom at Versailles. Murray's horses and carriage had been seized by the police on the outskirts of Paris. His friend Colonel Hooke implored him "to go yourself to M. de Torcy," who as secretary of state could sign the king's name and attach a seal (cachet) ordering his equipage freed. Murray hastened to Colbert de Torcy's hôtel on the rue de Vivienne only to find that the minister had departed for Versailles on business of state. Meantime, Hooke, who learned of Torcy's arrival at Versailles, intercepted the minister as he descended from his carriage and begged him to send a lettre de cachet to the Paris police on Murray's behalf. Torcy wrote the order himself but did not sign or seal it because he was summoned to the king's council. Hooke in a note to his friend confided that "it was not signed till this morning but it will go out this night's post." Murray and Crosby were fortunate indeed to have friends who could "make court" for them at Versailles.

One of Louis XIV's important accomplishments was to provide a permanent home for his ministers, councils, and commissions — offices and lodgings in the royal palace where they could receive suitors, assemble documents, and dispatch orders. A map of Versailles drawn in 1705 by the dauphin's chief geographer Nicolas de Fer clearly shows the pavilions of the secretaries of state.[24] As the visitor looked from the windows at the center of the palace past the Cour de Marbre and the Cour Royal, he saw two long detached wings that formed the Aisle des Ministres. On the right-hand side were the pavilion of the chancellor and the meeting rooms of the Council of State, which were linked by corridors to the council rooms and apartments of the foreign ministry. On the left-hand side were the offices and apartments of the controller general, linked to those of the royal household and the marine. Behind the grand commun, on the rue de surintendance, was the

pavilion of the secretary of war. As a courtier observed, the king's councils are the court.

Although Versailles had by the 1690s become the home of the court and the accepted seat of government, Paris still housed the offices of many of the leading financiers and bureaucrats: the chancellery, the palace of the archbishop of Paris, the King's Library and the departmental archives, royal academies, the general tax farms, and the public treasury. Ministers and secretaries of state were obliged to shuttle back and forth between their bureaus at Versailles and their stately Parisian hôtels. In the mid- to late-seventeenth century,

VERSAILLES HAD BY THE 1690s BECOME THE HOME OF THE COURT AND THE ACCEPTED SEAT OF GOVERNMENT

there grew up near the Palais Mazarin a gilded ghetto for the greater civil servants that included the hôtels of the Colberts, Le Telliers, Phélypeaux, Desmaretz, Bignons, Chamillarts, and Charrons, to name but a few. This quarter was also the home of the newly constructed King's Library, located across the street from Mazarin's hôtel. Devoted to preserving the memoirs of the past and present reigns, scholars of the library included such eminent men as Nicolas Clément, Jean Boivin, Jean Buvat, the abbés Renaudot and Louvois, and the several Clairambaults. These scholars and librarians catalogued the king's collection, which by 1713 numbered over fifty thousand volumes and tens of thousands of manuscripts.[25]

Louis XIV urged his savants to scour Europe for rare books. Girardon, who traveled to the Ottoman Empire, purchased the library of Mathis Corvin in Budapest. Doms Mabillon and Montfaucon visited Italy several times between the mid-1680s and the beginning of the Spanish succession war in order to acquire for the king Greek and Latin manuscripts. In the Hôtel Colbert, whose gardens backed on the King's Library, Colbert's librarian Etienne Baluze catalogued the papers of Cardinal Mazarin. In a hôtel on the nearby Place des Victoires the Clairambault family prepared inventories of the Marine Ministry's manuscripts. The papers of the War Ministry were transferred in the early eighteenth century from the minister's home to a more permanent depository in the Invalides. At the same time, the older archives of the foreign ministry were moved from the Hôtels de Torcy and Pomponne to the upper stories of the Louvre, which served not only as an archive but as a meeting place for the royal academies and as a state-supported residence for artists and librarians.[26]

Louis was not only a passionate bibliophile but an avid collector of the plastic arts. A conjuncture of events made it possible for him to amass an enormous treasure of paintings and prints. The "inruptions" of war and civil strife in the early seventeenth century caused the scattering of some of the greatest collections of antique and Renaissance art. In the 1630s the duke of Mantua sold many of his paintings and objets d'art to, among others, Charles of England. But ten years later the great civil war in England caused King Charles in turn to offer many of his treasures for sale. Swedish armies meantime held the imperial capital of Prague to ransom. Many of the prize pieces of Emperor Rudolph passed into Queen Christina's collections or were scattered.[27]

In 1661 Louis XIV instructed his minister Colbert to obtain as many of these fugitive masterpieces as he could. Colbert soon thereafter paid an art entrepreneur, Everard Jabach, over 350,000 livres for a cache of paintings, including two Titians, one the famous *Entombment*; a Correggio, *The Exploits of Hercules*; and a Tintoretto and a Veronese. Several years later, while visiting the Louvre in the company of Colbert, Christiaan Huygens reported seeing the king's recent purchase of 300 prints, also acquired from Jabach. In 1671 Colbert bought over one hundred pictures, and 5,542 prints from the same dealer. To these gatherings were added a magnificent collection of engravings and prints sold to the king by the Abbé de Marolles, including the remarkable engravings by Albrecht Dürer of *The Three Heads of a Child*; *Adam and Eve* by Jan Van Eyck; drawings by Andrea del Sarto, Raphael, Michelangelo, Filippino Lippi, Leonardo de Vinci; and Peter-Paul Rubens' magnificent *Cavalier in Armor*, which was in fact a portrait of Louis XIV's great-great-grandfather, the Emperor Charles V.[28]

In December, 1681, Louis XIV, with his son the Grand Dauphin visited the Louvre to inspect the seven great galleries, including those built in the adjoining Hôtel de Grammont, which had been refurbished to house his collections. At that time Louis selected over thirty pictures for his apartments at Versailles and presented the Dauphin with Le Brun's *The Family of Darius*, one of the artist's finest.[29]

At Versailles Louis surrounded himself with art. Throughout the palace and in the famed gardens created by André Le Nôtre the majesty of kingship was enhanced by a profusion of vases, bronzes, and other objets d'art. The Salon of Hercules, one of the rooms of the state chambers, was embellished by two paintings of Veronese, *Eliezar and Rebecca* and *Feast at the House of Simon the Pharisee*. The Salon of Mars contained six portraits by Titian and Veronese's *Disciples on Their Way to Ammaus*. The Salon of Mercury boasted Van Dyke's very fine likeness of Marie-Anne of Hungary, two paintings by Carracci, and an *Entombment* by Veronese.[30]

Representations of immediate kingship were not slighted: Mignard's group portrait of *The Family of the Grand Dauphin*, completed in January, 1677, hung in the apartments of the queen until 1700, when the dauphin borrowed it for his own collection at Meudon. It was, however, the completion of the full-length painting of Louis XIV by Hyacinthe Rigaud that brought princely portraiture to its apogee.[31] Conceived in early 1701, the Rigaud portrait perpetuated in striking color and imposing stance what the marquis de Dangeau called "la goutte du roi" or the king's personal taste. A copy of the Rigaud work was packed off to Louis' grandson Philip V in early 1702. Philip presented his grandfather with a companion portrait of himself by Rigaud, which hung next to that of the king in the royal apartments at Versailles, renewing and enhancing the visual memory of kingship for a new generation of courtiers.[32]

Art served a practical as well as a symbolic purpose at the court of the king of France. In 1696, for example, Louis XIV, through his Introducer of Ambassadors, presented the papal nuncio with a gift of French art, including two silver figures on pedestals, four small gold vases, two chandeliers, twelve flambeaux, an oval basin, a cross of gold studded with diamonds and rubies — a treasure worth 18,000 livres, which represented in tangible form a reward for past services and future favors. Immediately after the signing of the Treaty of Utrecht with Great Britain, Louis XIV ordered his secretary of state Colbert de Torcy to send a complete register of the prints from the King's Library to the British Grand Treasurer Robert Harley, Earl of Oxford. As Torcy observed: "One must humor the Grand Treasurer. It is politic to do so." Even in one of the most calamitous years of the reign, 1709, Louis presented Cardinal

Ottoboni with a painting by Antoine Coypel, several Gobelin tapestries, and three silver figurines.[33]

The king was not only the bestower of largesse but the recipient of gifts from both foreign princes and his own subjects. The Republic of Venice sent him Veronese's *Feast at the House of Simon the Pharisee*; the Danish ambassador paid his homage to the king by offering him Segher's portrait of *Saint Francis*; the nuncio Delphino presented Louis with *Entombment* attributed to Veronese; and the descendants of Cardinal Richlieu "made their court" by adding Carracci's *Saint Sebastian* to the royal collections. But few of the acts of homage surpassed that of the nuncio Gualterio, who brought to Versailles "the mummified body of Sainte Victoire, martyr, magnificently encased with vases of porphyry at the head and a triptych at the foot" — a fitting tribute to His Most Christian Majesty.[34]

Louis was generous to his relatives as well as to foreign statesmen. To his son, his grandchildren, his legitimized children, and other members of the royal family he lent or gave paintings, prints, statues, furniture, coaches, jewels, and medals. He also helped his kin purchase palaces in the vicinity of Versailles: Meudon for the Grand Dauphin; Saint-Cloud for his brother Philippe; Sceaux for his legitimized son the duc de Maine; Rambouillet for another legitimized son, the comte de Toulouse. He even built a school at St. Cyr for one of the most celebrated schoolmarms of all times, Madame de Maintenon. In the early 1690s Louis purchased the Luxembourg Palace, but not before his superintendent of buildings had inspected and pronounced in good repair the great Rubens panels that depict in regal hues the life of his grandmother Marie de' Medici.

Near the end of his life Louis XIV received with his usual pomp and magnificent display ambassadors from Persia. The Hall of Mirrors was lined with tiers of carpeted benches and was diffused with the light of a thousand candles. At the far end of the gallery on a raised dais stood a silver throne under an ornately draped canopy. For the occasion the king lent the duc du Maine a set of diamond and pearl buttons. Louis' nephew the duc d'Orléans wore a blue velvet coat, "embroidered in a mosaic pattern, overlaid with pearls and diamonds." For himself, Louis chose "a coat of black and gold cloth . . . trimmed with the finest diamonds of the crown jewels" valued at over 12,000,000 livres. Near the throne the king placed the court painter Antoine Coypel and the secretary of the Académie des Inscriptions "to paint and describe the scene," perpetuating the memory for posterity.[35]

While thus surrounding himself with princely pageantry and pomp, Louis XIV made it possible for his relatives, his officials, and his subjects to make their court in a setting that was at once opulent and practical. As the duc de Saint-Simon observed: "The constant residence at Versailles caused a continual coming together of officials and persons employed, which kept everything going, got through affairs and gave more access to ministers and their business in one day than would have been possible in a fortnight had the court been in Paris. The benefit to the service of the king was incredible. It imposed orderliness on everybody and secured dispatch and facility to his affairs." One might recall Jean Racine's vision of princely duty:

High sovereignty may not be thus put off;
It's not a garment one may don and doff

. . . .

The interest of the State demands one king,
Who, with a constant order, rules his realms,
So that, home or abroad, his laws are
known.[36] ∎

FOOTNOTES

1. Emile Littré, *Dictionnaire de la langue française* (Paris, 1956), II, 994-97, in which Littré describes the art of making one's court.
2. To illustrate my point I will take only one picture, Rubens' *Coronation of the Queen* [Marie de' Medici] in Claudia Lyn Cahan, *Rubens* (New York, 1980), 14. Ms. Cahan notes that "the history in this painting is unembellished and very accurate. Princes and lords . . . could be identified by name."
3. André Campra in *Chefs d'Oeuvres Classiques de l'Opéra français* (Leipzig,

1880; reprinted New York, 1971), Vol. V: *Les Festes Vénitiennes*, 227-28, 290-93. André Raison's offer on the theme of "Vive le Roy" is discussed by Harry W. Gray in *Four French Organists-Composers* (Memphis, 1975), 49-51.
4. The poem has remained in manuscript. Archives des Affaires Etrangères, Mémoires et Documents, France 1202, fol. 96, dated Paris, October 3, 1714.

5. *Chefs d'Oeuvres Classiques de l'Opéra français*, V, 292. The ballet celebrates the signing of the peace of Ryswick, 1697.

6. Remy Saisselin, "Tivoli Revisited, or the Triumph of Culture," in *The Triumph of Culture: 18th Century Perspectives*, eds. Paul Fritz and David Williams (Toronto, 1972), 3.

7. The Medici were known not only for their love of painting and gardens but for music: an early opera, Pere's *Euridice*, was performed in 1600 to celebrate the wedding of Marie de' Medici and Henri IV of France. A recent and meticulously crafted book on the Pitti Palace is Malcolm Campbell's *Pietro da Cortona at the Pitti Palace* (Princeton, 1977). Charles Le Brun used the palace and its gardens as a model for the development of what Campbell calls "Academic Baroque Style of the French Court."

8. For Philip II, see Peter Pieson, *Philip II of Spain* (London, 1975), ch. IV, "The Court of Madrid and the Government of the Monarchy." A recent, excellent discussion of the Escorial is George Kubler, *Building the Escorial* (Princeton, 1982).

9. By a "conjuncture" — a word popularized in the literature of the *Annales* school of socio-historians — I mean a distillation and intensification of the historical process: the slow unfolding of the chance intersection of several cycles. See Samuel Kinser, "Annaliste Paradigm? The Geophysical Structuralism of Fernand Braudel," *American Historical Review*, LXXXVI (1981). On pp. 92-94, Kinser describes Braudel's concept of the conjuncture.

10. J. H. Elliott, "Revolts in the Spanish Monarchy," in Robert Forster and Jack P. Greene, eds., *Preconditions of Revolution in Early Modern Europe* (Baltimore, 1970), 109-30; Roland Mousnier, "The Fronde," ibid., 131-59.

11. *Mazarin: Homme d'Etat et Collectionneur 1602-1661. Exposition organisée pour le troisème centenaire de sa mort* (Paris, 1961), a richly annotated work describing 715 items from Mazarin's collections. There is an informative essay by Roger A. Weigert on "Mazarin Collectionneur" on pp. 145-75.

12. Francis Haskell, *Patrons and Painters. Art and Society in Baroque Italy*, revised and enlarged edition (New Haven, 1980), 181 ff; *Mazarin . . . Collectionneur*, 201-10. Giacomo Torelli reached Paris in 1645 just ahead of the Barberinis; most of his stage equipment was carried in the train of Francesco Barberini, who arrived in early 1646.

13. See Georges Durand, *Etats et Institutions, XVIe-XVIIIe Siècle* (Paris, 1969) 41-42, quoting from Pierre Clément, ed., *Lettres, instructions et mémoires de Colbert*, I, 535: "Mémoire dont le roy mesme dicta la substance au sieur Rose . . . [9 March 1661], "which records the notes of Mazarin's advice. John C. Rule, "Roi-Bureaucrate," in *Louis XIV and the Craft of Kingship*, ed. John C. Rule (Columbus, Ohio, 1970), 25, 40; John C. Rule, ed. *Louis XIV* (Englewood Cliffs, 1974), 43-44.

14. Luc Benoist, *Histoire de Versailles* (Paris, 1973), 15; F. Hamilton Hazelhurst, *Gardens of Illusion: The Genius of André Le Nostre* (Nashville, Tenn., 1980), 60-61; Rule, ed., *Louis XIV and the Craft of Kingship*, 40.

15. This paragraph and the following one are drawn from Pierre de Nolhac, *Versailles et la cour de France* (Paris, 1928), and Pierre de Nolhac, *La Création de Versailles, d'après les sources inédites* (Paris, 1901). An excellent summary of Louis XIV's reasons for abandoning Paris is given by Orest Ranum, "The Court and Capital of Louis XIV: Some Definitions and Reflections" in Rule, ed., *Louis XIV and the Craft of Kingship*, 266-69.

16. Duc de Saint-Simon, *Historical Memoirs: A Shortened Version*, ed. and trans. Lucy Norton, Vol. II: 1710-15 (London, 1968), 223.

17. Roger Guillemet, *Essai sur la Surintendance des Bâtiments du Roi sous le Regne personnel de Louis XIV* (Paris, 1912), 116-17. By 1680 Le Brun had enrolled on his record of "gages sur les fonds des Bâtiments" six painters and eleven sculptors. In the first inventory of the king's paintings, completed in the late 1680s, Le Brun, as *garde des tableaux*, lists 426 paintings dispersed among "diverses maisons royales" (p. 126). François Souchal, *French Sculptors of the Seventeenth and Eighteenth Centuries: The Reign of Louis XIV. An Illustrated Catalogue*, trans. Elsie and George Hill (2 vols., Oxford, 1977-81); Francis Haskell, "Famous but Unknown" (review of Souchal's volumes), *New York Review of Books* (April 15, 1982), p. 32; *Collections de Louis XIV: Dessins, albums, manuscrits*, 307. Yves Laissus speaks of the care with which Louis XIV arranged his collections; he also notes that these collections were "consacrée au goût du grand Roi, à la gloire et son temps." A distinction is made by Remy Saisselin between the *grand goût* of Louis XIV and the *goût modern* of the eighteenth century in his *The Rule of*

Reason and the Ruses of the Heart: A Philosophical Dictionary of Classical French Criticism and Aesthetic Issues (Cleveland, 1970), 276.

18. Quoted in Rule, ed., *Louis XIV and the Craft of Kingship*, 42, 41; an adaptation of the translation.

19. The description of the civil *Maison du Roi* is adapted from Marcel Marion, *Dictionnaire des Institutions de la France aux XVIIe et XVIIIe Siècles* (Paris, 1923), 346-52.

20. Michel Antoine, *Le Conseil du Roi sous le régne de Louis XV* (Paris, 1970), 45-77, affords the reader an excellent overview of Louis XV's reign. Also consult Roland Mousnier's comprehensive *Les Institutions de la France sous la Monarchie Absolue, 1598-1789, II: Les organes de l'Etat et la Société* (Paris, 1980), 152-60, "Chanceliers, Conseils, Ministres: 1661-1715."

21. Saint-Simon, *Memoirs*, II, 104.

22. Bibliothèque Nationale, Manuscrits français, Nouvelle Acquisitions 7492, October 2, 1692, fols. 406, 410.

23. Nathanial Hooke, *Correspondence* (2 vols., London, 1854), II, 424-26.

24. An excellent map by Nicolas de Fer, dated 1705, revealing the "pavillons" of the secretaries of state on either side of the Aisle des Ministres and in the palace itself; reproduced in Catherine Valgone, *Louis XIV et Louise de La Vallière à Versailles* (Paris, 1964), 15.

25. J[ean] Gillet, *Camille Le Tellier de Louvois: Bibliothécaire du Roi* (Paris, 1884), 229-31, which discusses the *cercle* of scholars attached to the King's Library; also Lionel Gossman, *Medievalism and the Ideologies of the Enlightenment* (Baltimore, 1968), 219 ff.

26. Maarten Ultee, *The Abbey of St. Germain des Prés in the Seventeenth Century* (New Haven, 1981), 28-34, for Montfaucon's Italian expeditions; Armand Baschet, *Histoire du Dépôt des Archives des Affaires Etrangéres* (Paris, 1875), 104-09, 140-43.

27. H. R. Trevor-Roper, *Princes and Artists: Patronage and Ideology at Four Habsburg Courts, 1517-1633* (New York, 1976).

28. The discussion of the king's collections is drawn from a magnificent work of scholarship cited before: *Collections de Louis XIV: dessins, albums, manuscrits*, especially pp. 10-31.

29. *Ibid.*, 20-21.

30. The description of the royal apartments is drawn from Claire Constans, "Les tableaux de Grand Appartement de Roi," *Le Revue du Louvre et des Musées de France*, III (1976), 157-73. In the same issue, which is devoted to Versailles, there is an article by Simone Hoog entitled "Le Goût du Roi: Les sculptures du Grand Appartement du Roi" (pp. 146-56).

31. *Tricentenaire du Rattachement de Lille à la France, Au Temps du Roi Soleil: Les Peintres de Louis XIV (1660-1715)* (Lille: Palais des Beaux-Arts, 1968), 58-60, for a description of the genesis of Louis XIV's portrait of 1702: "Avec cette composition, Rigaud a donné l'effigie la plus populaire du Grand Roi, celle qui traduit le mieux sa gloire et le pompe de sa cour." The portrait was probably inspired in part by Anthony Van Dyke's portrait of Charles I of England.

32. Constans, "Les tableaux," 172, fn. 64. Philip V presented the duc de Beauvilliers, while he was traveling to Spain with him, "une coppie du portrait du Roy d'Espagne sur l'original par Rigaud." It was a common practice for a painter to make multiple copies of his portrait so that the prince could reward the members of his entourage with a memento — a memory — of the occasion. See Archives des Affaires Etrangères, Correspondence Politique, Espagne 86, fol. 200, Desgranges to Colbert de Torcy, Amboise, December 12, 1700. Jonathan Brown and J. H. Elliott, *A Palace for a King: The Buen Retiro and the Court of Philip IV* (New Haven, 1980), 147 ff. Along with Campbell and Kubler this is a model for future work in the field. As the authors point out, there emerged in the sixteenth century a tradition for constructing a Hall of Princely Virtue, which borrowed from the "great cycles of glorification" of the Pope by Raphael. Louis XIV, rather than construct such a hall, chose to scatter contemporary royal portraits throughout the palace.

33. Bibliothèque Nationale, Manuscrits français 6679, fol. 141, which records the royal gift made to Cardinal-elect Cavalirini, March 14, 1696; Archives des Affaires Etrangères, Correspondence Politique, Angleterre 262, fol. 205ʳ, Torcy to d'Iberville, June 26, 1714, Marly.

34. Marcel Langlois, *Louis XIV et la Cour* (Paris, 1926), 266, drawn from the journal of Dangeau.

35. Saint-Simon, *Memoirs*, III. The description is adapted from pp. 404-405.

36. Rule, ed., *Louis XIV and the Craft of Kingship*, 42-43; Jean Racine, *Complete Plays*, trans. Samuel Solomon (New York, 1969), *The Theban Brothers*, Act I, Scene V, lines 203-04 and 206-08.

LOUIS XIV
AND
RELIGIOUS ABSOLUTISM
JULIUS R. RUFF

istorians frequently use the phrase "One king, one law, one faith" to summarize the goals of Louis XIV in creating his system of royal absolutism in France. By seventeenth-century standards the king certainly achieved the first two of his objectives. He exercised his personal authority without the aid of a first minister after 1661, and his codes regulating civil, criminal, and commercial law stood for over a century as monuments to the king's efforts at enforcing one law in his realm. The third of the Sun King's ends, in the opinion of most of his contemporaries, also was essential for absolute royal authority. Religious freedom was not a widely accepted doctrine in seventeenth-century Europe. The challenge of religious minorities to civil and ecclesiastical authorities in the recent past had caused civil warfare in France and in other countries. The enduring memory of that strife impelled the Sun King to seek the religious unification of his kingdom and his personal domination of its faith. Success in achieving religious unity, however, eluded Louis XIV and instead involved him in three bitter conflicts between church and state.[1]

The Huguenots, the largest Protestant group in France, were the greatest obstacle to the realm's religious unity. Modern historians estimate the number of these French Calvinists to have been between 850,000 and 1,000,000 persons in 1661, or about 4 or 5 percent of the kingdom's population. The influence of this minority, moreover, was greater than its numbers might suggest. Even though many of the powerful noble families who led Huguenot revolts in the past had returned to the Catholic fold, Huguenots still included in their ranks two Marshals of France,

Turenne and Schomberg, one of the king's great admirals, Duquesne, and many lesser officers of the crown. In addition, Huguenot financiers, merchants, and manufacturers wielded considerable economic power in some parts of France, and in the great port of Bordeaux they controlled the West Indian trade.[2]

The legal presence of these Calvinists in France rested on the protections accorded them by the Edict of Nantes. Issued in 1598 by the Sun King's grandfather, King Henri IV, that document represented an attempt to end the religious warfare of the sixteenth century by a policy of toleration. While Henri IV recognized Catholicism as France's official religion, he granted certain religious freedoms to the Huguenots, and he accorded them civil rights equal to those of his Catholic subjects. In an additional order, Henri IV also permitted the Calvinists to fortify about two hundred towns as insurance against the resumption of religious warfare.

This settlement maintained the religious peace during the reign of Henri IV, but in the reign of his son, Louis XIII, several Protestant revolts broke out. The response of Louis XIII's great minister was swift. Cardinal Richelieu, whose forcefulness is apparent in his portrait, destroyed the fortified strong points that had made the Huguenots "a state within a state," and had provided them with the means to defy the crown. At the same time, however, the cardinal reaffirmed Protestant religious rights at Alais in 1629 and thereby assured the monarchy of Huguenot loyalty even during the Fronde revolt of 1648-52.[3]

In the first years of his reign, Louis XIV moved slowly and sporadically against the Huguenots. Little of what we know of the king in this period suggests deep religious impulses for his action against the Protestants. Reasons of state instead seem to have motivated him, especially the wish to assure the realm's political stability by gradually enforcing religious uniformity. Consequently Louis' policy toward his Huguenot subjects prior to 1679 was one of strict enforcement of the narrowest limits of the Edict of Nantes. The king hoped, as he wrote in his *Mémoires* in 1671, that the Calvinists might be forced "thereby to consider from time to time by themselves, and without constraint, if they had any good reason for depriving themselves of the advantages that they could share with my other subjects."[4]

The Sun King defined the limits of the Edict of Nantes in a number of decrees. He decreed, for example, that Huguenots could maintain churches only in those locations where they had worshipped continuously since 1598. This law provided the legal justification for the destruction of perhaps two-thirds of all Calvinist sanctuaries. In addition, individual Huguenots were penalized for their faith by exclusion from certain public offices and by statutory limitations on their practice of certain professions, including law, medicine, and a number of skilled crafts. At the same time that the crown made Protestant worship more difficult and applied economic pressures on Huguenots to convert to Roman Catholicism, the king created positive incentives for members of the minority sect to adhere to the Church of Rome. Converts were enticed with offers of moratoria on their personal debts and, after 1676, even with outright payments through the Conversion Fund (Caisse de Conversions). Thousands accepted these offers and made at least superficial conversions.

In the 1680s royal policy toward the Huguenots became more stringent as Louis XIV initiated a final, harsh drive to create "one faith." Some historians have sought to find the reasons for this change of policy in a deepened royal piety that impelled Louis XIV to root out heresy. Certainly the aspect of a crusade is suggested by the commemorative medals and marbles in this exhibit. But much recent scholarship suggests instead that the king's policy again was dictated by reasons of state, not of faith. Foreign concerns propelled religious unity to the forefront of the king's attentions. The Dutch War (1672-79) seems to

have been a watershed event in the definition of royal policy toward the Huguenots. The Dutch War cost Louis some of France's traditional Protestant allies, and after the Peace of Nymegen Louis' attempt to push French boundaries eastward by the judicial action of his Chambres de Réunion cost him more non-Catholic allies. Henceforth, the king would have to seek allies in the Catholic states of Europe, and the Sun King's personal Catholicity would have to be beyond doubt. But just as circumstances dictated a Catholic foreign policy, the king's relations with Rome could not have been worse. Louis resolutely refused papal requests that he aid in the defense of eastern Europe against the Turks, and, as we shall see, the Sun King's conflict with the papacy over the rights of the Gallican Church pushed France almost to the point of a break with Rome. In order to appear a firm son of the Church in Catholic Europe, and to avoid a final schism, Louis therefore seems to have resolved on his final attack on his Protestant subjects.[5]

THE KING'S POLICY AGAIN WAS DICTATED BY REASONS OF STATE, NOT OF FAITH

The early 1680s witnessed increased pressure on the Huguenots to abjure their faith. Royal ordinances further restricted the religious freedoms of Huguenots and their pastors, closed still more careers to Protestants, and levied discriminatory higher taxes on them while reducing the imposts paid by members of the reformed faith adopting Catholicism. Other pressures on the Huguenots included the *dragonnades*, the forced quartering of royal soldiers in Protestant homes in an era in which the army was recruited from the lowest orders of society. The first *dragonnades*, in Poitou in 1681, achieved the desired effect of numerous conversions to the official faith.

The mounting pressure on the Huguenots culminated on October 17, 1685, when the king signed the Edict of Fontainebleau revoking the Edict of Nantes. In this document, the Sun King sought to destroy the Huguenot movement by ordering the destruction of its remaining sanctuaries, forbidding its religious assemblies, and enjoining the conversion or exile of its clergy. In order to eradicate all remnants of the faith, the edict forbade instruction in the Huguenot creed, required that children of Huguenot parents be baptized in the Roman Catholic Church, and levied penalties on new converts to Catholicism who relapsed into their former beliefs. Finally, the edict required punishment of all those who might try to flee France's new religious order.

Reactions to the Edict of Fontainebleau varied. French Catholics welcomed the edict, but it won Louis XIV no reconciliation with Rome. European Protestant powers responded with hostility. The Elector of Brandenburg issued his own Edict of Potsdam welcoming Huguenots to his realm, and by the end of the seventeenth century Berlin was reported to be one-sixth French-speaking in population. Some two hundred thousand Huguenots fled France in defiance of the law to accept religious asylum in Brandenburg and in other Protestant lands, including the United Provinces and North America.[6] The coreligionists of these refugees who remained in France found themselves subjected to *dragonnades* and other pressures to force the abjuration of their faith. Thousands abandoned their Calvinist creed, but it was soon apparent that the Edict of Fontainebleau had not reunified France in the Roman Catholic Church.

Court records for the years following 1685 reveal continued resistance to the new religious order. Many of the new Catholics fulfilled only the minimum spiritual duty of their new faith, the Easter obligation. Other Huguenots persisted illegally in their Protestant faith, continuing to assemble for services. In the years after 1685, some two thousand such individuals paid for their defiance of royal law in sentences to service on the royal galleys, generally for life terms. And there were countless individual acts of defiance as well, such as the militant group of Protestant women operating in the Bordelais near Sainte-Foy. These women, known as "The Strong Women," visited the homes of Huguenot poor in the 1680s with gifts of food to obviate the need for conversion for royal financial incentives. They also visited the deathbeds of converts to Catholicism to exhort them to one last act of defiance by refusing extreme unction and by dying in the Calvinist faith.[7]

The faith of many, though, seemed only strengthened by persecution. A new religious fervor among the Huguenots of the South led to the revolt of the Protestant Camisards of the Cévennes Mountains in 1702. This revolt engaged thousands of soldiers badly needed elsewhere during the War of the Spanish Succession, and Huguenot defiance

of the new religious order continued even when the royal army restored peace to the area. By the last days of Louis XIV, large Huguenot religious assemblies were being held in the old Protestant areas in defiance of the royal law. Held outdoors in isolated areas distant from the eyes of the authorities, these "Assemblies in the Desert" persisted until a freer religious climate returned to France on the eve of the Revolution of 1789.[8] The efforts of Louis XIV to extirpate Protestantism were a failure; the same result awaited the king's attack on Catholic dissent.

Jansenism threatened the unity of seventeenth-century French Catholicism. Its roots extended to the earliest centuries of Christianity because its main exponent, Bishop Cornelius Jansen of Ypres (1585-1638), drew from the writings of St. Augustine for his work *Augustinius*. Drawing on Jansen's work, Jansenists advocated a strict personal piety that they claimed was missing in the teachings of the seventeenth-century Church, and they advanced a principle of salvation in which the will of the individual counted for nothing and God's predestined grace was the soul's only justification. This aspect of Jansenist theology particularly was opposed by the Jesuits, who were proponents of a theology offering salvation to all believers.[9]

In France a number of eloquent advocates strengthened the Jansenist movement. The abbot of Saint-Cyran was its first great preacher, and the movement soon drew Mother Angélique Arnauld (1591-1661). Mother Angélique, the abbess of Port Royal-des-Champs, whose portrait appears with this exhibit, made her convent and its annex, Port-Royal in Paris, centers of Jansenism. Jansenism also attracted the abbess' brother, Antoine Arnauld. A theologian, Antoine Arnauld wrote a stinging attack on the Jesuits in *Of Frequent Communion*, a work condemning what the Jansenists saw as spiritual laxity in the offering of the sacrament to sinners who were not truly penitent. The most famous attack on the Jesuits, however, came from the pen of the brilliant mathematician Blaise Pascal (1623-62), whose portrait and writings appear in this exhibit. Pascal used the weapon of satire against the Jesuits in his *Provincial Letters*.[10]

Theological debate between Jesuits and Jansenists in France raged for some years before Rome acted to suppress the controversy. In his bull of 1643, *In eminenti,* Pope Urban VIII banned circulation of

the *Augustinius,* though the order had little effect in France since the pope died early the next year. An encyclical of Pope Innocent X in 1653 specifically condemned as heretical or false five propositions generally associated with the Jansenist position in their debate with the Jesuits. Pope Alexander VII strengthened this condemnation in 1657 by expressly declaring the five propositions to be present in the *Augustinius.* Jansenists responded by affirming that the propositions were indeed heretical, but they vehemently denied that the ideas formed part of Jansen's work.

This theological dispute still engaged Jesuits and Jansenists when Louis XIV commenced his personal rule in 1661. The Sun King had little understanding of the theological nuances of the debate, but he could not ignore the very real danger of Jansenism to French Catholic unity. Moreover, as recent studies of the contents of seventeenth-century personal libraries reveal, Pascal was only one of many educated and influential Frenchmen attracted to Jansenism. Jansenism also appeared to present a political danger to the crown. Although many disciples of the movement disavowed any role in politics, numerous Jansenists maintained ties to former leaders of the Fronde, a revolt crushed less than a decade earlier. This apparent link between religious dissidence and political subversion contributed to Louis' decision to enforce theological unity among French Catholics.

The authority of both the crown and the French clerical establishment therefore combined to seek the adherence of Catholic clergy to a formulary specifically condemning the five alleged Jansenist propositions. Even when reinforced by a papal decree, however, the formulary obtained the signatures of the most ardent Jansenists only with their reservation that the condemned ideas were not in the *Augustinius.* Louis XIV responded to this recalcitrance by ordering the arrest of Jansenist leaders and the burning of the *Provincial Letters.* For its part, the French Church denied sacraments to the nonconforming nuns of Port-Royal.

France, in fact, was approaching religious division when Pope Clement IX arranged a compromise in the Peace of the Church of 1669.

> THE SUN KING HAD LITTLE UNDERSTANDING OF THEOLOGICAL NUANCES, BUT HE COULD NOT IGNORE THE VERY REAL DANGER OF JANSENISM

Under this agreement, the formulary was signed by all clerics, but ecclesiastical authorities did not probe the signatories' doubts about the appearance of the condemned ideas in the *Augustinius.* The agreement did forbid the discussion of the issues raised by the Jansenists, but the ensuing religious peace permitted Jansenist leaders to emerge from prison or from hiding and allowed the nuns of Port-Royal again to receive sacraments.

The religious peace endured for over a decade. It ended briefly in 1679 when the king, freed from foreign concerns at the end of the Dutch War, resumed his persecution of the Jansenists. Louis banned postulants at Port-Royal in the hope that the existing generation of Jansenist nuns would be the last, and royal oppression drove Antoine Arnauld into exile in the Spanish Netherlands. But other concerns, including a conflict with the papacy in the matter of the *régale,* soon directed royal attention away from the Jansenists and granted them a few additional years' respite from harrassment.

Relieved of persecution, Jansenists spread their ideas between 1679 and the end of the seventeenth century. Jansenist influence particularly grew in the ranks of the parish clergy, among whom it came to be associated with Richerism. Richerists held that Church authority was not the sole province of the pope and the episcopate, but should involve the whole clergy, including the *curés.* This fusion of Jansenism with the disturbingly democratic ideas of Richerism alarmed the crown. Still more unsettling to the king and his advisers was the appearance of a new edition of a popular devotional work in 1693. In his *Moral Reflections on the New Testament,* the Oratorian Pasquier Quesnel (1634-1719) strongly stated both Jansenist and Richerist ideas.

Events in 1701 also fueled a growing concern at court about the influence of Jansenism. In 1701 a priest and nephew of Pascal, Louie Perier, died, espousing until the end the Jansenist position that the five propositions were heretical while maintaining a "respectful silence" on their presence in Jansen's work. When the Sorbonne faculty was asked if absolution could be granted to such an individual, the Jansenist issue grew more pressing since the theologians asserted that the deceased had a right to absolution. This decision by theologians of the kingdom's premier university coincided with a new foreign crisis, the War of the Spanish Succession, and it seems to have helped persuade Louis XIV and his advisers of a renewed danger of religious division. The arrest of Quesnel resulted from this conviction, and reinforced it as well, since the theologian's captured papers convinced the crown of the existence of widespread Jansenist subversion.

The first step in Louis' renewed campaign against the Jansenists was to secure the bull *Vineam Domini* in 1705 requiring all French churchmen to acknowledge the presence of the five propositions in the *Augustinius*. Again the Jansenists resisted, and in 1709 Louis XIV secured papal permission to close Port-Royal. By royal decree the convent's nuns were dispersed, and to prevent Port-Royal from becoming a Jansenist shrine, the bodies of deceased nuns buried at Port-Royal-des-Champs were reburied elsewhere and the nunnery's buildings were razed.

To complete the attack on Jansenism, Louis obtained in 1713 yet another bull, *Unigenitus,* specifically condemning a number of ideas in Quesnel's *Moral Reflections.* This bull, like its anti-Jansenist predecessors, was never completely accepted in France, and it remained a political issue for much of the eighteenth century. That it became such an issue, frustrating royal efforts to stamp out Jansenism, is ironic indeed. Many in France found the bull hard to accept, because to them it represented an infringement of traditional French ecclesiastical independence from Rome. That freedom, embodied in the liberties of the Gallican Church, had once been defended by Louis XIV himself in the third of his church-state conflicts.[11]

The liberties of the Gallican Church commanded considerable support in France, though there was little concensus on the exact meaning of these freedoms. For French bishops, Gallican liberty meant a decentralized Church in which primacy rested with Church councils rather than the pope. To the king, the Sorbonne, and the lower clergy, Gallican rights represented the royal leadership of the Church established in the Concordat of 1516. That agreement between king and pope provided for royal appointment of bishops, abbots, and priors and accorded the papacy only confirmation of the sovereign's nominees. The young Louis' vision of

his power within the French Church manifested this strain of Gallicanism in the extreme. The king had little regard for the Papacy, and he wrote in his *Mémoires* for the dauphin's instruction that: "You should, therefore, first rest assured that kings are absolute lords and naturally have free and full disposition of all of the goods possessed by clergymen as well as by laymen." Such a view led Louis XIV into conflict with one of the most implacable pontiffs of the age, Pope Innocent XI, and brought France to the point of schism with Rome. The issue in this conflict over royal prerogatives within the Church was the *régale.*[12]

The French crown long had possessed the *régale temporelle* — the right to receive the revenues of most French dioceses while they were without bishops. This power applied to all French sees except those in territories recently added to the realm, but in 1673 a royal edict extended the *régale temporelle* to the newly acquired dioceses. The issue for the king in thus extending his rights was not a financial one. The monarchy returned two-thirds of the revenues so collected to the diocese and retained one-third in a fund to aid in the conversion of Protestants. Rather, Louis seems to have sought the extension of royal power and the administrative unification of the realm. The king's simultaneous claim of new appointive power in the *régale spirituelle* also suggests that reasons of state again motivated royal actions. The *régalle spirituelle* would have endowed the king with enhanced authority in the Church by permitting him to appoint holders of certain convents and other Church offices in the absence of a bishop.

The first resistance to royal pretensions came from the Jansenist bishops of Alet and Pamiers, who refused to apply the new royal orders in their dioceses. The bishops soon found support in Pope Innocent XI, a pious and uncompromising pontiff chosen in 1676. Louis' response to papal intervention in the matter of the *régale* in 1682 was the convocation of an assembly of French clergy supporting the king's position. Initially the assembly sought a settlement of the royal dispute with Rome, but when Innocent XI proved unwilling to compromise, the assembly adopted the four articles of Gallican religious liberty on behalf of the French Church. In these articles, the assembly joined the disparate elements of Gallican rights into a strong denunciation of papal supremacy in the Church. The assembly declared that kings were not subject to popes in secular matters; that councils, rather than the pope, held primacy in the Church; that the pope could do nothing contrary to the liberties of the French Church; and that papal decrees on matters of faith could not be final until they received the general approval of the Church. The adoption of these articles, strongly challenging papal authority, left France perilously close to schism.

The four articles brought papal condemnation and with it Innocent's refusal to confirm any French bishop accepting this statement of Gallican liberties. The result of this latter papal action was thirty-five vacant sees by 1688. Compromise seemed impossible for both sides in the struggle, and even Louis XIV's revocation of the Edict of Nantes failed to soften papal intransigence. Instead, the king's differences with Rome reached a crisis point in a dispute over diplomatic immunities. In 1684 Pope Innocent XI deprived foreign embassies in Rome of the franchise — the privilege of granting asylum to anyone on embassy grounds — claiming that such a right impaired Roman law enforcement. Only the French embassy refused to obey the papal order, and Louis XIV, to protect French prestige, continued to claim the franchise. The arrival in Rome of the marquis de Lavardin, newly appointed French ambassador to Rome, with a small army to defend the Sun King's claim to the franchise, elicited the final blow in the struggle between the Sun King and the pope. Innocent XI excommunicated Louis XIV and his advisers on November 18, 1687.

Louis appealed his excommunication to the next Church council, seized the papal enclave at Avignon, and launched a campaign of printed vilification of the pope. But Innocent XI remained impervious to such attacks until his death in August, 1689. With a new pope, Innocent XII, settlement of the quarrel became possible. Indeed, for France, the pressures of a new war, the War of the League of Augsburg, made compromise most desirable. In the final composition of the dispute, the papacy lifted the ban on Louis XIV and recognized the Sun King's right to the *régale temporelle* in all but two dioceses. For his part, Louis XIV pledged that the four articles would not be taught in France. Most important perhaps, the king abandoned his role as defender of Gallican rights and pursued an ultramontane policy for the rest of his reign.

Louis XIV died in 1715 at the age of seventy-six years. In his last days, had he chosen to do so, the king might have surveyed on every side the failure of his entire religious policy. The Huguenots still practiced their faith, albeit underground. The influence of the Jansenists continued to grow, and indeed they were instrumental in securing the expulsion of their old Jesuit enemies from France in 1762. And Gallican rights would never again be advanced as strongly by the French monarchy as in the four articles. France would never possess the Sun King's vision of "one faith." ■

FOOTNOTES

1. Basic studies of Louis XIV's reign include Pierre Goubert, *Louis XIV and Twenty Million Frenchmen*, trans. Anne Carter (New York, 1970), and John B. Wolf, *Louis XIV* (New York, 1968).

2. Samuel Mours, "Essai sommaire de géographie du Protestantisme réformé au XVIIᵉ siècle," *Bulletin de la Société de l'Histoire du Protestantisme français* (hereinafter cited as *BSHPF*), CXI (1965), 303-321; CXII (1966), 19-36. Also Jean Orcibal, *Etat présent des recherches sur la répartition géographique des "Nouveaux Catholiques" à la fin du XVIIᵉ siècle* (Paris, 1948).

3. The most accessible history of the Huguenots in English is George A. Rothrock, *The Huguenots: A Biography of a Minority* (Chicago, 1979). Standard French studies include Daniel Ligou, *Le Protestantisme en France de 1598 à 1715* (Paris, 1968), and Robert Mandrou, *et al.*, *Histoire de Protestants en France* (Toulouse, 1977).

4. Louis XIV, *Mémoires for the Instruction of the Dauphin*, ed. Paul Sonnino (New York, 1970), 56.

5. Jean Orcibal, *Louis XIV et les Protestants: "le Cabale des accommodeurs de religion," la Caisse des Conversions et la revocation de l'Edit de Nantes* (Paris, 1951), 91-94, 102-103. Orcibal's views are summarized in English in his "Louis XIV and the Edict of Nantes," in Ragnhild Hatton (ed.), *Louis XIV and Absolutism* (Columbus, 1976), 154-76. Sustaining Orcibal's interpretation are Emile G. Léonard, *Histoire générale du Protestantisme, II: L'établissement (1564-1700)* (Paris, 1961), 373; and Daniel Robert, "Louis XIV et les Protestants," *XVIIᵉ siècle*, Nos. 76-77 (1967), 39-52.

6. Warren C. Scoville, *The Persecution of the Huguenots and French Economic Development, 1680-1720* (Berkeley, 1960).

7. Samuel Mours, "Note sur les galériens protestants (1683-1775)," *BSHPF*, CXVI (1970), 178-231; Paul Bamford, *Fighting Ships and Prisons: The Mediterranean Galleys of France in the Age of Louis XIV* (Minneapolis, 1973), 182-83; Julius R. Ruff, *Crime, Justice, and Public Order in Old Regime France* (London, 1984).

8. On the popular mentality of the Protestants in the region see Emmanuel Le Roy Ladurie, *The Peasants of Languedoc* (Urbana, 1976), 265-86; and Henri Bosc, "La Guerre des Camisards. Son caractère. Ses conséquences," *BSHPF*, CXIX (1973), 335-55.

9. The best available English history of Jansenism is Alexander Sedgwick, *Jansenism in Seventeenth-Century France: Voices in the Wilderness* (Charlottesville, 1977).

10. A good biography in English is Jean Steinmann, *Pascal*, trans. Martin Turnell (New York, 1966).

11. On Jesuit-Jansenist conflict in the eighteenth century see Dale Van Kley, *The Jansenists and the Expulsion of the Jesuits from France, 1757-1765* (New Haven, 1975).

11. Paul Sonnino, *Louis XIV's View of the Papacy (1661-1667)* (Berkeley, 1966); Louis XIV, *Mémoires*, 165. The basic study of the conflict between Louis XIV and Innocent XI is Jean Orcibal: *Louis XIV contre Innocent XI: les appels au futur concile de 1688 et l'opinion française* (Paris, 1949).

LOUIS XIV AND EUROPE:
WAR AND DIPLOMACY
IN THE SEVENTEENTH CENTURY
JOHN T. O'CONNOR

n the introduction to his *Age of Louis XIV*, Voltaire assured his readers that he would not subject them to details of military campaigns and sieges; such events were inconsequential in the perspective of centuries when compared to cultural history. In political and military matters, he planned to concentrate only on "those great events which have determined the destiny of empires." Throughout the work he would include only information that might seize the attention of future generations and thus direct them toward "the love of virtue, the arts, and the fatherland."[1] Despite these clear intentions, in the writing of his history Voltaire was ineluctably drawn into fairly extensive coverage of the wars and alliances that were so much a part of the Sun King's reign. How could he have done otherwise when discussing a king who had brought into being the largest military force on the European continent since the armies of Ancient Rome?

It was predictable that Louis should have been frequently portrayed by artists and sculptors as a Roman emperor or in the guise of Mars. But still more appropriate is that in the pendant rooms dedicated to War and Peace at either end of the Hall of Mirrors at Versailles, the sculpture and decoration pertaining to war are distinctly superior as works of art when compared to those depicting peace. This artistic imbalance is reenforced by a most sobering statistic: "during the whole course of the seventeenth century there were only seven complete calendar years in which there was no war between European states, the years 1610, 1669-71, 1680-82."[2] As a munificent patron of the arts, Louis XIV was justly hailed by Voltaire. Yet for much of his reign, royal subsidies to artists and writers fluctuated according to the needs and fortunes of war — a familiar fact of life in today's world.

War is indisputably one of the major elements in state building, in the development of bureaucracies, in the streamlining of tax collection in early modern Europe. Certainly this was true in France during Louis XIV's extraordinarily long reign (1661-1715). Born in 1638 in the midst of the Thirty Years' War, Louis died in 1715 at the end of the longest and bloodiest war in his reign. Warfare was tragically and inextricably linked to the competitive state system that absorbed the attention and consumed the human and material resources of European rulers. Since one of the principal duties of the nobility of Europe was to fight for their country, warfare was also inseparably a part of the culture and assumptions of European aristocracies. As the first aristocrat of the realm, a king acted on the largest stage of all. It was axiomatic that a king would be the chief warrior, the protector of his people. In seventeenth-century France, this role was further bound up with the pursuit of *gloire* by members of the ruling class.

As a term or concept, *gloire* cannot simply be translated into English as "glory." It was thought of as a lifelong quest by an aristocrat, something well above the ambitions of mere commoners. In practice, it meant testing your mettle, rising to challenges, attempting to fulfill your potential. If you succeeded, it might be said of you at the end of your life that you had achieved your *gloire*. Your reputation would then resonate among your descendants, inspiring them to emulate your striving and your successes.

To achieve his own *gloire*, Louis XIV would have to fulfill his perceived obligations to God, man, and himself. The pursuit of *gloire* by a king commanding an army of 400,000 troops could be a chilling sight in that place and time. Yet Louis understood that if a king failed to protect a kingdom from foreign enemies, he would forfeit any hope of achieving his *gloire*. To be sure, "protecting a kingdom" could be variously interpreted. For Louis and numerous other rulers of that era, states might best be preserved through expansion. However we may wish to judge him, it is clear that Louis XIV did not have a monopoly on predatory initiatives.[3]

For centuries, a principal concern for French rulers and ministers was to extend the frontiers of the kingdom farther away from Paris. Louis would continue this tradition, seeking more buffer zones, more defensible frontiers. It must be emphasized that seventeenth-century Frenchmen did not seek "natural frontiers" (a major slogan in the French Revolution) but rather what the twentieth-century French historian Gaston Zeller has referred to as "strategic frontiers." Thus they were anxious to acquire territory and fortifications on the east bank of the Rhine or deep into the Holy Roman Empire as well as strategic sites in northern Italy. As Professor Zeller put it, "the ideal frontier was not only, nor even principally, that which sheltered the French from invasion; it was above all that which would permit them to carry their arms outside of the kingdom."[4]

Louis had been reared in the midst of a war that pitted the Habsburg dynasties of Spain and Austria against Bourbon France. For generations, the Spanish Habsburgs controlled territories that virtually encircled France; they were abetted by their Austrian cousins who possessed territory in Alsace and the Rhineland in addition to their holdings in Central Europe and who were repeatedly elected as Holy Roman Emperors. It is largely owing to this tradition that the king thought almost exclusively of land warfare, of expansion at the expense of land powers. Although he would accord funds for naval and colonial projects proposed by Jean-Baptiste Colbert and other ministers, the sea and colonies scarcely engaged his imagination. Indeed, he visited a French warship only once in his entire reign, during a tour of Dunkirk.

> FOR LOUIS AND NUMEROUS OTHER RULERS OF THAT ERA, STATES MIGHT BEST BE PRESERVED THROUGH EXPANSION

Louis XIV's preparation for kingship was most influenced by Cardinal Jules Mazarin, the Italian statesman who became principal minister of France in 1642 upon the death of Cardinal Richelieu. Young Louis' earliest memories included Mazarin's role in the negotiations to end the Thirty Years' War (Peace of Westphalia, 1648); the civil wars or Fronde, which lasted from 1648 to 1653; and the ongoing war between France and Spain that ended in 1659 with the Peace of the Pyrenees, a peace treaty that included Louis' betrothal to the Spanish princess Maria Teresa. Throughout the first two decades of his life, Mazarin's statecraft and instruction were to exert an overwhelming influence on the young man's perception of the world and the uses to be made of the power at the disposal of a monarch.[5]

One vital element in Mazarin's diplomacy — retained by Louis XIV during his personal reign — was the liberal use of subsidies and *gratifications*, cash and/or presents that were liberally dispensed across Europe so as to maximize French influence and advance French interests abroad. Historically, it was in France's interest to diminish the power of Spain anywhere in Europe and the power of the emperor in the German states. In the aftermath of the Thirty Years' War, Mazarin especially sought to cultivate a clientele of German princes in the western Empire whose territories might serve as a buffer zone as well as a salient for the furtherance of French designs, thus transforming foreign states into strategic frontiers. (This was especially so with the League of the Rhine, to be discussed below.) As puny as their military power may have been, these border territories had a strategic and political significance far in excess of their real power. Sovereigns of the electorates of Cologne, Mainz, and Trier, or of the principality of Liège — to provide only a few examples — were beset with internal difficulties, such as the attempt to win the assent of regional estates for new tax levies, the struggle to maintain even a small army, and the determined opposition of independent cities like Cologne. When such rulers allied with France, the subsidies they received were in large part earmarked for the building of armies that might fight next to French units when war came. But that same army might be used as well to dominate local opposition in a prince's territory, or to eliminate the possibility of effective representative assemblies in his lands. This trend toward "absolutism" was largely successful in the German states during the *ancien régime.*[6]

In addition to offensive-defensive alliances, pacts of neutrality were occasionally drawn up. But "neutrality" in seventeenth-century Europe was far different from what is understood by the term today. A treaty of neutrality might give a major power the right to peacable passage (*transitus innoxius*) through another state. The consequences of this right could be "the permission to buy — indeed, to carry off — provisions for the troops and the authorization to occupy strong points in the territory. Besides, the neutral state tolerated the recruitment of volunteers."[7] In some instances, the French were able to use the "neutral state" as a boulevard en route to the war front, recruiting troops, maintaining warehouses, and building pontoon bridges. In more recent times, such an arrangement would be tantamount to an offensive alliance.

Although political, military, and strategic considerations take up most of the space in the dispatches to and from the king and his ministers, they were far from lax in providing for the French economy as well as for trade benefits for French merchants. Occupied territories were expected to pay *contributions* for the upkeep of the French war machine. Annexed territories were subject to taxation and various forms of economic exploitation. The French tried to eliminate or reduce tariffs and tolls on their products in client states; Liège is a notable example here. Colbert was active in accumulating information on the trade relations between the Netherlands and the Rhineland, similar in kind to the inquiries made through ambassadors across Europe with an eye toward linking French economic interests more closely to her foreign policy.[8]

The first few years of Louis' personal reign, begun in 1661 after the death of Mazarin, were notable chiefly for administrative consolidation and the formation of working relationships with the team of ministers that would serve him in the next decade. These ministers, most of them aides or protégés of Mazarin, included Colbert for finances, Michel Le Tellier for war, and Hugues de Lionne for foreign affairs. Lionne helped to shape and execute the foreign policy of France and worked well with the young monarch. It was Lionne who early perceived that the king intended to occupy himself with the affairs of state, to devote many hours each day to the "*métier du roi*" — the craft of kingship.

What Lionne had observed was not immediately evident to spectators on the fringes of power. What they saw was a king engaged in a swirl of diversions that included tournaments, masked balls, ballets, and theatrical performances. As pleasant as these may have been, they were not enough: like many rulers of his age, Louis craved military exploits. The first such occasion came in 1664 when ten thousand French troops were sent to aid the Christian army in the Holy Roman Empire in a struggle against the Ottoman Turks. Of special interest here is that the itinerary worked out for those troops en route to the Eastern front was deliberately planned so that they would march through areas in Alsace that disputed French sovereignty as per the treaty terms of Westphalia and through territories in the Empire whose rulers hesitated in allying with France. Louis clearly aimed to frighten German princes into cooperation or submission.

The intimidation of princes (German and non-German alike) proceeded apace during the War of Devolution (1667-68) in which the French sought to gain territory in the Spanish Netherlands — the Belgian area — after the death of Philip IV of Spain in 1665. This war afforded Louis his first experience of battle as monarch. The opening of the campaign was famous for the leisurely royal progresses, with Louis in the company of his queen, his mistresses, and a splendidly caparisoned entourage. The rude shock of war was first felt when the enemy cut dikes and opened sluices to flood fields and roads in the path of the French army. Of still greater significance was the development of an alliance between the Dutch, the English, and the Swedes for the purpose of preventing a French seizure of the Spanish Netherlands. On the surface, the members of this Triple Alliance presented themselves as well-intentioned intermediaries between France and Spain. But in a secret clause they pledged to enter the war on the side of Spain if Louis XIV did not accept their good offices and come to terms. The king soon found out about this secret pact and determined to have his revenge. After reaching terms with the Spaniards — acquiring some territory in the Spanish Netherlands in the course of concluding a peace in 1668 — he set to work to isolate the Dutch from their allies before invading them.

As the Sun King's foreign policy was beginning to assume its characteristic form, the reaction of other states to Louis' rather peremptory manner began to follow an equally characteristic pattern. Such was the case with members of the League of the Rhine, an alliance fashioned by Mazarin in the 1650s. The league, which was renewable every three years, had as its object the protection of "German liberties." Membership was rather evenly distributed among Catholic and Protestant states; France, its most powerful member, gained entrance as a guarantor of the Treaty of Westphalia. Though the French saw the league as a means of checking Habsburg power, the alliance could only be truly effective when it served (or seemed to serve) the interests and aspirations of the German princes who were members. The league had been an integral part of Mazarin's system of French

Detail of Catalogue 51

diplomacy, but Louis XIV's quest for prestige and hegemony warped this system into a means of securing allies for offensive campaigns in western Europe. The league dissolved by 1668 as a result of French involvement in the Devolution War. Louis then tried to restitch the system together via bilateral treaties, offensive-defensive alliances, and neutrality pacts prior to the Dutch War. In this effort he was fairly successful since, in the words of a contemporary satirist, "money is a saddle that fits all horses."[9]

The reaction of German states toward France included elements of suspicion, even fear and dread; but there remained a fierce desire for Spanish and Dutch land along with fortifications, coveted objects that might be won as part of a French alliance. In the Dutch War, such princes soon found themselves in ruinous campaigns, drawn into the vortex of French ambitions and then faced with the riposte of allied coalitions resisting those ambitions. Greed and rapacity preceded anguish and disaster in the best tradition of medieval

morality plays.

Before the first shots were fired in the spring of 1672, French money proved sufficient to detach both England and Sweden from their union with the Dutch in the Triple Alliance. The Austrian Habsburg emperor, Leopold I, was willing to remain neutral — the Dutch were republicans and Protestant and surely might be taken down a few pegs with no damage to imperial interests — provided France did not invade Spanish lands in the march toward Amsterdam. In the opening months of the campaign, only Brandenburg-Prussia sided with the Dutch as the French commenced a series of sieges. Though the Dutch offered numerous concessions to win a peace, Louis' conditions proved impossible. He seemed determined to smash the Dutch, economically, politically, militarily. He seemed further determined not only to win victories against Brandenburg-Prussia in the Germanies but to occupy towns and territories in the Empire as well. What really did he want? How far did he intend to go? In the first year of the Dutch War, the English statesman Sir William Temple compared Louis to "a man that leaps into the water in strength and vigour, and with pleasure. [No one can say] how far he will swim; which will be, till he is stopped by currents or accidents, or grows weary, or has a mind to do something else."[10]

Soon enough, French troops were invading Spanish territory in the Netherlands. That course of action, coupled with French occupation of German territory even after Brandenburg made a separate peace with France, led Leopold I to declare war, a war joined by a number of German states including some that had until recently been allied with France. A war originally intended to punish the Dutch was now broadening into a war against a far-reaching coalition seeking to check French aggrandizement.

Within France itself, the strains of war and the attendant increases in taxation led to major revolts in Bordeaux and Brittany and to scores of uprisings across the kingdom. Such revolts were usually

crushed with considerable brutality, further exacerbating the grim atmosphere. Several plots against the king and his government were uncovered; some French conspirators, in league with the Spanish and Dutch, planned break-away movements of provinces in the north and south of France and the formation of separate states under the leadership of French Protestants, or Huguenots.[11] Effective police work and alert government surveillance of the movement of enemy ships sufficed to smash these conspiracies. Nevertheless, such schemes offered further evidence of the militancy, even desperation, in the domestic opposition against the regime.

While Louis' formidable army fought on several fronts, negotiations were pursued by his diplomats. The Dutch were the first to be detached from the allied coalition; they were offered generous economic advantages that they could willingly accept since it would be Spain's lot to make the major territorial concessions. The final treaty between France and the United Provinces was signed at Nymegen in the Netherlands in August, 1678. Spain came to terms in the following month, surrendering Franche-Comté to France and agreeing to an adjustment of the frontier in the Spanish Netherlands. The French thus eliminated some of their enclaves in Spanish territory and shaped a more compact northern frontier along the lines of the *"pré carré"* — a defensible geometric frontier — desired by Sébastien Le Prestre de Vauban, the leading designer of fortifications during Louis' reign. Vauban would subsequently oversee the construction of a network of fortresses, some with elaborate defensive perimeters, to ensure that Louis' frontiers and conquests might be preserved.[12]

At the end of the Dutch War, the elector of Brandenburg grudgingly admitted that Louis XIV had become "the arbiter of Europe" and that "at the present time, no prince will find security and success unless he remain a friend and ally of the king of France."[13] Yet amidst such tribute to "Louis le Grand," the king was not satisfied; his restless spirit was already plotting the next course of action: the "reunion" proceedings.

In various treaties stretching back to the conclusion of the Thirty Years' War, France had been awarded a number of towns and territories "along with their dependencies." Essentially, the word *dependencies* denoted the area that fell within the legal jurisdiction of a given town, but fixed limits seldom obtained. Indeed, since the early medieval period European princes had usually avoided treaties that involved crystal-clear limits, preferring to extend control and sovereignty via judicial interpretation and/or military might. As the royal legal machinery began to grind, disputed territories came under the jurisdiction of various bodies; one of them, the Chamber of Reunions at Metz, provided the name that soon would be applied to all such proceedings. With French archivists reporting to French judges who instructed French soldiers to occupy what was deemed French sovereign territory, consternation began to spread in neighboring lands since there was no clear sense of just when and where the process would end. The French assuredly did have legal claims to the territories in question, but the manner in which they conducted the affair led to alarm and hostility. As one historian has noted, "these 'reunions' reflect a concentration on immediate and petty aims befitting a second-rate medieval baron rather than the first power in Europe."[14]

At the very least, the reunion proceedings served to postpone any systematic implementation of Vauban's *pré carré*. The inhabitants of border territories might well have anxiously anticipated assimilation into a larger *pré carré* in the not-too-distant future. Tension intensified in September, 1681, when thirty thousand French troops surrounded the Imperial Free City of Strasbourg and forced it to capitulate. Close by Strasbourg was one of the most important bridges over the Rhine. During the Dutch War, the city of Strasbourg had allowed the enemies of France to enter Alsace on three occasions. Now the bridge as well as the city were secured. In the eyes of Germans, the tentacles were reaching farther and farther.

It is precisely at this juncture, with the end of reunions nowhere in sight, that one of the most crucial events of the seventeenth century occurred, the Turkish march on Vienna. By the summer of

> LOUIS CHERISHED THE PROSPECT OF VIENNA BEING OVERRUN BY THE TURKS, WITH THE REST OF THE CHRISTIAN EMPIRE RIPE FOR THE PICKING

1683 the city of Vienna was encircled and besieged by a Turkish army. Fervent and frantic pleas were addressed to Christian princes to aid the beleaguered city, to stop the onslaught of the Infidel against Christendom. No public figure was more eloquent or more effective in this cause than Pope Innocent XI. He viewed the Turkish challenge as a magnificent opportunity to launch a great Crusade whose ultimate objective was to drive the Moslems out of the Holy Lands and to seize Jerusalem for Christianity. The pope sent millions of florins to the king of Poland and millions more to the elector of Bavaria and to the emperor, Leopold I, in an all-out effort to equip a Christian army for battle.

Naturally, the pontiff beseeched the most powerful monarch in the Christian West to support this crusade. Louis XIV refused direct aid to the Christian cause since he viewed a defeat of Emperor Leopold as a victory for himself. He even had his ambassador at Constantinople urge the sultan to keep pounding away and held out the possibility that the French would open a second front in the West. Sure enough, while Vienna was under siege, a French army of 35,000 troops invaded the Spanish Netherlands on September 1, 1683.

What were Louis' motives? While we have no absolute proof, and while minutes of council meetings are lacking, it is likely that Louis cherished the prospect of Vienna being overrun by the Turks, with the rest of the Christian Empire ripe for the picking. At that point, the French army might step into the breach, smash the Turks, and send them scurrying back down the Danubian Valley. A discredited emperor might then be forced to abdicate with Louis XIV elected to replace him. Had that happened, the king would have achieved a *gloire* beyond the fantasies of his forebears. To repeat, the above is conjecture but it is by no means improbable. Mazarin had earlier sounded out German electors to discover whether Louis XIV might be acceptable as their emperor. In the face of opposition, the cardinal had not persisted, but a significant change of circumstances might well have produced a change in German receptivity.

If Louis ever did entertain such alluring dreams of conquest and power, imagining himself as the savior of Christendom, those dreams were dashed irrevocably upon news of the dramatic and overwhelming Christian victory over the Turks in

September, 1683. It was a complete rout, opening the way for incalculable gains in future campaigns. Such prospects were naturally obstructed by French belligerence in the West. After much negotiation, a twenty-year truce was signed between France and the Empire in the imperial city of Regensburg in August, 1684. The French gained sovereignty over all territories acquired in reunion proceedings before August 1, 1681; in addition, they retained Strasbourg and Luxembourg, which were not regarded by the French as part of the reunions. Furthermore, despite strenuous imperial efforts at the conference table, the French were allowed to strengthen and erect fortifications in the acquired territory. The imperial party underlined the provisional nature of the settlement, with the implicit assumption that future claims and adjustments — if not a total reversal — would be possible. On the French side, there was satisfaction since they would have ample opportunity to solidify their position in the course of twenty years.

In the year following the Truce of Regensburg, the Edict of Nantes was revoked: only Catholic public worship would now be legal in France. In that same year, 1685, the Catholic James II succeeded his brother Charles II as king of England. These events would later have political and military ramifications, especially since Protestant leaders such as the elector of Brandenburg and William III of Orange feared concerted Catholic action against the Protestants of Europe. Meanwhile, Louis was extolled in pamphlets and from pulpits across France. The painting by Antoine Coypel, executed at this time and entitled *Louis XIV Crowned by Glory Between Abundance and Peace,* conveys the mood of euphoria, or at least relief, in the aftermath of the truce with the Empire. With our hindsight, this almost appears as a willful exercise of wishful thinking. But contemporaries could not have known that the reign was only at the half-way mark, that longer and more grueling wars lay ahead.

An inkling of those future struggles — or at least a sense that they were probable — might then have been obtained on the battlefields of Hungary where the imperial army steadily advanced against the Moslem foe. The remarkable windfall of territory and resources harvested on the eastern front came largely under the control of the Austrian Habsburgs. The fields of Hungary with their bountiful crops of wheat and excellent grazing for horses provided essential components for a burgeoning war machine. For generations, Austrian rulers had repeatedly been elected as kings of Hungary. Now even the luxury of election was taken from the Hungarian ruling class: the kingship of Hungary would henceforth be a hereditary possession of the Austrian Habsburgs in the same way that the kingship of Bohemia had been absorbed during the Thirty Years' War. The extension of administrative control from Vienna was accompanied by a vigorous Catholicizing activity in the conquered territory, with a persecution of Protestants that has been less publicized but no less a fact than the persecution of Huguenots in France.

By the summer of 1688 the imperial army was on the verge of capturing Belgrade (it would fall in

and engaged in what appeared to be a vendetta against the Sun King. These accumulating dilemmas and frustrations, when added to the genuine fear of what recent Austrian gains portended, provoked the king and his ministers to adopt a bold course of action. In an atmosphere fraught with uncertainty, Louis' next decision led to the Nine Years' War.

The year 1688 is best remembered in the English-speaking world for the "Glorious Revolution": the expulsion of James II, the accession of William and Mary, the strengthening of Parliament, and a decline of the divine-right theory of kingship. The invasion of England by William III of Orange, who acted in concert with English political and military leaders, was closely intertwined with the history of Louis XIV's foreign

Detail of
Catalogue 208

September), thus confirming the French in their fears that the balance of power in Europe might be dangerously tipped in favor of their opponents. The aggressive exploitation of newly won territory by Emperor Leopold, coupled with the fact that he had at his disposal a combat-toughened army that might be utilized in a different theater of war, gave rise to alarm and fear at Versailles. There was no reason to believe that the Austrians would wait until twenty years had elapsed before making their move in the western Empire. In their place, would the French have exercised such forebearance? Matters were further complicated by a series of reversals in areas of the western Empire that the French expected to control, notably in the electorate of Cologne, reversals in which Pope Innocent XI openly sided with Austrian interests

policy and with the calculated risk taken by the French in invading the Holy Roman Empire in September. The plan, hammered out in a council meeting at Versailles in August, called for a quick strike against German states in the Rhineland. The projected campaign would be savagely destructive so as to force the people of the region to demand peace. At the end of a short war of perhaps several months, Louis expected the twenty-year Truce of Regensburg to be converted into a Peace of Regensburg, with the French retaining all of their reunion gains in perpetuity. The king knew of Dutch plans to invade England in the fall of 1688, which would effectively remove from the scene two of the strongest states in past anti-French coalitions. That, at least, was the theory. If all proceeded like clockwork, the fighting might cease before the imperial army could disengage itself from the Turkish front. The short war would thus strengthen French frontiers and offset the possible alteration in the balance of power.

The ensuing campaign included deliberate barbarities perpetrated by the French in the Germanies: villages were put to the torch and sections of cities shelled into rubble by cannon that were floated on barges from one site on the Rhine to the next. These atrocities led Germans to revile the French as "Huns," with Louis XIV frequently caricatured in the garb of Attila. Nonetheless, instead of collapsing according to a French schedule, the Germans resisted; the Empire officially declared war against France in February, 1689. The French timetable was likewise upset by events in England. Instead of a protracted civil war, James II fled the country and was declared to have abdicated; William and Mary were installed as monarchs; the English and Dutch joined a broad allied coalition. Louis' "sole and quite unintentional ally was the infidel Ottoman, still keeping the emperor and his best troops fully occupied on the borders of Hungary."[15]

The long and exhausting war extended to the farthest reaches of the globe. Like the future War of the Spanish Succession, to a notable extent it involved trade and the attempts made to oust French merchants from their positions in India and the Spanish New World. Though the French navy scored some signal victories against the combined Anglo-Dutch fleet (notably at Beachy Head in 1690), it was more often defeated. Naval action increasingly entailed interruption of trade and less open conflicts between rival fleets. The most successful French exploits at sea during the latter half of Louis' reign were those of the buccaneers, corsairs, and privateers in what has been referred to as "the golden age of privateering."[16] The war severely drained all the combatant powers, with the terrible famine in France in 1692-93 further sapping French strength. During the conflict, the Bank of England was founded, an institution that would be a mainstay in future English subsidies to allied coalitions.

As in the case of the Dutch War, Louis XIV began to extricate himself from the war by eliminating one of the members of the coalition. In the Treaty of Turin, concluded with the duke of Savoy in 1696, France gave up the fortifications of Casale and Pinerolo in northern Italy, emplacements fought for by Richelieu during the

Thirty Years' War. The remaining members of the alliance came to terms in the following year at the Treaty of Ryswick. The end of this ruinous war saw France come within an ace of surrendering Strasbourg. In the event, Louis gave up a number of reunion gains, as well as Luxembourg, Freiburg-im-Breisgau, Phillipsburg, and Breisach — the latter three key positions in the Holy Roman Empire on the right bank of the Rhine. Much of the strategic frontier in northern Italy and in the Empire, schemed for and fought for by Richelieu and Mazarin, was lost. In place of an alliance with well-intentioned German states, Louis XIV succeeded in alienating most of the Germanies and did more than Emperor Leopold ever could to bring about German unity. Not on the agenda at Ryswick was the most momentous issue of the day: the disposition of Spanish territories once the king of Spain, Carlos II, died without an heir.

Statesmen and diplomats had been expecting the sickly Carlos II to die for some thirty-five years when he finally expired in 1700. Since there was no prospect of an heir to control the far-flung Spanish possessions, it seemed prudent to arrange partitions of the Spanish inheritance in advance so as to obviate a war. Though several partition plans had been settled upon since the 1660s, each in turn became inoperative due to the casualties of war or the death of a principal figure. Just before Carlos II died, he signed a remarkable will leaving all of the Spanish inheritance to the grandson of Louis XIV, a seventeen-year-old boy who would become Philip V of Spain. If the Bourbons declined to accept this arrangement, then the entire inheritance would instead go to Karl, the son of Leopold I. Regardless of what was decided, Louis anticipated a war with Austria; at issue was whether the Dutch and the English could be kept out of the struggle. In a historic moment at Versailles, Louis introduced his grandson as the king of Spain. It was not long before Bourbon family connections were used to advance French merchant interests in the Spanish colonial world and to make military moves in the Spanish Netherlands that unsettled the Dutch. When the fighting began, Louis again found a broad allied coalition ranged against France; his only allies were Spain together with Bavaria and the electorate of Cologne.

An ocean of books and articles treats the manifold aspects of the Spanish Succession War. It was worldwide in scope, with European rivalries transported into distant colonial areas. As such, it served as a kind of prototype for the wars between European states throughout the eighteenth century. "This is a war about trade," said Louis XIV, and certainly merchant and colonial ambitions are central to any understanding of the war and the peace treaties that ended it.[17] Louis raised the largest army of his entire reign to fight multifront campaigns across Europe; his armies were trounced in the Empire, in the Netherlands, and in northern Italy in great open-field battles with unprecedented casualties for a single day of fighting. The tactics of the principal opposing generals — Eugene of Savoy in the service of Austria and John Churchill, duke of Marlborough — were soon imitated by the French, if only to keep the enemy at bay. Spain was invaded by Habsburg forces seeking to drive out the Bourbon Philip V. The result was civil war.

The lowest point of all in this tragic and draining contest came with the terrible famine of 1709, one of the worst in the history of France from the early medieval period to the present day. When Louis indicated a willingness to compromise, the enemy coalition raised its terms, even demanding that Louis participate in driving his grandson out of Spain. Enmeshed in what must have seemed an unending nightmare, the king wrote letters to bishops and to governors of provinces, letters that were printed and distributed broadside. The themes in these letters were recapitulated in a remarkable message to the people of France in which he pleaded for their understanding and support:

I have conducted this war with hauteur and pride worthy of this kingdom. With the valor of my nobility and the zeal of my subjects, I have succeeded in the enterprises that I have undertaken for the good of the state. . . . I have considered proposals for peace and no one has done more than I to secure it. . . . I can say that I have done violence to my character . . . to procure promptly a peace for my subjects even at the expense of my personal satisfaction and perhaps my *gloire* . . . but up to now my most important enemies have sought only to distract me, and have used every artifice . . . to deceive me as well as their own allies whom they oblige to make the great expenditures demanded by their unbridled ambitions. . . . I can no longer see any alternative to take, other than to prepare to

defend ourselves. To make them see that a united France is greater than all the powers assembled by force and artifice to overwhelm it, at this hour I have put into effect the extraordinary measure that we have used on similar occasions to procure the money indispensible for the *gloire* and the security of the state. . . . I come to ask for your councils and your aid in this encounter that involves your safety. By the efforts that we shall make together, our foes will understand that we are not to be put upon. The aid that I ask of you will oblige them to make a peace honorable for us, lasting . . . and satisfactory to the princes of Europe. This is the aim of my thoughts . . . the happiness and well-being of my people has always been and will always be to the last moment of my life, my most important and serious consideration.[18]

Some movement toward a solution of this exhausting war began in 1711 with the death of Emperor Joseph I, son of Leopold and brother of the Habsburg claimant to the Spanish throne. If Karl (the would-be Carlos III) succeeded as Holy Roman Emperor and at the same time was king of Spain, the sixteenth-century empire of Charles V would be revived with the likelihood of plunging all of Europe into a bloodbath for a generation and more. Joseph's death infused new fervor into the peace party in England and the final treaties at Utrecht, concluded in 1713-14, included an extensive reshuffling of territories connected with the partition of Spain's empire.

Philip V of Bourbon continued to rule in Spain and in Spain's American colonies, but the Spanish Netherlands as well as much of Spain's holdings in Italy were transferred to Austria. England obtained Gibraltar and Minorca from Spain as well as Canadian territories from France: Newfoundland, Nova Scotia (or Acadia, the origin of Louisiana's Cajuns), and vast tracts of land around Hudson's Bay. By virtue of the famous *Asiento* clause in the Utrecht treaty, the English received a monopoly in the provisioning of African slaves to Spanish colonies in the New World as well as the right to send a trading ship each year to Spanish America, opening up lucrative opportunities for smuggling. England thus received the lion's share of the spoils and had begun to undermine France's position in Canada. Both England and Austria made significant gains in power by comparison to the status that each had held *vis-à-vis* France at the beginning of Louis' reign in 1661. Not the least of the results of the coalition wars against France is that they established the basic guidelines for the balance of power in international relations in the eighteenth century.

At Louis XIV's death in 1715, France remained the most populous, and one of the most fertile, resourceful, and resilient states in Europe. The chain of fortifications designed by Vauban protected her frontiers and enclosed the territorial gains made during the reign, especially Franche-Comté and Alsace. By the standards of the times, Louis may be said to have achieved a great measure of the *gloire* that he pursued relentlessly throughout his long career. All the same, the king's quest for hegemony had fallen short of his aspirations. Moreover, that quest had exacted exorbitant human and material sacrifices from the French people. On his deathbed, Louis advised the successor: "Do not imitate me in war; try always to maintain peace with your neighbors, to spare your people as much as you can, which I have had the misfortune not to be able to do because of necessities of state."[19]

Some may view these words as the product of a harrowing awareness of the hardships he inflicted upon the French people. Others may assume that a man preparing to meet his Maker is in a mood to make amends to the living and the dead. There is also the possibility that he simply uttered words appropriate for a dying monarch, his mask for the occasion as it were. Perhaps one of these angles of perception contains a degree of truth. But we are left with the impression that by referring to "necessities of state" the king was still seeking to justify his choices, his actions, and all that flowed from them.

The Sun King's last words on his deathbed also included the famous phrase, "I depart but the state will always remain."[20] The state he bequeathed to his great-grandson, the future Louis XV, was significantly different from the France of Mazarin and the Fronde. During his long reign Louis XIV gave definitive form to the "bureaucratic, military, police state" that endured to the end of the *ancien régime*.[21] The structure of that state would be shaken by the Enlightenment, and then transformed and strengthened by the Revolution and Napoleon. ■

FOOTNOTES

1. Voltaire, *Le Siècle de Louis XIV*, in *Oeuvres Historiques* (Bibliothèque de la Pléiade) (Paris, 1957), 620.
2. Sir George Clark, *The Seventeenth Century* (New York, 1961), 98.
3. John B. Wolf, "The Formation of a King," *French Historical Studies*, I (1958), 70; Ragnhild Hatton, "Louis XIV et l'Europe: Eléments d'une révision historiographique," *XVIIᵉ Siècle*, XXXI (1979), 116.
4. Gaston Zeller, "Saluces, Pignerol et Strasbourg: La politique des frontières au temps de la prépondérance espagnole," *Revue Historique*, CXCIII (1942), 110. Other studies by Zeller on the subject include "La monarchie d'Ancien Régime et les frontières naturelles," *Revue d'Histoire Moderne*, VIII (1933), 305-33, and "Histoire d'une idée fausse," *Revue de Synthèse*, XI (1936), 115-31. For further discussion and bibliography, see John T. O'Connor, "Louis XIV's Strategic Frontier in the Holy Roman Empire," *Proceedings of the Third Annual Meeting of the Western Society for French History*, III (1976), 108-17.
5. A deft analysis of Mazarin's role in preparing young Louis for his future career is provided by Wolf, "Formation of a King," 40-72. This essay has been reprinted in John C. Rule (ed.), *Louis XIV and the Craft of Kingship* (Columbus, Ohio, 1969), 102-31. Wolf's ideas are more fully developed in the first part of his superb biography, *Louis XIV* (New York, 1968).
6. Bertrand Auerbach, Introduction to the *Recueil des Instructions données aux Ambassadeurs et Ministres de France depuis les Traités de Westphalie jusqu' à la Révolution française*, XVIII: *Diète germanique* (Paris, 1912), li-lii. See the fine study by F. L. Carsten, *Princes and Parliaments in Germany* (Oxford, 1959).
7. M. Huisman, *Essai sur le Règne du Prince-Evêque de Liège, Maximilien-Henri de Bavière* (Brussels, 1899), 13.
8. See Max Braubach, "Eine Wirtschaftsenquête am Rhein im 17. Jahrhundert," *Rheinische Vierteljahrsblätter*, XIII (1949), 51-86; and C. G. Picavet, *La Diplomatie française au temps de Louis XIV, 1661-1715* (Paris, 1930), 281-309.
9. Cited by Georges Livet, "Louis XIV et l'Allemagne," *XVIIᵉ Siècle*, XII (1960), 49, n. 26.
10. *Works of Sir William Temple* (London, 1757), II, 225.
11. For the conspiracies, see Klaus Malettke, *Opposition und Konspiration unter Ludwig XIV: Studien zu Kritik und Widerstand gegen System und Politik des französischen Königs während des ersten Hälfte seiner persönlichen Regierung* (Göttingen, 1976), including the invaluable archival material published in the appendices.
12. Gaston Zeller, *L'Organisation défensive des Frontières du Nord et de l'Est au XVIIᵉ Siècle* (Paris, 1928), 69. On the gradual evolution of the frontier in this region, see the solid study by Nelly Girard d'Albissin, *Genèse de la Frontière Franco-Belge: Les variations des limites septentrionales de la France de 1659 à 1789*. Bibliothèque de la Société d'Histoire du Droit des Pays Flamands, Picards et Wallons, vol. 26 (Paris, 1970).
13. Cited by Louis André, *Louis XIV et l'Europe* (Paris, 1950), 184, n. 2.
14. Andrew Lossky, "The General European Crisis of the 1680s," *European Studies Review*, X (1980), 178.
15. Hubert Gillot, *Le Régne de Louis XIV et l'Opinion publique en Allemagne* (Paris, 1914); Pierre Goubert, *Louis XIV and Twenty Million Frenchmen* (New York, 1972), 193.
16. Armel de Wismes, "The French Navy Under Louis XIV," in Ragnhild Hatton (ed.) *Louis XIV and absolutism* (Columbus, Ohio, 1976), 256.
17. Ragnhild Hatton, *Europe in the Age of Louis XIV* (New York, 1969), 100. The citation, from 1709, was drawn by Professor Hatton from E. W. Dahlgren, *Les Relations commerciales et maritimes entre la France et les côtes de l'Ocean Pacifique* (Paris, 1909), 561: "Le principal objet de la guerre présente est celui du commerce des Indes et des richesses qu'elles produisent."
18. Cited by Wolf, *Louis XIV*, 564-65.
19. Cited by William F. Church, "Louis XIV and Reason of State" in Rule (ed.), *Craft of Kingship*, 393.
20. *Ibid.*, 371.
21. This phrase was employed by Wolf in the preface to his *Louis XIV*, xi.

LOUIS XIV
AND THE COLONIES

THE COLONIAL POLICY
OF THE SUN KING
PHILIPPE JACQUIN

 haos reigned everywhere." In this single sentence Louis XIV depicted a striking image of the state of his kingdom upon his assumption of power in 1661, and left little doubt that this assessment also applied to the situation of the French colonies. In the first third of the seventeenth century, the facts seemed to prove him right. Despite its imposing Atlantic façade and the dynamism of its fishermen, France was slow in turning its vision toward the New World. When Cortez invaded Mexico, the Capetian kings were involved in Italian affairs; while the destiny of Europe was at stake on the shores of America, the French were still dreaming of a Continental empire. Nevertheless, conflict with Spain soon opened everyone's eyes, for they saw the gold of the Aztecs invested in the dreaded infantry regiments of Charles V. The power of a nation, they began to realize, no longer depended on the courage of its nobility but on the strength of its finances. American gold had effectively overthrown the economy of the Old World. But how can one explain the "colonial backwardness" of France vis-à-vis Spain, which weighed so heavily upon the young Louis XIV? What means were at his disposal to change the policy of his predecessors? Would the France of the Sun King become a colonial power capable of commanding respect in the forests of Canada as it did on the frontiers of Europe?

Before Louis XIV's accession to power in 1661, the word "colony" in its current political definition was never used. It can be found neither in administrative acts nor in the memoirs and contracts for chartering sailing vessels. Richelieu, although preoccupied with the French domain abroad, never used it in his *Political Testament* or in his *Letters.* If the term was virtually unknown, it is due to the fact that for contemporaries it did not refer to a tangible and identifiable reality.

Once Europe learned of Spanish colonial gains and the benefits they brought to the crown, Frenchmen embarked on the colonial venture. Thus in 1534 Jacques Cartier left with orders from King François I: "to discover certain islands and countries where, it is said, great quantities of gold and other valuable things are to be found."[1] Dreams of Eldorado still filled the heads of the noblest and the humblest alike! Moreover, François I had violently contested the pope's decision in 1493 to divide all discovered territories between the Spanish and Portuguese and had demanded "to see the last will and testament of Adam to know how he had divided the world." In an effort to ingratiate himself with both the papacy and the French clergy, François I reminded explorers and navigators to give some thought to the conversion of the indigenous populations.

During the Wars of Religion that ravaged the kingdom from 1560 to 1598, few men of politics were concerned about faraway lands. Nonetheless, the Protestant Admiral Coligny, in the service of Charles IX, hoped to combat the Spanish in America while founding Protestant settlements that would not only serve as refuges for persecuted Huguenots but also contribute to the greatness of the realm. This intention to found colonies for the purpose of settlement, known as "la peuplade," was later taken up again by Henri IV. But with France laid waste by religious conflict and the royal government unable to finance such expeditions at the end of the sixteenth century, the king accorded the fur trade monopoly first to La Roche and then to Chauvin on the condition that they construct forts and houses and transport settlers to New France. In such a way were born the monopolistic companies of the private sector that possessed a free hand in the colonization and exploration of the country. But the hoped-for results did not materialize. Instead, colonization in Brazil, Florida, and Canada clustered around a few forts headed by noblemen who did not encourage the development of the land and limited their efforts to sporadic trading with the Indians, especially for foodstuffs. In truth, the nobility was more concerned with chivalric adventures and noble deeds than with profits, agriculture, or commerce.

If in the sixteenth century the French Court and financiers were uninterested in colonial expansion, a change began to take place in the early seventeenth century. More than a transformation of mentalities, this change arose from a new vision of the role of the state and from a reexamination of the origins of economic power. The monetary flood that inundated Europe not only made possible the Golden Age of Spain but also stimulated countries less advantageously positioned on the European chessboard. The rise of the Republic of the United Provinces, which developed an excellent navy and grew rich from its commerce, provoked considerable reflection on the part of French intellectuals. In 1615 Montchrestien, drawing on the Dutch example, recognized in his *Treatise on Political Economy* only one way to enrich the kingdom: to export as much as possible and import as little as possible, therefore necessitating the founding of colonial settlements to serve as natural outlets for French products. Finally, he believed the kingdom would have little trouble undertaking colonization given the plethora of individuals ready for adventure. The mercantilism of Montchrestien would later find its application with Colbert, but the notion of state power being linked to commerce and colonization was well received in a century when kings sought above all else to assert themselves in Europe and the world. The grandeur of the kingdom was to be the obsession of the seventeenth century.

Another factor intervened to influence the

colonial policy of kings: the resolve of sailors and soldiers. Samuel de Champlain is the best example of the dynamism of these individuals. Upon his return from Canada in 1603, he brought to Henri IV an inventory of the human and natural resources of the Saint Lawrence region that greatly impressed the sovereign. On his second voyage in 1602, Champlain was accompanied by Pierre de Mons, who was named lieutenant general and also placed in charge of commerce. The letter the king sent to de Mons reveals the objectives of colonization: "our greatest concern and task since our accession to the Crown has always been to maintain and preserve its ancient dignity, grandeur, and splendor and to extend and enhance their limits as much as legitimately possible," and, the king adds, "to convert, win over and educate the people who inhabit this country."[2] Thus royal grandeur was inconceivable without religious action on the part of "The Most Christian King" — all the more so given Henri IV's desire to efface the memory of his Huguenot past! But the commercial monopoly granted to de Mons angered the merchants in the French ports. Despite these difficulties, de Mons founded a colony in Acadia while Champlain extended the limits of New France, made alliances with the Hurons, and dreamed that "our young men will marry your [Indian] daughters and we will become but one people."

Richelieu pursued these same objectives but preferred that the state direct the colonial effort. In order to accomplish this, in 1626 he assumed control over "the navigation and commerce of France." Confronted with the menacing European situation, the state refused to commit itself financially abroad and continued to manage the colonies via company monopolies. Nevertheless, the beginnings of a public/private mixture began with the creation in 1627 of the Company of One Hundred Associates for North America, in which the usual merchants were joined this time by members of the upper nobility and by individuals drawn from the upper echelons of the state bureaucracy. Thanks to the company, funds arrived

THE NOTION OF STATE POWER BEING LINKED TO COMMERCE AND COLONIZATION WAS WELL RECEIVED IN A CENTURY WHEN KINGS SOUGHT ABOVE ALL ELSE TO ASSERT THEMSELVES IN EUROPE AND THE WORLD

in New France at the same time as the first Jesuits. The year before, Richelieu had created the Company of the American Islands. In the Antilles, then under Spanish control yet the scene of operations for Norman and Breton corsairs, piracy was gradually displaced by commerce and colonists. Martinique, Guadeloupe, and neighboring islands, occupied by the French between 1625 and 1635, became with their seven thousand white inhabitants the most imposing colony of the kingdom. Finally, the slave trade appeared as the "indispensable" complement to the development of the sugar economy in the Antilles.

But the vulnerability of France to the colonial enterprises of its more powerful neighbors, notably Holland, also resulted from the reluctance of French merchants to engage their capital in overseas expeditions or business ventures. Each port, one could even say each family, adopted a policy that it would do nothing to displease its commercial partners. Thus La Rochelle was hostile to all initiatives that might displease the Dutch. Bretons and Normans quarreled over the profits to be had from the Grand Banks of Newfoundland and from the fur trade.

This distrust, even hositlity, on the part of private investors toward colonial ventures weighed heavily on the conduct of the men surrounding Louis XIV. From the death of Richelieu (1642) until the end of the series of revolts against the extension of royal power that is known as the Fronde, internal disorder and European diplomacy absorbed all the energy and financial resources of the state. Mazarin, during the minority of the young king, spent little time on colonial affairs. The colonies, virtually abandoned to their own resources, struggled merely to survive. Sacrificed to European concerns, their only hope for resuscitation lay in the renewal of royal commitment, until then sadly lacking.

In 1661, upon the death of Mazarin, Louis XIV was twenty-three years old. He had passed part of his youth being packed off between Paris and the several towns where the royal entourage found refuge from the violent riots of the Fronde. His political education was dominated by Mazarin, "l'Italien," a fine diplomat surrounded by competent financiers, among them a certain Jean-Baptiste Colbert. Unfortunately, colonial policy was far from being the cardinal's greatest concern. The young king, schooled in European affairs, knew little about France's foreign possessions. Two ideas obsessed him: the lingering Spanish threat and the economic success of the Republic of the United Provinces. He readily appreciated the vigor of the Company of Amsterdam which, in 1655-58, retained a force of fifteen thousand soldiers and eighty thousand sailors. The Dutch had just chased the Portuguese out of Ceylon and installed themselves on the west coast of India. English foreign policy also gave the monarch cause to reflect, notably with the creation in London of the Council of Foreign Plantations, which directed all of the American colonies. Moreover, the rising power of the English in the New World further manifested itself in 1661 with the fall of New Amsterdam, which then entered history under the name of New York. In the preamble of the Edict of August, 1664, the king invoked "the experience of our neighbors" while laying the foundations of his own colonial policy:

among all the means we have often examined to achieve such a desirable goal, and after having reflected a great deal on such a far-reaching matter, we have adhered to the policy of long-range commerce in the certainty that natural and ordinary reason as well as the experience of our neighbors demonstrate that the profit derived therefrom will infinitely surpass the effort needed to penetrate such faraway countries, and because such a policy conforms to the genius and glory of our Nation.[4]

The text reveals very clearly the sovereign's thinking at the outset of his reign, for one finds therein the notion of grandeur and the importance of commerce, the two being inseparable in the minds of contemporaries.

The king lived only for glory, although the means to attain it became more difficult to procure when France was severely put to the test. Well before his assumption of power in 1661, Louis XIV had taken notice of Mazarin's secretary, Colbert. A native of Champagne, Colbert cultivated connections with financial circles in Paris and Lyon. His experience as a merchant familiarized him with international commerce. He had read Montchrestien and was also acquainted with the works of the economist Du Noyer de Saint-Martin, who argued that the wealth of France lay in maritime commerce and called for the creation of a single company and a bank in order to promote it.[5]

An excellent bureaucrat, an indefatigable worker, this great civil servant became the confident and majordomo of the king, supervising everything, and devoted himself to the application of his mercantilist ideas. Like many of his contemporaries, Colbert was convinced that the State — that is, the prince — had to be strong and that power was based on wealth; wealth, in turn, meant gold and silver, both of which France sorely lacked, and only foreign commerce could procure the specie necessary for grandeur. Therefore, France necessarily had to manufacture at home whatever goods buyers sought abroad, thereby preventing "the flight of specie." And in order to derive the maximum profit from these goods, French commerce and shipping had to be supervised, regulated, and protected. France had to obtain from its overseas possessions the precious colonial goods it bought elsewhere and monopolize them for itself. The interests of the colony must coincide with those of the mother country. The colonies would sell their raw materials to France and purchase from her all necessary goods, particularly manufactured objects. In order to prevent the flight of specie, all exchanges would occur in the form of barter. Finally, Colbert held that all maritime transportation had to take place under the French flag and that only French merchants would be allowed to participate in the slave trade. This system, put into effect by Colbert, reserving commerce exclusively to the French, was dubbed "l'Exclusif" and later the "Pacte Colonial."

Under Louis XIV and Colbert, colonial policy thus underwent a radical change. The directing authorities downplayed the apostolic justification of colonization and instead emphasized that colonization was essentially a commercial venture. The colonies, it was argued, represented "the source and the principle of abundance." Colbert himself took over the direction of colonial affairs. Controller general since 1661, he became minister of the Marine in 1669 and in this position held sway over the colonies, formulating policy until his death in 1683. Events would soon provide the king and his minister the opportunity to display the new direction of their policy.

Louis XIV had only recently assumed the throne when he received at court two visitors from New France, Monseigneur de Laval and Pierre Boucher,

UNDER LOUIS XIV AND COLBERT, COLONIAL POLICY THUS UNDERWENT A RADICAL CHANGE

who came to expose to him all of the colony's complaints about Governor d'Avaugour. In May, the king placed Louis Gaudais-Dupont in charge of a royal inquest to go to Canada and report on the state of the colony, its resources, and the Iroquois menace. A royal edict of March, 1663, withdrew from the Company of One Hundred Associates its proprietorship of the colony along with its commercial monopoly and placed New France under direct royal administration. The king also reorganized the seigneurial regime: seigneurs who had abandoned their fiefs or allowed them to remain uninhabited were stripped of their proprietary rights, which were then awarded to more dynamic seigneurs who promised to promote settlement. Montreal, which until then had enjoyed administrative independence, was forced to submit to the authority of the colonial governor.

But the greatest innovation occurred in the new administration put into place. Following the example of the kingdom, New France received a governor responsible for military affairs and foreign relations and an intendant charged with the administration of justice, public order, and finances. By means of this duality of power, the sovereign hoped to limit the abuse of authority, but in reality the personality of those in power weighed heavily on the management of affairs in the colony. Not content to reform the upper echelons of the judiciary, Louis XIV also suppressed the seigneurial court of justice and replaced it with the Sovereign Council. One might with reason assume that its powers were limited to justice, but in fact the council was entitled to oversee many very diverse activities: it controlled the disbursement of public funds, supervised the fur trade and other commercial activities, and even concerned itself with police matters and questions of morality. The Sovereign Council, unique among all the colonies of the epoque, was in charge of the day-to-day administration of the colony under the supervision of the governor. The council was composed of the governor, the bishop, five counselors, a prosecutor general, and a scribe. One of its first decisions, in 1664, was to establish the customary law of Paris: law, weights, and measures were therefore uniform throughout Canada while in France they still varied

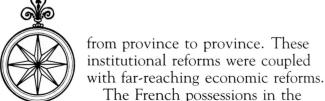

from province to province. These institutional reforms were coupled with far-reaching economic reforms.

The French possessions in the Antilles, the Islands as they were then called, offered the advantage of fitting perfectly into the mercantilist system constructed by the state. They not only exported to the kingdom tropical products that did not compete with the products of the mother country, but also produced tobacco, dyestuffs, and sugarcane, which were readily reexported to the rest of Europe. Finally, the colonists required grain, wine, meat, textiles, and tools — an excellent outlet for French manufactured goods.

From the beginning of the seventeenth century, the Dutch handled all commerce with the Islands, served as intermediaries between them and the mother country, and brought them slaves from Guinea. Consequently, the displacement of these fierce competitors was all the more urgent. In September, 1664, the king forbade entry into French ports in the Antilles of any vessel of the United Provinces and obliged the small private companies of the planters to conform to the new legislation — that is, to depend entirely on the Company of the West Indies created by Colbert in 1664 to regulate all commerce with the New World. To that the sovereign added an administrative measure: he replaced the proprietors in charge of each of the more important islands with a governor directly responsible to Paris. At roughly the same time the Company of One Hundred Associates in Canada was suppressed and, as in the Antilles, commerce was entrusted to the new Company of the West Indies.

Fascinated by the success of the Dutch, Colbert hoped to reform both the management and organization of commercial activities in the Atlantic and therefore was instrumental in the creation of the Company of the West Indies. The king's taste for glory and that of Colbert for centralization accustomed both men to thinking on a large scale. Therefore, the minister was convinced, and the Dutch and English precedents seemed to confirm, that only an undertaking well supplied with men, ships, and capital could succeed on the international scene.

Colbert was equally innovative in the way he raised capital, the company no longer being an association of proprietors but a joint-stock company, in fact a state company. In effect,

despite the noisy publicity in its favor, the commercial bourgeoisie maintained a great distrust for this most recent offspring of the new regime. Colbert therefore began to offer shares to members of the royal family, dukes, and the tax farmers. Finally, he himself appointed the directors and filled all positions of authority, not hesitating to name members of his own clan, his family, and his close friends. At the same time, he never ignored the advice of influential merchants. In order always to favor mercantilism, tariff duties were maintained on imported and exported colonial goods, but a premium per unit was paid by the state to the company. Nor were goods held in French warehouses exempted from the duties.

But it did not suffice to place the colonies of the New World under royal authority; in addition, it was essential to supervise their economic development and reinforce their productive capacity. Qualified men were therefore needed, and Colbert proved to be very concerned with the settlement of Canada and the Islands. In both territories women were scarce, and the colonists married Indians or lived with black women. The first thing always asked of arriving ship captains was whether they had brought any women, and it was said that "the islands were hell for men, but paradise for women." Colbert asked the governors to encourage marriage between young people, but that was not enough. The state therefore had recourse to forced emigration and indentured servitude. Penal deportation was nothing new and, in the eyes of the populace, America and the Islands had bad reputations. Tradition had it that ports and other cities would regularly purge themselves of beggars, vagabonds, and other idlers by sending them to America. Under the reign of Louis XIV, notably at the end of the seventeenth century, this practice was used more and more often. Women of ill-repute, libertines, smugglers, and the sons of families in decline all found themselves together on the king's ships![6] All that was asked of them was to work and to populate America. Only under Colbert's successor, Pontchartrain, was this policy put to a halt.[7] French Protestants, who were quite numerous in the Islands since the early seventeenth century, were never encouraged to leave France. In fact, the "Most Christian King," loyal to his own religious policies, forbade their emigration to the colonies in March, 1685. Those already in the Antilles soon left for the British colonies along the east coast of

America.[6]

Indentured servitude was another means of providing manpower for the colonies. Poor people, attracted by the prospect of owning their own land, could reach the Islands by hiring themselves out under contract to work for three years for a plantation owner in exchange for the price of their passage. At the expiration of his term, the "servant" received a plot of land and sometimes a bit of money. The system had given rise to abuses, and many servants became veritable slaves, unable to settle and eventually escaping to join freebooters. In order to breathe new life into the practice of indentured servitude, Colbert promulgated a decree in February, 1670, against "the trickery of merchants, ship captains and others." Servants had to be well treated, allowed to attain their freedom, and awarded their land at the expiration of their service. But plantation owners opposed the settling of potential competitors and instead preferred to encourage the importation of a black labor force. In light of the considerable growth of the slave population since 1640-50, Colbert attempted to regulate slavery. Published in 1685, the Black Code prepared by Colbert required owners to respect Sunday's rest, to limit daily work, and to provide sufficient nourishment, clothing, and lodging for their "ebony." Nevertheless, corporal punishment was not abolished and owners could still dispose of their "personnel" at will.

Settlers, indentured servants, and slaves all had to devote themselves to the production of agricultural goods and raw materials. The plantations of the Antilles offered an exemplary model that Louis XIV and his minister would have liked New France to imitate. In his instructions to the intendants, the preoccupation with the exploitation of the land was a constant theme. Colbert blamed the underdevelopment of New France on the refusal of the colonists to clear and cultivate the land. He recommended that the intendant Talon be exacting: "the said inhabitants will be obliged to clear all land granted to them; otherwise, their grants will be reduced by one-tenth or one-fifteenth each year and given to new settlers."[7] He added further on that "one of

Canada's greatest needs is to attract artisans capable of providing much needed day-to-day objects." Moreover, fewer imports would mean the loss of less specie. Finally, the country also needed to exploit its forests: "a treasure that we must carefully preserve and in time use to found shipyards for the construction of the King's vessels" but from which in the immediate future it could export "a great quantity of wood suited to all purposes, even for the construction of ship components." When one considers that the construction of a ship of seventy-four cannons required four thousand oaks, one can well understand the minister of the Marine's interest in such a country.

In addition to the economic question of New France, the royal government was confronted with the delicate problem of Indian policy. In this domain Colbert followed the lead of Champlain and Richelieu. The latter had affirmed in 1628 that "the savages educated and converted to the true faith will be considered as reputed natural Frenchmen and as such will be entitled to come live in France whenever they please and there acquire, bequeath, succeed to and accept donations and legacies." Colbert favored such assimilation: "the savages can be persuaded to join with the French by marriages and the education of their children." He even viewed conversion as an instrument that would lead to assimilation and confirmed as much in 1674 to Frontenac, the governor of New France: "His Majesty believes that it would be much more advantageous to the welfare of religion and his service to apply oneself to what is close at hand. Therefore, while they [the Jesuits] convert the savages they should also persuade them to join civil society and abandon that manner of life which prevents them from becoming good Christians." His objective is clear: to strengthen the French possessions threatened by the English and Iroquois menace. Confronted with Iroquois incursions, the decision of the king was brutal: "The Iroquois, whose diverse nations are all perpetual and irreconcilable enemies of the colony, having impeded the further population of this country by the massacre of many Frenchmen and by the inhumane treatment of those who fall into their

THE WILL OF THE KING AND THE EFFORTS OF COLBERT THEREFORE TRANSFORMED IN THE COURSE OF A FEW YEARS THE STATUS OF THE FRENCH OVERSEAS POSSESSIONS

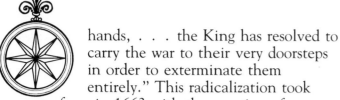

hands, . . . the King has resolved to carry the war to their very doorsteps in order to exterminate them entirely." This radicalization took concrete form in 1663 with the creation of a militia at Montreal and especially with the intervention in New France of more than one thousand soldiers of the Carignan-Salières regiment (1665), whose bayonets the Iroquois would soon come to fear.[8]

The will of the king and the efforts of Colbert therefore transformed in the course of a few years the status of the French overseas possessions. The implantation of an administrative structure copied after that of the realm achieved a certain degree of autonomy for the American colonies. These reforms were accompanied by the transformation of the administrative apparatus of the French state. Colbert was behind the unification of maritime and colonial affairs, but within the Department of State functions remained ill defined. His successor, Jérome Pontchartrain, would later develop the specialized offices headed by competent civil servants who often were his close relatives. In 1710 Pontchartrain succeeded to a degree in detaching the colonies from the Ministry of the Marine by creating a Bureau of the Colonies, a veritable independent department whose head was to all extent and purposes a minister of the colonies. At the same time appeared the financial institutions needed to support colonial policy. Colbert was the first to differentiate between ordinary and extraordinary departmental expenses; that is, he kept separate accounts for routine operating costs and for unusual and occasional expenditures. Each year, these accounts were audited and, at the beginning of the eighteenth century, a genuine accountability was established based on the financial statements sent by the colonies. The king in turn reviewed all accounts in his council and approved the direction of financial policy.

This administrative apparatus was under the direction of civil servants, qualified and zealous bureaucrats who handled the affairs of each colony. The highest ranking bureaucrat was really an office director with direct access to the minister and charged with studying reports, memoirs, and other letters that arrived in Paris. The minister took them under review, sought the advice of the king in serious problems, or simply decided along with his office director, who then drew up a response intended for the governor, the intendant, or the military authority. In this correspondence the most diverse questions touching on the life of the colony were dealt with, from the private life of individuals to the maintenance of public order, including religious and criminal affairs. To this testimony were added individuals' letters, merchants' petitions, and accounts of military expeditions, all of which permit the historian to discern the reactions and behavior of persons confronted with the newly implemented colonial policy.[9]

In practice, two obstacles paralyzed royal intentions: administrative understaffing and distance. In reality, a governor or an intendant had few men at his disposal to make orders from Paris respected. Of course, in the major cities the power of the government made itself felt, but what about beyond there? Colonists had their own habits and practices. Left for so long to their own resources, fiercely independent, they found it difficult to tolerate interference from a faraway administration. Because serious decisions had to be made in Paris, several months — even an entire year — elapsed before they were implemented in the colony. Nevertheless, these disadvantages could be partially eliminated if the "King's men," governors or intendants, knew how to make themselves heard, most often by relying on local pressure groups or "clienteles" linked to one or another powerful personage of the colony. Lineage and client-systems proved to be extremely efficacious in the constant battle for influence and power between the governor and intendant. Reading the colonial archives often reveals an endless succession of mutual recriminations, denunciations, embezzlements or other swindling that sometimes earned for the culprits prison sentences upon their return to the mother country. Another drawback was the absenteeism and disinterest of those placed in charge, who too often perceived appointment to the colonies as a disgrace. Nonetheless, some of them were devoted to their task and did eventually achieve success.

In the Antilles, Louis XIV and Colbert's goal of ending Dutch commercial domination provoked a grave crisis due to the inability of the French Company of the West Indies to keep the colonists supplied. Thus between February, 1665, and May, 1666, the company sent only forty ships — in contrast to the one hundred ships that ordinarily reached the Islands. As a result, scarcity ensued and the colonists, in need of everything, rebelled to the cry of "Long live the Dutch and Flemish."

The repression was terrible: Governor Clodoré hanged the rebels and reestablished order. Despite the protests, Colbert refused to allow Dutch ships to reappear in the ports, but in 1670 he admitted the partial check of the company and authorized independent French merchants to undertake the provisioning of meat and slaves. However, foreign products brought in more or less clandestinely, such as salted beef from Ireland, continued to enter the colony. This colonial rivalry with the Dutch was a key factor in the king's decision to declare war on the United Provinces in March, 1672. The maritime struggle, despite some French successes in the Antilles, was far from decisive, and the Continental victory of Louis XIV resembled a semi-defeat in the colonies since the Dutch regained the freedom to trade with the Islands (Treaty of Nymegen, August, 1678).[10] This setback was interpreted by Colbert as a disavowal not only of his anti-Dutch policy but also of his colonial policy in general. Thereafter the king would pay less attention to the advice of his minister and would instead fall under the influence of Louvois, minister of war, who had a profound aversion for the navy and colonies.

In New France there were no Dutch but there were Iroquois, no plantations but a great deal of land to clear! To turn this colony into a country of farmers and artisans was the goal of Colbert and his intendant, Talon, who wrote: "I propose that the King send here two weavers, two shepherds, two shoemakers and two hatters, each of whom will take on two young apprentices who, instead of dreaming of becoming *coureurs de bois,* will be educated and trained to be good workers." Both the intendant and governor found in Canada a populace deeply involved in the fur trade, with a taste for independence and highly intolerant of the new administrative regime. "One must not expect to make people here submissive and always respectful of the King's law and of those who represent his authority, since there has probably never been a country where so many people, even the foremost in every profession, have sought to deny it," the intendant reiterated. This task was all the more difficult because bad habits were inculcated early: "I cannot begin to describe to you, Monseigneur, the appeal that the life of a savage has for all the young men here, who want to do nothing, to be bound by nothing, to abandon themselves entirely to Indian life, and to place themselves beyond correction." The *coureurs de bois,* who engaged in the fur trade illegally since the Company of the West Indies alone held the monopoly, came to symbolize this incipient rebellion. The government took draconian measures: "His Majesty requests that the governors bring about a swift remedy to the harm caused by the *coureurs de bois,* who have increased in number because settlers provide them with the merchandise needed to continue their trade." The ordinances multiplied, notably in 1673, 1674, and 1682, and were renewed at the beginning of the eighteenth century, but the authorities ran a certain risk. In 1695, the intendant remarked that "200 or 300 men engaged in the fur-trade, being unaccustomed to fishing and agriculture and being without families, could easily defect to the English and by this means make them the masters of the trade with the Indians." But the adventurous life of the *coureurs de bois* provided the colony with excellent soldiers and with exceptional personnel for explorations, from Marquette to La Verendrye.[11]

Colbert had recommended to Talon that he extend the frontiers of New France and invade New Holland. This expansionist policy benefited from several assets: the taste for adventure of the *coureurs de bois,* the competence of men like Talon, Frontenac, and Iberville, and the resolve of exceptional personalities like Cavelier de La Salle. First Talon and then Frontenac, named governor, were well acquainted with the exploits and voyages of De Luth, Jean Nicolet, Radisson, Groseiller, and many other anonymous *coureurs de bois* who followed the waterways in their birchbark canoes and plunged further westward. The Great Lakes and Hudson Bay were opened to the French, while the Indians spoke of the "Vermillion Sea," the "Western Sea," and the longed-for passage to China. Whereas Talon gathered information but tried to restrain all initiatives, Frontenac encouraged them. In 1667 he directed Louis Jolliet and Father Marquette "to go discover the great river that the savages call Michissippi, which reputedly flows into the sea of California." Only

ONE MUST NOT EXPECT TO MAKE PEOPLE HERE SUBMISSIVE AND ALWAYS RESPECTFUL OF THE KING'S LAW

Jolliet returned to Montreal, but the Mississippi was inscribed on the maps. In November 1674, Frontenac presented to his minister a young Norman, Cavelier de La Salle, a man of spirit and intelligence capable "of all enterprises and discoveries one may wish to assign him." On May 13, 1675, Louis XIV ennobled La Salle and provided him with letters patent, "we have permitted and permit you by all present, signed in our name, to undertake the discovery of the western part of our said country of New France, and, in order to accomplish this enterprise, to construct forts wherever you deem it necessary." Cavelier de La Salle, animated by an unflagging resolve, traversed the Great Lakes and the Illinois country. Despite the setbacks and mistakes, he persevered and in April, 1682, took possession of the territory "along the River Colbert or Mississippi, from beyond the country of the Sioux all the way to its mouth." Louisiana was born. The following year, Colbert disappeared from the scene.[12]

The colonial policy implemented by Colbert was maintained by his son and successor Seignelay, with a new impulse supplied by the Pontchartrains, first Louis and then his son Jérôme, entrusted with the Department of State at the Ministry of the Marine between 1690 and 1715. The Pontchartrains were at the center of a veritable "pressure group" in which bankers, merchants, administrators, and nobles maintained close business and familial ties. Moreover, both for the Islands and Louisiana, the same men were found at the head of the commercial companies or acting as high-ranking civil servants of the central administration. The Pontchartrains would abandon the rigidity of Colbert's system due to the distrust that it provoked and the financial crisis it induced. The upper bourgeoisie and the merchants of the Atlantic ports were losing interest in colonization and wanted to continue trade with the Americas only if it proved profitable. Settlement, exploration, and wars only succeeded in ruining public finances.

Nevertheless, the Pontchartrains did not totally turn their backs on mercantilist ideas, for Louis de Pontchartrain placed at the head of Santo Domingo the excellent Ducasse who, from 1691 to 1700, developed the system of plantations and commerce that made of this colony a model of "the sugar island" in the eighteenth century. This success did not, though, prevent the minister from thinking that private companies ought to become involved again in America, and he and his son Jérôme initiated the French penetration of Spanish America in the years 1705-12. Underadministrated and given over to anarchy, the Spanish colonies

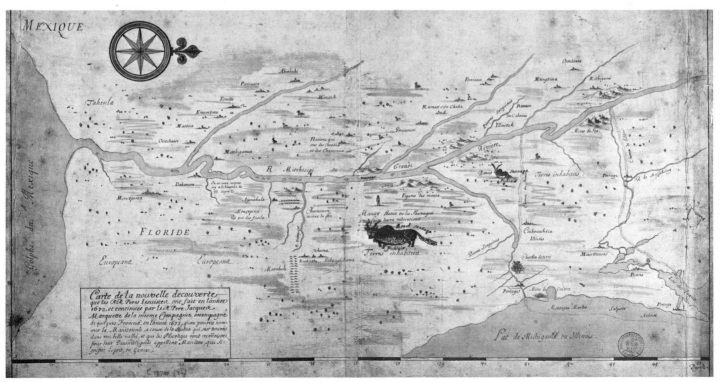

Catalogue 214

constituted an open market where only the British dared compete with the French. In August, 1701, the French easily obtained the privilege of the *Asiento* which, under the cover of providing blacks to the Spanish colonies, also allowed them to introduce other diverse merchandise. But hardly had a year passed before the War of the Spanish Succession (1702-13) broke out when Louis XIV placed his grandson, the duc d'Anjou, on the Spanish throne. The dynastic quarrel was only a pretext, for the sovereign himself wrote: "the principal object of the present war is the commerce of the Indies and the riches they produce."[13]

Well before the Spanish affair, Louis de Pontchartrain had dreamed that Louisiana might become a "French Mexico." His fear was that English ambitions would deprive the kingdom of the longed-for silver mines. The minister had entrusted to the Abbé Jean-Baptiste Dubos the mission of collecting throughout Europe all possible information on the valley of the Mississippi. Pontchartrain also received pressure from scholars, such as Claude Delisle, who favored the exploration of unknown lands to the west. The minister confided the task of exploration and settlement to an experienced sailor and excellent soldier, Le Moyne d'Iberville.

The French occupation of the coasts of Louisiana was far from easy. From 1698 to 1702 Iberville spared no efforts to bring about the creation of Mobile and to ensure good relations with the Indians. But the new colony hardly aroused much enthusiasm in the mother country, where the court was preoccupied with "the discovery of mines" and merchants refrained from investing so long as prospects of development remained uncertain. During the War of Spanish Succession the young colony suffered from isolation and financial distress despite the qualities of Iberville's successor, his brother Bienville. It was with resignation and in order to save the colony that Pontchartrain delivered it over to the monopoly of the financier Antoine Crozat, who created in 1712 the Company of Louisiana in order to promote the growth of trade. The country then had barely two hundred inhabitants, but the Indian diplomacy of Iberville and Bienville had permitted the establishment of friendly relations with the major tribes and, despite the low level of population, all of Lower Louisiana was acquired by the French. The financial and publicizing efforts of Crozat bore fruit: the royal entourage and merchants showed interest in the "country of the Sioux." In the field, the search for mines led especially to the exploration of the Missouri River and to incursions toward the west. At the end of the reign of Louis XIV, Louisiana was hardly more than a name on a map and formed along with New France, from Hudson Bay to the Gulf of Mexico, the "Empire of the French."

In 1715 the Sun King died. The Treaty of Utrecht (1713) brought a halt to French expansion: the Union Jack floated over Hudson Bay, Newfoundland, and Acadia, and the *Asiento* was tranferred to England. Despite these reverses, France was never stronger or better respected in America. This situation had resulted from the policy followed for a half century by the ministers, administrators, and officers of Louis the Great. Under his reign France asserted itself as a colonial power of the first order, a place it retained until the second half of the twentieth century. Their policy had also put into place the administrative apparatus that would endure and provide a decisive reinforcement to commercial capitalism, allowing an unprecedented development in the eighteenth century, notably in the Islands. But the despotism of the mother country and the imposition of strict mercantilist controls were greatly resented by the colonists. Large and small white landowners alike, from New France to Santo Domingo, violently objected to the new governmental restrictions. The prosperous colonies would yearn for independence from this yoke, and the assessment of the governor of Guadeloupe, the marquis de Mirabeau, was prophetic: "the New World will certainly shake off the yoke of the Old, and there is already evidence that this has begun in the strongest and most prosperous colonies, but once one of them has taken the plunge, the others will soon follow. In vain will we rack our brains, both in London and Paris, wondering how to prevent this from happening, but whatever we try will only hasten its accomplishment."[14]

Catalogue 221

FOOTNOTES

1. This essay was translated from the original French by Steven G. Reinhardt. Hubert Deschamps, *Les Méthodes et doctrines coloniales de la France* (Paris, 1953), 14.
2. Lescarbot, *Histoire de la Nouvelle France* (Paris, 1612), 432.
3. Deschamps, *Les Méthodes et doctrines,* 26-33 and Pierre Chaunu and Richard Gascon, *Histoire économique et sociale de la France* (Paris, 1977), I *(1450-1660).*
4. Cited in Philippe May, "Nicolas Fouquet et la politique coloniale de Louis XIV," *Revue d'Histoire Coloniale,* XXXIII (1940-41), 71.
5. Louis André Boiteux, "Un économiste méconnu: Du Noyer de Saint-Martin et ses projets (1608-1639)," *Revue d'Histoire Coloniale,* XLIV (1957), 28-38.
6. Charles Frostin, "Du peuplement pénal de l'Amérique française au XVIIᵉ et XVIIIᵉ siècles: hésitations et contradictions du pouvoir royal en matière d'interdiction," *Annales de Bretagne,* LXXXV (1978), 1, 67-94; Marcel Giraud, "Tendances humanitaires à la fin du regne de Louis XIV," *Revue Historique* (1953), 2, 217-37.
7. Instruction au Sieur Talon s'en allant en Nouvelle France, in *Lettres, instructions et mémoires de Colbert* (Paris, 1845), III (Pt. 2), 389-90.
8. Article XVII de la Charte de la Compagnie des Cent Associés, *Mercure de France,* XIV (1628), p. 245; Instructions pour M. de Bouterque s'en allant intendant (1668), in *Lettres, instructions et mémoires de Colbert,* III, 404; Instructions au Comte de Frontenac, in *ibid.,* III, 579; Instructions au Sieur Talon, in *ibid.,* III, 390.
9. This very valuable correspondence has been preserved at the Archives Nationales in Paris under the heading C 11A for Canada, C 9A for the Antilles, and C 13A for Louisiana. The responses of the minister were filed under the heading of Série A, Actes du Pouvoir souverain, and Série B, Ordres du Roi et Dépêches concernant les Colonies. Ottawa and Washington possess photocopies of the entire correspondence.
10. Pierre Renouvin, *Histoire des Relations internationales* (Paris, 1955), III, Vol. 2, 17-56.
11. Archives Nationales, C 11A, 6 f82; 4 f51; 7 f90; 4 f11; 13 f432.
12. Pierre Margry, *Origine française des Pays d'Outre Mer* (Paris, 1879), I, 337.
13. Marcel Giraud, *Histoire de la Louisiane française* (Paris, 1953), I, 34; Charles Frostin, "Les Pontchartrain et la pénétration commerciale en Amérique espagnole (1690-1715)," *Revue Historique* (April-June, 1971), 319.
14. Charles Frostin, *Les Révoltes Blanches à Saint-Domingue au XVIIᵉ et XVIIIᵉ siècles* (Paris, 1975); Henri Sée, "Les Economistes et la Question coloniale au XVIIIᵉ siècle," *Revue d'Histoire Coloniale,* XVII (1929), 384.

FROM NEW FRANCE TO LOUISIANA: POLITICS AND GEOGRAPHY
MONIQUE PELLETIER

In response to the request addressed to Louis XIV by Robert Cavelier, Sieur de La Salle, the king on May 12, 1678, issued letters patent commissioning him "to undertake the discovery of the western part of New France, and to construct forts there," all at the explorer's own expense — with the provision, however, that he be accorded the commercial monopoly in buffalo hides and with the recommendation that he not interfere with the savages who brought beaver and other pelts to Montreal.[1] The king did not wish to disturb the precarious equilibrium that existed and was wary of undertakings that risked upsetting the economic structure of Canada.

Even after La Salle had brought his mission to a successful conclusion, the king's concern resurfaced in his letter of August 5, 1683, addressed to the governor of New France, Monsieur de La Barre, who was hostile to the discoverer: "I am persuaded, like you, that the discovery of the Sieur de La Salle is worth very little; in the future one must prevent such undertakings, which only debauch the inhabitants with hopes of gain and diminish returns from beaver skins." The desire to limit the area of Canadian development had already been expressed by the minister of Louis XIV, Jean-Baptiste Colbert, who on April 5, 1666, wrote to the intendant of New France, Jean Talon:

The King has approved of your laying claim to the far reaches of Canada and, at the same time, your preparing legal acts of possession, because by these means you extend his sovereignty. I assume, though, that you have already discussed this matter with Monsieur de Tracy and other officials and realize that it would be better to limit settlement to an area that the colony can easily maintain rather than to take on too vast an area which one day we may be forced to abandon, diminishing the reputation of the King and of the Crown.

Eight years later, in 1674, Colbert expressed the same concern when he worried about the extension of Jesuit missions and the ambitious projects of the governor of New France, Louis de Buade, comte de Frontenac. The minister's advice was to concentrate on those regions close at hand, to clear and settle the most fertile lands only on the condition that they be located near the sea and thus in communication with France. Nevertheless, the preceding year Louis Jolliet, accompanied by the Jesuit father Jacques Marquette, descended the Mississippi to the Arkansas country, thereby showing the way to Cavelier de La Salle (Cat. 214). But Colbert, apparently uninterested in the newly-discovered regions or distrustful of their discoverer, wrote in 1677 to the intendant of New France, Jacques Duchesneau: "His Majesty does not wish to grant permission to the Sieur Jolliet to settle with twenty men in the Illinois country. We must multiply the number of inhabitants in Canada before we even think about other lands, and that must be your guiding principle in regard to the new discoveries made."

LOUISIANA AND LA SALLE

It was in these circumstances that in 1678 Cavelier de La Salle offered his services "to undertake the discovery of the western part of New France." This time the king seemed more open to projects of expansion — "there is nothing dearer to our heart than the discovery of this region" — but of equal importance to him was the prospect of opening a route to the riches exploited by the Spanish, because, he added, in this region "it appears that one can find the route to penetrate all the way to Mexico." In effect, Jolliet and Marquette had verified that the Mississippi did not flow into the Pacific but into the Gulf of Mexico, and had also emphasized the importance of the tributaries from the West, which would allow access even to the Vermillion Sea and California. From the outset of La Salle's expedition, the king was therefore interested in the location of the lower valley of the Mississippi and its proximity to the Spanish colonies.

But La Salle was not against colonial settlements; he had proved as much on the shores of Lake Ontario when he "formed settlements" on the lands the king had given him to clear by letters patent of May 13, 1675, and where he improved the defenses of Fort Frontenac. An account of the discoveries of La Salle presented to the king by one of La Salle's defenders, the Abbé Claude Bernou, before the outcome of the mission was even known described the development of this undertaking:

> Since the land along the shores of this lake is very fertile, the Sieur La Salle had several arpents planted in wheat, vegetables, and garden herbs, which thrived very well, although the wheat was damaged by grasshoppers, as ordinarily happens on newly cleared land in Canada due to the high moisture content of the soil. He raised fowl and cattle, of which he presently has more than twenty-five, and, since the trees are very fine and suitable for building houses and boats, and since the winter is much shorter than in Canada, there is reason to believe that a considerable colony will soon be formed there, thirteen or fourteen families and a Recollet mission already being established.

During this time, the narrator continued, "persons who were envious [of La Salle] . . . solicited the Sieur Jolliet to forestall him in his discoveries," but no settlements resulted from the voyage of the earlier explorer. In these first approaches, the

FROM LAKE ONTARIO AND FORT FRONTENAC ONE COULD GO BY CANOE ALL THE WAY TO THE GULF OF MEXICO

future of Louisiana was already outlined. Would it become an extension of inclement New France, or would it be the first step in new conquests toward the Southwest for more immediate profit?

Cavelier de La Salle left France in July, 1678, and arrived at Quebec in September. He followed in the footsteps of Jolliet and Marquette in order to accomplish Frontenac's optimistic plans for this "admirable" region where navigation was so easy that "from Lake Ontario and Fort Frontenac one could go by canoe all the way to the Gulf of Mexico, with only one portage to make." At the beginning of 1679, La Salle had a fort constructed on Lake Ontario at the mouth of the Niagara River. By way of Lake Erie, he went to Lake Huron and on September 12 entered Lake Michigan, reached Green Bay, and then constructed another fort at the southern shore of Lake Michigan, on the Miami River. By portage he reached the Illinois River and there constructed Fort Crèvecoeur. It was from there that La Salle, on February 29, 1680, sent Father Louis Hennepin, Michel Accault, and Antoine Auguelle on a reconnaissance mission toward the Mississippi River, which they followed upstream until captured by the Sioux on April 11. They would later return to Canada with Duluth by way of the Wisconsin River and Green Bay. As for La Salle, he decided to return to his base at Fort Frontenac, which he reached on May 6, leaving Henri de Tonti at Fort Crèvecoeur.

On August 10, La Salle again left for the Illinois country, passing directly from Lake Ontario to Lake Huron, but missing Tonti, who had not waited for him. During this time, war raged between the Iroquois and the Illinois Indians, for which La Salle was held responsible by the Intendant Duchesneau, who complained in 1681 of La Salle's mistreatment of the Iroquois: "after receiving permission to discover the mouth of the Great River of Mississippi, and, as he said, the concession of the Illinois country, he acted immoderately: he mistreated them [the Iroquois] and said he would supply arms and gunpowder to the Illinois Indians and would fight to the death." In November, 1682, the new governor of Canada, Antoine Le Febvre, sieur de La Barre, renewed the accusation that La Salle had touched off the war against the Iroquois.

The explorer was also reproached for having granted leave to his men to trade in forbidden territory.

Once the expedition was launched, it was still essential to convince the king of the necessity of colonizing the regions to be traversed by La Salle. The Abbé Bernou, a Parisian ecclesiastic linked to a coterie grouped around the *Gazette* and Eusèbe Renadot, grandson of the founder of this newspaper published from 1631 to 1914, dedicated himself to this task. Bernou dreamed of a bishopric in the newly discovered territories but failed to consider the territorial claims of the bishops of Quebec, who did not hesitate to promote their rights in expanding areas of New France. In his support of La Salle, Abbé Bernou spared no efforts: he presented three documents to the marquis de Seignelay, minister of the Marine and son of Colbert.

The first was a memoir that put forward the advantages of colonizing an area in which the French preceded the English. These new lands, the memoir claimed, would feed the settlers of Canada and give France the monopoly of the fur trade "because the savages who at present make every effort to flee from the Iroquois would settle in this fine region where they could hunt in peace under the protection of the French." One could also arm other tribes there against the Iroquois. Finally, such expansion would facilitate the serious conversion of the savages.

This promising picture was supported by two other documents that Bernou wrote without waiting for La Salle's return or even the latest news of the expedition of 1678-82 — a report accompanied by a manuscript map on which one important element was missing — the position of the mouth of the Mississippi in the Gulf of Mexico.

Bernou's account, entitled *Relation of the Discoveries and Voyages of the Sieur de La Salle (1679-1681)*, included an account of the expedition of Hennepin, Accault, and Auguelle, who had been sent from Fort Crèvecoeur on the Illinois River to reconnoiter the route to the Mississippi and then the course of the latter "above and below the mouth of the Divine [Illinois] River." La Salle did not restrict his ambitions to the lower course of the Mississippi but wanted to be the discoverer of the West of New France, of the upper valley of the Mississippi included as part of Louisiana on Bernou's map (Cat. 218);

moreover, he gave a complete description of it in one of his letters, although he himself had not participated in the expedition. But in this region La Salle competed directly with Duluth, a *coureur de bois* who could claim to have been there first.

The map, like Bernou's *Relation*, was incomplete: the lower course of the Mississippi was left blank. Nonetheless, the map was an influential document of large dimensions, executed with great care and art, drawn by Bernou to attract the attention of Seignelay. He designated two distinct regions: Canada or New France, and Louisiana, which followed the valley of the Mississippi all the way to the Ohio River. The *Relation* noted that the Iroquois used the Ohio, which "has its source thirty or forty leagues [one league = approximately 4 km or 3 miles] to the south of Niagara, flows toward the west for more than two hundred leagues and flows into the River Colbert [Mississippi] twenty-five leagues below the mouth of the Illinois River." Here was a potential new route to join New France to the valley of the Mississippi and the Gulf of Mexico on the condition that the Iroquois problem could be solved.

On his map, Bernou left between New France and Louisiana an intermediate zone formed by the Great Lakes and the Illinois country, and one can verify that the abbé did possess precise information on the Great Lakes. The valley of the Illinois, which had already tempted Jolliet, also seduced La Salle. Contemporary texts contained enthusiastic descriptions of it. One can read on the large globe that Father Vincenzo Maria Coronelli prepared for Louis XIV an inscription that praises the abundant resources of the Illinois valley: one finds there "all sorts of wild beasts, beavers, and game; fish are also abundant there; and during the winter the game from Canada migrates toward its confluence with the Mississippi." Tonti's text, although slightly different, also insisted on the attractiveness of the region: "The surrounding regions [of the Illinois River] are as delightful as they are fertile; one can see there all sorts of animals, deer, doe, lynx, elk, bison, goats, lambs, sheep, rabbits, and an infinity of others, but few beaver." Inclusion of the note was certainly a bit forced but necessary to attract the attention of the king and the French public to the value of the discoveries; it also expressed the very real joy that explorers felt while crossing these new lands so much more hospitable than the frigid valley of the Saint Lawrence. The propagandistic accounts of the period never failed to mention this

Catalogue 220

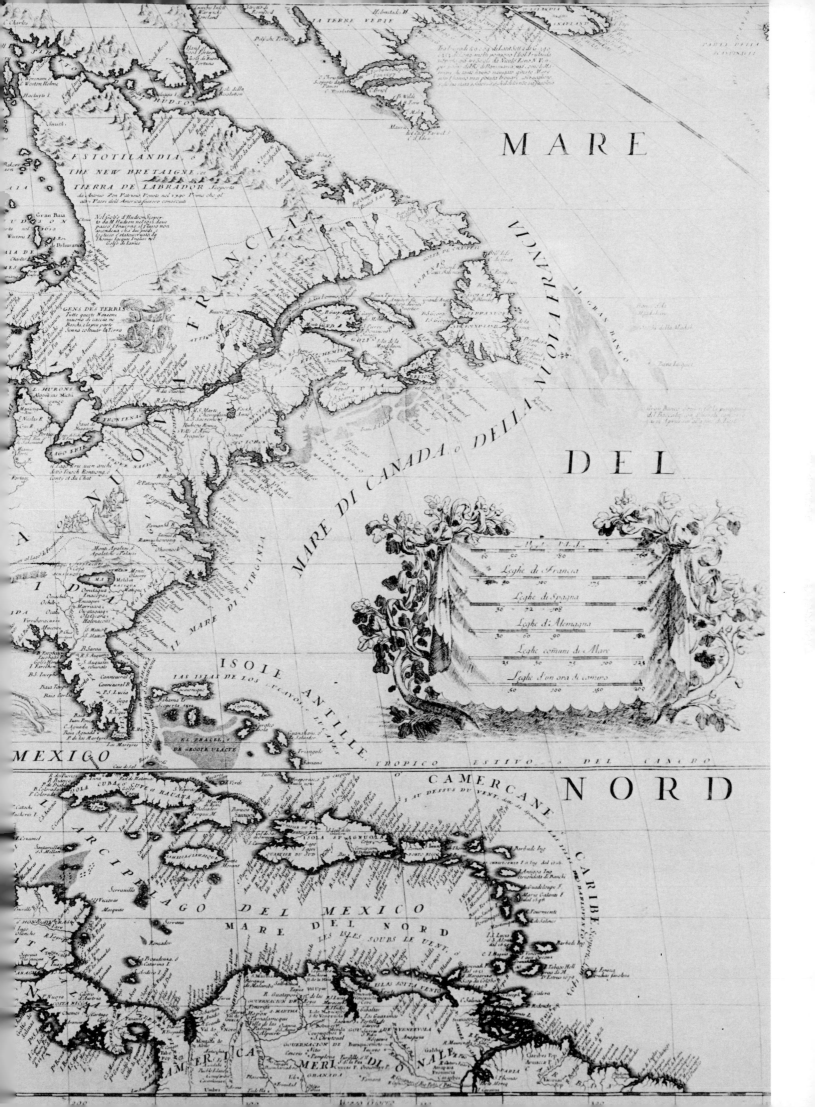

sharp contrast between the old and new lands.

Bernou was imitated by Captain Roussel, the author of the map published in Hennepin's *Description of Louisiana* (figure 1).

Because Hennepin claimed discoveries in the upper valley of the Mississippi for himself, he gave the name "Louisiana" only to the lower course of the river without even drawing it, for he had no more information about it than Bernou had.

Figure 1. *Carte de la Nouvelle France et de la Louisiane nouvellement découverte* par Roussel, 1683. (Publiée dans: Louis Hennepin, *Description de la Louisiane*) Cliché Bibl. nat., Paris.

THE POSITION OF THE MOUTH OF THE MISSISSIPPI AND THE FUTURE OF LA SALLE'S DISCOVERIES

It was then up to La Salle, from whom the latest news of the outcome of his expedition was awaited. A letter written in 1682, which is now preserved in the Bibliothèque Nationale in Paris with the papers of Bernou, gives a description of the course followed by the discoverer to the confluence of the Missouri River. In it, one can detect a change of opinion concerning the easiness of travel between Canada and the Gulf of Mexico: its author openly criticized the optimism of Jolliet, who "pretended that communication with Louisiana was very simple." One must not forget that the preceding year, before beginning his long journey, La Salle went to Montreal, where he found Frontenac had already left in May. Given his difficult relations with the Jesuits, this loss of important support must have caused La Salle to worry about future relations between the regions he would discover and New France, and undoubtedly made him cautious in the presentation of his findings and his plans for future projects.

In a letter that can be dated from October,

1682, he attempted to explain the reasons for his silence: "Although my discovery is made and I have descended the Mississippi River to the Gulf of Mexico, at 27 degrees of latitude north, it is impossible for me to send you this year either the account or the map. Upon my return, I was attacked by a deadly illness that held me in its grip for forty days, since May 10, in danger of my life, and left me so weak that it was impossible for me to think about anything for the following four months." Moreover, he depicts his expedition as a difficult undertaking. It required great skill and courage to cross territories occupied by belligerent tribes that had to be approached without antagonizing them. His wish was to be able to follow up by sea the discovery he had made by descending the Mississippi to its mouth. Everything, then, points to the fact that he knew the geographic position of the mouth and would be able to relocate it easily along the Gulf Coast. He declared it to be near the Spanish and the passage of their fleet, and he thought that the fertility of the region would permit the establishment of a strong colony well protected by an easily defended river mouth. Seven or eight rivers, he affirmed, flowed into the lower Mississippi, five of which came from New Biscay and New Mexico, where the Spanish had found so many mines. The new settlement would therefore serve as a base to "harass and even entirely ruin New Spain simply by arming the Savages." Thus La Salle fulfilled his contract: the strategic position of the lower Mississippi was without question.

All the same, the discoverer did not burn all bridges with New France, which could still supply aid, "Louisiana being only two days from Lake Erie which joins Lake Frontenac [Ontario]." Everything was set to develop this new project, as would be illustrated in the map drawn up in Paris in 1684 by the Québecois hydrographer Jean-Baptiste-Louis Franquelin and based on information provided by La Salle, who finally returned to France (Cat. 219). For the discoverer, the Mississippi must have replaced the Rio Escondido of former maps: its mouth was at the same latitude — he estimated it incorrectly at twenty-seven degrees — and its lower course flowed in the same direction. In the imagination of La Salle, the Rio Bravo, which he christened the "Seignelay River," became a tributary that joined the Mississippi "one hundred leagues west northwest of the spot where it [the Mississippi] flowed into the Gulf of Mexico.

One should note that the previous year another version of this geographic error had already been used; it relied particularly on the testimony of Father Zenobé Membré, a Recollet missionary who accompanied La Salle down the Mississippi and who argued that its mouth was located between twenty-seven and twenty-eight degrees of latitude, about thirty leagues from the Rio Bravo. Therefore, in 1683 Coronelli again relied on this thesis for the globe he was constructing for Louis XIV and revealed it by publishing maps drawn from his massive undertaking (Cat. 220). Whereas Franquelin's map remained more or less secret, the drawing of Father Coronelli received wide dissemination.

The project for a new settlement presented by La Salle in October, 1682, was not at all original. Abbé Bernou had already proposed a similar plan to Seignelay on January 18, 1682, in which he suggested a settlement in "Floride," at the mouth of the Rio Bravo, between twenty-five and thirty degrees latitude, with the support of freebooters from Saint-Domingue. By means of this new base, he planned to conquer New Biscay with its gold, silver, and lead mines worked by the Spanish. At first, Bernou hoped to entrust the operation to Count Diego de Peñalosa, a former governor of New Mexico who had been chased out by the Inquisition and who subsequently offered his services first to England and then to France. Peñalosa proposed the conquest of New Mexico and especially of the regions to the north, "Quivira" and "Thegayo." Bernou possessed a map of this region where the Rio Bravo had its source; he sent it to Coronelli, who reproduced it on Louis XIV's globe before publishing in France a map of New Mexico that used the same design (figure 2). The immense globe — almost four meters in diameter — was a marvelous instrument of propaganda whose contents were jealously guarded by Bernou, who was then in Rome.

On his globe, Coronelli responded to the wishes of Bernou and La Salle by according special attention to the mines of New Mexico, which served as inspiration for the artistic and realistic border of the globe's inscription. The evocation of the mineral riches of a weakened Spanish empire could not help but whet the appetite of Louis XIV, whose coffers had been emptied by war. The profits to be gained from such a conquest would surely be realized much more quickly than those to be had

from the long-term development of the too-vast Louisiana territory, whose resources were still so poorly known and whose main settlements were yet to be determined, even though the Illinois country had attracted great approbation. On Franquelin's map one can clearly discern the limits of La Salle's Louisiana. Whereas New France included the region of the Great Lakes, Louisiana extended mostly along the valleys of the Mississippi and Illinois Rivers — the latter region being called "colony of the Sieur de La Salle" — and included the tributaries to the west of the Mississippi, as well as the River Seignelay (Rio Bravo). To the east, Louisiana stopped at the Bay of the Holy Spirit, where Florida begins. (Earlier maps gave this bay impressive dimensions, but it was, in fact, the much smaller Galveston Bay.) To the north of Florida, Louisiana included the valley of the Saint Louis (Ohio) River, to which La Salle had not renounced his claim.

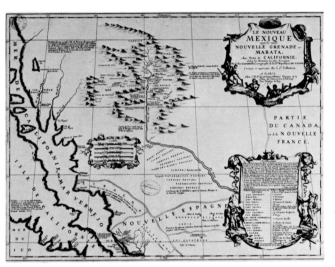

Figure 2. *Le Nouveau Mexique appelé aussi Nouvelle Grenada et Marata, avec partie de California selon les mémoires les plus nouveaux par le Père Coronelli. A Paris, chez J. B. Nolin, 168-, Cliché Bibl. nat., Paris.*

THE CONSEQUENCES OF A GEOGRAPHIC "ERROR"

La Salle's official position on the development of his discoveries can be found in the two memoirs he addressed to Seignelay. First of all, he proposed the founding of a fortified post sixty leagues above the mouth of the Colbert (Mississippi) River, from where the French could "harass the Spanish in the regions where they derive their wealth." This post would be easy to defend, given the narrowness of the river and the swampiness of the surrounding land; the savages won over by La Salle and the freebooters of Saint-Domingue would help him in this task. This first memoir was intended to win the support of the king; the second reveals La Salle's uneasiness about the future of the colony in the Illinois country, so dear to his heart but menaced by his enemy, the current governor of New France. The letters patent issued by the king on April 14, 1684, responded to La Salle's wishes since they placed him in command "in the regions in North America that again will be subject to our control, from Fort Saint Louis on the Illinois River to New Biscay." Nonetheless, one can ask if the geographic errors that helped La Salle obtain the support of the king were not committed on purpose or at least accentuated in order to gain royal approval for the new voyage by sea envisaged by La Salle since 1682, when the political situation in Canada had changed to his detriment.

Leaving France on August 1, 1684, La Salle stopped off at Saint-Domingue, where he fell ill. One of the members of the expedition, Minet, in an account unfavorable to La Salle, related how the discoverer, while delirious, believed "that everyone he saw had come to prosecute him, saying that he had fooled Monsieur le Marquis de Seignelay." According to the same source, at Cap Saint Antoine (Cuba), La Salle informed the captain of the fleet, the sieur de Beaujeu, "that his river was at 28°20′ at the top of the Gulf of Mexico, that one could recognize it by the natural jetty it extended into the sea, but that their rendezvous was in the Bay of Spiritu Sancto, where they first must go and then follow the coast."

La Salle held to the limits he had assigned to Louisiana on Franquelin's map and hoped that by skirting the coast he would be able to relocate the Mississippi. But he failed in his undertaking and was even reduced to looking for a decent port along the coast: he finally settled on Bay Saint Louis (present-day Matagorda Bay). Minet, in a letter to Seignelay, admitted his perplexity: "I cannot tell you with any certainty that the river flows into the lakes we have seen, for it could as easily flow into the Bay of the Holy Spirit or perhaps even the Rio Grande." It was by an overland route that La Salle finally reached the Mississippi on February 18, 1686; from there he wished to make a second trip to the Illinois country, but he was assassinated on March 19, 1687, on the shores of the Canots (Trinity) River. When in 1690 his brother, the Abbé Cavelier, presented a memoir showing the usefulness of continuing the work already begun, he made a point of proving that the Gulf of Mexico-Illinois connection was superior to the Montreal-Illinois connection, giving La Salle's last expedition a significance that the prospects for the conquest of New Biscay had partially obscured.

Figure 3. *Planisphère terrestre où sont marquées les longitudes de divers lieux de la Terre*, trouvées par les observations des éclipses des satellites de Jupiter par Mr de Cassini le fils. A Paris, chez J. B. Nolin, 1696. (Réduction gravée du grand planisphère de l'Observatoire) Cliché Bibl. nat., Paris.

THE REDISCOVERY OF THE MOUTH OF THE MISSISSIPPI AND THE ORIGINS OF A NEW LOUISIANA

The War of the League of Augsburg temporarily halted all colonial projects in America, but after the Peace of Ryswick of 1697 financial exigency again led to the search for deposits of precious metals. Nevertheless, the question of the Spanish Succession led Louis XIV to act prudently, for he did not wish to antagonize Charles II. It was in these circumstances that on June 23, 1698, the minister of the Marine, Louis de Pontchartrain, chose Pierre Le Moyne d'Iberville to rediscover the mouth of the Mississippi. The imprecise and misleading documentation of previous voyages was of little use to Iberville, who left Brest on October 24, 1698. Stopping off in Pensacola Bay, he made contact with the Spanish, who had recently built a fort there to ward off French expansion; while in Pensacola he undoubtedly learned that the Rio Palizada and the Mississippi were two names for what was in fact the same river. On March 2, 1698, a storm forced him to seek refuge behind some rocks where he found fresh water in a strong current: "These rocks are of petrified wood combined with mud," he asserted, "which made me know that here was the Palisade River, which to me seemed well-named because when one is at its mouth, which lies about one league and a half from these rocks, they appear to block the river completely." Iberville had fulfilled his mission: France had reconquered the mouth of the Mississippi, the natural outlet of Louisiana, of whose importance the negotiators of the Treaty of

Ryswick were reminded.

The second expedition of Le Moyne d'Iberville, which left France on October 17, 1699, was intended to assess the value and feasibility of a French settlement on the banks of the Mississippi. But when Iberville left Biloxi on May 28, 1700, he had not yet accomplished his mission, for he instructed those who stayed behind to catalogue the natural resources: pearls, wood, and mines.

With Iberville, the picture began to be clearer, more precise. The French would progressively have a much more exact image of Louisiana thanks to the simultaneous progress made by explorers and geographers. In France, calculations made by astronomers of the Academy of Sciences permitted the more accurate depiction of the world: the data were recorded on a large planisphere sketched on the floor of one of the towers of the Observatory in Paris (figure 3). Whereas geographers at the end of the seventeenth century, notably Claude and Guillaume Delisle, benefited from these data, Coronelli was unable to use them for Louis XIV's globe (1681-83); his guardian, Le Large, explains that "because it would have taken too long to redo all the individual maps he had chosen . . . he did not use any of them." In 1700 Guillaume Delisle published his map of *L'Amérique Septentrionale* (North America) (figure 4), on which there was no longer a Louisiana but a very large Canada, a Florida that extended along the Gulf of Mexico, and a New Mexico spread out on both sides of the Rio Bravo — Louisiana was still trying to establish itself, and designs on Spanish colonies had by then

dimmed. The author shows the route to the California or Vermillion Sea via northern New Mexico crossed by the Pekitanoni (Missouri) River, which was continued first by the Saint François River and then by the Saint Jérôme River. The source of the Saint Jérôme lay in the same mountains from which the Rio de Bona Guia (Colorado) flowed in the direction of the California Sea. In 1700 Claude Delisle, father of Guillaume, published in the *Journal des savans* a letter addressed to the celebrated astronomer Jean-Dominque Cassini concerning the position of the mouth of the Mississippi that aptly shows French scholars' interest in this subject. Cassini had developed a method for the calculation of longitudes based on the observation of the satellites of Jupiter, but Delisle avowed, "I will first of all declare that I was unable to derive any help from your observations, which had proved so useful to me before, because the satellites cannot yet be observed from that region, and because the eclipses of the moon, which had previously proved so useful in place of those of the satellites, are also unavailable to us. In truth, one can see a few of these lunar eclipses observed in Europe and at Vera Cruz, but they are useless for locating the mouth of the Mississippi." Delisle condemned Coronelli's map — published in France by Jean-Baptiste Nolin — "which cannot be relied upon." He stated that the coast of "Florida" north of the Gulf of Mexico "is one of the least known of America," its cartography being practically nonexistent. Therefore, one must rely only on accounts of voyages, primarily those of the Spanish, then those pertaining to the La Salle expedition. Delisle read what had been printed about La Salle's voyages and questioned his companions on the last voyage. Several of them explained the failure of this last expedition by the fact that "the coast of Florida is very low": the mouth of the Mississippi would therefore be easily lost "in the land and swamps." In contrast, Bernou asserted that it must be "wide and deep." Delisle, who studied the course then attributed to the river, did not believe it could be confused with the Rio Escondido of the Spanish. The last voyage of La Salle — who landed at Matagorda Bay and traveled 250 leagues to reach the Arkansas territory while walking "sometimes to the northeast and sometimes to the east northeast" and crossing about twenty rivers, "a few of which flowed into the Mississippi, but most of which flowed into the sea" — had "shown that there

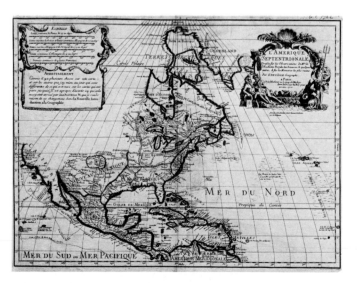

Figure 4. *L'Amérique septentrionale* dressée par G. Delisle, Paris, l'auteur, 1700. Cliché Bibl. nat., Paris.

must be a great deal of sea between the Mississippi River and Bay Saint Louis." Moreover, the shipwreck of the Spaniard Cabeza de Vaca to the west of the Mississippi and his long voyage along the coast to New Mexico led Delisle to argue that the mouth of the Mississippi was not as close to this province as the informants of Coronelli had thought. In addition, Delisle possessed a map of Le Moyne d'Iberville's voyage "to the southern coast of the Gulf of Mexico" sent to one of Iberville's friends, a copy of two of the explorer's letters, and finally another map drawn up by Monsieur de Chateaumorand. In light of all this evidence, the scholar concluded that the Mississippi flowed into the Gulf of Mexico at least one hundred leagues from the Rio Bravo. But he was not quite satisfied with his documentation: he entrusted to Iberville, about to leave on a second voyage, a map and memoirs that he himself had prepared, instructing the explorer to pay special attention to certain details. The Delisles' aproach to the difficult question of positioning the mouth of the Mississippi illustrates their meticulous methods: nothing escaped their attention, neither prior nor the most recent information. Dissatisfied with approximations, they demanded certitudes.

The Delisles would soon receive precise information on the course of the Mississippi from Charles Lesueur, who had discovered copper and lead mines on the Green River, a tributary of the Saint Pierre River, which flows into the Mississippi below the Falls of Saint Anthony of Padua. Lesueur was authorized by the minister of the Marine to take part in Iberville's second voyage in order to initiate the working of mines found in the "country of the Sioux." The mines continued and would continue to be the driving force behind expeditions, always directed towards the west. From March 2 to October 7, 1700, from 30° to 44°13′ of latitude, Lesueur went up the Mississippi River armed with a compass. He carefully noted its changing direction and at regular intervals measured the latitude, especially of villages and the confluence of tributaries.

As a result, Guillaume Delisle in 1702 was able to draw his *Carte de la rivière de Mississipi* (Map of the Mississippi River) which shows the river from its mouth to its source, on which, aside from a few exceptions (the Missouri River and the Moingona-Des Moines River), only the tributaries of the upper Mississippi were shown. The Red River, the Arkansas (Ossotoui) River, the Wabash

(Ouabache) River, and the Illinois River are only shown at their points of confluence with the Mississippi (Cat. 235). Delisle clearly illustrated Leseuer's 1699 remark that the French knew "perfectly all the rivers that flowed into the Mississippi all the way to the Illinois River." The extension of Canada toward the west and the southwest had not been halted; traders and *coureurs des bois* continued to explore the Sioux and Illinois countries in search of more hospitable living conditions than those found in the valley of the Saint Lawrence River.

Figure 5. *Carte de la Louisiane et du cours du Mississipi* dressée sur un grand nombre de mémoires entrautes sur ceux de Mr le Maire par Guillaume Delisle, Paris, 1718. Cliché Bibl. nat., Pais.

Sixteen years after the completion of this map, which remained in manuscript form, Delisle published his *Carte de la Louisiane* (Map of Louisiana), the sum of his research on the region (figure 5). This time Louisiana was accorded the place of honor: situated astride the Mississippi Valley, it was drained by a dense hydrographic network that was still crudely drawn, with the exception of the Mississippi River itself. The date of this document also gave it political significance: it was published just after the foundation of the Company of the West (August, 1717), the heir to Antoine Crozat's monopoly. The map highlighted not only the past by designating the itineraries followed by explorers since the sixteenth century, but also the future: Delisle called attention to the region included between the Missouri and Arkansas rivers, where he drew mountains with the promising notation "country rich in mines." It was the Canadian Jacques Bourdon, a settler in the village of Kaskaskia (on the Mississippi to the north of Cap Saint Antoine), who had pointed out the existence of gold, silver, copper, and lead mines in a radius of ten to twenty-five leagues to the west of the Mississippi, near the Meramec River. Delisle also presented a new tracing of the Missouri River by using notes sent by Etienne Véniard de Bourgmont. In a contemporary report of March 1, 1717, the missionary François Lemaire emphasized the significance of this river route whose upper course, he asserted, led to regions abundant in precious metals and whose sources adjoined those of the Rio Bravo and another river affording access to the Vermillion Sea, all of which the tracing of Delisle's 1700 map had anticipated.

One of the major difficulties encountered by La Salle and his successors was their poor knowledge of the coast of the Gulf of Mexico. After the death of Louis XIV, the duc d'Orleans (1674-1723) became regent and took an interest in the development of the sciences, notably geography. The Council of the Marine contributed to hydrographic progress by sending instruments to Dauphine Island. Father Antoine Laval made observations along the littoral of Louisiana, and several hydrographers, including the Sieur Valentin Devin, took surveys. As a result, the French came to know the coastline over a distance of 1,100 km (as the crow flies), at a scale of about 1:400,000. Cartographic work concentrated on the routes of access and penetration and on the sites for the first settlements. Once again in 1723 the exact longitude of the mouth of the Mississippi was the object of discussion at the Academy of Sciences, where Delisle contested the conclusions of Father Laval.

French expansion in North America under the reign of Louis XIV was therefore motivated by the following impulses: (1) the search for routes of communication leading to the Sea of California and Mexico; (2) the search for regions more hospitable than the cold valley of the Saint Lawrence; (3) the search for lands beyond English influence suitable for new settlements; and (4) the search for precious minerals needed to fill royal coffers emptied by wars. This expansion initially occurred under the control of New France, from whence the first explorers left for the West. When the direction of the course of the Mississippi became known, there then arose the question of locating its mouth in the Gulf of Mexico, whose coastline was still so poorly known: was it as close to the Spanish colonies as La Salle contended? The transformation of relations between France and Spain, the lack of interest shown by Louis XIV for overseas conquests, and personal conflicts of interest all slowed the progress of Louisiana, whose true founder was Le Moyne d'Iberville.

It would be pointless to debate the respective merits of Jolliet and La Salle, whose efforts were in vain due to the failure to provide them with the support needed to accomplish their true goal, the colonization of the lands they had discovered. The projected conquest of New Biscay gave new impetus to French expansion, but La Salle's personal failure in the Gulf of Mexico, renewed warfare in Europe, and the fear of displeasing Spain brought this second initiative to a halt. At the beginning of the eighteenth century, progress in geographic knowledge enabled the French to resolve the confusing situation so detrimental to their interests. If Louisiana affirmed its personality in relation to New France only after the death of its patron, Louis XIV, one must remember that the evolution of geographic knowledge, which began at the end of the seventeenth century, had been prepared by Colbert some twenty years before the end of the Great Century.

FOOTNOTE

1. This essay was translated from the French by Steven G. Reinhardt.

BIBLIOGRAPHY

Manuscript Texts

Papiers de l'abbé Bernou. Bibliothèque Nationale, Manuscrits, Clairambault 1016.

Lettres d l'abbé Bernou à Eusèbe Renaudot. Bibliothèque Nationale, Nouvelles acquisitions françaises 7497.

Inscriptions de globe terrestre de Louis XIV transcrites par François Le Large, garde du globe au château de Marly. (Bibliothèque Nationale, Fonds français 13 365.

Dossier Delisle. Archives Nationales de France, Séries 2 JJ 56.

Minet, *Journal de nostre voyage au golphe du Mexique.* Archives Nationales de Canada.

Printed Texts

Delisle, Claude. "Lettre de M. Delisle à M. de Cassini sûr l'embouchure de la rivière de Mississippi." *Journal des Savans* (1700), 211-17.

Le Clerq, C. *Premier établissement de la Foy.* Paris, 1691. (Containing the account, probably altered, of Father Zenobé Membré.)

Margry, Pierre, ed. *Découvertes et établissements des Français dans l'Ouest et dans le Sud de l'Amérique septentrionale, 1614-1698.* Paris, 1879, I-III.

Tonti, Henri de. *Dernières découvertes dans l'Amérique septentrionale de M. de la Salle.* Paris, 1697.

Principal Articles and Works Consulted

Delanglez, Jean. *Some Lasalle Journeys.* Chicago, 1938.
      Hennepin's Description of Louisiana. Chicago, 1941.

Frégault, Guy. *Pierre Le Moyne d'Iberville.* (Montreal, 1968.

Giraud, Marcel. *Histoire de la Louisiane française.* Paris, 1953-74, I-IV.

Pelletier, Monique. "Les globes de Louis XIV, sources françaises de l'oeuvre de Coronelli." *Imago mundi,* (1982), 72-89.

Villiers, Marc de. *La découverte du Missouri et l'histoire du fort d'Orléans (1673-1728.* Paris, 1925.

LA DÉLAISSÉE:
LOUISIANA DURING THE REIGN
OF LOUIS XIV
1699-1715
CARL A. BRASSEAUX

ouisiana is the namesake of Louis XIV, and well it should be, for the reign of the Sun King left an indelible stamp on the region. The French monarch's legacy, however, was not entirely beneficial. On the contrary, it might well be argued that Louisiana existed in spite of Louis XIV's colonial policies.

Indeed, the French exploration of the Mississippi Valley by Marquette, Joliet, La Salle, and others, which laid the groundwork for the colonization of Louisiana, was initially undertaken by adventurous individuals in contravention of a royal policy restricting French subjects to the St. Lawrence Valley.[1] Moreover, only by exaggerating both the proximity of the fabulous Mexican mines to the mouth of the Mississippi River and the ability of colonists to seize the source of Spain's wealth and thus replenish France's empty coffers was La Salle able to secure any royal assistance for his unsuccessful attempt in 1684 to colonize Louisiana.

The reluctance exhibited by the crown in funding La Salle's expedition reveals the low priority placed upon Mississippi Valley colonization by the king, and thus the expendability of the expedition should problems arise. Landing at Matagorda Bay, Texas, the colony was quickly overwhelmed by hostile Indians, disease, and internal dissension. Although aware of the expedition's crippling problems, the French monarchy was too beset with financial worries and too preoccupied with the War of the League of Augsburg to provide any assistance to the Frenchmen now stranded in Texas.[2]

The wealth promised by La Salle, however, proved too strong an attraction to be permanently forgotten by the increasingly impoverished Sun King, but the crown did not again underwrite a colonization expedition to the lower Mississippi Valley until the war's conclusion in 1698. Led by Pierre Le Moyne d'Iberville, the Canadian-born hero of the recent hostilities, this venture was plagued by the same fundamental problem that had crippled its predecessor — a lack of adequate royal support. Arriving off the Gulf Coast in 1699, Iberville duly explored the lower reaches of the Mississippi. Because of supply shortages, however, he was unable to reconnoiter sufficiently the neighboring coastline for a suitable colonization site. Iberville thus hastily selected an untenable location near present-day Biloxi, Mississippi. Far from the nearest anchorage, lacking a sanitary source of fresh water, plagued by mosquitoes, and surrounded by sterile soil, the settlement could not survive without assistance from France.[3] Fortunately for the eighty-man Biloxi colony, Iberville returned in 1700, but once again a lack of supplies forced the Canadian to curtail his exploration of the region and to withdraw without providing adequate supplies to the isolated garrison.

Iberville's voyages to the Gulf Coast demonstrated quite clearly that the crown must be prepared to make a heavier investment if a viable French presence was to be maintained in the region. This revelation was disheartening to the crown, particularly since Iberville's cursory explorations had suggested that the Mexican mines lay much further from the Mississippi than La Salle had suggested. The monarchy was thus forced to reassess its position regarding Louisiana.[4]

This reassessment came in the midst of calls for the abandonment of Louisiana on purely economic grounds. Particularly vocal was Sieur Bégon, the Intendant of Rochefort who had outfitted Iberville's expedition and who reported that the colony's economic prospects were bleak: the natives were primitive and "incapable of making any valuable contribution to the development of the land."[5] In addition, the region's indigenous products — poor-quality pearls, extraordinarily long reeds, and woolly but practically worthless buffalo hides — were of interest only to the realm's scholarly community.

Despite Louisiana's marginal economic value, the crown decided to maintain France's limited presence along the Gulf Coast. This decision was prompted by reports that the English had unsuccessfully attempted to plant a colony along the lower Mississippi River in 1700. Realizing that their occupation of the river's mouth would give the English strategic control over the North American interior, Louis XIV and Minister of the Navy and Colonies Jérôme Phélypeaux de Maurepas determined that France could not afford to abandon the outpost. Maurepas, who argued on behalf of Louisiana's retention, had been persuaded by Iberville that the colony must serve as a barrier to English expansion into the trans-Appalachian region. In addition, the impending accession of Philippe d'Anjou to the Spanish throne seemed to augur more congenial Franco-Hispanic relations and concomitantly the possibility of French expansion from Louisiana into Spain's North American possessions.[6]

To realize these objectives, Louisiana required substantial reinforcement. This was provided by the colonization expedition of 1702. Led by Iberville, the mission traveled to the Gulf Coast, transferred the existing garrison to a bluff along the Mobile River 27.5 miles above its mouth, and constructed on the new site a formidable fortress and a village of approximately seventy houses. The size and intent of this colonization venture seemed to presage a major expansion of the nascent French settlement, but the new post would soon decline due to the exhaustion of the French treasury and a woeful ignorance of Gulf Coast geography.

As with Biloxi, Mobile's location left much to be desired. Goods destined for the post had to be transshipped over forty miles from the nearest roadstead, the local water supply was poor, the colony's residential areas were subject to periodic flooding, and hostile Indians lived nearby. The

MASSIVE SUBSIDIES WERE ABSOLUTELY CRUCIAL TO LOUISIANA'S SUCCESS AS A ROYAL COLONY

problems posed by the physical environment were exacerbated by the reluctance of most settlers to make the colony self-sufficient. Indeed, the outpost was manned primarily by soldiers of fortune seeking only immediate wealth and return passage to France; they generally shunned physical labor, particularly cultivation of the soil, even for their own subsistence. Lacking farmers, the post was almost completely dependent upon the mother country for its provisions, but the colony was so poorly supplied that its store of provisions was consistently exhausted before the first relief expedition could arrive.[7]

Aware that this situation boded ill for the future of Louisiana, Iberville, who left the colony never to return in April, 1702, proposed a grandiose colonization scheme to the colonial ministry. Promoting Louisiana as a barrier to English expansion beyond the Appalachian Mountains, he urged the crown to augment the colony's existing, unstable population with more sedentary yeomen to be drawn from the impoverished masses of France's capital and rural provinces and transported to the Gulf Coast at royal expense. Massive subsidies were absolutely crucial to Louisiana's success as a royal colony, Iberville insisted, because, with the War of the Spanish Succession looming on the horizon, French merchants and financiers were understandably reluctant to invest in an unproven colonial venture. Hence, the king was obliged to assume full financial responsibility for the colony: staffing its garrisons, outfitting and transporting its colonists, and recruiting potential wives for the troops wishing to remain in Louisiana after their tour of duty. These settlers were to be clustered around Mobile and Fort Mississippi, a short-lived outpost established by Iberville in 1700.[8]

Although well organized, Iberville's scheme of establishing colonies of two to three hundred at Mobile and along the lower Mississippi Valley was doomed to certain failure. Conceived in a period of acute financial crisis, the plan was far too costly to stand any chance of blanket royal approval. Indeed, he was only permitted to transport, at government expense, the familes of the Louisiana-bound soldiers who requested them. Because of the prevailing mood of austerity at

court, Iberville subsequently revised his proposal, requesting that he be given a two-square-league *seigneurie* (fief) along the Mobile River, which he would develop with yeomen from France, Canadians for whom wives would be imported from the motherland, and black laborers whom he would purchase along the West African coast. But the minister rejected this proposal because the transportation costs would have accrued to the crown, and he informed the Canadian that he would receive a *concession* (land grant) only after "the land was developed." Rebuffed by the minister once again and personally unable to bear the cost of developing the colony, Iberville turned his attention to more promising, and lucrative, ventures.[9]

Neglected by its most influential advocate, forgotten by the French colonial ministry, the tiny French outposts in Louisiana languished and slowly disintegrated. Lacking provisions, the settlers were forced to adapt quickly to an alien, harsh, and unforgiving climate; yet this task was hampered by chronic shortages of the tools required to clear prime farmlands of the ubiquitous hardwood forests, by the vastly longer growing season, and by the oppressive heat and humidity that rendered their temperate zone crops and farming techniques useless. As historian Marcel Giraud has noted:

> On the "burning sand" at Biloxi, where . . . [Iberville] believed he could successfully raise the crops of France and the Antilles, heat and drought destroyed the peas, maize, sweet potatoes and yams he had planted. The winter cold and poor quality of the plants he brought from Saint Domingue [present-day Haiti] caused his experiments in growing sugar cane and banana trees to fail. The first crops planted around the Fort of the Mississippi were utterly destroyed by floods, and the satisfactory experiment that d'Iberville claimed to have made with barley and wheat . . . soon failed.

The colonists encountered similar problems in developing a viable livestock industry. Poorly fed and sheltered, cattle and hogs also adapted only slowly to the climate, and, preyed upon by wild predators and hungry Frenchmen, the colonial herds would remain pitifully small for at least two decades.[10]

Lacking an indigenous food supply, the colony was almost completely dependent upon France for its provisions, and whenever its source of supply was interrupted the colony faced starvation. In such situations, the colony was completely at the mercy of the peaceful agricultural tribes inhabiting the Gulf Coast. Indeed, between 1699 and 1715, colonial officials were forced to disband the Louisiana garrison on at least four occasions, permitting the troops to seek their livelihood as best they could among the Indians.

The colony's heavy reliance upon local Indian tribes demanded that the establishment and maintenance of amicable relations with the militarily powerful local tribes be given perennial priority. Alliances were forged with many villages by Iberville and his brother and successor, Jean-Baptiste Le Moyne de Bienville, but, because they were predicated upon the destitute colony's ability to provide friendly tribes with adequate supplies of guns, ammunition, and manufactured goods, the agreements were often nothing more than empty promises. Indeed, traders from the Carolinas, peddling British weapons and influence, worked ceaselessly to undermine French Indian diplomacy, and Louisiana's settlers lived in constant fear of a general Indian uprising. Only Bienville's personal influence over the major southeastern chieftains saved the colony from this fate.[11]

The settlers' existence was complicated still further by their own physiological difficulty in adapting to their new environment. Like their crops, they simply could not withstand the torrid and damp Gulf Coast summers, and the lack of sanitary water sources at the principal settlements made typhoid fever and dysentery ever-present dangers. The settlers' susceptibility to disease was also heightened by the monotonous and nutritionally deficient diet of corn and salt meat forced upon them by colonial supply shortages. These shortages, which had plagued the colony since its establishment, grew progressively worse after France's entry into the War of the Spanish Succession (1701-13).

The outset of the War of the Spanish Succession found France's navy in a terrible state of disarray. All available vessels — merchant and military — were pressed into service along the French coast or were incorporated into the convoys that sailed all too infrequently to the French sugar islands and Canada. These operations absorbed the meager resources of the French navy, and hence the nation's minor overseas possessions quickly lost all contact with the mother country. This is particularly true of Louisiana, which the ministry viewed as an unproductive outpost of only tertiary importance. Supply vessels, which carried a six-month supply of colonial provisions, called at Mobile only once a year in 1703 and 1704, and after 1704 shipments became even more infrequent, arriving in 1706, 1708, and late 1711.

The situation was aggravated by the fact that, because of wartime shortages, priority was given to domestic needs, with the colonies receiving inferior merchandise in inadequate amounts. Moreover, foodstuffs were usually rancid upon delivery as a result of careless packing or the failure of naval personnel to ventilate adequately the holds of their ships. But these problems were overshadowed by the increasing tendency of ship captains to engage in profiteering. Driven to desperate financial straits by the virtual collapse of the French treasury and the resulting nonpayment of military personnel in the latter stages of the war, naval captains replaced cargo destined for Louisiana with large quantities of manufactured goods that they hoped

Detail of Catalogue 228

to sell "for their own profit." Indeed, *L'Aigle*, which arrived at Mobile Bay in 1706, carried *only* merchandise belonging to the vessel's officers in lieu of the seed grain and flour destined by the naval ministry for the colony. The fact that Iberville was at least indirectly (and perhaps directly) responsible for the contraband placed aboard *L'Aigle* demonstrates the pervasiveness of this practice, the effect of which was devastating to the neglected outpost.[12]

Louisiana itself was not immune to the corruption born of France's economic chaos and the attendant administrative neglect of the minor colonies. Thwarted in their efforts to improve their fortune by serving the crown in the developing colonies, Louisiana's colonial officials were quick to follow the example provided by the naval personnel with whom they came into contact. Royal audits revealed that Iberville had grossly inflated the reported expenses incurred in establishing the Louisiana colony and had pocketed a sum roughly equivalent to the actual costs. Bienville, acting commander of the post in Iberville's absence, was accused of grievous malfeasance by Nicolas de La Salle, the colonial commissary, who charged his

governmental rival with appropriating provisions from the royal store houses, transporting them to Mexico aboard government boats, and selling them to Spanish merchants for his own profit. Responding to this accusation, Bienville suggested that corruption pervaded all elements of colonial society, including the civil bureaucracy and the clergy.

The intragovernmental feuding, precipitated by the charges lodged by La Salle against Bienville, was yet another product of royal neglect. The lack of contact with France during the War of the Spanish Succession, which condemned the already destitute colony to perpetual starvation, also created a crisis of authority in the beleaguered French outpost. In an age of authoritarian rule, neither Louis XIV nor his ministers were willing to designate significant authority to their governmental representatives overseas. Indeed, in an effort to protect its interests, the crown had imposed upon the colonies the realm's bipolar provincial governmental regime, which severely limited the power of the colonial authorities by dividing responsibilities between a military governor and a civil commissioner. In addition, by staffing these positions with members of rival social classes and endowing them with overlapping powers, thereby creating an atmosphere of mutual suspicion, the crown assured itself of administrative accountability, for, in the bickering that inevitably characterized French colonial governments, abuses were exposed.

The effectiveness of this royal safeguard, however, hinged upon a responsive colonial ministry, and in the War of the Spanish Succession Louisiana commanded little attention in Paris. Lacking instructions and unsure of their respective responsibilities, the colony's leaders experienced a crisis of authority. Controversies arose over intracolonial policies, and factions developed around Bienville and La Salle. Factionalism, which divided the colony into Canadian and French camps, soon pervaded all elements of Louisiana society, eventually involving trappers, soldiers, and the clergy.

Factionalism shook Louisiana's rickety foundations and threatened the colony with disintegration. Realizing that the strategic settlement would indeed collapse if the situation were not remedied, Minister of the Navy and Colonies Maurepas took drastic action in 1708. Bienville, who had fallen into royal disfavor because of his brother's recent defalcation with government funds as well as because of the allegations of his own misconduct, and La Salle, whom the acting commander had discredited, were relieved of their duties, and replacements were dispatched from France. But replacement of the colonial administration, Maurepas astutely realized, was merely a stop-gap measure and fundamental changes were required if France was to maintain its tenuous presence along the Gulf Coast. Because of the crown's financial embarrassment, the colonial minister realized that the colony's salvation must necessarily lie with a nongovernmental agency. Therefore, in late October, 1708, Maurepas ordered Michel Bégon, Intendant at Rochefort, to encourage merchants in the neighboring ports to organize a mercantile company to exploit the as-yet-undetermined resources of the Mississippi Valley.[13]

Although the commercial monopoly offered by the government was undoubtedly attractive to potential investors, the attendant responsibilities of populating, defending, and developing the outpost precluded any possibility of short-term profitability. Moreover, French merchants knew only too well that proprietary ventures in New France and Acadia during the preceding century had proved dismal failures, partially because of the enormous amounts of capital required by these enterprises and partially because of the tremendous difficulty incurred by colonizers in recouping their investments. The problems that had beset New France and Acadia now plagued Louisiana, and French naval personnel circulated reports that the lower Mississippi Valley was a wretched land, devoid of valuable resources. Consequently, businessmen saw quite clearly that the prospects of realizing a profit in Louisiana were marginal at best. Thus, Bégon's proposals were greeted politely but unenthusiastically.[14]

Rebuffed by the realm's commercial interests, Maurepas could do no better than to seek an entrepreneur to outfit a royal vessel for Louisiana — a minor undertaking that the impoverished government could no longer afford. Yet, despite the expedition's small scale and the need for all types of French goods in the long-neglected colony, the minister encountered great difficulty in finding a merchant willing to underwrite the voyage. Antoine Alexandre de Remonville finally stepped forward to accept responsibility for the voyage in hope of obtaining a colonial governorship from a grateful monarch. The continuing wariness of the French business community was amply justified by the unhappy fate of the outfitter, who was financially ruined by the venture and failed to obtain any compensation from an unsympathetic king.

The monarchy's blatant exploitation of Remonville effectively discouraged further assistance from the private sector at the time when such assistance was crucial to Louisiana's survival. Indeed, the deplorable condition of royal finances in the twilight stages of the War of the Spanish Succession dictated an expedient *rapprochement* with France's commercial interests, through drastic means if necessary. Since the merchant class was now well aware of the hazards of investing in Louisiana, Maurepas, upon whose shoulders fell the onerous task of salvaging the colony's remains, resorted to subterfuge to procure a colonial proprietor. Indeed, the minister recruited Antoine Laumet, alias Lamothe Cadillac, the flamboyant former commandant of Detroit and an adroit liar, to extol the virtues of Louisiana with Antoine Crozat, a nouveau-riche businessman in whom the crown saw a potential investor. Cadillac's persuasive rhetoric and unqualified praise for the colony, which he had never visited, eventually wore down Crozat's resistance, and in June, 1712, the wealthy Frenchman reluctantly agreed to assume control of Louisiana. In return, Crozat received a fifteen-year monopoly on the colony's commerce and the lion's share of all mineral wealth discovered and exploited under his proprietorship.[15]

Although the Crozat proprietorship was viewed by the crown as the salvation of Louisiana, the new regime only magnified the problems already existing in the struggling colony. Under the terms of the transfer, Crozat was obligated to develop the colony economically and to expand its population, but Louisiana's new proprietor lacked sufficient financial resources to accomplish these ambitious objectives over an extended period. Moreover, fully cognizant that Louisiana's known resources were of only marginal value in France's depressed economy, he realized that the only hope of making the colony financially solvent was to establish and maintain trade with Louisiana's Spanish neighbors at Pensacola, Havana, and Vera Cruz. However, these prospective Spanish markets were officially closed to French trade, largely through the efforts of local merchants who raised the cry of mercantilism to protect their interests, so Crozat's proprietary venture was uncertain of success.

This uncertainty obviously militated against the subsidized growth of the colonial population and particularly the establishment of farmers necessary to support the immigrants. Indeed, Crozat flagrantly ignored the terms of the agreement, and, whereas the colonial garrison that remained the responsibility of the crown grew slightly, the civilian population remained static. In fact, between 1702 and 1715, Louisiana's overall population grew from 140 to only 215.[16]

Louisiana's economy also stagnated under Crozat's proprietary regime. The efforts of Crozat's representatives to open the Spanish markets to French commerce quickly proved to be unqualified disasters, and, desperately needing an alternate source of income, Crozat began to exploit the practically pennyless colonial

Detail of Catalogue 242

population. The long years of neglect by France had deprived Louisiana's farmers, artisans, and trappers of markets for their goods, and the production of food, boats, lumber, and furs had consequently declined. The artificially low prices offered by Crozat for Louisiana's merchandise and the inflated cost of goods sold at Mobile by the proprietor further suppressed production and forced many Louisianians either to engage in smuggling or to participate in a black-market economy in order to survive.

Dissatisfaction with the proprietor's economic activities seriously undermined the effectiveness of his political representatives. Cadillac, commissioned to govern Louisiana under Crozat, possessed a particularly abrasive personality, and his authoritarian outlook brought him into immediate disfavor with the equally haughty royal officers whom he replaced, as well as with his fellow proprietary officials. The result was the creation of a vocal anti-Cadillac faction led by Bienville, who had been demoted to lieutenant of the garrison after the recent scandal, and by Jean-Baptiste du Bois du Clos, the chief colonial administrator who engaged in contraband commerce to supplement his

meager income. Through his position as commissioner, du Clos challenged Cadillac at every turn, and when the Superior Council, the colony's chief judicial and legislative body, was established in 1714, he used his influence as first judge to promote legislation effectively negating Crozat's monopoly in a bid to open the colonial economy to free enterprise. Only through personal intimidation of the councilors was Cadillac able to block the motion. The governor's triumph proved to be a hollow victory, for du Clos, with the assistance of Bienville and much of the colonial population, undermined the proprietary regime by selling the commissioner's goods on the black market and by smuggling provisions stolen from the proprietary warehouse to Spanish authorities at Pensacola.[17]

These illicit activities produced a flurry of bitter intragovernmental disputes that effectively paralyzed the colonial administration. No longer able to implement its policies or enforce its monopoly, unable to wring any profits from Louisiana's beleaguered economy, and overwhelmed by the expenses of operating its commercial outpost, Crozat's regime collapsed in 1715, the year of Louis XIV's death, although the proprietary charter was not officially revoked until the following year.

The failure of the Crozat proprietorship brought to an end the crucial formative stage of Louisiana's development. The course of this development was determined by the virtual collapse of Louis XIV's government in the waning years of his rule. The establishment and reinforcement of a French colony along the Gulf Coast between 1699 and 1702 seemed to augur the rise of an era of French imperial domination in North America at a time when France's newly-gained influence over the Spanish throne seemed to afford the Bourbons hegemony over western Europe. The Bourbon dream of European domination, however, was dashed by the costly War of the Spanish Succession, which virtually destroyed France's struggling economy and emptied the royal coffers. Bankrupt, the French monarchy was forced to address only the most pressing domestic problems, while the colonies — particularly the minor colonies — were set adrift.

The rapid decline of France in the twilight years

of Louis XIV's reign produced a corresponding deterioration of conditions in Louisiana. The colonists were chronically plagued with famine, soldiers were forced to adopt Indian dress and to hunt with the Indians to support themselves, and officials often went years without receiving their salaries.

The cession of Louisiana to a proprietary regime at first seemed to resolve the colony's problems: new officials were appointed, the garrison was enlarged, the empty storehouses were filled, and the anticipated trade with Spanish North America promised a revitalization of the colony's moribund economy. Once again, however, problems spawned in France brought Louisiana to its knees. The proprietor's commercial policies, while expedient, were not feasible and, when trade with the Spanish colonies failed to materialize, Crozat attempted to drain off the colony's remaining resources, while simultaneously refusing to meet the basic needs of the settlement.

Virtually abandoned by France while under private and royal domination, the colony was forced to survive as best it could. Since the colony was manned by adventurers and soldiers who refused to support themselves through agriculture and who generally lacked the skills necessary to endure the harsh and unhealthy environment of the southeastern frontier, survival of the outpost was contingent upon the economic assistance of the local Indian tribes, upon whom the French also relied for military protection. Hence, the astute Indian diplomacy conceived by Iberville and implemented by Bienville was crucial to the colony's success.

Bienville, however, was far less successful in other areas of colonial administration. Haughty, highly opinionated, stubborn, and vindictive, the colonial commandant consistently alienated most of his governmental colleagues. The resulting intragovernmental feuding soon pervaded all segments of colonial society, polarizing the settlers into pro- and anti-Bienville factions. The factionalization, which was underscored by pronounced ethnic (Canadian-French) cleavages in the colonial population, paralyzed the government, and the chronic lack of ministerial directives and the absence of centralized authority in Louisiana prevented any resolution of the problem. Indeed, even a change of government failed to eradicate the feuding.

Torn by factional strife, chronically neglected by the mother country, and perpetually poised on the brink of collapse, Louisiana somehow weathered the chain of crises that marred the declining years of Louis XIV's reign and survived despite the low priority assigned to the colony in the Sun King's imperial designs. Nonetheless, the legacy of administrative neglect, factionalism, and economic and demographic stagnation continued to plague Louisiana throughout the entire period of French rule (1699-1769). ∎

FOOTNOTES

1. W. J. Eccles, *France in America* (New York, 1972), 86. For a listing of the major works treating the French exploration of the North American interior, see Carl A. Brasseaux, "French Louisiana," in Light Townsend Cummins and Glen Jeansonne, eds., *A Guide to the History of Louisiana* (Westport, Ct., 1982), 3-16.
2. On the fate of La Salle's colony, see Robert S. Weddle, *Wilderness Manhunt: The Spanish Search for La Salle* (Austin, Tex., 1973).
3. Iberville to Pontchartrain, September 7, 1700. in Archives de la Marine (Paris), Series B 4, Vol. 20, fol. 427vo.
4. For accounts of Iberville's voyages, see Carl A. Brasseaux, trans. and ed., *A Comparative View of French Louisiana: The Journals of Pierre Le Moyne d'Iberville and Jean-Jacques-Blaise d'Abbadie* (Lafayette, La., 1979); and Richebourg Gaillard McWilliams, trans. and ed., *Iberville's Gulf Journals* (University, Ala., 1981).
5. Quoted in Marcel Giraud, *A History of French Louisiana*, Vol. I, *The Reign of Louis XIV, 1698-1715*, trans. Joseph C. Lambert (Baton Rouge, La., 1974), 42.
6. Iberville's memoir on the settlement of Mississippi, 1706, in Archives de la Service Hydrographique (Paris), Cartes et Plans, Vol. 67, no. 4; Giraud, *History*, I, 44.
7. On the establishment of a French colony at Mobile, see Jay Higginbotham, *Old Mobile: Fort Louis de la Mobile, 1702-1722* (Mobile, Ala., 1977).
8. Giraud, *History*, I, 93-94. On the short-lived French outpost in present-day Plaquemines Parish, Louisiana, see Mauries Ries, "The Mississippi Fort, Called Fort de la Boulaye," *Louisiana Historical Quarterly*, XIX (1936), 846-55.
9. Giraud, *History*, I, 95. Iberville purchased a captaincy in the French coast guard, the income from which permitted him to recoup his personal expenses from the Louisiana expeditions. In addition, in 1700 he purchased an estate near La Rochelle, France. *Ibid.*, I, 107-108.
10. Higginbotham, *Old Mobile*, 45-120; Giraud, *History*, I, 99.
11. Giraud, *History*, I, 214-21.
12. *Ibid.*, I, 111, 119.
13. De Muy, Bienville's replacement and commandant of the post, died while en route to Mobile. Bienville thus continued to govern the colony, pending the outcome of the investigation into his alleged malfeasance. La Salle, however, was replaced by Dartaguiette. *Ibid.*, I, 131.
14. See Carl A. Brasseaux, "The Image of Louisiana and the Failure of Voluntary Immigration," *Proceedings of the Fourth Meeting of the French Colonial Historical Society* (Washington, D.C., 1979), 47-56.
15. Giraud, *History*, I, 248-50.
16. Of the 215 persons residing in Louisiana in 1715, 160 were members of the colonial garrison. *Ibid.*, I, 97, 277.
17. Carl A. Brasseaux, "Private Enterprise vs. Mercantilism: The Cadillac-Duclos Affair," in Mathé Allain and Carl A. Brasseaux, eds., *A Franco-American Overview* (Cambridge, Mass., 1981), V, 55-64.

LOUIS XIV:
PATRON OF THE ARTS AND SCIENCES

IVPITER APPLAVDENS LODOICO FVLMINA CESSIT.
IAMQVE NOVVM MVNDVS SENSIT ADESSE IOVEM

LOUIS XIV
AND THE
MIRROR OF ANTIQUITY
ROBERT WYMAN HARTLE

To a century that is accustomed to keep its gaze fixed on the future with a belief that technology will keep marching on, and that believes that the new and the different are qualities inherent in the creation of beauty; to a century that equates creativity with difference, where the potter is careful not to make his creations too perfect lest they be mistaken for machine-made products, it is difficult to understand an age that saw itself in the context of Antiquity, where artistic creation began with an imitation of the Ancients, where the Ancients of Greece and Rome were daily invoked as the standards of perfection that one must try to live up to. Today creativity means breaking the mold, occasionally actually throwing the paint at the canvas to produce random results. In the seventeenth century, the most talented artists were sent to Rome in order to spend their time perfecting their craft in the copying of ancient statues. (The Romans themselves had spent much time copying the perfection of the Greeks, and most Greek statues are known to us today through Roman copies of Greek bronzes.)

As a result, we do not have the standardized symbolic references available to the artists of the seventeenth century. We deal in the newly created. Two companies merge, and the new organization promptly hires someone at a rich fee to create a "logo" that will tell the story of the company. Much corporate executive time is spent on pondering the appropriate form for the "logo." Needless to say, at the next merger the process is repeated, and the general public is not really affected in its perceptions by these exercises. Not so in the seventeenth century. In the first place, for centuries the public had been reading the commonly accepted symbols of Christian worship. The cathedral was the layman's encyclopedia of this world and where it came from, as well as where it was going. In French, for instance, when one wants to speak of someone who is really ugly, one says "ugly as the seven capital sins." The expression, probably unbeknownst to the speaker, comes right out of the Middle Ages, when the capital sins were represented in the churches in such a way as to make them repulsive to the layman. Thus the public was accustomed to see representational meaning in traditional terms. With the Renaissance came also the rebirth of the use of ancient mythology and legend as the shorthand of the artist; and poems, novels, and the visual arts were suddenly populated with nymphs, fauns, and Arcadian shepherds.

Texts that had lain dormant for centuries were suddenly translated and published in astonishing quantities. A recent scholar wishing to use the historian of Alexander, Justin, was obliged to use an edition published in Paris in 1823, whereas in the seventeenth century Cauvigny's translation of Justin, first published in 1616, was reprinted in 1617, 1627, 1644, 1650, 1654, 1661, 1666, 1669, 1672, and 1675 — an extraordinary literary success[1] — and in 1693 Louis Ferrier published a new translation.

Throughout the whole seventeenth century there were some quarrels about the authority of the Ancients, some sniping to the effect that the rules of the Ancients were all right in their day, but that times had changed and required different styles.[2] Regularly, however, painters were compared with Apelles, Molière was said to have revived Plautus and Terence, Racine to reincarnate Sophocles, and Boileau deliberately set out to imitate the career of

Horace, first with satires, then with odes, and eventually with his *Art poétique.* To be compared with an Ancient author was the highest form of praise for the seventeenth century. The voices of dissent were largely drowned out by the majority until the time of one of the polemics that aroused the fiercest passions, the Quarrel of the Ancients and the Moderns, provoked by a book that claimed that the authors and artists of the seventeenth century were superior to the Ancients.[3] The quarrel continued into the eighteenth century, when it was resolved in favor of the Idea of Progress and the perfectibility of Man. Let there be no mistaking, however, the seventeenth century had an idea of its just worth; it felt — quite correctly to my mind — that it had arrived at one of those peaks of civilization and culture that occasionally occur throughout history as in the Age of Pericles or Augustus. They were particularly sure of the greatness of their monarch and regularly compared him with the greatest heroes of Antiquity.

"Hail to the Chief" does not stir too many emotions today when the president appears, and so we can only dimly imagine the emotions of the subjects of the boy who was to become the Sun King. Even the British enthusiasm for their royal family can furnish only the most pallid basis for comparison. Four days after his father's death, the four-and-a-half-year-old Louis held his first Bed of Justice in the Parlement of Paris. Omer Talon, the Judge Advocate General, opened the session by saying to him: "Your Majesty's seat represents for us the throne of the living God. . . . The orders of the kingdom render unto you honor and respect as to a visible divinity." Louis was regularly referred to as God's lieutenant on earth. Thus the words of the *Gazette* seem almost modest when they record the procession on August 25, 1649, the feast of Saint Louis, when the young king, almost eleven years old, went on a small white horse to the Church of Saint Louis. This was during the early days of the four-year insurgency known as the Fronde. In the words of the *Gazette,* the horse "appeared as proud as Bucephalus could have been beneath this young Alexander, whose grace and majesty depicted on his face an august temperament, capable of making him equally loved and feared." The year before

that, a painting shows the ten-year-old boy sweetly holding a thunderbolt in his right hand, while at his feet is the eagle of Zeus and in the background Vulcan is forging arms for him. By way of comparison, in Alexander's day the sculptor Lysippos blamed Apelles for drawing Alexander's picture with a thunderbolt in his hand.[4]

If we can only dimly imagine the emotions of Louis' subjects, it is even more difficult to imagine what must have been his own inner thoughts and emotions. It is certain that he had early determined to rule in his own right, and the decision that he took on the day following Cardinal Mazarin's death to rule as his own minister was rightly considered the primary event of his reign. Not only that, to everyone's surprise he actually carried out his functions, attended Council every day (a medal was later struck commemorating "The King's Assiduity at the Council"),[5] and, as an observor who was not too impressed with the king's native intelligence grudgingly admitted, "by dint of application he became clever."

It is safe to say that another characteristic of Louis was premeditation and the consciousness that his every gesture was being studied — fortunes at court were made and lost by a smile or a frown from the king; he knew it and rationed them out with prudence and frugality. Whereas Alexander had gained the loyalty of his men by fighting and drinking alongside them, Louis based his power on maintaining a distance between himself and his courtiers. He never relaxed or caroused with anyone. He had no familiars.

Louis was not a dictator; the time of the republican Cincinnatus was long past, and the invention of totalitarianism was reserved for our own time. He did understand that there were certain rights and privileges of the nobility that he could not abolish, but he intended to be a monarch in the etymological sense of the term: one alone was to rule, and it was to be himself. It was an inevitable part of his thinking that he must arrest a man, Fouquet, the Superintendent of Finances, whose resources were so great that on occasion the Queen Mother had recourse to him for loans. This decision had been made before the famous visit in August, 1661, when Fouquet entertained the king and the whole court with a

> WE CAN ONLY DIMLY IMAGINE THE EMOTIONS OF THE SUBJECTS OF THE BOY WHO WAS TO BECOME THE SUN KING

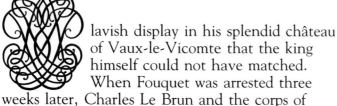

lavish display in his splendid château of Vaux-le-Vicomte that the king himself could not have matched. When Fouquet was arrested three weeks later, Charles Le Brun and the corps of tapestry workers working for Fouquet under his direction found themselves without a patron.

ALEXANDER THE GREAT AND THE CAREER OF CHARLES LE BRUN

In October, Le Brun must have been overjoyed to receive an invitation to Fontainebleau, where the king invited him to paint a picture for him.[6] But the subject must have posed a dilemma for the artist. Louis wanted a painting from the life of Alexander the Great. This must have been an embarrassment to Le Brun, for, according to the allegorical code of the time, the picture must allude to or represent in some way the sponsor of the picture. To portray the greatest conqueror of all time and allude to a king who had been at peace since the much-celebrated Treaty of the Pyrenees of 1659 must have presented quite a problem. Le Brun's solution was to remember the paintings by Sodoma and Veronese of Alexander the Great coming upon the Tent of Darius wherein were his wife and family.

There is some disagreement among the historians, both ancient and modern, as to whether Alexander ever set eyes on the wife and daughters of Darius, who were his captives after the Battle of Issus. For my own part, I would consider it indeed strange that a man of Alexander's omniverous curiosity would not even *look* at Darius' wife, who was reputed to be the most beautiful woman in all Asia. Those ancient historians who allow that he did make the visit are unanimously extravagant in their praise of Alexander's self-control, as he treated them royally and did not molest them. As Tarn comments, "their praise of what he did throws a dry light on what he was expected to do."[7] That Le Brun should have chosen to paint an allegory about Louis' self-control with respect to women may strike some as paradoxical, if not downright foolhardy; however, flattery of a monarch rarely stumbles against ridicule. As a matter of fact, Louis' behavior toward women was always marked by an outward show of the greatest respect and courtesy, and he prided himself on his self-control in his actions.

Many examples of this self-control survive, such as when he was operated on for an anal fistula — without anesthesia, of course — and then continued about his duties as if nothing had happened. In the *Memoirs* that Louis wrote for the instruction of the Dauphin he wrote, "Very little can resist the one who knows how to master himself."[8] These words echo what Plutarch says at precisely the moment of the discovery of the family of Darius: "But Alexander, deeming, in my opinion, it to be a more royal thing to conquer himself than to defeat his enemies, did not touch them, nor any other girls or women before marrying them."[9] Le Brun had hit precisely the point on which Louis liked to be praised — his self-control. On Edelinck's engraving of the painting, the inscription reads, "It is a kingly thing to conquer oneself" (figure 6). On the tapestry made from this painting under Le Brun's supervision, the Latin inscription reads, "Sui victoria indicat regem" ("The victory over himself proclaims the king"). The historical reference is to Alexander's clemency, but the phrase can also be translated to say that self-control is the mark of a king. Who knows, perhaps the king himself had suggested the subject.

Whatever the case, Le Brun had hit the target. When the picture was hung in the Royal *Cabinet des peintures*, the king remarked that "in the midst of so many rare paintings it maintained a brilliance and power that nothing was capable of effacing."[10] Perhaps the fact that the great conqueror bore a certain idealized resemblance to Louis himself had something to do with the king's appreciation. The king's pleasure in the painting touched off a wave of critical appreciation that made it the single most famous painting of the century, and made allusions

Figure 6

to Louis XIV as Alexander an almost obligatory exercise for those who would succeed at his court.[11]

Félibien des Avaux wrote an interesting pamphlet on this work, for we can see therein how the seventeenth century, at the same time as it thought that it was translating directly from the Ancients, took care to polish up the mirror into which it gazed. Writers and artists felt no compunction at improving on Antiquity, almost seeming not to notice that they were doing so. Le Brun took great care to model his painting on the ancient historians: he makes Alexander and Haephestion enter alone, and he makes Sisigambis, the mother of Darius, at first take the lieutenant for the king, because Alexander was slightly shorter than Haephestion. These details all come from Diodorus Siculus, Arrian, and Quintus Curtius. Félibien explains that Haephestion is

> taller and straighter than ALEXANDER, nevertheless these two figures are so well treated and the figure of ALEXANDER arranged in such a noble and pleasing way that one easily sees that it represents that king, and that it is the most important of all.

> It is in that way that one recognizes the excellence of a workman when he knows how to arrange his subject so well, & instead of bringing out the natural defects of the person he is painting, he disguises them cleverly without nevertheless taking away from the true resemblance.[12]

Le Brun was named First Painter of the King, which game him a virtual dictatorship over all works of art produced for the royal household. The Gobelins Manufactory of Furnishings was established with him as its director, and he brought with him the nucleus of weavers who had worked under him for Fouquet; he even brought some of the tapestries made for Fouquet. He coolly removed the latter's emblem and replaced it with a sun and the motto "nec pluribus impar," meaning that Louis the Sun King was "not unequal to many [suns]." Le Brun was just what the king needed: he combined energy, a multiplicity of talents, and organizational ability. By 1663, when the king made a formal visit to the Gobelins, there were

more than two hundred workers in the establishment! In the tapestry commemorating this event, one can see the diversity of objects made under Le Brun's supervision.[13]

Given this success, is it any wonder that Le Brun immediately set out to complete the series of the deeds of Alexander the Great in heroic proportions? He did the Crossing of the Granicus, the Battle of Arbela, the Presentation of the Defeated Porus, and Alexander's Triumphal Entry into Babylon, all of them some forty feet long. He immediately set his weavers to making tapestries of these same subjects. The series of Gobelins tapestries from the History of Alexander was the best-known set done there in the seventeenth century. The main scenes stand fifteen and three-quarters feet high (4m.80) and are somewhat more than twenty feet long. To these are added a Left Wing and a Right Wing for each of the battles — of the same height but only one-third as long — and in some of the series an *entre-fenêtre*, thus making a total of eleven or twelve hangings for each series. During the seventeenth century, this series was produced at the Gobelins alone eight times; all but once gold thread was interwoven in the cloth. If one remembers that a master weaver could do only about one square yard per year, one can appreciate the magnitude of the task. In the 1670s, some of the best engravers were set to making copies of the tapestry cartoons. These engravings enjoyed a very wide dissemination, and the ateliers in Brussels, Aubusson, and Felletin used them as models to produce their own sets of tapestries. Perhaps because of the slight resemblance between his own features and those of Le Brun's Alexander, or perhaps as part of his well-calculated politic of self-aggrandizement, this series was a favorite gift of Louis: he gave copies of it to the duc de Lorraine, to his brother the duc d'Orléans, to a minister of the king of Denmark, and to Mademoiselle de Montpensier.[14]

THE LESSON OF VERSAILLES

In the midst of this work, Le Brun was called to supervise the decoration of the little château that

> WE MUST TAKE VERSAILLES SERIOUSLY, NOT ONLY AS A WORK OF ART IN ITSELF, BUT ALSO AS THE OUTWARD MANIFESTATION OF A KING

Louis XIII had built as a hunting refuge near Versailles, which Louis XIV had decided to make into a palace that would surpass anything seen before. It was to be the secular cathedral erected to his own greatness. Like a cathedral, all the decorations would have an allegorical meaning. It is no exaggeration to say that everything in Versailles was meant to explain its resident divinity and to extol his virtues. A historical explanation of Versailles published by Laurent Morellet explains:

> The subjects of painting which complete the decoration of the Ceilings, are of the Heroes & illustrious men, taken from History and Fable, who have deserved the titles of Magnanimous, of Great, of Fathers of the People, of Liberal, of Just, of August & Victorious, & who have possessed all the Virtues which we have seen appear in the Person of our Great Monarch during the fortunate course of his reign; so that everything remarkable which one sees in the Château & in the Garden always has some relationship with the great actions of His Majesty.[15]

Thus we must take Versailles seriously, not only as a work of art in itself, but also as the outward manifestation of a king who has continued to fascinate posterity, as the seventeenth century was itself fascinated by the heroes of Antiquity.[16] As the Romans made the Greek gods and their own into personifications of qualities, eventually supplanting the autochthonous and sometimes self-contradictory individual characters of the Greek gods, so too did the seventeenth century. Historical events were also to be read allegorically as contemporary events.

A visitor to Versailles in the latter part of the seventeenth century would come upon the Cour de Marbre, the small central courtyard outside the Royal Apartments. There, on the balustrade, he could see graceful statues representing Magnificence, Justice, Wisdom, Prudence, Diligence, Peace, Europe, Asia, Renown, Abundance, Force, Generosity, Wealth, Authority, Fame, America, Africa, and Victory. Flanking the central clock were Hercules and Minerva. The message conveyed was clear: here Power was guided by Virtue, thereby deservedly gaining wealth and fame.

An important visitor to Versailles would have entered by the great Ambassadors' Staircase, which Le Brun worked on from 1672 to 1678. Unfortunately it was demolished in 1752 by Louis XV, but, fortunately for us, the original copper plates of engravings of the staircase still exist in the Chalcographie du Louvre.[17] (A visitor can still today order relatively inexpensive engravings from these centuries-old plates.) One of the plates tells us that the purpose of the staircase was "to impress on a Foreigner respect for the Prince whom he was going to see on the Throne", and one can easily imagine that a visitor would be impressed:

> Over the Cornice extends a Balustrade bearing Vases decorated with festoons, which serves as a base for four solid stone Statues, each one eight feet high; these Statues represent allegorically some of the Royal Virtues: the first . . . is Diligence; she holds in her hand a branch of thyme on which is a Bee; at her feet is a Cock. The 2nd . . . is Prudence, characterized by a serpent twisted around an arrow. The 3rd . . . is Pallas leaning on her shield. Finally, the 4th . . . is Justice holding the Sword and Scales. . . . the decoration of the 2 backgrounds of . . . [the] vault . . . the Club with the Caduceus, the great Trophies and the other symbols show that when Force and Prudence are united in the person of an enlightened King, Victories are frequent and the Kingdom becomes rich and flourishing.

Later, Wisdom and Force are represented on a grand scale by Minerva and Hercules once again. Louis' preceptor as a youth, Hardouin de Péréfixe, had composed for him an *Institutio principis,* in which he recommended four cardinal principles — traditionally royal virtues — Prudence, Justice, Temperance, and Force. Alexander often disregarded Prudence — Louis did not.[18]

The Royal Apartments were decorated with the actions of other monarchs of Antiquity, many of whose actions were read directly as allusions to specific acts of Louis. In the Salle de Vénus one notices Augustus presiding over the Circus (Louis XIV at the Carrousel of 1662), and Nebuchadnezzar and Semiramis building the Gardens of Babylon (Versailles). Since the Hanging Gardens of Babylon were one of the Seven Wonders of the Ancient World, one gets some notion of the scope of Louis' ambitions for Versailles. One sees Alexander the Great marrying

Roxane (Louis' marriage with Marie-Thérèse), and Cyrus arming himself to go to the aid of a princess (the War of Devolution for the queen's rights in 1667).

The Salle de Diane celebrates the goddess as not only the patroness of the hunt — a passion with Louis — but also as patroness of a practical art, navigation. Thus we see Jason and the Argonauts, and Julius Caesar sending a colony to Carthage (America?), as well as Alexander hunting a lion and the Sacrifice of Iphigeneia. (Racine's play on this subject was played for the first time at the sumptuous fête given by the king at Versailles in 1674 to celebrate the Second Conquest of Franche-Comté.)[19]

In the Salle de Mars, in addition to allegories of Mars, Hercules, Terror, Fury, and Wrath, we see Cyrus haranguing his troops, the Triumph of Constantine, and some pointed pedagogical reminders to officers in the form of Caesar reviewing his legions (Louis' tightening up on false musters), Alexander Severus reducing an officer, and Mark Antony making Albinus a consul.

Mercury was celebrated as protector of the Arts and Sciences and also as the god of Commerce. In his room were Alexander receiving an embassy of Indians, Ptolemy talking with scientists in his library (the founding of the Academy of Sciences?), Augustus also receiving an embassy of Indians, and Alexander receiving animals from all over the world so that Aristotle could write their natural history.

Upon arriving in the Throne Room, one would see at first the enormous silver throne, 2.60 meters high, and later one would remark on the ceiling Apollo on his chariot, lyre under his arm, with France and Navarre beneath and the four continents in the corners. Beneath that, four paintings: Coriolanus lifting the siege of Rome at his mother's entreaty (Louis' filial piety), Vespasian giving orders to complete the Coliseum (the building of Versailles), Augustus building the port of Misenum (the fortification of Rochefort), and Porus being brought before Alexander (Louis victorious and clement).

Everywhere Alexander appears, he is counterbalanced by Augustus. Likewise, in the Hall of Mirrors, "The Second Conquest of Franche-Comté" is balanced by "The King Governs by Himself." Other warlike acts are balanced by acts putting order into the administration of the kingdom.

ALEXANDER AND THE CAREER OF JEAN RACINE

The subject of the clemency of Alexander toward the Indian king Porus had an interesting history in the seventeenth century. The young Jean Racine used it as the subject of his second tragedy.

Racine, now known as one of the small handful of the world's great writers of tragedy, did not start out with that reputation. Left an orphan at an early age, he was taken in by the Jansenist school at Port-Royal because his closest relative was an aunt who was a nun in the convent there. As a result, he received the finest education that the age had to offer. But when it came time for him to think of making a living, he had to decide what he would do with that splendid education. *He* wanted a career as a man of letters, but the Jansenists, who still continued in their role *in loco parentis*, considered the theater as a school of vice in which the more honestly the passions were depicted, the more insidious they became. So they packed him off to Uzès, to await an ecclesiastical benefice that his uncle, a canon there, might be able to garner for him. He had to play the hypocrite, dress in a cassock, read St. Thomas, and otherwise look the part of a deserving candidate, while slyly ogling the local girls. After a year and a half of impatient waiting, the ecclesiastical benefice fell through, and Racine went back to Paris to do various errands for a cousin who was the majordomo for a Jansenist nobleman. At the same time he was able to place his first play with Molière, who suddenly needed a new play and turned it into a passable success, enough to encourage Racine to continue.

The young *arriviste* knew, as did all France, that the king's approbation was an invincible means of success. The king's approbation *was* success. Looking around, Racine saw the magnificent career that Le Brun had made for himself with the Alexander motif, and in 1663 he read Félibien's account of Le Brun's painting of the Queens of

> RACINE'S POETIC GENIUS HAD BEEN FORMED BY MEN WHO LOOKED AT THE WORLD IN THE CONTEXT OF ETERNITY AND SAW IT AS VANITY

Persia, the Tent of Darius.[20] Quite unsurprisingly he decided to do a play on Alexander, but *what* Alexander motif? He faced the same problem that had been Le Brun's: Louis was still at peace. He scoured the ancient sources in the original and found in Arrian and Plutarch the story that when, after a desperate battle, Alexander asked the Indian king Porus, captive and wounded, how he wished to be treated, the latter answered with one word that meant "as a king" (basilikōs).[21] Instead of being angered, Alexander was so struck with admiration by the firmness of this answer that he reestablished Porus as satrap over his former kingdom and even extended its boundaries. Here was the same note struck by Le Brun: self-control, self-mastery, and magnanimity.

Racine would improve on the original Alexander by making him have a credible (for the time) motive for the conquest of India and the rest of the world: Alexander would be in love with an Indian queen, Cléofile — he had come all that way to lay his glory at her feet! The play is filled with a namby-pamby sequence of conceits about the Victor captive, the Conqueror defeated by love, etc., but Racine does bring off the great scene with Porus fairly well, and all ends happily. The king liked the play; it was one of the great successes of the century, played often before the court, and for the rest of the century Racine was known as the author of *Alexander the Great.* Today the play lies unread and unperformed. The finest poetry is that which is spoken *against* the idea of military conquest and lays bare the vanity, the bleak emptiness of conquest. Racine's poetic genius had been formed by men who looked at the world in

Detail of Catalogue 18

the context of eternity and saw it as vanity, and worldly glory as so much smoke founded on ashes. The love interest being dominant, the prevailing sense of the plot is at odds with the prevailing sense of the poetry. The love interest flatly contradicts, as Racine well knew, what his sources had to say about Alexander's susceptibility to love, but the seventeenth century didn't care; it was in love with Alexander, it was in love with its king, and its king was in love with love. The audience saw in Racine's play a purified image of itself, a king's dream.[22]

Crowning Racine's success was the fact that the king accepted the Dedicatory Epistle. In writing the epistle, Racine fell into the same trap of first judging military conquest from the viewpoint of eternity and then going on to praise it. Racine's problem was still how to dedicate to Louis a play about a military genius without making him feel the comparison too keenly. He decided to strike boldly. Without trying to soften the comparison, he made it the basis of the epistle. In order to make Louis feel superior to Alexander, Racine began by adopting a lofty moral point of view: Louis' greatness and preeminence did not need to be "imposed by the force of arms," they were not "built on ashes and ruins" but were founded on the spontaneous admiration of his wisdom and prudence. Louis had "arrived at the peak of glory by a newer and more difficult road than Alexander. . . . It is not extraordinary to see a young man win battles, to see him set the whole earth on fire. It is not impossible for youth and luck to sweep him victorious to the depths of India." Racine recalls that among the Ancients there was a question as to whether luck or virtue had the greater part in Alexander's conquests. Racine's duplicity is clearly revealed by the fact that *in the play* he makes much of Alexander's virtue as the key to his success, but when comparing him to Louis *in the Epistle* he says loftily that "history is full of young conquerors," but that the world has never before seen "a king who at the age of Alexander had displayed the conduct of Augustus, who without moving away from the center of his kingdom, had spread his radiance to the ends of the earth, and who had begun his career at the point which the greatest princes have tried to attain at the end of theirs." Very sweet

LOUIS HAD DECIDED *HIMSELF* THAT HE WOULD BE CALLED "LOUIS THE GREAT"

flattery of a king who owed "the flourishing state of his kingdom to his own counsel" (an allusion to Louis' decision to be his own prime minister), but what if Louis had warlike ambitions? What would that do for Racine's denigration of conquest? The king was already beginning to growl in the traditional direction of Spain. Perhaps, Racine continues smoothly, His Majesty will cover himself with a brand new glory, "perhaps we shall see Him at the head of an army complete the comparison which can be drawn between Him and Alexander, and add the title of conqueror to that of the wisest king on earth. Then his subjects will consecrate their evening watches to the telling of so many great actions."[23] Very neat sleight-of-hand, but it does not satisfy upon reflection. After speaking contemptuously of epic conquests as the result of "youth and luck," after having morally condemned them for being founded on "ashes and ruins," it is simply not consistent to go on to an apotheosis of military glory.

No one noticed. The following year Louis took personal command of the conquest of Flanders and the year after that of Franche-Comté. La Fontaine had an easier time of it in the dedicatory epistle to the *Fables* in 1668: he could say, "upon . . . [Louis'] return from that expedition, where he conquered like an Alexander, you see him govern his people like an Augustus."[24]

Racine did not notice the inconsistencies, for with dazzled eyes he was in the process of stepping out of the somber religious atmosphere of his childhood and youth, where the controlling vision was that of eternity, into the very worldly world of the theater and the court. He engaged in a rather tawdry anonymous polemic with his former masters about the theater. He also became the lover of the most beautiful actress of the time and at the same time had his entrée at court.

One of the delicious ironies of the story is that, in a document of 1667, a few weeks before the triumph of his third play *Andromaque*, Racine is referred to as prior of the Priory of Saint Petronilla in the Diocese of Angers.[25] In other words, the worldly triumph of his *Alexander* had brought him the ecclesiastical benefice that all his wearing of the cassock in Uzès had not been able to produce. Best of all, he didn't even have to go near Angers — he could stay in Paris with his mistress, draw

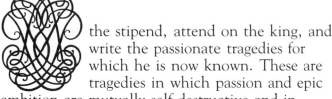 the stipend, attend on the king, and write the passionate tragedies for which he is now known. These are tragedies in which passion and epic ambition are mutually self-destructive and in themselves ironically self-defeating. Racine had duplicated the success of Le Brun. In the world and of the world he could see through it. Now that he had attained with his *Alexander* the success that no one could have foreseen, he was free to write plays that body forth a tragic vision where passion is poison, and glory, smoke and ashes. They prove his Jansenist masters correct.

In 1677 Racine and Boileau were ordered to quit all other occupations in order to become the King's Royal Historiographers. This cost posterity many other great tragedies, but for Racine it was a great step upward. Scholars have argued at great length about the spiritual and psychological reasons for his leaving the theater, but how could he have done otherwise? We project our regrets backwards and assume that Racine must have felt the same, or that he must have undergone a great conversion. When the king conferred this honor upon the orphan from La Ferté-Milon, Racine was, quite properly for the time, overwhelmed. Later, he became a member of the Petite Académie working on the medals struck to proclaim Louis' greatness to the subsequent centuries. Why should Racine not have felt sincerely that it was a task at least equal to his genius? Why should he not have felt a sincere admiration for the king? He was no crypto-democrat. Although the words were another's, why should he not have felt, as he said in the Dedicatory Epistle to *Alexander the Great,* unequal to the task of praising Louis until he had practised on the heroes of Antiquity?[26]

HOW TO BECOME GREAT

Most French kings had some sort of appellation, like Charles the Bald, Louis the Lazy, Louis the Fat, or Charles the Affable. Only two of them had been called "the Great" — Charlemagne (Carolus Magnus), and our Louis' grandfather, Henri IV. On the medals struck for the glorification of the events of the reign of Louis XIV, the title Ludovicus XIIII is replaced in 1673 by the title Ludovicus Magnus, and the Porte Saint Denis, dedicated in the same year, bears the inscription LUDOVICO MAGNO.[27] A bit of research in the Archives of the City of Paris revealed that, after the great

victories in the North and the Crossing of the Rhine in 1672, the body that today we would call the City Council proposed to give Louis a triumphal entry like the one given to Henri the Great and the one given to Louis XIII after the siege of La Rochelle. The Provost of the Merchants also noted that the gates of the city were in a condition to be decorated, and in the margin it says "in honor of a king who might justly be entitled Louis the Magnanimous." The Provost of the Merchants and the Provost of the Magistrates would wait on the marquis de Seignelay, Colbert's son, and ask him to present the resolution to His Majesty. Almost a year later the answer came. The result was that the king had been pleased by the resolution, but that he was willing to dispense the city from a triumphal entry. Nevertheless, that should not prevent

> the city from giving some mark of the gratitude it owed to the glorious labors of this hero who bore the honor of His Crown and of the French name far above his illustrious predecessor, that ancient Rome had consecrated by triumphal works the memory of Julius Caesar and that it was fitting that the Capital of the state should pass on to posterity by some public Monument the memory of the Astonishing Exploits of the King Louis the Great, that the construction of the new Saint Denis gate gave a good occasion for it, and that one could make thereon a bas-relief which would show the Crossing of the Rhine and all the Conquests over all Holland and with the inscription Ludovico Magno and to preserve its memory that there should be struck medals with the same inscription, begging the Company to deliberate on this proposition.[28]

The King's Counsel moved the resolution; as one can readily imagine, it was carried without dissent, and the provosts were empowered to proceed with its implementation. Whereas all previous medals had born the legend "LUCOVICUS XIIII REX CHRISTIANISSIMUS," this one said merely "LUDOVICUS MAGNUS REX." And despite centuries of revolution, the Porte Saint Denis still bears the inscription LUDOVICO MAGNO.

After wading through the tortured indirect discourse of the secretary's recording the report of the provost of the merchants' report of what the marquis de Seignelay reported to him on what the king had said to *him,* it comes through quite clearly

 that the City of Paris had proposed that Louis be called "Louis the Magnanimous," and that Louis had decided *himself* that he would be called "Louis the Great."

In the year 1673 or 1674 Louis paid a formal visit to the great Jesuit establishment of learning in Paris known as the Collège de Clermont. Over the doorway was the inscription *Collegium Societatis Jesu,* for it had started as a Jesuit community house that quickly turned into a great school. Such diverse figures as Saint François de Sales and Molière had studied there. It was indeed a great honor that the king was conferring upon the collège to make the visit. Some time after the visit — the exact date is in dispute — the name was changed to the Collège Louis-le-Grand, and some pious souls were quietly scandalized when the name of Jesus over the entrance was removed and replaced by that of Louis the Great.[29] Later secularized, the collège is now the Lycée Louis-le-Grand, the finest and most competitive institution of secondary education in France, despite the anomoly of the royal name under a Socialist government.

The gift that the king made to the collège to commemorate his visit is one of the most eloquent silent indicators of Louis' reason for calling himself "the Great." He gave the collège a painting by Jouvenet that is a direct copy of Le Brun's "Tent of Darius." (The painting still hangs today in the office of the principal.) We can reasonably infer from this commemorative gift that Louis had decided that in fact he did deserve to be compared to Alexander. In all of this, Louis had quite deliberately used the tools of bureaucracy to grant to himself the attributes of heroism to pass on to posterity.

In his *Art poétique,* Boileau exhorts the writer of heroic poems to recount "amazing deeds worthy of being heard / Let him be like Caesar, Alexander, Louis." Father Michel Le Tellier in dedicating an edition of Quintus Curtius to the dauphin says that, whereas Alexander had before his eyes the far-off pictures of Hercules and Achilles, the dauphin did not need such images to become another Alexander, for he had before his own eyes his father's example. But one wonders by what alchemy this is compared to the exploits of Alexander. Louis had become astute in many ways, including the art of warfare, but he was too intelligent to take it out of the hands of his skillful

generals.[30] He knew that, and he knew that he had to be prudent with his own life, yet he evidently liked Boileau's comparing him to Caesar and Alexander or he would not have named him to be one of the two Royal Historiographers. Louis could give himself the appellation "the Great" in imitation of Alexander, but he earned it by his mastery of bureaucratic detail, his imposition of a complex ritual surrounding his person, and by keeping himself at a great distance from his subjects.

IMAGE AND REALITY

To what extent do the symbols of an age reflect the feelings of its actors and to what extent do they in turn mold the actors themselves? To what extent did the constant repetition to Louis that he had surpassed all prior heroes — that he combined Alexander and both Julius and Augustus Caesar — mold his conduct, and to what extent did he consiously manipulate those symbols? Was it wishful dreaming or conscious posing? And to what extent did he actually come to believe in whichever one it was? Or was it a curious ritual that took on its own reality? Alexander had a son whom he named Heracles; his posthumous son was named Alexander IV. Louis had five sons, all named Louis, and three daughters, two of whom were named Louise. The three sons by Madame de Montespan were called Louis Auguste (b. 1670), Louis César (b. 1672), and Louis Alexandre (b. 1678). They were all legitimized and, Louis César having died in 1683, Louis Auguste and Louis Alexandre were placed in the line of succession to the throne.

One also wonders to what extent the symbols of Prudence and Wisdom and the peaceful pursuits of Augustus were the creatures of Colbert's suggestions to Le Brun in order to influence the thinking of Louis? These are no doubt novelistic questions that will admit of no absolute answer. But it was surely the élan of self-confidence, the sense of creating an epoch that was an ideal mirror — and rival — of Antiquity, that made the seventeenth century one of those culminating points of culture that happen on rare occasions in history.

It would be niggardly to deny to Louis the appellation he gave himself — certainly the fact that this state bears his name is in itself a proof of his greatness. In comparing Louis with Alexander one could legitimately wonder whether Alexander ever would have been able to quiet his wanderlust and settle down to reigning like an Augustus or a Louis.

But we cannot help noting that after a quarter of a century it began to be apparent that the king had dreamed himself to be Alexander too often, at the expense of the other side of his character, which was that of a prudent manager. By 1694 the great Gobelins Works were forced to shut down for three years because of the terrifying state of finances in the kingdom. Most of the fine-wrought silver was melted down for coin to finance warfare, thus reversing Isaiah: masterpieces were beaten into (money to make) swords.

In 1696 the king, harassed and sick, unable to

sleep, used to send for Racine to sleep in his chamber and read to him during the long hot nights of August and September. There, under Le Brun's painting of Porus and Alexander, Racine read to him from Plutarch's *Lives*. One can picture them reading the life of Alexander the Great and coming to the passage where it says that Alexander "loved glory better than rule or even his own life." At this the old monarch, perhaps remembering the day at the siege of Ghent when a stray cannonball passed within seven feet of him, would straighten his noble profile, and a lofty smile would flicker over his lips as he felt he heard the echo of a kindred spirit across the centuries. ∎

FOOTNOTES

1. Robert W. Hartle, "The Image of Alexander the Great in Seventeenth Century France," in Basil Laourdas and Ch. Makaronas (eds.), *Ancient Macedonia* (Thessaloniki, 1970), 391. I should like to take this opportunity to thank the A. W. Mellon Foundation and the administrators of the grant at Queens College for granting me research time to write the present study.
2. For example, François Ogier's Preface to Jean de Schelandre's play *Tyr et Sidon* (Paris, 1608 and 1628), reprinted in *Ancien Théâtre François* (Paris, 1856), VIII, 9-23.
3. Charles Perrault first read his poem *The Century of Louis the Great* before the Academy in 1687. Later, he published four volumes between 1687 and 1697, entitled *Parallel of the Ancients and the Moderns*. Amusingly enough, some of those who actually were arguably the equals of the Ancients were the staunchest defenders of the Ancients' superiority: the names that come immediately to mind are Racine, Boileau, and La Fontaine, whereas the proponents of the Moderns are those that are no longer read with much frequency. See E. B. O. Bergerhoff, *The Freedom of French Classicism* (Princeton, N.J., 1950), 3-4, and *passim*.
4. Georges Lacour-Gayet, *L'Education politique de Louis XIV* (2nd ed.; Paris, 1923), 262 (all translations are mine); Henri Carré, *L'Enfance et la première jeunesse de Louis XIV* (Paris, 1944), 84; Plutarch, *De Iside et Osiride 24*, p. 360D, cited by Margarete Bieber, *Alexander the Great in Greek and Roman Art* (Chicago, 1964), 37.
5. Josèphe Jacquiot, *La Médaille au temps de Louis XIV* (Paris, 1970), 182, medal no. 261.
6. Much of this material was published in different form in Robert W. Hartle, "Le Brun's *Histoire d'Alexandre* and Racine's *Alexandre le Grand*," *The Romanic Review*, XLVIII (1957), 90-103, and in Hartle, "Image."
7. W. W. Tarn, *Alexander the Great* (Cambridge, 1950), I, 28.
8. Louis XIV, *Mémoires pour l'année 1661* (Paris, 1923), 131.
9. Translated from Amyot's Plutarch, which is what the seventeenth century continued to read, *Alexandre le Grand, XXXIX*.
10. Quoted by André Félibien des Avaux, *Les Reines de Perse aux pieds d'Alexandre: Peinture du Cabinet du Roy* (Paris, 1663), reprinted in *Recueil de Descriptions de peintures et d'autres ouvrages faits pour le Roy* (Paris, 1689), 52.
11. Charles Perrault considered it the masterpiece of Le Brun — and he placed Le Brun above Raphael! — because of "the honor he had of painting it under the eyes of the King." *Parallèle des Anciens et des Modernes en ce qui regarde les arts et les sciences* (Paris, 1688; facsimile ed., Munich, 1964), I, 231-32.
12. *The Tent of Darius Explained*, translated from the French of M. Félibien by Colonel Parsons (London, 1701), 10-12 (my translation from this bilingual edition). Note that the date and place of publication give evidence of the painting's continuing importance. Note also that Félibien uses the term "ouvrier" (workman) rather than "artiste." A good indication of the point that the artist is not supposed to show his originality, but rather his craftsmanship.
13. Fouquet's emblem was a squirrel, from the Old French meaning of his name, with the motto "Quo non ascendam?" which meant "How high shall I not rise?" He found out. See the portrait of Fouquet, also the painting of Vaux-le-Vicomte. Anthony Blunt, *Art and Architecture in France: 1500-1700* (2nd ed.; Baltimore, 1970), 93.
14. Heinrich Göbel, *Wandteppiche*, II. Teil: *Die romanischen Länder* (Leipzig, 1928), I, 132; Maurice Fenaille, *Etat général des tapisseries de la Manufacture des Gobelins, depuis son origine jusqu'à nos jours* (Paris, 1903), II, 184-85 (unfortunately some of these tapisseries were burned during the Revolution in order to extract the gold and silver.

15. Laurent Morellet, *Explication historique de ce qu'il y a de plus remarquable dans la maison royale de Versailles et en celle de Monsieur à Saint-Cloud* (Paris, 1681). Much of this material has appeared in different form in Robert W. Hartle, "The Allegory of Versailles: Then and Now," *Laurels*, 52 (1981), 9-18.
16. Hartle, "Allegory," 9.
17. I wish to express here my gratitude to the Research Foundation of Princeton University for making it possible for me to spend a summer of research mainly at Versailles, the Chalcographie du Louvre, and other museums in and around Paris. I wish also to thank the many curators of the Museum of Versailles, and the guards who showed me unfailing courtesy. The same was true of the curators of the Chalcographie du Louvre.
18. Chalcographie du Louvre, CN10, 2528-2529; Carré, *L'Enfance*, 105-106.
19. See Félibien, *Les Divertissemens de Versailles, donnés par le Roy à toute sa cour, au retour de la conquête de la Franche-Comté, en l'année 1674*.
20. Racine actually copied some of Félibien's prose in his Dedicatory Epistle to the king. See Hartle, "Le Brun's *Histoire*," 102.
21. Plutarch, *Alexander*, LX; Arrian, V, xix.
22. In 1672, after Racine had already produced the masterpieces of *Britannicus, Bérénice*, and *Bajazet*, Madame de Sévigné wrote that "Racine will never go beyond *Alexander* and *Andromaque*." Quoted in Racine, *Oeuvres* (Paris, 1865), I, 497, n.2. All references to Racine are from this edition.
23. Racine, *Oeuvres*, I, 515. In particular this passage is taken from Félibien; see above, note 26.
24. Jean de La Fontaine, *Fables, Contes, et Nouvelles* (Paris, 1948), 6. The phrase "take personal command" should not be taken too literally. Louis and the Royal Household would go out to a spot near a siege, but he did not interfere in the details of command. That did not stop him, however, from taking credit for the victories. "Louis' own military experience in the field was largely confined to titular command over an army besieging fortifications; he never commanded a field battle." John B. Wolf, *Louis XIV* (New York, 1968), 179-80.
25. Raymond Picard, *Supplément au Corpus Racinianum* (Paris, 1961), 10.
26. Object #37 is the order for the pension to be paid to the two Royal Historiographers. The official name of the "Petite Académie" was the Académie des Incriptions et Médailles. In 1694 it was placed under the direction of the conte de Pontchartrain. Racine's admiration for Louis was apparently reciprocated. He had become the perfect courtier and was frequently among the very select company invited to Marly.
27. See Robert W. Hartle, "The Image of Alexander the Great in Seventeenth-Century France, II. Royal Parallels," in *Ancient Macedonia*, II (Thessaloniki, 1977), 528. See especially Josèphe Jacquiot, *Médailles et jetons de Louis XIV, d'après le manuscrit de Londres* (Paris, 1968), I, xlix-1, n. 4. Mlle. Jacquiot was the first to track down the date precisely.
28. *Registre du bureau de la ville de Paris*, 16 août 1670-13 août 1673, in Archives Nationales, Série H 1823, folios LXXXVIᵛ, LXXVIIʳ, LXXVIIIʳᵛ, CCCLXXXIᵛ, CCCLXXXIIʳ, CCCLXXXIIʳᵛ. I should like to thank Mlle. Jacquiot for material assistance in facilitating access to these archives and for her erudition in deciphering them. Dr. Serban Andronescu, then a graduate student, was patient enough to sift through these documents in the places I had indicated.
29. Some Latin verses on the subject circulated clandestinely. I am grateful to Monsieur Paul de Heuvels, *Proviseur* of the Lycée Louis-le-Grand, for access to this information.
30. Wolf, *Louis XIV*, 180: "This was partly because of his firm conviction that a king should rely upon the advice of men better informed or more experienced than himself."

FROM POLITICS TO COLLECTING: LOUIS XIV AND PAINTING
ANTOINE SCHNAPPER

ouis XIII loved the arts and from time to time even worked with pastels. Critics and art historians, who first appeared in France around 1650, reverently describe for us the lessons the king deigned to receive from Simon Vouet, whose return to France in 1627 — at the behest of Louis XIII — marks the symbolic rebirth of French painting, somewhat abandoned since the death of Henri IV in 1610. Nonetheless, royal interest in painting appeared only intermittently, notably in commissions awarded to Vouet or his collaborators for decorative work at the Louvre, Saint-Germain-en-Laye, Vincennes, or Fontainebleau. The king did not collect works of art. The Superintendent of Buildings, Sublet de Noyers, undoubtedly with Cardinal Richelieu's encouragement, considered enlisting the arts, especially painting, in the service of royal glory, or at least making them contribute to it. The precise reasons for the foundation of the Académie Française in 1634 remain controversial, but the idea that the cultivation and perhaps control of the arts was indispensable to a powerful monarchy certainly figured therein. In 1640-41 the ministers of Louis XIII arranged for the return to Paris of the most famous of French-born painters, Nicolas Poussin, whom they were unable to retain. They then invited, also without success, the sculptor François Duquesnoy and the painter Pietro da Cortona. The return of Poussin was probably linked to a project for the creation of an academy of painting and sculpture, which would only be realized in 1648.

All the same, the king remained basically indifferent, which can be explained in part by the almost constant political difficulties of the realm and by the king's own character. Out of a sincere modesty, it seems, Louis XIII did not even use traditional *entrées* — the well-known royal corteges that marched in procession along temporary decors replete with allusions to the noble deeds and virtues of the prince, festivities whose memory was preserved and assured of wide diffusion by one or several engravings — to enhance his own glory.

In contrast, members of Richelieu's circle displayed a true interest in the arts and a real appreciation for their political use. Nothing would have been easier than to renew the lapsed tradition exemplified by Henri IV's decoration of the chapel at Fontainebleau and especially of the Petite Galerie of the Louvre, embellished in 1607 with effigies of the kings and queens of France in an effort to affirm the dynastic continuity of a controversial king only distantly related to his predecessor, Henri III. One also finds this tradition in Richelieu's first protector, Queen Marie de Medici, whose Florentine origins accustomed her to patronage. In order to enhance her own glory and that of the late king, she had Rubens paint one of the galleries of the new Luxembourg Palace, a task in which Richelieu took a keen interest. The cardinal guided royal incursions into the domain of the arts primarily through his own lively interest in works of art, which he collected avidly (paintings, classical sculptures, porcelains), but also through his patronage; thus he had galleries decorated to glorify both the royal dynasty and his own government, not only in his Parisian palace (the Gallery of Illustrious Men) but also in the Richelieu family château in Poitou. The ministers and protégés grouped around him, Pierre Séguier, Louis Phélypeaux, the marquis de La Vrillière, and especially Jules Mazarin, all imitated him in this respect.

Paradoxically, it seems that the humiliations experienced by the French monarchy during the Fronde played a determinant role in its return to protection and political use of the arts. In 1649 the city of Paris welcomed the king with a solemn *entrée* of a kind rarely seen since 1623. In 1654 Louis XIV was consecrated with great pomp at Reims, and the Chevalier Avice was charged with the task of "producing plates for engravings to be distributed in the farthermost lands as visible proof to confirm for people's eyes what they may have only heard from rumor."[1] Accordingly, three large plates appeared the following year.

But only after the death of Mazarin in 1661 and Louis XIV's assumption of personal power did everything really begin, prompted by the king himself and particularly by Jean-Baptiste Colbert. One then witnesses a veritable explosion of artistic energy in all fields.

Let us first consider the realm of collecting. It behooved royal magnificence to gather artistic treasures in order to impress visitors with their splendor. Reviving the tradition begun by François I and aspired to by Henri IV during his brief reign, Louis XIV gathered in a few years the immense collections that still form the core of French museums and the Bibliothèque Nationale. This *curiosité,* in the seventeenth-century sense of the term, extended to the realm of knowledge as well as the arts. Colbert, himself an avid book-lover, was feverishly busy assembling books and manuscripts in the Royal Library that he established on the Rue Vivienne. There as elsewhere the king benefited from a decisive event: the death in 1660 of his uncle Gaston d'Orléans, who left his collections to him. In addition to his library, Gaston had two areas of specialization: works of classical antiquity and botany. He had collected a great many antique busts and statues, several of which, according to Henri Sauval, were drawn from the royal collection itself, so neglected by its proprietor, plus many engraved stones and especially medals which, in accordance with usual practice, were connected to the library.[2] Around this core collection Louis XIV assembled by means of legacies, gifts, and purchases an enormous mass of small antique objects, which without question constituted at the time of his death the most important collection in the world.

A botanist and great lover of flowers and birds, Gaston d'Orléans had created at Blois an aviary and a botanical garden equal in importance to the one opened in Paris at about that time. Although the garden itself barely outlived its creator, traces of Gaston's passion for botany live on in the form of hundreds of miniatures of birds and plants that he commissioned artists (principally Nicolas Robert) to paint on vellum. In turn, the miniatures were bequeathed to Louis XIV, preserved by subsequent kings of France, and today are known as the "vellums of the museum." In the realm of the traditional arts, the king joined the ranks of great collectors by obtaining thirty celebrated canvases, antique statues, and tapestries from the collection of Mazarin and by purchasing from Jabach in 1662 a sizable lot of paintings, almost all of which were Italian. This lot was followed in 1671 by a second lot, accompanied by more than five thousand drawings, which today comprise the core collection of the Cabinet des Dessins of the Louvre. Without going into unnecessary detail, one should note that during this time the king also obtained a great many other paintings; for example, in 1665 he acquired the duc de Richelieu's first-rate collection, so rich in paintings by Poussin.

From this time onward, the major outlines of royal taste in painting began to take shape. The king inherited from his predecessors Richelieu and Mazarin the traditional respect for "classical" Italian painting: Leonardo da Vinci, Raphaël, and their followers on the one hand; Correggio and the Venetian masters Bassano, Titian, Tintoretto, and Veronese on the other. Modern (but not contemporary) Italian painting was also well represented by members of the Caravaggio school, as well as by the Bolognese group of painters in the line of Annibale Carracci, whose work the king particularly liked. Following numerous acquisitions at the end of the century (notably the rich bequest of André Le Nôtre in 1693), the royal collection became extraordinarily strong in Bolognese, especially Albani, to the point that today the French national collections are the richest in the world outside Italy.

In contrast, the king showed little interest in Dutch or Flemish painting, aside from Van Dyck, or even in French painting, with the notable exception of Poussin. The work of the latter

ONE WITNESSES A VERITABLE EXPLOSION OF ARTISTIC ENERGY IN ALL FIELDS

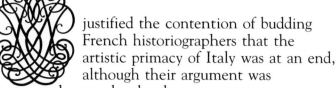

justified the contention of budding French historiographers that the artistic primacy of Italy was at an end, although their argument was attenuated somewhat by the near-permanent nature of Poussin's stay in Italy. The prime candidate for titular head of a truly French school was Charles Le Brun, who not only acted as Colbert's collaborator and representative to the artistic world, but who also held the position of First Painter of the King. His role in the decoration of the royal châteaus, principally at Versailles, was immense. In regard to painting alone, he directed the ornamentation of the Grands Appartements and the upper floor, as well as the decoration of the Ambassadors' Stairway, the Grande Galerie, and the Salons of Peace and War. Does that mean that Louis XIV, to whom Le Brun gave paintings in a pointed effort to retain royal favor after the death of Colbert, was ever very interested in his work? The king managed to address a few kind words to Le Brun when Louvois emphatically abandoned him, but he still allowed his war minister to transfer his favor to Le Brun's old enemy Pierre Mignard. Here was one sign among many others of a certain indifference on the part of the king to contemporary painting. His true passion was architecture and interior decoration, as demonstrated by his important role in the construction of the Grand Trianon in 1687.[3]

Many signs point to the fact that Colbert — rather than the king himself — played the determinant role in the implementation of the very active arts policy initiated in 1661, even before he officially became Superintendent of Buildings. Arguing from the contrary, the decisiveness of his role, especially in the question of painting, becomes readily apparent in light of the change of policy — or rather, the collapse of policy — that occurred upon his death. Although the king had only just recently settled at Versailles, he developed a passion for the smaller, more comfortable châteaus such as Trianon and Marly, and neglected the Grands Appartements and the imposing decor of Versailles at a time when Mignard, in the Petite Galerie, competed with Le Brun, who was completing the Grande Galerie and the Salons of War and Peace. The painted decor of the Grand Trianon would, after 1688, give way to decorative paintings — mythologies as well as flowers and landscapes — without, however, there being a conscious program of royal iconography.[4] The exaltation of the monarchy and the traditional concern of a dynasty with relatively uncertain origins to link itself with Saint Louis and Charlemagne are certainly evident in the painted ornamentation of the church of the Invalides or in the chapel of Versailles. But it is only under Colbert and not afterwards that one observes the marked political resolve to exploit art to enhance the glory of the sovereign.

The memoirs of Charles Perrault place this turning point at the end of 1662, when Colbert prepared to assume the post of Superintendent of Buildings:

He hoped to work not only toward the completion of the Louvre but also to supervise the construction of many monuments to the glory of the king, such as triumphal arches, obelisks, pyramids, mausoleums: for there was nothing great and magnificent he did not propose to accomplish. He foresaw the need to strike a great many medals to consecrate for posterity the memory of the great deeds the king had already performed and, Colbert believed, those even greater deeds he would accomplish in the future. Moreover, he anticipated that all these great exploits would be combined with divertissements worthy of a prince, with festivals, masquerades, carrousels and other similar diversions, all of which would need to be described and engraved with verve and intelligence for distribution in foreign countries, where the manner in which they are received will be only slightly less honorific than the events themselves.[5]

In fact, beginning in 1661 Colbert was involved in the transactions that led to the acquisition by the king of the important works from the Mazarin collection. In August, 1662, a few months after the acquisition of very important paintings from the collection of Jabach, the scholar Louis Douvrier agreed to collaborate with Colbert on the inscriptions planned for the monuments to be erected to the glory of the king.[6] The same year, upon the occasion of the Carrousel, Douvrier invented the famous motto of Louis XIV: *Nec pluribus impar.* By the end of the year, a commission of erudite members of the Académie Française existed around the writer Jean Chapelain and was charged with the task of writing the inscriptions to be engraved on medals and monuments. This commission came to be known as the Petite Académie and formed the core around which would soon grow the Academy of Inscriptions and Belles-Lettres, one of whose first tasks was the reproduction of the Carrousel of 1662.

To ensure the glory of the king in the eyes of foreigners and especially of posterity, nothing was more suitable than architecture: "Your Majesty knows that aside from brilliant military actions, nothing better testifies to the grandeur and spirit of princes than buildings, for all of posterity takes the measure of princes by the size and beauty of the residences they constructed during their lifetime."[7] Resistance to the ravages of time was an equally important characteristic of medals, and Colbert had more than one hundred thirty struck to the glory of the king. The "other laudable means of spreading and sustaining the glory of his Majesty" — tapestries, paintings, and printed works — were recognized "to be less durable than the others, precluding their long conservation" (Chapelain).

NOTHING BETTER TESTIFIES TO THE GRANDEUR AND SPIRIT OF PRINCES THAN BUILDINGS

There is no need to dwell on the glorification of the monarchy and of the king himself undertaken by the painters commissioned to decorate the Tuileries and Versailles. Such artistic efforts were primarily indirect, such as Le Brun's immense canvases depicting the life of Alexander, or the obligatory Mount Olympus drawn by a team of artists on the ceilings and walls of the Tuileries. But contemporary texts, most often written by André Félibien, who became Historiographer of the Buildings of the King, enable us to decipher these allusions to royal splendor.[8] Van der Meulen avoided this traditional language when he directly glorified recent royal conquests in his paintings on the walls of the Ambassadors' Stairway and especially in those for the vault of the Hall of Mirrors. Renouncing his original plans, Le Brun decided not to depict Hercules and Apollo but instead the great deeds of the king since his accession to power in 1661; allegorical language found itself subordinated to royal glorification.[9] Le Brun and his team, with Van der Meulen in the first rank, also furnished the models for tapestries made at the new workshops of the Gobelins, created by Colbert in 1662. Accordingly, in 1665 work began on a hanging, *History of the King*, whose title aptly illustrates this program.

The disadvantage of a painting resides in its uniqueness; even tapestries could not easily be reproduced. In contrast, therein lay the immense advantage of the engraving and consequently its capital role under Colbert in the diffusion of the king's glory. A team working out of the Gobelins factory and including Israël Silvestre, Sebastien Le Clerc, François Chauveau, and Jean Le Pautre, would produce a great number of plates that can be divided into two principal categories. On the one hand, were those glorifying the kingdom: its loveliest spots, old and especially new royal residences, royal fêtes, and the artistic treasures that Louis XIV either obtained or created, particularly at Versailles. This was the task assigned to Silvestre, commissioned as engraver to the king in March, 1663, to engrave "all his palaces and royal residences, the loveliest views and perspectives of his gardens, public assemblies, carrousels and surroundings of the cities."[10] These plates appeared either individually or in collections accompanied by a dithyrambic text, generally written by André Félibien. Thus, beginning in 1670, there appeared several series reproducing the famed Carrousel of 1662, the Fêtes of Versailles in 1664, 1668, and 1674, the tapestries *The Four Elements* and *The Four Seasons*, paintings from the royal collection and antique statues, the Labyrinth and Grotto of Versailles, etc. These collections, often privately sponsored, continued to appear after the death of Colbert and spread the fame of the Gallery of Apollo at the Louvre, the Ambassadors' Stairway, the Hall of Mirrors, a great many statues, vases, and fountains from the park of Versailles, etc. The wonders of the reign received equal coverage in the monthly issues of the *Mercure Galant*, which also reported the publication of engravings.

Félibien explained in his own words the value of these prints:

Through them posterity will one day see, in the guise of appealing figures, the history of the great deeds of this August Monarch, and from this day forward peoples in faraway lands will benefit as we do from the new discoveries made in the Academies. . . . Moreover, by means of these prints all nations will admire the sumptuous edifices that the King constructed regardless of cost, as well as the rich ornaments that embellish them. And because the paintings and statues this great prince so carefully sought out are priceless and remarkably beautiful, His Majesty also insisted that the person charged with executing his orders select the most excellent engravers of his Kingdom to engrave them and form collections, so that by means of the published prints the works themselves will, if necessary, be seen by the most backward nations unable to view them in the original.[11]

The other essential aspect of these engravings was the representation of the "great deeds" of the king — in other words, his military conquests, especially of fortresses. In sum, the fruits of war came after those of peace. These views of battles and conquered places pursued and developed a recent precedent, the large collection of the *Glorious Conquests of Louis the Great*, begun in the 1640s by Sebastien de Pontaut, chevalier de Beaulieu, an engineer of the king wounded at the siege of Philipsbourg. His undertaking, in which Stefano della Bella and Nicolas Cochin also participated, was pursued after his death in 1674. But the central player in this military glorification was Van der Meulen, active from 1664 until his death in 1690. Just as Israël Silvestre had done in 1665, Van der Meulen followed the king's armies on several campaigns, sketching the encampments, the uniforms, the site of towns. The Gobelins frequently drew upon his talent and experience, but his most important work in this respect was the series of large paintings done in the 1680s for Marly, known under the name of *Conquests of the King*, and soon reproduced in engravings. And when, before too long, the Superintendence neglected this activity, Van der Meulen himself and then his widow took on the task. Louis XV later purchased the ensemble of plates, which presently belong to the Chalcographie du Louvre. The painted representation of the king's conquests, which by the end of the seventeenth century had taken on a somewhat anachronistic aspect, was nonetheless continued at Marly at the initiative, one could say, of the collaborators and students of Van der Meulen, Jean Paul, Sauveur Le Comte, and the Martins.

These representations of towns, like the celebrated series of relief maps begun in 1668, were also of great military value. More generally, they evidenced the king's desire to know and possess his realm in a real and tangible way, a desire one also finds in the intense cartographic activity of the century.

In art as in other domains, the personal reign of Louis XIV can be divided into two distinct periods, before and after 1685. The first twenty-five years of the reign were dominated by large-scale projects directed by Colbert and Le Brun. This was the epoch of the veritable creation of Versailles, an immense task in which painters played an important role. But from the very moment of its completion in the Hall of Mirrors and two adjoining salons, the grandiose celebration of the virtuous peace imposed by Louis XIV on Europe was moribund. The political situation deteriorated, leading to the difficult War of the League of Augsburg, which provoked such financial troubles that the budget of the Superintendence of Buildings was sacrificed and the king's own silverware was sent to the foundry. Moreover, the king had already tired of the ponderous showiness of Versailles. In addition, the installation of the Hall of Mirrors and the Salons of War and Peace had brought about the destruction of a portion of the Grands Appartements of the king and queen and, along with it, of their grandiose iconographic program, inspired by the Pitti Palace, of the planets associated with the gods of Olympus. In addition, the shift of the king's Grand Appartement to the eastern portion of the château in 1679-83 made available several new ceilings (second Salon of Venus, Salon of Abundance) painted by Houasse, a

Catalogue 103

123

loyal student of Le Brun, which did not fully match the earlier ceilings in style or iconography.[12]

At the same time, Houasse worked on the decoration of a new room, the Cabinet des Curiosités, a veritable symbol of turn-of-the-century Versailles: the king became a collector. Since 1661 the enrichment of the royal collections had been prodigious due to the prompting of Colbert, but with little evidence of personal interest on the part of Louis XIV. In contrast, beginning in about 1684 his collections became one of his principal distractions at Versailles. Once the collection of medals was transported there, the king visited it almost daily after Mass, and Oppenord constructed a dozen sumptuous cabinets to house the collection. In 1684-89 alone, the king spent more than 560,000 livres to purchase medals, "crystals, agates and other rarities."[13] The entire eastern portion of the Petit Appartement, to which two new rooms were added in 1692 (the Salon Ovale and the Cabinet des Coquilles), was transformed into a kind of museum, particularly the Petite Galerie that Mignard, in untimely revenge on his old rival Le Brun, had just redecorated. Having rejected a project of amazing luxuriousness relying primarily on tortoise shell and lapis lazuli, the king insisted that the walls receive a more sober treatment suitable for hanging pictues.[14]

This evolution of royal taste explains in part the sad fate of Le Brun, who not only saw Louvois the war minister systematically prefer Mignard over himself, but who also completed the solemn painted decoration of Versailles just when the king was losing interest in his ponderous allegories, which time would render obsolete. Beginning around 1685, as already noted, royal taste turned to small châteaus, where one could pass the day among carefully selected company, savoring the charms of the countryside as well as the good food.

Flowers, landscapes (quite numerous among the paintings hanging in the royal collection at Versailles), and pleasant mythological scenes supplanted monumental paintings. Even Marly, for which so many warlike canvases were painted, was invaded by paintings of flowers and by small canvases, often of Flemish or Dutch inspiration, drawn from the reserves of the royal collection or painted on command. The Grand Trianon was entirely filled with these sorts of paintings. There the king employed alongside the loyal students of Le Brun, Houasse and Verdier, an old notable like Noël Coypel as well as the best representatives of the new generation, the painters born around 1640, such as Charles de La Fosse, the Boullogne brothers (Bon and Louis), Jean Jouvenet, and Antoine Coypel.

Although all of these painters remained in ascendance until the death of Louis XIV, nothing indicates that the king paid much attention to them. The position of First Painter of the King was left vacant after Mignard's death in 1695, despite the hopes of the active and ambitious Antoine Coypel, who would have to await the Regency to hold that post immediately prior to his death. For example, nothing suggests that Louis XIV concerned himself with the choice of painters employed in the Grand Trianon, otherwise so dear to his heart: between 1688 and 1714 one finds the most diverse range of painters working there, from one room to the next — if not in the same room. Everything was conducted as if the king were more interested in his orange trees.

The distance the king maintained between himself and the best painters at the end of his reign clearly appears in the register in which the architect Jules Hardouin-Mansart noted the orders of the king from 1699 to 1703.[15] When it was necessary to commission new paintings — even for a location as prestigious as the central salon of Marly — the king never specified a painter but limited himself to vague formulas: one will choose "the most adept painters," "the best masters," or "the painters must be well chosen."

This lack of interest in contemporary painting, when the king no longer had beside him a superintendent of the caliber of Colbert or even of Louvois, who personally protected Mignard, appears equally clearly in the intrigues and confusion surrounding the orders for the decoration of the new church of the Invalides. For over a dozen years, hesitations and errors followed one another in the decoration of every feature: should it be confided to a painter or to a sculptor? If to a painter, which one? Several important works, in the course of their execution or even once completed, were destroyed (pendentives first sculpted then turned over to La Fosse; a chapel painted by Charles François Poërson then by Bon Boullogne), before the decor, shared among a group of artists, was finally completed in 1706.[16]

The monarchy still possessed all the means of controlling and stimulating artistic life that Colbert had created (the Gobelins) or reformed (the

Academy of Painting and Sculpture), but it had lost the determination so characteristic of that great minister. Henceforth artistic life took place in Paris rather than at Versailles. One would have to wait until the middle of the eighteenth century and the arrival of superintendents such as Lenormant de Tournehem and Marigny before the monarchy would resume its role as promoter of the arts. ∎

Catalogue 8

FOOTNOTES

1. This essay was translated from the French by Steven G. Reinhardt, *La pompeuse et magnifique cérémonie du sacre du roy Louis XIV, fait à Rheims, représentée au naturel par ordre de Leurs Majestés* (Paris, 1655). See Madeleine Lauraine-Portemer, "Opposition et propagande: Paris au temps du sacre de Louis XIV," *Etudes européennes. Mélanges offerts à Victor-L. Tapié* (Paris, 1973), reprise in *Etudes mazarines* (Paris, 1981), 155-74.
2. Henri Sauval, *Histoire et recherche des Antiquités de Paris* (Paris, 1724, reedited 1733), II, 55.
3. Bertrand Jestaz, "Le Trianon de Marbre ou Louis XIV architecte," *Gazette des Beaux-Arts* (November, 1969), pp. 259-86.
4. Antoine Schnapper, *Tableaux pour le Trianon de Marbre, 1688-1714* (Paris, 1967).
5. *Mémoires de Charles Perrault*, ed. Paul Lacroix (Paris, 1878), 20.
6. Bibliothèque Nationale, Manuscrits, Mélanges Colbert 110, f° 313-14, cited in the catalogue of the exhibition *L'Académie des inscriptions et Belles-Lettres, 1663-1963*, Paris, Archives de France, 1963, n° 3.
7. Pierre Clément, *Lettres, instructions et mémoires de Colbert* (Paris, 1861-65), V, 269.
8. Among the numerous texts of Félibien, see his description of the paintings of Nicolas Loyr at the Tuileries, *Entretiens sur les vies et sur les ouvrages des plus excellens peintres anciens et modernes* (Paris, 1685-88), II, 633-41.
9. See Johannes Langner, "Le Brun interprète de l'histoire de Louis XIV: A propos d'un tableau de la Galerie des Glaces à Versailles," *Formes* (Spring, 1982), pp. 21-26.
10. Published by E. de Silvestre, *Renseignements sur quelques peintres et graveurs des XVIIe et XVIIIe siècles Israël Silvestre et ses descendants* (Paris, 1868), 109.
11. André Félibien, *Tableaux du Cabinet du Roy, Statues et Bustes Antiques des Maisons Royales* (Paris, 1677).
12. Antoine Schnapper, *Jean Jouvenet, 1644-1717, et la peinture d'histoire à Paris* (Paris, 1974), 59-64.
13. See the recapitulative memoir of 1690 published by Clément, *Lettres . . . de Colbert*, V, 567 ff.
14. Antoine Schnapper, "Two Unknown Ceiling Paintings by Mignard for Louis XIV," *The Art Bulletin*, LVI (1974), 82-100.
15. Archives Nationales, 0¹ 1809.
16. Schnapper, *Jouvenet*, 109-119.

Le Duc de Guise Roy Ameriquain

MONUMENTAL ART,
OR THE POLITICS OF ENCHANTMENT
DANIEL RABREAU

ith *The Fountains of Versailles*, a great secular cantata created in 1681, Michel-Richard de La Lande celebrated the victorious return of the king, hero of the Army of the Rhine. But there was little of a military nature in this musical tribute to the pleasures of the court. The repose of the warrior inspired a setting commensurate with his tastes, one of delightful relaxation and bountiful renown. "Apollo and Ceres sing the glory of the young conqueror of hearts and France's enemies, and praise the charm of the places planned with his advice." Moreover, in hommage to the great horticultural architect Le Nôtre, "the text of this work enabled the principal mythological personnages of the basins of the park at Versailles to proclaim that it was not the return of Spring but rather the return of the Sun King which rejuvenated nature and made the flowers bloom in Le Nôtre's gardens."[1] On the adjoining side suddenly appeared the new Alexander, on the court side arose Phoebus-Apollo: fiction attached to the person of the monarch dictated, in a sense, the "monuments program." The nature of the location inspired a certain respect for convention: in town, trophies, triumphal archs, and equestrian statues were erected; in residences, the divinities of Olympus sipped nectar in complete equality with the owner.

Monumental statuary, whether in Paris or at Versailles, represents more than a symbol. It is a permanent *mise en scène*, a living spectacle for the pleasure not only of the eyes, but of all the senses. Each statuary group reflects, like a faceted mirror, the image of the king's personal radiance. "Yesterday Madame de Lafayette was at Versailles," wrote Madame de Sévigné in the month of April,

1674, "where she was well received, indeed, very well received, meaning that the King had her seated in his own calèche with the ladies, and took pleasure in showing her all the beauties of Versailles, as would any proud owner of a country house."[2] Fifteen years later, Louis himself wrote his celebrated *Manner of Showing the Gardens of Versailles*, almost a choreographed promenade for the use of admirers, the guide to an incessantly repeated "ritual." Could one today understand the monumental art of the Grand Siècle, frozen in marble, stone, and bronze, without first recalling to mind the significance of a gesture, a glance, the arrangement of a cortège, the impact of a hymn or fireworks?

Two stunning but very different fêtes, both of which have remained famous, marked the debut of the personal reign of Louis XIV. The first, in 1660 at Paris, preceded the death of Mazarin and celebrated the marriage of the king and the Franco-Spanish alliance. The second, in 1664 at Versailles, was entitled *The Pleasures of the Enchanted Island* and dedicated a select spot that the king would constantly remodel to suit the activities of his court.

Other fêtes could also be evoked, such as the famous Carrousel of Paris (1662): the Entrée of 1660, punctuated with allegorical triumphal arches, gave way to games borrowed from the chivalry of the Middle Ages, cloaked in Roman style for the occasion. Louis, as emperor, personally led the classical quadrille, whereas the princes led the other groups meant to evoke different civilizations and parts of the world. For example, the duc de Guise commanded the quadrille of the "American Savages." In this grandiose "urban" ballet of the aristocracy, a representation of the hommage paid

Detail of Catalogue 149

France by surrounding nations, historians already recognize the illustration of the solar myth employed in the vivid royal iconography. The only thing needed was for Louis XIV to establish, by means of monuments, this ephemeral imagery and give it significant political meaning. Relegated to the role of intermediaries for monarchical absolutism, the nobility, like birds in a gilded cage (the court), would have no further purpose than to reflect "the solar image of the sovereign placed in their midst."[3]

In devoting himself to the development of the virtues of "monumental art," Louis XIV could not help but personalize its application. Such is the sense of the creation of Versailles. Its recognized supremacy over all other creative aspects of the century can be explained by the exceptional means placed at the disposal of the artists, to the detriment of the planned or hoped-for accomplishments in the capital. The dynamism of the centralizing French state which, from the eighteenth to the twentieth century, nourished the Paris/province conflict, had its origin to a certain extent in this opposition of Paris and Versailles under Louis XIV. And in contrast to the capital of the popes, crucible of European baroque, the capital of the Sun King did not yet undergo the monumental development appropriate to its rank in the seventeenth century. One must await the following century, the "Century of Enlightenment," to see the myth of Paris as the "New Rome" take on a tangible meaning. But would this efflorescence of monumental urban art in the eighteenth century have been possible in France without the example of Versailles? Nostalgic defenders of Colbert would undoubtedly reply in the affirmative, as did Lafont de Saint Yenne in his pamphlet entitled *The Shadow of the Great Colbert*, or even Voltaire, who in *The Age Of Louis XIV* contended "that the minister must share the glory of the master" — not without recognizing that the former would have been nothing without the will of the king. Such is the paradox that governs the blossoming of monumental art in France after 1661: the "team" of Colbert and Louis XIV was drawn in opposite directions, on the one hand toward Paris, on the other toward Versailles. And to the provinces, the king — aided by the ingenious Vauban — personally bestowed monuments of war, particularly citadels and bastions. Only by translating the very essence of absolute monarchy would artists and institutions in the service of the king and the nation bring about a new, independent achievement benefiting the contentious yet submissive masses. The Academies, like the Royal Manufactures, were founded with this primary — yet not exclusive — goal in mind. The eighteenth century, in turn, would develop this sumptuous heritage beyond all expectations.[4]

The Parisian fêtes that crowned the policy of Mazarin (in 1660), like Colbert's later projects for the Louvre and the beautification of Paris, illustrate a governmental art that was "national" but not "cosmic." Bernard Teyssèdre, in an inspired book that reexamines the personal artistic role played by Louis XIV in the creation of French classicism, very ably characterized the Versailles ideology, its iconographic principles, and its opposition to Paris:

> In opposition to this governmental art, "national" but not "cosmic," the King placed courtly art. He was the first servant of the State, and he worked assiduously; he was also sovereign by divine right, imperceptibly yet inevitably united with Nature and the Creator. He was at the head of his people, and gazed beyond, towards the Months and the Seasons governed by thesun, towards the Elements, the Continents, the Temperaments which make a Cosmos out of Chaos. "His court is an elect society, and his terrestial Olympus an arcadian nature, ordered, civil, and obedient to the wise guidance of man." Absolute, he directs the government of his people, but remains essentially different. He cannot reside in the capital.[5]

THE MONUMENTAL COURT: VERSAILLES

If Louis XIV, leaving Paris behind, abandoned the great plans for the Louvre, it was in order to devote himself entirely to a much more spectacular undertaking that would emerge solely from his own will: the creation of the "palace of the sun." Symbolism, naturally attached to the residence of the sovereign, acquired at Versailles a dimension theretofore unknown, not only by the amplitude and quality of the site, the buildings, and the decor, but also by the cohesion of an iconological program that was simultaneously stimulating yet represented the materialization of a harmonious fairy-land that has remained the symbol of classicism.

The transformation of the small "brick and

stone" château of Louis XIII (1624-38) into a vast palace of stone and marble was accomplished in several stages, under the personal supervision of the king. And if at first this transformation was essentially the adaptation of what was originally a hunting lodge into a permanent royal residence, it soon turned into a complete renovation when it became a question of lodging the court there. At that time the development of the gardens, waterways, and the new town of Versailles (1671), which sprung up around the royal *appartements*, gave the vast complex the appearance of a microcosm.

The network of avenues in the park and the immense crossroads that leads, beyond the Place d'Armes, to the Cour de Marbre onto which the King's bedchamber opened, are tangible evidence of the royal desire for centralizing power, as is the orthogonal web of alleys of the gardens and streets of the town. This structuring of space, whether considered baroque or classical — according to a currently obsolete debate — reflected absolute power so aptly that all the sovereigns of Europe adopted it during the eighteenth century in the great many châteaus copied after Versailles. The urbanism of Baron Haussmann's Paris two centuries later, as well as Pierre L'Enfant's plan of Washington, also drew inspiration from this universally applicable model.

The architect Le Vau, the painter Le Brun, and the gardener Le Nôtre — the creators of the famous château of Vaux-le-Vicomte (1656-61) — were chosen by Louis XIV to carry out the work at Versailles. The work, which fluctuated with the fortunes of the reign, can be divided into three large continuous periods: 1661-66, 1666-83, and 1683-1715.

Between 1661 and 1666 Le Vau remodeled Louis XIII's little château from top to bottom, decorated the walls with busts, marble columns, and gilded grills, adding nuances to the delicate coloration of the brick. He also constructed the commons on either side of the château's entrance, as well as the first orangerie and menagerie (both later destroyed) in the park, for which Le Nôtre laid out new parterres and basins. At the same time, the sculptors Lerambert and M. Anguier executed an ensemble of terms in stone, figures of "Roman divinities" a dozen feet high. Versailles was still primarily a place of fêtes, where the decor would only gradually become fixed. For example, it was not until the fête of *The Pleasures of the Enchanted Island* in 1664 that the decor of the Cour de Marbre assumed its definitive form.[6]

Between 1666 and 1683, radical transformations took place that not only moulded a new space but also reduced the scale of the architecture and park. The old château was doubled in size on the side of the gardens by three groups of buildings that retained the U-shape of the original building. The new façade by Le Vau, in blond stone from Saint-Leu, extended majestically in a sober and elegant style, while the royal *appartements* displayed all the sumptuousness of gold, polychrome marbles, mirrors, and paintings applied to the walls by *marouflage*. The decoration of the Grands Appartements (1661-81), which preceded the definitive installation of the court at Versailles in 1682, was accomplished under Le Brun's personal supervision by a great many artists: René Antoine Houasse, J. Rousseau, C. Audran, and Jean Jouvenet painted the ceilings and vaults of the Salons of Abundance, Venus, Diana, Mars, etc. The ensemble culminated with the Ambassadors' Stairway (later destroyed), the Throne Room (Salon of Apollo), and finally the Hall of Mirrors, constructed by Jules Hardouin-Mansart (the successor of Le Vau, who died in 1670) in the center of the façade facing the garden, between the Salon of War and the Salon of Peace. Here Le Brun executed a program of admirable paintings framed in the stuccos of Girardon, Regnaudin, and the Marsy brothers. The episodes in the life of the king were illustrated in an allegorical iconography borrowed from the legendary cycle of the history of Alexander and from the mythological cycle of Apollo.

The latter cycle is repeated on a vast scale in the gardens in order to glorify the Sun King. Phoebus, the seasons, and the elements (water, in particular) all appear in the fountains and sculptures of gilded lead or marble arranged here and there on the lawn and along the lagoons, following the axis of the Grand Canal. Between 1670 and 1683, Tuby sculpted the group for the Basin of Apollo; the Marsy brothers created those for the Basin of Latone, the Encelade, and Autumn; and Girardon produced for the Grotto of Thetis the group *Apollo Served by the Nymphs* — the equivalent in a round relief sculpture of the most famous of the "classical" group compositions of Poussin — as well as the Basin of Winter, the Bath of the Nymphs, and the Pyramid. The naturalist inspiration shows through, as evidenced by all the works in which fantasy does not exclude the perfect rigor of spiritual yet tempered forms.

The immense monarchical complex thus constituted would once again be expanded during the last years of the reign. The architect Hardouin-Mansart took over from the painter Le Brun the task of organizing the work and embellishment. One could say, then, that in place of the colorful and fairylike Versailles there emerged a Versailles of marble, a worthy rival of antiquity, an eternal model of deliberate classicism.

Between 1683 and 1715, while the town of Versailles developed to the east, Hardouin-Mansart extended the west façade of the château by two long set-back wings and constructed the stables, orangery, the grove of the colonnade, and the chapel (completed in 1710 by Robert de Cotte). Finally, as the last original touch of this vast undertaking that witnessed the triumph of lengthy porticos in colonnades, the Grand Trianon, a sort of pleasure château alongside the principal residence, was erected at the far end of the park (1687-88). The program of sculptures for the garden was completed by a new series of works owed to Girardon, Desjardins, and Guérin, while the famous native of Marseilles, Pierre Puget, an impetuous baroque figure envied at the court, contributed first his *Milon de Crotone,* followed by his group of *Persée et Andromène* (1685). By then, Versailles had emerged as the foremost site of monumental sculpture, where the expressionist work of this great Provençal baroque figure found its place alongside the naturalist genius of Girardon and the Marsy brothers. Antoine Coysevox, who dominated the last period of the reign (see his bas-relief *Nymphe à la Coquille* in the Salon of War), would soon accentuate the return to antique style that characterized the Versailles school.

ARCHITECTURE AND URBAN ART

The sixteenth century, with P. Lescot, De l'Orme, Goujon, or the Du Cerceaus, had created a new and original style created from an amalgamation of Italian influences and French practices and traditions. An expressive style, rich and exuberant, had gradually been purified, then systematized around 1600. The great architects of the reigns of

Henri IV and Louis XIII, Salomon de Brosse, Le Mercier, Le Muet, and especially François Mansart, made possible to an extent the blossoming of art at Versailles under Louis XIV. The progressive refinement of forms, the "nobility" of the architectonic language of a Jules Hardouin-Mansart, correspond to a propitious heritage whose exemplariness cannot be limited to courtly art or to the radiance of Versailles. The monumental art of the Grand Siècle also contained its moments of glory in private, religious, and public architecture. In regard to a finicky and status-conscious hierarchy, the zealous servants of the monarchy were able to apply the advice that Colbert whispered to Louis XIV: "Your Majesty knows that aside from striking military actions nothing better marks the grandeur and spirit of Princes than buildings."[7]

Private construction during that period was restricted primarily to a very narrow range of client, especially in Paris. Nobles, humbled by the king, constructed little; they remained on their lands and adopted a relatively discreet position. In addition, by an edict of October 31, 1660, the king forbade the initiation of "any new buildings or of any repairs to property, both in his good city and suburbs of Paris, as well as within a radius of ten leagues, without express permission." This interdiction, which would be more or less respected, put a halt not only to aristocratic but also to bourgeois construction. Normal activity would resume after 1668, but in much more modest and simpler proportions than in previous reigns.[8] The vanquishers of the Fronde were the crown and high finance. The only ambitious architectural projects, aside from those of triumphant royalty, originated with his immediate entourage: ministers, bankers, big businessmen. These projects would be realized by a few great architects already recognized by the king and very sought-after by those anxious to construct dwellings commensurate with their social position. The morphological and aesthetic characteristics of architecture were thereby modified.

As a general rule, châteaus lost all fortified characteristics as a consequence of royal policy. Their architectural plans, patterned after those of François Mansart (the château of Maisons, 1642-51), were greatly simplified and often reduced

THERE EMERGED A VERSAILLES OF MARBLE, A WORTHY RIVAL OF ANTIQUITY, AN ETERNAL MODEL OF DELIBERATE CLASSICISM

to a single main dwelling flanked by pavilions. Châteaus and *hôtels* had their outbuildings, with their bothersome noises and smells, pushed out of view or cleverly disguised (Le Vau's Vaux-le-Vicomte and the Hôtel Lambert). More and more frequently, *hôtels* came to be located "between court and garden" (Le Vau's Hôtel de Lionne, Hardouin-Mansart's Hôtel de Noailles). The façades of these private edifices were marked by a certain simplicity, an assertive symmetry, and a distinct gracefulness. The motif of cornerstones, for example, took on a great importance, whereas bands (single and double) continued to demarcate the different floors. Architects took it on themselves to purify somewhat the richness of preceeding generations: superimposed arrangements disappeared and were readily replaced by a more colossal style. The influence of official, public architecture on private architecture is quite evident here. Sculpted decoration became much lighter. Rhythms became much simpler, marked in the sixteenth century by systems of successive traves or systems inspired by Sebastiano Serlio (the Venetian or Palladian window); as in Italy, they were reduced in the epoque of Louis XIV to alternating frontons or dormer windows. Slate roofs abandoned their "broken" character inherited from the Renaissance and became unified to cover the ensemble of the edifice in a single expanse. The uniformity of surfaces, of masses — in short, the silhouette — carried the day both in Paris and at Versailles. Repetitive rhythm set the tone for tempered classicism.

Floorplans evolved along similar lines, and from the end of the century the art of "distribution" came to be recognized throughout Europe, including Italy, as a French specialty. The stairway, which traditionally occupied the center of the edifice, was relegated to an angle where it would not impede internal traffic. Ideas of comfort progressed, as did the belief in the clear separation of the different funcions of the dwelling: entertaining, living, working. To take only one example, bathrooms became less and less rare. Even the shape of the rooms adopted multiple variations: at the Château Du Val at Saint-Germain-en-Laye, Jules Hardouin-Mansart grouped four rooms around a central stove that heated the ensemble and gave them the shape of a rectangle, a circle, an octagon, and a square with rounded corners. At the Hôtel Lambert, Le Vau designed an octagonal bedchamber and an oval vestibule; at the Hôtel Crozat, Pierre Bullet interjected a note of fantasy into the shape of the vestibule, chamber, bedroom, and gallery. The architects of the beginning of the eighteenth century, the creators of "rococo," would elaborate further on this French-style floorplan. More than one feature in private architecture prefigured Versailles. Even if the Palace of the Sun was in turn imitated throughout Europe, it would be unfair to neglect the models.

Certain *hôtels* also possessed sumptuous interior decoration. Le Vau, at the very beginning of his career, decorated the Hôtel de Lauzun. But the true master of such artistic works for more than thirty years was the painter Le Brun. At the Hôtel Lambert (whose gallery prefigured, on a much smaller scale, those of the Louvre and Versailles) and at Vaux-le-Vicomte, he displayed his genius with immense variety and richness. The château of Vaux, given the central place it occupies in seventeenth-century art, merits special mention. Its owner, the Superintendent of Finances Nicolas Fouquet, had wanted to accomplish something stunning, a symbol of his position — and of his wealth. Everything there prefigures Versailles: we already know the well-deserved jealousy of the young king and the subsequent disgrace without appeal of the minister. Louis Le Vau, André Le Nôtre, and Charles Le Brun, already associated in this work, created a château equal to Fouquet's lofty ambitions and tastes. Although he poured his fortune into the work, he was hardly able to derive any benefit from it before his arrest in 1661, which brought a halt to all interior decoration. The artistic work of the king was about to begin.

Less forceful and rigorous than François Mansart, Louis Le Vau nevertheless represents the genius of French architecture which, even before Versailles, attempted to free itself from Italian tutelage. Still very baroque in its vocabulary and syntax, the art of Le Vau acquired a suppleness and variety that his predecessors had not shown. After Vaux-le-Vicomte, Le Vau completed in Paris a work noted for its importance not only to architecture but also to urbanism: the Collège des Quatre Nations (today the Palais de l'Institut, seat of the Academies). Constructed between 1660 and 1670 in accordance with Mazarin's last will and testament, this elegant edifice raises its dome of slate and gold above a curvilinear courtyard facing the quai of the Seine.

The presence of this monument on the bank of the river, just across from the Louvre and up from the Pont-Neuf with its dividing island and equestrian statue of Henri IV, marks the desire to incorporate the Seine into the Parisian cityscape — which was quite a novelty in the seventeenth century. Under Louis XV, the "basin" of Paris would become the privileged site of nautical fêtes and a great many fireworks, all linked to events of dynastic or military significance. Another monument, even more imposing and replete with plans for grandiose avenues and esplanades, would continue the ordered structuring of the capital begun to the west, on the Left Bank: the Royal Hôtel des Invalides, a vast army hospital erected by Libéral Bruant and Jules Hardouin-Mansart between 1670 and 1691. In the chapel of the Dôme, a French masterpiece of the *plan centré* translated into volume by pure gracefulness of mass and a quasi-contrapuntal interplay of composition, Hardouin-Mansart was inspired by a project undertaken by his great-uncle François Mansart for a funeral chapel for the Bourbons at Saint-Denis (the burial site of the kings of France). The project for a royal mausoleum on a site in the center of Paris dedicated to victories as well as to the war-wounded had long been discussed. Of course, the magnificent Dôme des Invalides was destined to receive, at a much later date, the ashes of Napoleon I!

The monumental art of Paris, always anxious to glorify the state and the person of the king by emphasizing their power, was nevertheless part of a wider progressive program of public works. One should, for example, mention the immense hospital of La Salpêtrière (Le Vau and Libéral Bruant, 1656-70), the astonishing Observatory due to Claude Perrault, as well as a good number of convents and churches which, to a lesser degree in the religious domain, continued the initiatives of preceding reigns (the Church of the Assumption, by C. Errard).

But the great royal project that Colbert hoped to achieve in Paris remained incomplete due to the king's departure for Versailles. He had hoped to expand the Louvre, to connect it with the Palais des Tuileries (today destroyed), and, according to a vast plan, to create a central axis for the

COLBERT PLANNED A SOLEMN FAÇADE WORTHY OF THE REIGN'S PRESTIGE

development of the capital on the Right Bank. The layout of the Avenue des Champs-Elysées, by extending the gardens of the Tuileries, for which Le Nôtre had designed parterres and basins peopled with statues according to the principles previously established in his parks, would only assume its true importance in the eighteenth century with the creation of the Place Louis XV (1753-63, presently the Place de la Concorde).

The opening of the city toward the west was first accomplished by the disappearance of the restraining city walls, replaced by the Grands Boulevards destined for promenades. Extended to the north and east, they were embellished with admirable gates sculpted as triumphal arches: Porte Saint-Denis and Porte Saint-Martin, the former by F. Blondel, the latter by P. Bullet, between 1672 and 1674. At the eastern entrance of Paris, in the faubourgs, a gigantic tree-lined avenue was created with a roundabout and pathways that balanced the Champs-Elysées: the Court of Vincennes. The royal axis of Paris was thus initiated. The Louvre was the monumental "hub," but one would have to await the laying-out of the interminable Rue de Rivoli in the nineteenth century before the axis would assume material form and traverse the old center of Paris. Monumental Paris, abandoned by the king, was thus gradually laid out thanks to the initiative of Louis' two ministers: Colbert, intent on pursuing the completion of the Louvre and perfecting the institutions and regulations governing architecture and urbanism; and Louvois, instigator of the creation of the Place Louis le Grand (the Place Vendôme today) and promoter of private initiative in Parisian urbanism, which would expand under the Regency — one thinks of the speculations of John Law when, after the death of Louis XIV, the court migrated to Paris.

At the Louvre, under the reign of Louis XIII, Jacques Lemercier had constructed the Pavillon de L'Horloge, which dominates the Cour Carrée with its great caryatids sculpted by J. Sazzarin. Upon the death of Lemercier, Le Vau was charged with the completion of the north wing and the remodeling of the royal *appartements* (1661-63). The most remarkable ensemble of this epoque remains the Gallery of Apollo, where the paintings of Le Brun are integrated with the stucco of Girardon, Regnaudin, and the Marsy brothers. This team (now at full strength) of architect, painter, and sculptors, prefigured that of the first work undertaken at Versailles. But before Louis XIV definitively abandoned this new Louvre in "gestation," one last accomplishment was undertaken at the personal prompting of Colbert, who hoped to retain the king in his capital: the celebrated colonnade facing the city.

Colbert planned a solemn façade worthy of the reign's prestige. The pope's architect, the Cavalier Bernin (Gian Lorenzo Bernini), perceived to be one of Europe's most famous creators of the age, brought his plans to Paris in 1665. But Bernini's project was refused not only because it was insufficiently studied in regard to arrangement, but also for reasons of national prestige. The new façade, conceived as a calm, antique frontispiece, was begun in 1667 on the basis of plans emanating from a veritable artistic council headed by Claude Perrault — the author of the exemplary translation of Vitruvius' *Ten Books of Architecture* (Paris, 1673) and the champion along with F. Blondel of the famous Quarrel of the Ancients and Moderns. Thanks to the originality and perfection of this emblematic colonnade, Perrault succeeded in creating — alongside Versailles — *the* monument of architectural classicism. Succeeding generations would sing its praises, and it would remain an inexhaustible source of inspiration until the Universal Exposition of 1900.[9]

However, abandoned by the sovereign, the Louvre lost forever its function as a royal residence, for under the Revolution the Palais des Tuileries served that purpose. But the political intentions of Louis XIV and especially of Colbert precluded the abandonment of this architectural marvel. Always en route to completion, the Louvre was destined for a new purpose, no less symbolic than the former: to become the Palace of Arts of the realm. The immense structure housed not only important collections of works of art, but also the administrative and "cultural" services. From 1640 onwards, for example, the Royal Printing House was located there, joined in 1672 by the Academies, which would meet there throughout the eighteenth century. The century of the *Encyclopédie* would further determine the fate of the edifice by creating the Salons of Painting, the royal school for state-sponsored students, and soon a museum, the ancestor of the modern Museum of the Louvre.

Artistic institutions, such as the administration of buildings, evolved rapidly in the eighteenth

Catalogue 96

century. The impact of French art on Europe, founded on the splendor of Versailles, was also due to the exceptional quality of the institutions founded during the reign of Louis XIV. Colbert's role in the development of the Academies, the Royal Manufactures, the teaching of the arts, and, through the use of by-laws regulating construction, his recognition of the function of the architect, must not be forgotten in this brief overview of monumental art under the reign of the Sun King.

In the seventeenth century, the Superintendent of Buildings of the King was also Director of the Arts, Tapestries, and Manufactures of France. The position corresponded to a veritable ministry whose offices were organized on a nationwide scale. Under Colbert, beginning in 1664 the different architectural services had at their disposal a staff of officers which, in addition to the First Architect of the King (Le Vau, then Hardouin-Mansart) and his customary architects, included many artists and master workmen (from the roofer to the gardener). A vast ensemble of trades, directed by the architects, thus prefigured the Department of Civil Buildings of the modern state. Royal policy in the domain of the arts, as in other areas, manifested its absolute authority: the weakening of trade associations was the natural corollary of this expansion of official monumentalism.

The prestige of the profession of architect in the service of the king was definitively recognized in 1671 by the creation of the Royal Academy of Architecture. Its members, architects of the king who formed a sort of permanent advisory council to the superintendent and his staff, were especially commissioned to elaborate a doctrine and to transmit it to students. While institutionalizing the theoretical aspects of the training of architects, their education did not neglect practical knowledge, most often directly taught in the office of one of the king's architects. In place of the traditional apprenticeship, which was individualized and above all practical, with on-the-job training (as it had been since the Middle Ages), the Century of Louis XIV substituted a systematic education generative of a uniform culture. This institutionalization — at once hierarchical and centralized — of a "craft" at the summit of the liberal professions would develop throughout the realm wherever urban civil architecture would be called upon, after 1700, to replace religious, aristocratic, or military architecture, especially in the provinces.[10]

During this epoch of triumphant royal policy, the art of fortifications also attained a sort of apogee. New towns created all at once along the frontier, garrisons, citadels, as well as Atlantic and Mediterranean ports, presented Vauban with the opportunity to display his genius for building. Among the sites that have since become famous tourist attractions, although once regarded as menacing fortresses, can be named, between 1679 and 1692: the new towns of Sarrelouis, Montlouis, Montdauphin (all royal names), and Neufbrisach (1698) in the plan of a checkerboard enclosed within a bastion; the citadels of Besançon, Blaye, Briançon, and Lille, which Vauban considered his masterpiece; the ports of Rochefort, Brest, Lorient, Sète, and Toulon (project of the Arsenal, 1678).

Alongside Perrault and Vauban, Jules Hardouin-Mansart appears as the third directing genius of the monumental art of the realm at the apogee of monarchical power. To him belonged the privilege of illustrating the major urban theme of the epoque, in Paris as in more than one provincial city: that of the Place Royal, a sort of architectural showcase dedicated to the pedestrian and equestrian statue of the sovereign. Isolated in his court, the king had himself represented in effigy in the heart of his "good city" and in certain provincial capitals (one knows the fate of the theme throughout Europe in the eighteenth century!). Jules Hardouin-Mansart designed two very different models in Paris: the Place Louis le Grand and the Place de la Victoire. He designed the Place des Etats (1686) of Dijon and prepared the megalomanic plans for the Place Bellecour of Lyon (later completed in an altered form by his successor R. de Cotte).

"Monsieur de Louvois, wishing to distinguish himself in the Superintendence of Buildings of the King as he had done in the Ministry of War, inspired in the King the plan to create a great square."[11] Such is the origin of the Place Louis le Grand, which opened onto the land of the Hôtel de Vendôme (1685). An ambitious "civil" program had to accompany the erection of the bronze equestrian statue executed by Girardon: behind the uniform elevations of the square, conceived as a plastic decor, Louvois hoped to install the King's Library, the Academies, the Mint, and the Hôtel of the Ambassadors Extraordinary. But the death of the minister in 1691 caused this administrative program to fall through and freed the construction space behind the facades for real-estate speculation.

Even more representative was the Place des Victoires, also the emanation of a personal wish, but one much more astonishing than that of the minister. In effect, it was a courtier, the maréchal de la Feuillade, who took the initiative of opening a curvilinear square arranged by Hardouin-Mansart (1684-86) around an ostentatious monument: "The statue of this prince (Louis XIV), and that of Victory, here constitute a group all the more brilliant because it is of gilded bronze. The former is dressed in the grand attire used for the ceremony of the Consecration, clothing unique to our kings, and which distinguishes them from all other kings. The statue is trampling underfoot the three-headed dog Cerberus, which represents the Triple Alliance formed at that time by the enemies of France."[12] This group, which can be attributed to the sculptor Desjardins, also included bas-reliefs and four statues of chained slaves. Four lanterns born by freestanding columns acted as beacon lights at the far ends of the square and accentuated beyond measure the solemnity of the scene: the Place Royale became a sort of open-air chapel dedicated to the adoration of the divine-right monarchy. Never before had the "cult of the monarchy" been raised to such an art. And it was no longer a question of pleasant mythology or an hommage to the "culture" and magnificence of the century. If Versailles was the fascinating spot from which the king cast his "spells," the adulation of a courtier, translated into monumental urban art, seemed to have embellished Paris as if with a magic wand.

The dedication of the Place des Victoires took place on March 28, 1686. "On that day, the Maréchal Duc de la Feuillade, on horseback and at the head of the Regiment of French Guards of which he was the colonel, went around the statue three times." The inscription, in Latin, which seems to betray the motives of such a ceremony, summarizes in itself the political function of monumental art. On the Place Royale, the simulated presence of the king operated as a sort of physical presence: it reassembled and breathed life into the entire body of the state and left its mark on his subjects:

> TO LOUIS THE GREAT
> The Father and Leader
> OF ARMIES,
> Always successful.

After having vanquished his Enemies. Protected his Allies. Added very powerful Peoples to his Empire. Assured the Frontiers by Impregnable Fortresses. Joined the Ocean to the Mediterranean. Chased the Pirates from all the Seas. Reformed the Laws. Destroyed Heresy. Compelled by the sound of his name the most barbarous Nations to revere him from the far corners of the Land, and ruled perfectly all things within and without by the Grandeur of his courage and genius.

> FRANÇOIS VICOMTE D'AUBUSSON
> Duke de la Feuillade, Peer and
> Marshal of France
> Governor of Dauphiné, and
> Colonel of the French Guards.
> IN PERPETUAL MEMORY
> to posterity[13]

FOOTNOTES

1. This essay was translated from the French by Steven G. Reinhardt. H. L. Sarlit, presentation text for the recording of the *Fontaines de Versailles,* Collection "Fastes et divertissements de Versailles," III, Philips A 00 347 L (C. 1956).
2. Cited by R. Girardet in the preface to Louis XIV's *Manière de montrer les jardins de Versailles* (Paris: Plon, 1951).
3. J. M. Apostolidès, *Le roi-machine: Spectacle et politique au temps de Louis XIV* (Paris: Editions de Minuit, 1981), 46.
4. Lafont de Saint Yenne, *L'Ombre du Grand Colbert* (1752), cf. *Les Actes du Colloque de Strasbourg* (October, 1981), *Pouvoir, ville et société en Europe, 1650-1750* (Paris: Editions Ophrys, 1982); cf. Voltaire to M. le maréchal de Richelieu, Berlin, August 31, 1751; Voltaire to Mme. Denis, Potsdam, December 24, 1751; Voltaire to M. le Président Hénault, Berlin, January 8, 1752, all in Voltaire, *Lettres choisies* (Paris: Editions Hatier, 1947), II.
5. B. Teyssèdre, *L'Art au siècle de Louis XIV* (Paris: Editions du Livre de Poche, 1967), 41.
6. P. de Nolhac, *Versailles et la cour de France: la création de Versailles; Versailles résidence de Louis XIV* (Paris: Editions Conard) and *Les jardins de Versailles* (Paris: Editions Manzi, Joyant et Cie, 1911; P. Francastel, *La sculpture à Versailles* (Paris: Editions Morancé, 1930).
7. Cited by Teyssèdre, *L'Art au siècle de Louis XIV,* 41. Louis Hautecoeur, *Histoire de l'architecture classique en France* (Paris: Editions Picard, 1948), T. II, vols. I-II.
8. A. Blunt, *Art and Architecture in France, 1500-1700* (London: Pelican History of Art, 1953).
9. W. Hermann, *La théorie de Claude Perrault* (Brussels: Editions Mardaga, 1980). Cf. P. Francastal, *L'Urbanisme de Paris et l'Europe, 1600-1680* (Paris: Editions Klincksieck, 1969), and P. Lavedan, *Histoire de l'urbanisme: Renaissance et Temps modernes* (Paris: Editions Laurens, 1941).
10. The architects of the king were more and more involved in civil architecture in the provinces; among the celebrated works of the First Architect, Jules Hardouin-Mansart, one should note the Hôtel de Ville of Arles (1668) and the remodeling of the Hôtel de Ville of Lyon (1700).
11. Germain Brice, *Nouvelle description de la ville de Paris* (Paris, 1725), III, 1.
12. *Ibid.,* 61.
13. *Ibid.,* 65.

Catalogue 153

THE POLITICS OF ROYAL OPERA
IN THE REIGN OF
LOUIS XIV

ROBERT M. ISHERWOOD

o king before him or in later years was more devoted to building his self-image than Louis XIV.[1] He was determined to inspire a vision of a monarchy so awesome and brilliant, a court and country so unified, affluent, and powerful, that its enemies, foreign and domestic, would not challenge it. Indeed, the king wanted his contemporaries and the generations who came later to revere him, as Voltaire would, and to emulate his reign as the most radiant moment in the history of civilization. The task of image-building was entrusted to the dozens of artists, musicians, and writers who enjoyed Louis' patronage. Teams of poets and historians, sculptors and engravers, ballet masters and architects, landscape gardeners and painters created the godlike attributes of a ruler at once heroic, benevolent, wise, mighty, just, and devout. Why was this mystique of kingship so important to the young man who began his personal reign in 1661, and how could the arts, opera in particular, serve his grandeur?

A glance through Louis' eyes at French history in the century preceding his reign helps to provide an answer. In the sixteenth century, France had been torn apart by rival factions of nobles divided by religious ideology who wanted to control the French monarchy. Catherine de Medici, the mother of France's last three Valois rulers, struggled in vain to conciliate and pacify the religious factions. Her inept sons were pawns of the powerful nobles. France's internal turmoil was an irresistible temptation to Habsburg Spain, which invaded. The last of the Valois, Henri III, was assassinated in 1589. The era lasting from the 1560s until the 1590s, when Henri IV finally brought peace to the country by converting to Catholicism and then granting religious toleration to the Huguenots, was one of the bloodiest and most anarchical in French history.

Henri's strong reign was only a brief respite. Following his assassination in 1610, France was again riddled with factionalism during the regency of Marie de Medici. Rising to power definitively in 1624 as Louis XIII's first minister, Cardinal Richelieu shaped the institutions and policies that would characterize the absolute state for more than a century. But even Richelieu's success in centralizing authority, defusing the Protestant problem, and curbing the nobility could not conceal the deep divisions within France. There were constant intrigues and conspiracies at court, most of them led by Princes of the Blood who were angry at being excluded from power. The supreme court of the realm, the Parlement of Paris, also resisted the onset of absolutism; it remonstrated against royal decrees and began claiming sovereign authority. In the provinces, nobles led revolts of peasants and townsmen against royal officials. Abroad, France became entangled in another struggle with the Habsburgs during the Thirty Years' War. The Richelieu years, in short, did not bring an end to the factionalism, discord, and rebellion in French society. Instead, the growth of the absolute state inflamed the resentments of nobles, magistrates, peasants, and others. Upon his death in 1642, Richelieu might very well have uttered the words attributed to Louis XV: "après moi, le déluge."

And it came. Revolution broke out in 1648, again in a period of regency government headed by Louis XIV's mother Anne of Austria and Cardinal Mazarin. Nearly every element of French society was in revolt. The robe nobles (magistrates) and sword nobles (Princes of the Blood) who led the Fronde were not fighting for a more democratic regime: they did not represent the people. They sought to dismantle the government of Richelieu and Mazarin in order to gain power for themselves.

Revolution fomented by power-hungry nobles, some of whom were guilty of treason, was thus the foremost event of Louis XIV's life between the ages of ten and fifteen. The Fronde was a terrible specter to him. At one point, he had been forced to leave Paris for his own safety. When Louis began his personal rule after Mazarin's death in 1661, he looked back on a century of chaos. For decades France had been ravaged by civil war, regicide, conspiracy, foreign invasion, and revolution. Louis was determined to end all that. The state, the society, the culture that he created were all geared to making himself the absolute master of his country and of Europe.

Louis excluded the great nobility from positions of authority in a centralized state run by officials of bourgeois background. He stifled provincial authority and reduced the power of Parlement. He exerted his authority over the French Catholic Church and abolished toleration of Protestants. The economy was regulated and controlled in the interest of mercantilistic self-sufficiency and supremacy. Beyond France, Louis' policy was based on securing what Richelieu had called the "frontier gates" — the zones of past and potential invasion — and to do so, he built the most powerful army in Europe and pursued an agressive foreign policy.

In all of these political, social, and economic goals, pursued with such tenacity by a monarch appalled by the barbarity of the past and the ineptitude of his predecessors, the arts played an essential role. Excluding the traditionally rebellious nobility from office had to be accompanied by taming them and making them servile. Thus, Louis built Versailles, that colossal shrine to Apollo, his personal image. His artists made every tapestry, fountain, and allegorical painting into a shimmering commemoration of his power and virtue. The nobles lived in a deliberately contrived atmosphere of ceremony, pomp, and luxurious entertainment. The performing arts — music, theater, the dance — were the vehicles by which this atmosphere was perpetuated. The nobility was under the king's eye, competing for his favor, living in a controlled, make-believe world. Most important, Louis kept it harmlessly occupied, passive, and submissive. He gave gargantuan

Catalogue 21

banquets, lavish balls, fireworks displays, and a myriad of recreations. The nobles attended Lulli's operas and Molière's plays, and participated in spectacular *grands divertissements* often lasting several days. The French historian Roland Mousnier has written: "In a series of marvelous, fairylike festivals, the king appeared attired as the Olympian god, with the courtiers as lesser divinities or heroes. In this way, they were able to transmute their vain dream of power and greatness in this imitation of the life of the immortals, exalted above common humanity, and, if they must obey, they would at least obey the Lord Jupiter, the King god. Etiquette habituated them to seeing a superhuman being in the king."[2]

In addition to helping the king to solve a social problem, the arts were useful for Louis' foreign policy objectives. Staging the sumptuous operas of Lulli and the glittering *grands divertissements* amidst the splendor of Versailles enabled Louis to display France's wealth, security, and contentment during wartime. Throughout the late years of the reign with war raging constantly, the *Mercure galant,* the principal organ of court news, emphasized that Versailles and Paris continued their pleasures as always, and that France's artistic life was undiminished. In 1708, during the dark days of the War of the Spanish Succession, the *Mercure* noted the extravagant balls given by the king and observed that "the foreigners who are here . . . have been surprised to see what things have occurred in a manner quite contrary to what is published in their countries about the situation in which France finds herself."[3] The point is that the pageantry of the court gave an appearance of the affluence of the realm and of its tranquility in time of war. These were wars of attrition, so the regular presentation of costly *divertissements* was a useful psychological weapon against Louis' enemies.

Thus, the arts served important political objectives of Louis XIV. French history was a record of civil war and revolution fomented by the nobility, and a record of foreign policy setbacks until mid-century that resumed in the later years of Louis' reign. The king, determined to reverse the trends of the past, used the performing arts to divert and occupy the nobility, to represent France as a flourishing, fun-as-usual society to his foreign enemies in wartime, and above all to project an image of himself as a superhuman deity.

Reason of state alone, however, does not account for Louis' great personal devotion to the arts and particularly to music. His mentality and that of his age were still greatly under the influence of one of the strongest and most enduring intellectual currents in Western civilization — Neo-Platonism.[4] Plato believed that musical harmony imitated and expressed the harmony of the highest part of the human soul, the rational soul, where understanding, will, and abstract truth were lodged; that in making music, men were not just amusing themselves, but were literally imitating the harmony of the celestial spheres and the harmony of the soul. Plato held that music not only duplicates and reflects, it has the power to induce harmony, to restore order to a soul filled with discord. In the *Timaeus,* Plato wrote that "harmony, which has motions akin to the revolutions of our souls, is not regarded by the intelligent votary of the Muses as given by them

with a view to irrational pleasure . . . but as a means to correct any discord which may have arisen in the courses of the soul, and to be our ally in bringing her into harmony and agreement with herself."[5] In conjunction with a text, a poem, music goes swiftly and directly to the sensible level of the soul, where the imaginative faculty that organizes sense information is lodged, and from there it is transmitted to the highest level of the soul where it induces harmony, stimulates understanding, and profoundly affects our temperament and behavior.

Music can also provoke discord. It can affect a wide range of emotions in man including joy, sadness, anger, and melancholy. It can induce moral and physical responses that are injurious and detrimental to the soul. In fact, Plato identified each mode of ancient music and each meter of ancient poetry with a particular kind of behavior, some of which he claimed were harmful because they caused softness of character and indolence.

Plato drew one very important conclusion from these reflections: music must be carefully controlled by the state. Since music can instill vice or virtue, it must not be left to chance. There must be laws governing it and governing the musical education of young people. Some of the modes must be banished from the republic. The proper relationships between the rhythms of music and the meters of poetry must be regulated by laws. The state must ensure that music and poetry appeal to the highest level of the soul through the imaginative faculty of the sensible soul, rather than to the vegetable soul where sensual pleasure is lodged. Thus, Plato's belief in the enormous affective power of music and poetry to induce harmony in the soul led him to call for legislators of music.

Plato's convictions about music became deeply ingrained in Western thought over the centuries. They can be found in Plutarch, Saint Augustine, and Boethius, and later in the Renaissance humanists such as Marsilio Ficino and Pierre de Ronsard. In France, the most notable expression of Neo-Platonism came from the first French academy, the Academy of Music and Poetry, established in 1570 by Charles IX. Jean-Antoine de Baif, the founder of the academy, not only subscribed to the ideas of Plato and his intellectual descendants, he also believed that the ancient Greeks created musical and poetic forms that actually produced the powerful effects Plato and others had described. Baïf and his fellow academicians were convinced that they in turn could create music that would reflect the harmony of the soul, appeal to its highest faculties, and stir people to virtuous behavior. The secret, Baïf believed, lay in a perfect coordination of music and poetry, so he invented what he called *musique et poésie mésurée,* in which the meters of ancient classical verse were adapted to French poetry and musical rhythms were adapted to verse meters.

The extent to which Neo-Platonism was accepted in sixteenth-century France can be seen by the fact that the academy was established as an institution of the state. In the documents establishing the academy, Charles IX referred to the ancient philosophers and reasoned that because of the power of music, the academy must be under the monarchy's control.

Although Baïf's academy passed from existence in the later years of the sixteenth century because of the religious wars, the Neo-Platonic tradition remained strong in the seventeenth century. Major writers such as Marin Mersenne continued to espouse the basic beliefs of Neo-Platonism. Seventeenth-century writers also shared with Plato the belief that music must be presented with a poem, which provided an element of rational control. This conviction helps to explain why France's first operatic composer, Jean-Baptiste Lulli, and his librettist, Philippe Quinault, put so much emphasis on the text, and why opera, which united music and text, was probably the most important musical form of the baroque era.

Although many seventeenth-century philosophers of music continued to believe that music and poetry ought to appeal to the soul's highest faculties, it is apparent that most people by Louis XIV's time no longer believed that it was possible or necessary to actually revive, as Baïf tried to do, the music of antiquity. Most no longer believed that music actually duplicated the harmony of the spheres or that it so elevated the mind as to lead it to a perception of abstract truths. The basic convictions of Neo-Platonism remained as the strong intellectual underpinning for opera, but writers made the old doctrines more pragmatic. Platonic metaphysics were stressed less than the morally useful and instructive power of

MUSIC MUST BE CAREFULLY CONTROLLED BY THE STATE

music and poetry. Music could help curb the passions, instill good temperament, and induce order. The texts could instruct people in such virtues as justice, honesty, courage, loyalty, and kindness. Thus, it was only logical that music and poetry could serve image building. That is why opera was so important to Louis XIV. He used opera, with all its Neo-Platonist assumptions and connotations, for political aims. The effects of music could be planned carefully through the skillful use of rhetorical devices to instruct the French people in the virtues and deeds of their king.

Louis put all of the arts under his personal protection and supervision by establishing a group of academies. The arts, he believed, had to be controlled if they were to be used to evoke the flattering image he sought and if they were to dazzle foreign dignitaries and play a role in court pageantry. Moreover, supremacy in Europe entailed self-sufficiency and leadership in the arts; the Italian domination of European culture must be ended, and France must set the artistic standards for Europe and must export rather than import her culture. Jean-Baptiste Colbert's mercantilistic policies of self-sufficiency and regulation were applied to the arts, and Colbert personally attended to the establishment of the academies — an Academy of Dance, an Academy of Painting and Sculpture, an Academy of Inscriptions, an Academy of Architecture, and an Academy of Music. Louis and his minister viewed the artistic projection of royal grandeur through the academies as a necessity of state, not as an expression of vanity.

It is notable that the first of these institutions was the Academy of Painting, originally formed in 1648 and recognized as a crown institution in 1661, because it shows the monarchy's role in raising the visual arts out of their old, inferior status as crafts. They had never enjoyed the prestige of music and poetry in the Neo-Platonist scheme of knowledge, not even in Renaissance Italy or in Baïf's academy. By Louis XIV's time, however, many artists and intellectuals had begun to relate the Neo-Platonist doctrine of the affective power of music to the visual arts. For example, the architect François Blondel speculated about applying the principles of musical harmony to an

architectural structure. He held that the emotional impact on the soul produced by certain musical intervals could be duplicated by similar combinations of architectural proportions. Blondel actually tried through mathematics to work out an equivalence of architectural and musical proportions. Thus, the affective powers of music and poetry were also attributed to the visual arts in the seventeenth century, eradicating the traditional separation of the arts.

Moreover, seventeenth-century Neo-Platonists believed that visual symbols, like music, were reflections of divine truth. They contended that profound truths which were concealed in ancient fables and myths could be represented in art as in poetry through symbols and images. Like music, these images could penetrate the highest faculty of the soul in a flash, having much greater power than logical discourse. These Neo-Platonist beliefs help to account for the allegorical and mythological imagery found in baroque art, especially in painting. Possessing enormous expressive power analogous to the affective power of music, allegorical figures could represent and induce the virtues of courage, justice, love, and charity. They could direct the imaginative and rational faculties of the soul toward the ideas and values represented in art. Seventeenth-century Neo-Platonists also moved toward a more pragmatic view of the instructional or propagandistic utility of the visual arts similar to their conception of music and poetry. Rhetorical devices were developed that could be used for didactic purposes. The rhetorical process involved establishing a central idea or moral and the images related to it. The source of this idea or moral came either from nature or from classical mythology or literature such as the Bible and Homer. During the century, certain conventional themes evolved, including the conflict between love and duty and the defeat of discord and evil. It was commonly accepted by Louis XIV's time that devices used in one art had equivalents in all the others. Musical keys had corresponding colors, gestures, poetic meters, and the orders of architecture.

This conception of the arts was highly useful to Louis XIV. He took as his personal symbol Apollo, the ancient sun god, and his artists, poets, and musicians made the most of it. Apollo was a familiar image of the harmony of the universe. He had been represented in antiquity in the dual role

of ruler of the planets and leader of the Muses. For Christian Neo-Platonists, Apollo was equivalent to the sun and represented God. The Neo-Platonists converted the three pagan Graces who attended Apollo into an image of the Trinity or, alternatively, an image of the three Christian virtues of faith, hope, and charity. Finally, Apollo was also the god of music and therefore, in the Platonic sense, an image of the universal harmony that music was thought to reflect. So, Apollo the sun god was the center of the universal harmony of the world, just as Louis XIV was the center of French unity and order. The image of Apollo appeared in every sort of art produced in Louis' reign. In the ballets of the 1650s Louis danced the role of Apollo, dressed in a costume that simulated the flames of the sun. The image of Apollo appeared in all the ceremonies, pageants, and musical dramas of the court. At Versailles the god is depicted in one of the great fountains charging on his chariot out of the surging water toward the palace. He symbolized the king springing to life to enlighten the world. In the interior of the palace, the Hall of Mirrors is a grand gallery of Apollo surmounted by Charles Le Brun's staggering depiction through allegory and mythology of the great events of Louis' reign.

Newly imbued with Neo-Platonist thought and elevated to the level of monarchical academies, the visual arts thus took their place alongside music and poetry. But the crowning achievement of the academic movement was the Royal Academy of Music, founded in 1669 and directed by the composer Jean-Baptiste Lulli, because lyric tragedy, which was the academy's exclusive concern, united all the arts. Lulli's operas combined music and poetry, as the Neo-Platonists had insisted, but the visual arts were also vital to opera. All of the images employed by painters and sculptors were united with literary and musical media in opera. In Lulli's operas, all the rhetorical devices used by Nicolas Poussin and codified into rules of expression by the Academy of Painting, all the allegorical creatures of Le Brun's paintings and decorations, all the imagery of Coysevox's sculptures came to life on the stage. As in Le Brun's paintings, the operas of Lulli and Quinault depicted figures representing Louis crushing the forces of discord, triumphing over foreign enemies, and basking in the accolades of the Graces and Muses. And, as music was still the highest expression of man's moral being and his affinity with the heavens, so opera was the quintessence of musical expression and artistic unity.

The subjects of most of Lulli's operas were drawn from classical sources, chiefly from the Roman poet Ovid, whose verse provided opportunities for Quinault to introduce glorious scenes of combat, sacrifice, and celebration in which the heroic virtues of courage, pride, gallantry, and magnanimity were portrayed. These were the virtues attributed to the king. In nearly every opera the hero confronts insurmountable obstacles; he triumphs over gods and tyrants; he foils the evil powers of sorcery; he slays dragons and monsters; he crosses mountains and oceans. Despite the torments he must endure, the hero is always charitable to his enemies. His reward is a woman's love. Bold in the face of danger, the hero is tender, chivalrous, and faithful to his lover. Quinault's characters were not complex. They express clear emotions. Love dominates the hero's behavior, and, conforming less to the reality of conduct in the seventeenth century than to its aspirations, the hero personifies fidelity. He deals with love's rivalries and jealousy, and he occasionally falls victim to human frailty. In the end, however, he is loyal and recommends constancy to the audience. The hero's love is seldom passionate or profound; it is delicate and discreet, in keeping with the play of manners in vogue at Louis' court.

The operas of Lulli and Quinault began with prologues that were transparent allegorical tales acted out by gods, nymphs, and demons, in which the official history of Louis' reign unfolded. They not only presented encomiums to the monarch, they also alluded to Louis' latest military exploits. They literally interpreted his foreign policy and the wars to audiences, always stressing the evil designs of his enemies and the heroism, courage, magnanimity, and justice of the king of France.

Lulli's first opera, *Cadmus* (1673), illustrates the image-building, didactic use of a prologue incorporating mythology and symbolism in the framework of a lyric tragedy. The subject is the birth of the serpent Python in the warm mud of the earth after the Deluge, and his death at the hands of the Sun. Palès, goddess of the shepherds, and Mélisse, divinity of forests and mountains, join the chorus in a song about the brilliant glow of the sun as it rises over a marshy field. The rustic spirits scatter, however, as the stage darkens and

Catalogue 156

subterranean voices are heard. The shepherds sing: "The day grows pale, the sky is troubled; let us flee, save us." Envy emerges from the darkness to unleash the monstrous serpent Python, who, springing from the marsh, spits flames as Envy releases the Winds in a storm. Challenging the Sun's powers, Envy vows to fill the land with horror. She distributes serpents to the Winds who dance around her in fury. Suddenly, flaming bolts of light pierce the storm, striking Python, who flounders and sinks back into the ooze. Envy and her Winds are eradicated in a rain of fire from the sky. She sings: "You triumph, Sun; everything surrenders to your power. . . . What despair!" Palès, Mélisse, and the rustic folk hail the Sun's conquest of Envy and Python, as he appears in the sky in a chariot singing: "It is not for a pompous sacrifice that I am pleased to see my efforts rewarded. . . . I make the sweetest of my vows in order to render the whole world happy." The Sun commands the Muses to provide songs and games, as a forest deity sings: "Love is content, all is well. In the beautiful days of our life, the pleasures are in their season, and the little follies of love are often

Catalogue 157

worth more than reason."

The meaning of this prologue was clear to French audiences. Louis, seeking to gain a defensible frontier in the Spanish Netherlands, had gone to war with the Dutch who stood in his way. The Dutch foiled his advance in the summer of 1672, however, by opening the dikes and flooding the land. In Lulli's prologue the United Provinces are the marsh. The Dutch are represented by Envy and her Winds. The many-headed serpent Python symbolized the Dutch threat. Victory does not come easily when one's successful march through a country is countered by opening the dikes, or when, after one head of the serpent is cut off, others pop out for battle.

Louis opened peace negotiations with William of Orange in the spring of 1673, but, to show his strength, at the same time he joined the French army for a successful attack on the City of Maestricht in June, 1673, and the war resumed. Thus, in the prologue to *Cadmus*, the Sun, obviously meaning Louis and all the symbolism associated with Apollo, cut through the storm and defeated Python and Envy. The rustic spirits

singing Louis' priases were the French people. And Quinault cleverly provided the Sun with an aria expressing Louis' claims that he fought to secure his subjects' happiness, not to satisfy his pride. The prologue eulogized the monarch and interpolated a synopsis of the king's war for the edification of the French people. It was thinly veiled allegorical and musical propoganda designed to impress audiences with the power and rectitude of the king.

All of the subsequent operatic prologues by Lulli and Quinault were similar to *Cadmus*. Their third opera, *Thésée*, first performed for Louis in January, 1675, celebrated Turenne's defeat of the Imperial army in the Palatinate and Alsace. The prologues of *Thésée* and of Lulli's next opera, *Atys*, developed the theme of the compatibility of love and courtly pleasure, represented by Venus, and military victory, represented by Mars. In *Isis* (1677), Louis' realm was likened to Neptune's aquatic kingdom, and the king of the sea joined Fame, Apollo, the Muses and the Arts to warn "the enemies of peace against a conqueror whose navy equals the strength of his army." Neptune referred to the French engagement of the Dutch and Spanish fleets in the Mediterranean in the spring of 1676.

In the summer of 1678 Louis concluded the war with Holland and Spain by the Treaty of Nymegen and was close to signing a peace with the emperor. The opera *Bellérophon* commemorated the event with some interesting imagery. In defeating the chimera of a lion, a dragon, and a goat, Bellérophon represents temperance and self-control. The reference was, of course, to the king's display of restraint and moderation in dealing with his enemies. The opera ran for nine months in the Palais-Royal, and Louis was so pleased with it that at its performances for the court at Saint-Germain-en-Laye in October, 1769, and January, 1680, he interrupted it several times to have choice sections repeated.

Peace was also the theme of *Proserpine*, first performed in the fall of 1680. In the prologue Discord, encouraged by Hatred, Rage, Jealousy, Grief, and Despair, chains Peace, Felicity, Abundance, the Games, and the Pleasures to the walls of her den. But Discord's aria boasting of her ability to entice conquered nations to new, rash aggressions is interrupted by trumpet fanfares and the descent of Victory from the sky. Discord plunges into an abyss in the earth opened by Victory who joins Peace in the final duet: "The conqueror is covered with glory; people must admire him forever. He has served himself with Victory in order to allow Peace to triumph."

The shift in Louis' foreign policy tactics in the early 1680s from war and diplomacy to the use of pseudolegal commissions (the Chambers of Reunion), which simply declared certain territory in Alsace to belong to France, was suggested in the opera *Persée*. Instead of eulogizing him as a gallant warrior and benevolent peacemaker, Lulli and Quinault presented the king as a man of justice and virtue. In his dedication of the opera, Lulli referred to Persée as a faultless hero of divine birth. "I understand," Lulli declared, "that in describing the favorable gifts which Persée has received from the gods and the astonishing enterprises which he has achieved so gloriously, I am tracing a portrait of the heroic qualities and the wonderful deeds of Your Majesty."

In 1683 Louis XIV's armies were once again on the move. The campaign on the northeastern frontier resumed in the fall; a siege was conducted at Courtrai in the Netherlands in November; Catalonia was subsequently invaded, and the duc de Créqui conquered Luxembourg. It was time to change Louis' operatic image from an embodiment of the benevolent and pacific virtues and to depict him once again as the glorious warrior in a struggle against envious enemies. In a prologue to the opera *Amadis*, presented in Paris in 1684, the enchantress Urgande and her husband Alquif have fallen under a spell resulting from the death of the great hero Amadis. The appearance of a new hero breaks the spell, however, and Urgande sings: "In vain thousands of envious arm themselves on all sides. With one word, with one of his glances, he knows how to bend their useless fury to his will. It is up to him to teach the great art of war to the masters of the earth. It is he who must teach the great art of ruling. The whole universe admires his exploits; let us live happily under his laws." *Roland* in 1685 also portrayed the king as the heroic defender of France's security against envious warmongers. In addition, Quinault worked two contemporary events into his opera. The Siamese ambassadors had arrived in France in October, 1684. The poet made the queen of Cathay his heroine and inserted a scene for "oriental natives." Moreover, the French navy had conducted a campaign against Barbary pirates off the coast of Tripoli and had bombarded Algiers in the fall of 1684. Quinault made Médor, a follower of one of the African kings, his secondary hero.

Catalogue 155

Finally, the opera *Armide*, performed in 1686, hailed Louis for striking down a monster "who for so long was thought to be indestructible." The reference was to Louis' Revocation of the Edict of Nantes, ending religious toleration. *Armide* was Lulli's last opera with Quinault. He composed one more with another librettist before his death in 1687. The lyric tragedies of Lulli and Quinault constituted an apothesis of the king's power, virtue, and grandeur. They kept before the court and the public the most flattering scenario possible of the monarch's military exploits. None of Louis' artistic imagemakers served the king better than they.

Lulli's personal success was enormous. He became the wealthiest composer in history and, thanks to Louis' support, one of the most powerful as well. Louis gave the Royal Academy of Music a monopoly over the lyric theater in France. In 1681 Lulli's position at court was so high that he could ask for the title of secretary of the king, which Louis conferred over the protest of the court nobility. Lulli was a rare example of a man who leaped all the ranks of the social structure in a single lifetime. He began as a lowly servant, a cook's helper, and finished with a royal title and noble status.

Louis XIV played a very direct role in the affairs of the academy. Her personally selected the subjects of the operas from lists provided by Quinault. Lulli also played parts of the score for the king. Most of the operas were performed in lavish, spectacular productions in the gardens of Versailles for Louis and the court before being staged for the general public in Paris at the Palais-Royal. Members of other artistic academies participated in the creation and production of Lulli's operatic spectacles. Quinault's texts, for example, were submitted to the Academy of Inscriptions for modification and approval, because the academy specialized in the study of antiquity. Thus, in just about every respect, opera constituted the first unity of the fine arts, joining music and poetry with their affective power over the human soul in the Neo-Platonist sense, to the greatly upgraded arts of painting, sculpture, and architecture with their persuasive rhetorical devices and vivid imagery. The Royal Academy of Music was the preeminent cultural institution of a monarchy determined to impose order on all aspects of society, a monarchy renowned throughout Europe for its artistic brilliance, and a ruler who sought to inspire a godlike image of himself for reasons of state. ■

Catalogue 161

FOOTNOTES

1. This essay is reprinted from Robert M. Isherwood, *Music in the Service of the King: France in the Seventeenth Century,* ©1973 by Cornell University. Used by permission of the publisher, Cornell University Press.
2. Roland Mousnier, *Les XVIe et XVIIe siècles,* Vol. IV of *Histoire générale des civilizations* (Paris, 1954), 235; quoted in *The Greatness of Louis XIV – Myth or Reality?* ed. William F. Church (Boston, 1959), 95.
3. *Mercure galant,* February, 1708, pp. 294-95, 297-306.
4. Isherwood, *Music in the Service,* 1-54. Readers are also urged to consult Frances A. Yates, *The French Academies of the Sixteenth Century* (London, 1947), and H. James Jensen, *The Muses' Concord: Literature, Music, and the Visual Arts in the Baroque Age* (Bloomington, Ind., 1976).
5. Plato, *The Collected Dialogues of Plato Including the Letters,* ed. Hamilton and Cairns (New York, 1964), *Timaeus* 1175.
6. Isherwood, *Music in the Servicc,* 150-203.

BELLES-LETTRES UNDER THE SUN KING: AN AGE OF CLASSICISM

MARCEL GUTWIRTH

riters who adorned the long reign of Louis XIV (1651-1715), even counting only those who garnered some renown, do not invariably come under the heading of classicism. Many were, in fact, reckoned under the contrary rubric of *les irréguliers,* flouters of the belief that art is subject to strict rule (one thinks of Cyrano de Bergerac [1619-55] — the author, not the Rostand creation!). Yet the most original and enduring as well as the most steadily influential creation of the age is the classical achievement,[1] briefly and provisionally defined as the set of writings consciously or unconsciously shaped by admiration for, or emulation of, the literary best of classical antiquity.

French classicism falls easily into three parts: early and late classicism bracketing what has come to be known as the classical period, which coincides with the rising fortunes of the Sun King's reign, dated from the death of Mazarin in 1661 to the completion of Versailles around 1685.

Early classicism, the formative period, coincides largely with the reign of Louis XIII, or better, the iron-fisted rule of his chief minister, Cardinal de Richelieu (1624-41); although, in the person of the poet Malherbe (1555-1628), it reaches as far back as the court of Henri IV, assassinated in 1610. Four names will be cited here, sufficient for our purpose, which is principally to give an idea of the state of letters under Louis XIV: Malherbe, Corneille, Descartes, Pascal.

The last three are among the giants of the century; the first a martinet of letters, must be thought of as the incarnation of the classical resolve that literature forego irresponsible fantasy, that the rules of logic and prosody form the backbone of even its wildest freedom. In a day of extravagant conceit mongering, a stern adherence to the purity and simplicity of what today our philosophers call "everyday language" set up Malherbe as a reformer to whom classicism was to owe its unparalleled clarity of diction. Where Montaigne (1533-92) in the last decades of the preceding century accurately foresaw the damage that a language in flux was to do to the future accessibility of his *Essays,* Racine (1639-99) is so transparently available to the speaker of modern French as to make one quite forget that he wrote in the days of Milton!

Pierre Corneille (1606-84), *le grand* Corneille, is for all practical purposes the creator as well as the most versatile and indefatigable practitioner of classical drama in all its genres. Thirty plays rolled off his pen in the space of forty-five active years, half a dozen of them immortal masterpieces. His career spanned the reigns of both Louis, but his specific gift to classical art was its depiction of a crisis in the inner lives of its protagonists.

Psychological drama alone could fit the severe requirements of a plot that had to be resolved within the span of twenty-four hours dictated by the creative misreading of Aristotle's *Poetics,* upon which classical doctrine was grounded. Pitting a nobleman's self-affirmation against a nobleman's ideal of all-for-love — *gloire* against *flamme* — Corneille shaped the peculiarly French classical inner tension, whereby aristocratic nature turned on itself to fashion greatness out of its agony. An exalted idea of self, a view of love founded in admiration and leading to self-sacrifice (*générosité*) fused with elevated diction to constitute a model of heroic tragedy, the subversion of which would furnish an equally great successor, Jean Racine, with the elements of a tragic absolute.

René Descartes (1596-1650) and Blaise Pascal (1623-62), major scientists both — one the founder of postscholastic metaphysics, the other the most eloquent spokesman for a radical Augustinian view of our fallen nature since Augustine himself — complete our brief survey of early classicism by their exemplification of its catholicity. Descartes' *Discourse on Method* (1637) and Pascal's *Pensées* (1670) are landmarks of French classical prose — one a philosophical treatise, the other a set of notes that were to lead to the composition of an Apology of the Christian Religion cut short by death before it was properly begun. For all its insistence on the airtight distinction between comedy and tragedy, on the distinctiveness of the genres generally, and for all its piety toward the inherited modes of literary utterance pedigreed all the way back to classical antiquity, French classicism must not be equated with its own narrowest pronouncements. The French Academy, Richelieu's creation and a bastion of defensive purism, always numbered among its members a social elite of dukes and high clergymen rubbing elbows with mere men of letters, signaling that the condition of the man of letters, in France, is inseparable from an awareness of other spheres of human activity and social existence. Long before Jean-Paul Sartre gave the term currency, back all the way to an authoritarian monarchic regime and an aristocratic mind set, French literature was, in the best sense, *engagé*. Pascal's views on concupiscence, Descartes' on the split between matter and spirit, penned with vigor and grace, were no less "literary" than an ode or a sonnet.

Late classicism, to take a leap of four or five decades, evokes figures like La Bruyère (1645-96), Fénelon (1651-1721), Perrault (1628-1703), Fontenelle (1657-1757), and Saint-Simon (1675-1755). With the exception of La Bruyère, they all tend, these late comers, to look forward toward the century to come, to the Age of Enlightenment, for they are often numbered among its precursors. Of Saint-Simon this has to be said both literally and quite paradoxically, because that cantankerous peer of the realm indeed penned his memoirs of the court of Louis XIV well into the reign of that monarch's great-grandson, Louis XV,

AN ARRAY OF NAMES TO CONJURE WITH, A HARVEST OF MASTERPIECES

but in a spirit so savagely retrograde, in a style so heedlessly headlong and dense as to hark back to quite an earlier epoch. Fontenelle's elegant scientific popularization, *Conversations on the Plurality of Worlds* (1686), Perrault's venture into folklore, *Tales of Mother Goose* (1697), and bishop Fénelon's didactic romance, *The Adventures of Telemachus* (1699), both extend the already widened horizons of literary undertaking and point to a modernist concern with the growth of knowledge and the betterment of the human condition — a concern that peeps beyond the staunchly immovable outlook of pure classicism. La Bruyère, on the other hand, though wedded to such a conservative outlook, indicts his own age in *The Characters* (1688, 1694) too specifically and in a style too self-consciously stiletto-carved to be counted in the body of classicism proper.

The first fact to take in about the quarter century of the classical era itself is the sheer unexampled abundance of writers of a stature whose like, in such numbers, would never be seen again. An array of names to conjure with, a harvest of masterpieces — this is our first impression of what Voltaire was to term the Age of Louis XIV, an era to be placed alongside the Periclean and the Elizabethan ages in the honor list of humankind. Just consider: Molière (1622-73), Racine, La Fontaine (1621-95), Boileau (1636-1711), Madame de Sévigné (1626-96), La Rochefoucauld (1613-80), Bossuet (1627-1704), Madame de La Fayette (1634-93). Or again, *Tartuffe* (1669), *The Misanthrope* (1666), *The Imaginary Invalid* (1673); *Andromache* (1667), *Phaedra* (1677), *Athalia* (1691); La Fontaine's *Fables* (1668-94); Madame de Sévigné's *Letters* (published in the next century); Boileau's *Satires* (1668); La Rochefoucauld's *Maxims* (1665); Bossuet's funeral orations (1666-87); and that forebear of the modern psychological novel, Madame de La Fayette's *La Princesse de Clèves* (1678). Such transcendent achievement, an unsurpassed plenty of capital creations, each setting up a model of a kind of perfection, poses the very real question of the reasons for such an abundance, not merely of talent of the first rank but of genius.

Genius was a word not much in fashion in the classical era, or at any rate not regarded in the

light that Romantic promotion of the extraordinary, supremely gifted individual was later to shed upon it. Classical doctrine defined genius more as a matter simply of natural endowment, and, while granting the needfulness of it, rather emphasized its conscious cultivation, which it called *art*. Genius nonetheless is what confronts us in the enumeration we set down above, a listing that outshines even the quite remarkable outpouring of great names in the sister arts (Le Nôtre, Mignard, La Tour, Coysevox, Mansard, Lulli, to cite a few) to give the age of the Sun King its most enduring luster. Interestingly enough, the brilliant array of Louis' generals — Condé, Turenne, Villars, Vauban — is most nearly a match for it.

To account for such a harvest, one explanation — the one that springs to mind — is surely the least adequate: royal policy. Louis' first political gesture upon assuming personal control of his government was the elimination of that ardent patron of the arts, Nicolas Fouquet, his superintendent of finances. The man who could entertain his sovereign in truly royal style in his Château de Vaux — that prototype of Versailles — amid gardens shaped by the same Le Nôtre who would labor so unforgettably on that later creation, gave umbrage but also set an example. The hard-working Colbert took over Fouquet's sponsorship of the fine arts as well as his oversight of the nation's economy. A policy of magnificence entailed, in addition to a building program and the most lavish round of court entertainment, active encouragement (and control) of the domain of letters. The superannuated poet Chapelain (1595-1674) was set the task of drawing up the list of the worthy recipients of royal largesse, the so-called *gratifications*. Aside from granting himself the top award — double that of Molière — Chapelain accomplished little in the way of genuine promotion of the writers we remember today. Of the writers we do remember, Racine and Molière alone — successful playwrights both and so in little need of it — came in for some support from the royal *cassette*. And surely this support could have made little difference to a marquise, a duke, or a bishop like Sévigné, La Rochefoucauld, and Bossuet. Boileau was a personal enemy of Chapelain, and La Fontaine far too independent (he had the audacity to deplore the unmerited severity of Fouquet's fall from grace!) to qualify for

patronage. It came down, finally, to the very active protection afforded by Louis to the theater, which he viewed in the light of his own royal entertainment — invaluable "cover" for the boldness of Molière's infringement of all the taboos.

But even if royal policy had been comprehensive and sustained — which it was not — it could at best have kept genius alive where support was needed; it could not have brought it to life. The birth of so many writers of the first rank in a given epoch remains a mystery for which our science is inadequate. A semimystical answer, in fact, may be in order. It may not be unreasonable to posit that cultures grow as do individuals, and that the culture of France, under the long-triumphant rule of Louis XIV, reached its point of full maturity. Two developments lend this notion verisimilitude: the stamp of definitiveness set upon the classical age by the consensus of succeeding generations that accepted its achievement as a model of greatness; and, as mentioned before, the stabilization of the French language itself, coming to a point of maturity in that same epoch. This is less an explanation than a metaphorization, to be sure, but our explanations so often are not much more than that.

There was an abundance of genius, then, but also a considerable variegation of the literary endeavor. Tragedy, comedy, satire, fable, and the novel (albeit a totally unprecedented antiromantic novel) certainly represent time-honored genres inherited from classical and postclassical antiquity. But what are we to make of Madame de Sévigné's inspired journalism? of La Rochefoucauld's and La Bruyère's social anthropology? of Pascal's indictment of the human condition? of his Christian apologetics? of Fontenelle discoursing on Galileo and Descartes? of Bossuet setting down the universal history of mankind on a biblical model? of La Fontaine encompassing such a variety of tonalities in endowing his animal world with wit, finesse, humor, tenderness, and pathos as to have earned for himself the unlikely appellation of a French Homer? What has been called "the classical moment" is a matter, then, not only of a heightened perfection, of the poise, elegance, and roundedness that we almost unthinkingly associate with the term *classical*, but of a notable freedom to roam the length and breadth of significant possibility in the realm of letters, from laughter to tears, from the systematic to the fragmentary, from the topical to the universal, from the sacred to the profane.

The same variegation is decidedly not present in the social composition of the literary set. Two dukes (one a peer of the realm), a countess, a marquise, and two bishops, with a smattering of personages issued mostly from the lower rungs of the magistracy (under the *ancien régime* a combination of court officers and civil servants) such as Racine, Boileau, and La Fontaine, delineate the range of social milieus represented. Molière alone — but what an exception! — as Jean-Baptiste Poquelin, son of an upholsterer, albeit the king's own, was pure middle class, a Parisian bourgeois. A mere inspection, therefore, of the class composition of the authors' phalanx reveals the aristocratic bias of that literature. Classicism is, among other things, the embodiment of the esthetic preferences of an elite.

More than the social origins of its writers, however, the singular esthetic cohesion and social homogeneity of its public defines the enterprises of classicism. *La cour et la ville*, court and town, encompassed the ideal viewership of its plays, the readership of its books. The court, as the assemblage of the ruling elite of the nation, consisted of high officers of the realm, the great ladies who set the tone of civilized discourse, the upper echelons of the officer corps, men of fashion, men of wit — all those who groomed themselves in readiness for weighty and prestigious assignment, who plumed themselves on their birth, their rank, their capacities, who backbit, backstabbed, groveled, and curtsied their way to eminence and favor — a choice public indeed! An author needed to take care to exhibit the human heart in its true light to an audience whose members owed their political survival to the art of discerning motives and seeing through masks. The author's diction had to come up to standards of refinement judged not unworthy of that seat of elevated discourse and decorous demeanor. The author could not with impunity violate the sacrosanct proprieties, *les bienséances*, which in an aristocratic milieu imposed rules of deportment no less stern than the requirements of gradation and tone to be observed in a work of art. This public, in other words, nurtured and reinforced the sense of rule and fitness, of elegance and restraint, of ease under constraint that characterize the classical manner.

To this, the other side of the equation, *la ville*, added a note of middle-class seriousness and middle-class learning. *Les doctes*, the men of learning, were the severest critics of any lapse from the true spirit of antiquity. The magistracy, as the first segment of the laity to attain literacy back in feudal times, had from the beginning been identified in France with the cultivation of belles-lettres. Theirs was the love of learning that turned the lighthearted precepts of Horace and the observations of Aristotle into immutable law. An author could not appeal to the best of *that* public if he lacked the solid grounding in the thought and example of the ancients that was necessary to give his (or her) utterance weight.

Indeed, "the ancients," *les anciens*, is what the authors we call classical were called in their own time. To reach a sense of what French classicism is truly about, we must turn to the clearest of their avowed common preoccupations: the example set by classical antiquity, the study of the ancients.

Intimate familiarity from schooldays on with the literature of Rome especially, and of Greece, and a rejection of their immediate literary forebears (though Molière and La Fontaine each fashioned his own synthesis) afford these writers a significant measure of creative discontinuity. They did not so much vie with their Renaissance antecedents to make their mark; they took on antiquity unmediated. Their models were far-off, near buried in a defunct civilization of which they represented the most perfected achievement, brought back to the consciousness of a later age by the miracle of the Renaissance. These works were, then, both near and far. Deeply assimilated, they still displayed a formal perfection arisen in a distant time and place that lent their perfection an aura of the forbidding. A creative imitation set in, on the one hand bridging the gap as it naturalized the Latin and the Greek into equally felicitous French, and on the other hand, inspiring emulation — the devising of a perfection that both mirrored and contested the perceived perfection of the ancient originals and might even be said to have surpassed

> IT WAS AN ART STRIVING AFTER MODELS, KEEPING ITS SIGHTS ON PERCEIVED PERFECTION, SETTLING FOR NO LESS THAN THE BEST IT KNEW

Detail of Catalogue 78

component of the learning that the major writers of the seventeenth century saw as a requirement of their craft. The sense of an art ruled by rules, of plays that must observe unities of time, place, and plot to earn a compression that gains them credibility, arises out of a daunting faithfulness to the precepts of these lawgivers (*législateur du Parnasse* is the proud title wherein Boileau, as their self-conscious emulator, mantled himself). High moral seriousness, in turn, was gained from the application of Horace's precept that art must instruct as well as delight. In a society strongly under the sway of Counter-Reformation zeal, the artist felt it incumbent upon himself to justify the pleasure that he sought to give by the benefits it could bestow in the form of moral uplift, however implausible. Although La Fontaine was urged to renounce, and on what he thought was his deathbed did renounce, his erotic tales derived from Ariosto and Boccaccio, he made much in his prefaces of the exemplarity of his fables, of their informativeness, their cautionary import, and their contribution to animal lore. On the other hand, *castigat ridendo mores*, "a laughing reproof," was Molière's rejoinder to those who impugned the moral worth of comedy as they quailed at his irreverence. Whatever degree of credence we attach to such protestations, the coloration is there of an art that held itself accountable to moral stricture. Antiquity thus left a perhaps unforeseeable mark on the practice of those who held it in such high esteem.

Timelessness, finally, descended on an art that found its models in another time and place. The most widely shared tenet of those authors in seventeenth-century France whom we dub classical is their adherence to the notion of a universal human nature. Those who sought, and found, invaluable insights into the human heart and the unpredictableness of human behavior in Vergil and Euripides — in the writings, that is, of fellow mortals two millenia in their graves — could not but hold that human nature was one across time and space, and that the study of the human heart was a search after universal truths. A psychology so based made for a sort of rueful serenity, a sense also of the immutability of human affairs quite removed from our own feverish, ever-frustrated meliorism, our post-Enlightenment faith in progress.

Finally, it must be said, French classicism, by the end of the century and in the days when the Sun King's high zenith, unbeknownst to him, was

it. Set by the side of Terence and Plautus, and perhaps even Aristophanes, does not Molière tower over them both? or all three? His own age, at any rate, came to be of that opinion.

The consequence of this high indebtedness for their art was twofold. It was an art striving after models, keeping its sights on perceived perfection, settling for no less than the best it knew — and that best the fine flower of a civilization that gave pride of place to the sense of beauty. And it was an art that looked upon nature as already presented in and filtered through the medium of art. Art as a study of models is an art that believes in a disciplined nature, a nature shorn of its warts — *la belle nature*. Idealization may have come to represent to us, the heirs of the Romantic revolution and its Realist sequel, the worst sin of so-called academic art, but it must be remembered that this can happen only insofar as an idealized nature is hardest to achieve, easiest to pastiche. In classical art, the word *Ideal* and the word *Nature* are held in genuine tension — a naturalness in refinement that culminates in grace.

The art of antiquity produced its own brand of reflection on art (one thinks primarily of Aristotle's *Poetics* and Horace's *Ars poetica*, but also, importantly, of Longinus' *On the Sublime*), and these reflections constitute the specifically learned already past, appears to have won its wager, to have established itself as the equal of its models, to have turned its own authors into classics. The paradox of that condition is that the authors so consecrated viewed themselves firmly within the camp of the Ancients, and that they found themselves embroiled in a celebrated quarrel with those Moderns who vociferously proclaimed them winners in a contest they had not entered in a spirit of possible victory. Both sides in the heat of argument badly overstated their case, Perrault speaking up principally for relegating the Ancients to the dustbin of history, Boileau proclaiming unchallenged their self-evident supremacy. It matters little in the end. French classicism, willy-nilly, had to take its place alongside the models that French schoolchildren thenceforth would be made to absorb, be invited to emulate, be driven at last to want to forget or overthrow.

Before we take our leave of the landscape of that achievement, we may well once more invoke the two great names that foreshadow its accomplishments, the names of Descartes and Pascal, not to claim for either the paternity of that loose ensemble, the French classical tradition, but in a purely emblematic capacity. Descartes, whose name is synonymous with logic, method, rigor, and lucidity, as the apostle of unbending reason in its abode of perfect clarity can stand in our minds for that side of classicism that craves regularity, that shuns the vague and the unformed, that shies away from the abyss. Pascal, on the other hand, with a rigor and a lucidity scarcely to be outdone even by his illustrious fellow mathematician, stressed the truth of the heart — "the heart has its reasons," he wrote, "that reason knows not of" — and the intuition that alone can grasp the supernatural truth of divine love and divine Grace. The theoreticians of classicism gave a name to these imponderables — those truths of the heart and the grace that classicism both sought after and knew how to prize — that breathe life into what would otherwise remain a merely faultless achievement — *le je ne sais quoi,* the I-know-not-what. A view of classicism that scants either side of the equation is faulty. Compounded of rigor and grace, a relaxed decorousness, a mettlesome ease is a description that comes close to doing it justice.

A last word. The idea of classicism almost irresistably calls up an image of symmetry, of grandeur, of monumentality. Let us remember then, in order to take in fully the figure of the

Detail of Catalogue 79

French classical age — the age, as Perrault termed it, of Louis *le Grand* — how many of its masterpieces are made up of fragments — *les Lettres de* Mme de Sévigné, *les Maximes de* La Rochefoucauld, *les Pensées de* Pascal — and that, in the view of its most authoritative critic, Nicolas Boileau, the greatest of its writers (and posterity heartily concurs) was an acrobatic slapstick comedian named Molière.

FOOTNOTE

1. *Classical* is what it is called in French usage, which will be followed here. The English label *neoclassical,* while technically more exact, since these writers enacted a revival of the literature of classical antiquity, muddies the waters in two ways. It is an appellation that properly belongs to the writers indebted to these French classics — French (and English) authors of the subsequent Age of Voltaire. It robs French classicism, moreover, of that stamp of authority that made it less the reflected glory of an earlier time — as these same writers, in their modesty, would have claimed — as the shining exemplar of a specifically French achievement, *the classical moment* of that tradition.

LOUIS XIV:
PATRON OF SCIENCE
AND TECHNOLOGY
E. STEWART SAUNDERS

ouis XIV during the fifty-five years of his personal reign (1661-1715) created the institutional foundations for the science and technology of France. These institutions were outwardly an attempt both to meet the needs of the French state for technical advice and to provide professional scientists with the necessary support for pure scientific research. In a less obvious sense, the origin and evolution of these institutions represented an attempt on the part of the monarchy to disentangle the pursuit of knowledge from the prevailing system of political patronage and from the political and religious speculation that fed the social conflicts of the period. By the end of the seventeenth century, Louis XIV and his ministers had attained these goals and set French science and technology on the high road of success for the duration of the eighteenth century.

The institutions of science and technology took several forms. The Royal Academy of Sciences was established in 1666. Within the Ministry of the Navy and Colonies, several technical advisory bureaus were created, among them the Bureau of Maps and Plans in 1696. A large corps of professional engineers emerged within the Service of Fortifications in the 1670s and 1680s. Of these institutions, the Royal Academy of Sciences was preeminent in terms of its research in the sciences and the advisory role it assumed for the major technological enterprises of the government.

ORIGIN OF THE
ROYAL ACADEMY OF SCIENCES

The fifty years preceding Louis' personal reign were both a period of scientific discoveries that changed the fundamental notions about physical reality and a time of general freewheeling intellectual speculation that tested the boundaries of political and religious orthodoxy. In 1610 Galileo had used a crude telescope to discover the mountainous terrain of the moon, and in 1644 Torricelli performed a number of convincing experiments to demonstrate the existence of a vacuum. Both discoveries challenged the accepted Aristotelian explanation of physical phenomena. In 1628 William Harvey proposed the theory that blood circulates in the body. For the first time perhaps in the history of mankind, a number of man's most perplexing questions seemed capable of definitive answers. The temptation to extrapolate this mode of inquiry into the realms of faith, law, and society was irresistible.

During the 1640s and 1650s, various groups in French society engaged in acrimonious debate and confrontation, often supporting their positions with either the ideas of the new learning or the traditional knowledge of the past.[1] At stake was not just the truth of their arguments but the correctness of a body of knowledge that justified the special privileges accorded these interest groups. The Paris Faculty of Medicine defended the traditional Galenic medicine against new ideas on the circulation of blood and the use of metallic compounds for medicinal cures. By law only graduates of the Paris Faculty of Medicine were allowed to practice in the northern part of France around Paris, yet proponents of the new medicine and graduates of other medical schools were attempting to establish themselves in the vicinity of Paris. The theologians of the Sorbonne strongly opposed the implications of Cartesian philosophy, especially the implications of the dualism of mind and body for the doctrine of the sacraments and Thomistic theology in general. Such a philosophy greatly undermined the prerogatives of the ordained clergy in the administration of the Eucharist, and the Sorbonne was eventually able to create legislation forbidding the teaching of Cartesianism in the universities.

The most pervasive ideologically based conflict of the 1650s and 1660s was between the Jesuits and the Jansenists. The points of conflict were not just theological but ranged over moral conduct, philosophy, and the rights of the French Church. A number of Jansenists embraced the new ideas of Copernicus and Galileo, while the Jesuits in general supported a traditional cosmology. The danger of this conflict for society and the state was that other groups such as the Parlement of Paris, the Sorbonne, and the parish clergy in general all became engaged in the conflict.

Much of the debate and turmoil was centered in Paris, which was something of a magnet for many natural philosophers and intellectuals. They congregated in groups to discuss and argue Cartesian science, the meaning of comets, medical remedies, the proper functions of music and literature, or whatever came to mind. One such group was the Bureau of Address, which was a sort of public forum at which all types of topics were debated. More learned in approach were small groups that met in private homes.

Although these meetings were well suited to the discussion of history, philosophy, and literature — the host nearly always had a large personal library for the convenience of his guests — they did not serve the needs of experimental scientists. As a consequence, questions of science often degenerated into philosophical wrangling. The Montmore group finally disbanded because of the ill feelings generated from this type of pettiness. The more experimentally minded scientists began to meet at the home of Melchisédech Thevenot, but the very expense of experimental equipment limited the scope of their work.[2]

Many scientists and literary men sought protection and financial support from the leading figures of the realm. The death of Cardinal Richelieu in 1642 and of Louis XIII in 1643, followed by the revolts of 1648-52 known as the Fronde, had opened the way for a number of these leading figures, some of whom were related to the king or in the king's government, to build independent bases of political power apart from the king himself. The financial support offered by these "grandees" to scientists and intellectuals, while often motivated by a genuine interest in the state of knowledge, was seldom disinterested or untainted by the political uses to be made of such patronage. Gaston, Louis XIV's uncle and a rebel during the revolts of the Fronde, subsidized a large number of intellectuals and took a special interest in the science of botany. Nicolas Fouquet, Louis XIV's Superintendent of Finances, whom Louis later imprisoned, gained a reputation in the 1650s for his generous support of literature and scholarly research.

To counter the political power of these "grandees," Louis XIV in 1661 assumed responsibility for the daily business of government and surrounded himself with a select group of loyal advisers and ministers of state. The most prominent advisor to emerge at this time was Jean-Baptiste Colbert (1619-83), Secretary of State for the Navy and Colonies, Controller General of Finances, and Superintendent of Royal Buildings.

Colbert worked hard, not only to assert the authority of the king but to rationalize the procedures of government finance, the legal system, and the administrative bureaucracy. Colbert was not, however, ignorant of the fundamentals of politics. Hence he took steps to create a loyal group of supporters, both within the government administration and at court, to advance the cause of his policies, to offer advice on policy, and to gather information.

Colbert had grasped the importance of supporting the scientific and literary community, not only as useful servants of the government but as agents of his personal political career. In 1655, while still in the service of Cardinal Mazarin, he had commissioned Pierre Costar and Gilles Menage to prepare a list of scholars worthy of royal financial support. The list was prepared, but it was Colbert's political rival, Nicolas Fouquet, not Colbert, who was successful in obtaining a number of government pensions for this group. Fouquet, who was Superintendent of Finances from 1655 to

COLBERT HAD GRASPED THE IMPORTANCE OF SUPPORTING THE SCIENTIFIC AND LITERARY COMMUNITY

1661, created a clientele of intellectuals beholden to him for patronage. They would often gather at Fouquet's country estate, Vaux-le-Vicomte, or at his Paris townhouse in St. Mandé. Among Fouquet's clients were the mathematician Pierre Carcavi, the physician Marin Cureau de La Chambre, and the physiologist Jean Pecquet.

Fouquet's ambition was to replace Cardinal Mazarin as the first minister to the king, and his patronage of the intellectual community was a stratagem to gain their support. On Mazarin's death in 1661, however, Fouquet was blocked in his goal by Colbert, who convinced Louis XIV that Fouquet had embezzled state funds and was a threat to the king's own power. Fouquet's arrest in 1661 and his subsequent trial were a blow to the scholarly community. In 1662 no scholars or men of letters received their pensions. Colbert became Controller General of Finances and let it be known that he was in a position to find pensions for deserving scholars and men of letters. Most of those who had received pensions by the good graces of Fouquet now switched their allegiance to Colbert. Those who remained loyal to Fouquet during his trial received no financial support and a few even went to prison with Fouquet.[3]

In 1663 Colbert created a group of scholars who advised him on the arts, scholarship, and the distribution of pensions. At this time Colbert received correspondence from several quarters, all suggesting that it would be well to organize the king's support of the intellectual community into some sort of academy. The suggestions varied in the type of scholarship they emphasized, but all agreed that such an institution would benefit the king with good advice and greatly enhance his reputation among the nations of Europe. They also agreed that questions of government policy and articles of faith should not be discussed and that the principles of reason and objective discourse should govern the exchange of ideas.

Following the design for an academy suggested by Charles Perrault, a member of Colbert's advisory group, Colbert created in 1665-66 a General Academy composed of scientists, historians, linguists, and philosophers. This caused a good deal of opposition from the established professional academic groups, notably the Sorbonne and the Faculty of Medicine. After considering the consequences of doing battle with these groups, Colbert disbanded the General Academy and created in its place the Royal Academy of Sciences.

Having originated as a response to the political context of the intellectual community of France, the Royal Academy of Sciences and the technical institutions that were created after it now responded to the needs of the state. These in turn were dictated by the policy concerns of the particular ministers of state who handled cultural affairs. In the period 1661 to 1715, three ministers of state dealt directly with scientific and technical matters. They were Jean-Baptiste Colbert (1661-83), François Michel Le Tellier, the marquis de Louvois (1683-91), and Louis Phélypeaux, the comte de Pontchartrain (1691-1715). Each pursued different policies for the state of France, policies that in turn reflected the wishes of Louis XIV himself, and had direct effects on the demands made of the new institutions of science and technology and the work they produced.

Catalogue 70

SCIENCE AND TECHNOLOGY DURING THE COLBERT YEARS

The creation of the Royal Academy of Sciences in December of 1666 was but a first step in the institutionalization of science and technology. From a view of a contemporary in 1667, no structural changes had really occurred. Colbert had simply replaced Fouquet and Mazarin as the principal power of the government and had managed to pension the more prominent lights of the intellectual community in such a way as to favor his own political cause. Colbert selected the members of the academy and determined its program. In the mind of the court, they were "his men" and dedicated to supporting "his program." It was several years before they were even referred to as the Royal Academy of Sciences, and at his death the academy had no legal basis that would assure its continued existence.

The relationship of scholars, and scientists in particular, to their patron had in fact changed. Colbert, despite his concern for building his own base of power, was not an independent "grandee" but very much Louis XIV's minister. Colbert saw to it that Louis received the *gloire* for the accomplishments of this coterie of scientists. The services performed by the academy supported Colbert's program, but that program was to make France a great maritime power — a goal that certainly transcended maintaining his personal power. In addition, by the creation of the academy Colbert had succeeded in compartmentalizing the speculative process. The members of the academy were free to investigate and were protected from the slings of the vested academic groups so long as they did not stray into politics and religion. In this respect, some of the spirited battles that had set one group against another and had so disquieted Louis XIV's attempts to moderate the various factions of society were brought under control.[4]

Some flavor of the work performed by the scientists of the academy may be glimpsed from their daily program. Colbert had created pensions for sixteen to eighteen scientists. Half of the scientists worked in mathematics or astronomy and the other half in anatomy, botany, or chemistry. They met twice a week in the Royal Library, alternating in subjects between the physical and biological sciences. A typical meeting might include the dissection of a crocodile, a report on the distillation of a particular medicinal herb, or a discussion of a recent essay on the moons of Saturn. When not meeting, the scientists devoted themselves to full-time research or to work on government engineering projects. To facilitate astronomical observations, Louis XIV had an observatory built on the outskirts of Paris. Anatomical and chemical laboratories were established in the Royal Library, and botanical research was conducted at the Royal Botanical Gardens. By the end of his reign, Louis XIV had spent between two and three million pounds to support the research of the academy and to build the Paris Observatory, a truly remarkable commitment.[5]

THE PRINCIPAL SCIENTIFIC AND TECHNICAL ACCOMPLISHMENT OF THE REIGN OF LOUIS XIV WAS ACCURATELY MAPPING THE WORLD

Whatever may have been Colbert's dedication to the enrichment of the mind, there is little doubt that his greatest enthusiasm was for those aspects of mathematics, mechanics, and astronomy that would improve the art of navigation. Colbert was at that time engaged in a plan to strengthen the French navy and expand France's commercial relations around the world. The principal obstacle to open-sea shipping was the inability to calculate longitudes with less than one degree of error. Reckoning latitudes was no problem, but navigation could be considerably improved from maps with accurate longitudes. An error of just one degree in reckoning the location of a ship or port resulted in a sixty-nine-mile error at the equator. Existing maps of the Mediterranean Sea, for instance, were in error by as much as six hundred miles in depicting its length.

The principal scientific and technical accomplishment of the reign of Louis XIV was nothing less than a revolution in the means of accurately mapping the world. The Mercator map of the world represented the best map of the mid-seventeenth century. It was accurate in helping mariners plot directions but distorted the shapes of land masses and the distances between them. The astronomers of the Academy of Sciences made two major advances in geodetics that laid the cornerstone for all future cartography. First, they determined the distance represented by one degree of latitude; and second, they developed a method for the precise determination of longitudes.

Abbé Jean Picard, an original member of the academy, was able to calculate correctly the number of miles represented by one degree of the earth's circumference. In 1669 he began to survey an eighty-mile stretch of open country north of Paris, which lay on a meridian of longitude. The astronomers of the period assumed the earth to be a perfect sphere so that any degree on a meridian would equal any other degree on a meridian. A degree on a meridian would also equal a degree of longitude at the equator and a degree north of the equator could be calculated using spherical trigonometry. Picard's first task was to measure accurately the distance between two points on the meridian. He chose the Pavillon in Malvoisine and

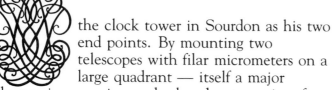

the clock tower in Sourdon as his two end points. By mounting two telescopes with filar micrometers on a large quadrant — itself a major advance in surveying — he layed out a series of thirteen triangles between them. One side of the first triangle was very carefully measured with a rod, and the sides of the other twelve triangles were computed from trigonometric tables. By using telescopes on the quadrant, Picard determined the angles of the triangles very precisely. Having measured the distance between these two points, his next task was to calculate the degrees between the two points. He used a zenith sector to determine the angle of elevation of a particular star from both these points and from this determined the arc between Malvoisine and Sourdon to be 1°11′57″. Picard took two years to make the measurement, but the value of one degree of latitude had been accurately established at 69.07 miles.[6]

Having determined the value of a degree of the earth's circumference, the only remaining obstacle to an accurate mapping of the earth was the determination of differences in longitudes between major cities and ports of the world. As early as 1663 Colbert had been in contact with the Dutch mathematician and inventor Christiaan Huygens concerning Huygens' progress in perfecting a pendulum clock capable of maintaining accurate time aboard ship. Were Huygens to accomplish this, it would be possible to determine precise longitudes not only for distant ports of the world but for ships at sea. By 1665 it appeared that Huygens had perfected his clock, and Colbert invited him to France with the offer of a large pension, a patent on his clock, and membership in a future group of scientists. Huygens' clock erred less than a minute over long stretches of time, but in order to be useful for navigation, it would have to maintain this accuracy during the rolling of a ship. The clock could be set to the local time of a port in France from the zenith of the sun. This clock aboard ship would thus always be set to the time of that port, and the time of a distant port or a ship at sea could be determined from the zenith of the sun. The difference in time between the clock set for the time of the port in France and a clock set for another port or a ship at sea represented the difference in longitude. Colbert sent Jean Richer, a member of the Academy of Sciences, on a tour with the Atlantic fleet in 1668 and to Acadia in 1670 to test Huygens' clock. The pendulum clock proved unsatisfactory in these tests at sea. Although Huygens continued to work on the clock, Colbert turned his support to other projects.

Since Huygens' clock had failed at sea, the most promising alternative means of determining longitudes was the simultaneous observation and timing of a predictable celestial event from two different points of the globe. In 1669 Colbert prevailed upon Jean D. Cassini, an Italian astronomer, to come to Paris to head the astronomical program of the Academy of Sciences. Cassini had published periodic tables of the moons of Jupiter that made it possible for two astronomers to observe simultaneously their eclipses from two distant points. In 1672 Cassini sent Jean Richer to Cayenne on the coast of South America to establish the longitude of Cayenne with respect to Paris. Cassini at the Observatory in Paris and Richer in Cayenne made several simultaneous observations of the eclipses of Jupiter's moons. Each had set a clock to local time by determining the sun's zenith at each observation point, and from the exact time of the eclipses they calculated the difference in degrees of longitude between the two places. Never before had two such distant points of the world been so accurately measured. Twentieth-century measurements have shown that Cassini and Richer erred by only three minutes of one degree. In 1679, when Louis XIV asked the academy to make a new map of France, Colbert was able to dispatch astronomers of the academy to the ports and borders of the country to establish longitudes using the methods developed by Cassini. Over the next fifteen years accurate coordinates were determined for a number of points around the world, and in 1696 Cassini was able to publish a new map of the world showing accurate locations and distances for forty-three locations in Europe, Asia, and the Americas.[7]

Colbert did not neglect the research program in the biological sciences, although it was clearly secondary in his own view. Matheticians and astronomers had been included in his original General Academy but not anatomists, botanists, or chemists. Colbert had created the Academy of Sciences by appointing as academicians the mathematicians and astronomers of the defunct General Academy and by adding to them a handful of "physicians" to round out the research program in the biological sciences.

The anatomists led by Claude Perrault began to dissect and compare the structures and functions of the anatomical parts of various exotic animals. Their work was possible because Louis XIV gave dead animals from the Royal Menagerie to the academy. In 1681 Louis XIV himself visited the laboratory to watch the dissection of an elephant. The results of this work were published in the two well-illustrated volumes (1671 and 1676) under the title, *Memoirs on the Natural History of Animals.* The use of species that had evolved in other parts of the world helped to dispel fanciful ideas about these animals and provided a better understanding of the functions of the bodily parts. The work in anatomy was also used to support research in physiology. In one instance, however, this led Jean Mery to conclude that blood flowed to the lungs of a human fetus. His conclusion was based on a false comparison of the heart of a sea tortoise with the heart of a human fetus, but fortunately his ideas were rejected by other anatomists of the academy.[8]

The botanists and chemists worked together to define the differences between plants and to specify their uses. In the *Memoirs on the Natural History of Plants,* published by the academy in 1676 and 1679, one would find first a description of the parts of a given plant, its flower, roots, etc., followed by a list of the various salts and oils to be obtained by distilling the parts of the plant. Botany and chemistry had traditionally focused on finding the medical uses of plants, and this concern is quite prominent in determining the work and methodology used by the academicians. Within the context of the academy, however, they were also searching for more fundamental principles. They were seeking a foundation, both anatomical and chemical, by which plants might be classified; they wished to know what salts and oils were unique to plants — that is, which were produced by the plant and which were absorbed from the earth through the roots; and in the long term they hoped to find empirical verification of the corpuscular theory of natural philosophy. Chemical analysis through distillation yielded results beyond the analytical methods at their disposal, and after 1700 the chemists abandoned this type of analysis and turned to pneumatic chemistry.[9]

> LOUVOIS INITIATED SOME NEW DIRECTIONS IN THE ACTIVITIES OF THE ACADEMY THAT HAD MAJOR REPERCUSSIONS

SCIENCE AND TECHNOLOGY UNDER THE MARQUIS DE LOUVOIS

When Colbert died in 1683 and his rival, the marquis de Louvois, became the new Superintendent of Buildings, it was not at all certain that Louvois would extend his protection to the Academy of Sciences — the academy, after all, had been the personal creation of Colbert, and Louvois was bent on driving from office the protégés of his former rival. However, Louvois accepted the role of protector to the academy and became involved in its affairs. He held summer soirées at Meudon for the academicians and he made plans for the academy to meet in new quarters, proposed but never built, in the Place Vendôme.

Louvois, however, initiated some new directions in the activities of the academy that had major repercussions on the effectiveness of this institution over the next eight or more years. In an age when scientific discoveries in astronomy, physics, mechanics, and mathematics were revolutionizing Europe's view of the universe and its laws, Louvois directed most of the energies of the academy into natural history and withdrew practically all support for the physical and mathematical sciences. We can see this new policy unfolding during the first months of Louvois' protectorship in his reactions to projects that had been initiated by Colbert before his death.

During his last years as protector of the academy, Colbert had organized an expedition of members to Gorée and to the French West Indies to determine their longitudes, and at about the same time he arranged for the other astronomers to extend the meridian of Paris both north and south in order to have an accurate foundation for a new map of France. He had also agreed to finance three publications, one on the voyages of the academy, one on the astronomical observations of Tycho Brahe, which members of the Academy had been verifying and correcting, and one on the natural history and anatomy of rare animals that had recently been dissected in the laboratory of the academy.

The two astronomers who had been sent to

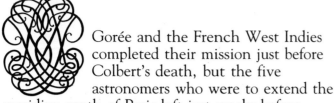Gorée and the French West Indies completed their mission just before Colbert's death, but the five astronomers who were to extend the meridian south of Paris left just weeks before Colbert's death and were recalled. Cassini broached the project to Louvois a few months later but could get no support to complete it. Louvois cancelled the publication of Brahe's observations, although ninety-six pages had already been pulled at a cost of over ten thousand pounds.

Louvois did agree to finance the publication of a book on the voyages of the academy and a book on the anatomy and natural history of rare animals. The actual support he gave to these two projects, however, was quite different. He gave a strong personal endorsement to the publication on anatomy and natural history. During 1684, the first year of Louvois' administration, the number of presentations on anatomy and natural history discussed at the biweekly meetings increased threefold. The book on the voyages of the academy, on the other hand, seems to have been a matter of indifference to Louvois. This book described the attempts of the astronomers to establish the longitudes and other geodetic data about distant places around the world. Louvois gave no endorsement to the project, and within several months it was no longer being discussed in the academy's meetings. The number of presentations on astronomy discussed at the academy decreased 38 percent over the next eight years, and those on mechanics and mathematics disappeared almost entirely.[10]

The marquis de Louvois had no particular desire to promote French overseas commerce or to expand its navy. He was Secretary of State for the Army and considered the fortunes of France to be tied to its forces on the land and the strength of its borders. For better than fifteen years he had competed with Colbert and the navy for funds to support the army; now after Colbert's death he was still competing with Colbert's son, the marquis de Seignelay, who had succeeded his father as the new Secretary for the Navy and Colonies, for the same funds. Within the context of these policies Louvois had little need for astronomers and mathematicians. Rather, he relied on a corps of around two hundred highly skilled military engineers for technical expertise.

Engineers had held important functions in both the army and the Service of Fortifications since the time of Henri IV or earlier, but the increasing necessity of fortified places for the control of the terrain and the grand strategy of warfare raised them to major positions of responsibility in the mid-seventeenth century. A series of well-placed fortifications could secure a frontier. An army of that day could not bypass a fortified place for fear of being attacked on its flanks or having its supply lines cut. Louis XIV was a conservative warrior and gave special attention to the art and strategy of fortification. The correspondence between Louis XIV and Louvois reveals that both men had a good grasp of the technical requisites of fortification and siege warfare. Sometimes Louis XIV even argued with his engineers over the technical details for the construction of the fortress. In developing their war plans for the defense of France, Louis and Louvois preferred the advice of their chief military engineer, Sebastien Vauban, to that offered by Louis XIV's field marshals.

Sebastien Vauban was the preeminent military engineer of the seventeenth century. He did not invent the science of fortification but took its parts and drew them together into a rational system. His perfection of this science was so complete that his principles were considered the state of the art for two hundred years and were not superceded until the use of cannon with rifled bores became common in the late nineteenth century. Vauban's science of fortification is best understood from three aspects: his redesign of the bastion and detached outworks; his creation of a system of zigzag and parallel trenches for sieges; and his systematic location of fortresses on the frontier.

The design of the rampart walls themselves had been greatly advanced by Vauban's predecessor, Blaise de Pagan, in the 1650s. These walls were built to withstand the battering of heavy cannon and to position the defensive artillery in such a way as to shower the attackers with a crossfire. Using geometrical principles and good surveying techniques, Pagan planned a new fortress by establishing first an outer perimeter measured from the outermost points of the bastions, those arrowhead-shaped projections from the walls of the fortress. This procedure reversed past procedure, which laid the inner perimeter of the ramparts first and then worked outward, but often failed to have the bastions properly situated for covering its sides with musket and cannon crossfire. Vauban's advance over Pagan was to change the angle of the sides forming the points of the bastion in such a way that a projection of a line from one bastion's side intersected the rampart walls precisely where the neck of the adjacent bastion touched the walls. This gave gunners situated on the neck of one bastion a clear view and range of fire across the sides of the adjacent bastion without hitting the other bastion with shot or ricochet fire. This made it nearly impossible for infantry to approach the base of the ramparts in order to scale the wall.

Siege tactics prior to Vauban were haphazard and often ineffective. Vauban devised a logical system of attack using parallel and zigzag trenches to move the attacking forces from the distant hills around the fortress to a protected trench right on the edge of the moat. The attack would begin under the cover of darkness. Sappers would dig a trench parallel to one of the walls of the fortress, and when dawn broke the defenders would see enemy cannon protected by a trench some six hundred yards from the ramparts. The cannon would then begin a bombardment, and sappers would dig several trenches from the parallel trench toward the

rampart walls. These trenches snaked their way forward in a zigzag pattern, always at a forty-five-degree angle to the rampart walls to protect those digging the trenches from gunfire. After the zigzag trenches had advanced several hundred yards, another parallel trench would be dug and the cannon brought into closer range. Vauban would repeat these steps until he had placed cannon just across the ditch from the ramparts. At this close range, the twenty-four-pound cannon could easily knock holes in the walls through which the infantry could enter. During his lifetime, Vauban directed fifty-three sieges and never failed in a single one.[11]

In the course of his career, Vauban built thirty-three new fortresses, rebuilt around three hundred older fortresses, and razed many more that had lost their strategic importance. The extent to which Vauban was a leading strategist has been debated by historians. Some historians point out that for the most part he merely rebuilt existing fortresses and thus did not shape any grand

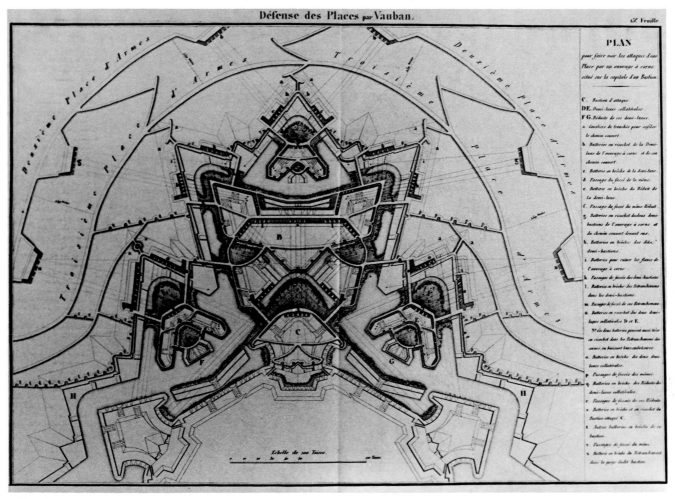

Detail of Catalogue 52

strategy; others counter that he selected for rebuilding only those that conformed to his ideas of a strategic frontier and razed all the others. Prior to Vauban, fortresses had been built to defend a particular bridgehead or river junction but did not reinforce each other to create a "fortified zone." During the Dutch War, Vauban asked Louis XIV to acquire certain cities on the northern frontier in order to secure a more defensible line and to give up other fortresses in Flanders. Vauban conceived of the Rhine as a natural frontier for France and projected a double line of fortified places across the northern frontier, but his strategic ideas were still evolving and he never arrived at a comprehensive concept of a "fortified zone" before his death.[12]

Engineers in the royal service in the mid-seventeenth century were identified by a certificate from the government, but they had no institutional structure that advanced the practice and profession of engineering. This was partly in the nature of their work: during wartime they served mostly in the army; during peacetime they were attached to other projects. The institutional foundations for French military engineering were given their basic form during Louis XIV's reign. Louvois created a special reserve-officer commission in the army for engineers that gave them a special status as engineers and protected their military careers. When not engaged in the army, most engineers worked on various fortification projects. In 1690 Louis XIV consolidated several sections of the Service of Fortifications into one administration. These two institutional changes together had the effect of creating a professional structure for engineers through which they might advance their careers and perfect their skills.

Except for the problems of fortification, Louvois tended to leave other scientific and technical needs unresolved. Matters of particular concern to Louis XIV himself were exceptions. Supplying enough water for the gardens of Versailles and Marly was one of those concerns, and both Louvois and his predecessor Colbert had to deal with water for the royal gardens. Some 1,400 fountains were built at Versailles and Marly, not to mention the canals and cascades. The half-dozen pumps that had supplied the water when Versailles was just a hunting lodge for Louis XIII were totally inadequate. Colbert in his capacity as Superintendent of Buildings was responsible for resolving this problem until his death in 1683. It

had been suggested that an aqueduct be constructed to bring water from the Loire River, but when Jean Picard of the Academy of Sciences surveyed the area in 1674, he found that the level of the Loire was some sixty feet lower than Versailles. In 1678 Arnold de Ville presented Colbert with a plan to build a pumping station on the Seine that would supply all the water needs for Marly and Versailles. His ideas were accepted and work began immediately.

The "Marly Machine," as de Ville's scheme came to be called, has been praised as a model of ingenuity and labeled the first hydraulic system to pump water through metal pipes under high pressure. It has also been damned as one of the most inefficient white elephants ever built. De Ville claimed that his design for a pumping station could move around eight thousand cubic yards of water per day from the Seine to a reservoir 502 feet above the level of the Seine and a mile from its bank. From this reservoir, water would flow by gravity through viaducts to run all the fountains at Versailles and Marly. One major problem in pumping water to any height in the seventeenth century was that the terra cotta and lead pipes of that day would burst at pressures greater than three or four atmospheres. Iron pipes were just coming into use at this time, and their first extensive use was at Versailles. Some twenty-four miles of iron pipe were laid in the 1680s, and when much of it was excavated in 1939 it was found to be still in good condition. The more critical limiting factor at Versailles, however, was that there was not a sufficiently tight fit between the piston and the cylinder of the pumps of that day to produce the pressure required to raise the water 500 feet.

The "Marly Machine" resolved these technical problems by generating large quantities of power and then transmitting that power across long distances. Fourteen undershot paddle wheels, each thirty-nine feet in diameter, were installed on the Seine, and the river was dammed to force the water under the wheels. Six wheels were used to drive sixty-four lift-and-force pumps to raise the water from the Seine to a reservoir 150 feet above the river. At this reservoir, another seventy-nine pumps raised the water to still another reservoir 175 feet higher in altitude, and here yet another set of pumps raised the water to the final reservoir. The pumps at the two intermediate reservoirs were driven by a string of rocker arms stretching for almost a mile up the slope from the river and

Catalogue 123

receiving their power from the other eight wheels on the river. It has been estimated that 90 percent of the power was expended in friction and inertia to drive the rocker arms and only about 10 percent was actually available to drive the pumps at the reservoirs above the river. The whole system created a horrible racket. Although designed to raise eight thousand cubic yards of water to the top reservoir, it in fact never exceeded a capacity of four thousand cubic yards. Consequently, most of this water was used for the fountains at Marly and only the surplus reached the fountains at Versailles.[13]

Louis XIV was disgruntled over this state of affairs. It was a common practice to turn the fountains on just before Louis arrived at a particular point and then to turn them off as he moved on to another area of the gardens. It was not uncommon for them to fail to work altogether. Louvois proposed to bring the water of the Eure River to Versailles. The Eure was at a level higher than Versailles, but transporting the water across the valley at Maintenon was a major problem. Louvois asked Vauban for a plan, and the latter proposed the construction of a tube on the floor of the valley that would operate like a siphon to raise the water on the far side of the valley. Louvois, however, believed that a siphon would be too costly in that it would require nine miles of cast iron pipe one foot in diameter. Members of the Academy of

Sciences had been doing the necessary surveying for the project in 1684 and suggested that a aqueduct be built across the valley. Louvois chose the academy's plan and used army regiments to undertake the construction. In the end, the aqueduct was never completed because the war with Europe beginning in 1688 drew money away from such a costly undertaking.

The Academy of Sciences had become moribund during the eight years under the direction of the marquis de Louvois. The reasons are not hard to determine. Colbert had aligned the scientific program of the Academy of Sciences too closely with his own projects and policies and by extension with the politics of his career. Consequently, the sudden shift in policy and technical projects that resulted when Louvois assumed control of the academy was reflected in a radical alteration in the scientific program of the academy. The result was a decline in the academy's scientific research.

PONTCHARTRAIN AND REFORM

Louis Phélypeaux, comte de Pontchartrain, assumed control of the Academy of Sciences in 1691 on the death of Louvois. His position in 1691 was in many ways analogous to Colbert's position in the 1660s and 1670s. He was Controller General for Finance and Secretary of State for the Navy and Colonies. He resolved the dilemmas of scientific research and government policy inherited from his predecessor through a judicious separation of the research functions of science from those necessary to implement government technical projects. In 1696 he created the Bureau of Maps and Plans within the Ministry of the Navy and Colonies to deal with the technical and strategic problems of overseas commerce and exploration. In 1699 Louis XIV, at Pontchartrain's request, gave the Academy of Sciences a set of regulations that redefined the goals of the academy in terms of scientific research and provided for a separation of functions that insulated the academy from changes in policy. Yet the academy did not completely disengage itself from the government. It remained in the background as a group of experts ready to advise the government on projects of a technical nature, but it was no longer a springboard for the execution of projects.

When Pontchartrain assumed responsibility for the academy in 1691, his first task was to restore the vitality of the research program. Not only had most of the activity in the astronomical and mechanical sciences been curtailed by his predecessor, Louvois, but in 1689, two years before his death, Louvois had ordered a complete halt in all publications of the academy. Pontchartrain realized that publication was a necessary stimulus to research, and in 1691 he established a monthly, *Mémoires,* to publish the academy's research. He followed this up with the appointment of his nephew, the Abbé Jean-Paul Bignon, as president of the academy. The result was a growth in the new research reported at the biweekly meetings of the academy and a resurgence of work in astronomy and mechanics. Cassini and the other astronomers were campaigning to resume the unfinished project of extending the meridian south of Paris, but Pontchartrain was unable to support this project until 1700. Still, the *Mémoires* offered the scientists an incentive for research and the Abbé Bignon, who had Pontchartrain's confidence, was able to procure from his uncle the financial support needed for the academy's program.

Having the Academy of Sciences once again linked to the same administrative direction as the Ministry of the Navy was doubtlessly beneficial for the academy's research in astronomy and the mathematical sciences. Yet the war of the League of Augsburg (1688-97) was jeopardizing all of France's North American possessions. What was needed was immediate action, and in this

atmosphere Louis Pontchartrain and his son Jérôme created in 1696 the Bureau of Maps and Plans within the Ministry of the Navy and Colonies to focus France's scientific and technical expertise on the problem of empire. This bureau drew together a group of engineers, cartographers, and military strategists who planned France's ventures into the Louisiana Territory. Parts of the Mississippi had already been explored in the 1680s. With the treaty of peace signed in 1697, the immediate problem was to explore and fortify the Mississippi and its tributaries before the English could establish a foothold and cut the link between France's Canadian and Caribbean possessions. Based on the plans of this bureau, Iberville set sail in 1698 to find the mouth of the Mississippi and establish a fort there. The maps for the expedition were prepared by Guillaume Delisle, and Vauban offered his strategic ideas.[14] Several members of the Academy of Sciences prepared memoranda for the bureau. In 1699 Vauban became an honorary member of the academy, and in 1702 Delisle became Cassini's "student astronomer." The new interest in empire was certainly beneficial to the astronomical and mathematical research of the academicians, but the creation of a new bureau with the express mission of exploration facilitated the implementation of government policy and gave sharper focus to the research-oriented goals of the academy.

The academy, however, needed something more than a revived program in astronomy and the support of a sympathetic administrator. Despite the stimulus to research given by Pontchartrain in 1691, the academy was hard-pressed to maintain the momentum of these changes. The 1690s were years of war and famine for France, and research fell behind. The end of the war in 1697 offered a new opportunity for reform, and Louis XIV took this period to make some necessary institutional changes to repair the stresses of many years of war and dearth. These latter years had revealed the weaknesses of the older institutional arrangements. In order to give the academy more realistic goals and a greater institutional stability, Louis XIV promulgated in 1699 a set of fifty regulations.

How did the regulations of 1699 put scientific research on a firm institutional foundation? First, they outlined the work of the academicians in terms of research in specific scientific disciplines and limited their work on applied projects designed to forward national policies to an advisory role

rather than an implementive role. Second, they gave legal recognition to the academy's existence and gave it a fixed place in the government's budget. Third, new appointments to the academy were based on nominations made by the members themselves, thus reducing the opportunity for government officials to appoint family and friends. Fourth, the scientists were organized into a hierarchy. A young scientist starting at the bottom of the ladder could advance through diligence to a fully pensioned position. Fifth, fully pensioned members were required to present the results of their research at regular intervals or face dismissal from the academy. Sixth, each of the six major areas of science was guaranteed an equal number of scientists; thus all areas of science advanced on an equal footing. Seventh, the size of the academy was increased to sixty active members. The assumption behind Pontchartrain's reforms was that a well-balanced program of scientific research, determined by the scientists themselves and propelled forward by promises of advancement and recognition, would best serve the interests of public and government.

Louis XIV's fifty-five-year reign is perhaps best characterized as the period when the sovereignty of the monarch was transformed into institutions that embodied the sovereignty of the state and would survive independently the life of the monarch and even the institution of monarchy itself. The institutionalization of science and technology also occurred in Louis' reign. Colbert accomplished the first stage in 1666 with the creation of the Academy of Sciences, an act that disengaged the activities of scientists from the independent milieu of the Parisian salons and from the speculative traditions of philosophy. Yet, although Colbert redirected the scientific enterprise to the concrete empirical questions of nature, the answers to which also served the practical needs of Colbert's national policies, the program and personalities of the academy became representative of his own political ambitions and party. The worst features of ministerial patronage and policy surfaced during Louvois' direction of the academy, and it became apparent that a successful program in science and technology needed some sort of insulation from the changes of ministerial policies and a new definition of goals. The regulations of 1699 served this purpose. Louis XIV's ministers were concurrently creating other scientifically informed government units. These groups, most notably at this time the corps of engineers and the Bureau of Maps and Plans, were created to furnish the technical support for the more precisely defined national objectives. While independent of the Academy of Sciences, their work was to come under its scrutiny and review.

Louis XIV's patronage of science and technology established a pattern of government institutions that was to grow in the eighteenth century and to endure in a modified form down to the present. What was emerging was a constellation of scientific and technological institutions with the Academy of Sciences at the center. Each was devoted to a specific task and responsible to a particular governmental agency but was reviewed by the academy for quality and professionalism. This preeminent role assigned to the Academy of Sciences gave it considerable authority over the scientific and technological development of France.[15] This institutional arrangement provided for France a golden age of sustained scientific growth and technical expertise unrivaled by any other European nation in the eighteenth century.

FOOTNOTES

1. Robert Mandrou, From Humanism to Science, 1480-1700 (Middlesex, England, 1978), 228-83.
2. Harcourt Brown, Scientific Organizations in Seventeenth-Century France, 1620-1680 (Baltimore, 1934).
3. E. Stewart Saunders, "Wealth and Politics in Scholarship: The Library of Nicolas Fouquet and the Collège Royal," Journal of Library History (forthcoming).
4. E. Stewart Saunders, "The Decline and Reform of the Académie des Sciences à Paris, 1676-1699," Ph.D. dissertation, Ohio State University, 1980), 11-36.
5. John M. Hirschfield, The Académie Royale des Sciences, 1663-1683 (New York, 1981).
6. Tom B. Jones, The Figure of the Earth (Lawrence, Kan., 1967).
7. Lloyd A. Brown, Jean Domenique Cassini and His World Map of 1696 (Ann Arbor, 1941).
8. Francis J. Cole, A History of Comparative Anatomy from Aristotle to the Eighteenth Century (London, 1944), 393-442.
9. Alice Stroup, "Wilhelm Hombert and the Search for the Constituents of Plants at the 17th Century Académie Royale des Sciences," Ambix, XXVI (1979), 184-201.
10. Saunders, "Decline and Reform," 65-104.
11. Christopher Duffy, Fire and Stone: The Science of Fortress Warfare, 1660-1860 (London, 1975).
12. Henry Guerlac, "Vauban: The Impact of Science on War," in Makers of Modern Strategy: Military Thought from Machiavelli to Hitler, ed. Edward M. Earle (Princeton, 1944), 26-48.
13. Paul Gille, "Hydraulic Works and Water-Supply Systems," in A History of Technology and Invention, ed. Maurice Daumas (New York, 1969), II, 511-30.
14. John C. Rule, "Jérôme Phélypeaux, Comte de Pontchartrain, and the Establishment of Louisiana, 1696-1715," in Frenchmen and French Ways in the Mississippi Valley, ed. John F. McDermott (Urbana, 1969), 179-97.
15. Roger Hahn, The Anatomy of a Scientific Institution: The Paris Academy of Sciences, 1666-1803 (Berkeley, 1971).

NOTES ON THE CONTRIBUTORS

CARL BRASSEAUX, a native of Louisiana, received his doctorate from the Université de Paris and is currently Director of the Colonial Records Collection at the Center for Louisiana Studies, University of Southwestern Louisiana. The author of numerous books and articles on colonial Louisiana, Dr. Brasseaux recently published *Selected Bibliography of Scholarly Literature on Colonial Louisiana and New France* (Lafayette, 1982).

MARCEL GUTWIRTH is chairman of the Romance Languages Department at Haverford College. He has served as visiting professor at The Johns Hopkins University, Queens College, Bryn Mawr College, and was named visiting Mellon Professor in Humanities at Tulane University (Fall, 1980). Professor Gutwirth, who received his doctorate from Columbia University, is an internationally-recognized specialist on Molière and Racine and the author of numerous books, articles, and reviews in French and English.

ROBERT WYMAN HARTLE, professor of romance languages at Queens College of the City University of New York, received his doctorate from Princeton University. A distinguished and internationally-recognized scholar of seventeenth-century French literature, he has published extensively. Professor Hartle participated in the Tulane University Symposium on the legend of Alexander held in April, 1982, where he presented a paper entitled "Alexander the Great and the Conquest of Versailles."

ROBERT M. ISHERWOOD received his doctorate in history from the University of Chicago and is presently associate professor of history at Vanderbilt University. In addition to his book, *Music in the Service of the King: France in the Seventeenth Century* (Ithaca & London, 1973), Professor Isherwood has recently published the results of his research on fairs and popular entertainment in eighteenth-century Paris.

PHILIPPE JACQUIN has done extensive research in the colonial archives of France, Canada, and the United States. He is a noted expert on French-Indian relations in New France and Louisiana from the sixteenth to the eighteenth centuries and the author of many publications on this subject. Currently he holds the position of professor of history at the Université de Lyon III.

JOHN T. O'CONNOR received his doctorate in history from the University of Minnesota and presently holds the position of professor of history at the University of New Orleans. A noted specialist on diplomatic affairs in the reign of Louis XIV, Professor O'Connor has worked in archives and libraries in several European countries. He is the author of a number of publications, most notably *Negotiator out of Season: The Career of Wilhelm Egon von Furstenburg, 1629-1704* (Athens, Georgia, 1978).

MONIQUE PELLETIER is Director of the Department of Maps and Plans at the Bibliothèque Nationale in Paris, one of the richest cartographic collections in the world. She is an expert in paleography and most recently the author of "Des globes pour le Roi-Soleil, Les origines des 'globes' de Marly," *Revue de la Bibliothèque Nationale* (December 1981).

DANIEL RABREAU currently holds the position of professor of art history at the Université de Paris-Sorbonne. For more than ten years Professor Rabreau has done research on art and architecture under Louis XIV and published numerous articles on the subject. Recently, he co-edited *Apollo dans la ville – Essai sur le théâtre en France au XVIIIe siècle* (Milan-Paris, 1983).

STEVEN G. REINHARDT is Curator of French Manuscripts at the Louisiana Historical Center of the Louisiana State Museum. He holds a doctorate in history from Northern Illinois University and is the author of "Crime and Royal Justice in Ancien Regime France: Modes of Analysis," *The Journal of Interdisciplinary History* (1983).

JULIUS R. RUFF, assistant professor of history at Marquette University, holds a doctorate from the University of North Carolina. Currently conducting research on the legal status and judicial treatment of Huguenots, Professor Ruff is also the author of *Crime, Justice, and Public Order in Old Regime France* (London, 1984).

JOHN C. RULE, who holds a doctorate in history from Harvard University, is currently professor of history at Ohio State University. The author of numerous publications on seventeenth-century France, Professor Rule edited and contributed to the highly-praised *Louis XIV and the Craft of Kingship* (Columbus, Ohio 1969).

E. STEWART SAUNDERS received his doctorate in history from Ohio State University and is presently Reference Librarian for History and Foreign Languages at Purdue University. He has done extensive research in the Bibliothèque Nationale and Archives Nationales on the decline and reform of the Academy of Sciences in Paris in the late seventeenth century and is the author of "The Archives of the Académie des Sciences," *French Historical Studies* (1978).

ANTOINE SCHNAPPER, professor at the Université de Paris-Sorbonne, is a well-known authority on art during the reign of Louis XIV. He has published extensively on the subject, notably

Tableaux pour le Trianon de Marbre (1688-1714) (Paris, 1968) and *Jean Jouvenet (1644-1717) et le peinture d'histoire à Paris* (Paris, 1975).

JOHN B. WOLF, professor emeritus of the University of Illinois at Chicago Circle, is one of the foremost scholars of Louis XIV. His widely-acclaimed *Louis XIV* (New York, 1968) is generally considered the best biography of the king available in any language. Professor Wolf, who received his doctorate in history from the University of Minnesota, presently resides in Jupiter, Florida.

THE SUN KING

PART II
THE EXHIBITION

LOUIS XIV AND THE NEW WORLD

FRACTORUM BELLO PATER

THE SUN KING:
LOUIS XIV AND THE NEW WORLD
AN INTRODUCTION TO THE EXHIBITION
VAUGHN L. GLASGOW AND PIERRE LEMOINE

he Sun King: Louis XIV and the New World is the product of an international partnership between the Louisiana State Museum and its sister institutions in France. Realization of the exhibition involved the active cooperation of over one hundred professional colleagues and agencies. Essential to this effort was the enthusiastic support and assistance of curators and administrators at every level of the Réunion des Musées Nationaux; the Association Française d'Action Artistique; numerous museums, other repositories such as the Bibliothèque Nationale, the Archives de France and the Archives of the Ministère des Relations Extérieures as well as private collectors.

In May 1982 the Louisiana State Museum presented the concept of the exhibition to the leadership of French museums, archives, and appropriate governmental offices in Paris. Meetings were arranged with directors and curators whose institutions held materials important to the subject. A collaborative structure was created with the appointment of American and French commissioners.

Between October, 1982, and January, 1983, meetings were held in Paris with curators of pertinent French collections and private collectors. Curators and collectors responded enthusiastically and suggested objects from their collections that would be important to the project and could travel. Because of the nature and importance of the Sun King project, curators and collectors agreed to lend major works. Some items such as the Courses de Testes et de Bague[1] and the Peace of Utrecht[2] are not normally on public view. Works such as Philippe de Champaigne's portrait of Cardinal Richelieu[3] rarely leave the Louvre, nor does

Hyacinthe Rigaud's great Louis XIV[4] often venture from Versailles. The interaction between exhibition commissioners and curators took on its own momentum and lesser known resources were uncovered and tapped.

As objects became available to the exhibition, preliminary scripting was undertaken. Pieces were categorized, documented and placed within the context of the exhibition themes: Louis XIV the man, Louis XIV the patron, and Louis XIV and Louisiana. They were evaluated by the criteria of historic significance, artistic importance, and symbolic value.

As the interrelationships of objects became apparent, the organizers recognized that together the materials of the exhibition related a fuller and clearer message than they did separately. It was rewarding to illustrate the Peace of the Pyrenees[5] with a handsome seventeenth-century Nevers platter,[6] thereby joining history, technology and art. It was significant to reunite Sébastien Le Clerc's engraved plate of the construction of the Louvre colonnade[7] with an original seventeenth-century impression pulled from it. Associating documents, paintings and decorative arts brought life and insight to austere and forbidding personalities and events of the past. An additional sense of discovery came from the unearthing and study of several previously obscure seventeenth-century treasures. As a result, Louis XIV, his court, his Louisiana colony, and his times have emerged in a revealing human dimension.

In February, 1983, the exhibition script and object selection were completed. During the following six months they were refined and this catalogue was prepared from the contributions of French and American curators and the staff of the

Louisiana State Museum. Catalogue essays were written by an international selection of scholars. In a remarkably short period, the Sun King has shrugged off a cocoon of time, and an American audience will have the opportunity of meeting an historic personality who has contributed significantly to their own cultural heritage.

The exhibition reveals the king to have been a very hard worker at the "craft of kingship," never depending on a first minister as had his predecessors. He assumed control of government upon the death of Cardinal Mazarin[9] and never released it. His strength of character was such that he could attract the best administrative minds he could locate and employ them in developing and serving his government.[10] Many branches of French civil service today have descended from offices created during his reign.

Louis XIV was the first king to centralize and administer the arts in modern times. The arts were harnessed in the service of the state through the creation of the Royal Academy of Painting and Sculpture[11] and the French Academy in Rome,[12] which trained artists to serve the Bâtiments du roi (or Department of Works) in creating architectural masterpieces, their settings and decor for the crown. Certain aspects of the fine and decorative arts became industries. France, formerly an importer of Italian and other luxury goods, became an exporter of its own national products and design. French tapestries and French furniture achieved world renown and imitation. Paris became a center of fashion and arbiter of taste and retained this preeminence until the twentieth century.

An official style came into being, which is called Baroque Classicism or the Classical Baroque, and it completed the break with the French medieval past in the visual arts. Its seeds had begun to sprout during the reign of Louis XIII, particularly in painting. Both Poussin[13] and Vouet[14] had integrated aspects of ancient Rome and the Renaissance into their creations.

Under the influence of Le Brun,[15] a tireless administrator and designer, these were amalgamated into all the arts, encompassing even architecture and sculpture. We see the influence of the Classical Baroque in the imperious monuments of the nineteenth century and the hotel lobbies of

LOUIS XIV WAS THE FIRST KING TO CENTRALIZE AND ADMINISTER THE ARTS IN MODERN TIMES

today.

When the king built, he did it on a grander scale than any of his contemporaries. The construction of Versailles, of the colonnade of the Louvre, of the Invalides, of the great gates of Paris and myriad other projects were undertaken during his reign. They were used to impress. The French took pride in these achievements, and foreign powers, through their embassies, were awed. Other monarchs adopted the "Louis Style" at courts throughout Europe for several succeeding generations.

Music and dance gained in importance. The works of Lulli, Couperin[16] and others are played today. Ballet began to assume its modern classical form, and in his youth the king himself appeared on the stage.[17] Opera was codified and directed toward its triumphant nineteenth-century expressions. Royal academies of dance and music guided these art forms in their seventeenth-century developments and trained performers and creators.

French literature and language made enormous advances, governed by the forty members of the French Academy and the Academy of Inscriptions and Belles-Lettres. The legacy we have received from the Sun King's patronage includes the works of Racine[18] and of Molière[19] and a host of others. Even some idea of the appearance of their stage productions and court spectacles can be judged from drawings that were saved by the office of the menu plaisirs.[20]

The sciences, not so well defined or subdivided as in our times, advanced from alchemy to research with the king's creation and support of the Academy of Sciences and the Observatory of Paris[21] and the programming of the Royal Botanical Gardens.[22] Cartographers were able to couple astronomical observations and discoveries with ground measurements to increase enormously their knowledge of virtually all parts of the globe.[23] Their efforts were occasionally used for political ends.[24]

The Sun King created a nation. His early wars were concerned with establishing natural and defensible frontiers. His later wars attempted to expand the French sphere of influence, and his power, real or imaginary, frightened smaller European states into a variety of coalitions against

THE SUN KING: LOUIS XIV AND THE NEW WORLD

him. His centralization of administration reduced the power of the provinces and directed French thought toward the birth of a national consciousness, something that would not happen in the neighboring German and Italian city states and principalities until the nineteenth century. The king's high degree of visibility through his monuments and daily ceremonies gave this new nationalism a natural focal point in his person.

Comfortable with the defensible French frontiers established by the Peace of Nymegen ending the Dutch War,[25] the Sun King began to turn an expansionist eye on the New World. Always jealous of the Spanish and Portuguese empires, French monarchs had made previous efforts to claim, explore, and settle in Brazil, in French Florida (actually South Carolina), and various Caribbean islands.

The most successful French effort in the Western Hemisphere had been made in Canada. There a colonial population had built respectable forts, cities, ports, and farms. Second and third generations of colonial families had developed New World pride, identities, and fortunes. An excellent trade had been established in furs and timber, but the French had enjoyed little success in mining, particularly of precious metals. Spanish gold had captured the minds and imaginations of all Europe. It was from a Canadian base that the French would push southward, ever closer to Mexico, the American Southwest, and El Dorado.

The Church, and particularly the Jesuits, took a leading and active part in the push southward and westward. Charged with the conversion and religious instruction of the Native Americans, this mission served as justification for many expeditions of exploration and conquest. Because of the Gallican Liberties, which placed the king at the head of church administration in France, these religious explorers preached in the name of Christ and claimed in the name of Louis.

The earlier forays of the 1670s passed through the areas below the Great Lakes into the "Illinois Country" and the "Arkansas," named for their aboriginal inhabitants, or westward across the upper Great Plains.[26] They established missions and fortified outposts that were of particular value in checking the westward expansion of British colonies from New England and the Atlantic seaboard. They established trade and sought mines. Lead, copper, and other minerals appeared, but El Dorado kept his shining face still further to the south and west, and spoke Spanish, not French.

Although European wars intervened, French attention always reverted to expanded New World exploration and exploitation. In the late 1670s La Salle obtained the king's permission,[27] and descended the full length of the Mississippi. He arrived at the Gulf of Mexico in early 1682, claiming the entire river valley for the French crown and naming it "Louisiana" in the Sun King's honor. La Salle's second great voyage, by sea, was a failure. The mouth of the Mississippi was not relocated by a water route. The early maps of La Salle's discoveries placed the mouth of the river too far west or were mutilated,[28] perhaps for political purposes in order to extend the French claim ever westward, ever closer to the gold and silver of Spanish Mexico.

The War of the League of Augsburg prevented further exploration in the later 1680s.[29] Shortly thereafter, members of the colonial Le Moyne family[30] began their exploits, successfully finding the elusive gulf outlet of the river, exploring the lower Mississippi Valley, dotting the landscape with French names, and founding the first permanent European settlements.

The last years of the Sun King's life were taken up by the War of the Spanish Succession[31] and its aftermath. Unable to bear the expenses of maintaining or developing his namesake colony, the Sun King assigned it by letters patent to Antoine Crozat,[32] in whose hands it remained until after the monarch's death.

Louis XIV would have been astonished and intrigued by the blast furnaces of Gary, the skyscrapers of Chicago, the ragtime of St. Louis, and the jazz of New Orleans. Yet he and his times are intimately linked with all of them. Of the thirteen states carved from this vast territory after it was sold by Napoleon, only one retains the original designation "Louisiana." But hundreds of place names recall the French explorers of the seventeenth century and their followers during the succeeding three quarters of a century. Thirteen states developed from the colonies of England and thirteen states were made from the single colony of the Sun King. If America looks to her founding kings, Louis XIV must be recognized.

Although Louis XIV was a valiant military leader, none of his wars ended in unqualified victory. Warfare was an integral part of diplomacy and nearly continuous throughout the seventeenth century. Able early generals resisted the king's efforts to be his own commander-in-chief and his efforts to provide chains of command and overall direction to military operations. Those who came up in the ranks to replace the Condés and the Turennes seem to have had neither the fire nor the genius of these old war horses. One shining star appeared in the person of Vauban, who made important contributions in military engineering, offensive and defense fortifications,[33] and technical concepts, some of which served until the twentieth century.

With little happening in Spain, despite its New World gold, France was *de facto* the largest and most powerful of the Western European nations. Unchecked, Louis XIV and his ministers would have crushed the Dutch whose burgeoning commerce they envied, and done it garbed in the moralistic cloak of the Catholic Counter-Reformation. Every French effort, however, was checked by Protestant alliances that included some uneasy Catholic participants. These alliances were the nemesis of the Sun King. Seldom invading French territory, they pecked away at its flanks on all sides. Louis XIV, perhaps because his power was so frightening, was never able to conclude successful alliances himself. France was isolated in every major conflict. Even during the War of the Spanish Succession, France supported Spain rather than vice versa.

Late in the Sun King's reign these wars drained the national coffers and France verged on bankruptcy, although during an earlier period Colbert had managed to balance the French budget. To face those allied against him, the king fielded the largest armies ever seen in Europe and paid enormous military costs. He sent an alleged 55,000 pounds of gold and silver from the royal residences to the smelters and asked the nobility to follow his example. Even this was not enough. The system of taxation, which took from those least able to afford it, coupled with bad weather, poor crops, and resultant near-starvation, had a crushing effect on the national morale. Despite brilliant beginnings, neither the Sun King nor his reign can be considered successful from a military standpoint.

AS HE GREW OLDER THE SUN KING BECAME DEVOUT, CONCERNED WITH THE SALVATION OF A SOUL THAT HAD ENJOYED A PROFLIGATE YOUTH

The king dealt with religion awkwardly. Despite his youthful association with the worldly Cardinal Mazarin, he paid little more than lip service to the French Church until well into middle age. As he grew older the Sun King became devout, concerned with the salvation of a soul that had enjoyed a profligate youth. The traditional Gallican Liberties allowed the Sun King great freedom from Rome in naming French prelates, and his diplomatic relations with the papacy were not always the best.[34] Internally, Jansenism, Quietism, and Molinism split the French Church. The Jesuit faction triumphed on the surface. Jansenism was condemned as Calvinism in Catholic clothing, and the famed convent at Port-Royal was razed.[35] Such moves inspired passive resistance among the devout, and Louis left more Jansenists in France than he had found at the beginning of his reign.

His warlike attitudes toward Protestant nations and his treatment of Protestants at home did little to endear the Sun King to Northern Europe. And in the South, even the pope considered the overzealous Edict of Fontainebleau (revoking the religious freedoms granted by the Edict of Nantes) to be more harmful than effective. He was proven right by the mass departure from France of valuable citizens who had contributed substantially to the development of the economy and the advancement of industries and trades at a time when the country could ill afford their loss. But the king had the courage of his convictions, or of what he took to be his convictions, and the majority of his recorded contemporaries were in support of his stance.

Louis XIV was carefully raised to be a king by Anne d'Autriche[36] and Cardinal Mazarin, and he took kingship as his divine right very seriously. He reigned for over seventy years, living his life as a public symbol of his office. He learned sacrifice early, when, as part of the Peace of the Pyrennes, he was married to Marie-Thérèse d'Autriche[37] instead of his heart's desire, Marie-Anne Mancini.

The young king adopted the sun as his personal symbol[38] shortly after his marriage. He likened it to a monarch attended by a court of stars reflecting its

176

light. He wrote of "equal and just distribution" of that light, its "perpetual and regular movement" and its "constant and invariable course" which made it "the most dazzling and the most beautiful image" a prince could choose and one to remind a ruler of his duties.

The Sun King delighted the French, who adulated him as a near-divinity, inspiring a popular personal loyalty that is difficult to imagine or comprehend in today's society. He ruled alone, but with the advice of councils. The splendor of his château at Versailles was open to the public day and night, few rooms were not on view. He rose in the morning in public ceremony and retired each evening in the same manner. He conducted his own death as he had led his life, as a public pageant.[39]

The exhibition *The Sun King: Louis XIV and the New World* has been shaped to provide both an aesthetic and humanistic experience to Americans separated from the Sun King by space and time. It gives a glimpse of the character and accomplishments of a unique and complex man. If Louis XIV did not say "L'Etat c'est moi," he should have. ∎

NOTES

The following notes take the form of citations to works which appear in the exhibition to which the reader is referred for fuller information.

1. Cat. 149, *Courses de Testes et de Bague Faittes par le Roy et par les Princes et Seigneurs de sa Cour en l'Année 1662*, hand-painted book, Bibliothèque Municipale de Versailles.
2. Cat. 239 and 240, *Peace of Utrecht* with (respectively) England and Prussia, manuscripts, Archives of the Ministère des Relations Extérieures.
3. Cat. 14, *Armand Jean du Plessis, Duke and Cardinal of Richelieu*, oil on canvas, Musée du Louvre.
4. Cat. 209, *Louis XIV King of France and of Navarre*, oil on canvas, Musée National du Château de Versailles.
5. Cat. 25, *Nuptial Chant for the Marriage of the King* and *Treaty of Peace Between the Crowns of France and Spain with the Marriage Contract of the King*, bound in one printed volume, archives of the Ministère des relations extérieures.
6. Cat. 22, *Round Platter*, faïence, Musée National de Céramique.
7. Cat. 97, *Representation of the Machines That Served to Lift the Two Large Stones That Cover the Pediment of the Principal Entrance of the Louvre*, engraved copper, Musée du Louvre.
8. Cat. 96, *Representation of the Machines That Served to Lift the Two Large Stones That Cover the Pediment of the Principal Entrance of the Louvre*, etching, Musée Carnavalet.
9. Cat. 19, *Jules, Cardinal Mazarin*, oil on canvas, Musée National du Château de Versailles.
10. Cat. 38, *Jean-Baptiste Colbert*, oil on canvas, Musée National du Château de Versailles and Cat. 41, *Chancellor Séguier*, marble, Musée du Louvre.
11. Cat. 87, *Establishment of the Royal Academy of Painting and Sculpture*, printed document, Archives Nationales.
12. Cat. 86, *Draft of "Statutes and Rules That the King Wishes and Orders to be Observed in the Academy – That his Majesty has Resolved to Establish in the City of Rome,"* manuscript, Archives Nationales.
13. Cat. 204, *Saint John Baptizing*, and Cat. 205, *The Young Pyrrhus Saved*, both oil on canvas, both Musée du Louvre.
14. Cat. 11, *Louis XIII Between "France" and "Navarre,"* oil on canvas, Musée du Louvre and Cat. 16, *Louis XIII, Louis XIV enfant, Anne d'Autriche and Monsieur*, tapestry, Mobilier National.
15. Cat. 103, *Charles Le Brun*, marble, Musée du Louvre; Cat. 167, *Visit of Louis XIV to the Gobelins*, tapestry, Mobilier National and Cat. 203, *Jesus Carrying His Cross*, oil on canvas, Musée du Louvre.
16. Cat. 154, *Charles Couperin and the Daughter of the Painter*, oil on canvas, Musée National du Château de Versailles.
17. Cat. 156 and 157, *Costumes for "War" and a "Fury,"* both gouache on vellum, both Musée Carnavalet.
18. Cat. 158, *Jean Racine*, oil on canvas, Musée National du Château de Versailles.
19. Cat. 159, *Jean-Baptiste Poquelin, Called Molière*, oil on canvas, Musée National du Château de Versailles.
20. Cat. 161, *Scene of Glory or Transfiguration*; Cat. 162, *Festival on Water* and Cat. 163, *Theatre Scene*, all black stone, ink and wash on paper, all Archives Nationales.
21. Cat. 70, *The Establishment of the Academy of Sciences and the Observatory*, oil on canvas, Musée National du Château de Versailles.
22. Cat. 83, *Declaration of the King to Have the Experiments in the Royal Botanical Gardens Continued*, printed document, Archives of the Ministère des Relations Extérieures.
23. Cat. 72, *The Terrestrial Globe Represented in Two Hemisphere Plans*, hand-colored engraved map, Louisiana State Museum.
24. Cat. 238, *Maps and General and Specific Descriptions Regarding Knowledge of Events of the Times on the Subject of the Succession of the Crown of Spain in Europe, in Asia, Africa and America, Addressed and Dedicated to His Catholic Majesty Philip V* (the "De Fer Atlas"), book, Louisiana State Museum.
25. Cat. 53 and 54, *Peace of Nymegen* with (respectively) Holland and Spain, manuscripts, Archives of the Ministère des Relations Extérieures.
26. Cat. 214, *Map of the New Discoveries That the Reverend Jesuit Fathers Made in 1672* (that were) *Continued by Reverend Father Jacques Marquette of the Same Company, Accompanied by Some French in the Year 1673*, manuscript, Bibliothèque Nationale.
27. Cat. 216, *Permission to the Sieur de La Salle to Discover the Western Part of New France*, manuscript, Archives Nationales.
28. Cat. 220, *America Settentrionale*, printed map, Louisiana State Museum, and Cat. 219, *Map of Louisiana in North America From New France to the Gulf of Mexico, Upon Which are Described the Lands Which the Sieur de La Salle Discovered . . . .*, manuscript (mutilated), Bibliothèque Nationale.
29. Cat. 222 and 223, *Peace of Ryswick* with (respectively) England and the Empire, manuscripts, archives of the Ministère des relations extérieures.
30. Cat. 224, *Pierre Le Moyne, Sieur d'Iberville* and Cat. 228, *Jean-Baptiste Le Moyne, Sieur de Bienville*, both Coll. Le Moyne de Martigny.
31. Cat. 237, *Philippe de France, Duc d'Anjou*, oil on canvas, Musée National du Château de Versailles.
32. Cat. 242, *Antoine Crozat, Marquis de Chatel*, oil on canvas, Musée National du Château de Versailles.
33. Cat. 52, *Fortifications*, engraving, Louisiana State Museum.
34. Cat. 63, *The Pompous and Magnificent Entrance of Flavio, Cardinal Chigi, Lateran Legate in France . . . .*, engraving and etching, Musée Carnavalet.
35. Cat. 65, *Jacqueline-Marie, Mère Angélique Arnauld*, oil on canvas, Musée du Louvre.
36. Cat. 12, *Anne d'Autriche, Queen of France and of Navarre*, oil on canvas, Musée National du Château de Versailles.
37. Cat. 26, *Marie-Thérèse d'Autriche, Queen of France and of Navarre*, oil on canvas, Musée National du Château de Versailles.
38. Cat. 1, *Apollo Mask*, bronze doré, Musée de la Marine.
39. Cat. 208, *Louis XIV Crowned by Glory Between Abundance and Peace*, oil on canvas, Musée National du Château de Versailles and Cat. 212, *Last Words of King Louis XIV)Spoken) to King Louis XV, His Great-Grandson*, printed document, reproduced from the collections of the Bibliothèque Nationale.

LENDERS TO THE EXHIBITION

Anonymous Private Collectors
Archives Nationales de France, Paris
Bibliothèque Historique de la Ville de Paris
Bibliothèque Municipale de la Ville de Versailles
Bibliothèque Nationale de France, Paris
Domaine de Vaux-le-Vicomte, Maincy
Monsieur le Comte Jacques-Pierre LeMoyne de Martigny, Maincy
Louisiana Museum Foundation, New Orleans
Louisiana State Museum, New Orleans
Manufacture Nationale de Sèvres
Metropolitan Museum of Art, New York
Ministère de la Culture (Direction du Patrimoine Mobilier), Paris
Ministère des Relations Extérieures (Archives), Paris
Mobilier National, Paris
Musée de l'Armée, Paris
Musée des Arts Décoratifs, Paris
Musée Bricard, Paris
Musée Carnavalet, Paris
Musée de la Céramique de la Ville de Rouen
Musée de la Chasse et de la Nature, Paris
Musée du Louvre, Paris
Musée de la Marine, Paris
Musée LeSecq des Tournelles de la Ville de Rouen
Musée National de Céramique, Sèvres
Musée National du Château de Versailles
Musée National de la Légion d'Honneur et des Ordres de Chevalerie, Paris
Service Historique de la Marine, Vincennes
Monsieur le Comte Patrice de Vogüé, Maincy

A NOTE ON GALLERY CHANGES AND OBJECT CONSERVATION

Through the generosity of the lenders, many rare and fragile pieces appear in "The Sun King: Louis XIV and the New World." Therefore, not all objects that appear in this catalogue will be found in the exhibition galleries at any one time. International standards governing the display of light-sensitive and fragile materials mandate that exposure time be limited. In some instances, lending institutions were unable to release objects in excess of certain periods. For these reasons, selected objects are replaced with comparable pieces every ninety days. Pages are regularly rotated in exhibition cases and galleries. In this way, the exhibition remains complete in itself at all times, and the catalogue provides an even broader overview and record. Perhaps more important, fragile and light-sensitive objects are placed under the least possible stress in order to assure their preservation for future audiences.

Catalogue 1

THE ROYAL ICONOGRAPHY

he symbol that I adopted and that you see all around you represents the duties of a Prince and inspires me always to fulfill them. I chose for an emblem the Sun which, according to the rules of this art [heraldry], is the noblest of all, and which, by its unique quality, by the brightness that surrounds it, by the light it lends to the other stars that constitute, after a fashion, its court, by the equal and just distribution of this light to all regions of the world, by the universal good it does, endlessly promoting life, joy, and growth, by its perpetual and regular movement, by its constant and invariable course, is assuredly the most dazzling and the most beautiful image of the monarch.

— LOUIS XIV

1. APOLLO MASK
Unidentified artist
17th century
Copper/bronze *doré*
39-3/8" (dia.) x 3-1/2" (100 x 9 cm.)

Loaned by the Musée de la Marine / 49.0A.1

Louis XIV adopted the Sun as his special symbol in the early 1660s. He personally set the date at 1662, on the occasion of the famed carrousel of that year. After this time, many sun symbols were used to represent the king. The mask of Apollo, ancient God of Light, became a favorite and was rendered in many media.

This exceptional mask was thought, during the disbursement of collections at the time of the French Revolution, to be an element of marine *décor*, although modern analysis suggests otherwise. In all probability it was used as an architectural *trophée* (see #125 and #126) and may have been employed in the decoration of one of the royal houses or garden pavilions.

French art during the Sun King's reign tended toward the principles of Classicism. The double system of bilateral symmetry of the face linked with radial symmetry of the sunburst give the mask a balanced, calm grandeur.
VLG

2. MONOGRAM OF INTERLACED L's

Unidentified blacksmith
Late 17th or early 18th century
Wrought iron
14-1/8" x 11-3/8" (36 x 29 cm.)

Loaned by the Musée Lesecq des Tournelles of the City of Rouen / INV 121

Royal initials in the form of stylized monograms are traditional symbols of French monarchs. Mirrored interlacing L's in single or multiple pairs, sometimes surmounted by a crown, were used by Louis XIV and by his descendants. They appear on bookbindings, carved in paneling, wrought in iron, and in other media.

These interlaced letters were probably used as the motif or the central medallion of a balcony or gate crown. The beautifully handled crossing iron elements, drawn from calligraphy, are the expression of great technical prowess.
CV/VLG

3. PORTIERE DE MARS (The Royal Arms)

Gobelins after Charles Le Brun (1619-90)
Ca. 1670
Wool and silk, 20 threads per inch (8 per cm.)
129-7/8" x 100-3/8" (330 x 255 cm.)

Loaned by the Département des Objets d'Art of the Musée du Louvre / OA 5403

The Sun King ordered the creation of this tapestry, a door hanging, to be used in the royal residences. Its complex symbolism centers on shields with the arms of Bourbon lilies (*fleurs-de-lys*) representing France and interlocking chains standing for Navarre, his two kingdoms. Below them is suspended the badge of the Order of the Holy Spirit. The arms are flanked by military *trophées* of weapons, flags, and standards. Mars and Minerva are seated below with instruments of war and cornucopias of abundance and peace. The globe between the figures is enlightened by the Sun Mask shining above the arms. The whole is surmounted by a crown and placed in a *trompe l'oeil* architectonic frame.

The design for this portiere was made by Charles Le Brun when he was engaged in the service of Nicolas Fouquet at Vaux-le-Vicomte in 1659 and 1660. It was woven several times, first at Maincy for Fouquet, who was at that time Superintendent of Finance, and later at the Gobelins for the king, where it continued to be woven until the end of his reign.
AL/VLG

Catalogue 3

4. EQUESTRIAN STATUE OF LOUIS XIV

Jean Gobert the Younger (active 1685-1723)
17th century
Bronze
29-1/2" x 33-1/8" (75 x 84 cm.)

Loaned by the Département des Sculptures of the Musée du Louvre / MR 1623

In the tradition of the Italian Renaissance, the Sun King was often portrayed in armor on horseback for monumental bronze sculptures to decorate public squares and commemorate victories (see #93). In this statuette the rearing horse not only provided the sculptor with a difficult technical challenge but also suggests a more dynamic, baroque passion than the trotting horses typical of classical sculpture.
VLG/GB

Catalogue 2

Catalogue 4

5. APOLLO TAPESTRY

Attributed to Beauvais, after Jean Bérain the Elder
(1640-1711)
Ca. 1690-1700
Wool and silk 20 threads per inch (8 per cm.)
136-5/8" x 107-1/8" (347 x 272 cm.)

Loaned by the Mobilier National / GMTT-411

Apollo, god and personification of light, poetry, music, prophecy, healing, and manly beauty, was one of the most important symbols of the Sun King. Isolated elements of Apollo's iconography, such as the lyre or laurel wreath, were also used to represent Louis XIV, who had a strong personal interest in music. The ideal physique of Apollo of mythology implied the many aspects of perfection that apologists wished to attribute to the king. Bérain was also a designer of theatrical settings and ephemeral *décor* (see #161).

Just as Charles Le Brun characterized and dominated the first period of the decorative style of Louis XIV, Bérain symbolized the second: "Nothing was made," wrote Mariette, "of any sort whatever, without its being in his style, without him having made the designs."

The famous tapestry suite of "Grotesques," on a yellow ground, woven at Beauvais at the end of the seventeenth century, was directly taken from Bérain's engraved work, as was the suite of "The Great Gods," of which the Mobilier National possesses "Mars" in addition to this "Apollo."

At the feet of the statue of the god, musicians in costumes drawn from the Italian commedia dell'arte are grouped; on their side, medallions evoke (on the right) the story of the poet Arion. The architecture, with caryatids, pilasters, and balustrades arranged to give fleeting perspectives, emphasized by multicolored marbles, heavy draperies, and floral garlands, recalls opera and ballet settings which, from 1680 onward, Bérain was charged with executing for the Royal Academy of Music. In this capacity in 1681 he created the costumes and scenery of the ballet "Impatience," in which the king, who danced quite well, appeared as Apollo.

Although still subject to the laws of rigid symmetry, the compositions of Bérain presage, by their elements of fantasy, the art of the eighteenth century. New elements make their

Catalogue 5

appearance, such as shells and dolphin heads gushing sheets of water. Figures are integrated into groups that are above all ornamental and no longer narrative: tapestry retrieved the decorative character that it had grown away from over the course of the preceding decades.
JC/ID/VLG

Catalogue 6

6. APOLLO CROWNED BY MINERVA
Noel Coypel the Elder (1628-1707)
Ca. 1663 (?)
Oil on canvas
84-1/4" x 40-5/8" (214 x 115 cm.)

Loaned by the Département des Peintures of the Musée du Louvre / INV 3461

This picture was ordered for the small apartments of the king in the Tuileries Palace (destroyed), and is a pendant to "Apollo Crowned by Victory" now at the Louvre. A cloud-borne Minerva, goddess of war, wisdom, and the arts, carries a palm of peace and a laurel crown, traditional attribute of Apollo, which she is about to place on his brow. The idealized god of light and music, poetry, prophecy, healing and manly beauty strongly resembles portraits of the young Louis XIV (see #17 and #20).

Coypel's work is noted for its reflection of the classicism of his first teacher Poussin. Closed form and linear clarity characterize "Apollo Crowned by Minerva." The figure of Apollo recalls ancient Roman classical statuary, to which an idealized portrait head of the young Sun King has been grafted.
VLG

7. LOUIS XIV AND HIS FIRST NURSE, LADY MARIE LONGUET DE LA GIRAUDIÈRE
Unidentified artist
Ca. 1638
Oil on canvas
33-1/8" x 26-3/4" (84 x 68 cm.)

Loaned by the Musée National du Château de Versailles / MV 5272

Louis XIV was born at the Château of St. Germain-en-Laye near Paris in September, 1638. He entered the world to great ceremonial rejoicing, assuring the continuation of the French throne in the Bourbon dynasty. Like most royal and aristocratic infants, he was suckled by a wet nurse — an honored position at court. This earliest painted portrait of the future Sun King depicts the elaborate lace-trimmed garments of both baby and nurse. The royal infant is swaddled and wears the ribbon of the Order of the Holy Spirit (see #56). The *mémoires* of the Royal Academy of Painting and Sculpture report that a portrait of the King at the age of eight days was ordered from the Beaubruns. Another version of this picture bears a Beaubrun signature and the date 1638.
CC/VLG

YOUTH, 1638-1659

Catalogue 7

184

Catalogue 8

8. ADORATION OF THE SHEPHERDS

Charles Le Brun (1619-90)
1689
Oil on canvas
59-1/2" x 84-5/8" (151 x 215 cm.)

Loaned by the Département des Peintures of the Musée du Louvre / INV 2879

Royal propagandists consciously paralleled the birth of Louis XIV to the Nativity. This painting, created many years later, was ordered by the Sun King personally.

Throughout his long career Charles Le Brun remained a favorite artist and designer of the Sun King. "Adoration of the Shepherds" is one of several religious works ordered for the royal collections during the last years of the artist's life. This preference for religious subjects may reflect the king's growing interest in salvation encouraged by Madame de Maintenon.
VLG

9. LOUIS XIV *ENFANT*

Unidentified artist
Ca. 1643
Bronze on marble socle
23-5/8" with socle (60 cm.)

Loaned by the Département des Sculptures of the Musée du Louvre / RF 2508

Although formally crowned with laurels and draped *à l'antique*, this portrait bust is among the most casual and lifelike presentations of the royal infant. Louis XIV's childhood days as dauphin were near an end; the bust was created at about the time of his father's death.

The bust has been traditionally attributed to Jacques Sarrazin (1592-1660), the best Parisian sculptor during the reign of Louis XIII. After a long Roman sojourn, he established with François Mansart and his relative, the painter Simon Vouet, the bases of French classical art, oscillating between the poles of the Italian baroque and respect for ancient art. It is known that Sarrazin executed for the queen a bust cast in bronze of Louis XIV at a very young age, and that she had placed it in her apartments at the Palais-Royal. This commission may have been linked to the project of decoration for the Pont-au-Change, for which Sarrazin prepared a maquette about 1643.

However, it is also known that the sculptor and goldsmith Jean Varin (1607-72) also made a very fine bronze bust of the young king. In 1643 Varin, as chief of the Royal Mint at Moulin, executed a large medal commemorating the accession of Louis XIV and his mother as regent. In the medal the king is shown in the same pose, same costume, and same hair style as the bust. This image was used on all the royal *écus* minted in 1643 and 1644. An analysis of the casting does not assist in determining the authorship, as both artists are known to have used the same founder, Henri Perlan, who was the best in Paris at the time.
GB/VLG

Catalogue 9

Catalogue 11

11. LOUIS XIII BETWEEN "FRANCE" AND "NAVARRE"
Simon Vouet (1590-1649)
Ca. 1640
Oil on canvas
64-1/4" x 60-5/8" (163 x 154 cm.)

Loaned by the Département des Peintures of the Musée du Louvre / INV 8506

Louis XIII (1601-43), father of the Sun King, died in 1643 leaving the throne to his four-year-old heir. Sickly and ill-favored, Louis XIII governed through his powerful prime minister, Cardinal Richelieu (see #14), who was delighted with the birth of the dauphin in 1638, answering the prayers of the king and queen after two decades of childless marriage. Louis XIII spent little time with his firstborn and even less with the queen, who had charge of the infant Sun King and proved to be a zealous mother.

The painter Simon Vouet was a favorite of Louis XIII, and gave the king art lessons; under his tutelage, Louis XIII became a competent pastellist. The two female figures in the painting are personifications of the two kingdoms ruled by the Bourbon dynasty. A second version of this picture exists in the collections of the Musée National du Château de Versailles. Vouet is credited with firmly transmitting the classicizing influence of Raffaelo Sanzio (1483-1520) into French art of the seventeenth century.
VLG

Catalogue 10

10. ANN D'AUTRICHE AND LOUIS XIV (obverse) and CHURCH OF THE VAL-DE-GRÂCE (reverse)
Attributed to Jean Varin (1604-72)
1638
Silver
3-5/8" dia. (9.1 cm.)

Loaned by the Cabinet des Médailles of the Bibliothèque National / SR-3073

Among her personal projects, Queen Anne d'Autriche (see #12) was patroness of the construction of the Church of the Val-de-Grâce in Paris. Symbolically, she had the cornerstone of the structure, begun in 1638, laid by her infant son, Louis XIV. She built the church in thanksgiving, fulfilling a vow to do so if her childless marriage was blessed with progeny.
VLG

Catalogue 12

12. ANNE D'AUTRICHE, QUEEN OF FRANCE AND NAVARRE
Unidentified artist
17th century
Oil on canvas
54" x 43-3/4" (137 x 111 cm.)

Loaned by the Musée National du Château de Versailles / MV-7074

After a frivolous youth, Anne d'Autriche (1601-66) became a devoted mother with the birth of Louis XIV in 1638. She was the daughter of Philip III (1578-1621) and Margaret of Styria and sister of Philip IV, king of Spain (1605-65) with whom France was at war when the Sun King was born.

By fulfiling the most important obligation of a royal princess — providing an heir to the throne — she gained respect and acceptance as part of the reigning dynasty, whereas previously she had been mistrusted as a suspicious foreigner. She made the infant Sun King the center of her universe, suppressing all else, including her second son Philippe, traditionally known as Monsieur (1640-1701), see #134), in the interest of the future monarch.

Her poor personal relationship with her husband Louis XIII, whom she had married in 1615, made her suspicious of the officers of his government and members of his family. During the regency following his death, she made Cardinal Mazarin (see #19) her powerful first minister. Historic gossip reports him to have been her lover or secret husband as well.
CC/VLG/JM

13. THE CHÂTEAU OF ST. GERMAIN-EN-LAYE WITH LOUIS XIV AND TURENNE IN THE FOREGROUND

Adam-François Van der Meulen (*ca.* 1632-90)
1669
Oil on canvas
22-1/8" dia. (56 cm.)

Loaned by the Musée National du Château de Versailles / MV-2144

The Château of St. Germain-en-Laye near Paris was the birthplace and childhood home of the Sun King. Here, protected, indulged, and fostered by a doting mother, he spent what may have been the happiest times of his life.

The painting was created when Louis XIV was 31 years old, just after the Peace of Aix-la-Chapelle (1668). The king's foreground companion is Henri de la Tour d'Auvergne, vicomte de Turenne (1611-75), one of the greatest French military leaders and strategists of the seventeenth century.
VLG

Catalogue 13

Catalogue 14

14. ARMAND JEAN DU PLESSIS, DUKE AND CARDINAL OF RICHELIEU

Philippe de Champaigne (1602-74)
Ca. 1635
Oil on canvas
87-3/8" x 61" (222 x 155 cm.)

Loaned by the Département des Peintures of the Musée du Louvre / INV 1136

Cardinal Richelieu (1585-1642), who achieved this ecclesiastic rank in 1622, was primary advisor to and first minister for Louis XIII, father of the Sun King. The cardinal died when Louis XIV was only four, reportedly not from the ailment but from the treatment to which he was subjected in an attempt to cure an anal fistula. Though Richelieu had little direct contact with the Sun King, the shaping that the cardinal gave to French administration and politics influenced Louis XIV and royal thinking for many decades after his demise. The magnificent and incisive portrait is among the best known of all seventeenth-century French paintings.

Champaigne was one of the first members of the Royal Academy of Painting and Sculpture, founded in 1648 (see #87). His personal mysticism was reinforced by his friendship with Jansenist leaders, and his youngest daughter became a nun at Port-Royal. Many of his works were painted for the Jansenist convent there.
VLG

187

15. MAXIMS OF STATE OR POLITICAL TESTAMENT OF THE EMMINENT ARMAND, CARDINAL DUKE OF RICHELIEU

Unidentified scribe
1639 (?)
13-1/4" x 9-1/2" x 1-1/4" (33.5 x 23.6 x 3 cm.)
closed

Loaned by the Archives of the Ministère des Relations Extérieures / MD France, Vol. 84

Prior to his death in 1642, Cardinal Richelieu wrote out his philosophy and achievements as a reference work for future leaders. This autobiographical "political testament" was published in the seventeenth century and avidly read by civil servants and aristocracy alike.

This volume was part of the personal archive of the cardinal, sent upon his death to Marie-Madeleine de Vignerot, duchesse d'Aiguillon, his niece and heir. These materials remained in the family until 1710, when Jean-Baptiste Colbert, marquis de Torcy (1655-1746), had them transferred to the Louvre on the order of the king in anticipation of the creation, in 1710, of the Repository for Foreign Affairs.

As opposed to the cardinal's *Mémoires*, which were meant for publication, the *Political Testament* was certainly conceived by Richelieu as a work destined only for Louis XIII. The cardinal, in poor health and fearing he would die well before the king, seems to have wanted to leave him a sort of manual of government.

The authenticity of the *Testament* has been disputed for many years, notably by Voltaire, who denied it any value. Montesquieu attributed it to the erudite Abbé de Bourzeis, who probably worked on Richelieu's papers and supervised the completion of this work, but who died before giving it a definitive review.

The publication by Hanotaux of the *Maxims and State Papers*, which served for the editing of the *Testament*, seems to establish its authenticity. It is incontestable that Richelieu, sick and bedridden, unable to use his right arm, turned to a staff of collaborators to write it, as he had done for the *Mémoires*. Louis André, author and editor of the most recent edition of the *Testament*, advances that a certain Father Joseph Le Clerc (1577-1638) was the head of this staff, since the work seems to have been abandoned after Father Joseph's death.

No original manuscript of the *Political Testament* is known, but seventeen copies from the seventeenth and eighteenth centuries are held in various libraries and archives. It is possible, although not likely, that other manuscripts are still in private hands. The known copies belong to two traditions. Fifteen of them seem to have been made from the example shown here. The seventeenth, at the Sorbonne, may perhaps be considered the oldest of all, since it includes some incomplete sections.

During the seventeenth and eighteenth centuries, the *Testament* was published or reprinted at least eighteen times. It has appeared three times in the nineteenth and twentieth centuries. MC/VLG

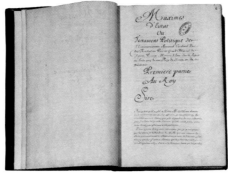

Catalogue 15

16. LOUIS XIII, LOUIS XIV *ENFANT*, ANNE D'AUTRICHE AND MONSIEUR

Savonnerie after Simon Vouet (1590-1649)
Woven in the studio of Pierre Dupont, 1643
Wool
88-5/8" x 88-5/8" (225 x 225 cm.)

Loaned by the Mobilier National / GOB 1335

Executed in the year of the death of Louis XIII, the tapestry is a remarkable symbol of the transfer of power and the continuation of the reign of the Bourbon dynasty.

To the left of the composition, King Louis XIII already belongs to history, the open book of which the figure of Fame holds before her. Shown with the attributes of Hercules, he transmits to his son a terrestrial globe, symbol of monarchial strength, which the young Louis XIV reaches to receive. Standing in an antique costume covered by a mantle strewn with *fleurs-de-lys*, the infant king leans on a group formed by his brother Philippe, duc d'Orleans, and his mother. Shown as Minerva, the queen dominates the right side of the composition. With a finger she designates the portrait of Louis XIII in the book, recalling the origin of her authority as regent.

The troubled events of the times, which are represented by the hydra trampled by the two kings, made such an affirmation of the monarchy necessary. This composition is not without relationship to the monument created by Simon Guillain between 1643 and 1647 at the end of the Pont-au-Change in Paris (later removed), where Louis XIII and Anne d'Autriche were sculpted in ceremonial robes presenting the young Louis XIV crowned by Fame, while the queen accepted the responsibilities of the regency.

Simon Vouet is traditionally considered the author of this composition. Protected by Louis XIII, from whom he received a pension and lodgings in the Louvre upon his return from Italy, he depicted the sovereign on several occasions and executed numerous tapestry cartoons for the Parisian manufactories.

The history of the Savonnerie tapestry works began in the early years of the seventeenth century, and with it truly began the history of carpet weaving in France. Founded by Henri IV, who established it in the galleries of the Louvre, the Manufactory of Carpets "in the fashion of Persia and the Levant" was augmented under the reign of Louis XIII by studios installed on the banks of the Seine in Paris, at the foot of the Chaillot Hill, in the buildings of a former soap factory. Called a *savonnerie* in French, the "soap factory" appellation remained attached to the site.

This high warp panel is among the rare examples surviving of the early Savonnerie works and was probably executed in the Louvre studios.
JC/ID/VLG

Catalogue 16

17. LOUIS XIV *ENFANT*
Unidentified artist
Ca. 1644
Oil on canvas
17-3/4" x 14-5/8" (45 x 37 cm.)

Loaned by the Musée National du Château de Versailles / MV 3439

The first sugar cane plantations were being established in the Caribbean Islands of the Antilles when this portrait was painted. Affairs of state, including the Sun King's education, were being handled by his mother, Anne d'Autriche, with the aid of her first minister, the able Cardinal Mazarin. The Thirty Years' War was drawing toward a conclusion, and the horrors of the Fronde were still a few years in the future. The picture is among the last to endow the Sun King with the innocence of childhood.
CC/VLG

Catalogue 18

Catalogue 17

18. AUGUSTUS BEFORE THE TOMB OF ALEXANDER
Sébastien Bourdon (1616-71)
Ca. 1660
Oil on canvas
43-3/4" x 54-3/4" (111 x 139 cm.)

Loaned by the Département des Peintures of the Musée du Louvre / INV 2810

This painting, eventually acquired by the Sun King, was painted during his youth. It depicts the moral, if apocryphal, lesson of one great ruler imbibing the wisdom of another by a mysterious process of graveside osmosis. Louis XIV was frequently compared to and shown as Caesar or Apollo, a theme of Alexandrian imagery. His most distinguished recent ancestor, grandfather Henri IV, set numerous examples for him to emulate.
VLG

189

Catalogue 19

19. CARDINAL MAZARIN
In the manner of Philippe de Champaigne
(1602-74)
Ca. 1650 (?)
Oil on canvas
55-1/8" x 46-1/8" (140 x 117 cm.)

Loaned by the Musée National du Château de
Versailles / MV 6062

Jules, Cardinal Mazarin (1602-61)
assumed the cardinal's hat upon
Richelieu's death in 1641, only months
before the death of Louis XIII. Anne
d'Autriche left virtually all governmental
functions in his hands during the
regency (1642-61), which ended with
his death. It is thought that they were
secretly married. Mazarin was charged
with directing the young king's
education and served as a father figure
for him to emulate. The cardinal guided
the royal family through the difficult
years of the Fronde (1648-54) and went
into a brief self-imposed exile (1651-53).
Mazarin used his immense fortune in the
interests of the king when necessary and
eventually gave it to Louis XIV, who
later returned it to the cardinal. Mazarin
introduced Jean-Baptiste Colbert (see
#38), a fiscal specialist on his own staff,
and recommended his talents to the
king. The cardinal's brilliant political
maneuvering set the example that the
Sun King attempted to emulate during
his personal reign (1661-1715).
CC/VLG

190

20. LOUIS XIV, VANQUISHER OF THE FRONDE

Unidentified artist
1652-61
Oil on canvas
65-3/8" x 56-1/4" (166 x 143 cm.)

Loaned by the Musée National du Château de Versailles / MV 8073

The weakness of Louis XIII as a ruler had left an open door for the family of his brother, Gaston d'Orléans (1608-60), to amass power. A segment of the nobility led by the ambitious Orléans attempted a revolt, known as the Fronde, during the minority of Louis XIV. This near civil war (1648-54) was successfully quashed by the faction of the reigning monarch led by Anne d'Autriche and Mazarin. The young king's restored authority was underlined by images portraying him as conquering hero. In this picture, he is shown in the guise of Jupiter with Vulcan's forge in the background.

Jupiter was the legendary god whose name meant "heavenly father." As a deity of the heavens he controlled weather and used thunderbolts as weapons. He was noted as the prime protector of the state in ancient Rome; generals brought him the spoils of war and magistrates made sacrifices to him.

In this picture, Louis XIV as Jupiter places his foot on a shield bearing a Medusa mask (see #150 and #151). Medusa was the best known of the Gorgons and was killed by Perseus, who gave her head to Athena. Consequently the hideous Medusa mask appeared on the shield of Athena and on other shields because of its power to frighten or petrify.

The forge recalls Vulcan, the mythical fire god, also associated with the Greek artisan-god Hephaestus. In this connotation, Vulcan is the protector of smiths and other craftsmen who employ fire to the good of mankind.

By combining all these references the picture may easily be interpreted as the Divine-Right King (heavenly father) trampling the Fronde (evil Medusa) and using fire (thunderbolts and forge) to enforce and rebuild the authority of the monarch for the good of the nation. Elaborate allegories of this sort are common in baroque art and drew on a long Western tradition. Educated

Catalogue 20

viewers were expected to recognize and understand allegories and their editorial statements. On occasion, patrons wrote out the symbolic content for very complex allegories that they wished artists to realize for them.
VLG/JM

21. LOUIS XIV ADOLESCENT, TRAMPLING THE FRONDE

After Gilles Guérin (ca. 1606-78)
Ca. 1654
Bronze
20-7/8" x 13" x 7-1/8" (53 x 33 x 18 cm.)

Loaned by the Musée Carnavalet / S. 3420

Paris was the scene of great unrest and support of the anti-Louis XIV movement during the Fronde (1648-54). After the revolt was defeated, Parisians were reminded of the young king's restored authority by a large marble placed in the courtyard of the Town Hall. The marble was eventually removed in 1689 as an unnecessary reminder of an unhappy time and replaced by another statue. Today it is located at Chantilly.

This small bronze was made about the same time the larger work was installed in Paris in 1654. Contemporary bronze reductions of large seventeenth-century works are rare and prized *objets d'art.*

It was to make honorable amends, to obtain the king's pardon for their participation in the Fronde that, in 1653, the provost and the sheriffs of Paris commissioned from Guérin a figure of the king trampling a hydra representing the revolt. On the socle, an engraved text accompanying the dedication recalled the visit the young king made to the municipal body in 1653. Louis XIV did not go back to the Town Hall until 1689, at which time he expressed his desire to see the statue removed. It was replaced by a bronze by Coysevox, which is today in the entrance court of the Musée Carnavalet in Paris.

This reduction has been somewhat simplified in detail in comparison to Guérin's large work. In his personal works Guérin oscillated between an attraction to movement, seen in this statute, and a realism without extremes, as seen in the tomb of Charles de la Vieuville and his wife (now in the Louvre). He expressed the hesitations of French sculpture in the face of the Italian baroque before it definitively took on the character of the classicism of Versailles.
FF/VLG

Catalogue 21

PEACE OF THE PYRENEES/ MARRIAGE OF THE KING (1659-1660)

22. ROUND PLATTER
Nevers, 1660-70
Tin-glazed earthenware (faïence)
19-7/8" dia. (50.5 cm.)

Loaned by the Musée National de Céramique / MNC 21576 / Gift of the Société des Amis du Musée, 1949

On November 7, 1659, the conclusion of the Peace of the Pyrenees put an end to the Franco-Spanish War begun in 1635. Negotiations had been conducted by Cardinal Mazarin (shown to the left) and Don Luis de Haro (at the right) on the Isle of Pheasants in the Bidassa, the river that was the western part of the frontier between the two countries. Spain submitted to important territorial concessions, while France pardoned the Grand Condé and Louis XIV was married to the Infanta Marie Thérèse, daughter of King Philip IV. The purse that Mazarin designates by a finger evokes the dowry of 500,000 écus that the Infanta was to bring to the French crown and the clause that Mazarin had skillfully foreseen to draw up, stipulating that nonpayment of this sum would cancel Marie Thérèse's renunciation of her rights to the Spanish throne. Mazarin knew that an exhausted Spain would not be able to pay this amount, and thus he laid the foundations for the War of Devolution (1667-68).

The depiction of a contemporary event is rare in faïence until the eighteenth century and particularly so at Nevers. "Historiated" décors represented biblical, mythological, and literary scenes or episodes drawn from ancient classical history. The date of the Peace of the Pyrenees as well as the style of the décor, notably the sprinkling of birds, flowering branches, and trophées of the genre de Savone, which ornament the lip, permit the dating of this platter in the decade of the 1660s.
EF/VLG

23. THE SWEARING OF THE PEACE BY THE TWO KINGS OF FRANCE AND SPAIN and THE ENTRY OF THE KING AND QUEEN INTO THEIR GOOD CITY OF PARIS, AUGUST 26, 1660
Nicolas de Larmessin II (Ca. 1638-94)
1661
Engraving
32-7/8" x 21-5/8" (83.6 x 55 cm.)

Loaned by the Musée Carnavalet / Almanach 1661 (G:20311)

As a result of the Peace of the Pyrenees, shown in the upper scene, Louis XIV was married to the Spanish crown princess or Infanta Marie-Thérèse d'Autriche as a part of Mazarin's foreign policy. Her official entry into the French capital is recorded in the lower register. Popular calendars or almanacs of this sort were illustrated with depictions of important events of the previous year. They often have a quickly executed "folk" character.
VLG

Catalogue 22

Catalogue 23

24. BUST OF LOUIS XIV
Unidentified artist
Ca. 1660
Plaster
39-3/8" x 31-1/2" (100 x 80 cm.)

Held at the Musée du Vieil-Zix; loaned by the Division du Patrimoine Mobilier of the Ministère de la Culture. Gift of Mlle. Marie d'Estienne de Sain-Jean, 1933.

The Sun King traveled to the Spanish border for the signing of the treaty of peace that ended the turmoil begun by the Fronde. France strengthened her position by annexing Roussillon and Artois and ending Spanish intervention in French affairs. As a sign of good faith, Spain offered the crown princess as bride to Louis XIV.

It has been recorded that the Sun King offered a bust to Aix-en-Provence as he passed through as a token of royal favor. After a disappearance of many years the bust has been recently rediscovered and restored. Tradition indicates the bust was given to André Estienne, who was president and treasurer-general of France in Provence from 1639 until his death in 1681. Historians at Aix-en-Provence record, however, that the king lodged at the hôtel of the Baron de Chateaurenard, nearby that of the Estienne de Saint-Jean family.
VLG/T

Catalogue 25

25. NUPTIAL CHANT FOR THE MARRIAGE OF THE KING and TREATY OF PEACE BETWEEN THE CROWNS OF FRANCE AND SPAIN WITH THE MARRIAGE CONTRACT OF THE KING
Various authors
1660
Full calf binding
14-1/2" x 9-1/2" (37 x 24 cm.) closed

Loaned by the Library of the Ministère des Relations Extérieures / 34-G-2

The bitter necessity of sacrificing personal interest to affairs of state was learned by the Sun King at the age of twenty-one. Marriage to his cousin Marie-Thérèse d'Autriche, Infanta of Spain, was negotiated in 1659 as an integral part of the Peace of the Pyrenees. On June 7, 1660, the French and Spanish delegates met again on the Isle of Pheasants to ratify the terms of the treaty and to celebrate the king's marriage.

Although there was great legitimate public interest in all events of the monarch's life, the Sun King often promoted such interest and documented his own career by fostering publication about it. For the safety of the book, it will be shown opened to various sections at different times during the exhibition.

The *Nuptial Chant for the Marriage of the King* was written by Hippolyte Jules Pilet de la Mesnardière (1610-63), who had been named to the French Academy in 1655. Pilet de la Mesnardière had studied medicine and became Ordinary Physician to both Cardinal Richelieu and to Gaston-Jean-Baptiste, duc d'Orléans, brother of King Louis XIII. He abandoned the practice of medicine to become Maître d'Hôtel to the King and Ordinary Reader of the Chamber. PE/VLG

Catalogue 24
(Detail)

26. MARIE-THÉRÈSE D'AUTRICHE, QUEEN OF FRANCE AND OF NAVARRE

Attributed to the Beaubruns (Charles Beaubrun, *ca.* 1604-92 and/or Henri Beaubrun, *ca.* 1603-77)
Ca. 1670
Oil on canvas
70-7/8" x 55-1/8" (180 x 140 cm.)

Loaned by the Musée National du Château de Versailles / MV 2042

Marie-Thérèse d'Autriche (1638-83) became the bride of Louis XIV as part of the Peace of the Pyrenees. She was the Infanta (crown princess) of Spain and eventually and inadvertently brought the Spanish crown to the French Bourbons. Marie-Thérèse was also the double first cousin of the Sun King, being the daughter of the brother of Anne d'Autriche and the sister of Louis XIII. She bore six royal children; only the dauphin lived beyond infancy. At Versailles her apartments were on the main floor in the southern part of Le Vau's "envelope" in rooms that are a picture gallery today.

Although she handled public occasions well and was devoted to the king, Marie-Thérèse had neither the mind nor spirit to be a queen in the style the Sun King appreciated. She enjoyed playing with dogs and dwarfs (entertainers at the Spanish court), never learned proper French, had short legs and bad teeth. The queen luxuriated in long hot baths with olive-oil soap and was enormously jealous of the royal mistresses. Noted for her piety, she also loved gambling. She played badly and lost enormous sums. Louis XIV treated her in a fatherly way and upon her death is reported to have said, "Poor woman, it's the only time she has ever given me any trouble."
VLG

27. OFFICE FOR HOLY WEEK

Unidentified bookbinder
1662 (date of publication)
Ink on paper, bound in tooled leather
8" x 5-3/8" x 1-1/8" (20.2 x 13.8 x 3 cm.)

Loaned by the Musée des Arts Décoratifs / INV 18780

The royal family was expected to set good examples to their subjects by confessing during Holy Week preceding Easter. This Holy Week missal was the personal property of Queen Marie-Thérèse d'Autriche and is sumptuously bound with her monogram and arms.
VLG

Catalogue 27

Catalogue 26

THE KING AT WORK

28. LOUIS XIV, KING OF FRANCE AND NAVARRE

Unidentified artist
Ca. 1675
Oil on canvas
77-1/4" x 61" (196 x 155 cm.)

Loaned by the Musée National du Château de Versailles / MV 8369

The Sun King assumed personal direction of the government in 1661 upon the death of Mazarin. By serious application to the duties of kingship, Louis XIV quickly became the most powerful man in Europe and probably the most powerful in the world. This portrait was painted during the Dutch War (1672-79) and the ship seen through the window may refer to an important French naval victory over the Dutch in the Antilles in 1674. Royal portraits often flattered the king's youthful figure and strong legs, of which he was proud. He holds a *bâton* of military command, and beside him are crown, scepter, and feathered helmet. The Sun King often wore an ostrich-plumed hat in preference to a crown.
VLG

Catalogue 28

29. THE CHÂTEAU OF FONTAINEBLEAU

Gobelins after Charles Le Brun (1619-90)
Woven in the De La Croix Studio, *ca.* 1680
Wool, silk and gold, 20 threads per inch (8 per cm.)
126" x 70-7/8" (320 x 180 cm.)

Loaned by the Mobilier National / GMT 3009

The site of court and governmental activity changed with some frequency, especially before the transfer to Versailles in 1683. The Sun King inherited numerous royal residences. The pattern of living in various places resulted from the earlier tradition of such peregrinations of the monarch to dispense justice throughout the kingdom. Fontainebleau, with its beautiful Renaissance interiors, usually welcomed the court and the administration for several months each year. This tapestry takes the form on an *entrefenêtre*, meant to be hung between windows. Such hangings often traveled with the royal household when it was on the move.

Charles Le Brun took up the theme of the twelve months of the year in this famous tapestry suite, for which he provided the first drawings beginning in 1668. If the "History of the King" suite is consecrated to the offical pageantry and military events of the early years of the Sun King's reign, the suite of "Months" evokes the relaxations and pleasures of the court. Spectacles, promenades, hunting parties, and the like are each associated with a royal dwelling which appears in the background of the composition in an architectonic frame.

Full scale models of the tapestries were made, following drawings by Le Brun, by the staff of painters who worked at the Gobelins under his direction; the landscapes, notably, are due to A. F. Van der Meulen (*ca.* 1632-90).

The low-warp studios of the Manufactory of the Gobelins, directed by De La Croix and Mozin, executed three series of eight "golden" *entrefenêtres* (using thread of gold), the subjects of which were drawn from the principal pieces of the suite.

This low-warp *entrefenêtre* of Fontainebleau shows several peculiarities; the view of the château (seen from the side of the Great Parterre, the boxwood edgings of which can been seen) is not the same as in the large corresponding tapestry from

Catalogue 29

the suite. At the left, the wing of the Belle Cheminée (beautiful mantlepiece) or Ancienne Comédie (old theater) is recognizable as is the Pavillon of the Porte Dorée (gilded door) with its superimposed loggia, the Ball Room, and the Apse of the Saint Saturnin Chapels. The arms of France appear in the upper border.

Throughout his reign, Louis XIV enjoyed sojourning at Fontainebleau. He had his own room remodeled, made up an apartment for Madame de Maintenon, and had Le Nôtre design the parterres.

On the balustrade, a silver vase and a heavy damask drapery evoke the rich décor of the staterooms. The birds, painted by Pieter Boel (1622-74), recall the Ménagerie of Versailles, completed in 1663, where the king kept rare animals that he received from the most distant lands.

Of the twenty-four *entrefenêtres* woven about 1680, six were given away by the king from 1682 onward. Fifteen still remain in the French national collections.
JC/ID/VLG

196

30. TOUSSAINT ROSE, SECRETARY TO THE KING
François de Troy (1645-1730)
17th century
Oil on canvas
50-7/8" x 38-5/8" (129 x 98 cm.)

Loaned by the Musée National du Château de Versailles / MV 5479

Louis XIV's success depended on efficient bureaucratic administration. Among the most valued and faithful in the retinue of the Sun King was his secretary Toussaint Rose (1611-1701). Rose was probably more an office manager than a scribe, taking the king's dictates and distributing and supervising the work among a clerical staff.

Rose began his court career as secretary to Cardinal Mazarin. He was placed in charge of the Chambre des Comptes or accounting section in 1661, at about the time of the king's marriage. As "Secretary of the Hand" Rose was allowed to sign documents for the king. It is often difficult to distinguish his authorized signatures from those actually written by Louis XIV.
VLG/JM

Catalogue 30

Catalogue 31

31. LETTER ON THE AFFAIRS OF EUROPE ANNOTATED BY LOUIS XIV
Hugues de Lionne (1611-71)
Paris, 7 July 1667
Ink on laid, watermarked paper
12-1/4" x 7-5/8" (31 x 20 cm.) each page

Loaned by the Archives of the Ministère des Relations Extérieures / MD France, Vol. 415, fol. 205-207

The Sun King read voraciously. He often spent several hours daily in his office, annotating reports and correspondence that were given to his secretary and ministers for necessary follow-up work. This legendary attention to detail kept the royal staff on its toes. The writer, Hugues de Lionne, was head of the king's Foreign Office.

This letter alludes to the election of Clement IX (Giulio Rospigliosi, 1600-69), in May, 1666, and to his proposal of mediation between the king of France and his adversaries engaged in the War of Devolution. The annotations appear to be in the autograph hand of the king as Toussaint Rose, Secretary of the Hand, "isn't here." The principal notations of the king are:
"It has been decided regarding this not to do so [i.e., have a *Te Deum* sung for the exaltation of the Pope] because one was sung for the last one and that would change it into a custom."
"Good" [i.e., to accept the proposition of mediation by the Pope]
"No" [i.e., to accept a request for armistice presented by the Pope]
"I will give no commission to the Arch[bishop] of Lyon for neutrality [of the Franche-Comté], the manner of

treating it has not yet been resolved. I have ordered that orders be given to tell him to live at Bordeaux or at Toulouse in case he goes there."
The writer, Hugues de Lionne, was born in Grenoble in 1611, son of Artus de Lionne, Counsellor of the Parlement of Grenoble and Bishop of Gap after his widowhood, and of Isabelle, sister of the Secretary of State Abel Servien (*ca.* 1593-1659). He left for Italy after the disgrace of this famous uncle and while there met Cardinal Mazarin, who had him named secretary to Anne d'Autriche. As Ambassador Extraordinary to Rome in 1655, he attended the election of Alexander VII (Fabio Chigi, 1599-1667, elected pope in 1655) whom he succeeded in bending toward the favor of France, despite the intrigues of Jean-Francois-Paul de Gondi, Cardinal de Retz (1614-79).

De Lionne was one of the French negotiators of the Peace of the Pyrenees (1659) and the marriage of the king. He was named Secretary of State for Foreign Affairs in 1663 after having effectively directed the department for two years. He died in Paris in 1671.

De Lionne symbolizes the triumphant diplomacy of the first years of the personal reign of the Sun King. His *Mémoires to the King* went through numerous editions in the seventeenth century. D'Argenson said of them, "There is the book which those who are destined to politics must read to learn of business and negotiations." The most famous editions are those that appeared in the Low Countries after the seizure of diplomatic dispatches at Lille.

MC/VLG

36. ORDER OF LOUIS XIV TO GÉDÉON DE METZ TO PAY 162,000 *LIVRES* TO BEARER

Unidentified scribe, possibly Toussaint Rose (1611-1701)
Fontainebleau, 20 September 1679
15" x 9-7/8" (38 x 25 cm.)

Loaned by the Archives Nationales / K-119-B, No. 40[26] (Musée AE II 876)

The king personally directed large expenditures of funds. Bearer notes from the monarch were used when the recipient was to remain anonymous or when the monies were to be employed for secret purposes.

This document is an "Order to Cash" — an act that put funds at the direct disposition of the king, not only for secret affairs of this sort, but also for gratuities (see #37) and other unforseen expenses. It is written on the recto of a single sheet of paper and is signed "LOUIS."

Above and to the left of the signature Louis XIV has written two marginal postscripts in his own hand. By the first, which reads "good," he authorized the pledging of the expenditure. The second, which says, "I know the use of this sum," is posterior and attests that the funds had been employed following the king's intentions, but to what end could not be revealed. At the same time this later note was written, the signature was barred, which signifies that the expenditure had been verified by the king himself in his Council of Finance, the "cashed" order having been returned by the treasury after execution.

In this manner the detail of secret business escaped regulation or control by the Chamber of Accounts of Paris, which had supreme jurisdiction over the accountants of the treasury.

Below the date, the charge of the sum against "casual revenues" — that is, irregular and extraordinary resources of the treasury — has been written by Jean-Baptiste Colbert, Controller General of Finance.
JB/VLG

37. ORDER OF LOUIS XIV TO GÉDÉON BERBIER DE METZ TO PAY 12,000 *LIVRES* TO BOILEAU AND TO RACINE

Unidentified scribe, possibly Toussaint Rose (1611-1701)
Fontainebleau, 11 September 1677
14-1/2" x 9-5/8" (37 x 24.5 cm.)

Loaned by the Archives Nationales / K-119, No. 36[14] (Musée AE II 873 A)

The king personally directed large expenditures of funds. He had named the recipients as the official historians of the kingdom; the payment was for their annual stipends. Louis XIV was always concerned that an appropriate record of his reign be created for posterity.

The order is written on the recto of a single sheet of paper and has been signed "LOUIS" twice and countersigned "COLBERT." The notation "good" is found in the hand of the king above the signature, which has been barred and later replaced and indicates the king's authorization to pledge the expenditure, while the barring of the signature shows that it was later verified (see #36).

Jean-Baptiste Colbert, Controller General of Finance, has written a second upper postscript, marking that the charging of the expense has been done.

Nicolas Boileau-Despréaux (1636-1711) and Jean Racine (1639-99) were named historiographers to the king thanks to the intervention of one of the sisters of the marquise de Montespan (1641-1707, see #128), the king's mistress. Both were famed poets and representatives of literary classicism. Nevertheless, one is amazed (rather like the marquise de Sévigné) that the duties of historiographer had not been confided to a gentleman with more competence in recording the military achievements of the king. Historiographer was apparently one of those marks of preference for non-military functions reserved by Louis XIV to the bourgoisie.

In any event, Boileau and especially Racine conscientiously fulfilled their task, which as a result gave them nearly uncontested dominance in the world of letters. Unfortunately, the greatest part of their work as historiographers perished in a fire in 1726. From 1684 onward, they were members of the "Little Academy," forerunner of the Academy of Inscriptions and Belles-Lettres, and thus contributed to the composition of inscriptions and devices for the glory of the king, with Racine playing the role of historical expert.
JG/VLG

Catalogue 36

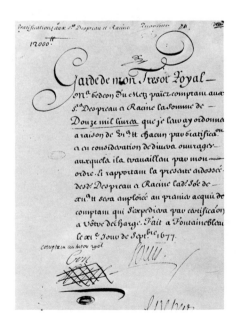

Catalogue 37

30. TOUSSAINT ROSE, SECRETARY TO THE KING

François de Troy (1645-1730)
17th century
Oil on canvas
50-7/8" x 38-5/8" (129 x 98 cm.)

Loaned by the Musée National du Château de Versailles / MV 5479

Louis XIV's success depended on efficient bureaucratic administration. Among the most valued and faithful in the retinue of the Sun King was his secretary Toussaint Rose (1611-1701). Rose was probably more an office manager than a scribe, taking the king's dictates and distributing and supervising the work among a clerical staff.

Rose began his court career as secretary to Cardinal Mazarin. He was placed in charge of the Chambre des Comptes or accounting section in 1661, at about the time of the king's marriage. As "Secretary of the Hand" Rose was allowed to sign documents for the king. It is often difficult to distinguish his authorized signatures from those actually written by Louis XIV.
VLG/JM

Catalogue 30

Catalogue 31

31. LETTER ON THE AFFAIRS OF EUROPE ANNOTATED BY LOUIS XIV

Hugues de Lionne (1611-71)
Paris, 7 July 1667
Ink on laid, watermarked paper
12-1/4" x 7-5/8" (31 x 20 cm.) each page

Loaned by the Archives of the Ministère des Relations Extérieures / MD France, Vol. 415, fol. 205-207

The Sun King read voraciously. He often spent several hours daily in his office, annotating reports and correspondence that were given to his secretary and ministers for necessary follow-up work. This legendary attention to detail kept the royal staff on its toes. The writer, Hugues de Lionne, was head of the king's Foreign Office.

This letter alludes to the election of Clement IX (Giulio Rospigliosi, 1600-69), in May, 1666, and to his proposal of mediation between the king of France and his adversaries engaged in the War of Devolution. The annotations appear to be in the autograph hand of the king as Toussaint Rose, Secretary of the Hand, "isn't here." The principal notations of the king are:

"It has been decided regarding this not to do so [i.e., have a *Te Deum* sung for the exaltation of the Pope] because one was sung for the last one and that would change it into a custom."
"Good" [i.e., to accept the proposition of mediation by the Pope]
"No" [i.e., to accept a request for armistice presented by the Pope]
"I will give no commission to the Arch[bishop] of Lyon for neutrality [of the Franche-Comté], the manner of treating it has not yet been resolved. I have ordered that orders be given to tell him to live at Bordeaux or at Toulouse in case he goes there."

The writer, Hugues de Lionne, was born in Grenoble in 1611, son of Artus de Lionne, Counsellor of the Parlement of Grenoble and Bishop of Gap after his widowhood, and of Isabelle, sister of the Secretary of State Abel Servien (*ca.* 1593-1659). He left for Italy after the disgrace of this famous uncle and while there met Cardinal Mazarin, who had him named secretary to Anne d'Autriche. As Ambassador Extraordinary to Rome in 1655, he attended the election of Alexander VII (Fabio Chigi, 1599-1667, elected pope in 1655) whom he succeeded in bending toward the favor of France, despite the intrigues of Jean-Francois-Paul de Gondi, Cardinal de Retz (1614-79).

De Lionne was one of the French negotiators of the Peace of the Pyrenees (1659) and the marriage of the king. He was named Secretary of State for Foreign Affairs in 1663 after having effectively directed the department for two years. He died in Paris in 1671.

De Lionne symbolizes the triumphant diplomacy of the first years of the personal reign of the Sun King. His *Mémoires to the King* went through numerous editions in the seventeenth century. D'Argenson said of them, "There is the book which those who are destined to politics must read to learn of business and negotiations." The most famous editions are those that appeared in the Low Countries after the seizure of diplomatic dispatches at Lille.

MC/VLG

32. FRAGMENT OF A LETTER ANNOTATED BY LOUIS XIV

Attributed to Hugues de Lionne (1611-71)
Compiègne, 18 July 1667
6-3/4" x 7-7/8" (17.3 x 20 cm.)

Loaned by the Archives of the Ministère des Relations Extérieures / MD France, Vol. 415, fol. 229

The author of the letter was in all probability Hugues de Lionne, Secretary of State for Foreign Affairs from 1663 until his death. He asks to be kept up to date about everything happening with the army so as to inform the government and to fight the "false noises" that are going about. The annotation, in the hand of the king, confirms, "I will have word sent to you of all that happens."

The letter was written on both recto and verso sides of the sheet of laid, watermarked paper. It is in the hand of a professional clerk.

In addition to his many other achievements, de Lionne did the diplomatic groundwork to prepare Europe to take a pro-French stance for both the War of Devolution and the Dutch War. He had become a diplomatic advisor to Cardinal Mazarin as early as 1643 and was Mazarin's Parisian agent during the Fronde. Upon Mazarin's death, he had become a member of the *Conseil d'en Haut*, the king's innermost advisory body. The collapse of de Lionne's complex and skillfully built network of communications and alliances at his death in 1671 made the French position much more difficult during the Dutch War.
MC/JM/VLG

Catalogue 32

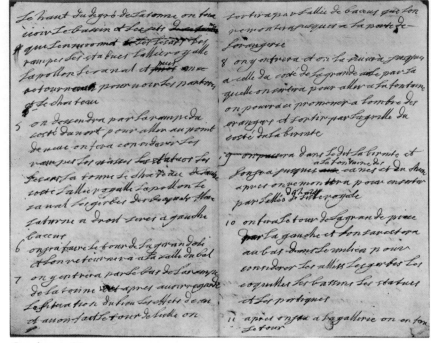

Catalogue 33

33. MANNER OF SHOWING THE GARDENS OF VERSAILLES

Louis XIV
17th century
12-3/4" x 16-3/8" (32.5 x 41.5 cm.)

Loaned by the Réserve of the Cabinet des Estampes of the Bibliothèque Nationale / VE 1318 Réserve

The arts figured prominently in the work of the king. Louis XIV utilized the buildings and gardens of Versailles to entertain and to impress foreign visitors with French creations and French products. His personal interest was so strong that he hand-wrote this "visitor's guide" to the elaborate garden complex.
VLG

34. TOPOGRAPHIC JOURNAL OF THE KING IN FLANDERS DURING THE YEAR 1680
François de La Pointe
1680
Ink and watercolor on paper, bound in leather
19-5/8" x 14-3/8" (49.8 x 36.3 cm.)

Loaned by the Cabinet des Estampes of the Bibliothèque Nationale / Ve 162 a

The Sun King was greatly concerned with creating a record of his activities for posterity. When he traveled to the Low Countries at the end of the Dutch War, he was accompanied by a topographic artist who portrayed all major stops on the royal route and all locations of possible strategic military interest. This served the double purpose of royal documentation and future reference for military use. To prevent overexposure to damaging light, the journal will be shown opened to different pages during the exhibition.
VLG

Catalogue 34

35. PROJECT FOR A PAINTED FAN ANNOTATED BY LOUIS XIV
Unidentified artist
Ca. 1692
Various pigments on paper
12-1/4" x 23-1/8" (31 x 58.7 cm.)

Loaned by the Réserve of the Cabinet des Estampes of the Bibliothèque Nationale / Qb³ Réserve 1692

The arts were an important consideration in the work of the Sun King. In many cases he personally inspected preliminary drawings for buildings, gardens, fortifications, and even decorative arts, giving designers his critical opinions prior to execution of the work in question. He suggested, for example, that the number of dwarfs be reduced before this fan was made. It was probably intended as a royal gift. As such, it was part of the king's duties to assure its perfection.
VLG

Catalogue 35

36. ORDER OF LOUIS XIV TO GÉDÉON DE METZ TO PAY 162,000 *LIVRES* TO BEARER

Unidentified scribe, possibly Toussaint Rose
(1611-1701)
Fontainebleau, 20 September 1679
15" x 9-7/8" (38 x 25 cm.)

Loaned by the Archives Nationales / K-119-B, No.
40[26] (Musée AE II 876)

The king personally directed large expenditures of funds. Bearer notes from the monarch were used when the recipient was to remain anonymous or when the monies were to be employed for secret purposes.

This document is an "Order to Cash" — an act that put funds at the direct disposition of the king, not only for secret affairs of this sort, but also for gratuities (see #37) and other unforseen expenses. It is written on the recto of a single sheet of paper and is signed "LOUIS."

Above and to the left of the signature Louis XIV has written two marginal postscripts in his own hand. By the first, which reads "good," he authorized the pledging of the expenditure. The second, which says, "I know the use of this sum," is posterior and attests that the funds had been employed following the king's intentions, but to what end could not be revealed. At the same time this later note was written, the signature was barred, which signifies that the expenditure had been verified by the king himself in his Council of Finance, the "cashed" order having been returned by the treasury after execution.

In this manner the detail of secret business escaped regulation or control by the Chamber of Accounts of Paris, which had supreme jurisdiction over the accountants of the treasury.

Below the date, the charge of the sum against "casual revenues" — that is, irregular and extraordinary resources of the treasury — has been written by Jean-Baptiste Colbert, Controller General of Finance.
JB/VLG

37. ORDER OF LOUIS XIV TO GÉDÉON BERBIER DE METZ TO PAY 12,000 *LIVRES* TO BOILEAU AND TO RACINE

Unidentified scribe, possibly Toussaint Rose
(1611-1701)
Fontainebleau, 11 September 1677
14-1/2" x 9-5/8" (37 x 24.5 cm.)

Loaned by the Archives Nationales / K-119, No.
36[14] (Musée AE II 873 A)

The king personally directed large expenditures of funds. He had named the recipients as the official historians of the kingdom; the payment was for their annual stipends. Louis XIV was always concerned that an appropriate record of his reign be created for posterity.

The order is written on the recto of a single sheet of paper and has been signed "LOUIS" twice and countersigned "COLBERT." The notation "good" is found in the hand of the king above the signature, which has been barred and later replaced and indicates the king's authorization to pledge the expenditure, while the barring of the signature shows that it was later verified (see #36).

Jean-Baptiste Colbert, Controller General of Finance, has written a second upper postscript, marking that the charging of the expense has been done.

Nicolas Boileau-Despréaux (1636-1711) and Jean Racine (1639-99) were named historiographers to the king thanks to the intervention of one of the sisters of the marquise de Montespan (1641-1707, see #128), the king's mistress. Both were famed poets and representatives of literary classicism. Nevertheless, one is amazed (rather like the marquise de Sévigné) that the duties of historiographer had not been confided to a gentleman with more competence in recording the military achievements of the king. Historiographer was apparently one of those marks of preference for non-military functions reserved by Louis XIV to the bourgoisie.

In any event, Boileau and especially Racine conscientiously fulfilled their task, which as a result gave them nearly uncontested dominance in the world of letters. Unfortunately, the greatest part of their work as historiographers perished in a fire in 1726. From 1684 onward, they were members of the "Little Academy," forerunner of the Academy of Inscriptions and Belles-Lettres, and thus contributed to the composition of inscriptions and devices for the glory of the king, with Racine playing the role of historical expert.
JG/VLG

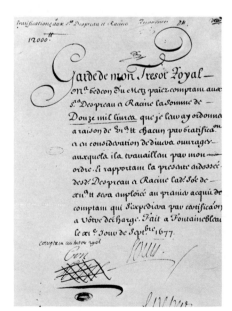

Catalogue 37

Catalogue 36

Catalogue 38

38. JEAN-BAPTISTE COLBERT
Claude Le Febure (or Le Febvre)(1632 - *ca.* 1680)
1666
Oil on canvas
54-4/8" x 44-1/2" (138 x 113 cm.)

Loaned by the Musée National du Château de Versailles / MV 2185

Colbert (1619-83) began his court career as financial manager on the staff of Cardinal Mazarin, who recognized his brilliance and commended him to Louis XIV. As leading minister Colbert managed the national economy, created protective tariffs, established industries, and created the French policy of Mercantilism. He strongly supported the arts as luxury goods to be sold abroad and was instrumental in founding the various royal academies. He supported the amelioration of Paris as opposed to the creation of Versailles, but organized and financed the construction and furnishing of the immense château when it became evident that the royal will could not be swayed.

Colbert was the son of a draper and was trained in business. The king first assigned him to the Finance Department in 1665. As controller general Colbert reduced the national debt and, for a time, balanced the state budget. In conjunction with the War of Devolution and the ensuing Dutch War, he became Secretary of State for the Marine in 1669. His upgrading of the French navy was useful not only to military endeavor, but also encouraged the development of commerce and colonization. Colbert held a wide range of offices during the remainder of his lifetime and played one of the most dynamic roles in French economic and political life.

VLG/JM

39. MÉMOIRE ADDRESSED TO LOUIS XIV

Jean-Baptiste Colbert (1619-83)
1670 (undated)
12-5/8" x 8-1/8" (32 x 20.5 cm.)

Loaned by the Archives Nationales / K-899, No. 4
(Musée AE II 863)

In this mémoire, Colbert advised the Sun King against continuing the extensive construction program at Versailles. The minister was overruled and brought his financial genius to play in financing the enormous undertaking. Although Colbert was nineteen years older than the king, the authority of age was frequently required to bend to the royal will.

Colbert urgently begs the king to limit annual expenditures to sixty million pounds. Ill-disposed to the great works at Versailles, he advises the king to give priority to projects in Paris, notably to complete the Louvre and to begin construction of the Observatory and the tapestry factory at the Gobelins. The document consists of autograph notes written on fifteen of the sixteen octavo pages of the notebook.

Jean-Baptiste Colbert, who had organized the arrest in 1661 of Superintendent of Finance Nicolas Fouquet, replaced him and assumed the title of Intendant of Finance. Then in 1665 he became Controller General of Finance, which was henceforth the official title until the Revolution brought an end to the ancien régime. To these duties Colbert added other governmental functions in such a way that, without being prime minister in name, he was essential in all elements of the royal government, with the exception of foreign affairs and war, until his death on September 6, 1683.

Colbert's powers encompassed finance, the economy, industry and commerce, part of the interior, cultural affairs, the marine, and overseas affairs. An extraordinary worker, he reestablished order in the sector of finance and for a time managed to balance the budget so that receipts equaled expenditures, all the while applying himself to procuring the means to assure the glory of the king and of France in every field of endeavor.
JG/VLG

Catalogue 39

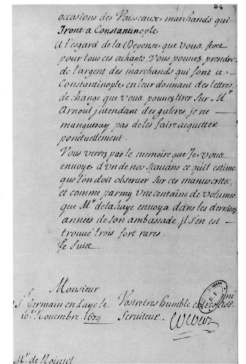

Catalogue 40

40. LETTER TO THE MARQUIS DE NOINTEL

Jean-Baptiste Colbert (1619-83)
St. Germain-en-Laye, 10 November 1674
12-7/8" x 8-1/8" (32.7 x 20.6 cm.) each page

Loaned by the Archives of the Ministère des Relations Extérieures / CP Turquie, Vol. II, fol. 52-54

Colbert took an active part in assembling the royal collections and his own holdings. In this letter he asks the French ambassador at the court of the Ottoman Empire to assist in obtaining rare, ancient, and beautiful Islamic manuscripts for both the king and for himself. His descriptive information addressed to Charles-François Ollier, marquis de Nointel, is precise. Colbert is concerned with acquiring "very old manuscripts, or books of history of the Levant or books of belles-lettres, or of doctrine by authors known in Antiquity; and which have not yet been published in Europe."

Colbert recommends that Nointel look into the library of the First Dragoman of the Grand Vizir, which was for sale, and that of the Marionite Monastery of Saint Catherine of Mount Sinai. He enclosed a note from a scholar on the interest in publishing these manuscripts in order to advance the sciences and trades in France. It was Nointel who acquired the most precious oriental manuscripts now held by the Bibliothèque Nationale. Nointel was himself a collector and according to legend broke with Colbert in an argument over the purchase of an antique cameo.
MC/VLG

THE KING AT WORK: WAR AND DIPLOMACY

41. CHANCELLOR SÉGUIER
Gérard-Léonard Errard, called Hérard (ca. 1631-75)
Ca. 1670
Marble
40-3/8" x 36-1/4" (102.5 x 92 cm.)

Loaned by the Département des Sculptures of the Musée du Louvre / MR 2163

Pierre Séguier (1588-1672) was among the grand old men whom the Sun King inherited from his father's reign. Séguier was a shrewd administrator with a clear grasp of international affairs and served as chancellor of the Foreign Office for many years. Séguier was the first to recognize the talents of Charles Le Brun and placed him in the studio of Simon Vouet to study. He also backed Colbert in promoting the interests of Paris. The sculptor Hérard has portrayed Séguier with a compactness that is frequently characteristic of the French classical baroque. Such a marble bust of Séguier was ordered from the artist by Louis XIV in 1671, and final payment was made for it in August, 1673. It was placed in the "Room of Antiquities" in the Louvre, precurser of the current museum.

Hérard's bust shows the celebrated chancellor in a profoundly realistic manner. The chancellor was about eighty-two when it was made. The artist may have masked the age, but he did not idealize. He has surrounded his sitter with the signs of prestige: a heavy curled wig and cap, an imposing mantle with deep folds embroidered with the Order of the Holy Spirit, which reappears on the sash around his neck, and the simple neckband or *rabat* of a man of the law.

The magnificence of the bust sets one of the principal political personages of the reign of Louis XIII and the youth of Louis XIV in a fine light. Séguier was also a member of the French Academy and succeeded Cardinal Mazarin in 1654 as protector of the Royal Academy of Painting and Sculpture. His large library, now in part at the Bibliothèque Nationale, evidenced his intellectual tastes.
GB/VLG

Catalogue 41

42. THE GREAT BOOK FOR PRECIOUS STONES

Unidentified scribes for Jean-Baptiste Colbert, marquis de Seignelay (1651-90)
15 November 1677 - 1 September 1684
17" x 12" x 2" (43 x 30.5 x 5 cm.)

Loaned by the Archives of the Ministère des Relations Extérieures / MD France, Vol. 2042

The Sun King employed lavish gifts as part of his diplomacy. This custom impressed and overpowered foreign ambassadors and reminded his own nobility of the largesse of the king. The use and expense of precious stones were recorded in this ledger. In order to prevent overexposure to damaging light, the ledger will be shown opened to different pages throughout the exhibition.

The Great Book, bound in tooled vellum, is divided into eight parts: (1) general inventory of the stones of the king; (2) state of funds coming from orders sent for the payment of the king's stones; (3) state of payments made for the purchase of stones with funds coming from these orders; (4) state of works in (precious) stones delivered to H(is) M(ajesty) or given (away) by his order; (5) state of orders sent to be employed for the payment of gold purchased from goldsmiths and of funds used in these payments; (6) general state of gold purchased from goldsmiths; (7) state of gold chains given (away) on behalf of the king; and (8) state of orders of gratuities sent to Sirs Piton, Alvarez, and Montarsy, goldsmiths.

These precious stones or works by goldsmiths were given by the king as presents to persons he wished to thank or to honor, to foreign ambassadors, or on the occasion of a happy event, something like decorations in our times. The register was approved by the king in these terms, "I have approved the following accounting and I wish that Du Mets continue responsibility, as he had done until the present, for the funds for these stones and of the distribution following my orders and that in the future he leave in the hands of goldsmiths and jewelers only those which are being worked." Du Mets, mentioned by the king, has not been identified.

The Great Book was kept under the direction of Jean-Baptiste Colbert, marquis de Seignelay. He was the eldest son of the great Jean-Baptiste Colbert and was born in Paris in 1651. The marquis became Secretary of State for the Marine in 1676 and succeeded his father in all his offices except that of Superintendent of Works. Colbert de Seignelay became Minister of State in 1689 and died November 3, 1690.
MC/VLG

Catalogue 42

43. CODED DISPATCH FROM CONSTANTINOPLE

Pierre Puchot, comte des Alleurs (ca. 1643-1725) and an unidentified cryptographer
Constantinople, 19 May 1714
13-1/4" x 8-1/4" (33.5 x 21 cm.)

Loaned by the Archives of the Ministère des Relations Extérieures / CP Turquie, Vol. 53, fol. 101-102

Coded dispatches were frequently employed by French diplomatic correspondents. Interlineal translations were made before such documents were given to the king or chancellor.

The author of this dispatch, after having recounted the disappearance of the principal artisan of the broadcloth manufactory in Constantinople, confesses in numbered code that he himself, after three years of effort, had persuaded the craftsman to enter the service of the king of France, and had sent him to Marseilles!

It was Jean-Baptiste Colbert who, taking up the policy of Maximilien de Béthune, duc de Sully, and of Cardinal Richelieu, had created or resuscitated the manufacture of textiles in France — the broadcloth of Abbeville, the serges of Aumale, the linen of Burgundy, and the woolens of Poitou — by peopling these regions with "workers enticed from abroad," according to Roman d'Amat. The dispatch shows that the policy was followed throughout the reign of Louis XIV, who needed skilled artisans to replace Protestants who left France after the Revocation of the Edict of Nantes in 1685.

Pierre Puchot, comte des Alleurs, was born in either 1643 or 1645. He began with a meteoric military career. He rose from ensign in the French Guards in 1672 to Brigadier of the Infantry in 1693 and was named Commander of the Order of St. Louis (see #58, #59, and #60) upon its inception. But he was financially ruined, so he was forced to sell his company and abandon the army for diplomacy.

Louis XIV launched him on a colorful diplomatic career by sending him as ambassador without portfolio to the Elector of Brandenburg in December, 1697, and recalled him in January, 1701, when Frederick I was crowned King of Prussia. Des Alleurs was then sent to Cologne. In 1703 he refused the embassy to Portugal and was sent as secret advisor to the Hungarian Racoczy who had rebelled against the Emperor. In January, 1704, des Alleurs was officially charged with French affairs in Transylvania and made Lieutenant Commander of the Order of St. Louis on May 1. He received the Great Cross on April 8, 1707. Des Alleurs' astonishing career is reported to have been aided by the intrigues conducted on his behalf by his wife Marie-Charlotte de Lutzelbourg (b. 1668) at Versailles.

In 1709 des Alleurs accepted the embassy to Constantinople. Old and ill, he asked for his own recall in 1713, but his successor, Jean-Louis Dusson, marquis de Bonnac, named at the end of the year, could not get to his post until June, 1716. Des Alleurs was given the governorship of Laval upon his return to France and he died in Paris on April 25, 1725. The following year his heart was sent to the Capuchin Church of St. Louis in Constantinople. His son Roland was also ambassador in Turkey, serving from 1747 to 1754, and was buried in the same church.
MC/JM/VLG

44. CODED DISPATCH FROM ADRIANOPLE
Pierre-Antoine de Castagnery, marquis de Châteauneuf (1647-1728), and an unidentified cryptographer
Adrianople, 27 March 1693
11-3/4" x 8-1/8" (30 x 20.5 cm.)

Loaned by the Archives of the Ministère des Relations Exterieures / CP Turquie, Vol. 24, fol. 262-269

In this document, Castagnery explains that the Grand Vizir of the Ottoman Empire has been deposed. In the coded portion he describes the new replacement as a man of "mediocre mind." As a whole, the dispatch mainly concerns the peace negotiations conducted between the allied Christian monarchs of Europe and the Ottoman Empire through the mediation of Holland and the king of England. The war was begun in 1682 and ended by the Peace of Carlovitz on January 28, 1699. The document consists of eight pages written on both recto and verso of each sheet of laid, watermarked paper. It is in the hand of a professional scribe and has been signed by Castagnery.

Pierre-Antoine de Castagnery, marquis de Châteauneuf, was born at Chambery. His family was originally from the Italian Piedmont, and he was naturalized as French in 1675. He was the eldest son of Jacques-Louis, baron de Châteauneuf, Senator for Savoie, and of Françoise-Marie de Regard. He served as counselor-clerk from 1674 and from 1680 was lay counselor at the Parlement of Paris. In April of 1680 he acquired the lordship of Marolles.

Castagnery was named ambassador to Constantinople in 1689. Very close to high Musulman officials, he went everywhere with the sultan. He organized a new and rapid system of information and transport. Castagnery was responsible for the restitution to the Catholics of the Church of the Holy Sepulchre.

Recalled in 1699, Castagnery was sent to Lisbon in 1703 after that post had been refused by Pierre Puchot, comte des Alleurs (see #43). After the rupture between France and Portugal over the Spanish Succession, he replaced Jean, Abbé d'Estrées, as French Ambassador o to Madrid, to the satisfaction of the Princess Orsini. Castagnery returned to Paris in 1704.

Designated in 1713 as ambassador to The Hague, Castagnery was involved in the negotiations of 1715 between Spain and Portugal. He was a signatory of the Triple Alliance of 1717 and of the Franco-Russian treaty of commerce of the same year.

Castagnery retired to France in 1718. He was named Councilor of State in August of the following year and Provost of the Merchants of Paris in July, 1720. He died March 12, 1728.

Castagnery's brother, François, abbé de Châteauneuf (d. 1709), also played a diplomatic role. He was sent in 1697 to Melchior, abbé de Polignac, ambassador to Poland, to have François-Louis de Bourbon, prince de Conti (1664-1709), elected king, but the mission was a failure.
MC/JM/VLG

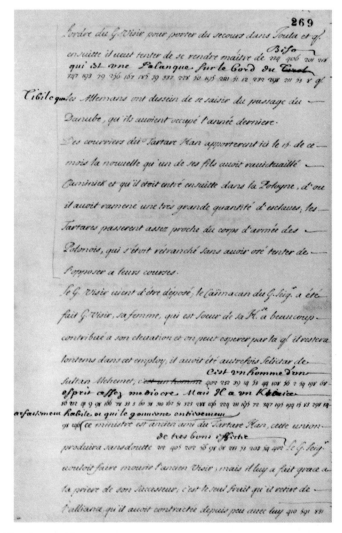

Catalogue 44

Catalogue 43

45. LETTER TO LOUIS XIV
Mehmed IV, Sultan of the Ottoman Empire (*ca.* 1642-92)
1669
37-3/4" x 18-1/2" (96 x 47 cm.)

Loaned by the Archives of the Ministère des Relation Extérieures / CP Turquie, Vol. 27 sup., fol. 36

Throughout his reign the Sun King maintained regular contact with the heads of foreign states. The formal correspondence he received from Eastern potentates was elaborate and ceremonial. Crumbled gold or silver leaf was often used to pounce damp ink, giving their letters a glittering effect.

This extraordinary document is written on glazed, laid paper and pounced with powdered gold. It is dated at the beginning of the Moon of Muharrem of the Hegira 1080 (1669 according to our calendar). The gist of this letter can be stated in these terms:

> The Great Lord (sultan) wished to know the reasons that have engaged the King of France to recall his Ambassador from Constantinople. He sends Soliman to France to ask for explanations in this regard.

In effect, the excellent Franco-Turkish relations of the sixteenth century existed only in memory during the seventeenth. The discord between the two countries, which culminated in the first ten years or the personal reign of the Sun King, had several causes: piracy in the Mediterranean; competition with the English and the Dutch; the fact that France had spread its system of alliances against the Austro-Spanish bloc throughout Northern Europe; and certainly the deplorable choice of French ambassadors to the "Door," as the Ottoman throne was called.

Commerce with the Levant had been completely disrupted. It was the era of the "outrages," those arbitrary fines imposed upon foreign traders. In addition, the pope sought to involve the Sun King in the crusade being planned by the Holy Roman Emperor. Louis XIV refused this rupture because of traditions and because of Colbert's projects to resuscitate trade with the Levant and to spread French commerce throughout the Far East.

However, the French ambassador, La Haye-Vantelet was so badly treated when he arrived in Constantinople in 1665 that the king recalled him at the beginning of 1669 before sending

François de Vendôme, duc de Beaufort, Vivenne, and Philippe de Montault de Benac, duc de Navilles, to relieve the Venetian island of Candia (Crete), which had been attacked by the Turks. Nevertheless, a merchant was left in Constantinople, charged with looking after French interests.

After the Cretan expedition was checked by the death of Beaufort, who was killed upon his arrival, and the opening of peace negotiations between the Venetian Republic and the Door, Louis XIV felt himself free of obligations and agreed to accept the Turkish ambassador. The ambassador, a man of modest origins, debarked at Toulon in early August, 1669. After many difficulties he obtained an audience with Hugues de Lionne at Suresnes in mid-November. There they fixed the conditions for resumption of diplomatic relations between the king and sultan.

Charles François Ollier, marquis de Nointel (see #40), was designated ambassador to Constantinople and left with a large entourage including Antoine Galland, future translator of the *Thousand and One Nights.*

Mehmed IV, born about 1642, became sultan in 1649. Reaching his majority in 1655, he undertook his first military efforts in Dalmatia in 1658. He declared war on the Poles in order to defend the Cossacks, who had pledged fealty to him, and personally commanded the siege of Caminiek in 1672 (or the Hegira 1083). He imposed an annual tribute on Poland, which John Sobieski refused to pay. Mehmed IV then reopened hostilities, but with less success, and signed a peace in 1676.

Another disastrous war, with Russia, ended in 1680. In 1681, to relieve the rebellious Hungarians, Mehmed IV broke the truce concluded with the Holy Roman Emperor in 1664. He failed at Vienna in 1683 and was beaten by Sobieski. In 1687 rebellious Janissaries deposed him; he died five years later.
MC/VLG

Catalogue 45

Catalogue 46

46. LETTER TO LOUIS XIV
Amoudja Zadhk Hussein Koprili, Grand Vizir of the Ottoman Empire (d. 1702)
25 January 1700
31-1/8" x 20-1/8" (79 x 51 cm.)

Loaned by the Archives of the Ministère des Relations Extérieures / CP Turquie, Vol. 36, fol. 77

The Grand Vizier's letter is written on the recto of a sheet of glazed, laid paper and is pounced with powdered gold. The invocation in gilded lettering is written around his seal. According to the translation made in Paris by Petis de La Croix in 1700, the letter concerns the arrival of the comte de Ferriol as French ambassador in Constantinople.

Amoudja Zadkh Hussein Koprili, governor of Belgrade, was given the Imperial Seal as Grand Vizir on September 17, 1697, and negotiated the Peace of Carlovitz in 1699. He resigned his duties in 1702 and died shortly afterward.
MC/VLG

47. THE ROYAL AND MAGNIFICENT AUDIENCE GIVEN TO THE VERY ILLUSTRIOUS AMBASSADORS OF THE MAGNIFICENT KING OF SIAM

Nicolas de Larmessin II (*ca.* 1638-94)
1687
Engraving
35-5/8" x 22-1/4" (90.5 x 56.5 cm.)

Loaned by the Musée Carnavalet / Almanach 1687
(G: 20300)

Frenchmen of the seventeenth century were fascinated by the presence of exotic foreign envoys. The Sun King received the Siamese embassy in the Hall of Mirrors at Versailles with great pomp in 1686, and the event was recorded in this popular calendar or almanac for the following year. The Siamese presented the king with banded silks and cottons. These fabrics, called *siamoises,* were widely imitated by French textile producers. Their mirrored banding patterns survived in French folk traditions and were woven by Louisiana Acadians of French descent as late as the early twentieth century.

Franco-Siamese relations had as objectives the countering of the commercial preponderance of Holland in Southeast Asia and the opening of Siam to evangelical missions. They were facilitated by the nomination, as First Minister of Siam, of Constance Phaulkon, an adventurer of Greco-Genovese origins who was favorable to France. The arrival of three Siamese ambassadors to France, prepared by the chevalier de Chaumont, ambassador to Siam, and the Abbé de Choisy, enflamed the popular imagination. The event amused the *gazettes* of the time, and no less than six almanacs for 1687 depicted it.

The Siamese ambassadors arrived at Brest on June 18, 1686. Accompanied by twenty mandarins, they were received by Louis XIV at Versailles on September 1. In addition to gifts, they brought a message to the French sovereign from Prah Haraï, king of Siam. "They gave the king respect which ran nearly to adoration and in departing did not wish to turn their backs and went out backwards," wrote the Abbé de Choisy.

With the death, in the following year, of Minister Phaulkon, accompanied by internal revolts, the relations of France with Siam were broken and remained ephemeral. This diplomatic episode resulted in nothing but a dazzling memory of the exoticism of the visitors, the strangeness of their mores, and the marvels of their costumes.

The cartel in the lower section of the print shows, in a free view, the site and the battle of Buda with the Ottomans. The liberation of the Hungarian capital from Turkish hegemony took place in September, 1686, after a long siege and the death of Abdurrahman, ninety-ninth and last Pasha of Buda, who is shown vanquished in the left corner.

The end of Turkish occupation in Hungary, coming after the check in 1683 of the Grand Vizir Kara Mustapha beneath the walls of Vienna at the hands of the army of John Sobiesky, the king of Poland, marked the annihilation of the Turco-Musulman menace that had raged on land and sea for two centuries. The victory at Buda of Charles de Lorraine, commander-in-chief of a multinational army, represented the ultimate success of the European coalition.
RH/VLG

Catalogue 47

48. INFANTRY HELMET
Unidentified armorer
17th century
Iron

Loaned by the Musée de l'Armée / INV G-202

From 1666 to 1668 the Sun King fought the War of Devolution, claiming for France the Spanish Netherlands. His wife's father, Philip IV of Spain (1605-65), had left the Spanish throne to her sickly half-brother Charles II (1661-1700) and named her half-sister Marguerite-Thérèse (1651-73), then engaged to Leopold I (1640-1705), as second to inherit. This excluded the French Bourbons from the Spanish succession. Although Marie-Thérèse had renounced her claim to the Spanish throne upon marrying Louis XIV, he felt no compunction about usurping the Spanish Netherlands in lieu of her unpaid dowry; and the resultant squabble was as much dynastic as political.

The Sun King's army was the strongest on earth, well equipped and under the able military command of Henri de La Tour d'Auvergne, vicomte de Turenne. Turenne's strategy of sieges on three fronts produced many conquests, and the French advanced as rapidly as logistics would allow. Transportation and food posed the greatest problems in moving over seventy thousand men across Europe, as supplies were handled by the marquis de Louvois with success.

Louis XIV spent many months with his troops as a well-conducted military leader, showing personal bravery and inspiring high morale. He paraded leading beauties of the court through conquered cities, showing Netherlanders their new queen, impressing them with gorgeous costumes and elaborate trappings, thereby gaining their new-found loyalties through his understanding of seventeenth-century showmanship.
VLG

Catalogue 49
(Detail)

49. MATCHLOCK MUSKET
Unidentified gunsmith
17th century
Wood, iron and other materials
51-1/8" (130 cm.)

Loaned by the Musée de l'Armée / INV M-40

The threat of the victorious, well-equipped French army gave rise to fears that the Sun King would not stop with the Netherlands but would take Holland and Germany as well. France's enemies England, Holland, and Sweden formed the Triple Alliance to seek a peace and secretly agreed to fight France back to her frontiers of 1659 if negotiation was not successful.

Hugues de Lionne, chancellor of the French Foreign Office, won a bloodless diplomatic victory in fearful Brandenburg and Bavaria. Austria agreed to a partition of the Netherlands upon the anticipated death of the ailing young Charles II of Spain, thus partially vindicating Marie-Thérèse's claim. Unexpectedly, Charles outlived most of the negotiators.
VLG

Catalogue 50

50. DESIGN OF FIREWORKS GIVEN BY THE DUC DE CHAULNES
Attributed to or after Gianlorenzo Bernini (1598-1680)
1668
Ink and wash on laid paper
11" x 8-1/8" (28 x 20.5 cm.)

Loaned by the Archives of the Ministère des Relations Extérieures / CP Rome, Vol. 192, fol. 49

The Treaty of Aix-la-Chapelle ended the War of Devolution in 1668. The entire French world celebrated, and the French ambassador in Rome held an elaborate display of fireworks, thought to have been designed by Bernini. He enclosed this sketch with his report to the French Foreign Office.

The Sun King settled for a boundary based on his military conquests of 1667. This created an enviable frontier from any standpoint but made the king appear reasonable and gained time for military preparations for the ensuing Dutch War, which Louis XIV foresaw even as the treaty was being signed at Aix. Louis XIV had used as justification for the war his wife's claim to Brabant and diverse fiefdoms of the Spanish Netherlands. "Devolution" was a concept and custom that favored children "of the first bed" in cases of inheritance.

Catalogue 48

Catalogue 51

Charles d'Albert d'Ailly, duc de Chaulnes (1625-98), was born in Amiens. He followed a military career, achieved the rank of lieutenant general in 1653, and served as governor of Doullens. The duke was French ambassador to Rome for the election of Clement IX in 1667, of Clement X in 1670, and of Alexander VIII in 1689. Intermingled with these diplomatic missions, de Chaulnes continued his military endeavors, was governor of Brittany in 1670, and became famous for his cruel repression of the "stamped paper" insurrection. He died in Paris in 1698.

Spectacular fireworks were practically a hallmark of elaborate French festivities, and detailed descriptions were sometimes written to record these ephemeral wonders. De Chaulnes did well to employ a designer of Bernini's fame. Bernini had traveled to France in 1665 and executed both a bust and an equestrian statue of Louis XIV. The display in Rome featured a flattering figure of the pope surmounting a globe, flanked by personifications of War (with sword) and Peace (with palm). The globe appeared over a bed of cloud, smoke, and flame.
MC/VLG

51. CROSSING THE RHINE
Adam-François Van der Meulen (ca. 1632-90)
1672
Oil on canvas
19-3/8" x 43-3/4" (49 x 111 cm.)

Loaned by the Département des Peintures of the Musée du Louvre / INV 1490

The Sun King espoused the concept of the Rhine as the natural northern frontier of France. He met the Dutch at Tolhuis on June 12, 1672, and won a great victory despite an impetuous and premature charge led by Louis II de Bourbon de Condé and his son. The theme later figured widely in the fine and decorative arts.

The badly frightened Dutch cut the dikes, flooded Holland, and isolated Amsterdam in an impassible quagmire. The French waited for a winter freeze to drag their cannon across the ice, but mild weather prevailed. The Dutch refused the crushing French terms for peace, which reflected Colbert's

vengeance on their mercantile success, and the war entered a new "European" stage that was far less successful for the French on either military or diplomatic fronts. De Lionne's diplomatic isolation of Holland began to fail. The Grand Alliance of 1673 united the Empire, the Dutch Netherlands, Spain, and Lorraine against Louis XIV.

During the Dutch War the king was forced to remove certain marshalls of France who refused to obey his field commander Turenne, saying they took orders only from the king. Subsequently Louis XIV began to act as a modern chief-of-staff, coordinating the activities of a large army on several fronts when it became evident that field commanders, isolated from each other, could not work effectively without centralized control. Older commanders such as Condé and Turenne did not react well to this new form of military management.
VLG

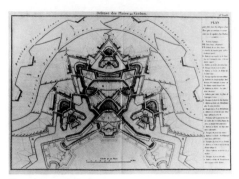

Catalogue 52

52. FORTIFICATIONS

After Sébastien Le Prestre, marquis de Vauban
(1633-1707)
1737-1742
Engraving
21" x 16-3/4" (50.8 x 42.5 cm.)

Louisiana State Museum / T.172.1983.15

Many aspects of the art of modern warfare were crystallized by the French during the Dutch War. Numerous victories were due to the efforts of Sébastien Le Prestre, marquis de Vauban. He perfected siege techniques and the design of fortifications with the effect of making engineering an important part of warfare. Vauban also championed the concept of "lines of defense," an idea that has remained standard in military conflict through the twentieth century. His theoretical plans for offensive and defensive fortifications on different terrains were published at The Hague beginning thirty years after his death.
VLG.

53. THE PEACE OF NYMEGEN
(Treaty with Holland)
Various scribes and signatories
Nymegen, 10 August 1678
14" x 9-1/4" (35.5 x 23.5 cm.)

Loaned by the Département des Traités of the Archives of the Ministère des Relations Extérieures / No Acc. No.

Nymegen was selected in 1676 as the site for peace negotiations, but it took a full year to settle questions of protocol before the talks got underway. By 1677 hard times in France resulting from heavy war taxes and poor harvests called for a quick settlement. The northern frontier had been largely straightened out into a defensible line in the campaigns of 1676. The king decided that one stupendous victory would force the negotiators to conclude a peace. He selected Ghent as the target, obtained the victory, and built a public image of himself as the conquering hero, despite the inconclusive campaigns of the mid-1670s.

This treaty concluded the Dutch War and was negotiated at Nymegen in 1678. France annexed the Franche-Comté and parts of Flanders, providing a defensible northern frontier. Despite these gains, the initial goal of crushing Dutch commercial dominance was not met.

Individual treaties were drawn up between the French and each major participating party in the conflict (Holland, Spain, and the Empire). The last version, that with the Empire, was not signed until early 1679. The series of treaties came at the apogee of the reign of the Sun King. Louis XIV consolidated his northern frontiers, while the Dutch won a repeal of the customs duties of 1667, which had been one of the causes of the war.

The French plenipotentiaries included Godefroy Louis, comte d'Estrades, who had been the French agent in Holland before becoming a lieutenant general in 1650. He was sent as ambassador extraordinary to England, where he obtained the restitution of Dunkirk from Charles II in 1662. D'Estrades was then sent to Holland in 1663. He was promoted to Maréchal de France in 1675 and became governor of the king's nephew Philippe II, duc de Chartres, in 1686.

The second French representative was Charles Colbert, marquis de Croissy, brother of Jean-Baptiste Colbert. Colbert de Croissy had been the first president of

the Sovereign Council of Alsace and then president of the Parlement of Metz in 1662, before being sent as ambassador to London, where he served from 1668 to 1674. He replaced Simon Arnauld, marquis de Pomponne, as Secretary of State for Foreign Affairs.

Jean-Antoine de Mesmes, comte d'Avaux, was the third French signatory. From a diplomatic family, his great uncle had negotiated the Treaty of Munster in 1648. D'Avaux served as French ambassador to both Holland and Sweden. The Dutch delegation included Jerome of Beverningk, William of Nassau, and William of Haren.
PE/VLG

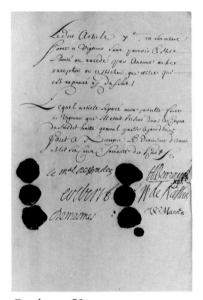

Catalogue 53

Catalogue 54

54. THE PEACE OF NYMEGEN
(Treaty with Spain)
Various scribes and signatories
Nymegen, 17 September 1678
13/1/4" x 9-1/8" (33.5 x 23 cm.)

Loaned by the Département des Traités of the
Archives of the Ministère des Relations Extérieures

By the treaty drawn up with Spain,
France made important territorial gains.
Spain gave up the Franche-Comté,
Valenciennes, Bouchain, Condé,
Cambrai, Maubeuge, Aire, and
Saint-Omer, as well as several places in
Flanders. France ceded Charleroi, Ath,
and Coutrai to the Spanish crown.

The Spanish treaty was signed for
France by the same plenipotentiaries
who had place their seals on the
agreement with Holland the preceding
month (see #53). Spanish signatories
were Don Pablo Spinola-Doria; Don
Gaspardo de Tebes y Cordova-Tello;
Don Pedro Ronquillo, marquis de la
Fuenta; and Jean-Baptiste Cristin.
PE/VLG

Catalogue 55

THE KING AT WORK: ORDERS AND HONORS

55. THE ROYAL RECOMPENSES OF LOUIS THE GREAT
Nicolas de Larmessin II (ca. 1638-94
1676
Engraving
32-1/4" x 20-1/4" (82 x 51.5 cm.)

Loaned by the Musée Carnavalet / Almanach 1686
(G:20292)

Rewarding loyal courtiers and military
leaders was an important duty of the
king. It helped bind them to him
personally as the result of recognition
and flattery.

The Sun King bestowed titles,
marshal's *bâtons*, and knighthoods in the
Royal Orders each year to his subjects
and occasionally to outstanding
representatives of foreign governments.
Medals and jewelry were dispensed at
other times as marks of royal favor.

In this image, the Sun King appears

as master of the armies of the most
powerful country in Europe. Although
presented seated, by symbolic scale he is
larger than the courtiers who surround
him. To his right stands the dauphin,
while the queen is shown behind the
king. The other figures are important
functionaries of state, including the
chiefs of the army who will receive the
marshal's *bâton*. The scene opens onto a
perspective of the Army of the Rhine,
grouped in regiments and squadrons. It
is commanded by the Grand Condé,
who was called after the death of
Turenne to replace him and said "If
only God would allow me a quarter of
an hour to speak with the ghost of
Monsieur de Turenne."

Turenne's portrait, in a medallion, is
carried into the Heavens by a

personification of Fame. The great
strategist, the savior of Lorraine and
Champagne, began the campaign of the
Rhine against his old and esteemed
enemy Montecuccoli, a famed tactician
who served the Emperor Leopold, after
the cruel campaigns of the Palatinate
and of Alsace. On July 27, 1675, an
errant cannon ball at Salzbach carried
off Turenne. His death was a heavy loss
for France.

Among the six laureates at the
ceremony of promotion shown in the
engraving, which took place July 30,
1675, was François-Henri, duc de
Luxembourg, a worth emulator of the
great Turenne and Condé, and not the
least of the architects of the Peace of
Nymegen.
RH/VLG

211

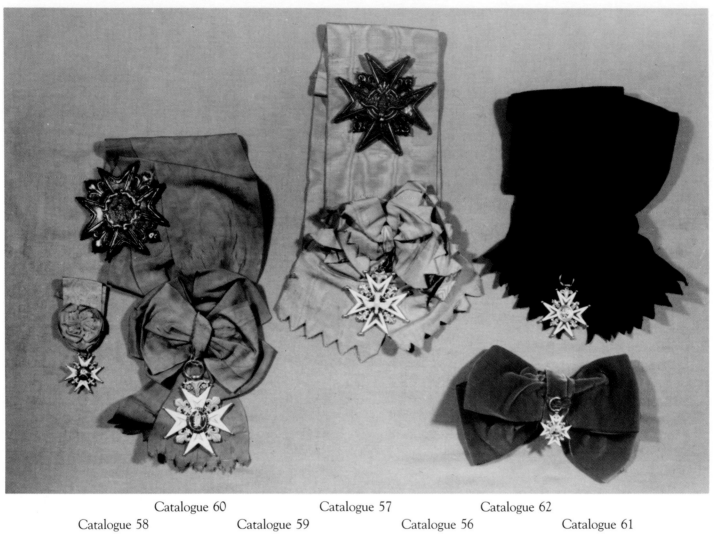

Catalogue 60
Catalogue 58   Catalogue 59   Catalogue 57   Catalogue 62   Catalogue 61
Catalogue 56

56. CROSS OF THE ORDER OF THE HOLY SPIRIT
Unidentified goldsmith
18th century
Gold and enamel with sash
2-3/4" dia. (7 cm. dia.)

Loaned by the Musée National de la Légion d'Honneur et des Ordres de Chevalerie / Gift of Lady Deterding / INV 04726

Membership was prized in this, the most prestigious of orders. Knights of the Order of the Holy Spirit generally displayed their crosses or badges prominently in their painted portraits.

The Order of the Holy Spirit was created by Henri III on December 31, 1578. Membership was limited to one hundred Frenchmen of at least three generations of nobility. "Chapters," or ceremonies, were held annually on New Year's Day and were the occasion for sumptuous proceedings. The seat of the order was located at the Convent of the Grands Augustins in Paris; the king served as Grand Master. The Order of the Holy Spirit and the other royal orders were abolished in 1830 when Louis-Philippe came to the French throne.
duP/SR/VLG

57. BADGE OF THE ORDER OF THE HOLY SPIRIT
Unidentified artisan
18th century
Thread of silver and other fibers
4-1/8" dia. (10.6 cm. dia.)

Loaned by the Musée de la Légion d'Honneur et des Ordres de Chevalerie / Gift of Lady Deterding / INV 04728

Badges of metallic thread, worked in relief with the symbol of the order, were sewn to outer garments.
duP/VLG

58. CROSS OF A KNIGHT OF THE ORDER OF SAINT LOUIS
Unidentified goldsmith
17th century
Gold and enamel with ribbon
1-1/2" dia. (4.0 cm. dia.)

Loaned by the Musée National de la Légion d'Honneur et des Ordres de Chevalerie / Gift of Lady Deterding / INV 04742

The military Order of Saint Louis was created by Louis XIV in 1693. Membership was limited to Catholic officers who had served a minimum of ten years in the royal army, but noble birth was not required for admittance. This first "democratic" order had three grades of membership: Great Cross, Commander, and Knight.
duP/SR/VLG

59. GREAT CROSS OF THE ORDER OF SAINT LOUIS
Unidentified goldsmith
18th century
Gold and enamel with sash
3" dia. (7.5 cm. dia.)

Loaned by the Musée National de la Légion d'Honneur et des Ordres de Chevalerie / Gift of Lady Deterding / INV 04741

60. BADGE OF THE GREAT CROSS OF THE ORDER OF SAINT LOUIS
Unidentified artisan
18th century
Thread of silver and other fibers
3-7/8" dia. (9.8 cm. dia.)

Loaned by the Musée National de la Légion d'Honneur et des Ordres de Chevalerie / Bucquet Bequest / INV B-960

61. CROSS OF THE ORDER OF SAINT LAZARUS AND OUR LADY OF MOUNT CARMEL
Unidentified goldsmith
18th century
Gold and enamel with ribbon
1-1/4" dia. (3.2 cm. dia.)

Loaned by the Musée National de la Légion d'Honneur et des Ordres de Chevalerie / Gift of Lady Deterding / INV 04739

The former Order of Saint Lazarus of Jerusalem was united by Henri IV with the papal military Order of Our Lady of Mount Carmel, instituted in 1608. It was limited to a membership of one hundred knights of high birth and placed under the authority of Grand Masters selected by the king.
duP/SR/VLG

62. CROSS OF THE ORDER OF SAINT MICHAEL
Unidentified goldsmith
18th century
Gold and enamel with sash
2" dia. (5.2 cm. dia.)

Loaned by the Musée National de la Légion d'Honneur et des Ordres de Chevalerie / Gift of Lady Deterding / INV 04723

The Order of Saint Michael was the oldest. It was instituted by Louis XI in 1469, who named thirty-six knights. After the Wars of Religion, the cross lost much of its prestige due to being too widely awarded. Louis XIV reorganized the order, but limited membership to one hundred.
duP/SR/VLG

RELIGION:
THE KING AND THE CHURCH

63. THE POMPOUS AND
MAGNIFICENT ENTRANCE OF
FLAVIO, CARDINAL CHIGI,
LATERAN LEGATE IN FRANCE
Nicolas de Larmessin II (ca. 1638-94)
1665
Engraving and etching
33-5/8" x 2" (plate mark) (85.2 x 53.3 cm.)

Loaned by the Musée Carnavalet / Almanach 1665

The relationship between the Sun King
and the Catholic Church resembled an
uneasy truce. The king wished to
maintain the historic Gallican Liberties,
including the right to name prelates
within France. The papacy hoped to
gain rather than lose ground within the
Sun King's lands. In addition, the king
and the Church sometimes took
opposing views with regard to doctrinal
and interpretive issues such as
Jansenism, Quietism, or with regard to
the various religious orders. When he
was not at odds with Rome, the king
was pitched against religious groups
within France, such as the Protestants or
the Jansenists.

The affiar of the ambassadors of
France and Spain in London in 1661
— a quarrel over precedence that
resulted in the recognition by the king
of Spain that the ambassadors of the
king of France had precedence over his
own — had shown Louis XIV's will to
affirm himself as the first sovereign of
Europe. Another incident the following
year confirmed this wish and showed
that even the pope had to submit. The
ambassador of France to Rome, Charles

III, duc de Créqui, in order to parade
French royal authority to the eyes of all,
extended diplomatic immunity from his
official residence, the Palazzo Farnese, to
the entire surrounding quarter. This
provoked numerous brawls between
partisan "Romans" and "French," which
culminated when the Corsican Guard of
the pope, at the instigation of his
nephew Don Mario Chigi, laid veritable
siege to the Palazzo on August 20, 1662,
and fired at the French ambassador for
his insolence. The sovereign pontiff
refused to make up for the insult, and
diplomatic relations were broken
between the two courts. Shortly
afterward, Louis XIV seized Avignon,
which had been a papal possession. The
king was only restrained from mobilizing
against Alexander VII (Fabio Chigi,
1599-1667, elected pope 1655) by a
promise that the Corsican Guard would
be disbanded; a sculptural pyramid,
engraved with a history of the incident
including the pope's remorse, would be
erected in Rome; Avignon would be
ceded to the French; and the pope's
nephew would travel to France and read
a full apology to the assembled French
court.

The principal theme chosen for the
almanac of 1665 was the luxurious
entrance of the Cardinal Chigi, the
Lateran legate, into Paris on October 9,
1664. The engraving gives a precise and
evocative image of one of these grand
entries, the details of which were
minutely regulated by official etiquette.
The cardinal, under a canopy, was

preceded by a crucifix and mace bearers
and was followed by a cortege of
prelates, trumpeters, pages, and baggage
carriers; afterward came the nobility,
then the constables of the town
preceding the municipal officers, and
finally the clergy.

In the lower medallion, surrounded by
the cardinal virtues that form a "noble
support" for the procession, the cardinal
receives the compliments of the
Parlement of Paris in the person of its
First President, Monsieur de Lamoignon.
The two upper medallions, which flank
the portrait of the king, present two
scenes that are not related to the
cardinal's entry: to the left, the birth on
November 16, 1664, of Princesse
Marie-Anne, who died several weeks
later and for whom the queen had asked
the intercession of Saint Geneviève,
patron of Paris; to the right, an
evocation of the victory of Raab in
Hungary, one of the numerous episodes
in the struggle with the Turks, endemic
throughout the seventeenth century,
where "the French showed their worth."

While the print evokes the
ceremonial aspects of the entry of a
sovereign into a city, de Larmessin's
plate is also, by allusion, a reminder of
the conflicts between Rome and the
"Eldest Daughter of the Church" (i.e.
France) that agitated the whole of
the seventeenth century and resulted, in
1682, in the *Declaration of the Assembly
of the Clergy of France*, a veritable
manifesto of Gallicanism.
J-MB/VLG

Catalogue 63

64. UNIGENITUS
Giovanni Francisco Albani, Pope Clement XI
(1649-1721)
Papal bull
Rome, 8 September 1713 (printed shortly
afterward)
10-1/2" x 8" (26.7 x 20.3 cm.)

Loaned by the Archives of the Ministèe des
Relations Extérieures / CP Rome, Vol. 529, fol.
198-203

The papal bull, Unigenitus, condemned over one hundred propositions set forth in the *New Testament in French with Moral Reflections on Each Verse* published by the Jansenist Father Pasquier Quesnel (1634-1719), priest at the Oratory in Paris, in 1671. The bull was issued at the urging of Louis XIV in an effort to reduce the influence of Quesnel, who led Jansenist opposition to the king first from Brussels where he had lived since 1685, and then from Amsterdam after 1703. Quesnel had been arrested in 1702 by order of Philip V (duc d'Anjou, grandson of Louis XIV) on the Sun King's request, but had escaped.

The bull was poorly accepted in France. On this occasion when the Sun King obtained papal support, it worked against him. The Parlement of Paris refused to register the bull, and it met with passive resistance from most French bishops and resolute opposition from some.

Pope Clement XI was born in Pesaro. In Vatican service, he was Secretary of Briefs and was created cardinal in 1690. Albani was elected pope in December, 1700, and died March 19, 1721.

The document is printed on laid, watermarked paper and consists of six pages printed on both sides. The title page bears the papal arms framed by Saints Peter and Paul in oval medallions. It was printed shortly after September 10, 1673, date of its official registration.
MC/VLG

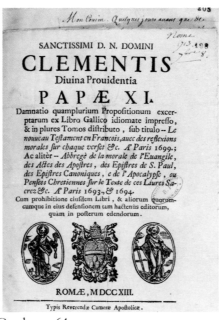

Catalogue 64

65. JACQUELINE-MARIE, MÈRE ANGÉLIQUE ARNAULD

Philippe de Champaigne (1602-74)
1654
Oil on canvas
51-1/4" x 38-5/8" (130 x 98 cm.)

Loaned by the Département des Peintures of the Musée du Louvre / INV 2035

The longest of the Sun King's religious squabbles was with the Jansenists at Port-Royal, not far from Versailles. The leaders at the Cistercian establishment came from the Arnauld family. Jacqueline-Marie, Mère Angélique Arnauld (1591-1661), was named coadjutrix to the abbess at the age of seven by Henri IV and was confirmed by papal bull giving a false age. Mère Angélique became nominal abbess in 1602 and found her nuns too worldly, especially after her inner conversion in 1608 brought on by a serious illness in the previous year. She began a heartfelt and long career of housecleaning, restoring the full Cistercian rule at Port-Royal and other convents.

The Dutch priest Cornelius Jansen (1585-1638) began as early as 1616 to attack the Jesuit-espoused concept of free will and preached a form of mystical puritanism, accepting predestination. His incomplete manuscript *Augustinus* was published in 1640 and was promptly accepted as the doctrinal basis for Port-Royal. *Augustinus* was papally condemned at Jesuit insistence, first in 1642 and again roundly in 1653, as Calvinism in Catholic clothing. During most of this period the nuns were in Paris, where they went in 1626 to escape the unhealthy damp environment of Port-Royal; they returned in 1648 to escape the Fronde.

During their absence, the buildings were occupied by "solitaires," pious men leading a monastic existence without the benefit of vows, dedicated to scholarship and religion. From 1638 onward, the solitaires had conducted excellent schools for young children.

The Sun King entered the Jesuit-Jansenist fray in 1661 by promulgating a papal order that all French clergy sign a statement condemning Jansenism. Mère Angélique soon died, her demise partially brought on by this stressful situation. Seventy nuns at Port-Royal refused to sign and were effectively excommunicated. Louis XIV never fully forgave them for their defiance, although they were welcomed back to the fold by a nicely ambiguous

Catalogue 65

papal bull in 1668 giving enough latitude for Jansenist coexistence with the Jesuits.

Louis XIV continued to frown on Port-Royal despite the fact that numerous courtiers had relatives at the convent and visited there with some frequency. The king's confessor was always a Jesuit; a new one arrived in 1709 and convinced him that the fate of his immortal soul depended upon the extermination of the Port-Royal Jansenists. In that year, troops were dispatched to the convent with orders to give the few remaining nuns fifteen

minutes to pack up and get out. The following year, the buildings seen over Mère Angélique's shoulder were razed to the ground.

The king's ploy did not work. Papal antipathy toward Jansenism polarized the French clergy into a nationalistic Gallican camp opposed by a smaller ultramontaine ("over the mountains") faction that preached strict adherence to Rome. There were far more Jansenists in France at the king's death than at his birth.
VLG

66. RELIGION TRAMPLING HERESY
Jean Hardy (1653-1737)
1688
Marble
31-7/8" x 29-7/8" (81 x 76 cm.)

Loaned by the Département des Sculptures of the
Musée du Louvre / MR 2729

The Edict of Nantes, decreed by Henri IV in 1598, had assured freedom of religion, within certain limits, to French Protestants who had enjoyed this liberty and flourished as bourgeois merchants and shipowners for nearly a century. The Huguenots were regarded with increasing suspicion by Louis XIV, the "Very Christian [i.e. Catholic] King," due partly to their economic prosperity and partly to their sympathies toward the Protestant Dutch, traditional enemies of France.

The Edict of Fontainebleau revoked the freedoms of the Edict of Nantes and was promulgated by Louis XIV in 1685. It was one of the most controversial actions of his reign, although loudly approved by many influential contemporaries. It subjected Protestants to a variety of persecutions and required their conversion to Catholicism.

This was a popular subject in Catholic Counter Reformation contemporary art, although the papacy in the person of Innocent XI regarded the revocation as a pointless act of folly.
VLG

Catalogue 66

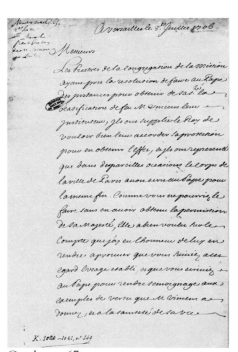

Catalogue 67

67. LETTER TO THE PROVOST OF MERCHANTS AND THE SHERIFFS OF PARIS
Jean-Baptiste Colbert, marquis de Torcy (1665-1746)
Versailles, 8 July 1706
12-5/8" x 8-1/4" (32 x 21 cm.)

Loaned by the Archives Nationales / K-1020-1021, No. 149

Vincent de Paul (1581-1660) was one of the principal architects of the Catholic Reformation in France. During the reign of Louis XIII, he created the Congregation of the Mission (called the Lazarists), and had measures adopted for the training of the clergy and for aid to orphans. He followed a personal creed based on the poverty of Christ.

This letter was written at the request of the Congregation of the Mission and informs the Parisian city fathers that the Sun King has approved their actions to secure the beatification of de Paul. It was a long process. Beatification was achieved in 1729, and St. Vincent de Paul was canonized in 1737.

The letter was written by Jean-Baptiste Colbert, marquis de Torcy (1665-1746), nephew and godson of the great Colbert. De Torcy was Secretary of State for Foreign Affairs from 1696 to 1715. The document consists of a sheet of paper folded into four pages, two of which have been utilized.
JG/VLG

Catalogue 68

68. EDICT OF THE KING ESTABLISHING THE GENERAL HOSPITAL
April 1656
10-3/8" x 8-1/4" (26.5 x 21 cm.)

Loaned by the Archives Nationales / AD + 329

The General Hospital established by this edict and the thirty-nine subsequent articles included but was not limited to a health-care facility for the poor. It encompassed the supervision of all vagabonds and beggars, healthy and infirm, and consisted of a variety of facilities ranging from hospices for the elderly poor to prison workshops to house errant citizens. The edict attempted to turn over spiritual care of marginal citizens to the Congregation of the Mission (the Lazarists) led by Vincent de Paul. This charge was ultimately refused by the Congregation, which equated contemporary poverty with the historic poverty of Christ and would not accept the incarceration of the poor.

The Lazarists did participate in the public health care programs of the General Hospital, which provided the institutional prototype for similar facilities elsewhere, including Charity Hospital in New Orleans.

Vincent de Paul was noted for an extraordinary variety of good works throughout his lifetime. The city fathers of Paris sought his beatification in 1706 with the blessing of the Sun King (see #67).

This copy of the edict was printed in Paris by Prault in 1765. The printed text is over forth pages in length.
JG/VLG

69. THE COLBERT DE VILLACERF CHAPELLE
Nicolas Dolin
Paris, 1666-67
Chased and repoussé silver
Altar cross: 27-7/8" (70.7 cm.)
Pair of candelabra: 22-3/8" (56.8 cm.)
Ewer: 10-1/8" (25.7 cm.)
Platter: 18" x 13-1/4" (45.8 x 33.6 cm.)
Chalice: 12" (30.4 cm.)
Patin: 7-1/2" dia. (19.2 cm.)
Pair of cruets: 6-3/8" (16.0 cm.)
Basin: 9-1/4" x 6-3/4" x 2-3/4" (23 x 17.3 x 7.6 cm.)
Bell: 5-3/4" (14.7 cm.)
Host Box: 4-1/4" x 5" dia. (10.8 x 12.8 cm.)
Held at the Treasury of the Cathedral of Troyes; loaned by the Division du Patrimoine Mobilier of the Ministère de la Culture

Sumptuous homes and private châteaus generally had chapels or altars. Edouard Colbert, marquis de Villacerf (1628-99), was a powerful court figure, serving as superintendent and director of the Department of Works and of Gardens. In 1680 he acquired the Château de Villacerf to the west of Troyes.

This remarkable ensemble of precious metal constituted the liturgical furnishings of the Château de Villacerf; its elements bear the Colbert de Villacerf arms in cartouches. After the French Revolution these pieces were assigned to the Cathedral of Troyes.

Repoussé scenes decorate the major elements of the *chapelle*. The foot of the chalice depicts the Flagellation, Christ and Veronica, and the Crucifixion; on the stem are found the Good Shepherd, the Virgin and Child, and Saint Michael and the Dragon; the cup shows the arrest of Christ, Christ before the Caliph, and the Crown of Thorns. The Pentecost appears on the Patin. The cruet for wine depicts the Wedding at Cana, while that for water shows Moses Striking the Rock. The accompanying basin bears scenes of Christ and the Samaritan and the Washing of the Feet. The Miracle of the Fishes appears on the ewer, and its platter shows the Baptism of Christ and the Healing of the Cripple.

Standing pieces from the *chapelle* follow the heavy dramatic baluster silhouettes seen in seventeenth-century French furniture and decorative arts, ornamented with *rinceaux* of foliage. The bases of the chalice, the cruets, and the basin are enriched with open-work acanthus leaves.
VLG

Catalogue 69

Catalogue 70

THE KING AND PARIS: ACADEMIES AND EDUCATION

70. THE ESTABLISHMENT OF THE ACADEMY OF SCIENCES AND THE OBSERVATORY

Henri Testelin (1616-95), after Charles Le Brun (1619-90)
17th century
Oil on canvas
20-1/2" x 35-1/2" (52 x 90 cm.)

Loaned by the Musée National de Château de Versailles / MV 6344

In the spirit of the Enlightenment, the Sun King was responsible for the establishment of many educational and professional institutions in the arts and sciences, and the construction of a number of imposing buildings to house them. The majority of these organizations were seated in or near Paris.

The Royal Academy of Sciences was created at the urging of Jean-Baptiste Colbert in 1666 for the study and promotion of mathematics, physics, and natural history. The Paris Observatory was organized in the following year, and the building was constructed from 1668 to 1672 by Claude Perrault (1613-88), also credited with the design of the East Front of the Louvre.

This painting is the preparatory sketch for the cartoon of a tapestry that was never woven.
VLG/CC

Catalogue 71

71. VIEW OF THE OBSERVATORY AND ITS SURROUNDINGS
Attributed to Jean Millet, called Francisque
(1666-1723)
Early 18th century
Oil on canvas
52" x 73" (132 x 185.5 cm.)

Loaned by the Musée Carnavalet / P.237

The Paris Observatory has functioned for over three hundred years. The austere and monumental structure has housed many pioneers in astronomy, horology, cartography, and related fields.

The Meridian of Paris forms the axis of the square pavilion of the Observatory. The sides of the octagonal towers are aligned to the summer and winter solstices and to the spring and fall equinoxes. The astronomer Jean Dominque Cassini (1625-1721), first director of the Observatory, requested even more elaborate astrological orientations, but his demands were ignored by the architect.

The Observatory of Paris was created in 1667 at the initiative of Colbert and the recently established Academy of Science, itself organized at Colbert's urging. The site selected for the Observatory was in the Faubourg Saint Jacques, then outside Paris. Claude Perrault, brother of the writer and architectural theorist, was selected as architect for the building, which was completed in 1672.

This view of the Observatory was taken from the Butte aux Cailles ("Quail Hill"), a rise with windmills, as the view shows. Behind the observatory the Convent of Port-Royal is visible, and farther on the dome of the Val-de-Grace. The picture represents an extension into the eighteenth century of the Flemish scenographic formula, using lateral groups of trees to translate depth and alternating light and dark zones. While the background is a faithful presentation of the topography, both realism and convention are employed in the foreground, where real and make-believe shepherds appear. The "false" shepherd is seen inviting a pastoral idyll with a young woman who has escaped from a troop of laundresses, who were taking their wash to the Bièvre, a small river nearby.
FF/de la H/VLG

72. THE TERRESTRIAL GLOBE REPRESENTED IN TWO HEMISPHERE PLANS
Map: Jean Baptiste Nolin (1657-1725)
Color: Nicolas Bocquet
1700
Hand-colored engraving
37" x 49" (94 x 124.5 cm.)

Collections of the Louisiana State Museum / Gift of Mr. and Mrs. Solis Seiferth / 1982.77.114

Among the prominent geographers, publishers, and engravers of the Sun King's era was Jean-Baptiste Nolin, who was born and died in Paris. A student of François de Poilly, he traveled to Rome to perfect his art. Returning to Paris, Nolin opened a boutique selling prints in the Rue Saint-Jacques, at the sign of "la Place des Victoires." He soon turned to selling geographic maps and acquired a reputation for the decorative embellishment of his maps. In 1693, Nolin became a royal geographer and usurped the title of "Engraver to the King and Geographer to the Duke of Orleans."

In 1700 Nolin plagiarized Guillaume

Catalogue 72

Delisle's globe of 1699. Delisle, holding the privilege of the king, brought suit against Nolin in the royal court, charging that Nolin had in large part reproduced his innovations in cartography. Experts were called in from the Academy of Sciences and held that Nolin was guilty of plagiarism. Delisle was given the right to destroy Nolin's printing plates. However, Delisle was moderate in his execution of the sentence and only effaced those portions of the plates which copied his globe.

The map shows the routes of several explorers, French and English, around the world. Of particular interest in the Western Hemisphere is evidence of the continued hope of finding a Northwest Passage to the Orient. Across the top of the map are six scenes of Adam and Eve in the Garden of Eden, their expulsion, and Cain and Abel at their respective altars offering up the fruits of their labors to God. Surrounding the two hemisphere portions of the map are scenes showing the six days of creation, all in brilliant color.
JDC

73. MODEL OF CORONELLI'S CELESTIAL GLOBE

Jean Baptiste Nolin (1657-1725), after Arnould de Vuez (1644-1720)
Restrike engravings

Loaned by the Louisiana Museum Foundation

Royal encouragement to the sciences in France attracted foreign experts such as the Franciscan Vincenzo Maria Coronelli (1650-1718). He was the founder of the Academia Cosmografo degli Argonauti and official cartographer to the Serene Republic (Venice). His French works consist largely of beautiful celestial and terrestrial globes. A spectacular pair, over fifteen feet in diameter, was made for the Sun King and installed at the Château de Marly. Coronelli's smaller globes, three and one-half feet in diameter, completed in 1688, are considered his most important works.

Coronelli's celestial globes present thirty-eight constellations in the Northern Hemisphere and thirty-three in the Southern Hemisphere and include 1,092 individual stars. The curvilinear globe form was projected into odd-shaped flat surfaces for printing. The prints were trimmed, glued over a three-dimensional frame, and hand colored.
JM/VLG

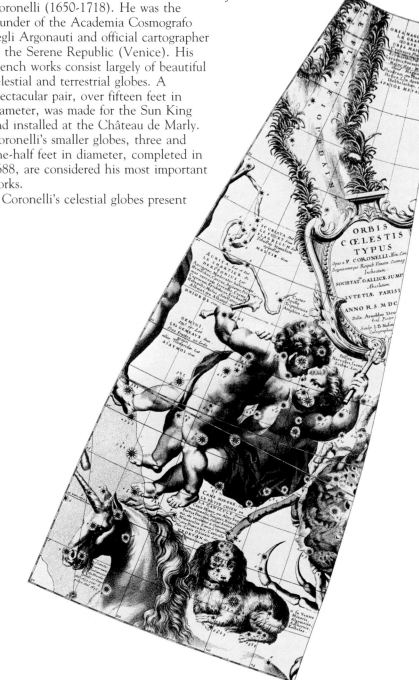

Catalogue 73

74. INSTRUMENT FOR CALIBRATING SUNDIALS
Unidentified maker
Late 17th century or early 18th century
Brass and silver
5-1/4" x 5-3/8" x 2-1/8" (13.4 x 13.7 x 5.4 cm.)

Loaned by the Department of European Sculpture and Decorative Arts of the Metropolitan Museum of Art / 03.21.17 / Gift of Mrs. Stephen D. Tucker, 1903

Catalogue 75

Horology, or the science of measuring time, was an aspect of astronomy. Paris time is still announced from the famous "talking clock" at the observatory.

Michael Butterfield, an Englishman who worked in Paris between 1678 and 1727, is believed to have been the inventor of a class of pocket sundials that bears his name and became the standard French model. These are small horizontal dials made of brass or silver with a recessed compass and engraved with three or four circles or chapters of hour lines for use in several latitudes. They have folding styles that adjust to the correct angle of latitude indicated by the characteristic little bird beak. This instrument, however, is more than a simple Butterfield-type portable sundial. Nicolas Bion, author of the most popular treatise on scientific instruments of the eighteenth century, the *Traité de la Construction et des Principaux Usages des Instruments de Mathématique*, first published in Paris in 1709, explained its use. By adjusting the revolving circular plate and the screw feet, and by extending a thread from the center hole through the appropriate hour lines to a series of points on a surface beyond the edge of the square baseplate, the instrument can be used to calibrate various kinds of sundials without the necessity of having to calculate the positions of their hour lines mathematically.

The maker of this instrument is unknown, but its applied silver decoration are characteristic of the latter part of the reign of King Louis XIV. While most of the better French sundial makers of this period did identify their work, this instrument may have remained unsigned because it belonged to a larger set of various instruments of which only a few would customarily have been signed.
Cl. V

Catalogue 74

75. BRACKET CLOCK (of the "Religious" Type)
Jacques Huguet
Ca. 1690
Wood, tortoise shell, bronze *doré*, enamel and various metals
24-3/8" x 10-5/8" (62 x 27 cm.)

Loaned by the Musée des Arts Décoratifs / INV. 5353

Devices for measuring time, based on astronomical discoveries, became very elaborate. Decorative dials and complicated cases housed intricate mechanisms. Complex metal inlay was the hallmark of the cabinetmaker André-Charles Boule (1642-1732), and examples are generically called by his name.

76. WATCH
Movement probably by Nicolas Gribelin (1637-1719)
Paris, *ca.* 1680
Signed (on the backplate of the movement): Gribelin
Case and dial of painted enamel on gold; movement of gilded brass, silver, and steel, partly blued
2-3/8" dia. (6 cm. dia.)

Loaned by the Department of European Sculpture and Decorative Arts of the Metropolitan Museum of Art / 17.190.1559 / Gift of J. Pierpont Morgan, 1917

Jean Toutin (1578-1644), a goldsmith of Châteaudun, is believed to have been the inventor of a type of painting in colored enamels on a white enamel ground exemplified by the miniatures on the case of this watch. No example of Jean Toutin's work is known, but a watchcase painted by his son Henri (b. 1614) in Paris and dated 1641 is in the collection of the Rijksmuseum in Amsterdam. Painted enamel watchcases continued to be a French specialty throughout the reign of Louis XIV. The miniatures on the base and dial of this watch depict Anthony and Cleopatra, and they appear to belong to a group illustrating the same subject found on at least one other watch case that is probably by the same enamel painter. They were once attributed to Robert Vauquer (1625-70), but in fact their source remains obscure and rather difficult to date on the basis of style

Catalogue 76

alone.

The dating of this watch rests therefore on evidence provided by the movement, which is fitted with a balance spring. An invention of the Dutch mathematician Christiaan Huygens in 1675, the balance spring made the addition of a minute hand to a watch practical. The presence of a chapter of minutes on the outermost ring of the painted enamel dial of this watch indicates that the watch originally had a minute hand and that the balance spring is not a later addition. Furthermore, the movement lacks a *fusée*, the device traditionally used to even out the force of the mainspring as

it unwinds. *Fusées* were abandoned during a brief period when watchmakers tried to employ the balance spring alone to regulate their watches. The results were rather unsatisfactory, and fusées soon became standard in watches with balance springs. The watch is probably a rare survival of that brief period of experimentation.

The maker was probably Nicolas Gribelin, a member of a prominent family of clockmakers active in Blois in the sixteenth and seventeenth centuries. He is recorded as early as 1674 working in Paris as clockmaker to the Grand Dauphin.
Cl. V

Catalogue 77

77. WATCH

Movement by F. L. Meybom
French (Paris), *ca.* 1675
Signed (on the backplate of the movement):
F. Meybom à Paris/St. Germain
Case of gold, silver, blued steel, rock crystal, and
diamonds; movement of gilded brass and steel,
partly blued
1-1/4" x 1-1/4" x 7/8" (3.1 x 3.1 x 2.2 cm.)

Loaned by the Department of European Sculpture
and Decorative Arts of the Metropolitan Museum
of Art / 17.190.1600 / Gift of J. Pierpont Morgan,
1917

This watch is a fine example of French craftsmanship at the height of the reign of Louis XIV. Its case is decorated with tiny pierced and engraved floral patterns of gold, strengthened by gold wires that complete the design, and mounted on panels of blued steel. The hinged cover is made of polished rock crystal set in a silver and diamond bezel, and the face of blue and white enamel is painted with black numerals and miniature pink and blue floral designs. The growing independence of the makers of gold watchcases from French goldsmiths' guilds during the course of the seventeenth century resulted in the establishment of such craftsmen in their own separate and specialized workshops. It may account for the relative freedom of choice of media employed in making watchcases, and it probably also explains why few cases are marked by their makers in a way that is comparable to ordinary goldsmiths' work.

The anonymous maker of the Metropolitan Museum's watchcase probably made a second one for another movement by Meybom, which is now in the Fitzwilliam Museum in Cambridge. A third case, now in the Louvre, has a movement signed "Baltazar Martinot à Paris." Practically nothing is known about Meybom, but the second watchmaker seems to have been Balthazar Martinot l'Aîné (1635-1716), who came to Paris from Rouen before 1683 and became clockmaker to both Anne d'Autriche and the king. The movement of the Metropolitan Museum's watch has no balance spring, and it is unlikely that it would have been made without one after about 1680. The watch is probably not very much earlier in date, for the design of the case finds its closest comparisons in ornamental engravings of the decade 1670-80.
CL

224

78. RENÉ DESCARTES

Sébastien Bourdon (1616-71)
Before 1650
Oil on canvas
35-5/8" x 28" (88 x 71 cm.)

Loaned by the Département des Peintures of the Musée du Louvre / INV 2812

René Descartes (1596-1650) was among the leading mathematical researchers of his time, discovering negative roots, exponential conventions, cartesian coordinates, and cartesian curves, making milestone contributions to analytical geometry. He also made advances in optics, physical theory, and psychology. His numerous publications were widely read and studied in France and abroad.

Descartes developed a philosophy of Dualism, maintaining that the physical world is mechanical, separate, and entirely different from the mind; the

meeting point of the two lay in God. He adopted as his motto "*Cogito, ergo sum*" ("I think, therefore I am").

Descartes was educated by the Jesuits at the Collège de la Flèche of the University of Poitiers, after which he pursued a short military career in the service of Prince Maurice of Nassau. In 1628, he left the army and established himself briefly in Paris and then in Holland, where his major work was accomplished. Queen Christina of Sweden invited him to her court in 1649. Descartes died in the following year, suffering from the hostile northern climate.

The painter Sébastien Bourdon (1616-71) also lived briefly in Sweden at Queen Christina's invitation. He served as First Painter to the Swedish Crown from 1652 to 1654.

VLG

Catalogue 78

79. BLAISE PASCAL

Unidentified artist
17th century
Oil on canvas
27-5/8" x 22-1/8" (70 x 56 cm.)

Loaned by the Musée National du Château de Versailles / MV 5527

The scientist-philosopher Blaise Pascal (1623-62) contributed many advances to calculus and the physical sciences, particulary hydraulics. René Descartes (see #78) disagreed with Pascal's ideas concerning vacuums, saying that the only perfect vacuum in existence was in Pascal's head. Pascal's law states that pressure applied to a fluid at any point is transmitted throughout the fluid in all directions and acts equally and at right angles on all surfaces of the confining vessel.

Pascal was an ardent Jansenist; his sister Jacqueline was in the convent at Port-Royal. Pascal studied as a young man with his father and later with the Jansenists. By the age of sixteen he had written a paper on conic sections which received favorable attention and, at nineteen, he invented a calculating machine. He is credited with originating the modern theory of probability.

Pascal's best-known philosophical works are his *Provincial Letters,* defending the Jansenists against Jesuit attack, and his *Thoughts,* published posthumously in fragmentary form, which hold faith to be above rather than contrary to reason.

The majority of known portraits of Pascal are variants on the engraving by

Gérard Édelinck (1640-1707), made after the picture by François II Quesnel (1637-99) done several years after Pascal's death, but which, according to certain contemporaries, was quite

accurate. This painting, inversed from the engraving, is perfectly true to the model but cannot be attributed to any identifiable painter.
CC/VLG

Catalogue 79

Veüe du College des quatre Nations　*Prospectus Collegij quatuor Nationum*

Catalogue 80

80. THE COLLEGE OF THE FOUR NATIONS
Israël Silvestre the Elder (1621-91)
Restrike engraving
22-1/2" x 30" (57.2 x 76.2 cm.)

Loaned by the Louisiana Museum Foundation

Three days before his death, Cardinal Mazarin (1602-61) wrote into his will a provision for a large legacy to create a college for the education of sixty young men from the aristocracy of four newly annexed provinces of France — Artois, Alsace, Roussillon, and Pignerol. The design, inspired by the Church of St. Agnes in Rome, was drawn by Louis Le Vau (1612-70). Construction was not completed until after Le Vau's death.

The imposing Italianate baroque structure with curved wings is located directly across the Seine from the Square Court of the Louvre. Mazarin's tomb by Antoine Coysevox (1640-1720) was originally located in the central domed chapel. The cardinal's magnificent library had been maintained in the building, which now houses the Institut de France, composed of the five official academies.
VLG

81. FORMALITIES TO BE OBSERVED ON THE PART OF PENSIONERS FOR ADMISSION TO THE COLLÈGE MAZARIN

Unidentified scribe
Paris, 31 December 1686
9-5/8" x 7-1/8" (24.5 x 18 cm.)

Loaned by the Archives of the Ministère des Relations Extérieures / MD France, Vol. 1594, Fol. 395-396

Following the wishes expressed in the will of Cardinal Mazarin, admission to the College of the Four Nations (also called the Collège Mazarin) required that students be of families of at least one hundred twenty years nobility on the paternal side and be originally from the provinces of Artois, Alsace, Roussillon, or Pignerol. They had to be between the ages of ten and fifteen, "capable of at least the first class in grammar," and without deformities or chronic illnesses, in addition to other requirements. The school opened to its first class in 1668, seven years after the Cardinal's death.

The document consists of two sheets of laid, watermarked paper on which a letter had been started before this manuscript of the "Formalities" was composed. Both sheets have been employed on both sides.
MC/VLG

82. STATE OF THE YOUNG ORIENTALS SUPPORTED AT THE COLLÈGE LOUIS LE GRAND BY THE LIBERALITY OF THE KING

Unidentified scribe
August, 1705
8-3/4" x 6-5/8" (22.2 x 17 cm.)

Loaned by the Archives of the Ministère des Relations Extérieures / MD Turquie, Vol. 155, fol. 17-19

Hoping to sway future foreign leaders favorably by educating them in France, the Sun King underwrote the expenses of students from Eastern Europe and the Near East. A report of their progress was written; its first entry reads:

"Pantaleon Xavier Lomaca. Greek by Nationality, Native of Pera, twenty-three years of age, arrived in France June 16, 1700. He has completed a year of Theology and will begin the second next year. He is destined for an ecclesiastic career. It is proposed by his Latin bishop to send him back to Constantinople at the end of 1706 to receive Orders, and [was] sent by the Holy Congregation. He is of spirit [mind] and capability."

These students helped spread the French language and admiration for French culture throughout the diplomatic centers of Europe and the East.

By decree of November 18, 1669, Louis XIV fixed the "Statute of the Dragomans [i.e. interpreters] in the Steppes of the Levant" and created language schools for French children in the convents of the Capucins in Constantinople and Smyrna at the expense of the Chamber of Commerce of Marseilles. These were the antecedents of the School of Living Oriental Languages, now in Paris.

In order to meet the competition of the English, who had started a free seminary at Oxford for twenty young Greeks, Père Portier proposed in 1698 to found a competitive establishment at the Abbey of St. Victor in Marseilles. The idea was taken up the following year by Cardinal Janson and Père François de La Chaise (1624-1709), the king's confessor at Versailles. The project was studied and then put aside during the War of the Spanish Succession.

The final decision was to enroll a certain number of young Christian Orientals at the Collège Louis le Grand, supported by the kings' privy purse. This institution, now a well-known preparatory high school, is still found in the Rue Saint-Jacques in Paris.

The document gives a listing of the young people being educated in this fashion in 1705, and it establishes some general principles to be used to guide the selection of future students. It consists of three sheets of laid, watermarked paper.
MC/VLG

Catalogue 81

Catalogue 82

83. DECLARATION OF THE KING TO HAVE THE EXPERIMENTS IN THE ROYAL BOTANICAL GARDENS CONTINUED

Jean-Baptiste Colbert (1619-83)
Paris, 20 January 1673
9-7/8" x 6-5/8" (25 x 17 cm.)

Loaned by the Archives of the Ministère des Relations Extérieures / MD France, Vol. 1594, fol. 323-324

Experiments and public demonstrations in the fields of botany, chemistry, and anatomical dissection were carried out at the Royal Botanical Gardens in Paris. The garden and its programs were established by an edict of Louis XIII in January, 1626. They were started as a collection of medical plants and herbs, patterned after that of Henri IV at Montpellier, which was considered an exemplary prototype. Specimen plants and exotic species were introduced in the late seventeenth century.

The programs of the gardens were expanded in 1635 by the introduction of three doctors instructing in medicine, and again in 1671 by the creation of an improved and enlarged administration. The Sun King by this decree expressed his wish that these scientific and educational programs should be continued, especially those dealing with dissection and surgery.
MC/VLG

84. PHARMACEUTICAL URN

Unidentified potter, Nevers
17th century
Tin-glazed earthenware (faïence)
19-5/8" x 16-1/8" (50 x 41 cm.)

Loaned by the Musée Carnavalet

Among the medicinal concoctions prepared from herbs in the seventeenth century was *theriaque* or *theriaca* (sometimes called treacle in English). This potion was a baroque cure-all, prescribed to fortify the heart, cure ulcers, dropsy, and jaundice, and as an antidote to poisons and snakebite. Variant recipes called for such ingredients as juniper and ground vipers. The invention of *theriaca* is traced back to Galen, and the composition, held secret, varied according to the epoch and the country. Its use ceased progressively with the advances of medical science in the nineteenth century.

A theriaca urn in the seventeenth century, and especially at Nevers — an important center of production along with other towns such as Lyon — was a vase of monumental aspect in the form of an urn with handles and a lid. Although this form continued in use in the following century, the *décor* of this urn is very specific to Nevers production in the seventeenth century: the birds and foliage, ringed in dark strokes, painted in copper green on a ground of white enamel, are characteristic, along with the dark blue and yellow orange grounds of the "Persian" *décor*. This oriental style seems to have been inspired by Iranian vases of the fifteenth and sixteenth centuries, which came to France by way of Venice and Genoa. It was probably perfected before 1650 in the manufactory of Pierre Custode and enjoyed great popularity during the

second half of the century. The green *décor*, rather rare in comparison to blue grounds, had been used for vases — whether they were apothecary or not (forms differed but little) — and also for the gourds (or bottles) of pilgrims. It was often associated with a motif of black *rinceaux*, giving an appearance of the *niello* (inlaid enameling) of goldsmithing. This motif is executed on a yellow ground and is laid out in horizontal bands. On this piece the ornamentation appears on the foot as well as the base and collar of the vessel. The twisted arms, dappled on a manganese violet ground, are less typical of a precise style because they are also allied to the *décor* called "Italo-Nevers."

Two masks, one of which is provided with wings, isolate the cartouche surrounding an inscription indicating the use of the urn, according to correct design for pharmaceutical faïence.

The ceramics of Nevers reached their apex in the seventeenth century, before declining at the end of the reign of Louis XIV. The first Trianon in the Versailles complex, called the Trianon de Porcelaine, was ornamented in 1672 with Nevers faïence, along with that of Delft and Rouen. At Nevers, the production of faïence imitated Italian majolicas and began in the manufactory of the Conrade brothers, natives of Albissola, near Savona, Italy, who had been attracted to France by the Italian Luigi Gonzaga, duc de Nevers. The royal monopoly accorded by Henri IV to Augustin Conrade expired in 1630, after which date rival manufactories multiplied, among them the famous one of Pierre Custode. French makers then departed from the imitation of Italian majolicas to create a series of original styles, the "Persian" *décor* being one of the more remarkable.
FF/VLG

DECLARATION DU ROY,
POUR FAIRE CONTINUER
les Exercices au Jardin Royal
des Plantes.

*Regiſtrée au Parlement & Chambre des Comptes,
le 23. Mars 1675.*

A PARIS,
Chez FREDERIC LEONARD, Imprimeur du
Roy, ruë S. Jacques, à l'Ecu de Veniſe.
M. DC. LXXIII.
AVEC PRIVILEGE DV ROY.

Catalogue 83

Catalogue 84

Catalogue 85

85. JEPHTÉ

Abbé Claude Boyer (1618-98) and an unidentified bookbinder
1692
Printed book, bound in gold-tooled leather
10" x 7-1/2" x 5/8" (25.4 x 19 x 1.5 cm.)

Loaned by the Musée des Arts Décoratifs / INV D-18881

Educated women in the seventeenth century were either convent schooled or privately tutored. Under the auspices of Madame de Maintenon, a special school for two hundred fifty young women from ages six to nineteen was created at the Convent of St. Cyr, near Versailles. Highly original in concept, the school prepared young women for the world rather than for the veil (Madame de Maintenon herself had married Paul Scarron to escape the nunnery). The large complex at St. Cyr was designed by Jules Hardouin-Mansart to Madame de Maintenon's specifications.

Among its unusual programs, the school produced theatrical entertainments with students playing all the parts. This copy of *Jephté*, a tragedy by the Abbé Claude Boyer (1618-98), is bound in the arms of St. Cyr. Madame de Maintenon exerted her personal influence to persuade Racine to write *Esther* (1689) and *Athalie* (1691) for the school. The first headmistress, the Ursuline Madame de Brinon, wrote the verse "Grand Dieu Sauvez le Roi" in honor of Louis XIV. It later became the British national anthem in translation as "God Save the King."

The school had a checkered existence. From a brilliant beginning it passed from progressive to reactionary phases and was involved in religious scandals concerning the doctrine of Quietism.
VLG

86. DRAFT OF "STATUTES AND RULES THAT THE KING WISHES AND ORDERS TO BE OBSERVED IN THE ACADEMY . . . THAT HIS MAJESTY HAS RESOLVED TO ESTABLISH IN THE CITY OF ROME"

Jean-Baptiste Colbert (1619-83) and clerical assistants, 11 February 1666
13-3/4" x 9-5/8" (35 x 24.5 cm.)

Loaned by the Archives Nationales/ O-1935, pièce 1

France was a leader in arts education. The Royal Academy of Painting and Sculpture was founded in Paris in 1648, during the youth of the Sun King. As the great schemes for Versailles were developed and Colbert began to conceive his ideas for Mercantilism, it became evident that France lacked sufficient and sophisticated artists to produce all that was needed. It was determined that the most promising students at the Academy would benefit from direct contact with ancient, Renaissance, and possibly recent Italian art.

The French Academy in Rome was created to direct the Italian experience of students who won an annual competition for the Rome Prize. The Roman institution (now housed at the Villa Medicis) was conducted according to this able set of regulations promulgated by the king.

Academy enrollment was limited to twelve students, who were to spend their full time copying antique Roman statuary and Italian painting and drafting plans of Italian landmark structures. They were forbidden to work for private individuals; because their expenses were paid by the king, their work was considered property of the French crown.

The statutes were actually decreed by Jean-Baptiste Colbert, then Controller

Catalogue 86

General of Finance and Superintendent of the Department of Works, Arts, and Manufactures. In an autograph postscript, Colbert requests Charles Perrault to have the statutes recorded and to see him about them.

In addition to the French Academy in Rome, Colbert was involved in the founding or reauthorization of the Royal Academy of Painting and Sculpture, the Royal Library (now the Bibliothèque Nationale), and the Paris Observatory. All of these institutions had a common goal — to place artists, scientists, and men of letters within a framework to serve the king and France with maximum efficiency.

The document consists of eight pages of paper, of which seven are used. It is an unidentified hand, with the exception of Colbert's note.
JG/VLG

87. ESTABLISHMENT OF THE ROYAL ACADEMY OF PAINTING AND SCULPTURE

1692
9-7/8" x 7-1/2" (25 x 19 cm.)
[This object is not illustrated]

Loaned by the Archives Nationales / AD VIII 1

The Sun King's reaffirmation and reorganization of the Royal Academy of Painting and Sculpture in 1692 is headed by the original edict creating the Academy in 1648, when he was ten years old. It was the first state-sponsored fine arts training institution of its kind. Academicians or faculty were named from artists practicing in appropriate styles. Nomination to the Academy was the sign of royal recognition and tantamount to financial success. Promising students were rigorously trained to produce works worthy of France. The most promising, selected by annual competition, were sent to the French Academy in Rome (founded in 1666) to benefit from the Italian arts of ancient Rome and the Renaissance. The École Nationale Supérieure des Beaux-Arts in Paris is the descendant institution of the old Royal Academy of Painting and Sculpture.

Creation of the Academy came about because Charles Le Brun, Painter to the King since 1641, and numerous other artists no longer wished to be confused with artisans (such as gilders, marble polishers, color grinders, and the like) and decided to found an academy limited to the best painters and sculptors, who would teach these arts. They obtained a Council decree on January 27, 1648, reserving membership in the Academy to the master painters and sculptors of Paris and ruling that Frenchmen and distinguished foreigners would be admitted to this academy if they were judged worthy by the twelve members of longest standing.

In addition to this decree (pp. 3-5 of the document, erroneously dated January 20, 1648, in the title), the brochure includes the first statutes of the Royal Academy of Painting and Sculpture (first official mention of this title) and thirteen articles confirmed by letters patent from Louis XIV in February, 1648 (pp. 6-14); twenty-one articles added on December 24, 1654, at the king's order to establish the positions of a director and four rectors, to give the title of professor to the twelve members

Catalogue 88

88. SELF-PORTRAIT

Elizabeth-Sophie Chéron Le Hay (1648-1711)
1672
Oil on canvas
34-5/8" x 28-3/4" (88 x 73 cm.)

Loaned by the Département des Peintures of the
Musée du Louvre / INV 3269

Each artist received as a member of the
Royal Academy of Painting and
Sculpture was required to submit an
example of his (or her) best work as a
morceau de réception ("reception piece").
Elizabeth-Sophie Chéron was welcomed
into the Academy in June of 1672 and
presented this self-portrait.

There were relatively few women
artists in the seventeenth century, and
not many of them were named as
Academicians. Widely talented,
Mademoiselle Chéron was a painter,
engraver, musician, and woman of
letters. She was the daughter of the
painter-engraver Henri Chéron. Born
Protestant, she converted to
Catholicism, probably because of the
Revocation of the Edict of Nantes
(1685). At the age of sixty (1708), she
married Jacques Le Hay, a royal
engineer of the same age.
VLG

of longest standing, to admit the best
engravers to the Academy, and to
organize an annual competition among
Academy students for a preliminary
drawing for a painting on the theme of
the heroic actions of the king (pp.
38-45); and definitive statutes and
twenty-seven articles decreed by the
king on December 24, 1663, confirming
a new organization of the Academy and
giving thirty members the same
privileges as the forty members of the
French Academy (pp. 83-93).

Charles Le Brun, the protégé of

Jean-Baptiste Colbert, was the first
chancellor of the Academy, where he
reigned as a virtual despot, governing
the work of artists and their choice of
themes. The annual competition
established in 1654 was the origin of the
competition for the Rome Prize, which
permitted winners to study at the French
Academy in Rome (see #86).

The document was printed in Paris by
the Widow Jean-Baptiste Coignard and
Jean-Baptiste Coignard, Jr. It consists of
a brochure of 104 pages covered in
marbled paper.
JG/VLG

THE KING AND PARIS: THE URBAN ENVIRONMENT

Catalogue 90

90. MAP OF PARIS TAKEN AT THE ORDER OF THE KING
Pierre Bullet (1639-1716)
1676
Engraving
76-3/8" x 76-3/8" (194 x 194 cm.)

Loaned by the Bibliothèque Historique de la Ville de Paris / Rés. A 1504ª

The map approved by the king (see #89) was engraved and published in 1676 and sold by Blondel. The published map was illustrated with views of the Porte Saint-Bernard and the Porte Saint-Denis at the upper left, the Porte Saint-Antoine and the Porte Saint-Martin at the upper right, a plan of fountains and drains of the public water system of Paris at lower left, and a map of the surrounding area at the lower right.
HV/VLG

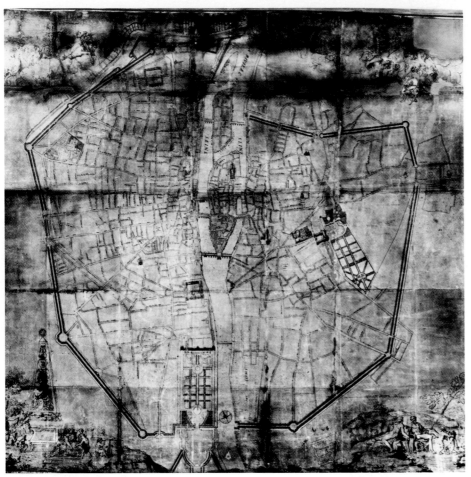

Catalogue 89

89. PLAN (of Paris) TAKEN BY ORDER OF THE KING
Pierre Bullet (1639-1716)
1676
Ink and graphite on paper
95-1/4" x 93" (242 x 236 cm.)

Loaned by the Département des Cartes et Plans of the Bibliothèque Nationale / Ge A 54

The France of Louis XIV had an estimated population of twenty million. Paris was both the capital and largest city, although much smaller than it is today. During his reign, the Sun King built many of the monumental structures that comprise its current landmarks. But the king preferred the country and open space, so he transferred the court and governmental functions to nearby Versailles in May, 1682. We do not often hear of the king in Paris, but many of his courtiers enjoyed its theater and other urban attractions whenever possible.

The Sun King's projects, which can be seen on the map, include the destruction of the ancient northern walls of the city and the establishment of broad, tree-lined boulevards (some over thirty-five yards wide) marked with monumental gates in the form of triumphal arches such as the Porte Saint-Denis (1672), the Porte Saint-Antoine (1674), the Porte Saint-Martin (1674), and the Porte Saint-Bernard (1670). The Cours de Vincennes and the Grand Cours (later the Champs Élysées) had been started, as well as an urban lighting system, increased from 2,736 lanterns in 1667 to 6,000 by 1679.

The map was ordered in 1673 and took two years to complete. This manuscript copy was executed in 1676 for Louis II de Bourbon, prince de Condé (1621-86), whose arms are seen at the upper right.

On June 30, 1673, the Provost of Merchants and the Sheriffs of Paris ordered Pierre Bullet (1639-1716), architect of the Department of Works, and two geometricians, Jean Vibert and François Fastière, to make a plan of the town and suburbs of Paris. The work was completed at the beginning of 1675. It was presented to the City Council in March of 1675 and to Louis XIV in July of 1676, who accorded it letters patent.

Such royal favor is not surprising, since the map shows as much of the great projects of royal city planning as it does of the actual state of Paris. Projects that are shown but had not been achieved were boulevards, begun in the north, which were to encircle the whole town; the quais along the River Seine, which were to be completely opened to circulation; a number of streets that were to be widened; and new streets that were projected in order to facilitate communication between various parts of town.
JB/VLG

232

91. THE PONT-NEUF, THE LOUVRE, AND THE COLLEGE OF THE FOUR NATIONS
Unidentified artist
Ca. 1670
Oil on canvas
22-1/4" x 51-3/4" (56.5 x 131.5 cm.)

Loaned by the Musée Carnavalet / P.700 bis

The River Seine linked Paris with the coast of Normandy and the sea. The original city (Lutetia, an ancient Roman foundation) occupied the island visible in the distance (the Île de la Cité) and grew during Medieval times to encompass the Latin Quarter (to the right) and the Right Bank (to the left in this view). The College of the Four Nations (now the French Academy) was among the last commissions of the architect Louis Le Vau, who directed the first stages of the enlargement of Versailles for the Sun King.

The Pont-Neuf, completed in 1606, proved to be an ideal spot from which to admire the city as well as a convenient crossing point over the Seine. Parisians were charmed by views of the aristocratic new quarter on the left bank, the administrative center of municipal life on the Île de la Cité, and the royal residence of the Louvre on the right bank. Artists quickly sensed the interest in this new urban scenery as a pictorial theme and views from or of the Pont-Neuf appeared so rapidly that their production was almost an industry comparable to that of Venetian *vedute* in the eighteenth century.

This view was made from the Pont-Rouge (later the Pont-Royal). In the foreground are the extensions of modern Paris toward the west: to the left, the *grande galerie* linking the Louvre to the Tuileries, built during the reign of the Sun King's grandfather Henri IV, who broke through the old walls of Charles V, and the Porte Neuve ("New Gate"), which is seen on the riverbank; to the right, between a series of newly built *hôtels* and the high roofs of the Hôtel Guénégaud are the buildings under construction of the College of the Four Nations, an institution founded by Mazarin's will. Their state of completion allows the picture to be dated about 1665. In the distance, beyond the Pont-Neuf and the modern Place Dauphine, the whole of old Paris appears: from left to right are the Tower of Saint Jacques, the roofs of the Châtelet, the Town Hall, the towers of Saint-Jean-en-Grève, and the tall facade of Saint Gervais-Saint Protais, which partially hides the dome of Saint Louis. After the Pont-au-Change and the tower of the Palace of Justice, the spire of Sainte Chapelle and the towers of Notre Dame can be seen. This unique urban ensemble was among the most admired views of Paris. It gained great fame in the seventeenth century and has been widely admired ever since.

The river itself provided no less pleasure to the eyes. It served as a very active port, as seen from the large number of barges and lighters that encumber it. In the foreground two richly ornamented boats add an unusual note. To the left is the *Royal*, which took the king for outings on the Seine, and toward the center is the *Royale*, a galley that towed it.
J M B/de la H/VLG

Catalogue 91

92. THE BREAD AND POULTRY MARKET ON THE QUAI OF THE GRANDS AUGUSTINS (Painted Fan)
Unidentified artist
17th century
Gouache on paper
10-5/8" x 17" (27 x 43 cm.)

Loaned by the Musée Carnavalet / D.7780

A thriving urban life flourished in Paris, a center of trades, industries, and education. Small merchants maintained open-air markets, and their frequent and rambunctious disputes provided lively subject matter for genre painters. Elaborate painted fans were an important accessory to feminine costume and their decoration was often scenic in nature (see #140 and #35).

Markets and fairs played an essential role in Parisian life in the seventeenth century, assuring a diversification of foodstuffs and a multiplication of commodities, necessary in an epoque of frequent scarcities. Although home production of bread was important, flour was difficult to preserve. The purchase of bread was an ordinary and widespread custom, at least among ordinary people, who were the most susceptible to want. Parisian bakers with shops and hawkers both sold in the markets. At the beginning of the eighteenth century, there were no less than fifteen bread markets in Paris, about six hundred resident bakers, and over fifteen hundred hawkers. Bread made in the environs of Paris, particularly at Gonesse of Saint-Germain-en-Laye, was particularly sought.

The poultry or game market was held in a single place, but the widespread public works and construction in Paris in the seventeenth century caused it to move several times. It was probably located on the Quai of the Grands Augustins about 1660. However, it was only by a Council decree of 1697 that it was officially placed there and united with the bread market of the Pont Saint-Michel. It is possibly shortly after this time that the fan should be dated.

In the background, on the other side of the Pont-Neuf, the Louvre can be seen at the extreme left, then the Ile de la Cité with the equestrian statue of Henri IV, the facades of the houses in the Place Dauphine overlooking the Quai des Orfèvres, and finally Sainte Chapelle.
MM/VLG

Catalogue 92

93. LEFT FOOT OF LOUIS XIV
(Fragment of an Equestrian Statue)
François Girardon (1628-1715)
Cast by the Keller Brothers, 1692
Bronze
26-3/4" (68 cm.)

Loaned by the Département des Sculptures of the Musée du Louvre / MR 3448

Among the best-known urban monuments of eighteenth-century France was the equestrian statue of Louis XIV in the Place Louis le Grand (later the Place Vendôme). The square was created largely due to the initiative of François Michel Le Tellier, marquis de Louvois, in an effort to please Louis XIV, to beautify the city, and to leave his own mark on Paris. The land was ceded to the City of Paris, which undertook completion of the square in 1699, following the designs of Jules Hardouin-Mansart, honoring Louis XIV as Warrior King. The Place Louis le Grand was occupied by figures associated with Louisiana history: Antoine Crozat and John Law both later lived there. In the nineteenth century, one of its houses was occupied by the mother of the Baroness Pontalba.

In 1792, during the French Revolution, Girardon's great bronze in the Place Louis le Grand was torn down. All that remains of the original sculpture is this fragment.
VLG

Catalogue 93

Catalogue 94

94. ELEVATION OF THE PRINCIPAL FACADE OF THE LOUVRE ON THE SIDE OF SAINT-GERMAIN L'AUXERROIS, BUILT UNDER THE REIGN OF LOUIS XIV AND THE MINISTRY OF JEAN-BAPTISTE COLBERT, ON THE DESIGNS OF CLAUDE PERRAULT OF THE ROYAL ACADEMY OF SCIENCES

Jacques-François Blondel (1705-74)
18th century
Engraving
19-5/8" x 45-5/8" (49.7 x 116 cm.)

Loaned by the Musée Carnavalet / Topo GC IV D

Completion of the Palace of the Louvre by providing a monumental facade for the exterior of the Square Court was deemed necessary during the early years of the Sun King's reign. Although Louis XIV ultimately chose to live at Versailles, Colbert urged him to make the Louvre and Paris into a palace and capital worthy of the monarch.

After the official rejection of Bernini's projects for the Louvre, Colbert had, in April, 1667, brought together a "Little Council" composed of Louis Le Vau, his assistant François d'Orbay, Charles Le Brun, and Claude Perrault, confiding to them the task of elaborating a design for the single eastern facade. This commission supplied in fact two designs: one, probably by Le Brun, adapted without difficulty to the pre-existing construction; the other was by Claude Perrault, according to the opinionated *mémoires* of his brother Charles.

A classically balanced series of three pavilions connected by long colonnades of freestanding paired columns was selected. The combined grandeur and severity of this facade, begun in 1667, gained it instantaneous recognition as the epitome of the Louis XIV style in architecture.

Claude Perrault (1613-88) was given credit for the design. There were, however, considerable contributions in thinking from Charles Le Brun (1619-90), Louis Le Vau (1612-70), and François d'Orbay (1634-97), as well as the influence of the designs made by Gian Lorenzo Bernini (1598-1680) in 1665. Influenced perhaps by the anterior suggestions of Houdin (made in 1661) and of Le Vau (1664), Perrault had proposed a colonnade, the principle of which was accepted on May 14, 1667, by Louis XIV, and the cornerstone of which was accpeted on May 14, 1667, by Louis XIV, and the cornerstone of colonnade satisfied the needs of monumentality but *ipso facto* created a disparity in style with the quite recent south facade (on the Seine) built between 1660 and 1663 by Le Vau, which harmonized perfectly with the east wing of the Square Court to the point of repeating its dome. To this problem of aesthetic order was added the financial impossibility of obtaining, at the price of numerous demolitions, sufficient visual privacy for the king's apartment, which was to be placed in the colonnade wing.

The solution that was adopted consisted of enlarging the former apartment in the south wing by doubling its depth and by building, at a distance of fifteen meters in front of it, a new facade in harmony with the colonnade. This made the colonnade too short, so it was elongated by widening the *avant-corps*, which compensated for the thrusting forward of the south wing. As it was no longer destined to receive the king, the east wing had its windows blinded and the colonnade became a facade screen with no other justification than an ideology of grandeur.

The respective roles taken by the different architects in these complex transformations remain difficult to evaluate. It seems that d'Orbay (Le Vau's collaborator, for whom he directed the construction yards after 1660) built the south facade (possibly with Perrault) and amended the initial design of the colonnade, of which Perrault was not the exclusive author. Liberties were taken with the canonical proportions of the Corinthian order, which the purist Perrault would not have permitted. Although the intervention of d'Orbay is indisputed fact, it seems just to credit Perrault for at least the original conception and the experimental use of the iron framework.

Louis XIV's decision to abandon Paris for Versailles led to suspension of work on the colonnade, which was only finished under the Empire. The print shows it in an idealized state of completion, including the presence of statues, in niches that were changed into windows in the nineteenth century and the four parts of the world on the piers of the central body. Likewise the garlanded ovolos (wide convex moldings) never received the projected reliefs (scenes from the life of the king in allegorical form), but during the Restoration simple knottings were supplied. Finally, the tympanum of the entrance was not carved until the period of the Empire.

The colonnade constituted, vis-à-vis the projects of Bernini, a sort of manifesto of French architecture, freed of the formal rules and games of the Italian baroque, reaching toward an aesthetic of "a noble simplicity and a calm grandeur." Certainly the rationalists of the nineteenth century blamed it for a lack of rigor in constructional techniques (multiple overhangs in the assembly of stones necessitating the use of iron braces — heterogeneous material that quickly rusted from infiltration of moisture). They also underlined the absence of logic of a conception for an ensemble, which made a sort of *trompe l'oeil* of this facade — an insensitive veneer against the buildings of the Square Court.

Nevertheless, the colonnade was widely admired in its time and was reproduced as a model in the "Course" by François Blondel (theoretician and architect of the Porte Saint-Denis). A century later, it retained its reference value since it was the admitted model of Gabriel for his palaces in the Place Louis XV.
FF/VLG

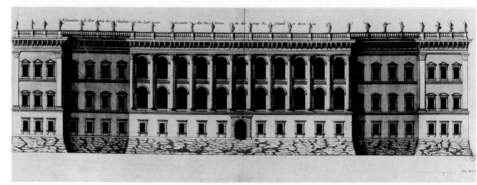

Catalogue 95

95. ELEVATION OF THE ENTRANCE OF THE TUILERIES SIDE, DESIGN BY CAVALIER BERNINI
Jean Marot (1619-79)
Ca. 1665
Engraving
17-5/8" x 21-7/8" (44.7 x 55.7 cm.)

Loaned by the Musée Carnavalet / Topo GC IV A

Gian Lorenzo Bernini (1598-1680) was probably the most famous living artist-architect in the mid-1660s. Bernini was summoned from Rome to Paris at the behest of the Sun King to design the major entrance to the Louvre; his visit recalled that of Leonardo Da Vinci to the court of François I.

Bernini's personality did not please the French, who found him arrogant. His designs, with deeply projecting Italian baroque components, were too dramatic for reserved French taste, and Bernini finally returning to Italy, laden with gifts, at the end of 1665. The ultimate rejection of his plans in 1667 may have been as much the result of French jealousies as of French tastes. While in France, Bernini executed a magnificent bust of Louis XIV and in Italy made an equestrian statue of the Sun King that was later delivered to Versailles.

Dissatisfied with earlier French proposals for the Louvre, Colbert had addressed, in April, 1664, those

prestigious promoters of the Italian baroque Carlo Rainoldi, Pietro da Cartona, and Bernini. Bernini sent a proposal that would join to the existing construction an eastern facade with an alternation of convex and concave projections. Colbert's criticisms induced Bernini to furnish new propositions, which in their turn were severely examined by the minister. It was at this point, thanks to diplomatic pressures applied to the Holy See, in whose service Bernini worked, that Louis XIV had the artist brought to Paris. Bernini's visit began happily. Presented to the king in June, 1665, Bernini submitted a third design, which was accepted in September.

The western facade of Bernini's final proposal, shown in this print, presented an elevation similar to that of the east: rustication, channeling, and the colossal Corinthian order, crowned with sculpture. The cornerstone was laid by the king on October 17, 1665, and three days later Bernini left for Rome.

Colbert kept the work at a slow pace from 1665 to 1667 and on July 15 of that year announced to Bernini that military expenses had obliged him to suspend construction. However, in April Colbert had called together the "Little Council," composed of Le Vau, Le Brun, and Claude Perrault, which ultimately resulted in the realization of the existing colonnade.
FF/VLG

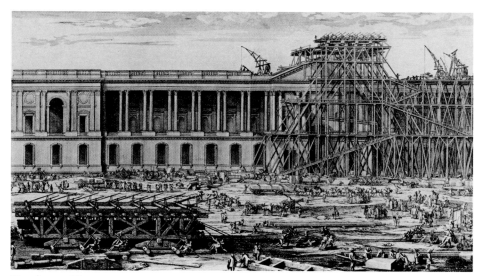

Catalogue 96

97. REPRESENTATION OF THE MACHINES THAT SERVED TO LIFT THE TWO LARGE STONES THAT COVER THE PEDIMENT OF THE PRINCIPAL ENTRANCE OF THE LOUVRE
Sébastien Le Clerc the Elder (1637-1714)
1677
Engraved copper
15" x 24-7/8" (38 x 63 cm.)
[This object not illustrated]

Loaned by the Chalcograpie of the Musée du Louvre / 2825

This elaborately detailed copper plate depicting the final stages of the construction of the East Front of the Louvre was used in 1677 to print the etching that accompanies it (see #96).
VLG

96. REPRESENTATION OF THE MACHINES THAT SERVED TO LIFT THE TWO LARGE STONES THAT COVER THE PEDIMENT OF THE PRINCIPAL ENTRANCE OF THE LOUVRE
Sébastien Le Clerc the Elder (1637-1714)
1677
Etching
15-3/4" x 25-3/8" (39.9 x 64.5 cm.)

Loaned by the Musée Carnavalet / Topo GC IV D

Construction of the massive East Front of the Louvre was a major technological achievement. It was completed by capping the pediment of the central pavilion with two immense stones that had to be moved onto the site and lifted into position.

The pediment was put up in 1672. The monolith from which it was made had been brought to Paris from the quarries at Meudon on the transport wagon seen in the foreground of the print. It was sawed into two pieces and raised using a complicated scaffold equipped with block and tackle and cranes. This stupendous achievement caught the popular fancy, as this image testifies. Even in the following century the artist Restout depicted this facade in his painting "Semiramis Building Babylon."
RH/de la H/VLG

98. BUST OF LOUIS XIV
Attributed to Antoine Coysevox (1640-1720)
Ca. 1675(?)
Marble
43-1/4" x 39-3/8" x 18-1/2" (110 x 100 x 47 cm.)

Anonymous lender

The inscription on the socle of this bust identifies Louis XIV as Patron or Father of the War-Wounded. It is thought that the bust was commissioned for the Hôtel Royal des Invalides (built in two stages, 1671-76 and 1679-1706) and removed from the building complex during one of the several subsequent remodelings.

The Sun King was very proud of his achievement. In his testament he said, "Among the different establishments that have been created during my reign, there are none more useful to the State than that of the Hôtel Royal des Invalides."

During the time of his grandfather

Catalogue 98

Henri IV, the military hospital had been located at the Maison de Charité in the Rue de Lourcine. His father Louis XIII had planned to enlarge the Château de Bicêtre for this facility but only partially completed the extensions and renovations.
VLG

237

Catalogue 99

99. THE KING ACCOMPANIED BY HIS COURT VISITS THE HÔTEL OF THE INVALIDES AND ITS NEW CHURCH

Nicolas Langlois (b. 1640)
1707
Etching
35-1/4" x 22-1/4" (89.4 x 56.3 cm.)

Loaned by the Musée Carnavalet / Almanach 1707 (G:20310)

The Invalides was officially created in 1670 to house and care for poor officers and soldiers who were disabled or who had grown old in the royal service. The main body of the complex and the first church were built by Libéral Bruant (ca. 1635-79), architect of the Church of the Salpêtrière. The cornerstone was laid in late 1670 and the structure completed in 1676 with a capacity to house over six thousand military personnel around a vast peristyle court complex. Bruant was overshadowed by Jules Hardouin-Mansart (1646-1708), who added the impressive domed Church of St. Louis to the structure.

Among those foundations attached to the name of Louis XIV, that of the Invalides appeared to contemporaries as the most justified because it responded to an urgent social need. The facilities provided by his father and grandfather were insufficient, and when the war-wounded could not be accepted into convents, they were often reduced to vagabondage, which generated disorder.

In 1670 Louis XIV, made aware of this problem because of the War of Devolution with Spain, decided on the advice of Louvois, Minister of War, to group the soldiers wounded in his service in a special establishment. It was the equivalent of the Hospital of the Salpêtrière, created by Mazarin to "close up" the beggars of Paris and its environs.

The Invalides was built on the Plain of Grenelle, beyond the Faubourg Saint-Germain, at the city limit. Bruant gave it the form of a quadrangle of buildings divided by a deep court of honor flanked on both sides by two square courts. The *hôtel* was oriented to the north, toward the Seine. The principal wing, reserved for the governor, the intendant, the doctors and surgeons (all named by the king), opened toward the river. The huge entrance court was ringed by four dining halls on the ground floor; lodgings for the soldiers were situated on the upper floors and around the lateral courts. At the rear of the main court and on its

axis opened the soldiers' church. The infirmary was outside the main complex (to the right in this free view). It was composed of a quadrangle divided into four courts by a cross of buildings.

The construction of the edifice was hardly achieved when Louvois asked Jules Hardouin-Mansart to add a choir for parish usage to the soldiers' church. Mansart conceived a centrally planned church crowned by a dome that was perhaps based on François Mansart's proposal for the funerary chapel of the Bourbons at Saint Denis. Begun in 1680, construction dragged on because of military expenditures until 1691. The *décor* was not terminated until 1706.

Following the consecration of the new church by the archbishop of Paris, the king went to hear a mass there on August 28, 1706. Followed by the Princes and Princesses of the Blood, he received the key from the hands of Mansart, who was accompanied by his collaborator Robert de Cotte. This is the moment chosen by the engraver to represent in the central part of the print.

Below this scene, several vignettes offer partial views of the edifice and certain episodes of the life led by its occupants. The central cartouche, crowned by the royal arms, reveals an interior view of the royal church with its baldequin designed by Mansart. Inspired by that of the Val-de-Grâce, it was carried on six salamonicas (twisted columns) placed on an oval plan. The angels ornamenting its summit were sculpted by Guillaume Coustou.

From right to left, grouped under a *trophée* of arms and ecclesiastical symbols, cartouches explain the functioning of the royal institution. The three vignettes to the left offer views of a room in the infirmary, of the open ground in front of Bruant's facade that served as recreation space for the sick, and, below, one of the dining halls decorated with paintings by Van der Meulen.

The vignettes on the right show a meeting of the governor and executive personnel of the Invalides deliberating beneath the effigy of Louis XIV, a parade that took place on the esplanade between the hospital and the Seine, and the interior of the soldiers' church with the baldequin of the royal church, with which it intercommunicated, visible at the termination of the sight lines.
FF/VLG

238

Catalogue 100

100. VIEW OF THE CHURCH OF THE ROYAL HÔTEL OF THE INVALIDES AT THE TIME OF THE VISIT OF LOUIS XIV

Pierre-Denis Martin the Younger (1673-1742)
1701
Oil on canvas
43-3/8" x 63" (110 x 160 cm.)

Loaned by the Musée Carnavalet

The Sun King, shown standing by his carriage and wearing his hat, made several visits to the Invalides while it was being built. He enjoyed touring construction sites. This particular inspection occurred on July 14, 1701.

The new Church of St. Louis, appended to the older soldiers' chapel, was designed by Jules Hardouin-Mansart (1646-1708). Construction began in the late 1670's; the building was inaugurated by the king in 1706.

Construction of the royal church of the Invalides had been completed in 1691, and in the following year Mansart presented his work to the Academy. The *décor* was finished in 1706; Jouvenet and Lafosse collaborated on the cupola; the Boullognes, Michel Corneille, and Poerson painted the peripheral chapels.

When the king visited in 1701, the gilded dome and the sculptural *décor* of the facade had been completed. Part of this sculptural program disappeared during the Revolution. In this view, the dome dominates the Grenelle Plain at the right of the picture toward the slopes of the Montmartre, which was then still sprinkled with windmills. Today, the Invalides complex has been engulfed by the city of Paris.
FF/VLG

THE KING AS BUILDER: VAUX-LE-VICOMTE

101. NICOLAS FOUQUET
Charles Le Brun (1619-90)
Ca. 1660
Oil on canvas
38-7/8" x 52" (98.8 x 132 cm.)

Loaned from the Collections of the Château of
Vaux-le-Vicomte

Nicolas Fouquet (1615-80) was part of
the Mazarin legacy left to Louis XIV,
consisting of Hugues de Lionne, Michel
Le Tellier, and Colbert, among others.
Upon Mazarin's death in 1661 the Sun
King himself assumed the role of first
minister. Fouquet alone, of the Mazarin
"bequest," had the subtlety, nerve, and
poor judgment to aspire to Mazarin's
position. Fouquet was quite rich and had
a strongly fortified château at Belle-Isle
as well as the showplace of
Vaux-le-Vicomte.

Although he named Fouquet
superintendent of finances, Louis XIV
also appointed Colbert to the same
department, probably to keep an eye on
the superintendent. Fearing a new
Fronde as the result of Fouquet's
ambition, the king decided as early as
June, 1661, to arrest him, laid his secret
plans carefully, and struck in September.
At that time he wrote to his mother
Anne d'Autriche, "By whatever artifice
he might attempt, I was not long in
recognizing his bad faith."

Without sufficient evidence of treason
or outright theft of public funds, the
court appointed by the king was only
able to banish Fouquet. The Sun King
reversed this sentence and sent him to
the fortress of Pignerol, where he was
kept under close scrutiny.
VLG

Catalogue 101

**102. VIEW OF THE CHÂTEAU OF
VAUX-LE-VICOMTE, SEEN FROM
THE GARDEN SIDE**
Jean-Baptiste Martin the Elder, called Martin des
Batailles (1659-1735)
1728
Oil on canvas
83-7/8" x 152-3/4" (213 x 388 cm.)

Loaned from the Collections of the Château of
Vaux-le-Vicomte

The Sun King first visited the newly
built Château of Vaux-le-Vicomte on
his return from signing the Peace of the
Pyrenees in 1660. He came again for the
lavish party given in his honor by
Nicolas Fouquet in August of 1661,
already knowing that Fouquet's downfall
was imminent.

The château that Fouquet built has
been called the most beautiful house in
France. Created under the direction of
decorator Charles Le Brun by the
architect Louis Le Vau and landscape
designer André LeNôtre, it represented
the epitome of nationalistic French
classical baroque design, largely free of
Italian influence. It became a prototype
for the king's plans for Versailles,
utilizing the creative group genius of the
three master artists. The Château of
Vaux-le-Vicomte was begun in 1656 and
fully completed in 1661, just prior to the
king's second visit.
VLG

Catalogue 102

103. CHARLES LE BRUN
Attributed to Antoine Coysevox (1640-1720)
Ca. 1670(?)
Marble
35-1/2" x 25-5/8" (90 x 65 cm.)

Loaned by the Département des Sculptures of the
Musée du Louvre / MR-2489

Charles Le Brun (1619-90) was the son of a sculptor, who apprenticed him to François Perrier to learn painting. The young artist came to the attention of Cardinal Richelieu and the Chancellor Pierre Séguier, who placed him in the studio of Simon Vouet for further training. His work impressed Nicolas Poussin, and Séguier sponsored Le Brun's trip of four years to Italy to study with Poussin.

Nicolas Fouquet employed Le Brun's services at Vaux-le-Vicomte, where the artist met Cardinal Mazarin, who introduced Le Brun's work to the Sun King. Le Brun's multi-faceted skills and talents led Colbert to name him director of the Royal Manufactory of the Gobelins, where Le Brun supervised and designed for studios creating tapestries, furniture, gold and silver, locks and hardware, mosaics, and marquetry.

Le Brun received many honors and executed enormous commissions for the king and various courtiers. Colbert's death in 1683 brought Le Brun considerable troubles, since Louvois repudiated his predecessor's protégé as *Surintendent des Bâtiments*. Le Brun's last years saw his withdrawal from court life (despite the king's continued favor and patronage), and he died in 1690 after a lingering illness.

The bust is typically that of an artist: the sitter is shown with his head turned three-quarters to the left, the gathered shirt is liberally open, leaving the neck exposed. The left shoulder is draped with a richly embroidered mantle.

There is some question as to the date of this work. The youthful appearance suggests a date of *ca.* 1670. However, the supple execution, the vigorous wig, the high and mighty expression, the care taken in animating the marble skin and the folds of the shirt, and the brocade of the mantle all suggest a considerably later date. Perhaps this is Coysevox's hommage to Le Brun, shown in his fullest independence and authority, made at the time Coysevox carved Le Brun's tomb, which included a bust in a similar pose.
GB/VLG

Catalogue 103

Catalogue 104

104. LOUIS LE VAU
Unidentified artist
17th century
Oil on canvas
59-7/8" x 49-5/8" (152 x 126 cm.)

Loaned by the Musée National du Château de Versailles / MV-4346

Louis Le Vau (1612-70) was "expropriated" from Vaux-Le-Vicomte by the Sun King, along with Le Brun and Le Nôtre. From 1661 until his death nine years later, Le Vau's principal energies were expended creating the "envelope" at Versailles for the Sun King, surrounding the hunting lodge of Louis XIII with the early stages of the château of Louis XIV.

Le Vau was named "First Architect to the King" in 1654. He collaborated with Le Brun at the Hôtel Lambert in Paris before working with him at Vaux-le-Vicomte. Le Vau was involved in all the major royal building projects for the remainder of his life, including the Louvre, Vincennes, and the Collège des Quatre Nations (which now houses the Institut de France, composed of the Academies and the Mazarin Library) just across the Seine from the Louvre, which was completed from his drawings after his death.

In this picture, Le Vau holds a plan for the portion of the Louvre arranged as apartments for Anne d'Autriche to the southwest of the Square Court. He is shown in front of the pavilion that terminated the Apollo Gallery.

In Paris, Le Vau played an important part in the reconstruction of the Île Saint-Louis, where he resided, and provided the plans for the Church of Saint Louis. At Versailles, assisted by François d'Orbay, he directed the enormous undertakings of the Orangerie and the "Envelope" that contained the two large suites of apartments of the king and queen, practically creating an architecture the purity of which would influence the largest European building projects of the eighteenth century. CC/VLG

105. ANDRÉ LE NÔTRE
Carlo Maratta (1625-1713)
1679
Oil on canvas
44-1/8" x 33-1/2" (112 x 85 cm.)

Loaned by the Musée National du Château de
Versailles / MV-3545

From a family of professional gardeners,
André Le Nôtre (1613-1700) became
the most famous of all French landscape
architects. He was "found" by the Sun
King at Nicolas Fouquet's
Vaux-le-Vicomte and was promptly
removed to Versailles, where he laid out
the new town in the early 1660s and
created the great garden complex of
terraces, groves, fountains, vistas, and
allées (see #111).

Although twenty-five years older than
his royal master, Le Nôtre was a
personal favorite of Louis XIV. Many
stories illustrate their *comraderie*,
including the possibly apocryphal
account in which Le Nôtre refused a
coat-of-arms offered by the Sun King.
The First Gardener said he already had
one — three slugs crowned by cabbage
leaves!

Le Nôtre designed other royal
gardens, including that of the Château
of Clagny for Madame de Montespan,
and many parks for noble clients. The
formal "French" garden, subjecting
nature to the architectonic vision of
man, remains firmly attached to his
name.

Le Nôtre visited Rome in 1679 and is
believed to have commissioned this
portrait from Maratta at that time. In
the picture, Le Nôtre wears the cross of
the Order of Saint Lazarus (see #61).
This was added to the painting after it
was completed, since LeNôtre was not
decorated with this order until 1681.
CC/VLG

Catalogue 105

THE KING AS BUILDER: VERSAILLES

106. VIEW OF THE CHÂTEAU OF VERSAILLES FROM THE AVENUE DE PARIS

Adam-François Van der Meulen (ca. 1632-90)
Ca. 1664
Oil on canvas
22-7/8" x 26-3/4" (68 x 68 cm.)

Loaned by the Musée du Château de Versailles / MV 5752

As a child Louis XIV had visited and hunted at his father's "lodge" outside Paris, toward Chartres. During the early years of his personal reign he had staged *fête champêtre*-like parties on its grounds. It was a place of special childhood memories to the Sun King, but too small to accommodate court entertainments or to serve as a proper royal residence. Louis XIV conceived a plan to retain this original structure, while making Versailles the official seat of both court and government.
VLG

107. VIEW OF THE ORANGERIE OF VERSAILLES

Attributed to Jean-Baptiste Martin the Elder, called Martin des Batailles (1659-1735)
Late 17th or early 18th century
Oil on canvas
45-1/4" x 65" (115 x 165 cm.)

Loaned by the Musée National du Château de Versailles / MV 6812

By the end of his reign, the Sun King had transformed the "lodge" at Versailles (see #106) into the largest and most splendid royal residence in Europe. The park had been enlarged and made over into the most gigantic of all "French" gardens. To accomplish this, Louis XIV used the financial talents of Colbert and the artistic energies of Le Brun, Le Vau, and Le Nôtre, as well as the administrative skills of an enormous bureaucracy.

Versailles became the showplace of French taste and French products to impress foreign visitors and develop a pan-European market for French goods. It also became the seat of French government, housing the king, court, and administration under a vast series of roofs.

The first Orangerie was built by Louis Le Vau in 1663 and was then destroyed. The Orangerie by Jules Hardouin-Mansart (1646-1708), shown here, was constructed between 1684 and 1686 under the Parterre du Midi. The organization of its facade, the center slightly emphasized by columns, recalls those by Le Vau and Mansart, which dominate the parterre. The principal gallery, ornamented with a centrally placed standing statue of Louis XIV by Martin Desjardins (ca. 1640-94), is oriented to the south.

The two complementary side galleries lower as they pass under the staircases of the "Hundred Steps." A large number of orange trees, brought even from Fontainebleau, were sheltered here in the winter and brought out during the summer onto the parterre composed of "six large compartments of lawn with scrolls [i.e., plantings] and a large pool in the middle." The statues depicting scenes of abduction are now in the Louvre.
CC/VLG

Catalogue 106

108. VIEW OF THE CHÂTEAU OF VERSAILLES AND ITS TWO WINGS SEEN FROM THE GARDEN SIDE
Israël Silvestre the Elder (1621-91)
Restrike engraving

Loaned by the Louisiana Museum Foundation

The transformation of Versailles took two decades. Two architects determined its final form. Louis Le Vau directed the first major building campaign, encasing the old "lodge" in a new "envelope." Jules Hardouin-Mansart became chief architect in 1679 and enlarged Le Vau's elegant creation into the vast chateau that stands today.

On May 6, 1682, the Sun King declared Versailles the official seat of French government. Courtiers desiring proximity to the royal person lived in the château if favored, or in nearby *hôtels* if less fortunate. Despite its size, space at Versailles was at a premium. Nobles living away from the king were without influence or favor, but those residing with him were often ruined by the expense of life at the new capitol. VLG

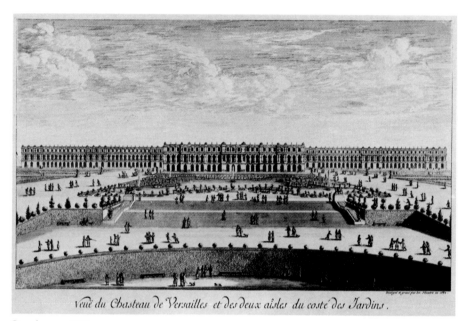

Veuë du Chasteau de Versailles et des deux aisles du costé des Jardins.

Catalogue 108

Catalogue 107

109. VIEW OF THE CHÂTEAU OF VERSAILLES SEEN FROM THE LARGE SQUARE
Israël Silvestre the Elder (1621-91)
Restrike engraving

Loaned by the Louisiana Museum Foundation

At the center of the "new" Versailles lay the "lodge" of Louis XIII (see #106). The Sun King wished to preserve his father's "play house" as a pious memory, but the combined Le Vau and Mansart building campaigns left only a vestige of the old building visible at the rear of the vast double entrance court.
VLG

Chasteau de Versailles, veu de la grande place.

Catalogue 109

110. THE MAGNIFICENT BUILDINGS OF VERSAILLES
Jean Arnould (1621-?) and Pierre Le Nègre (?-?).
after Pierre Mignard (1612-95)
Ca. 1686
Bronze
30-1/2" dia. (77.5 cm.)

Loaned by the Département des Sculptures of the Musée du Louvre / RF 3466

The elegant Place des Victoires in Paris was created in 1685 under the auspices of Marshall de La Feuillade, embellishing the space in front of his *hôtel* (townhouse) with a horseshoe-shaped *place* designed by the architect Jules Hardouin-Mansart. The new square was officially inaugurated by the unveiling of a statue of the king in 1686. The king was no doubt properly flattered.

Shortly after this inauguration, in August, 1686, de La Feuillade ordered bronze ornaments from the sculptor Arnould and the founder Le Nègre for the columns supporting the lights of the *place*. This medallion was among the first group installed; it was paid for in October, 1686. In 1699 the lighting system was taken down, and in 1718 the supporting columns were dismantled.

The medallion shows the château with the Orangerie in the foreground. The nymph of Versailles presides over the waters serving the château and its gardens; behind her, an aqueduct recalls the canalization of the waters of the Seine to the "Marly Machine." In the background, the earlier building of Louis XIII is seen with a shepherd grazing his sheep. The whole is a precious witness to the importance and prestige of Versailles.

Catalogue 110

246

111. GENERAL PLAN OF THE CHÂTEAU AND GARDENS OF VERSAILLES
Unidentified draftsman
Ca. 1710
Inks, wash and watercolor on paper
17-7/8" x 23-3/8" (45.5 x 59.5 cm.)

Loaned by the Archives Nationales / Vers. Archit. XXVI, No. 110

The magnitude of "house" and "gardens" envisioned by the Sun King for Versailles is shown by numerous drawings prepared by the offices of Le Nôtre, Le Vau, and Mansart. As a country residence set in a formal park, Versailles was known as a château, although the scale exceeded that of any European palace.

This drawing was prepared by a staff draftsman of the Department of Works under the direction of Robert de Cotte (1656-1735), Mansart's brother-in-law, who succeeded him as First Architect to the King in 1709. It is drawn at a scale of 7 millimeters to the *toise*, or fathom, a measurement of about 6.4 feet. It shows the château and gardens as far as "Little Venice" in a free view. A numbered legend appears in a cartouche. "Little Venice" was the housing area built by the Sun King for the Venetian gondoliers who took courtiers for jaunts on the Grand Canal.
DG/VLG

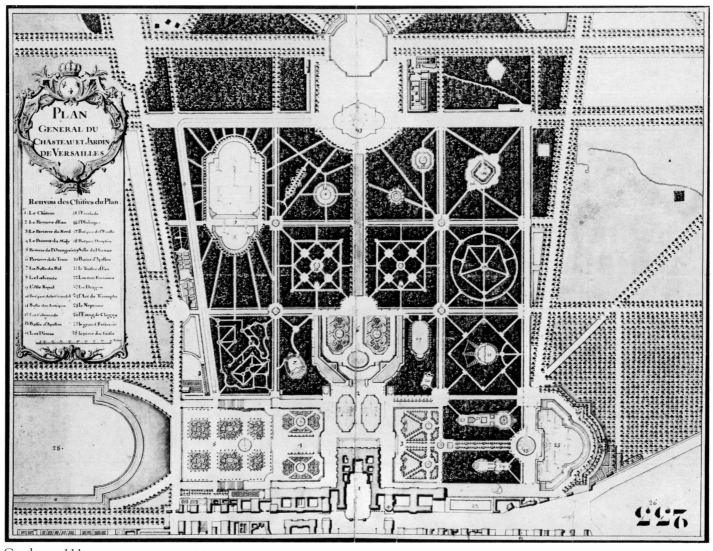

Catalogue 111

112. SECTION THROUGH THE VESTIBULE OF THE CHAPEL AND THE SALON D'HERCULE (of the Château of Versailles)
Unidentified draftsman
Ca. 1712
Ink, graphite, wash, and watercolor on paper
22-1/2" x 50-3/8" (57 x 128 cm.)

Loaned by the Archives Nationales / O[1] 1768, No. 1

Among the last additions to Versailles during the Sun King's lifetime was a permanent chapel, complete with royal tribune. It was certainly encouraged by Madame de Maintenon, well known for her pious, good works and concern for the king's salvation. In form the chapel, built between 1699 and 1710 according to the plans of Jules Hardouin-Mansart (1646-1708), recalled Gothic structures such as Sainte Chapelle in Paris. In decoration, it was a sumptuous, if reserved, representation of the French classical baroque.

Decoration of the Salon d'Hercule was begun in 1712 according to the designs of Robert de Cotte (1656-1735) and was interrupted by the death of the Sun King in 1715. Under de Cotte's direction, the project was resumed in 1729. The bare vault was filled with an "Apotheosis of Hercules" commissioned from the painter François Lemoyne (1688-1737) in 1733 and was completed in 1736. This large apartment, which measures eighteen and one-half meters by seventeen meters, served as a ballroom during the reign of Louis XV (1710-74), great-grandson of

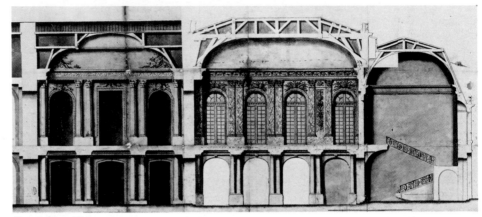

Catalogue 112

the Sun King.

The drawing was executed by an unidentified draftsman of the Department of Works under the direction of de Cotte, and is drawn at the scale of 45 millimeters to the *toise*. It shows two stories going to the gallery of the north wing as far as the Royal Court. The vestibule is seen from the chapel side; the windows of the Salon d'Hercule are those that open onto the High Court of the Chapel. The marbles actually employed (rance, Pyrenees,

Sérancolin, and campan) are not those shown in the drawing. The grilles closing the passage beneath the Salon d'Hercule were never executed. Some of these changes were measures of economy instituted by Louis XIV because of the grievous state of French finances due to the War of the Spanish Succession; others were the result of aesthetic considerations under the reign of his successor.
DG/JM/VLG

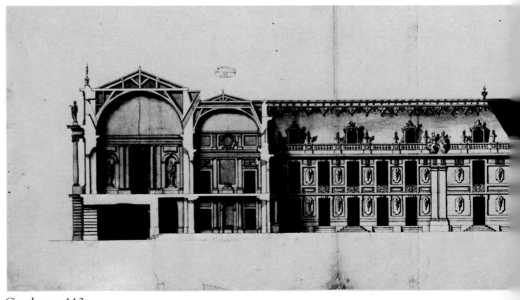

Catalogue 113

113. ELEVATION OF THE GOVERNMENT WING AND SECTION THROUGH THE ROYAL APARTMENTS AND THE HALL OF MIRRORS (of the Château of Versailles)

Unidentified draftsman
After 1682
Inks, wash, and watercolor on paper
14-1/2" x 57-1/2" (37 x 146 cm.)

Loaned by the Archives Nationales / 0¹ 1768¹, no. 1

The major functions of Versailles are shown by this drawing. The building complex housed the French administration, the court, and the royal family and provided spaces for official functions and court activities. To house the enormous bureaucracy, forerunner of France's contemporary civil service, a large government wing had to be constructed beyond the stables.

The drawing was prepared by an unidentified draftsman of the Department of Works under the direction of Jules Hardouin-Mansart. The elevation of the government wing depicts the side on the Marble Court and Royal Court and shows projects for the roofs and the alignment of the ridges. A band across the vestibule of the ground floor shows a proposal to lower the level of the Marble Court by one step. At the extreme left, the profiles of the semi-circular windows of the Hall of Mirrors can be seen. The King's Parlor, even in section, became the King's Bedroom in 1701.
DG/VLG

114. PROJECT FOR THE KING'S BEDROOM: THE ROYAL ALCOVE (at the Château of Versailles)

Unidentified draftsman
Ca. 1699
Ink, graphite, wash, and watercolor on paper
17-3/4" x 17" (45 x 43 cm.)

Loaned by the Archives Nationales / 0¹ 1768², No. 31

The decoration of the Royal Apartments was of particular interest to the Sun King. This drawing was prepared for his inspection with several "standup" flaps, showing alternate schemes for the recess in which the State Bed would rest.

The drawing was prepared by an unidentified draftsman in the Department of Works under the direction of Jules Hardouin-Mansart. It was drawn on the scale of 57 millimeters to the *toise* and is a project to transform the King's Parlor, referred to as the "Salon where the King dresses," into the King's Bedroom. The room, on the main floor at the center of the Marble Court in the old château of Louis XIII, was remodeled for this purpose in 1701.

The portion of the drawing hidden by flaps shows the internal walls on the Hall of Mirrors side of the room, with its three doors and Corinthian pilasters of 1680. The first flap proposes an alcove for the State Bed with stretched fabric. The second shows the design that was actually used: a bed alcove in a large shallow arcade with a canopied State Bed trimmed with heron's plumes.

For the crown of the arch of the alcove, the drawing presents three

Catalogue 114

schemes, two of them on small flaps. The king could choose the Arms of France set between *trophées* of weapons or two personifications of Fame, or an oval painting between two figures representing Genius. As executed, it was "France Triumphant" by the sculptor Nicolas Coustou (1658-1733, see #122) that watched over the king's sleep. In the reveals are two "Fames" sculpted by François Lespignola (1644-1705).
DG/VLG

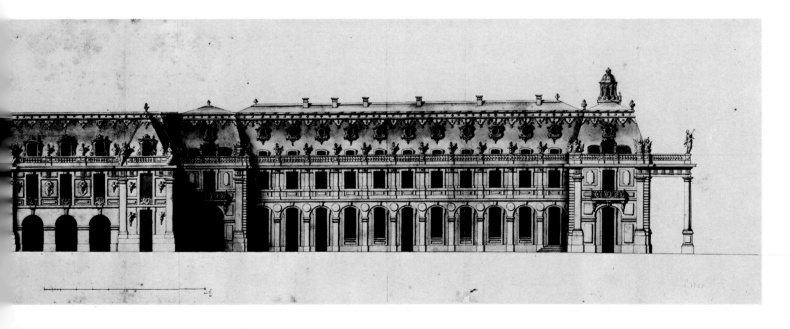

Catalogue 116

115. PLAN OF THE KING'S APARTMENT OF THE CHÂTEAU OF VERSAILLES

Unidentified draftsman
Early 18th century
Ink and wash on paper
22-1/2" x 33-1/2" (57 x 85 cm.)

Loaned by Archives Nationales / 0¹ 1768², No. 1

Each member of the royal family occupied a separate apartment at Versailles. Courtiers scrambled for the remaining residential spaces. The king's personal suite was divided into several rooms of varying degrees of public access.

The drawing was prepared by an unidentified draftsman of the Department of Works under the direction of Jacques V. Gabriel (1667-1742) at the scale of 21 millimeters to the *toise*, and shows the King's Apartment on the main floor, opening onto the Marble and Royal Courts and to interior courts.

The Royal Apartment is presented as it was inhabited by Louis XIV. It includes the King's Bedroom of 1701 (see #114), the Council Room, the Wigging Room, the Wardrobe or Dressing Room, the "Chair" (euphemism for toilet), the Billiard and Dog Room, a parlor or antechamber on the Small Stair, a Painting Room, a Shell Room (for the display of natural history curios), an Oval Salon, and a Small Gallery. The Royal Apartment maintained this configuration until 1738 when a new King's Bedroom was created on the Court of Stags for Louis XV. DG/VLG

116. THE HALL OF MIRRORS (of the Château of Versailles)

Unidentified draftsman
Ca. 1680
Wash, ink, and watercolor on paper
7-1/2" x 37-3/8" (19 x 95 cm.)

Loaned by the Archives Nationales / 0¹ 1768², No. 19

Jules Hardouin-Mansart's most famed contribution to Versailles was the Hall of Mirrors. Crossing the rear of the old "lodge" and occupying a terrace created by Le Vau, it served for official events, state occasions, diplomatic receptions (see #47), and court entertainments. The lavish use of mirrors (a striking technological achievement in the seventeenth century) gained it an instant reputation.

This drawing was prepared by an unidentified draftsman in the Department of Works under the direction of Jules Hardouin-Mansart at the scale of 23 millimeters to the *toise*. It shows an internal elevation of the long wall of the apartment side of the Hall of Mirrors.

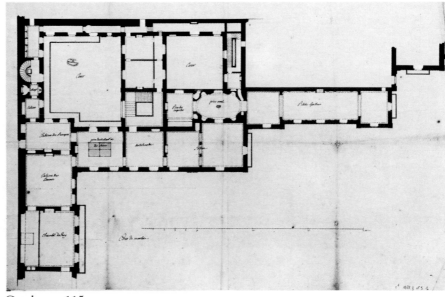

Catalogue 115

The mirrored bays, each composed of many small rectangular mirrors, correspond to the seventeen arched windows of the exterior wall that they face. The mirrored bays are grouped by threes, alternately separated by pilasters or by niches of unequal width, and are surmounted by *trophées*. The niches were intended to hold the finest ancient Roman statuary that the king possessed; "Diana of the Doe" is recognizable in the drawing. Four busts of Roman emperors on socles complete the *décor*.

The mirrors filled the long gallery with light and perhaps made a subtle allusion to the sun of the Sun King. A suite of highly reflective solid silver furniture, including a large throne, was commissioned to furnish the Hall of Mirrors but was melted down to pay military expenses at the end of the Sun King's reign.
DG/VLG

117. THE HALL OF MIRRORS (of the Château of Versailles)
Unidentified draftsman
17th century
Graphite on paper
13-3/4" x 40-1/4" (35 x 102 cm.)

Loaned by the Archives Nationales / 0^1 1768^2, No. 18

The drawing was prepared by an unidentified draftsman of the Department of Works under the direction of Jules Hardouin-Mansart at the scale of 23 millimeters to the *toise*. It shows the exterior or window wall of the Hall of Mirrors. Sculptural detailing includes the trumeau panels, reveals, capitals, a cornice surmounted by *trophées*, and busts of Roman emperors on stands. In the right margin is a profile of the molding of a pilaster and the base of a column. On the reverse is a sketch of a single bay with notes on the marbles to be used, which were rance, white vein and campan green.
DG/VLG

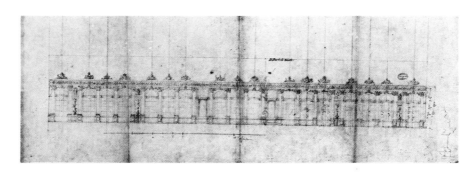

Catalogue 117

118. DRAWING FOR LOUIS XIV'S MIRRORED CABINET, CHÂTEAU OF VERSAILLES
Unidentified draftsman
1684
Ink and wash on paper
11-1/2" x 26-3/8" (29 x 67 cm.)

Loaned by the Archives Nationales / 0¹ 1768², No. 33

Catalogue 118

In addition to the Hall of Mirrors, the Sun King had a more private mirrored salon in the château. Less grandiose in scale and less accessible than the "Hall," it attracted less attention. Unfortunately, the handsome room was remodeled in the rococo style of Louis XV in the next century.

The drawing was prepared by an unidentified draftsman of the Office of Plans of the Department of Works under the direction of Jules Hardouin-Mansart (1646-1708). It was drawn at the scale of 55 millimeters to the *toise*. The King's Mirrored Parlor was located between the King's Parlor and the Wigging Room and was "the Room where the King holds Council" (see #115). Two sections are shown, one along the length of the room, the other through the width. The walls were completely covered in small mirrors framed and held in place by ironwork and decorative bronze moldings by Demenico Cucci (1635-1705). Small consoles supported precious vases in agate or jasper from the royal collections (see #192, 198, 199). The spring points of the arching on the right offered two locations for fireplaces.
DG/VLG

Catalogue 119

119. PROJECT FOR THE PAVING OF THE CHAPEL (of the Château of) VERSAILLES

Unidentified draftsman
Early 18th century
Wash, ink, and watercolor on paper
42-1/8" x 28-3/8" (107 x 72 cm.)

Loaned by the Archives Nationales / O¹ 1782⁵, No. 11

Among the last additions to Versailles during the Sun King's lifetime was a permanent chapel, complete with royal tribune. It was certainly encouraged by Madame de Maintenon, well-known for her pious good works and concern for the king's salvation. The chapel was consecrated by Louis Antoine, cardinal de Noailles, on June 5, 1710.

In form, the chapel recalled Gothic structures such as Sainte Chapelle in Paris, In decoration, it was a sumptuous if reserved representation of the French classical baroque. Due to financial problems resulting from his late seventeenth-century wars, the Sun King was forced to simplify this elaborate flooring scheme before the chapel was built.

The drawing was prepared by an unidentified draftsman of the Department of Works under the direction of Robert de Cotte (1656-1735) at the scale of 45 millimeters to the *toise*. The paving was executed by Lisqui and Tarle, who received a first payment of 13,600 pounds on August 4, 1709.
DG/VLG

Catalogue 120

Catalogue 121

120. PANEL FROM THE ROYAL APARTMENTS OF THE CHÂTEAU OF VERSAILLES

Unidentified craftsman
17th century
Carved wood
59-1/8" x 23-5/8" (150 x 60 cm.)

Loaned by the Musée National du Château de Versailles / V-3821

Sumptuous carved panels served as wainscotting in the Royal Apartments of the château (see #115), and their iconography was an omnipresent reminder of the Sun King's glory. The crowned interlaced *L*'s of the royal monogram (see #2) surmount Apollo's lyre in this example.
VLG

121. PANEL FROM THE ROYAL APARTMENTS OF THE CHÂTEAU OF VERSAILLES

Unidentified craftsman
17th century
Carved wood
59-1/8" x 23-5/8" (150 x 60 cm.)

Loaned by the Musée National du Château de Versailles / V 3820

A "French" globe (coverd with *fleurs-de-lys*) is enlightened by a symbolic Sun Mask in the upper portion of this wainscot panel. Below is the French shield featuring Bourbon lilies (see #3). The dolphins and crown above the shield suggest a connection with the dauphin or crown prince.

The balanced design of these panels is typical of the French classical baroque and precedes the more playfully shaped and curvilinear paneling of rococo cabinetry.
VLG

122. HERCULES (The Emperor Commodus as Hercules)
Nicolas Coustou (1658-1733)
1683-85
Terra-cotta
31-1/2" x 13" x 9-1/8" (80 x 33 x 23 cm.)

Loaned by the Département des Sculptures of the Musée du Louvre / RF 199

Immense quantities of garden statuary were required as focal points, fountains for parterres, and defiles (parades) in the huge park at Versailles. The Royal Academy of Painting and Sculpture (founded 1648, see #87) and the French Academy in Rome (founded 1666, see #86) trained young artists to produce them. The work of pensioners funded by the king was then considered crown property.

In 1683, Nicolas Coustou won the Rome Prize and was sent to the French Academy as a pensioner. He executed this terra-cotta *bozzetto* (sketch or model) from the ancient Roman statue "The Emporer Commodus as Hercules." It was approved, and he repeated the work in a larger-than-life-size marble version that is now on the Parterre of Latona in the Versailles gardens.
VLG

Catalogue 122

123. THE BASIN OF LATONA
Jean Le Pautre (1618-82), after Balthasar Marsy
(1628-74)
Restrike engraving

Loaned by the Louisiana Museum Foundation

Water played an important part in animating the Versailles gardens. Immense and impressive jets, misting sprays, sparkling cascades, and reflecting pools glittered throughout the park. They operated as a result of a huge pump at Clagny and the famed "Marly Machine," which were triumphs of seventeenth-century hydraulic engineering.

Many elements of the immense garden complex reflected various aspects of the Apollo theme. The Parterre of latona separates the Parterre d'Eau from the Tapis Vert and focuses on a fountain group of "Latona and Her Children" by Balthasar Marsy. It represents a legendary incident in which Latona, mother of Apollo and Diana, begs Jupiter to take revenge on disrespectful peasants. Obligingly, he turned them into frogs. The group was installed in 1670.
VLG

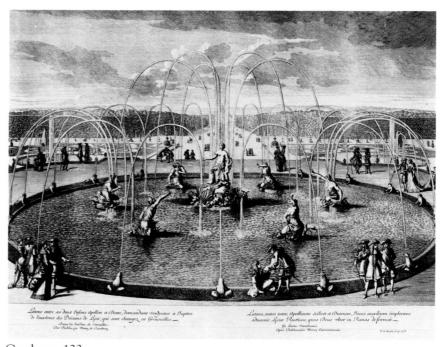

Catalogue 123

124. THE FOUNTAIN OF FAME
Israël Silvestre the Younger (1621-91)
Restrike engraving
22-3/8" x 30" (57 x 76.2 cm.)

Loaned by the Louisiana Museum Foundation

Designed by Le Nôtre in 1675, the Bosquet des Dômes was constructed by Jules Hardouin-Mansart in 1677 and was among his earliest constructions at Versailles. Its original name, "Fountain of Fame," was due to the gilded lead statue that served as its focal point.

The notions of *gloire* and *renommée* (glory and fame) were important to French monarchs. The traditional personification was a female figure with horn, trumpeting forth the fame of the person being honored. This one, naturally, broadcast the fame of the Sun King until the *bosquet* was transformed in later years.
VLG

Catalogue 124

125. TROPHÉE IN THE FORM OF A HELMET
Unidentified artist
17th century
Bronze *doré*
22-7/8" x 14-5/8" (58 x 37 cm.)

Loaned by the Musée National du Château de Versailles / MV 8462

The *bosquets* or groves in the Versailles gardens often contained architectural features. These were decorated with a variety of sculpture, including *trophées* or wall plaques. This example from the pavilions of the Bosquet des Dômes (grove of the verdant arches) takes the form of a warrior's helmet with a cock representing ancient Gaul in place of plumes, and an Apollo mask representing the Sun King on the visor. Unfortunately the pavilions were destroyed by Louis XVIII.

Most of the *bosquets* at Versailles could be illuminated for evening events. Indeed, they were often furnished with tables, chairs, buffets, and other pieces and served as outdoor salons, supper rooms, and even dance pavilions.
VLG

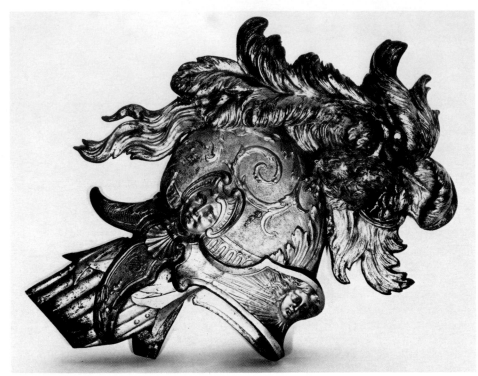

Catalogue 125

Catalogue 126

126. TROPHÉE IN THE FORM OF AN ALLEGORY OF AMERICA
Unidentified artist
17th century
Bronze *doré*
31-1/8" x 20-1/2" (79 x 52 cm.)

Loaned by the Musée National du Château de Versailles / MV 8460

Also from the Bosquet des Dômes, this *trophée* represents "America" as an Indian maiden (of decidedly African features) with an alligator at her feet. This symbol is cast in relief on a large turtle shell resembling a shield. The plume-skirted Indian with a feather crown was derived from images of Brazilian natives that the French brought back from their colonial efforts in South America in the mid-sixteenth century. This figure later came to represent North America as well in European imagery. In 1805 a similar device was selected by W. C. C. Claiborne as the coat-of-arms of the City of New Orleans.

THE KING AND THE COURT: FAMILY AND FRIENDS

127. LOUISE DE LA BAUME LE BLANC, DUCHESSE DE LA VALLIÈRE
Jean Nocret the Elder (1615-72)
1663
Oil on canvas
50-7/8" x 37-3/8" (129 x 96 cm.)

Loaned by the Musée National du Château de Versailles / MV 3539

The Sun King's affections were attracted by Louise de La Baume Le Blanc (1644-1710) in the early 1600s. He had been flirting with his sister-in-law, the first "Madame" (Henrietta of England); to avoid gossip, she suggested he pretend to be courting Louise. Louise was tactfully kept out of sight until the death of Anne d'Autriche (1666), after which she was promptly recognized as the titular mistress and bestowed with the title of duchesse. She quickly became very rich by sponsoring *placets* (petitions) to the king, from which she drew a percentage if the petitioner was successful.

Louise de La Vallière was a simple and melancholy person and excellent horsewoman. Although beautiful, she did not have the public personality necessary to the role of official mistress. She provided the king with at least three children. Their son Louis de Bourbon (1663-66) died in infancy. Marie-Anne de Bourbon, princesse de Conti (1666-1739), became a longtime court favorite. A second son, Louis de Bourbon, comte de Vermandois (1667-83), died at sixteen.

The *divertissement* of 1668 celebrated the end of the War of Devolution and signaled the end of the duchesse's "reign." At that event the king was attracted to another beauty from Madame's household (known henceforth as the nursery garden of the mistresses), and Louise's favor declined. She fled to the Convent of Chaillot in 1671; the king sent Colbert to negotiate her return with the mother superior. After traveling with the king, the queen, and Madame de Montespan in the military campaign of 1673, the duchesse retired from court, taking the veil as a Carmelite at the age of thirty.
CC/VLG

Catalogue 127

128. FRANÇOISE ATHÉNAÏS DE MORTEMART, MARQUISE DE MONTESPAN

Unidentified artist
17th century
Oil on canvas
27-1/8" x 22-1/2" (69 x 57 cm.)

Loaned by the Musée National du Château de Versailles / MV 4265

Intelligent, witty, entertaining and beautiful, Athénaïs de Mortemart (1641-1707) was introduced to the king by the duchesse de La Vallière, who found her irresistible. So did Louis XIV. It is said she invoked black masses to win his interest, and she became the royal mistress during the military campaign of 1667 from which La Vallière was excluded. Her husband objected vociferously, finally pretending that his wife was dead and thus infuriating the king.

Athénaïs produced a number of children for the king, and retained his relatively undivided attention until about 1676. During the early 1680s she was implicated in the poison scandals of Paris, and by 1684 she was turned out of her apartment in Versailles and relegated to rooms on the ground floor. CC/VLG

Catalogue 129

Catalogue 128

129. MADEMOISELLE DE BLOIS AND MADEMOISELLE DE NANTES

Philippe Vignon (1638-1701)
17th century
Oil on canvas
31-1/2" x 35-1/2" (80 x 90 cm.)

Loaned by the Musée National du Château de Versailles / MV 3645

Louis XIV, despite the duties of kingship, was a remarkable family man who adored his children and gave them every possible advantage. Mademoiselle de Blois (1677-1749) and Mademoiselle de Nantes (1673-1743) were respectively his youngest and eldest daughters by Françoise Athénaïs de Mortemart, marquise de Montespan.

Mademoiselle de Blois (Françoise-Marie de Bourbon, duchesse d'Orléans) married Philippe II, duc d'Orléans (1674-1723), in 1692. She was a bedside witness at her father's death in 1715. Her husband became regent of France, and the City of New Orleans, founded in 1718, was named in his honor.

Mademoiselle de Nantes (Louise-Françoise, duchesse de Bourbon) married Louis II de Condé, duc de Bourbon (1688-1710), heir to one of France's most powerful aristocratic families. VLG

Catalogue 130

130. FRANÇOISE D'AUBIGNÉ, MARQUISE DE MAINTENON
Pierre Mignard (1612-95)
Ca. 1694
Oil on canvas
50-3/8" x 38-1/4" (128 x 97 cm.)

Loaned by the Musée National du Château de Versailles / MV 3637

Françoise d'Aubigné (1635-1719) was born Protestant in a respectable if somewhat erratic family. Converted to Catholicism, she married Paul Scarron (1610-60) in order to avoid the nearly obligatory convent existence of unmarried women of good birth but no fortune. Upon his death, an allowance from Queen Mother Anne d'Autriche permitted her to maintain meager lodgings. She attended the *divertissement* of 1668 with Françoise Athénaïs de Mortemart, marquise de Montespan, who first introduced her to the Sun King. The king and the marquise later called her into service as governess of their first children, housing her in Paris where she was active in salon society.

In 1673 Madame Scarron and her young charges were moved to court, and in the following year she began the "long struggle for the king's soul" in which she pitted the king's children against his titular mistress. Madame de Montespan retaliated with plans to marry off Madame Scarron or send her to a nunnery. These failed when the king purchased the Maintenon estate and gave it to Madame Scarron with the title Marquise de Maintenon. The ladies appeared to have reached a stalemate,

and the king indulged himself in a final fling with Anne de Rohan-Chabot, princesse de Soubise (1648-1709), and Marie Adélaïde de Scorailles de Roussilhe, duchesse de Fontanges (1661-81), among others.

By 1682 the marquise de Maintenon had triumphed, and she secretly married the king shortly after the death of Queen Marie-Thérèse d'Autriche. She was never publicly recognized, held to her own circle of religious and literary friends, and directed the king toward sober salvation. Life at Versailles was less lively during her sway, and many governmental activities during this period took place in her apartments.

A faithful wife, she remained in the king's presence during his extended terminal illness of 1715 until shortly before his death.
VLG

Catalogue 131

131. LOUIS, DAUPHIN DE FRANCE
After Hyacinthe Rigaud (ca. 1659-1743)
Late 17th century or early 18th century
Oil on canvas
42-1/2" x 35-1/8" (108 x 89 cm.)

Loaned by the Musée National du Château de Versailles / MV 3597

The Grand Dauphin (1661-1711), so designated because of his size and height, was the only one of the Sun King's six legitimate children to survive beyond 1672. Louis XIV consigned his education to Jacques Bénigne Boussuet,

bishop of Meaux (1627-1704), and his general supervision to Charles de Sainte-Maure, duc de Montausier (1610-90), who exerted such strict discipline and corporal punishment that the young prince developed a strong aversion to all forms of book learning. He became a famed collector and patron of performing arts, and his apartments at Versailles were a must on visitors' itineraries.

A great hunter, the Grand Dauphin kept one of the six packs of hounds in the royal kennel and is credited with making the wolf an extinct species in the Île de France. Called "Monseigneur" ("My Lord") at court, he was kept out of government by his father and preferred to live at his Château de Meudon.

Noted for his taste for unattractive women, he was married to Marie-Anne Christine-Victoire de Bavière (1660-90). The difficult birth of their son Louis, duc de Bourgogne (1682-1712), was the first event of note after the official transfer of the court to Versailles in May of 1682. The marriage was graced with two additional sons before the Dauphine's death in 1690. The Dauphin was then secretly married to Marie Thérèse Joly de Choin (ca. 1670-ca. 1732), even less of a court beauty.

The Grand Dauphin strongly defended the rights of his second son, Philippe, duc d'Anjou (1683-1745), to the Spanish throne upon the death of the childless Charles II (1661-1700). Acceptance of this inheritance set off the War of the Spanish Succession (1700-13), the last great military conflict of the Sun King's reign.

In 1711 the Grand Dauphin came down with smallpox. He appeared to recover, then collapsed and died of circulatory failure from the bleedings prescribed by his attending doctor, thus fulfilling the possibly apocryphal prophecy "son of a king, father of a king, never a king."
CC/VLG

132. PROCLAMATION OF THE PUBLIC CRIER ANNOUNCING THE DEATHS OF THE DAUPHIN AND OF THE DAUPHINE

The Crier de Voulges
Paris, 1712
17-3/4" x 21-1/2" (45 x 54.5 cm.)

Loaned by the Archives Nationales / K-10003, No. 19

The death of the Sun King's grandson and heir, Louis de France, duc de Bourgogne (1682-1712), frightened the aging monarch, who at the age of seventy-three began to fear that he would have no legitimate heirs. He was truly saddened by the death of his granddaughter-in-law, Marie-Adélaïde de Savoie, duchesse de Bourgogne (1685-1712), whom he had adored. He was also prompted to issue a decree according the French crown to his illegitimate children in the event that his sole surviving great grandson, aged two, died before him. The child lived to become Louis XV (1710-74). Had he not lived, it is debatable that the French would have allowed the throne to go to one of the royal bastards.

François de Salignac de la Mothe Fénelon (1651-1715) was appointed tutor to the young duc de Bourgogne in 1689. He succeeded in subjugating the impetuous character of his student, but because of his involvement with Quietism, Fénelon was stripped of his charge and exiled from the court in 1697. Bourgogne, however, remained attached to Fénelon, who had inculcated in him his political notions, especially the idea of re-establishing the aristocracy in all of its ancient privileges.

In 1696 Bourgogne married his cousin Marie-Adélaïde de Savoie, who was also grandniece of the Sun King, since she was the daughter of Victor-Amédée II, duc de Savoie (1666-1732), and Anne-Marie d'Orléans (1669-1728), who was the daughter of the king's brother "Monsieur." Of a lively and spritely character, the new duchesse de Bourgogne woke up the court at Versailles, which had become morose under the regime of Madame de Maintenon. The couple became the hope of partisans seeking governmental change, especially when Bourgogne became dauphin upon the death of his father in 1711.

The duc and duchesse de Bourgogne were probably victims of an epidemic of malignant measles and were entombed in the Abbey of Saint-Denis. They had three children. The first of the surviving sons, the duc de Bretagne (1707-1712), became dauphin but died less than twenty days after his father, just after having been baptised under the name of Louis.

JG/VLG

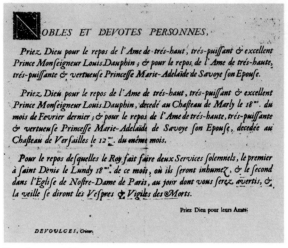

Catalogue 132

133. EDICT ACCORDING THE CROWN OF FRANCE TO THE ROYAL BASTARDS

Louis XIV and clerical assistants
Marly-le-Roi, July, 1714
13-1/4" x 9-7/8" (33.5 x 25 cm.)

Loaned by the Archives Nationales / K-136-No. 1 (Musée AE II 943)

Among the Sun King's least popular measures was this decree, which was prompted by the untimely deaths of four of his heirs. It is doubtful that the decree could have been enforced, which would have made Louis Auguste, duc du Maine (1670-1736), his eldest son by the marquise de Montespan, the king of France. Fortunately, Louis XIV's great-grandson, a child of four when the decree was promulgated, lived to become Louis XV (1710-74).

At the time this edict was rendered, Louis XIV was in grave danger of not having a legitimate male heir. Three dauphins had successively died in less than a year, between April 14, 1711, and March 8, 1712 — his son the Grand Dauphin (1661-1711); his grandson the former duc de Bourgogne (1682-1712); and one of his last two great-grandsons, the duc de Bretagne (1707-12).

The current dauphin (the future Louis XV, king from 1715 to 1774) was born February 15, 1710, and was titled Duc d'Anjou. He was the third and last child of the duc de Bourgogne and Marie-Adélaïde de Savoie and barely escaped the malady that carried off his elder brother the duc de Bretagne, with whom he had been baptised on March 8, 1712. His health, however, remained frail.

In addition, the king had already lost five legitimate children at birth or in early infancy, including a son who died in 1671. His grandchild Philippe, duc d'Anjou (1683-1746), became king of Spain in 1700 and in 1712 renounced all rights to the crown of France (see #239 and #240). The third and last grandson, the duc de Berri (1685-1714), died on May 4, 1714.

With the exception of the Grand Dauphin, the king had only two male descendants, both illegitimate — Louis-Auguste de Bourbon, duc du Maine (1670-1736), legitimized in 1673, and Louis-Alexandre de Bourbon, comte de Toulouse (1678-1737), legitimized in

1681. Both were sons of one of the king's principal favorites, the marquise de Montespan. Louis XIV, who had a lively affection for his bastards, strove to have them play great roles in the kingdom.

In the remainder of the royal family, there was only a nephew, Philippe II d'Orléans (1674-1723), sole surviving son of the king's brother. The king was not pleased with this nephew, who led a debauched life and was suspected by some of attempting by poison to eliminate the obstacles separating him from the throne. The nephew had only one legitimate son, who was not yet married.

The edict is lengthy, consisting of a booklet of twelve pages of parchment, eleven of which are filled with the text and signatures, folio numbered from one to six. It is signed "LOUIS," countersigned "Phélypeaux," and bears the visa of Voysin. The edict was registered by the Parlement of Paris and with the courts on August 2, 20, and 31, 1714.

Jérôme Phélypeaux, comte de Maurepas and later comte de Pontchartrain (1674-1747), who countersigned the edict, succeeded his father Louis Phélypeaux, comte de Pontchartrain (1643-1727), in 1699 as Secretary of State for the Marine and the Royal Household. The two large lakes near New Orleans were named in their honor by Pierre Le Moyne d'Iberville in 1699. The elder Pontchartrain resigned his post as chancellor on July 2, 1714, as it seems he strongly disapproved of this edict. He was replaced by Daniel-François Voysin de la Noiraye (1654-1717), who signed the document.

During the following month, on August 2, Louis XIV wrote a will that placed the regency after his death in the hands of a council. Both his legitimized sons were to be members, with his nephew as president. On April 13, 1715, he added a codicil that at the behest of Madame de Maintenon limited his nephew's powers still further, but he seemed to have had few illusions as to the fate of this testament (see #210). JG/VLG

Catalogue 134

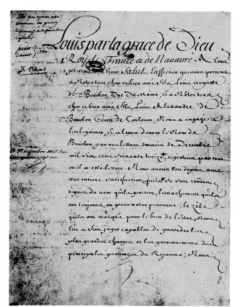

Catalogue 133

134. PHILIPPE DE FRANCE, DUC D'ORLEANS
Attributed to Pierre Mignard (1612-95)
17th century
Oil on canvas
28-3/4" x 22-7/8" (73 x 58 cm.)

Loaned by the Musée National du Château de Versailles / MV 8368

The Sun King was the center of court life. In all probability, no monarch in modern history has lived as much in public. From the established routines of *lever* (the morning rising and dressing) to *coucher* (the evening undressing and retirement), Louis XIV conducted his authoritarian and self-controlled existence as a symbol. Courtiers were honored to participate in these daily cycles and gravitated to the Sun King like fillings attracted to a magnet.

Among the most colorful of all court

characters was the king's brother, Philippe de France, duc d'Orléans (1640-1701), known as "Monsieur." Raised by Anne d'Autriche and Cardinal Mazarin in ignorance of public affairs, he could not compete with the king and posed no ambitious threat to the throne as had his uncle, Gaston d'Orléans, brother of Louis XIII. The Sun King loved "Monsieur" and treated him well. He was the only man allowed to sit and dine with Louis XIV. He was given the Château de Saint Cloud, a magnificent apartment at Versailles, and the Palais Royal, former residence of Cardinal Richelieu.

"Monsieur" has been called the "grandfather of Europe." By his first wife, Henrietta of England (1644-70), whom he married in 1661, there were eight children. The two who survived beyond birth were Anne-Marie d'Orléans, duchesse de Savoie (1669-1728), and Marie-Louise d'Orléans, queen of Spain (1662-80), who was married to Charles II in 1679. The second "Madame" was Elizabeth-Charlotte de Bavière, the Princess Palatine (1652-1722), whom he married after a year as a widower. She rivaled her husband as a colorful court fixture. Of their three children only Philippe II d'Orléans, duc de Chartres (1674-1723), survived, marrying Françoise-Marie de Bourbon, called Mademoiselle Blois, the youngest daughter of Louis XIV and the marquise de Montespan. "Monsieur" also had a liking for gentlemen. His three best-known paramours were Philippe-Julien Mancini, duc de Nevers; Philippe de Lorraine-Armagnac, called chevalier de Lorraine; and the marquis d'Effiat.

"Monsieur" was a brave warrior and a good military strategist. He arrived on the battlefield overly dressed and overly made up but was an excellent military leader. He was the most important member of the Sun King's court until the dauphin grew up. He did not participate in strenuous activities such as hunting, although both his wives took part enthusiastically. He died in 1701 of a stroke brought on by a quarrel with the king about his treatment of Monsieur's son the duc de Chartres, who later became regent of France upon the death of Louis XIV in 1715.
VLG

Catalogue 135

135. ELIZABETH-CHARLOTTE DE BAVIÈRE, PRINCESSE PALATINE, DUCHESSE D'ORLÉANS

Attributed to (or after) Hyacinthe Rigaud (ca. 1659-1743)
Ca. 1700
Oil on canvas
58-1/8' x 40-3/8" (147.5 x 102.5 cm.)

Loaned from the Collections of the Château of Vaux-le-Vicomte

"La Palatine" (1652-1722) was among the most colorful court fixtures. Second wife of "Monsieur," she came to France in 1671. The second "Madame" wrote long, scathing letters describing life at Versailles to royal relatives throughout Europe. She rode and hunted well and loved theater. Born Protestant, "Liselotte" was converted to Catholicism to marry a French prince, giving up her strong claim to the English throne.
VLG

Catalogue 136

136. ANNE MARIE LOUISE D'ORLÉANS, DUCHESSE DE MONTPENSIER

Attributed to Beaubrun (Charles, ca. 1604-92, or Henri, ca. 1603-77)
17th century
Oil on canvas
51-1/4" x 38-5/8" (130 x 98 cm.)

Loaned by the Musée Carnavalet / P. 2198

The "Grande Mademoiselle" (1677-93) earned her nickname from her height and strength and from her unusual military activities. The daughter of Gaston d'Orléans (1608-60), brother of Louis XIII, and Marie de Bourbon, duchesse de Montpensier, she was an active participant in the Fronde, "taking" the town of Orléans with a company of ladies in 1652. Her wish to marry her young cousin Louis XIV came to naught. Her second choice, Antoine de Caumont, comte de Lauzun, was denied her by the king in 1670, who imprisoned him ten years. She finally married Caumont in 1680.

Jean-Baptiste Lulli was "given" to her as a "present" at the age of seven. She employed him as a scullery boy in her kitchens until his musical genius was recognized. At the king's insistence, she left large landholdings, part of her inheritance of the immense Montpensier fortune, to Louis Auguste de Bourbon, duc du Maine, the king's son by the marquise de Montespan. An intelligent woman who participated in the salons of her day, she said, "I am of birth that does nothing that is not great and noble."
VLG

Catalogue 137

137. ANNE-LOUISE BÉNÉDICTE DE BOURBON-CONDÉ, DUCHESSE DU MAINE

Attributed to Pierre Gobert (1662-1744)
Ca. 1691
Oil on canvas
50-7/8" x 38-1/4" (129 x 97 cm.)

Loaned by the Musée Carnavalet / P.679

Balls were an integral and frequent feature of court life, demanding elaborate costumes and coiffures. During the late years of the Sun King's reign, a new generation of courtiers provided a lively and frivolous element at these events.

Anne-Louise Bénédicte de Bourbon-Condé (1676-1753) was the daughter of the old *frondeur* Louis II de Bourbon de Condé (1621-86), called the "Grand Condé," who had been forgiven and reinstated by the Sun King. In 1691 she married Louis-Auguste de Bourbon, duc du Maine (1670-1736), favorite son of Louis XIV and Françoise Athénaïs de Mortemart, marquise de Montespan.

The duchesse's children (the Sun King's grandchildren) were both born before the death of Louis XIV. They were Louis-Auguste, prince de Dombes (1700-55), and Louis Charles, comte d'Eu (1712-1775). Dombes was among the holdings Louis XIV coerced Anne-Marie-Louise d'Orléans, the "Grand Mademoiselle," into giving to the duc du Maine. The duc's name is remembered in New Orleans by Dumaine Street in the French Quarter.
VLG

138. MARIE-ADÉLAÏDE DE SAVOIE, DUCHESSE DE BOURGOGNE

Attributed to Pierre Gobert (1662-1744)
Late 17th century or early 18th century
Oil on canvas
50-3/4" x 38-5/8" (129 x 98 cm.)

Loaned by the Musée National du Château de Versailles / MV 2102

In 1696, twelve-year-old Marie-Adélaïde de Savoie (1685-1712) arrived at the French Court as child bride of Louis, duc de Bourgogne (1682-1712), son of the Grand Dauphin and Marie-Anne Christine-Victoire de Bavière, in direct line to inherit the Sun King's throne. She was her husband's second cousin and grandniece of the Sun King. Her own parents were Victor-Amédée, duc de Savoie, and Anne-Marie d'Orléans, daughter of "Monsieur" and the first "Madame," Henrietta of England, duchesse d'Orléans (1644-70).

Marie-Adélaïde charmed the Sun King, who spoiled her terribly, building her a private zoo and indulging her every whim. Other coutiers, jealous of the king's attentions, found her less pleasing — she behaved much as popular opinion claimed Marie Antoinette did in the next century. Marie-Adélaïde was sent to St. Cyr, the school sponsored by Madame de Maintenon, as a day student; as governess of the likely queen of France, the marquise thus acquired real power.

The duchesse was adored by her husband. Although she was not so enamoured of him, she had nine pregnancies, six of which ended in miscarriages. Of the three live births, the first child died at the age of one, the second, Louis (1707-12) died of measles, and the third, Louis, duc d'Anjou (1710-74), became Louis XV. Her personal favorites at court included Louis-Armand de Brichanteau, marquis de Nangis, who loved someone else; the marquis de Maulévrier who was "sent" to Spain to cure a pretended case of tuberculosis that he had invented to keep him at home near the duchesse; and Melchior, Abbé de Polignac, who was promptly reassigned to Rome.

Despite the Sun King's wish that court life continue as normal during the War of the Spanish Succession (1700-13), the duchesse ended balls at Versailles in 1710. She behaved soberly and well as dauphine, following the death of her father-in-law in 1711. She, her husband, and the eldest of their two surviving sons succumbed to an epidemic at Versailles in early 1712, leaving the Sun King desolated at her loss.
VLG

Catalogue 138

THE KING AND THE COURT: PASTIMES

139. THE TRIUMPH OF BACCHUS
Charles de Lafosse (1636-1716)
1700
Oil on canvas
61-7/8" x 53-1/8" (157 x 135 cm.)

Loaned by the Département des Peintures of the Musée du Louvre / INV 4537

The Triumph of Bacchus was ordered as an over-door decorative painting for the Château de Meudon, seat of the Grand Dauphin. The excesses of Bacchus made him a suitable subject for dining *décor*, and the various animals in the picture recall the Indian associations of this mythological personage.

Dining was an important part of court ritual and royal entertainment. All gentlemen, with the exception of the king's brother "Monsieur," were generally required to stand in the presence of the royal table. The Sun King's mealtime ceremonies were as elaborate and important as the daily *lever* and *coucher*.

Eating attained new elegance during the Sun King's reign. The fork was introduced at court, as well as the *surtout de table*, an elaborate gold or silver centerpiece. Precious metal services were replaced by ceramic vessels after the patriotic "great melt" during the War of the League of Augsburg and again during the War of the Spanish Succession, giving the French ceramics industry new life in the early eighteenth century (see #170, #178 and #181).
VLG

140. A PLAYING CARD FACTORY (Painted Fan)
Unidentified artist
Before 1685
Gouache on paper
9-1/2" x 18-1/8" (24 x 46 cm.)

Loaned by the Musée Carnavalet / D.7778

Gambling was a favorite pastime at Versailles, and nobles won and lost immense fortunes and properties at the gaming tables. Elaborate painted fans were presented as gifts to favored ladies and were carried as part of court costume. The interest in gambling is clearly evidenced by this fan depicting playing-card production.

Card games seem to have appeared in France at the end of the fourteenth century and enjoyed an increasing popularity from the sixteenth century onward. The first regulations governing card makers date from 1594. An edict of 1661 established a monopoly on card production for the benefit of eleven offices divided between Paris and provincial towns. Card makers worked in designated places under the supervision of state clerks in order to facilitate the collection of taxes imposed on this industry.

The fabrication of playing cards demanded an extraordinary number of steps. Card stock was made by gluing together several thicknesses of paper, which called for several repeated operations. The press, at the right in this scene, was used to fix the glue that was applied by workers with brushes. On the *étresses* obtained in this fashion, the card designs were printed. In the picture, a colorist is seen painting them with a brush. After having passed through the hands of the cutters, the cards were culled, sorted, and put in decks. All these operations were performed manually.

Catalogue 139

The factory in the scene was situated in a house in the Place Dauphine overlooking the Pont-Neuf in Paris, providing a view, highly reputed in the seventeenth century, downstream along the Seine from the Île de la Cité. In the foreground is the equestrian statue of Henri IV, to the right the Louvre, and to the left the Collège des Quatres Nations. In the background is the Pont-Barbier, made of wood, which was destroyed in 1685 to make room for the Pont-Royal, which allows the dating of the fan prior to that event.
MM/VLG

141. PLAYING CARDS
Unidentified craftsman
After 1678
Hand-tinted engraving
3-1/2" x 2-1/8" each (9 x 5.4 cm.)

Loaned by the Count Le Moyne de Martigny

Favorite card games at court were usually played in the *Grand Appartement* of the king, which often served as a general salon of those in royal favor. He preferred *reversi*, which was also enjoyed later by Napoleon. Most of the games resembled modern Twenty-One.

Cheating was common. Unless the king was present, losers tended to give free vent to their opinions of winners. Philippe de Courcillon, marquis de Dangeau (1638-1720), was reputed to be the best card player in France during this period. Many Versailles legends center on gambling, including one about the marquis de Beaumont, who was greatly admired because he lost all his worldly possessions with no show of emotion.

These cards descended in the Le Moyne family and were enjoyed by the brothers Pierre Le Moyne d'Iberville and Jean-Baptiste Le Moyne de Bienville, important figures during the exploration and early settlement of the Louisiana colony. The cards depict incidents from the "Popish Plot" of 1678, which created considerable concern in England after Titus Oates (1649-1705) appeared before Charles II and denounced the pope, Louis XIV, the archbishop of Armagh, and the Jesuits. According to Oates, the plotters were planning to assassinate Charles II and impose Catholicism on England by force. This allegation was partially confirmed by correspondence between Edward Coleman and Père La Chaise, the king's confessor at Versailles, and it led to a four-year anti-Catholic witch-hunt in England.

Such cards must have astonished and amused the Sun King and his English cousin James II, who spent the latter part of his life in exile in France.
VLG

Catalogue 140

Catalogue 141

142. ORDER OF PAYMENT OF LOUIS XIV TO COVER THE GAMBLING DEBTS OF THE QUEEN MARIE-THÉRÈSE D'AUTRICHE

Louis XIV and clerical assistants
Versailles, 16 October 1683
15-1/4" x 9-7/8" (38.5 x 25 cm.)

Loaned by the Archives Nationles / K-120, No. 6[27]

Queen Marie-Thérèse d'Autriche was an inveterate gambler and consistent loser. The king was often required to settle her gaming accounts.

The queen died at Versailles on July 30, 1683. Jean-Baptiste-Antoine Colbert, marquis de Seignelay, elder son of the great Colbert, was given the responsibility of organizing the funerary ceremonies and of inquiring into and settling the debts of the deceased. At the time he countersigned this order, he had just succeeded his father, who died September 6, as Secretary of State for the Royal Household and for the Marine. His signature strongly resembles that of his father.

The text of the order says that the sum of 159,610 pounds will be used for secret business concerning the service of the king, the nature of which could not be stated (see #36). However, a note added shortly afterward at the upper left reveals the use of the funds to pay the late queen's gambling debts. The autograph postscript of the king, which reads "good," appears beneath one of his two signatures. The order was executed and returned by the Treasury. At that time, the king's signature was barred and replaced by a second, showing that the expense had been verified by the king. A second, higher postscript in another hand concerns the charging of the expense.

The document consists of a single sheet of paper, of which the recto only has been used. It is signed "LOUIS" twice and is countersigned "COLBERT."
JG/VLG

143. NOTE FROM THE QUEEN REQUESTING 200 GOLDEN *LOUIS* TO PAY A GAMBLING DEBT

Marie-Thérèse d'Autriche (1638-83)
4 November 1681
6-1/2" x 4-1/2" (16.5 x 11.5 cm.)

Loaned by the Archives Nationales / K-120, No. 6[24]

The document consists of four sheets of paper, of which only the first has been used. The text is not in the hand of the queen. However, above her signature is an autograph postscript insisting on the urgency of the payment.
JG/VLG

Catalogue 142

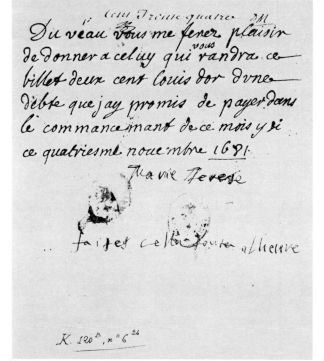

Catalogue 143

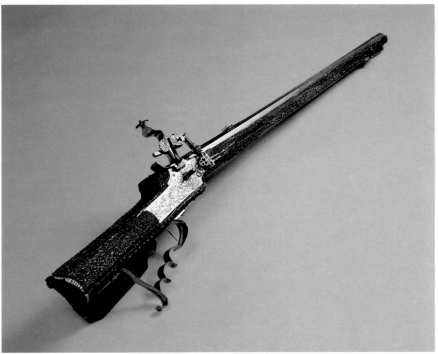

Catalogue 144

145. POWDER FLASK
Unidentified craftsman
17th century
Turtle shell mounted in chased silver with cord
5-5/8" x 3-1/2" x 2-3/8" (15 x 9 x 6 cm.)

Loaned by the Musée de la Chasse et de la Nature
/ INV 61.62

The well-appointed hunter at Versailles
was equipped with an elaborate or novel
powder flask. Some were made of
leather or velvet encrusted with gold or
ormolu. The "buccaneer" type was made
from the whole shell of a small turtle or
tortoise. Hollowed antlers (called "stag
wood") were also employed.
deQ-B/VLG

144. BLUNDERBUSS
Michael Buxbaum
Bohemia, 1680
Steel, wood, antler, and brass
40-1/8" (102 cm.)

Loaned by the Musée de la Chasse et de la Nature
/ INV P.O. 785 (on long term loan from the
Musée de l'Armée)

Hunting was a major pastime wherever
the court was located. The king was an
able horseman and an excellent shot.
He hunted nearly daily and shot from a
small carriage in later years. The Grand
Dauphin specialized in wolf hunting and
is said to have extinguished the species
in the Île de France. Many ladies of the
court rode and shot well, particularly
"La Palatine," second wife of
"Monsieur."

French gunsmiths were less adept than
their Central European competitors at
producing elaborate rifles and pistols for
such recreation. The maker, Michael
Buxbaum, signed and dated the gun on
the barrel. He was active in Bohemia in
the late seventeenth century.

The stock is entirely veneered in stag
horn.
deQ-B/VLG

Catalogue 145

146. "TANE" POINTING
PARTRIDGE
Alexandre-François Desportes (1661-1743)
Ca. 1700
Oil on paper
10-1/2" x 8-5/8" (26.5 x 22 cm.)

Loaned by the Musée de la Chasse et de la Nature
/ INV F#6-120 (on long term loan from the
Manufacture Nationale de Sèvres)

Six packs of hounds populated the royal
kennels, and favorite dogs lived in the
royal apartments so they would know
their master. In 1702, the Sun King
ordered "portraits" of his favorite dogs to
be used as overdoor decorations of the
antechamber of the Château de Marly.
This sketch was executed for the picture
of "Tane." The final painting, which
belongs to the Musée du Louvre, is on
long term loan at the Musée de la
Chasse et de la Nature in Paris.
deQ-B/VLG

Catalogue 146

147. STILL LIFE OF PARTRIDGE AND PHEASANT
Alexandre-François Desportes (1661-1743)
Before 1709
Oil on paper
12-5/8" x 21" (32 x 53.2 cm.)

Loaned by the Musée de la Chasse et de la Nature / INV Fp#2-86 (on long term loan from the Manufacture Nationale de Sèvres)

Best known of the artists specializing in sporting subjects was Alexandre-François Desportes (see #146 and #148). Many of his later animal pictures served as tapestry cartoons. Some of his early still lifes and *trophées* depicted game shot by the king. This work is said to bear an inscription, unfortunately covered over during an ill-planned restoration, that indicates "Pheasants killed by the King." A larger painting, now in the collections of the Musée de la Chasse et de la Nature, resulted from this sketch. It was painted before 1709 for the King's Apartment at the Château de Marly.
deQ-B/VLG

Catalogue 147

148. PHEASANTS
Alexandre-François Desportes (1661-1743)
Ca. 1700
Oil on paper
20-5/8" x 25" (52.5 x 63.4 cm.)

Loaned by the Musée de la Chasse et de la Nature / INV F#6-2 (on long term loan from the Manufacture Nationale de Sèvres)

French courtiers shot and ate a prodigious quantity of game. Their quarry included boar, stag, hare, pheasant, partridge, and other species. This sketch is a study for details of the painting "Diane and Blonde," hunting dogs of Louis XIV. It is inscribed at the lower right "Squatting pheasant and one in flight." The resultant picture was one of the series of four overdoors executed in 1702 for the antechamber of the Château de Marly. Like the sketch of "Tane," this preliminary work was part of the Desportes studio eventually acquired in 1785 by the Royal Porcelain Works at Sèvres.
deQ-B/VLG

Catalogue 148

149. COURSES DE TESTES ET DE
BAGUE FAITTES PAR LE ROY ET
PAR LES PRINCES ET SEIGNEURS
DE SA COUR EN L'ANNÉE 1662
Text: Charles Perrault (1628-1703)
Engravings: François Chauveau (1613-76); Gilles
Rousselet (1610-86); Israël Silvestre the Younger
(1621-91); and Claude Mellan (1598-1688)
Illumination: Jacques I. Bailly (*ca.* 1629-79)
Royal Printing Office, Paris, 1670
Ink and various pigments on paper, bound in
tooled leather
26" x 20-1/2", 41-3/8" open width (66 x 52 cm.,
105 cm. open width)

Loaned by the Bibliothèque Municipale of
Versailles / Reserve, Grand-in folio, A 21ᵃm, State
Holdings

Major events of the early years of the
Sun King's reign were celebrated by the
organization of court festivals, often
several days in length. The Carrousel
Festival of 1662 was given by Louis XIV
to celebrate the birth of the dauphin. It
was the first great festival of the Sun
King's reign. The celebration was held
in Paris in the garden between the
palaces of the Louvre and the Tuileries
(later destroyed) in the area that has
been known ever since as the "Place du
Carrousel."

In all, 12,197 people took part, all
fully costumed and divided into five
quadrilles. The quadrille of the Romans,
led by the king as emperor, was dressed
in red; that of the Persians, under the
orders of the king's brother "Monsieur,"
was garbed in carnation; the quadrille of
the Turks was in dark blue, directed by
Louis II de Bourbon, prince de Condé,
the duc d'Enghien; those of the East
Indians and of the Americans were
costumed in particolor and were
respectively led by Louis II de Bourbon
and Henri II de Lorraine, the duc de
Guise. In addition, the American
quadrille was accompanied by twelve
Moors carrying monkeys and leading
bears.

After having paraded through the
streets of Paris, the main participants
took part in the "Race of Heads," which
consisted of catching baubles with the
tips of swords according to the
customarily accepted rules. The next
day, a new parade was held followed by

LE DVC DE GVYSE, ROY AMERIQVAIN.

LA cuiraſſe étoit de peau de Dragons, dont les deux teſtes ſe rencontrant ſur les épau-
les, vomiſſoient les manches, dont celle de deſſus étoit de brocart vert, rebrodé de
même que l'habit, & celle de deſſous de toile d'argent qui deſcendoit juſque ſur le poignet,
étoit liée d'un bracelet de groſſes Emeraudes, & les quéües de Dragons faiſoient des lambrequins; le tout chargé d'une broderie de perles & de rubis, ainſi que les brodequins.

Sur la coeffure qui étoit un morion d'or, rampoit vn Dragon de même métal, qui ſoû-
tenoit deux cercles de brillans d'or, chargez de plumes vertes & blanches, ſurmontées de
trois bouquets de plumes en Aigrette, d'où ſortoient trois maſſes de Heron, qui donnoient
quatre pieds de hauteur à cét habillement de teſte, duquel une queüe de plumes encor deſcendoit ſur le dos du Chevalier.

Son Cimeterre étoit d'or garny de pierreries, le fourreau à la Chinoiſe enrichy de même, il portoit une maſſe d'armes à aîles dorées, & découpées à jour, dont le bâton étoit
entouré d'un Serpent au naturel.   Iii

Catalogue 149

the "Race of Rings," a joustlike event in
which the mounted competitors
attempted to lance a ring target.

This work, describing the festivities of
1662, was published in 1670. This copy
belonged to the Sun King and was

gouached for him by Jacques Bailly.

Because of its great light sensitivity,
the book will be shown opened to
different plates throughout the run of
the exhibition.
JMR/VLG

150-151. PARADE HELMET AND SHIELD
Unidentified armorer(s) and cabinet craftsman
Ca. 1700(?)
Blued steel, silver and gold
Helmet: 15" x 9" (38.1 x 22.7 cm.)
Shield: 23-1/8" x 15-1/4" (58.7 x 38.7 cm.)

Loaned by the Department of Arms and Armor of the Metropolitan Museum of Art / 04.3.259 and 14.3.260, Rogers Fund, 1904

These magnificent ceremonial objects, in an early Renaissance-Revival style, recall the elaborate costuming of the Carrousel of 1662 and may have been commissioned for that event. Their great weight suggests that they may have been carried in procession rather than worn. Ostrich plumes once garnished the elaborate dragon cockade of the helmet; a classical Medusa mask is featured on the shield. A similar helmet and shield appear in the painting "Louis XIV, Vanquisher of the Fronde" (see #20).

Scholars of ormolu have recently suggested that this type of decoration was made by cabinet craftsmen, and that the pieces may date from the eighteenth century.
VLG

152. FIREWORKS ON THE GRAND CANAL AT VERSAILLES
Jean Le Pautre (1618-82)
Restrike engraving
15" x 22-1/2" (38 x 57 cm.)

Loaned by the Louisiana Museum Foundation

Grandiose fireworks displays were a popular form of public entertainment in France, and intricate pyrotechnics were featured at numerous royal celebrations. Also favored in eighteenth-century England, they were the inspiration of the "Royal Fireworks Music" by Handel.

Several *divertissements* were given by the Sun King to amuse his courtiers and celebrate important events of the early reign. In 1668 France had conquered the Franche-Comté during the War of Devolution and did so again during the Dutch War. French title to this area, around Bescançon between Burgundy and Switzerland, was confirmed by the Treaty of Nymegen in 1678.
VLG

Catalogue 150 and 151

Catalogue 152

THE KING AND THE COURT: PERFORMING ARTS

153. POETRY AND MUSIC WITH THE BUST OF LOUIS XIV
Jean Rousselet (1656-93)
1686
Marble
36-1/4" x 28-3/8" (92 x 72 cm.)

Loaned by the Département des Sculptures of the Musée du Louvre / MR 2764

Contributions to literature and the performing arts are among the timeless achievements of the reign of the Sun King, who took a personal interest in such accomplishments. Many works created under his royal patronage have had profound influence on the development of these arts in the Western world.

The sculptor Rousselet commemorated the Sun King's patronage with this bas-relief, which was submitted by the artist as his *morceau de réception* upon his nomination to the Royal Academy of Painting and Sculpture. In addition to the bust of Louis XIV, Rousselet used Apollo's lyre as a secondary visual reference to the Sun King.
VLG

154. CHARLES COUPERIN AND THE DAUGHTER OF THE PAINTER
Claude Lefebure (or Lefebvre)(1632-ca. 1680)
1665-70
Oil on canvas
50" x 37-3/4" (127 x 96 cm.)

Loaned by the Musée National du Château de Versailles / MV 4280

Several members of the Couperin family were leading composers and musicians during the Sun King's reign. Best known among them was François Couperin (1668-1773), harpsichordist and composer, whose most famous compositions included *Les Papillions, Les Abeilles, La Voluptueuse* and others. His playing style influenced Johann Sebastien Bach. François Couperin was also known for his religious and organ music, and he served as organist at the church of St. Gervais in Paris from 1685 to 1733 (where various Couperins held the position from about 1650 until 1826). In 1693 François Couperin became organist for the royal chapel and was later named Music Master to the Royal Family and Harpsichordist to the Court.

Charles Couperin (1638-79), shown here, served as organist at St. Gervais from 1661 onward, where he succeeded his brother Louis Couperin, who had died. Shortly after signing his contract he married Marie Guérin, the daughter of a barber installed in the King's Stables. Charles in turn was followed at St. Gervais by his nephew François, the most famous member of the family.

Claude Lefebvre produced highly realistic flattering images of his sitters (see #38). The inclusion of his daughter in this picture suggests a family friendship with the Couperins.
VLG

Catalogue 153

Catalogue 155

155. CHARLES MOUTON, LUTE PLAYER

François de Troy (1645-1730)
1690
Oil on canvas
54-3/8" x 41-3/4" (138 x 106 cm.)

Loaned by the Département des Peintures of the
Musée du Louvre / RF 2469

The Sun King was enamored of music. A band played beneath his window at Versailles during the morning *lever,* and various musicians, suitable to his activities and schedule, followed the monarch and played throughout the Sun King's day. Louis XIV was himself an accomplished guitarist, as was his daughter Louise Françoise, duchesse du Bourbon, Mademoiselle de Nantes.

The lutenist Charles Mouton (1626-after 1699) was taught by Denis Gaultier, equally a composer, and spent part of his youth at the Courts of Savoie and of Turin. By 1678, Mouton was settled in Paris. In 1691, the year after this portrait was made, he is mentioned as a teacher. His students included several well-known musicians as well as the daughter of engraver Gérard Edelinck (1640-1707), who made an engraving of this portrait by de Troy. VLG/JM

Catalogue 154

273

156. COSTUME FOR "WAR"
Attributed to Henri Gissey (1621-73)
Ca. 1654
Gouache on paper vellum
13-3/8" x 9-1/2" (34 x 24 cm.)

Loaned by the Musée Carnavalet / D.8544 /
Jouvellier Bequest, 1977

Classical ballet took its modern form
(and terminology) from seventeenth-
century French productions. Louis XIV
was an enthusiastic supporter and
participant, appearing in the 1654
performance of Benserade's *Marriage of
Pelleas and Thetis*, and was acknowledged
as an accomplished dancer. Other
courtiers also took part in such
productions, ladies being obliged to
dance in long gowns, which
distinguished them from professional
male dancers who usually performed the
feminine roles. Dance as a profession
was greatly encouraged by the founding
of the Royal Academy of Dance in 1661
at the beginning of the Sun King's
personal reign.

One of the most original creations in
the arts during the reign of Louis XIV
was that of the French opera, with
highly defined characteristics that were
opposed to the Italianism triumphant
throughout the rest of Europe. It took
the form of lyric tragedy and made its
appearance in 1673 with *Cadmus and
Hermione* by Lully and Quinault. The
king, struck by ballet as were all the
French of his time (both as a performer
and as a spectator), gave up dancing at
this time, a decision that is perhaps not
entirely coincidental.

Hybrid spectacles proliferated during
the early years of the Sun King's reign,
due in part to Mazarin's efforts to adapt
Italian opera to France. These
performances made room for the French
ballet, thus prefiguring the opera-ballet
of Campra or Rameau. The *Marriage of
Pelleas and Thetis* was just such a
sumptuous, disparate spectacle — Italian
comedy set to music interspersed with a
ballet on the same subject in
contemporary terms. The librettist was
Buti and the composer Caproli, both
Italians. Benserade and the comte de
Saint-Aignon created the ballet
elements, and Saint-Aignon directed the
choreography. Torelli created the stage
sets and machinery.

The *Marriage* was premiered in the
Salle du Petit-Bourbon on April 14,
1654, and was one of the most striking
efforts in this vein. The fusion of Italian
opera and French court ballet was as

complete as possible. Each scene of the
"comedy" was sung in Italian by
professional performers and the ballet
sequences were danced by a mixture of
great names at the court and
professionals. It received unanimous
praise, particularly the appearances of
the king.

In the long spectacle of complex
intrigue, the king made no less than six
entrances. He was "Apollo" in the
prologue, a "Fury" in the first act, a
"Dryade" in the second, both an
"Indian" and a "Courtier" in the third,
and finally appeared as "War."
J-MB/de la H/VLG

Catalogue 156

157. COSTUME FOR A "FURY"
Attributed to Henri Gissey (1621-73)
Ca. 1654
Gouache on paper vellum
13-3/8" x 9-1/2" (34 x 24 cm.)

Loaned by the Musée Carnavalet / D. 8545 /
Jouvellier Bequest, 1977

The Sun King danced several roles in
the *Marriage of Pelleas and Thetis*. He
appeared in the second act as one of a
group of Furies, composed of the duc de
Joyeuse, the marquis de Genlis,
Monsieur Bontemps, and the Sieurs
Lorge, Vespré, Beauchamp, and others,
in addition to himself.

Isaac de Benserade (1612-91) was a
composer of ballets and masques. It was
for his *Marriage of Pelleas and Thetis* that
this costume was designed. During his
active career, which covered three
decades from 1651 to 1681, he produced
almost thirty royal ballets. In his
Cassandre, Louis XIV is depicted as the
rising sun, singing, "Je ne suis point à
moi, je suis l'univers" ("I am no longer
myself, I am the universe").

Wealthy and famous, Benserade was
noted for his wit and his light verse. He
collaborated with composers and
choreographers, working as a poet,
librettist and playwright. In his own day
he was ranked the equal of Pierre
Corneille. In 1674 Benserade was
elected to the prestigious French
Academy. The dispute over his
translation of Ovid's *Metamorphoses* was
a literary *cause célèbre* of the seventeenth
century.
J-MB/JM/VLG

Catalogue 157

158. JEAN RACINE
After Jean-Baptiste Santerre (1651-1717)
1673
Oil on canvas
24-7/8" x 20-1/2" (63 x 52 cm.)

Loaned by the Musée National du Château de
Versailles / MV 2926

The drama of Jean Racine (1639-99) remains a remarkable legacy of classical theatre to the modern world, employing Alexandrine verse and psychological realism of characterization. Racine was educated by the Jansenists at Port-Royal, but split with them over his love of theater. Professional jealousies pitted Racine against the machinations of Pierre Corneille and Jean-Baptiste Poquelin, called Molière; in these intrigues he was supported by Nicolas Boileau and the Sun King.

Louis XIV liked Racine personally and appointed Boileau and Racine as his official historiographers. In this capacity they followed the king, even to military fronts, but prudently avoided battle situations.

Racine's reputation was established with *Andromaque* in 1667. Many of his plays, such as *Britannicus* (1669), *Bérénice* (1670), and *Béjazet* (1672), regaled French audiences with his versions of contemporary scandals. Other works include *Mithridate* (1673), *Iphigénie en Aulide* (1674) and *Phèdre* (1677), written before his retirement in 1678. Madame de Maintenon used her influence to persuade him to write *Esther* (1689) and *Athalie* (1691) to be performed by students at St. Cyr, the school for young women under her patronage.

This portrait was made to hang in the French Academy, to which Racine was named in 1673. Each academician had such an official portrait in the Academy collection.
CC/VLG

Catalogue 158

159. JEAN-BAPTISTE POQUELIN, CALLED MOLIÈRE
After Antoine Coypel (1661-1722)
17th century
Oil on canvas
28-3/4" dia. (73 cm.)

Loaned by the Musée National du Château de Versailles / MV 5053

The plays of Moliere, a brilliant satirist, have entertained audiences in France and abroad for over three centuries. Son of an upholsterer to the king, Jean-Baptiste Poquelin (1622-73) trained with the Béjart troupe, marrying the proprietress' daughter in 1662. His own company, "The Illustrious Theater," was successful in the provinces but not in Paris until *L'Amour Médecin* was performed for Louis XIV. The king's favor established the troupe in the Palais-Royal, where it became the predecessor of the Comédie Française.

Molière was a universal man in theater, functioning as writer, actor, director, and stage manager. After winning the Sun King's favor, he produced all sorts of entertainments for the court. His best-known works are *L'École des maris* (1661), followed by *L'École des femmes* (1662) and *l'Impromptu de Versailles* (1663), and include such classics as *Le Tartuffe* (1664), *Don Juan* (1665), *Le Misanthrope* (1666), *Le Bourgeois Gentilhomme* (1670), and *George Dandin,* which premiered at the *divertissement* of 1668. VLG

160. THE ROYAL TROUPE OF ITALIAN COMEDIANS
Nicolas de Larmessin II (*ca.* 1638-94)
1689
Engraving
35-1/4" x 22" (89.5 x 56 cm.)

Loaned by the Musée Carnavalet / Almanach 1689 (G:20302)

The Italian *commedia dell'arte* provided a prototypical set of stock characters and situations that remained popular in France throughout the seventeenth century. The Italian comedians specialized in broad slapstick-like humor and ferocious satire. This engraving, a popular calendar or almanac, is of special interest for its detail of stage appearance and lighting.

Since the sixteenth century the Italian comedians had been popular at the French court. Queens Marie and Catherine de Medici had made the use of Italian widespread at court, thus language provided no obstacle to the success of the comedians who primarily utilized pantomime. The troupes, who came from a long tradition of popular theater in Italy, played at improvisations based on sketches. But borrowing from serious theater, the actors, who were also acrobats and musicians and sometimes highly cultivated, brought to France a taste for performances that mixed song, dance, and music, complex theater machinery and sumptuous settings.

A troupe of Italian comedians, at the request of Cardinal Mazarin, was permanently established in France in 1660 at the Hôtel de Bourgogne and are shown here. They are depicted just after the death in 1688 of their chief Dominique Biancolelli, who played the part of Harlequin. In the foreground is Angelo Constantini who created and played Mezzetin, the cunning valet. He is shown receiving the costume, mask, and slapstick of Harlequin, marking his change to this role and his accession to the function of chief of the troupe. MM/VLG

Catalogue 159

Catalogue 160

161. SCENE OF GLORY OR TRANSFIGURATION
Studio of Jean Bérain I (1640-1711)
1668(?)
Ink and wash over black stone on paper
17" x 25-1/4" (43 x 64 cm.)

Loaned by the Archives Nationales / Recueil de Décors, Vol. VI, 1ère partie, No. 3 (0¹-3242^B1, No. 3)

Notable special effects achieved by complicated stage machinery heightened the enjoyment of theater and opera produced for the Sun King. In this operatic scene the ascending figure is surrounded by nudes with floral crowns, in sharp contrast to the stage set of monsters intertwining the columns of the proscenium.
DG/VLG

Catalogue 161

Catalogue 162

162. FESTIVAL ON WATER
Unidentified artist
1664
Black stone, ink and wash on paper
23" x 35-1/4" (58.5 x 89.5 cm.)

Loaned by the Département des Cartes et Plans of
the Archives Nationales / Recueil de Décors, Vol.
VI, 1ère partie, No. 2 (0¹-3242^B1, No. 2)

The drawing depicts a scene from
Ariosto's *Orlando Furioso* performed for
the court during the third day of the
"Pleasures of the Enchanted Isle," the
divertissement of 1664. The legend
accompanying the engraving of this
scene by Israël Silvestre (1621-91)
describes it as "a theater set up in the
center of a large pond representing the
Island of Alcine, whose enchanted
palace emerges from a small outcrop of
rock on which a ballet of several scenes
was danced, after which the palace was
consumed by fireworks (see #152 and
#50) representing the rupture of the
spell after the flight of Roger."
DG/VLG

Catalogue 164

163. THEATER SCENE
Unidentified artist, possibly Jean Bérain I
(1640-1711)
1706
Black stone, ink and wash on paper
16-1/8" x 11-3/4" (41 x 30 cm.)

Loaned by the Archives Nationales / Recueil de
Décors Vol. VI, 1ère partie, No. 48²
(o¹-3242^B¹, No. 48²)

The drawing presents a scene from the
prologue of *Polyxene et Pyrrhus*, from the
script by Jean-Louis Ignace de La Serre
(1600-65). On the shore, Minerva
strikes the earth with a lance, making
an olive tree grow from the soil; near
her the new city is evoked by a tower
and fortified well. Neptune, on his side,
is about to strike the earth with his
trident to make a river spring forth. At
the rear of the stage the sea carries
Neptune's empty chariot, a huge shell
drawn by two horses.
   The Greek antecedent for this scene,
the dispute of Athena and Poseidon for
the foundation of Athens, was depicted
by an ancient cameo in the royal
collections (see #195). The legend of
Pyrrhus was among the many classical
subjects painted by Nicolas Poussin. His
picture of it was acquired by the king in
1665 (see #205) from the Richelieu
collection.
DG/VLG

Catalogue 163

164. THEATER SCENE
Jean Bérain I (1640-1711)
17th century
Black stone, ink and wash on paper
9-5/8" x 11-5/8" (24.5 x 29.5 cm.)

Loaned by Archives Nationales / Recueil de
Décors, Vol. VI, 1ère partie, No. 39¹ (0¹-3242^B¹,
No. 39¹)

This drawing of an enthroned divinity is
an excellent example of the special
effects employed in theatrical
productions in seventeenth-century
France. The drama for which it was
designed has not been identified.
DG/VLG

165. THEATER PERSPECTIVE

Unidentified artist
Ca. 1674
Black stone, wash, sanguine and ink on paper
10-1/2" x 14-1/8" (26.5 x 35.8 cm.)

Loaned by the Archives Nationales / Recueil de Décors, Vol. VI 1ère partie, No. 38[1] (0[1]-3242[B1], No. 38[1])

This theater setting evoked the French victories of the Dutch War of 1674. A prince is shown in his tent, surrounded by flags at the end of a lineup of military trophies. The exact production for which it was drawn remains unidentified. The elaborate perspective effects of seventeenth-century French stage settings are typified by the design. DG/VLG

Catalogue 165

Catalogue 166

166. THEATER PERSPECTIVE

Studio of Jean Bérain I (1640-1711)
17th century
Ink on paper
9" x 12-3/8" (23 x 31.5 cm.)

Loaned by the Archives Nationales / Recueil de Décors, Vol. VI, 1ère partie, No. 15[2] (0[1]-3242[B1], No. 15[2])

The drawing shows a public square designed for a heroic scene with a triumphal arch. It typifies the elaborate perspective effects often seen in seventeenth-century French theatrical set design. The exact production for which it was drawn remains unidentified. Ephemeral arches, pyramids, and other constructions were sometimes built for special processions, triumphal entries, and other occasions. DG/VLG

THE DECORATIVE ARTS

Catalogue 167

167. VISIT OF LOUIS XIV TO THE GOBELINS (October 15, 1667)
Gobelins after Charles Le Brun (1619-90)
Woven in the Le Blond Studio, 1729-34
Wool, silk, and gold, 20 threads per inch (8 per cm.)
147-5/8" x 228-3/8" (375 x 580 cm.)

Loaned by the Mobilier National / GMTT 98-10

The Gobelins manufactory under Colbert's administration produced not just tapestries but a wide variety of furnishing. This diversification was part of Colbert's mercantile policy of promoting the foreign sale of luxury goods as well as furnishing the royal residences.

Among the most spectacular of the Gobelins creations was the suite of silver furniture, including a throne over seven feet in height (see #47), made for the Hall of Mirrors at Versailles. When the Sun King visited the Gobelins, as seen in this tapestry, a variety of fine pieces, including silver, were brought out for his inspection and approval. The silver suite for the Hall of Mirrors was melted down to pay the enormous costs of the Wars of the League of Augsburg and the Spanish Succession.

This fine example is from the fourteen piece suite called "The History of the King." It is a low-warp tapestry and is the fourteenth piece of the sixth weaving of the series. In the upper border are the arms of France; there are *fleur-de-lys* in the corners and the king's monogram in the cartouches of the side borders. The inscription in the cartouche of the lower-border may be translated as:

The King Louis XIIII Visiting the //

Manufactory of the Gobelins where the //
Lord Colbert Superintendent of his //
Works Conducts him in All //
the Studios in Order to Show him //
the Diverse Works Which are Made There //

Since 1662, the year in which Colbert decided to group in a single location the diverse studios of Paris and of Maincy, near Vaux-le-Vicomte — which Louis XIV had just confiscated from Nicolas Fouquet — the Manufactory of the Gobelins played a role of exceptional importance in the decorative arts, and its history, particularly in the seventeenth and eighteenth centuries, is tied to that of French painting. Its name, synonymous with tapestry in many countries, is that of a family of "Dyers in Scarlet," the

Gobelins, who set themselves up in the mid-fifteenth century on the banks of the Bièvre, in the Saint Marcel suburb of Paris.

Colbert placed the new manufactory under the authority of the First Painter to the King, Charles Le Brun (1619-90). Director, organizer, and creator, Le Brun assembled a staff of painters who specialized in different genres, such as René-Antoine Houasse (ca. 1645-1710), Jean-Baptiste Monnoyer (1634-99), Guillaume Anguier (1628-1708), and Pierre de Sève (1623-95), who transformed his drawings into cartoons for the weavers. A.-F. Van der Meulen (ca. 1632-1690) was one of his principal collaborators, particularly for the landscape elements.

At the end of 1662 Le Brun conceived the plan of realizing a tapestry suite consecrated to the history of the king. For about ten years he worked on compositions that were intended to recall the principal facts of the life of Louis XIV. From 1664, Colbert had the newly created Academy of Inscriptions and Belles-Lettres compose the texts that were to be placed in the lower cartouches.

The model for the "Visit to the Gobelins" was painted by Pierre de Sève the Younger and was finished before March, 1673. In the preparatory drawing, which has been dated ca.

1672, Charles Le Brun, lightly sketching the ground of the scene he would assign to de Sève to complete, established the placement of the figures. The borders for the low-warp weaving were designed by Claude Audran (1639-84).

Louis XIV followed with interest the establishment of the manufactory, which he visited on several occasions from 1663 onward. This tapestry recalls his visit of October 15, 1667, which he made upon his return from the military campaign in Flanders. The Gazette of 1667 gave a detailed account of the visit.

The scene takes place in a courtyard of the Gobelins compound. To the left is the official party, at the center of which is seen the king, surrounded by his brother Philippe, duc d'Orléans, the duc d'Enghien (son of the Grand Condé), and Colbert. Charles Le Brun depicted himself as the three-quarter-size figure placed just below this group, hat in hand. In front of these illustrious visitors are the artists and craftsmen whose works Le Brun will present to the king. All the works were made at the Gobelins, which, in November, 1667, officially took the title of Manufactory of Furnishings of the Crown.

With few exceptions, it is certain that the tapestry shows neither a faithful image of the visit of October, 1667, nor the actual works shown to the king. It is

known that on the occasion of a previous visit in 1665 the king first saw the "Passage du Granique," a vast composition belonging to the ensemble of the "History of Alexander" painted by Le Brun and woven at the Gobelins. On either side of it are suspended two tapestries from the suite of "Months" or "Royal Houses"; that on the left can be identified as "June — Sign of Cancer — View of Fontainebleau," the high-warp weaving of which was begun in 1668 and completed in 1673.

The studies of the Manufactory of Furnishings of the Crown, installed until 1694 in the Gobelins compound, are represented by some of their most important productions. Some of the pieces of the famous silver furniture of Louis XIV are recognizable: a brancard (serving litter on stand), a vase, a guéridon, and a large oval platter. All these objects ornamented the grands appartements of Versailles until 1689, when they were sent to the foundry.

The "History of the King" suite was certainly the most famous and most brilliant set realized by the Manufactory of the Gobelins. From the first weavings of the set, begun in 1665, until 1741, the cartoons were ceaselessly replaced on the looms. A total of eighty-three pieces in either high or low warp, with or without gold, were woven.
JC/ID/VLG

168. ARMCHAIR
Unidentified cabinetmaker
Ca. 1680
Carved and gilded beechwood, gesso, and
upholstery (modern)
45-5/8" x 26-3/8" x 20-1/8" (116 x 67 x 51 cm.)

Loaned by the Musée des Arts Décoratifs / INV
3900

There was an elaborate protocol
involving furniture in
seventeenth-century France. Depending
on rank, a courtier might or might not
be entitled to be seated in an armchair.
To be offered one, particularly in the
presence of the king, was a signal honor
rarely accorded.

Few armchairs have survived from the
reign of Louis XIV. Especially rare are
those, such as this example, which have
not been rebuilt and regilded. This
particularly elegant chair features
balusterlike legs, reverse scroll diagonal
stretchers, and handsomely curved arms.
VLG

Catalogue 168

169. STOOL
Unidentified cabinetmaker
Ca. 1675
Carved and gilded wood, gesso, and upholstery
(modern)
15-3/4" x 20-1/8" x 14-5/8" (40 x 51 x 37 cm.)

Loaned by the Musée des Arts Décoratifs / INV PE
715

The mundane stool was considered a
quite honorable seat at the French
court. Few were entitled to them; most
courtiers were required to stand,
particularly in the king's presence. To be
accorded a stool was a mark of
distinction.

This is a typical stool in the Louis
XIV style, with baluster legs raised
above soclelike feet with shaped
stretchers.
VLG

Catalogue 169

170. PLATTER
Rouen
Early 18th century
Tin-glazed earthenware (faïence)
22-1/4" dia. (56.5 cm. dia.)

Loaned by the Musée des Beaux-Arts et de la Céramique de la Ville de Rouen / INV 683

Fine French earthenware of the seventeenth century was tin-glazed in brilliant white with decorative painting in scenic or geometric patters. Called *faïence,* it was much more elegant than the cheap stuffs, rudely thrown in mass quantities, that were used for much of the colonial trade.

Rouen, north of Paris in Normandy, became an important center of ceramic production. Located on the River Seine not far from the port of Le Havre, Rouen could send its products to the sea or to the capital and court.

Decorative motifs most frequently seen in Rouen wares are sophisticated repeating arabesques and garlands. Earlier pieces are decorated entirely in the characteristic "cameo" blue. Later wares added a brick red to the decorator's palette.

This very handsome serving piece is an excellent example of the "radiant" *décor* of Rouen faïence. It appears on a lightly blued enamel ground. The arabesquelike "scallops," which are characteristic of the reign of Louis XIV, are seen in their "radiant" phase. They project widely from the lip of the platter to extend toward the center, which is ornamented with a rosette.

These "scallops" — motifs alternated like pendentives — were among the most remarkable creations of the *faïenciers* of Rouen and were imitated by numerous French and European ceramic centers.

Rouen pottery manufacture began in the mid-seventeenth century. The major early figure was Edmé Poterat, whose production was from 1647 to 1697. Although Rouen wares never received royal patronage, they enjoyed great commercial success. Reminiscent of Delft wares, Rouen blue imitates the "Persian" blue of Nevers (see #178). Simple shapes of slightly heavy proportion are typical.
CV/JM/VLG

171. PLATE
Rouen
Early 18th century
Tin-glazed earthenware (faïence)
9-1/4" dia. (23.5 cm. dia.)

Loaned by the Musée des Beaux-Arts et de la Céramique de la Ville de Rouen / INV 530

This plate is a very good example of the blue-and-red *décor* of Rouen, with "scallops" on the lip and a basket of flowers on a console in the center. Red glaze appeared in Rouen faïence at the very end of the seventeenth century. It has a slightly grainy appearance and feel and varies from piece to piece, ranging in color from orange to vermillion. It is frequently applied in contiguous elements with motifs in "cameo" blue.
CV/VLG

Catalogue 170

Catalogue 171

Catalogue 172

172. EWER
Rouen
Early 18th century
Tin-glazed earthenware (faïence)
Height including handle 11-3/8" (29 cm.), base
5-1/4" dia. (13.5 cm.)

Loaned by the Musée des Beaux-Arts et de la
Céramique de la Ville de Rouen / INV 458

This ewer, in the form of an inverted
helmet (also seen in goblets), is typical
of the Louis XIV era, although its use
was prolonged beyond the Sun King's
reign well into the eighteenth century.
The "cameo" blue *décor* of this ewer is
divided into registers: festoons, fillets,
godroons, and a frieze of "scallops." An
Indian mask ornaments the undersurface
of the spout.
CV/VLG

173. SUGAR CASTER
Rouen
Early 18th century
Tin-glazed earthenware (faïence) with metal
fittings
Height 9-1/2" (24 cm.), width at base 3-1/8" (8
cm.)

Loaned by the Musée des Beaux-Arts et de la
Céramique de la Ville de Rouen / INV 455

After the 'great melt,' French ceramics
assumed a broad range of forms usually
associated with metals. Sugar casters
were used by the wealthy and were
commonly made of silver.

This sugar caster is made in two parts
with a threaded connector of pewter and
was used for powdered sugar. It is of
baluster form, with an alternation of
concave and convex elements raised on
a foot.
CV/VLG

Catalogue 173

174. SUGAR CASTER

David André (master 1703-pre-1743)
Paris, 1709-10
Silver
9-1/8" (23.2 cm.)

Loaned by the Department of European Sculpture and Decorative Arts of the Metropolitan Museum of Art / 48.187.73 a & b / Bequest of Catherine D. Wentworth, 1948

Although frowned upon by the king, the manufacture of silver hollowware continued after the 'great melt.' This example was made for an unidentified patron at the height of the War of the Spanish Succession.

Casters for powdered sugar began to appear on French tables in the second half of the seventeenth century. They were at first cylindrical or ovoid, the latter form appearing in a design of *ca.* 1697 for a caster believed to have been made for one of Louis XIV's services. This characteristic baluster model was developed between 1700 and 1710. At this period the caster appeared on the table as part of a *surtout de table* or centerpiece, to which reference is first made in Paris in 1692. Serving both a decorative and useful function, the *surtout* generally included a plateau fitted with a centerpiece (sculptural or in the form of a tureenlike vessel), girandoles, and a number of cruets, condiment pots, and casters. Two *surtouts* recorded in 1697 in the inventory of Louis XIV's table silver each included four sugar casters.

The maker's mark on the caster consists of a crowned *fleur-de-lys,* two *grains de remède,* DA, and a *device à harp.* The Paris charge mark for silver made between 1704 and 1712 is an A encircled by a crown. The Paris warden's mark from 1709 to 1710 is a crowned Q. In addition, there is the Paris discharge mark for 1704-12 for work made in more than one piece (*vaiselle montée*) — a crown with a scepter and hand of justice — and the Paris restricted warranty mark, 1838 to date — a boar's head.
LeC/VLG

Catalogue 175

Catalogue 174

175. EWER IN THE FORM OF A HELMET

Rouen, 1725-30
Tin-glazed earthenware (faïence)
11" x 9-7/8" (28 x 25 cm.)

Loaned by the Musée National de Céramique / MNC 10449 / Bequest of Albert Gérard, 1900

The form of this ewer precisely copies a goldsmith's model that appeared in the decade of the 1690s. The transposition into faïence of forms generally associated with silver and precious metals is linked to the sombre events that marked the end of the reign of Louis XIV. After the military reverses of the War of the Spanish Succession, the treasury was empty and the famous edict of 1709 enjoined the nobility to melt down its silver. The faïence industry was the beneficiary of these sad measures. Saint-Simon said in his *mémoires,* "All that was grand and noble was reduced to faïence in a week."

The decorative principle is also borrowed from goldsmith's techniques. The ground of "nielloed ochre" — so-called because of the *rinceaux* that recall the enamel inlays for which ornamentalists furnished designs to jewelers — outlined in blue, appeared in Rouen about 1725. It represents a luxury production, certainly very costly, and therefore seldom employed by itself. Most often it is associated, as seen in this piece, with blue and red *lambrequins.*
EF/VLG

176. EWER
Unidentified silversmith (I.V.)
Paris, 1698-99
Silver
10-3/4" (27.3 cm.)

Loaned by the Department of European Sculpture and Decorative Arts of the Metropolitan Museum of Art / 48.187.19 / Bequest of Catherine D. Wentworth, 1948

This silver ewer was made for an unidentified client at the end of the War of the League of Augsburg. It follows the traditional form, derived from Renaissance prototypes, which was widely imitated for less affluent patrons by French potters.

After the King ordered the 'great melt,' first in 1689 and again in 1709, some courtiers carefully hid their silver and ostentatiously used ceramic replacements. Despite this unpatriotic practice, few silver pieces from the period have survived.

By the end of the seventeenth century, ewers and basins were in use both at the dressing table and in the dining room, where the eating fork was only just coming into general use. A table service inventoried in 1684 among the dauphin's silver included a ewer and basin, and among the designs for French royal plate in the Nationalmuseum, Stockholm, is a ewer of this type made about 1690 for the duc d'Aumont specifically described as an "Eguière pour mettre sur le buffet." The Stockholm drawing documents what may be considered the earliest appearance of this so-called helmet type of ewer, which evolved in France about 1690 and became the standard model for the form in English and French silver until about 1720, as well as in faïence.

Engraved beneath the spout, at a slightly later date, are the arms of L'Estang du Rusquec. The maker's mark consists of a crowned *fleur-de-lys,* two *grains de remède,* IV, and the device of a lily. The Paris charge mark, 1697-1704, is an A with a scepter and hand of justice; the Paris warden's mark for 1698-99 is a crowned E, and the Paris discharge mark for work made in more than one piece *(vaisselle montée)* for 1697-1704 is a crowned lizard.
LeC/VLG

Catalogue 176

177. EWER
Probably Normandy (Rouen)
1690-1710
Glass
8-3/4" (22.2 cm.)

Loaned by the Department of European Sculpture and Decorative Arts of the Metropolitan Museum of Art / 81.8.164 / Gift of James Jackson Jarves, 1881

The glassblowers of Normandy were successful in developing a completely clear product with few inclusions, and their output included functional as well as decorative wares. Many of their forms were derived from those of the silversmith or potter.

An industry making superb clear and colored glass for use in stained glass windows flourished in Lorraine and Normandy from early medieval times. Utilitarian glass of a metallic green tint following the Roman formula was also made in many places in France, but for fashionable vessels of a clear crystal color of the type first produced in Italy in the late fifteenth century, the French were apparently content to remain dependent on imports from Venice, Germany, England, and the Low Countries until well into the eighteenth century. The exceptions to this pattern were a glasshouse founded in 1605 by François Garsonnet in the suburb of Saint Sever in Rouen, Normandy, which has been suggested as the source of a group of domestic pieces made in the later seventeenth century in a somewhat imperfect clear glass of Venetian type, and another at Nevers presumably owing its origin to the period of Italian influence under Ludovico Gonzaga, who became duke of Nevers late in the sixteenth century.

This ewer is the type known as a helmet ewer (a translation of the French term). The form, with its generous handle, baluster and domed pedestal feet, inverted bell shape, a string marking the lower third of the body, and a cuff of alternating concave and convex flutes applied to the base, is a precise equivalent in glass terms of contemporary ewers in silver. Such glass ewers are traditionally held to have been made in Normandy, but evidence connecting them directly with the glasshouse in Saint Sever, or with any other particular glasshouse is lacking. The three *fleurs-de-lis* stamped on applied pads on the foot, clearly an allusion to the French royal arms, may possibly point to its having been made as part of a large order to supply one of the royal residences.
McN

Catalogue 177

Catalogue 178

179. BOTTLE (GOURD) WITH FOUR TWISTED LOOPS
Nevers, 1688
Tin-glazed earthenware (faïence)
11-7/8" x 7-7/8" x 5-1/2" (30 x 20 x 14 cm.)

Loaned by the Musée de Céramique / MNC 3031 /
Acquired in 1842

The name of the owner of this piece, Georges Paille, is inscribed on the shoulder. The *décor* that ornaments the sides of this gourd — a Bacchus on a barrel on one side (a motif that had been employed by Rouen and Nevers manufactories in high relief for the fabrication of fountains) and the tools of the vintner on the other — explains the profession of the owner. The date 1688, which is found on the shoulder, is seemingly the year of the execution of the piece, but we cannot completely exclude that it might evoke an important event in the life of the said Georges Paille.

This work is a very precocious example of occupational *décor*, which was particularly practiced in the second half of the eighteenth century, a time when popular or "folk" faïence constituted the essential element of Nevers production. It has the special merit of bearing witness to the life of the *paysan* classes in France under the reign of Louis XIV.
EF/VLG

178. SHOP SIGN FOR A POTTER
Nevers, 1658
Tin-glazed earthenware (faïence)
13-3/4" x 13-3/4" (35 x 35 cm.)

Loaned by the Musée National de Céramique /
MNC 8330 / Acquired in 1885

The inscription CEANS SE FAICT ET VEND / DE TOUTE SORTE DE FA / IANCE 1658 ("Inside is made and sold all sorts of faïence 1658") attests to the purpose of this tile. However, shop signs in faïence are particularly rare, and, curiously, especially those of faïence merchants. The sign evokes one of the principal activities of this central French town where faïence has been made without interrruption for more than three centuries. In the seventeenth century Nevers was the major faïence production center, the only one functioning during the first half of the century, and the creator, in the 1650s, of a style that was able to detach itself from Italian influence to become properly French.

Scenes drawn from *l'Astrée,* the interminable novel by Honoré d'Urfé published between 1610 and 1627, which was illustrated with vignettes engraved by Michel Lasne after drawings by Rabel, enjoyed enormous popularity. The woman with the basket and the hunter shown on either side of a vase of flowers belong to this repertoire. However, the decorative principle is still completely in the Italian tradition; it is called *a compendiario,* an untranslatable term from the verb *compendiare* (to summarize), which involves a palette reduced to blue and yellow that had become fashionable at Faenza, Italy, in the mid-sixteenth century.
EF/VLG

Catalogue 179

Catalogue 180

180. PILGRIM BOTTLE
Nevers
Ca. 1670
Tin-glazed earthenware (faïence)
14-1/4" (36.2 cm.)

Loaned by the Department of European Sculpture and Decorative Arts of the Metropolitan Museum of Art / 02.6.274 / Gift of Alfred Duane Pell, 1902

The pilgrim bottle was the antecedent of the canteen. It was a flask with a round body, flattened sides, and a cylindrical neck, usually provided with loops for suspension from a beltlike girdle.

This large and ornamental pilgrim flask was doubtless made more for display than for use. It dates from the first decade of the personal reign of Louis XIV, a period when the encouragement given to the development of French art during his minority was bringing rich returns.

Made in Nevers, the pilgrim flask exemplifies this period in all its aspects. The Nevers faïence factory was founded by three brothers, majolica makers from Albissola near Savona, in 1585 — a time when the duchy was held by the Italian Lucovico Gonzaga. Their monopoly for making faïence ran out in 1632 when other faïence potteries were established in the city. One of these, the Ecce Homo pottery of Nicolas Estienne, provided faïence tubs for jasmine plants at Versailles in 1665, which shows that faïence from as far south as Nevers was appreciated in the court circle. This flask is one of a small group of related pieces that may have been made at the pottery of the Conrade family (descendants of the original Italian Corrado brothers), two members of which were favored by such titles as "faïencier ordinaire du roi" and "maitre faïencier de sa Majesté." The group to which this flask belongs is marked by an almost equal emphasis on sculptural and painted decoration derived directly from the engraved works of contemporary artists of the court, such as Vouet, Poussin, and Le Brun. Taking the place of the strapslots necessary on utilitarian pilgrim flasks are lions' masks with horns curling back over the heads and clusters of fruit and flowers hanging from rings held in their mouths. On each side is a scene from Greek mythology, both appearing in Ovid's *Metamorphoses* — the race between Atalanta and Hippomenes, and Venus chiding Adonis. The colors are the particularly subtle hues of high-temperature glazes found in this group — a pale lemon yellow, brilliant green, clear orange, soft misty blue, and light manganese purple. The latter color is used not only for painting areas of purple but also is effective for drawing the fine, thready outlines of the figures and landscape and for suggesting with the deftest of touches the compressed, tiny features of the faces. The same artist seems to have been responsible for all the pictorial painting on the group of highly elaborate wares from Nevers to which this flask belongs (other pieces are in the Louvre and in the Victoria and Albert Museum). Many of his subjects were based on engravings by Michel Dorigny and works by Vouet, but the two scenes on this piece have not yet been attributed.
McN/JM/VLG

Catalogue 181

181. GADROONED CUP AND SAUCER
Saint Cloud, between 1696 and 1722
Soft-paste porcelain with sun mark
Cup: 2-1/8" x 3-1/2" dia. (5.5 x 9 cm.)
Saucer: 5-1/4" dia. (13.3 cm.)

Loaned by the Musée National de Céramique / MNC 13402 / Gift of the Marquis de Brollier, 1908

In the seventeenth century, France, like all of Europe, had not yet penetrated the secret of making porcelain, the whiteness and translucency of which was fascinating. To try to remedy this lack, a substitute material was produced, called soft-paste or artificial porcelain, which contains no kaolin. The perfection of extremely complex soft-paste recipes was made in the faïence manufactories and met with success first at Rouen, then at Saint Cloud (about 1696).

Saint Cloud enjoyed the patronage of its powerful neighbor, Monseigneur, the duc d'Orléans, who was a rabid collector of Oriental porcelain. Thanks to his influence, the widow of Pierre Chicaneau and her sons obtained a license to establish a porcelain manufactory in 1702, renewed in 1712 and 1722. The mark, called "au soleil" (a rayed disc), was employed in honor or Louis XIV from 1696 until 1722 or 1724.

This cup with "sunken saucer" or "quaking" cup is completely typical of the earliest soft-paste production at Saint Cloud. The gadrooned form was obtained from a mold, because the soft-paste material, not very pliant, was difficult to turn. The *lambrequin* decoration was borrowed from the decorative repertoire of contemporary faïence.
EF/VLG

182. PHARMACEUTICAL VASE

Saint Cloud, *ca.* 1700
Tin-glazed Earthenware (faïence)
10" x 6-1/4" dia. (25.5 x 16 cm.)

Loaned by the Musée National de Céramique /
MNC 21361 / Bequest of Dr. Frombeure, 1948

In 1666 the Parisian merchant Claude Révérand purchased a house at Saint Cloud on the banks of the Seine near the château of Monsieur, the king's brother, to establish a faïence manufactory. It is known that between 1670 and 1673 this manufactory delivered a certain number of pieces for Versailles and the Trianon de Porcelaine. The business was subsequently rented to Pierre Chicaneau. After Chicaneau's death, his widow married Henri Trou, Bailiff of the Antechamber of the duc d'Orléans, whose son became director of the manufactory.

One of the principal activities of the Manufactory of Saint Cloud, which functioned until the mid-eighteenth century, was the production of pharmaceutical pots decorated with *lambrequins* painted in blue. This *lambrequin* or "embroidery" motif was created by ornamentalists and used by goldsmiths, cabinetmakers, tapestry producers, and book binders, and for "garden embroideries" or parterre patterns. In faïence it constituted an expression of the Louis XIV style and disappeared not long after his death.
EF/VLG

183. PAIR OF CANDLESTICKS

Unidentified silversmith (ID)
Paris, 1690-92
Silver
9-1/4" (23.5 cm.) ea.

Loaned by the Department of European Sculpture and Decorative Arts of the Metropolitan Museum of Art /48.187.249 and .250 / Bequest of Catherine D. Wentworth, 1948

In silver, as in the other fine and decorative arts, French designers of the seventeenth century tended to employ forms of classic derivation, often architectonic in character and frequently repeated in rhythmic, balanced patterns. In the restrained use of curve and counter-curve can be seen the seeds of the exuberance of the rococo design of the following century. Weight and volume are the baroque characteristics most often in evidence. The open form and dramatic composition of contemporary Italian design were generally avoided in favor of symmetry.

This is the earliest recorded example of this type of candlestick which survived, with modifications, until about 1730. Numerous pairs and sets of candlesticks were part of the royal silver for the dining table and for the personal apartments of Louis XIV and his family. With their finely detailed, small-scale decoration, candlesticks of this size were undoubtedly meant for personal domestic use. Each is engraved at one corner of the base with the combined arms of Adélaide-Charlotte du Deffand (1736-1820) and Eugène Eustache, marquis de Béthisy, who were married in 1767.

The unidentified maker's mark consists of a crowned *fleur-de-lys*, two *grains de remède*, ID, and the device of a lily(?). The Paris charge mark for 1687-91 is a crowned A flanked by reverse scrolls, and the Paris warden's mark for 1690-92 is a crowned X. There is also the Paris discharge mark for work made up in more than one piece (*vaisselle montée*) for 1687-91, a crown. The set bears the Paris counter mark for small work for 1691-96, interlaced C's.
LeC/VLG

Catalogue 182

Catalogue 183

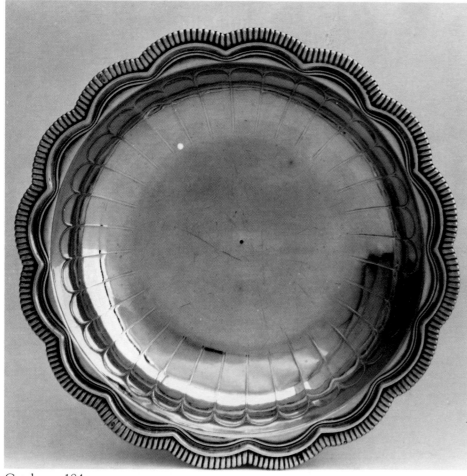

Catalogue 184

184. DISH
Simon Le Bastier (Master 1698/9, last recorded 1715)
Paris, 1710-11
Silver
10-1/4" dia. (26 cm.)

Loaned by the Department of European Sculpture and Decorative Arts of the Metropolitan Museum of Art / 48.187.36 / Bequest of Catherine D. Wentworth, 1948

Despite the Sun King's pleas that gold and silver be melted down to pay burgeoning war expenses, hollowware continued in vogue, even if somewhat clandestinely. This bowl was made during the War of the Spanish Succession, when French crown finances were at a particularly low ebb.

Plain surfaces and a rhythmic lobing of the lip give this bowl great elegance. It does not partake of heavy baroque ornamentation that could conceal flaws in the smith's workmanship.

The table service as a planned ensemble of eating and serving pieces of homogenous design originated at the French court and was in existence by 1664 when the first royal gifts of services made by Louis XIV are recorded. The composition of a service was not constant, and the usage of a given piece not always certain. Among the drawings of royal silver made in 1702 for the Swedish Court is a deep circular dish of this type, inscribed "assiette pottagere," and two dozen silver gilt soup plates are listed in 1671 in the inventory of Louis XIV's plate. By soup is not meant a broth or bouillon, which was served in a *pot* (a covered bowl with a handle, evidently the forerunner of the *écuelle*), but a ragoût chiefly of vegetables.

The piece carries a maker's mark of crowned *fleur-de-lys,* two *grains de remède,* SLB, and the device of a cross. The Paris charge mark for silver, 1704-12 is an *A* encircled by a crown, and the Paris warden's mark for 1710-11 is a crowned *R*. The Paris verification mark has been used in place of the discharge mark and is a fly. There is also the Paris restricted warranty mark, 1838 to date, a boar's head.
LeC/VLG

185. GRILL
Unidentified blacksmith
17th century
Wrought iron
38-5/8" dia. (98 cm. dia.)

Loaned by the Musée LeSecq des Tournelles of the City of Rouen / INV 20

Decorative architectural metalwork was highly developed during the Sun King's reign. French blacksmiths realized surprisingly three-dimensional motifs in handsome patterns following the balanced aesthetic of the classical baroque. Major architectural elements were designed and executed for churches, public buildings, and upper-class residences.

This large and handsome circular grill was made for a convent in the northern French town of Amiens in Picardy. Full scrolls and curves are enriched with stylized vegetal forms in eight radiating repeats. The design recalls the "radiant" style of the faïence of Rouen (see #170) and is an interpretation of the baluster motif (see #173) used in the seventeenth century in iron balconies and stair railings. At the center is a monogram composed of the letters GBM inscribed in a medallion. Such a grill would have been used above a door to admit light in the manner of a rose window.
CV/VLG

Catalogue 185

Catalogue 186

186. GRILL FROM AN IMPOSTE
Unidentified blacksmith
Late 17th or early 18th century
Wrought iron
25-5/8" x 49-1/4" (65 x 125 cm.)

Loaned by the Musée LeSecq des Tournelles of the City of Rouen / INV 293

Among the most elegant of iron architectural elements from the Sun King's reign is this grill. It plays a rigid internal geometry against delicate decoration to achieve great visual interest.

Following classical precepts, the grill is designed within an isosceles triangle, which features a central crowning stylized palmette. The palmette is symmetrically flanked with geometric semicircular elements supported from horizontal members connected to the palmette by scrolled C-curves. In turn, these lead to spiraling scrolls at the lower extremities of the triangle. The voids are filled with lacy, stylized vegetal elements throughout, which attest to the sophisticated control achieved at French forges.

The design is close to the compositions of Louis Fordrin, a master locksmith and ornamentalist active about 1700. The piece is transitional in style: the slender dentated elements of foliage have not achieved the fulsome quality of the eighteenth century, and the two stylized blossoms at the sides are well in the seventeenth-century tradition. However, the central five-branched palmette prefigures a motif that reached its fullest development in fine metalwork about 1720.

CV/VLG

Catalogue 187

187. KITCHEN GRILL
Unidentified blacksmith (IK)
17th century
Wrought iron
28-3/8" x 12-5/8" (72 x 32 cm.)

Loaned by the Musée LeSecq des Tournelles of the City of Rouen / INV 180

Mundane objects in metal were often the vehicles for exuberant decoration of a folk character. A fulsome play of reversing scrolls split from single bars of metal gives character and style to this open-work kitchen grill. The same technique has been employed for the handle as well as the four-part repeat of the circular support, resulting in stylized hearts and *fleurs-de-lys*.

The grill was an essential accessory in the French kitchen, where it was used for direct cooking on the brazier. Turning the grill on a central axis permitted a variety of exposure to the flame. Grills were frequently given on the occasion of a housewarming, known as "the hanging of the pot rack." They were customarily ornamented with symbols of love and marriage, often accompanied by the names of the recipients and the date of the event being celebrated. The stamped "IK" on the handle of this grill is the maker's mark.
CV/VLG

188. LOCK AND KEY FOR A PORTE-COCHÈRE

Unidentified locksmith
Late 17th century
Cut and chased wrought iron
Lock: 11-7/8" x 8-5/8" x 1-5/8" (30 x 22 x 4 cm.),
including attachments
Key: 5-1/2" (14 cm.)

Loaned by the Musée Bricard / INV 74.20.376 a
& b

The locksmith's art was highly refined
during the reign of Louis XIV,
developing traditions of the sixteenth
century. Elaborate form and internal
sophistication distinguish locks and keys
made for wealthy clients.

The general form of this lock is of a
typical French seventeenth-century
rectangular panel with an arched head
of reversing curves, placed on its side.
Three open-work palmette decorative
projections for attachment are appended,
as are two molded night-bolt buttons.
The key is of elaborate sectional profile,
the hollowed shank is heart-shaped, and
the bit splays. This specific profile, seen
in the keyhole as well, made the use of
the wrong key nearly impossible. The
internal complexities of the lock can be
judged from the steps of the key bit.
The bow of the key is of the "frog
thigh" type, composed of stylized
dolphin forms.
CP/VLG

Catalogue 188

189. COFFER LOCK AND KEY

Unidentified master locksmith
1680-1700
Steel (key with patinated head) and iron
Lock: 6-5/16" x 3-9/16" x 2" (16 x 9 x 5 cm.)
Key: 5-5/8" (14.3 cm.)

Loaned by the Department of European Sculpture
and Decorative Arts of the Metropolitan Museum
of Art / 57.137.7 a & b / Harris Brisbane Dick
Fund, 1957

"Masterpiece" objects were made by
skilled craftsmen of the seventeenth
century as a requirement for admission
to guildlike professional companies.
Membership in such organizations was
proof of master craftsman status. The
masterpiece creation was much like the
morceaux de réception demanded of visual
artists upon admission to the Royal
Academy of Painting and Sculpture. It
displayed the maker's highest degree of
technical skill and design.

This lock, probably a masterpiece or
test piece for admission to a guild of
locksmiths, is an example of a type of
chest or coffer lock with three catches.
In actual use, such a lock was fitted to
the inside of the coffer, where the major
portion of its decorative embellishments

remained hidden. Such locks were
described by Marthurin Jousse in *La
Fidèlle Ouverture de l'art De Serrurier* (La
Flèche, 1627), the most extensive
treatise on French locksmithing
published before the eighteenth century.
The maker of this lock has modernized
its traditional form with pierced foliate
scrolling from the decorative vocabulary
of French design of the last quarter of
the seventeenth century. The key, with
its intricately filed bit and hollow pipe
of triangular section, also derives from
earlier models illustrated by Jousse. The
heavy baroque S-scrolls of its bow,
however, place it firmly within the reign
of Louis XIV.

Neither lock nor key is signed or
marked in any recognizable fashion,
which is not unusual in this period,
even for locks and keys of such fine
workmanship. Evidence in the Archives
Nationales has been cited showing that
by 1620 locksmiths had already begun to
neglect their guild obligation to identify
their work; by the end of the century
they had all but abandoned the use of
such markings.
CLV/VLG-

Catalogue 190

190. GATE KNOCKER
Unidentified blacksmith
Late 17th century
Cut and chased wrought iron
15-3/4" x 7-7/8" (40 x 20 cm.)

Loaned by the Musée Bricard / INV 74.40.598

Excellent proportions, symmetrical solid form, and handsome execution mark this knocker. It is typical of those found on street gates of seventeenth-century houses of the Marais section of Paris. The fluid, stylized palmette in silhouette, from which the beater is suspended, suggests that it was made in the latter part of the seventeenth century. The beater is of the "frog thigh" type (see #188) also called a "game bag buckle."
CP/VLG

Catalogue 189

THE ROYAL COLLECTIONS: THE CABINET DU ROI

For a variety of reasons, Louis XIV became one of the world's greatest patrons and collectors of the fine arts. It was suitable to the royal magnificence to amass and to astonish, as manifested by the creation of Versailles itself, where the royal collections were installed.

In addition to his father's holdings, the Sun King inherited those of his uncle Gaston d'Orléans (1608-60). Colbert, who understood the power and political value of the royal hoard, began to play a decisive role with the acquisition of major portions of the collection of Cardinal Mazarin. In 1665 the holdings of the duc de Richelieu were acquired. After Colbert's death the king played an ever-greater and more personal role in the collecting process, and in 1693 came the magnificent gift of André Le Nôtre. By such wholesale methods and individual commissions and purchases the collection grew, ranging from Near Eastern manuscripts to botanical plates to Italian Renaissance masters to contemporary French works. These vast and all-encompassing collections have richly endowed France and form the basis of the Bibliothèque Nationale, the museums of the Louvre and Versailles, and other institutions – despite a dispersal during the Revolution that sent hundreds of works of art out of the country.

191. THE APOTHEOSIS OF GERMANICUS
Unidentified artisans
Ancient Roman cameo (carved sardonyx) in 17th-century mount (enameled gold set with brilliants)
5-1/8" x 5-3/8" (13 x 13.5 cm.), including mount

Loaned by the Cabinet des Antiquités of the Bibliothèque Nationale / INV 265

The Sun King had a strong affinity for cameos and other *objets d'art* from the ancient world, which may have reflected his use of the Apollo, Alexander, and Caesar themes in his personal public relations. He acquired such objects whenever possible and had them mounted for the *cabinet du roy*, or royal collection of *objets de vertu*. His holdings of small antiquities were regarded as the world's largest and finest.

The "Apotheosis of Germanicus" was collected by Louis XIV toward the end of 1684, just before the Revocation of the Edict of Nantes. It was purchased from the Abbey of Saint Èpure for seven thousand pounds. This enormous sum gives an idea of the value placed upon such pieces in the seventeenth century. Many such objects were found in the treasuries of French churches and religious foundations, where they had accumulatd during the middle ages.

Germanicus (15 B.C.-19 A.D.) was the nephew and adopted son of the Emperor Tiberius (ruled 14 A.D.-37 A.D.). Germanicus was a popular and successful military leader but never became emperor, due to his premature death. It is suspected that he was poisoned.

Apotheosis is a word of Greek origin that means "to deify" or "to make a god." Augustus has Julius Caesar deified, which started the tradition of deifying emperors and imperial favorites. As a divine-right monarch, Louis XIV certainly approved this concept from the ancient classical world.
VLG/JM

Catalogue 191

Catalogue 192

193. HENRI IV AND MARIE DE' MEDICI
Unidentified artist
1602 or 1607
Carved shell applied to sardonyx, set in enameled gold
3-1/8" x 2-3/8" (7.8 x 5.9 cm.), including mount

Loaned by the Cabinet des Antiquités of the Bibliothèque Nationale / INV 789

The king's collections contained "modern" as well as "ancient" art. "Modern" meant all postmedieval creations.

Filial piety no doubt played its part in motivating the Sun King to acquire this cameo of his paternal grandparents. He purchased it in 1699, between the War of the League of Augsburg and the War of the Spanish Succession, paying two hundred pounds for the piece. A date on the rim is partially obliterated and reads either 1602 or 1607. At about the same time he collected this piece, Louis XIV also acquired a cameo depicting his father (see #197).
VLG

192. FOOTED BOWL WITH SHAPED RIM
Unidentified craftsman
Hellenistic Greek
Carved sardonyx
2" x 6-1/2" dia. (5 x 16.5 cm.)

Loaned by the Cabinet des Antiquités of the Bibliothèque Nationale / INV 375

This delicate, translucent sardonyx bowl was brought to France from the Levant by the voyager and dealer Paul Lucas (1664-1737). The Sun King purchased it from him in 1708, during the War of the Spanish Succession. Such an acquisition at that time, when France was near bankruptcy, indicated both the bravado of the king in keeping up appearances and his esteem for such antiquities.

Lucas was one of the great adventurers of the seventeenth and eighteenth centuries. A native of Rouen, famed for its ceramic production, he ventured throughout Greece, Asia Minor, Egypt, Syria, and Spain. Several volumes of accounts of his travels appeared in the early eighteenth century.
VLG/JM

Catalogue 193

194. SEPTIMIUS SEVERUS AND HIS FAMILY

Unidentified artisans
Ancient Roman cameo (sardonyx) set in 17th-century mount (enameled gold)
2-7/8" x 4-3/8" (7.2 x 11.2 cm.), including mount

Loaned by the Cabinet des Antiquités of the Bibliothèque Nationale / INV 300

This cameo was an early acquisition of the Sun King, who purchased it from Achille de Harlay in 1674. Two small holes in the cameo indicate early attachments.

Septimius Severus (left front) was born in Leptis Magna (now Libya) in 146 A.D. and died in Eburacum (York, England) in 211 A.D. He became emperor in 193 A.D. and founded his own dynasty. He was governor of Pannonia (parts of Austria and Hungary) when the Emperor Commodus was murdered in 192 A.D. Commodus was succeeded by Publius Helvius Pertinax, who was promptly murdered by the Praetorian Guard. As a military leader, Septimius Severus then assumed power, dissolved the Praetorians and established his own trustworthy guard. His "military monarchy" was critical to the later Roman Empire.

The elder son Carracalla (right front)

Catalogue 194

ruled from 211 A.D. to 217 A.D. His younger brother Geta (right rear) ruled with him briefly from 211 A.D. to 212 A.D.
JM/VLG

195. THE DISPUTE OF ATHENA AND POSEIDON FOR THE FOUNDATION OF ATHENS

Unidentified artisans
Ancient Roman or Hellenistic Greek cameo (carved sardonyx) set in 17th-century mount (enameled gold)
3-3/4" x 3-1/8" (9.5 x 7.8 cm.), including mount

Loaned by the Cabinet des Antiquités of the Bibliothèque Nationale / INV 27

This elaborate cameo entered the royal collections about 1685 and was mistakenly thought to represent Adam and Eve. An engraving in Hebrew on its edge was added during the Renaissance from the beginning of the sixth verse of Genesis II: "And the woman considered that the fruit of the tree was good to eat, that it was agreeable to look upon, that it was appetizing" (as translated in the French). Close study and modern scholarship have revealed the true subject of the cameo.

Both Athena and Poseidon vied for the patronage of Athens at a time when Cecrops, an earthborn snake, ruled. Poseidon caused a salt-water well to gush forth on the Acropolis to show his power; Athena made an olive tree appear. Cecrops chose Athena's tree over Poseidon's well, and in a fit of rage Poseidon caused the city to flood.
JM/VLG

Catalogue 195

196. THE HOLY VIRGIN (and)
JESUS CHRIST
Unidentified craftsmen
16th century
Carved bloody jasper in open-work gold mounts
Both 3" x 2-5/8" (7.7 x 6.8 cm.), including mount

Loaned by the Cabinet des Antiquités of the
Bibliothèque Nationale / INV 416 and 408

The Sun King collected this superb pair of Renaissance cameos in mid-January of 1690, shortly after the outbreak of the War of the League of Augsburg. They were already mounted in Renaissance gold, and Louis XIV chose to preserve the original fittings, with suspension rings, rather than reset them.

The unidentified craftsman has shown imaginative Renaissance creativity in his choice and use of materials. Fine red graining in the bloody jasper has been raised to give the appearance of droplets of blood.
VLG

Catalogue 196

Catalogue 197

197. LOUIS XIII
Unidentified craftsmen
17th century
Carved carnelian set in gold
1-7/8" x 1-1/2" (4.7 x 3.9 cm.), including mount

Loaned by the Cabinet des Antiquités of the
Bibliothèque Nationale / INV 793

The Sun King acquired this cameo representing his father in March of 1699, on the eve of the War of the Spanish Succession. He paid two hundred pounds for the gold-mounted carnelian, which depicts a Cross of the Order of the Holy Spirit (see #56 and #57) on the reverse. At about the same time, a cameo of the king's paternal grandparents (see #193) entered the royal collections.
VLG

198. STANDING CUP

Unidentified artisans
Byzantine, bowl (carved sardonyx) set in 17th-century mounts (enameled gold)
4-7/8" x 5-1/4" x 2-7/8" (12.5 x 13.3 x 7.4 cm.)

Loaned by the Department of European Sculpture and Decorative Arts of the Metropolitan Museum of Art / 17.190.594/Gift of J. Pierpont Morgan, 1917

This spectacular standing cup was made up in baroque fashion in the seventeenth century from three separate elements of carved sardonyx. The base features an elaborate seal-like device on the under surface. The gold rim is missing.

The sensuous beauty of colored hardstone has been highly prized in a great many civilizations, and objects such as this low-footed oval cup of polished sardonyx are often found far from their place of origin. The similarity has been cited between the enameled leaf-ornament that adorns the mounts of this cup and the mounts of a number of other pieces of various origin that are known to have been part of the collections of Cardinal Mazarin, Louis XIV, and the Grand Dauphin, and were in all probability mounted by local French goldsmiths working during the first half of the seventeenth century. The sardonyx stem and foot of this cup were probably made at the same time as the mounts. The gold mount on the foot is engraved "427," the number under which it is described in an inventory of the possessions of the French crown (*Inventaire des Diamans de la Couronne, Perles, Pierres, Tableaux, Pierres Gravées et Autres Monuments des Arts et des Sciences existans au Garde-Meuble)* made by the Assemblée Nationale in 1791.
Cl.V/VLG

Catalogue 198

199. VASE

Unidentified craftsmen
Mid-17th century
Carved jasper mounted in silver-gilt
4-1/2" (11.5 cm.) high

Loaned by the Department of European Painting and Sculpture of the Metropolitan Museum of Art / 17.190.597/Gift of J. Pierpont Morgan, 1917

This beautiful small vase is of unknown provenance but is representative of the many *objets de vertu* in *pierre dure* (hard stone) which were prized by the king and wealthy collectors of the seventeenth century. The Sun King used pieces like this vase and the standing cup (see #198) to decorate his mirrored *cabinet* at Versailles (destroyed, see #118).

Small decorative objects made for royal patrons were nearly always mounted with enameled gold and often they were embellished with gems or pearls. The gadrooned silver-gilt mount on the rim of this vase would seem too modest for an object intended for one of the French royal collections. The vase itself, made of polished jasper, displays in its clarity of form and in certain similarities of technique a close resemblance to hardstone objects known to have belonged to King Louis XIV. Like those, the vase is probably the work of a French lapidary working around the middle of the seventeenth century, and it may once have adorned the *cabinet de curiosités* of a French nobleman or prince of the Church.
Cl.V/VLG

200. JUPITER AND JUNO
Attributed to the studio of François Girardon
(1628-1715)
Mid-17th century
Black patinated bronze
Jupiter: 25-5/8" x 13-3/8" (65 x 34 cm.), crown
inventory No. 191 engraved on the back of the
base
Juno: 23-5/8" x 10-1/4" (60 x 26 cm.), crown
inventory No. 192 engraved on the back on a
drapery fold

Loaned by the Département des Objets d'Art of
the Musée du Louvre / OA 5086 et OA 5087

This pair of pendant bronzes were first
acquired by the landscape architect
Andre Le Nôtre, a personal friend of the
Sun King, and they made up part of the
celebrated gift of art works that Le
Nôtre made to Louis XIV in 1693. They
are listd in the Collections of the
Crown, respectively Numbers 191 and
192, which are found engraved on the
backs, and have never left the French
national collections.

The attribution of these pieces to the
studio of Girardon (see #93) places
them in the milieu of Versailles sculptors
who combined the study of ancient art
and the living model with a taste for
rigorous execution of high quality. Their
presence in the royal collections
evidences the taste of the Sun King for
small bronzes, of which he possessed
several dozen and which he transmitted
to his son, the Grand Dauphin.
AL/VLG

Catalogue 200

Catalogue 199

201. JUPITER

Michel Anguier (1612-86), after Alessandro Algardi (1602-54)
Ca. 1660
Bronze
44-1/8" x 22-1/2" x 20-1/2" (112 x 57 x 52 cm.)

Anonymous Lender

The royal collections at Versailles contained works by or after selected "moderns" as well as ancients. Louis XIV owned, among others, a bust of Pope Urban VIII by the Italian "modern" Allesandro Algardi.

This Jupiter is in marked contrast to the French Jupiter (see #200) presented to the Sun King by André Le Nôtre. The serene stance of the classicizing French bronze is diametrically opposed to the jagged baroque composition and muscular tensions of the Italian example.

Algardi's Jupiter and Juno were executed 1653-54 on the commission of Philip IV of Spain. The same subjects were then made by Algardi in silver for Louis XIV and seem to have perished in the "great melt." Anguier used the original silver Jupiter to cast this bronze.
VLG

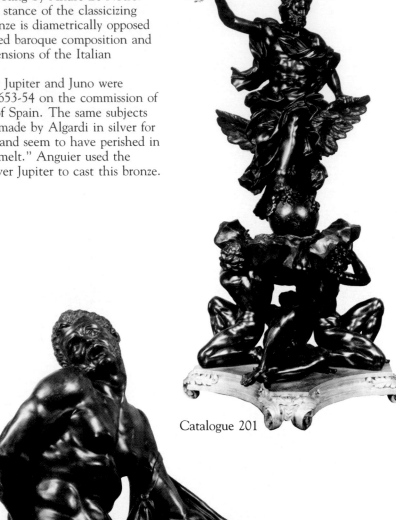

Catalogue 201

202. MILO OF CROTONA

After Pierre Puget (1620-94)
Ca. 1683
Bronze on wooden socle inlaid with brass
Bronze: 28-3/8" x 20-1/2" x 13-3/4" (72 x 52 x 35 cm.)

Anonymous Lender

The large marble of this subject by Pierre Puget was included in the royal collections of the Sun King and was shown at Versailles during his lifetime. It was ordered by Colbert for the gardens and was delivered in 1683 by François Puget (1651-1707), the sculptor's son. Louis XIV said of the artist's work, "There is no one in Europe who can equal Puget." Several additional works were commissioned from him for Versailles. The drama of the Italian baroque clearly influenced Puget's interpretation of Milo.

The subject, Milo, was a late sixth-century B.C. athlete from the Greek colony of Crotona in Calabria. He was a champion wrestler and won six Olympic and six Pythian games. He is said to have carried an ox through the Olympic stadium on his shoulders. At home in southern Italy he led the victorious army of Crotona against the Sybarites about 510 B.C.
VLG/JM

Catalogue 202

Catalogue 203

203. JESUS CARRYING HIS CROSS
Charles Le Brun (1619-90)
1688
Oil on canvas
60-1/4" x 84-1/4" (153 x 214 cm.)

Loaned by the Département des Peintures of the Musée du Louvre / INV 2884

Throughout his long career, Charles Le Brun remained a favorite artist and designer of the Sun King. "Jesus Carrying His Cross" is one of the several religious works ordered for the royal collections during the last years of the artist's life. This preference for religious subjects may reflect the king's growing interest in salvation encouraged by Madame de Maintenon.

The picture displays many of the characteristics of French baroque classicism. Space is organized by arranging compositional elements parallel to the picture plane, and deep space is avoided. Picturesque architectural fragments are composed of classical elements such as the round-headed arch. The composition is closed on either side by a *repoussé* tree. Figures are shown from a wide variety of viewpoints and in an equally wide variety of positions to demonstrate the artist's skills in portraying anatomy and drapery.
VLG

204. SAINT JOHN BAPTIZING

Nicolas Poussin (1594-1665)
17th century
Oil on canvas
37" x 47-1/4" (94 x 120 cm.)

Loaned by the Département des Peintures of the Musée du Louvre / INV 7287

During his early years of collecting, the king evidenced a preference for the works of Nicolas Poussin and acquired numerous examples. Poussin's "classical" compositions were considered the epitome of good taste in contemporary French art. This picture was given to the king in 1693 by the landscape architect André Le Nôtre and constituted part of the celebrated Le Nôtre gift (see #200).

Many scholars have studied this well-known picture and have disputed its date. Most suggest that it belongs to the period from 1635 to 1640.
VLG

Catalogue 204

Catalogue 205

205. THE YOUNG PYRRHUS SAVED

Nicolas Poussin (1594-1665)
1637-38
Oil on canvas
45-3/4" x 63" (116 x 160 cm.)

Loaned by the Département des Peintures of the Musée du Louvre / INV 7292

"The Young Pyrrhus Saved" was a very early acquisition by the Sun King after his assumption of personal rule. He obtained it from the collection of the duc de Richelieu in 1665 as part of a large addition to the royal holdings.

Pyrrhus of classical legend was the son of Athamus and Nephele. Athamus' second wife Ino inveighed upon her husband to sacrifice the children of his first marriage. As the boy was about to die the golden fleece appeared and carried off Pyrrhus and his sister Helle (who later fell off at the straits of the Hellespont). Pyrrhus survived, sacrificed the ram, and spread the fleece on the grave of Ares on the far side of the Black Sea. It was later sought by Jason and the Argonauts.
VLG/JM

206. ORPHEUS BEFORE PLUTO AND PROSERPINA

Francois Perrier (*ca.* 1584-1650), called le Bourguignon
17th century
Oil on canvas
21-3/4" x 27-5/8" (54 x 70 cm.)

Loaned by the Département des Peintures of the Musée du Louvre / INV 7163

Many of Perrier's paintings, such as "Orpheus Before Pluto and Proserpina" from the collection of Louis XIV, depict classical or mythological subjects. His study of Roman sculpture is often evident. In this picture the figure of Orpheus is clearly adapted from the Apollo Belvedere in the Vatican collections.

According to Greek legend, Orpheus, associated with Apollo, descended to Hades to retrieve his lost love Eurydice. By his musical talents he charmed Pluto, god of the underworld, Proserpina, daughter of the harvest goddess Ceres or Demeter, and the three-headed dog Cerberus, guardian of the gates of Hell.

Pluto agreed that Eurydice could return to the living world so long as Orpheus neither looked upon nor spoke to her until the journey was completed. Unable to resist, Orpheus peeked; Eurydice was instantly reconfined to the world of shades. Orpheus was reunited with her only in death after a long life of sorrow, mourning, and further adventures.
VLG/CH

Catalogue 206

THE KING IN RETREAT

Catalogue 207

207. THE CHÂTEAU DE MARLY
Pierre-Denis Martin (*ca.* 1663-1742)
1723
Oil on canvas
54" x 61" (137 x 155 cm.)

Loaned by the Musée National du Château de Versailles / MV 741

Marly was the last great house built by the Sun King. Architecturally it was most unusual. Rather than a single house with service buildings, Jules Hardouin-Mansart (1646-1708) created a central pavilion for the royal family, flanked by twelve smaller pavilions in two rows of six each in Palladianesque fashion, interlinked by plantings. Eleven of the pavilions housed guests, one was reserved for bathing facilities. Louis XIV later installed the enormous celestial and terrestrial globes created for him by Vincenzo Maria Coronelli (1650-1718, see #220) in two of them, sacrificing limited space to the astonishing spheres.

The complex included a fine French garden with reflecting pools and fountains by André Le Nôtre (1613-1700), which the king enjoyed renovating for many years. Unfortunately the château deteriorated so badly from neglect after the Revolution that it was razed in the nineteenth century. Only portions of Le Nôtre's park remain.

Construction began in 1679, and the house was in a state to be occupied in 1686. Not far from Versailles, Marly served — as did the Trianons — for intimate and relaxed occasions. The king spent as much time there as possible, and invitations to Marly were jealously sought by ambitious courtiers, one of whom replied to the king, "Sire, when it rains at Marly you don't get wet." The limited capacity of Marly meant that only the especially favored could be accommodated.

Marly was the retreat most frequently sought by the king after the deaths of close family members. On August 9, 1715, he left Marly for a hunt, proceeding to Versailles for the night. It was the last time he saw his elegant and favored second home.
VLG

208. LOUIS XIV CROWNED BY GLORY BETWEEN ABUNDANCE AND PEACE
Antoine Coypel (1661-1722)
1685
Oil on canvas
78" x 59-1/8" (198 x 150 cm.)

Loaned by the Musée National du Château de Versailles / MV 5273

As early as May, 1715, speculation in London rumored the imminent death of the Sun King. Throughout the summer he lost weight and appetite, becoming thin and withered. He complained of leg pains on August 11, and two weeks later was diagnosed as suffering from gangrene. He was ordered to immerse the infected leg in a wine bath and declined surgical treatment, realizing the end was near.

The Sun King suffered heroically for another week with the royal family and courtiers giving free vent to fashionable high volume grief in his antechamber. He conducted his death, as his life, with astonishing stoicism and self-control.

During his final days, the king received formal visits to make his farewells. He was attended first by a delegation consisting of his sister-in-law "Madame"; his daughters Marie-Anne de Bourbon, princesse de Conti; Louise-Françoise de Bourbon, Mademoiselle de Nantes, called Madame la Duchesse; and Françoise-Marie de Bourbon, Mademoiselle de Blois, duchesse d'Orléans, wife of the future regent.

The Sun King called for his great grandson, five-year-old Louis, duc d'Anjou, soon to be Louis XV, who arrived with his governess Charlotte Eléanore de La Mothe Houdancourt, duchesse de Ventadour. To them he made his famous deathbed address. They were followed by the Gentlemen of the Royal Household and then came the future regent, Louis XIV's nephew Philippe II, duc d'Orléans, to whom the king said, "You are about to see one king in his tomb and another in his cradle. Always cherish the memory of the first and the interests of the second."

The last visitor was Madame de Maintenon. To the duc d'Orléans the king had said, "She has been a great help to me, especially as regards my salvation." To her alone he observed, "I have always heard it was difficult to die, but I find it so easy."

Thereafter the king's rooms were filled with religious music and praying courtiers, with whom he recited the Rosary from time to time. Extreme Unction was administered by Armand-Gaston Maximilien, cardinal de Rohan. The king died quietly on September 1, 1715, at almost the age of seventy-seven, ending nearly three weeks of extraordinary emotional and physical torment and a spectacular reign of seventy-two years.

Coypel's allegorical picture presents a sort of "apotheosis of Louis XIV." Depicted as a Roman emperor, the Sun King is surrounded by the figures of War and Peace and crowned by Victory. The presence of figures representing fame, of animals symbolizing the countries of Europe (lions, eagles), and of captive rivers (the Rhine and Meuse) won for the kingdom by conquest, all show Coypel's great debt to Le Brun and the Hall of Mirrors.
CC/VLG

Catalogue 208

209. LOUIS XIV, KING OF FRANCE AND OF NAVARRE

Hyacinthe-François-Honoré-Mathias-Pierre-André Rigaud (ca. 1659-1743)
1701
Oil on canvas
108-5/8" x 76-3/8" (276 x 194 cm.)

Loaned by the Musée National du Château de Versailles / MV 2041

Several autograph versions of this picture were made; it is doubtless the most famous, but not necessarily the most representative, image of Louis XIV. This one was ordered by the king in 1700 to send to Spain with his grandson, the newly named Philip V, but it never left France. Another version, currently at the Louvre, was ordered by the king for himself because the first had pleased him enormously. The painting presents the king in majesty. There are surprisingly few images such as this one in which his crown and scepter are depicted.

Compositional and coloristic devices and conventions distinguish this picture as a great masterpiece of the late French baroque style. An animated play of scarlet draperies gives a crackle of reflected light in the upper portion of the painting, echoing and amplifying the personality and grandeur of the most powerful monarch. This aspect of ceremonial baroque painting is more frequently seen in Italian art than in French pictures, as is the almost blinding light focused on the subject. The red reappears as an accent color in the king's shoes. The remaining primary colors are also at work. The pale blue of the king's hose and the rich regal blue of his mantle fill the center of the canvas. Yellow completes the triad in both the ochre of the rear hanging and the gold of embroidery and tassels. A white flare of ermine carries the eye diagonally toward the upper left, where it is arrested at the king's face by the intense black of his wig.

Although Louis XIV lived for fourteen years after the painting was made, it stands as the last great image of the Sun King. The painter Hyacinthe Rigaud reached his zenith in this portrait, which by its appearance in countless publications has become as familiar as the Mona Lisa.
VLG/CC

210. PROCLAMATION OF THE PUBLIC CRIER ANNOUNCING THE BURIAL SERVICE OF KING LOUIS XIV

The Crier de Voulges
Paris, 1715
16-7/8" x 21-5/8" (43 x 55 cm.)

Loaned by the Archives Nationales / K-1003, No. 30 (Musée)

The king, suffering from gangrene, gave up walking on August 13, 1715. On the twenty-third or twenty-fifth he added a second codicil to his will of August 2, 1714, naming his son, Louis Auguste de Bourbon, duc du Maine (1670-1736), as the dauphin's governor. On the twenty-fourth he confessed and received the Last Rites. He died on the morning of September 1, at the Château de Versailles, at the age of almost seventy-seven, after a reign of seventy-two years, one of the longest in history.

Louis XIV was buried in the Abbey of St. Denis to the north of Paris, the traditional mortuary church and final resting place of the kings of France. His heart was taken to the Jesuit convent in the Rue Saint-Antoine in Paris and his entrails to the Cathedral of Notre Dame.

The death of Louis XIV was not greatly regretted by either the courtiers or the population. The day after his demise, September 2, 1715 — the Parlement of Paris, so long held in obeisance, broke the king's will and gave Philippe II, duc d'Orléans, sole responsibility for the regency by setting aside the royal bastards (see #133). The only portion of the will actually executed was the article of the second codicil relating to the naming of the dauphin's tutor, who was the future Cardinal de Fleury, first minister for Louis XV from 1726 to 1743.
JG/VLG

211. LETTER TO LOUIS XV

Ahmed III, Sultan of the Ottoman Empire
April, 1716
Ink and gold leaf on paper
26" x 43-1/8" (66 x 109.5 cm.)

Loaned by the Archives of the Ministère des Relations Extérieures / CP Turquie, Vol. 54, fol. 183

Just as the sultan had congratulated Louis XIV upon his ascension to the throne in 1643, so the sultan complimented his successor in the obligatory exchange of diplomatic letters following the Sun King's death.
MC/VLG

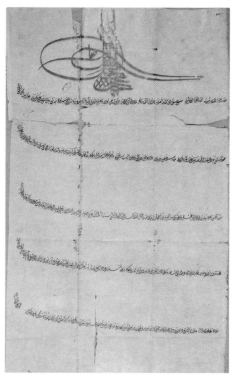

Catalogue 211

Priez DIEU pour l'Ame de Trés Haut, Trés Puiſſant, Trés Excellent Prince, LOUIS le Grand, par la grace de Dieu, Roy de France & de Navarre, Trés Chreſtien, Trés Auguſte, Trés Victorieux, Incomparable en Clemence, Juſtice & Piété.

Priez DIEU pour l'Ame de Trés Haut, Trés Puiſſant, Trés Excellent Prince LOUIS le Grand, &c.

Priez Dieu pour l'Ame de Trés Haut, Trés Puiſſant, Trés Excellent Prince, LOUIS le Grand, &c. Decedé en ſon Chaſteau de Verſailles le premier du mois de Septembre dernier.

Pour l'Ame duquel ſe feront les Prieres & Services ſolemnels le 23. de ce mois. dans l'Abbaye Royale de S. Denis en France, où il ſera inhumé. Et enſuite en cette Ville, le jour dont vous ſerez avertis. Et les veilles ſe diront les Veſpres & Vigiles des Morts.

Priez Dieu pour ſon Ame

Crieur De Voulges.

Catalogue 209

Catalogue 210

212. LAST WORDS OF KING LOUIS XIV (Spoken) TO KING LOUIS XV, HIS GREAT-GRANDSON
Broadside
11-5/8" x 7-1/8" (29.5 x 18.2 cm.)

Reproduced from the collections of the Réserve of the Département des Imprimées of the Bibliothèque Nationale / L37^b-4452

The Sun King's dying words to his five-year-old great-grandson were spoken in the presence of Charlotte Eléanore de La Mothe Houdancourt, duchesse de Ventadour. This deathbed address was recorded and quickly printed by the royal press. The document reads:

"My dear child, you will soon be King of a great kingdom; what I recommend to you most strongly is to never forget the obligations which you have to God. Remember that all that you are you owe to Him.

"Work to keep the peace with your neighbors.

"I loved war too much; do not imitate me in this; no more than in the overly great expenditures which I have made. Take counsel in everything and seek to know the best [way] so as to always follow it.

"Look after your people as much as you can, and do what I have had the misfortune never to be able to do myself.

"Never forget the great debt you owe to Madame de Ventadour. For myself, Madame," he added, turning toward her, "I am much upset to no longer be in a condition to make my gratitude known to you."

He finished by saying to Monsieur the Dauphin: "My dear child, I give you my blessings with all my heart." And then he kissed him twice with great show of feeling.

VLG

DERNIERES PAROLES DU ROY LOUIS XIV. AU ROY LOUIS XV.

SON ARRIERE PETIT-FILS.

 MON cher Enfant , vous allez être bien-tôt Roy d'un grand Royaume ; ce que je vous recommande le plus fortement , eſt de n'oublier jamais les obligations que vous avez à Dieu. Souvenez-vous que vous luy devez tout ce que vous êtes.

TASCHEZ de conſerver la paix avec vos Voiſins.

J'AY trop aimé la guerre ; ne m'imitez pas en cela ; non-plus que dans les trop grandes dépenſes que j'ay faites. Prenez conſeil en toutes choſes , & cherchez à connoître le meilleur pour le ſuivre toujours.

SOULAGEZ vos Peuples le plutôt que vous le pourrez, & faites ce que j'ay eu le malheur de ne pouvoir faire moi-même.

N'OUBLIEZ jamais les grandes obligations que vous avez à Madame de Ventadour. Pour moy , Madame, *ajoûta-t-il , en ſe tournant vers elle*, je ſuis bien fâché de n'être plus en état de vous en marquer ma reconnoiſſance.

Il finit , en diſant à Monſieur le Dauphin : Mon cher Enfant, je vous donne de tout mon cœur ma benediction ; *& il l'embraſſa enſuite deux fois avec de grandes marques d'attendriſſement.*

De l'Imprimerie du Cabinet du Roy , dirigée par J. COLLOMBAT Imprimeur ordinaire de SA MAJESTE'.

Catalogue 212

THE KING AND THE COLONIES: LOUISIANA — DISCOVERY

213. BUST OF LOUIS XIV
Unidentified artist
Ca. 1683
Marble
26-3/4" x 21-1/4" (68 x 54 cm.)

Loaned by the Département des Sculptures of the Musée du Louvre / MR 2680

The Sun King's efforts to discover, explore, colonize, and exploit in the New World were severely hampered by the financial drain of the War of the League of Augsburg (1686-97) and the War of the Spanish Succession (1702-13). In the years preceding the first of these conflicts, the Mississippi Valley was charted by the French and claimed and named for the Sun King. This marble relief was made at about the time news reached the court that René-Robert Cavelier de La Salle had successfully negotiated the great river linking New France with the Gulf of Mexico.

The king, in profile, appears to be about forty-five years of age. His slightly puffy features and fine mustache sugest a dating in the mid-1680s. Garbed in a breastplate covered with *fleurs-de-lys* over which a fringed mantle is knotted, he wears a great animated curled wig. Although numerous examples exist of other portrait medallions of the king, no other version of this work is known.
GB/VLG

Catalogue 213

214. MAP OF THE NEW DISCOVERIES THAT THE REVEREND JESUIT FATHERS MADE IN 1672 AND (That Were) CONTINUED BY REVEREND FATHER JACQUES MARQUETTE OF THE SAME COMPANY, ACCOMPANIED BY SOME FRENCH IN THE YEAR 1673

Unidentified cartographer
1673
Ink and watercolor on paper
17-3/4" x 30-3/8" (45 x 77 cm.)

Loaned by the Département des Cartes et Plans of the Bibliothèque Nationale / Rés. Ge C 5014

This map evokes the descent of the Mississippi made in 1673 by Louis Jolliet (*ca.* 1645-1700) accompanied by the Jesuit Jacques Marquette (1637-75), who since 1666 had undertaken his ministry to the Indians of the Great Lakes. Leaving from Green Bay (on Lake Michigan), they followed the Wisconsin River and then descended the Mississippi as far as the Arkansas territory at 33 degrees latitude, but then they retreated from fear of encountering the Spanish. They returned via the Illinois territory; in 1677 Colbert refused Jolliet permission to establish himself there with twenty men.

The document provides a census of the resources of these "new" lands: copper mines, soft coal, iron mines, and blood stone. The representation of two buffalo (called "Pichikiou" by the Indians) completes this initial economic inventory. While definitely the work of the Jesuits, this map was printed in the *Collection of Voyages* by Melchisedec Thévenot (1620-92) in Paris in 1681, about eight years after this manuscript was executed.
MP/VLG

Catalogue 214

215A. DESCRIPTION OF LOUISIANA NEWLY DISCOVERED TO THE SOUTH WEST OF NEW FRANCE

Father Louis (baptized Antoine) Hennepin (1626-*ca.* 1705)
Amable Auroy and Laurent Rondet [pub.], Paris, 1688
6-3/8" x 3-7/8" (16.1 x 10 cm.)
Reproduced from the Collections of the Réserve of the Bibliothèque Nationale / L¹² K-854-A

While René Robert Cavelier de La Salle was exploring the lower reaches of the Mississippi River, Louis Hennepin, a Belgian priest, was traveling through the upper Mississippi and Illinois River territory. He had been ordered by La Salle to explore this area and to make friends with the local Indian tribes for the purpose of establishing future trading posts. Hennepin left St. Ignace on September 2, 1679. On April 11, 1680, he was captured on the Mississippi River near the mouth of the Des Moines River and was taken by his captors to the village of Issati near Mille Lac. He escaped in July and returned to Québec. Hennepin then made his way to Paris, and there, in 1683, he obtained permission from the crown to publish his book, *Description de la Louisiane Nouvellement Découverte au Sud-Ouest de la Nouvelle France.* Other editions of this work were published over the next fourteen years in Dutch, English, Italian, and Spanish. The edition that appears here was published in 1688 with the permission of the king.

Hennepin hoped to convince the court to continue with the exploration of the new territory and to establish a colony there. He published his book not only in an attempt to further this cause

Catalogue 215A

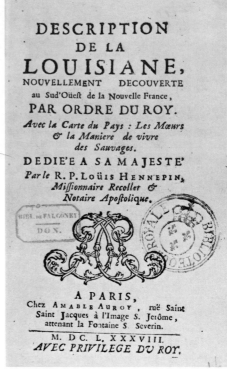

Catalogue 215B

but also to elevate the importance of his own role in the discoveries. Ordered by his superiors to return to America, he refused and was in consequence compelled to leave France. Falling in with Mr. Blauthwait, Secretary of War to King William III of England, prince of Orange, Hennepin passed to the service of the English king as a Spanish subject, by permission of his own sovereign and his clerical superiors.
JDC

215B. NEW DISCOVERY OF A VERY LARGE LAND SITUATED IN AMERICA . . .

Father Louis (baptized Antoine) Hennepin (1626-*ca.* 1705)
Guillaume Broedelet [pub.], Utrecht, 1697
6-1/8" x 3-7/8" (15.4 x 9.9 cm.)

Reproduced from the Collections of the Réserve of the Bibliothèque Nationale / P-Angrand - 998

Hennepin dedicated this and later editions to King William III since he was the pensioner of the king. The work begins with his own personal history and recounts his work as a "Missionaire Recollet & Notaire Apostolique" in Canada. In 1678, he went to Québec and soon after his arrival received orders to join La Salle's expedition. From this point his journal repeats the *Description de la Louisiane,* down to March 12, 1680. The reader is then informed that Hennepin actually went down the Mississippi to the Gulf but had not published the fact in order to avoid La Salle's hostility. There are many confusing "facts" in this part of the volume, such as Hennepin being in two places on the same day; covering the distance to the Gulf of Mexico in thirteen days; and returning upriver, reaching the Arkansas in twenty-four days; and then later stating that on the twelfth of April he was taken by the Sioux one hundred and fifty leagues above the mouth of the Illinois River, having travelled all that distance from the Gulf in eleven days. The confusion of dates and the utter impossibility of performing the trips within the times given are the glaring faults of this work.

The importance of this and the succeeding editions lies in the fact that the work convinced prominent English statesmen and merchants of the necessity of establishing a colony on the Gulf of Mexico in order to maintain and increase trade with the Indians in the Georgia-Alabama area and to prevent the French from cutting off English expansion from the east coast. One of these influential Englishmen was Dr. Daniel Coxe, one of the New Jersey Proprietors and a Patentee of Carolina. Dr. Coxe developed a scheme for establishing an extensive English colony west of the Carolinas. At the same time, King William III and his ministers were listening sympathetically to Hennepin. Building upon the English past tradition of trading with the Indians in the area of present-day Alabama, Dr. Coxe acquired a charter from King William to establish a colony on the Mississippi River.

In October, 1698, Dr. Coxe and several of his fellow Proprietors dispatched an expedition from England to settle the colony on the lower Mississippi. Arriving in Carolina, the expedition decided to winter over in Charleston before proceeding to the Mississippi. In the summer of 1699, a corvette under the command of Captain Lewis Banks traveled to the Mississippi. Upon entering the river and proceeding a short way upstream, Captain Banks encountered Jean-Baptiste Le Moyne, sieur de Bienville, below the area that is now the site of New Orleans.

Bienville boldly paddled his canoe up to the English warship and informed Captain Banks that he was in French territory, that he (Bienville) had a fleet a short distance upriver, that this was not the Mississippi, and that the English must leave immediately. Bluffed by Bienville's bold action, Captain Banks turned his ship around and sailed back down the river. This area in the river has been known ever since as "Detour des Anglais" or "English Turn."
JDC

216. PERMISSION TO THE SIEUR DE LA SALLE TO DISCOVER THE WESTERN PART OF NEW FRANCE
Louis XIV, and clerical assistants
12 May 1678
14-1/8" x 9-7/8" (36 x 25 cm.)

Loaned by the Archives Nationales / Colonies F³5, fol. 41-42

These letters patent were granted to René-Robert Cavelier de La Salle (1643-87), authorizing him to pursue his grand scheme of "working the discovery of the western part of New France, constructing forts . . . the whole at your expense. . . ." La Salle found backers to lend the necessary funds and was able to embark from La Rochelle for Canada on july 17, 1678, with arms, munitions, supplies, and thirty men including Henri, chevalier de Tonty (ca. 1650-1704).

Almost four years later, La Salle arrived at the Gulf of Mexico, having followed the entirety of the course of the Mississippi River. In a brief ceremony on April 9, 1682, he formally claimed possession of the vast land he had traversed for and in the name of Louis XIV.
PH/VLG

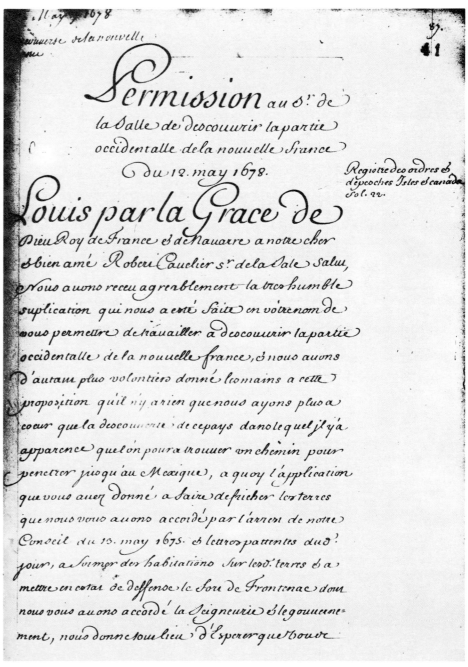

Catalogue 216

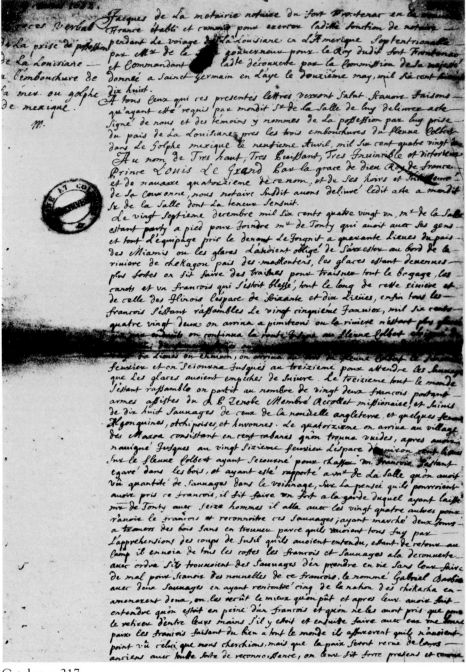

Catalogue 217

217. ACT OF POSSESSION OF LOUISIANA AT THE MOUTH (of the Mississippi River at) THE GULF OF MEXICO

René-Robert Cavelier de La Salle (1643-87)
9 April 1682 (modern facsimile)
13-3/8" x 8-5/8" (34 x 22 cm.)

Loaned by the Archives Nationales [No Acc. No.; original Colonies C13c3, fol. 28-29]

218. MAP OF NORTH AMERICA AND PART OF SOUTH AMERICA FROM THE MOUTH OF THE ST. LAWRENCE RIVER TO THE ISLE OF CAYENNE WITH THE NEW DISCOVERIES OF THE MISSISSIPPI

Abbé Claude Bernou
Ca. 1681
Ink and watercolor on paper
60-1/4" x 65" (153 x 165 cm.)

Loaned by the Département des Cartes et Plans of the Bibliothèque Nationale / S.H. pf. 122, div. 2, p.0

This map was a prestigious document destined to attract the attention of the Minister of the Marine, Jean-Baptiste Colbert, marquis de Seignelay, son of the great Jean-Baptiste Colbert. It was accompanied by a text designed to interest the minister in colonizing the territory discovered by La Salle and the *Relation of the Discoveries and Voyages of the Sieur de La Salle,* covering the period 1679-81. It preceded La Salle's return to France and thus does not show the full course of the Mississippi.

The author of the map and of the texts was the Abbé Claude Bernou, who would have liked to assume religious responsibility for these vast new territories, not counting on the demands and actions of the bishops of Québec. After La Salle's return, Abbé Bernou wanted him to complete the missing portions of the map, including the lower Mississippi. This never happened, and in 1684 La Salle had a rather different map made by the Franco-Québec cartographer Jean-Baptiste Franquelin (1653-after 1712, see #219), who was then in France.

This manuscript document is noted for the great beauty of its cartouche and the fine quality of its rendering. It is among the most handsome of such maps of the New World.
MP/VLG

219. MAP OF LOUISIANA IN NORTH AMERICA FROM NEW FRANCE TO THE GULF OF MEXICO, UPON WHICH ARE DESCRIBED THE LANDS WHICH THE SIEUR DE LA SALLE DISCOVERED IN A LARGE CONTINENT COMPRISED FROM 50° ELEVATION FROM THE POLE TO 25° IN THE YEARS 1679-80-81-82
After Jean-Baptiste Franquelin (1653-after 1712)
1684
Ink on paper
15-3/8" x 20-7/8' (39 x 53 cm.)

Loaned by the Département des Cartes et Plans of the Bibliothèque Nationale / Ge DD 2987 (8782)

This is an ancient manuscript copy of the map drawn in Paris by Jean-Baptiste Franquelin, based on information provided by Cavelier de La Salle. The lower part of the original document had been torn and lacked the configuration of the mouth of the Mississippi. On this version, the inscription of the name of Louisiana is not placed in the same fashion as on the modern copy made for Francis Parkman, on which are also shown the frontiers between Louisiana on the one hand, and New France, Pennsylvania, Virginia, Florida, New Mexico, and New Spain on the other. On the Parkman copy, Louisiana includes the Ohio Valley and thus extends widely on both sides of the Mississippi.

Franquelin, of French origin, went to do business in Canada in 1671. He soon devoted his full time to cartography, drafting maps from 1674 and 1693 that governors and intendants of New France had sent with their dispatches to France. At the end of 1683, Franquelin made a trip to Paris. It was then that he encountered Cavelier de La Salle and drew the original of the map shown here, which measured 140 x 180 cm. (55-1/8" x 70-7/8") and of which only reduced copies survive.

The map composed by Franquelin remained classified confidential, while the diffusion of the printed map drawn by Vincenzo Maria Coronelli (1650-1718, see #220) was broadly distributed. This last, much more schematic, faithfully reproduced the design of the manuscript globe that Coronelli built for Louis XIV between 1681 and 1683. It was Coronelli's map that Claude Delisle (1644-1700) attacked in 1700 in the *Journal des savans*; he contested the position of the mouth of the Mississippi, which La Salle had placed too far to the west.
MP/VLG

Catalogue 219

Catalogue 218

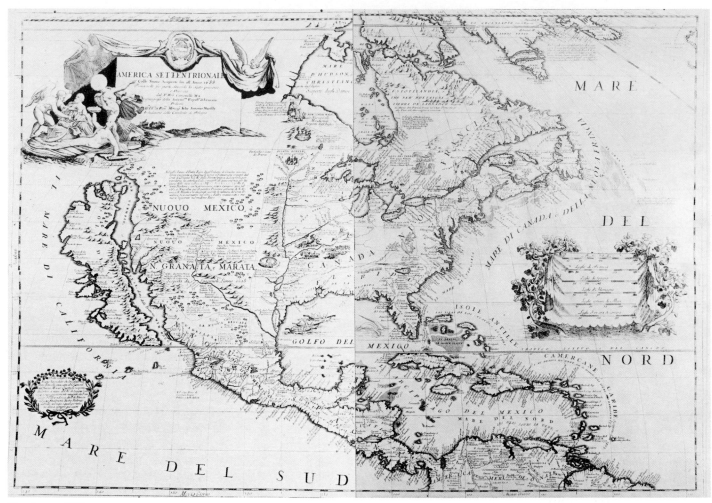

Catalogue 220

220. AMERICA SETTENTRIONALE
(North America)
Vincenzo Maria Coronelli (1650-1718)
1688
26" x 36" (66 x 91.5 cm.)

Collections of the Louisiana State Museum / Gift of the Friends of the Cabildo / 1981.147.2a & b

When La Salle returned to France, he reported that the Mississippi emptied into the Gulf of Mexico near Matagorda Bay (now Texas). It is almost certain that he intentionally falsified the location, placing it nearer the gold and silver of the Spanish colonies in order to interest the Sun King in colonizing the area over which La Salle would become governor. Cartographers working before 1700 had only La Salle's accounts from which to work, not having access to the suppressed Franquelin chart (see #219). The error was corrected only after Pierre Le Moyne, sieur d'Iberville, came to Louisiana in 1699 and subsequently reported the true position of the mouth of the Mississippi.
VLG

221. "FRANCE" PERSONIFIED AS "MINERVA"
Attributed to the workshop of Pierre Puget (1620-94)
Late 17th century
Carved wood
70-7/8" x 76-3/4" (180 x 195 cm.)

Loaned by the Musée de la Marine / INV 37.OA.22

Minerva was the Roman goddess of both wisdom and war, as well as of the arts, sciences, and inventions. In an era that looked to antiquity for inspiration, she was a laudable choice for a ship's namesake. In this fine poop sculpture, Minerva personifies France, enthroned beneath *putti* trumpeting her fame.
VLG

Catalogue 221

THE KING AND THE COLONIES:
THE WAR OF THE LEAGUE OF AUGSBURG —
THE PEACE OF RYSWICK (1697)

222. THE PEACE OF RYSWICK
(Treaty with England)
Various scribes and signatories
20 September 1697
Ink on paper with wax seals and ribbon
14-3/8" x 9-1/2" (36.5 x 24 cm.)

Loaned by the Département des Traités of the
Archives of the Ministère des Relations Extérieures
[No Acc. No.]

The League of Augsburg, composed of Sweden, Holland, several German states, Spain, and the Empire, was formed in 1686 to provide mutual protection against French agression. This conglomerate of Catholic and Protestant states feared the Sun King's religious policies against Protestantism, seen in the Revocation of the Edict of Nantes in 1685 and in his success in naming the bishops of Cologne, Hildesheim, and Munster in 1686. They feared his territorial pretensions as well, since he had claimed part of the Palatinate upon the death of the Elector in 1685 as the inheritance of his sister-in-law Elizabeth-Charlotte de Bavière, the Princess Palatine, duchesse d'Orleans, the second "Madame."

Pressing his German claims, the Sun King invaded in 1688 by marching on the Rhine, and in 1689 his troops sacked and burned major German cities to deprive enemy troops of sustenance. The cruelty of this move united England, the Empire, Spain, the United Provinces, Denmark, and Savoy in the first Grand Alliance. The Sun King was thus pitted against a unified Europe. Louis XIV then escalated his army to 450,000 men and his navy to 100,000 — the best equipped and largest force ever seen.

To pay for weapons and maintain his forces, the king ordered a melt of the royal silver and urged his courtiers to do likewise. As a result, large gold and silver objects from the reign of the Sun King are very rare. Coinage was reminted and depreciated by 10 percent, and heavy taxes were levied. Offices and titles were sold to the highest bidders. Louis Phélypeaux, comte de Pontchartrain, then Minister of Finance, told the king, "Every time your majesty creates an office, God creates a fool to purchase it."

French superiority on land was countered by French losses at sea. Famine and taxation in France brought great suffering. The deaths of François-Michel Le Tellier, marquis de Louvois, and of François-Henri de Montmorency-Bouteville, duc and marechal de Luxembourg, left the Sun King without great military leadership.

Separate peaces were concluded with each of the major powers. By this treaty with England, Louis XIV agreed to recognize William of Orange as William III of England but refused to expel his own exiled cousin, James II of England, from France. The principality of Orange was restored to William. Navigation and trade were to be free and unlimited between the countries, and the two kings returned captured territories to each other.

Through the series of treaties mediated by Sweden, France retained Strasbourg and the Franche-Comté and regained Pondicherry in India and Nova Scotia in North America. In view of the imminent death of Charles II of Spain (d. 1700), the treaties were really a truce prior to a foreseeable squabble over the rich Spanish Empire.

The treaty with England was signed for France by Nicolas-Auguste de Harlay, sieur de Bonneuil, Counselor of State; Louis Verjus, comte de Crécy, former Secretary of Writs to the Queen of Portugal, Secretary to the King, French representative to the Diet of Ratisbonne in 1679, negotiator at Trève in 1684, and member of the French Academy; and François de Callières, former negotiator for France in Poland and Savoy, Secretary of the Hand, and member of the French Academy.

The English plenipotentiaries were Herbert Thomas, eighth earl of Pembroke, Privy Keeper of the Seal; Edward Villiers, first earl of Jersey, baron of Hoo, and viscount of Dartford, former Master of Horse to the Queen, and Lord Justice of Ireland, who later served as ambassador to the Estates General and as Lord Chamberlain of the Household; Lord Robert Sutton of Aram, second baron of Lexinton, Gentleman of the Chamber and extraordinary envoy to the courts of Vienna and Spain; and Joseph Williamson, Counselor and Keeper of the Archives.

In addition, the document was witnessed by the Swedish mediator, Count Nils of Lillieroot. Although Lillieroot is considered one of the seventeenth century's finest diplomats, the king of England feared that he was pro-French. Lillieroot was the former ambassador to France and Swedish delegate to the Estates General.
PE/JM/VLG

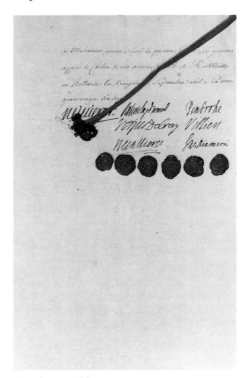

Catalogue 222

223. THE PEACE OF RYSWICK
(Treaty with the Empire)
Various scribes and signatories
30 October 1697
Ink on paper with wax seals and cords
15" x 9-5/8" (38.2 x 24.5 cm.)

Loaned by the Département des Traités of the
Archives of the Ministère des Relations Extérieures
[No Acc. No.]

By this treaty with the Empire, written
in Latin, France agreed to return all
captured imperial territories except
Strasbourg. The Emporer obliged himself
to defend the Catholic religion in these
recovered possessions. Lorraine, which
had been occupied since 1670, was
restored with the exception of Sarrelouis
and Longwy.

The treaty with the Empire was
signed by Nicolas-Auguste de
Harlay-Bonneuil; Louis Verjus, comte de
Crécy; and François de Callières for
France. The imperial plenipotentiaries
were Andreas von Kaunitz, Count
Henrich Johann von Stratmann, and
Baron Johann Frederich von Leilern.
The Swedish representative was Count
Nils of Lillieroot. The document was
witnessed by a large number of minor
German princelings.
PE/JM/VLG

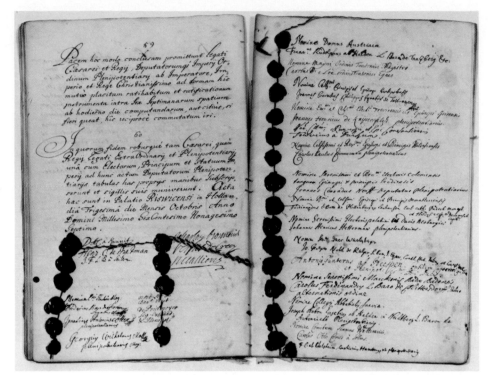

Catalogue 223

Catalogue 224

THE KING AND THE COLONIES: LOUISIANA — EXPLORATION

224. PIERRE LE MOYNE, SIEUR D'IBERVILLE
Unidentified artist
Ca. 1700
Oil on canvas
31-1/2" x 24-3/8" (80 x 62 cm.)

Loaned by the Count Le Moyne de Martigny

The first great expeditions of exploration to Louisiana in the respite between the War of the League of Augsburg and the War of the Spanish Succession were mounted under the direction of Pierre Le Moyne d'Iberville (1661-1706). The king's attention had been drawn to this French colonial Canadian by his excellent military record, particularly in the conquest of Fort Bourbon in the Hudson Bay territory during the War of the League of Augsburg.

Iberville's voyages of 1698 and 1700 relocated the water route to the Mississippi through the Gulf of Mexico and established the first French fortifications in the new colony. The topography of the complex multichanneled mouth of the Mississippi was explored and the alternate route inland by ways of Lakes Pontchartrain, Maurepas, and Borgne and Bayou Manchac was discovered. This new knowledge strengthened the French claim to the Mississippi Valley. Iberville was accompanied by his younger brother Jean-Baptiste Le Moyne de Bienville (1680-1767), who continued the family's exploits in Louisiana.

Pierre Le Moyne d'Iberville was the third son of Charles Le Moyne de Longueuil and Cathérine Thierry-Primot and was born in Montreal, Canada. His first service was with his brothers and took place in and around Hudson Bay, where he participated in the expedition of the chevalier de Troyes. Iberville distinguished himself by taking Carlaer in 1690 and returning to Hudson Bay to fight the English during the War of the League of Augsburg. He retook Fort Pemaquid on the Bay of Fundy and drove the English out of Nova Scotia.

During the early phases of the War of the Spanish Succession, following his Louisiana voyages, Iberville fought for France in the Antilles. He contracted malaria and died on route to Havana in 1706, at the age of forty-five.'
LeM/VLG

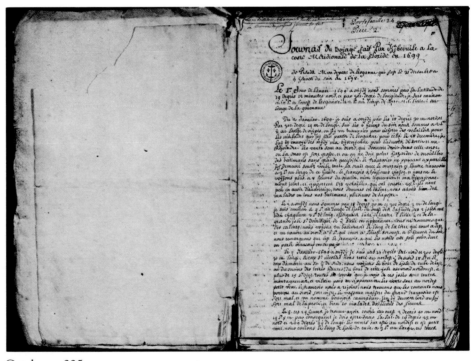

Catalogue 225

225. SHIP'S JOURNAL ON BOARD THE *BADINE*
Pierre Le Moyne d'Iberville (1661-1706)
1699
13" x 8-5/8" (33 x 22 cm.)

Loaned by the Archives Nationales / Marine 44-J-14, No. 2

Iberville's first voyage to Louisiana was as captain of the frigate *Badine* in 1698. His company consisted of 150 men, and the ship was laden with 20,000 francs worth of munitions, matériel and trading merchandise. He left from Brest with a flotilla of four ships and acquired a fifth at Cap François in the Caribbean.

Reaching North America at Santa Rosa, Florida, he proceeded westward to Mobile Bay; continuing west, he founded Fort Maurepas near Biloxi, Mississippi, in February, 1699.

The Mississippi River was reached on March 2, 1699, and the next day Iberville discovered Bayou Mardi Gras, named for the holiday on which it was found. He continued upriver, establishing contact with various Indian tribes and discovering and naming Lakes Pontchartrain (see #234), Maurepas; and Borgne. He returned to France in May 1700.
PH/RL/VLG

226. SHIP'S JOURNAL ON BOARD THE *RENOMMÉE*
Pierre Le Moyne d'Iberville (1661-1706)
1700
13" x 8-5/8" (33 x 22 cm.)
[This object not illustrated]
Loaned by the Archives Nationales / Marine
4-JJ-14, No. 3

Enthused by the discoveries of his first voyage, Iberville mounted his second Louisiana expedition at La Rochelle and departed in mid-October, 1700. By December, his two ships reached Cap François in the Caribbean and he was at Fort Maurepas, near Biloxi, Mississippi, in early January, 1701. He explored the lake route to the Mississippi River and on February 1 founded Fort de la Boulaye near the river's mouth.

Iberville met Henri, chevalier de Tonty (*ca.* 1650-1705), who had accompanied René-Robert Cavelier de La Salle in the 1680s, and together they went looking for the Lake Pontchartrain portage. The party continued upriver, negotiating French allegiance with various Indian tribes, including the Bayou Goula, the Houma and the Natchez. Iberville became ill and spent several days at the Tensas village near Newelton, Louisiana. In May, he returned to La Rochelle by way of New York.
PH/RL/VLG

227. CROSS OF THE ORDER OF SAINT LOUIS
Unidentified goldsmith
Ca. 1703
Gold and enamel
1-5/8" dia. (4 cm. dia.)
[This object not illustrated]
Loaned by an Anonymous Private Collector

Pierre Le Moyne d'Iberville was the first of the Louisiana explorers to be named a knight of the Order of St. Louis (see #59 and #60). His name was approved on the promotion list of 1703. Three other members of his family were accorded this honor during the regency following the death of the Sun King. Jean-Baptiste Le Moyne de Bienville (1680-1768) became a knight in 1717, the year before he founded the City of New Orleans. Joseph Le Moyne de Sérigny (1688-1734) was named in 1718, and Antoine Le Moyne de Chateauguay (1683-1747) was knighted in 1720.

This cross descended in the Le Moyne family of Montreal, Canada. It is thought to be the personal cross of Pierre Le Moyne d'Iberville.
LeM/VLG

228. JEAN-BAPTISTE LE MOYNE, SIEUR DE BIENVILLE
Unidentified artist
18th century
31-1/2" x 24-3/8" (80 x 62 cm.)

Loaned by the Count Le Moyne de Martigny

Jean-Baptiste Le Moyne de Bienville (1680-1768) accompanied his older brother Pierre Le Moyne d'Iberville on his voyages to Louisiana following the War of the League of Augsburg. On the first expedition, Bienville was left on the Mississippi while Iberville led a part of the expedition through Bayou Manchac. Descending the river, Bienville encountered an English flotilla, inspired by Hennepin's account dedicated to the king of England. Bienville adroitly convinced them of French strength upstream, and the English retreated. The site and the event are both known as English Turn. During his early career in Louisiana, Bienville also led an expedition upriver to quell the warlike Natchez tribe, which had massacred some early French colonists. At his

Catalogue 228

direction, the repentant Indians constructed storehouses and a fort for the French garrison, which Bienville named "Rosalie" in honor of Madame la Comtesse de Pontchartrain. This was later the site of the famed Fort Rosalie Massacre in 1729, when the Natchez again rose against the colonists.

After his brother's death, Bienville carried on the work of early colonization following the War of the Spanish Succession. He selected the site and founded the City of New Orleans in 1718, naming it for Philippe II d'Orléans, duc de Chartres (1674-1723), Louis XIV's nephew who became regent of France following the Sun King's death. Bienville remained commandant general of the colony until his recall in 1726 because of alleged professional jealousies. He was reinstated as governor general in 1732 and served in New Orleans for a decade. In 1743, he was named captain in the French navy and retired to Paris, where he died in 1768 at the age of eighty-eight.
LeM/VLG

Catalogue 229

229. CHALICE AND PATEN
Attributed to Claude de Poilly
Abbeville, *ca.* 1675(?)
Silver
Chalice: 11-1/8" x 6-3/8" dia. (28.3 x 16 cm. dia.)
Paten: 6-5/8" dia. (16.8 cm. dia.)

Loaned by an Anonymous Private Collector

These superb liturgical pieces descended in the Le Moyne family of Montreal, Canada, and are thought to have belonged to Pierre Le Moyne d'Iberville and his brother Jean-Baptiste Le Moyne de Bienville. They are representative of the fine belongings of early well-to-do colonial families; Bienville may have employed them in New Orleans. Large French silver of the Sun King's reign is rare due to the "great melt" encouraged by the monarch to defray the costs of the War of the League of Augsburg and the War of the Spanish Succession.

Fortunately, some silver in the colonies escaped the "great melt." Missionaries and explorers used such especially elaborate silver to impress native Americans with the magnificence of their king and his God. For the colonists themselves, these French pieces were a tangible, sentimental reminder of the Church and country they had left behind.

The decoration of these pieces illustrates scenes from the life of Christ. The cup of the chalice depicts the Crown of Thorns, the Flagellation, and Christ falled under the weight of the Cross. The three standing figures, separated by elongated cartouches around the stem or "knot," are Moses, David, and Melchisedec. On the base are the Washing of the Feet, the Mount of Olives, and the Last Supper. The Crucifixion is portrayed on the paten.

The chalice, consisting of a cup, liner, stem and base, can be disassembled. The liner is gold-washed; traces of the gilding remain. The set is comparable in style and construction to the chalice and paten depicting the Life of the Virgin at the Cathedral of Notre Dame de Québec, Canada.
LeM/VLG

230. TRAVELING CRUCIFIX
Unidentified silversmith and cabinet craftsman
Lille, *ca.* 1690
Silver, tortoise shell, and ebony
38" x 17-1/8" (96.5 x 43.5 cm.)

Loaned by an Anonymous Private Collector

This remarkable traveling crucifix was part of the *chapelle* or religious service of Marguerite Le Moyne de Martigny (1664-1746), third Superior General of the Congregation of Notre Dame, founded in Canada in 1659 by Saint Marguerite Bourgeoys. It descended in the family of her cousins, the Louisiana explorers and colonial officers, Pierre Le Moyne d'Iberville and Jean-Baptiste Le Moyne de Bienville. Iberville ordered a smaller one (height 17-3/4" [45 cm.]) from the master silversmith Jean-Baptiste Loir as an offering to the Redemptorist Fathers of Saint Anne de Beaupré in 1706, the year of his death.

The crucifix can be completely disassembled. By its dimensions, quality of execution, and richness of decor, it represents the tradition of large silver ordered from French smiths by powerful French colonial families in the seventeenth century.
LeM/VLG

Catalogue 230

231. LIDDED BOX FROM A TOILETRY SET
Unidentified craftsman
Dieppe, *ca.* 1690
Ivory, gold, and carnelian
4" x 3-1/8" x 5/8" (10 x 7.8 x 1.7 cm.)

Loaned by an Anonymous Private Collector

This highly decorative box descended in the family of Jean-Baptiste Le Moyne de Bienville and is thought to have been part of a *nécessaire de voyage* belonging to him. Made of ivory, the lid is finely embedded with gold-headed studs and red and black stones tracing large floral garlands. The style of work is associated with seventeenth-century craftsmen of Dieppe. The *nécessaire de voyage*, of which only the box remains, is thought to have been in Louisiana with Bienville in the early eighteenth century.
LeM/VLG

Catalogue 231

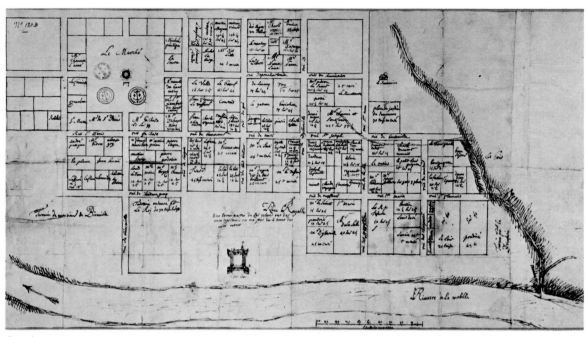

Catalogue 233

232. TOWN AND FORT OF MOBILE IN 1702
Unidentified cartographer
1702
Ink and watercolor on paper
39-3/8" x 23-5/8" (100 x 60 cm.)
[This object is not illustrated]
Loaned by the Archives Nationales / Dépôt fortif.
Colonies Louisiane, No. 119[A]

This rare early drawing is an idealized presentation of Fort Mobile made in the year of its founding, just at the outbreak of the War of the Spanish Succession, which would hinder further colonial development. In 1702, the French abandoned Fort Maurepas for the Mobile River where they established the first true town in the Louisiana colony. The site occupied an important strategic location because it permitted the colonists to hold the strong inland Indian tribes in check. They began with friendly relations, and the Indians regularly provided the French with various supplies such as corn, fowl, venison, and bear grease. Because of sandy soil, the site of the new fort was capable of producing only meager crops.
PH/VLG

233. PLAN OF THE TOWN AND FORT OF MOBILE, ESTABLISHED BY THE FRENCH
Unidentified cartographer
1711
Ink on paper
32-1/4" x 17" (82 x 43 cm.)

Loaned by the Archives Nationales / Dépôt des fortif. Colonies Louisiane, No. 119[B]

The first site of Mobile was not satisfactory because of constant flooding. Fort St. Louis de La Mobile consequently was relocated in 1711, date of this earliest map. The plan used on the new site was comparable to that of the first installation.

This plan was drawn quickly: the unidentified cartographer noted that he did not have the time to draw the houses. It shows only the lots, with the names of their occupants and their measurements, which gives the map the appearance of a survey, with the exception of the fort. However, the perspective drawing of the fort structure seems to have been added later; it is executed on a second piece of paper that is glued to the plan.

The plan consists of an ensemble of rectilinear streets that cross at right angles and define blocks, which are divided into lots. Names on the map include Bienville, Le Sueur, La Salle, and Le Vasseur, Canadians and soldiers at the very beginning of Louisiana colonization.
PH/VLG

234. LOUIS PHÉLYPEAUX, COMTE DE PONTCHARTRAIN
Robert Le Vrac de Tournières (1667-1752)
Late 17th or early 18th century
Oil on canvas
54-1/8" x 42-1/8" (137.5 x 107 cm.)

Loaned by the Musée National du Château de Versailles / MV 8232

Lake Pontchartrain, to the east of New Orleans, was named by Pierre Le Moyne d'Iberville for Louis Phélypeaux, comte de Pontchartrain (1643-1727), in 1699. At that time, Pontchartrain, former Minister of Finance, was serving as Minister of the Marine. It was deemed appropriate and politic to name the large body of water for this powerful court figure who had strongly supported Iberville's expeditions. Pontchartrain's office is indicated by the book, opened to an engraving of Neptune.

The ministry later passed to Pontchartrain's son Jérôme Phélypeaux, comte de Maurepas, for whom Lake Maurepas, the somewhat smaller body of water near Lake Pontchartrain, was named by Iberville on the same voyage. CC/VLG/RL

Catalogue 234

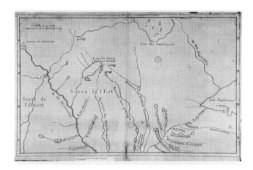

235. MAP OF THE MISSISSIPPI RIVER (Based) ON THE *MÉMOIRES* OF MONSIEUR LE SUEUR
Guillaume Delisle (1675-1726)
Ink on paper (5 sheets)
21-5/8" x 31-7/8", 21-5/8" x 31-7/8", 20-7/8" x 31-7/8", 21-5/8" x 31-7/8" and 22-1/8" x 31-7/8"
(55 x 81, 55 x 81, 53 x 81, 55 x 81 and 56 x 81 cm.)

Loaned by the Département des Cartes et Plans of the Bibliothèque Nationale / S.H., pf. 138 bis, div. 3, p.2[1]

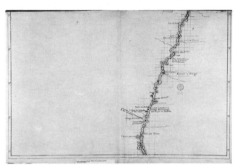

French knowledge of the tortuous course and complicated mouth of the Mississippi rapidly improved during the early eighteenth century. This map was made two years after Claude Delisle (1644-1700), father of Guillaume, published his article on the position of the mouth of the great river in the *Journal des Savans* in 1700. The Delisles, deeply involved in the still poorly developed cartography of the Gulf of Mexico, collected extensive documentation on the region. They gave a map and *mémoires* with precise questions to Pierre Le Moyne d'Iberville, who, after having relocated the mouth of the Mississippi by sea on March 2, 1699, left France on a second expedition in the company of Charles Le Sueur. Le Sueur had previously discovered the lead and copper mines of the Green River in Sioux territory and had been given the mission of exploiting them. On this occasion, Le Sueur went up the Mississippi armed with a marine compass and carefully noted the changes in direction of the course of the river. In addition, he measured the latitudes at regular intervals, particularly at Indian villages and tributary streams. On the basis of Le Sueur's information, Guillaume Delisle was able to draw a complete map of the river in 1702; however, with the exception of the

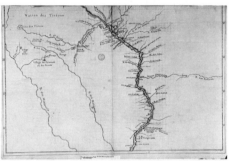

Missouri and Des Moines rivers, only the affluents of the upper valley were cartographically developed. In effect, the French then knew "perfectly all the rivers that empty into the Mississippi to the Illinois River," as Le Sueur said in 1699.

Basing his work on general maps that utilized a system of coordinates calculated with precision by the astronomers of the Academy of Sciences founded by Louis XIV, Guillaume Delisle created maps at much larger scale. For them he utilized ancient and contemporary documentation whose elements he verified with great care and clairvoyance. His work on Louisiana came to fruition in 1718 with the publication of a map of the region. MP/VLG

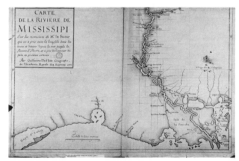

Catalogue 235

THE KING AND THE COLONIES:
THE WAR OF THE SPANISH SUCCESSION —
THE PEACE OF UTRECHT (1713)

**236. ENVIRONS OF THE
MISSISSIPPI (River)**
Attributed to Guillaume Delisle (1675-1726)
Before 1718
Ink and watercolor on paper
43 3/8" x 35-3/8" (110 x 90 cm.)

Loaned by the Archives Nationales / Marine
6-JJ-75, pièce 253

French knowledge of the tortuous course
and complicated mouth of the
Mississippi rapidly improved during the
early eighteenth century. Guillaume
Delisle and his father Claude Delisle
(1644-1700) were deeply involved in the
cartography of the Gulf of Mexico,
which was incompletely known. They
amassed considerable documentation on
the area from accounts of early explorers
and travelers.

   Guillaume Delisle studied with
Giovanni Domenico Cassini at the
Academy and became an associate
member in 1718. He served as
geographer to Louis XV. He began
compiling and publishing maps in 1700
and left blanks representing unknown
areas rather than fabricate hypothetical
features. The accuracy of his work,
especially the world map of 1700, which
eliminated the Error of Ptolemy and
which was plagiarized by Jean-Baptiste
Nolin (1657-1725, see #72), has earned
Delisle the reputation of "father" of
modern cartography.
PH/JM/VLG

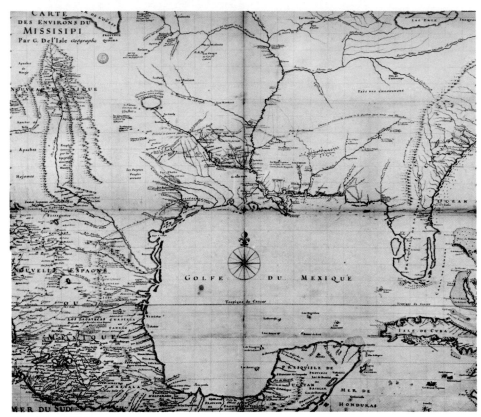

Catalogue 236

**237. PHILIPPE DE FRANCE, DUC
D'ANJOU**
Pierre Mignard (1612-95)
Late 17th century
Oil on canvas
39" x 29-1/2" (99 x 75 cm.)

Loaned by the Musée National du Château de
Versailles / MV 3629

In 1700, at the age of seventeen,
Philippe de France, duc d'Anjou
(1683-1746), grandson of Louis XIV,
became king of Spain and head of the
vast Spanish Empire by provision of the
last will of Charles II of Spain
(1661-1700), his distant relative.
European powers had secretly been
discussing the disposition of the Spanish
inheritance for years. It was evident that
it would go to either the Bourbons
(France) or the Hapsburgs (the Empire),
thereby badly upsetting the balance of
power and commerce, and various secret
treaties and negotiations were enjoined
before Charles II's death. By his first
important will (1698), the Spanish
monarch left his inheritance to
Joseph-Ferdinand, Electoral Prince of

Bavaria (d. 1699), grandson of the Emperor Leopold I (1640-1705). This child died shortly afterward, and on the advice of Pope Innocent XII, Charles II rewrote his will in favor of the young duc d'Anjou.

When the will was promulgated, it was accepted by Louis XIV despite his previous secret agreements to partition the Spanish holdings upon the death of Charles II. The new king was welcomed in Spain and quickly recognized by England, Denmark, Portugal, the United Provinces, Savoy, Bavaria, and several Italian and German states. However, Emperor Leopold I began to stir against the validity of the will, charging that Charles II had not been mentally sound when it was written and claiming the Spanish inheritance for the Hapsburgs.

Then events in France polarized Europe against the Sun King. In February, 1701, the Parlement of Paris registered a royal edict reserving the inheritance rights of the new Philip V to the French crown. This assured continuation of France under legitimate Bourbon rule by allowing Philip to return home if called to the French throne. It was not meant to unite France and Spain under a single crown, but it badly frightened the other countries.

Both England and the Empire began anti-French military activities in 1701. In September, the Treaty of The Hague, which constituted a Second Grand Alliance against France, was signed by England, the United Provinces, and the Empire. It supported the Emperor's claim to the Spanish inheritance and gave France the ultimatum of acceding within two months or facing a declared war.

The Sun King alleged himself bound to defend the will of Charles II. Then James II Stuart (1633-1701), pretender to the English throne exiled in France, died, and Louis XIV recognized his son as James III. This violated the Peace of Ryswick, by which Louis had recognized William III as king of England. Belatedly, the Second Grand Alliance officially declared war in May, 1702, and was soon joined by Denmark, Prussia, Hanover, Münster, Mainz, the Palatinate, Savoy, and Portugal.

Catalogue 237

A long and bloody conflict ensued, which drained France of men and money. Two decisive battles in 1704 virtually settled the outcome. In early August, an Anglo-Dutch fleet captured Gibraltar, and in mid-month the French military reputation was shattered by the English victory led by John Churchill, first duke of Marlborough, at Höchstädt (remembered by England as the Battle of Blenheim). The war dragged on for nine more bloody years. By 1706, France itself was endangered on all fronts, except on the boundary with Spain. With all Europe against him, the Sun King rallied his country and doggedly fought on.

His country decimated by famine, demoralized by defeat and nearing bankruptcy, the Sun King made two efforts in May, 1709, and March, 1710, to sue for peace. Both were rejected. In January, 1711, England sent a secret emissary to Paris and, as a result of further negotiations, got the United Provinces to call a congress of the warring countries at Utrecht, where a peace was signed in 1713, establishing a balance of power in Europe and the New World that would last until the Seven Years' War (1756-63).
VLG

329

238. MAPS AND GENERAL AND SPECIFIC DESCRIPTIONS REGARDING KNOWLEDGE OF EVENTS OF THE TIMES ON THE SUBJECT OF THE SUCCESSION OF THE CROWN OF SPAIN IN EUROPE, IN ASIA, AFRICA AND AMERICA, ADDRESSED AND DEDICATED TO HIS CATHOLIC MAJESTY PHILIP V
Nicolas De Fer (1646-1720)
1701
12" x 19-1/2" open (30.5 x 49.5 cm.)

Collection of the Louisiana State Museum / 2458

This atlas was published to aid Louis XIV's grandson, Philip V, in establishing his claim to the Spanish Empire. Maps were frequently used in this fashion by European monarchs in the seventeenth and eighteenth centuries to justify or substantiate territorial claims.
JDC

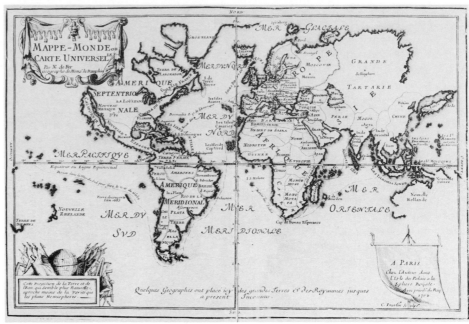

Catalogue 238

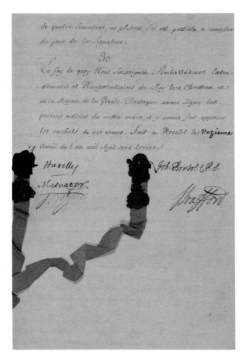

Catalogue 239

239. THE PEACE OF UTRECHT
(Treaty with England)
Various scribes and signatories
11 April 1713
Ink on paper with wax seals and ribbon
14-5/8" x 9-5/8" (37 x 24.5 cm.)

Loaned by the Département des Traités of the Archives of the Ministère des Relations Extérieures
[No Acc. No.]

England gained the most visible territorial and commercial advantages. France was forced to give up the Antilles, Hudson Bay, and Acadia as well as St. Christopher, thus radically altering the basis of New World power. In addition, France agreed to discontinue support of the Stuart pretender to the English throne. Philip V was allowed to retain the Spanish throne and much of the Spanish Empire.

The first French signatory of this document was Nicolas du Blé (or du Bled), marquis d'Huxelles, who had become a lieutenant general in 1688. He covered himself with glory at the defense of Mayence in 1689 during the War of the League of Augsburg and became Maréchal de France in 1703. In 1710 he was charged with negotiating with the Dutch at the conference of Geertruidenburg in concert with Melchior, Abbé de Polignac. He became president of the Council on Foreign Affairs during the regency following the death of Louis XIV, serving from 1715 to 1718.

The second French signer, Nicolas Le Baillif, comte de Saint Jean, called Le Mesnager, was the son of a shipowner from Rouen. In 1692 he purchased an office as secretary to the king. He was sent to Spain in 1704, 1706, and 1708-1709, then to England in 1710-11 to negotiate trade matters.

The English plenipotentiaries were John, bishop of Bristol, Privy Keeper of the Seal, and Thomas, count of Stafford, ambassador to the Estates General of the United Provinces and First Lord of the Admiralty. Stafford inadvertantly signed on the French side of the document. His name was scraped off and Le Mesnager signed over it.
PE/VLG

240. THE PEACE OF UTRECHT
(Treaty with Prussia)
Various scribes and signatories
11 April 1713
Ink on paper with wax seals and ribbon
14-5/8" x 9-5/8" (37 x 24.5 cm.)

Loaned by the Département des Traités of the
Archives of the Ministère des Relations Extérieures
[No Acc. No.]

The treaties of Utrecht brought a halt to
the War of the Spanish Succession,
provoked by the ascension of Louis
XIV's grandson to the Spanish throne.
Following two secret preliminary treaties
in London of October, 1711, England
constrained the United Provinces to call
a congress at Utrecht, which ultimately
concluded the six individual peaces
signed between the major powers and
France. The final treaty with the Empire
and the German princes was signed at
Restatt and Baden in early 1714.

By this document, France recognized
Frederick-William I, Elector of
Brandenburg, as King of Prussia and
ceded to him, in the name of Philip V
of Spain, Spanish Gueldre (Guelderland
in the Low Countries). France also
ceded the principality of Neuchâtel and
Valengin to the House of Orange. The
French plenipotentiaries were Nicolas du
Blé (or du Bled), marquis d'Huxelles,
and Nicolas Le Ballif, comte de Saint
Jean, called Le Mèsnager. The treaty
was signed for Prussia by Otto Magnus
of Dönhoff, Secretary of State and of
War, and Johann Augustus, Marshal of
Bieberstein.
PE/VLG

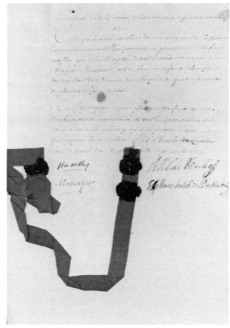

Catalogue 240

**241. LAYETTE OR TREATY BOX
FOR ENGLAND**
Unidentified craftsmen
Late 17th or early 18th century
Tooled leather over wood with steel hinges, handle
and lock
23-1/8" x 15-1/8" x 8-1/8" (53.5 x 38.5 x 20.5
cm.)

Loaned by the Département des Traités of the
Archives of the Ministère des Relations Extérieures
[No Acc. No.]

A series of "layettes" were made in the
form of large false books to hold original
treaty documents concluded by France
with major countries. This treaty box for
England certainly formerly held the
Peace of Utrecht with England (#239)
and possibly the Peace of Ryswick with
England (#222), which are alternately
shown during the exhibition. The red
leather of each box was tooled with the
arms of France and the name of a
different country. Today they are
preserved at the archives of the
Secretary of State for Foreign Affairs in
Paris. In the time of Louis XIV, they
would have been used to move essential
state papers which often traveled with
the king from one residence to another.
PE/VLG

Catalogue 241

Catalogue 242

242. ANTOINE CROZAT, MARQUIS DE CHATEL

Attributed to Alexis-Simon Belle (1655-1738)
Early 18th century
Oil on canvas
54-3/8" x 41-3/4" (138 x 106 cm.)

Loaned by the Musée National du Château de Versailles / MV 6150

Proprietary rights to the exploitation of Louisiana for fifteen years were granted to Antoine Crozat, marquis de Chatel (1674-1734), in 1712 (see #243). The king died three years later, leaving the vast land named in his honor in Crozat's hands.

Crozat retained proprietorship of Louisiana for five years. He voluntarily gave up his charter in 1717, discouraged because he saw no profit on his investment. He and his business associates had expended some 425,000 pounds and received a return of only 300,000, so he cut his losses.

Crozat is shown in the costume of an officer of the Order of the Holy Spirit, of which he was made treasurer in 1715, permitting him to wear the collar or ceremonial necklace of the order. Crozat, who was called "the richest man in France," was a financier and made the investment of part of his fortune in the Company of the Indies in 1710, thus obtaining a quasi-monopoly for his ships in French maritime commerce.
CC/VLG

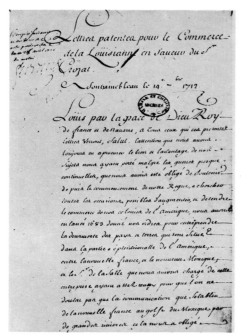

Catalogue 243

243. LETTERS PATENT FOR THE COMMERCE OF LOUISIANA IN FAVOR OF SIEUR CROZAT
Louis XIV and clerical assistants
14 September 1712 (registered)
14-1/2" x 9-7/8" (37 x 25 cm.)

Loaned by the Archives Nationales / Col. B 42 bis., fol. 1

As the War of the Spanish Succession neared an end, the Sun King's attention again focused on Louisiana, but the French treasury had no funds to continue settlement or exploitation of the colony because of huge war debts. Antoine Crozat, marquis du Chatel, and his associates had between 700,000 and 800,000 pounds available. By these letters patent, Louis XIV granted Crozat the immense region from Carolina to Mexico and from the Gulf of Mexico to the Missouri and Wabash Rivers, excluding the Illinois territory, as a proprietary colony. Crozat was given a fifteen-year monopoly on all trade, which was exempted from customs duties, as well as perpetual ownership of any lands, bodies of water, or industries that were improved or created during the fifteen-year period of proprietorship.
PH/VLG

244. LETTER TO NICOLAS DESMARETS
John Law (1671-1729)
24 December 1713
8-5/8" x 6-5/8" (22 x 17 cm.)

Loaned by the Archives Nationales / G⁷ 590, dossier 3, No. 182

John Law of Lauriston, a Scottish adventurer obliged to flee to the Continent following a murder, propounded the theory that the best money was that which circulated most easily, and for that reason paper money must replace gold and silver. Perhaps as early as 1701 or 1702, and surely by 1707, he had established contacts in France. Nicolas Desmarets (1648-1721), son of the sister of Jean-Baptiste Colbert, had become Controller General of Finance in 1708, at a time when the treasury was in dire straits, due largely to the expenses of the War of the Spanish Succession. A very capable man, he

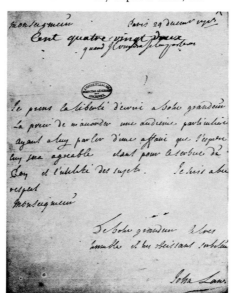

Catalogue 244

managed to avoid national bankruptcy which the powers coalesced against France were expecting.

In this letter, written in French, Law asks to speak with Desmarets "of a business . . . for the service of the King and the utility of his subjects." Desmarets has added in the margin above the date, "When he comes, I will speak with him." It is believed that this document served to introduce Law to the French court, less than two years before the death of the Sun King.

In July of 1715, Law sent Desmarets a project for letters patent creating a state bank. There had not been one prior to this time in France, which was behind the times in matters of credit and commercial financial methods. The State Council put off the proposition until August, just weeks before the death of Louis XIV, which was soon followed by the departure of Desmarets from office. However, Philippe II d'Orléans, duc de Chartres, had recommended Law to Desmarets, and when d'Orléans became regent, he accepted the project in modified form. It resulted in the creation of a deposit bank and financial clearing house, at first private and then royal, which became the keystone for Law's famous system (1716-20), an economic experiment that ended in failure and Law's flight. The crisis was brought on by the reckless sale of speculative stock in the Company of the West founded by Law for the exploitation of the Louisiana colony. The resultant scandal was called the "Mississippi Bubble."
JG/VLG

CATALOGUE CONTRIBUTORS

The catalogue notes are signed with the initials of contributors. In those instances when multiple signatures are given, the first initials indicate the major author, while subsequent initials indicate the contribution of supplemental information and/or editing and translating. Following is an alphabetical listing, by last name, of the scholars whom the organizers of the exhibition gratefully thank and acknowledge:

Jean Boutier (JB)
   Curator, Bibliothèque Nationale, Paris
Geneviève Bresc (GB)
   Curator, Département dès Sculptures,
   Musée du Louvre, Paris
Jean-Marie Bruson (J-MB)
   Curator, Musée Carnavalet, Paris
Joseph D. Castle (JDC)
   Curator of Maps, Louisiana Historical
   Center, Louisiana State Museum, New
   Orleans
Claire Constans (CC)
   Curator, Musée National du Château de
   Versailles
Monique Constant (MC)
   Curator, Archives, Ministère des Relations
   Extérieures, Paris
Jean Coural (JC)
   General Administrator, Mobilier National,
   Paris
Mlle. Isabelle Denis (ID)
   Technical Advisor, Mobilier National,
   Paris
Pascal Evan (PE)
   Curator, Archives, Ministère des Relations
   Extérieures, Paris
Franck Folliot (FF)
   Curator, Musée Carnavalet, Paris
Elizabeth Fontan (EF)
   Curator, Musée National de Céramique,
   Sèvres
Madame D. Gallet (DG)
   Curator, Archives Nationales, Paris
Vaughn L. Glasgow (VLG)
   Associate Director for Special Programs,
   Louisiana State Museum, and American
   Commissioner for the Exhibition, New
   Orleans
Jean Guérout (JG)
   Curator, Archives Nationales, Paris
Phillipe Henrat (PH)
   Curator, Archives Nationales, Paris
Carol Hester (CH)
   Volunteer Research Assistant, Louisiana
   State Museum, New Orleans
Debbie de la Houssaye (delaH)
   Sun King Project Assistant, Louisiana
   State Museum, New Orleans

Roselyne Hurel (RH)
   Curator, Musée Carnavalet, Paris
Rose Lambert (RL)
   Librarian, Louisiana Historical Center,
   Louisiana State Museum, New Orleans
Clare LeCorbeiller (LeC)
   Associate Curator, Department of
   European Sculpture and Decorative Arts,
   Metropolitan Museum of Art, New York
Amaury LeFebure (AL)
   Curator, Département des Objets d'Arts,
   Musée du Louvre, Paris
Michel Maucuer (MM)
   Curator, Musée Carnavalet, Paris
Count LeMoyne de Martigny (LeM)
   Collector and Independent Historian,
   Rubelles
Jessie McNab (McN)
   Associate Curator, Department of
   European Sculpture and Decorative Arts,
   Metropolitan Museum of Art, New York
Judy Miller (JM)
   Volunteer Research Assistant, Louisiana
   State Museum, New Orleans
Madame duPasquier (duP)
   Assistant Director, Musée National de la
   Légion d'Honneur, Paris
Monique Pelletier (MP)
   Director, Département des Cartes et Plans,
   Bibliothèque Nationale, Paris
Catherine Prade (CP)
   Curator, Musée Bricard (Paris)
Chantal de Quiqueran Beaujeu (deQB)
   Associate Director, Musée de la Chasse et
   de la Nature, Paris
Steven G. Reinhardt (SR)
   Curator of French Manuscripts, Louisiana
   Historical Center, Louisiana State Museum
   and Editor of the Catalogue *The Sun King:*
   Louis XIV and the New World, New
   Orleans
J.-M. Roidot (J-MR)
   Curator, Bibliothèque Municipale,
   Versailles
Mlle. Trouillet (T)
   Deputy Curator of Antiquities and Art
   Objects, Division du Patrimoine Mobilier,
   Ministère de la Culture, Aix-en-Provence
Catherine Vaudour (CV)
   Curator in charge of Ceramics and Metals,
   Musées de Rouen, Rouen
Clare Vincent (ClV)
   Associate Curator, Department of
   European Sculpture and Decorative Arts,
   Metropolitan Museum of Art, New York
Hélène Verlet (HV)
   Director, Bibliothèque Historique de la
   Ville de Paris, Paris

ILLUSTRATION CREDITS

Catalogue 1   B&W: Photographic Service of the Musée de la Marine; Color: Photographic Service of the Musée de la Marine; Additional Credit: Courtesy Musée de la Marine

Catalogue 2   B&W: Photo Ellebé; Color: None; Additional Credit: Courtesy Musée de la Céramique de la Ville de Rouen

Catalogue 3   B&W: Photographic Service of the Réunion des Musées Nationaux; Color: None; Additional Credit: Courtesy Musée du Louvre and the Réunion des Musées Nationaux

Catalogue 4   B&W: Maurice Chuzeville; Color: None; Additional Credit: Courtesy Musée du Louvre and the Réunion des Musées Nationaux

Catalogue 5   B&W: Photographic Service of the Réunion des Musées Nationaux; Color: Philippe Sebert; Additional Credit: Courtesy of the Mobilier National

Catalogue 6   B&W: Photographic Service of the Réunion des Musées Nationaux; Color: None; Additional Credit: Courtesy Musée du Louvre and the Réunion des Musées Nationaux

Catalogue 7   B&W: Photographic Service of the Réunion des Musées Nationaux; Color: None; Additional Credit: Courtesy Musée National du Château de Versailles and the Réunion des Musées Nationaux

Catalogue 8   B&W: Photographic Service of the Réunion des Musées Nationaux; Color: Photographic Service of the Réunion des Musées Nationaux; Additional Credit: Courtesy Musée du Louvre and the Réunion des Musées Nationaux

Catalogue 9   B&W: Photographic Service of the Réunion des Musées Nationaux; Color: None; Additional Credit: Courtesy Musée du Louvre and the Réunion des Musées Nationaux

Catalogue 10   B&W: Photographic Service of the Bibliothèque Nationale; Color: None; Additional Credit: Courtesy Bibliothèque Nationale

Catalogue 11   B&W: Photographic Service of the Réunion des Musées Nationaux; Color: Photographic Service of the Réunion des Musées Nationaux; Additional Credit: Courtesy Musée du Louvre and the Réunion des Musées Nationaux

Catalogue 12   B&W: Photographic Service of the Réunion des Musées Nationaux; Color: Photographic Service of the Réunion des Musées Nationaux;

Additional Credit: Courtesy Musée National du Château de Versailles and the Réunion des Musées Nationaux

Catalogue 13   B&W: Photographic Service of the Réunion des Musées Nationaux; Color: None; Additional Credit: Courtesy Musée National du Château de Versailles and the Réunion des Musées Nationaux

Catalogue 14   B&W: Photographic Service of the Réunion des Musées Nationaux; Color: Photographic Service of the Réunion des Musées Nationaux; Additional Credit: Courtesy Musée du Louvre and the Réunion des Musées Nationaux

Catalogue 15   B&W: Studio M. Tscherniak; Color: None; Additional Credit: Courtesy Ministère des Relations Extérieures

Catalogue 16   B&W: Photographic Service of the Réunion des Musées Nationaux; Color: Philippe Sebert; Additional Credit: Courtesy of the Mobilier National

Catalogue 17   B&W: Photographic Service of the Réunion des Musées Nationaux; Color: None; Additional Credit: Courtesy Musée National du Château de Versailles and the Réunion des Musées Nationaux

Catalogue 18   B&W: Photographic Service of the Réunion des Musées Nationaux; Color: None; Additional Credit: Courtesy Musée du Louvre and the Réunion des Musées Nationaux

Catalogue 19   B&W: Photographic Service of the Réunion des Musées Nationaux; Color: Photographic Service of the Réunion des Musées Nationaux; Additional Credit: Courtesy Musée National du Château de Versailles and the Réunion des Musées Nationaux

Catalogue 20   B&W: B&W: Photographic Service of the Réunion des Musées Nationaux; Color: None; Additional Credit: Courtesy Musée National du Château de Versailles and the Réunion des Musées Nationaux

Catalogue 21   B&W: Photographic Service of the Musée Carnavalet; Color: Photographic Service of the Musée Carnavalet; Additional Credit: Courtesy Musée Carnavalet

Catalogue 22   B&W: Photographic Service of the Réunion des Musées Nationaux; Color: None; Additional Credit: Courtesy Musée National de Céramique and the Réunion des Musées Nationaux

Catalogue 23   B&W: Michel Toumazet

Photographic Service of the Musée Carnavalet; Color: None; Additional Credit: Courtesy Musée Carnavalet

Catalogue 24   B&W: Henri Nicollas; Color: None; Additional Credit: Courtesy Ministère de la Culture, Direction du Patrimoine Mobilier and the Musée du Vieil-Aix

Catalogue 25   B&W: Studio M. Tscherniak; Color: None; Additional Credit: Courtesy Ministère des Relations Extérieures

Catalogue 26   B&W: Photographic Service of the Réunion des Musées Nationaux; Color: None; Additional Credit: Courtesy Musée National du Château de Versailles and the Réunion des Musées Nationaux

Catalogue 27   B&W: Dominique Bernard; Color: Dominique Bernard; Additional Credit: Courtesy Musée des Arts Décoratifs

Catalogue 28   B&W: Photographic Service of the Réunion des Musées Nationaux; Color: Photographic Service of the Réunion des Musées Nationaux; Additional Credit: Courtesy Musée National du Château de Versailles and the Réunion des Musées Nationaux

Catalogue 29   B&W: Photographic Service of the Réunion des Musées Nationaux; Color: Philippe Sebert; Additional Credit: Courtesy of the Moiblier National

Catalogue 30   B&W: Photographic Service of the Réunion des Musées Nationaux; Color: Photographic Service of the Réunion des Musées Nationaux; Additional Credit: Courtesy Musée National du Château de Versailles and the Réunion des Musées Nationaux

Catalogue 31   B&W: Studio M. Tscherniak; Color: None; Additional Credit: Courtesy Ministère des Relations Extérieures

Catalogue 32   B&W: Studio M. Tscherniak; Color: None; Additional Credit: Courtesy Ministère des Relations Extérieures

Catalogue 33   B&W: Photographic Service of the Bibliothèque Nationale; Color: None; Additional Credit: Courtesy Bibliothèque Nationale

Catalogue 34   B&W: Photographic Service of the Bibliothèque Nationale; Color: None; Additional Credit: Courtesy Bibliothèque Nationale

Catalogue 35   B&W: Photographic Service of the Bibliothèque Nationale; Color: None; Additional Credit: Courtesy

Service of the Réunion des Musées Nationaux; **Color:** None; **Additional Credit:** Courtesy Musée National du Château de Versailles and the Réunion des Musées Nationaux

Catalogue 127   B&W: Photographic Service of the Réunion des Musées Nationaux; **Color:** Photographic Service of the Réunion des Musées Nationaux; **Additional Credit:** Courtesy Musée National du Château de Versailles and the Réunion des Musées Nationaux

Catalogue 128   B&W: Photographic Service of the Réunion des Musées Nationaux; **Color:** None; **Additional Credit:** Courtesy Musée National du Château de Versailles and the Réunion des Musées Nationaux

Catalogue 129   B&W: Photographic Service of the Réunion des Musées Nationaux; **Color:** Photographic Service of the Réunion des Musées Nationaux; **Additional Credit:** Courtesy Musée National du Château de Versailles and the Réunion des Musées Nationaux

Catalogue 130   B&W: Photographic Service of the Réunion des Musées Nationaux; **Color:** Photographic Service of the Réunion des Musées Nationaux; **Additional Credit:** Courtesy Musée National du Château de Versailles and the Réunion des Musées Nationaux

Catalogue 131   B&W: Photographic Service of the Réunion des Musées Nationaux; **Color:** None; **Additional Credit:** Courtesy Musée National du Château de Versailles and the Réunion des Musées Nationaux

Catalogue 132   B&W: Photographic Service of Archives Nationales; **Color:** None; **Additional Credit:** Courtesy Archives Nationales

Catalogue 133   B&W: Photographic Service of Archives Nationales; **Color:** None; **Additional Credit:** Courtesy Archives Nationales

Catalogue 134   B&W: Photographic Service of the Réunion des Musées Nationaux; **Color:** Photographic Service of the Réunion des Musées Nationaux; **Additional Credit:** Courtesy Musée National du Château de Versailles and the Réunion des Musées Nationaux

Catalogue 135   B&W: Bernard Dupont, Graphic Photo; **Color:** Bernard Dupont, Graphic Photo; **Additional Credit:** Courtesy Count and Countess Patrice de Vogüé, Château de Vaux-le-Vicomte

Catalogue 136   B&W: Charles Delepelaire, Photographic Service of the Musée Carnavalet; **Color:** Photographic Service of the Musée Carnavalet; **Additional Credit:** Courtesy Musée Carnavalet

Catalogue 137   B&W: Lauros-Giraudon; **Color:** Lauros-Giraudon; **Additional Credit:** Courtesy Musée Carnavalet

Catalogue 138   B&W: Photographic Service of the Réunion des Musées Nationaux; **Color:** None; **Additional Credit:** Courtesy Musée National du Château de Versailles and the Réunion des Musées Nationaux

Catalogue 139   B&W: Photographic Service of the Réunion des Musées Nationaux; **Color:** None; **Additional Credit:** Courtesy Musée du Louvre and the Réunion des Musées Nationaux

Catalogue 140   B&W: Lauros-Giraudon; **Color:** Lauros-Giraudon; **Additional Credit:** Courtesy Musée Carnavalet

Catalogue 141   B&W: Bernard Dupont, Graphic Photo; **Color:** None

Catalogue 142   B&W: Photographic Service of Archives Nationales; **Color:** None; **Additional Credit:** Courtesy Archives Nationales

Catalogue 143   B&W: Photographic Service of Archives Nationales; **Color:** None; **Additional Credit:** Courtesy Archives Nationales

Catalogue 144   B&W: Dominique Bernard; **Color:** Dominique Bernard; **Additional Credit:** Courtesy Musée de l'Armée and the Musée de la Chasse et de la Nature

Catalogue 145   B&W: Photo Agraci; **Color:** Photo Agraci; **Additional Credit:** Courtesy Manufacture Nationale de Sèvres and the Musée de la Chasse et de la Nature

Catalogue 146   B&W: Photo Agraci; **Color:** Photo Agraci; **Additional Credit:** Courtesy Manufacture Nationale de Sèvres and the Musée de la Chasse et de la Nature

Catalogue 147   B&W: Photo Agraci; **Color:** Photo Agraci; **Additional Credit:** Courtesy Manufacture Nationale de Sèvres and the Musée de la Chasse et de la Nature

Catalogue 148   B&W: Photo Agraci; **Color:** Photo Agraci; **Additional Credit:** Courtesy Manufacture Nationale de Sèvres and the Musée de la Chasse et de la Nature

Catalogue 149   B&W: Photo Queste; **Color:** Photo Queste; **Additional Credit:** Courtesy Bibliothèque Municipale de la Ville de Versailles

Catalogue 150   B&W: Photograph Library, Metropolitan Museum of Art; **Color:** Photograph Library, Metropolitan Museum of Art; **Additional Credit:** Courtesy Metropolitan Museum of Art, Rogers Fund, 1904.

Catalogue 151   B&W: Photograph Library, Metropolitan Museum of Art; **Color:** Photograph Library, Metropolitan Museum of Art; **Additional Credit:** Courtesy Metropolitan Museum of Art, Rogers Fund, 1904.

Catalogue 152   B&W: Photographic Service of the Réunion des Musées

Nationaux; **Color:** None; **Additional Credit:** Courtesy the Chalcographie of the Musée du Louvre and the Louisiana Museum Foundation

Catalogue 153   B&W: Photographic Service of the Réunion des Musées Nationaux; **Color:** None; **Additional Credit:** Courtesy Musée du Louvre and the Réunion des Musées Nationaux

Catalogue 154   B&W: Photographic Service of the Réunion des Musées Nationaux; **Color:** Photographic Service of the Réunion des Musées Nationaux; **Additional Credit:** Courtesy Musée National du Château de Versailles and the Réunion des Musées Nationaux

Catalogue 155   B&W: Photographic Service of the Réunion des Musées Nationaux; **Color:** Photographic Service of the Réunion des Musées Nationaux; **Additional Credit:** Courtesy Musée du Louvre and the Réunion des Musées Nationaux

Catalogue 156   B&W: Lauros-Giraudon; **Color:** Lauros-Giraudon; **Additional Credit:** Courtesy Musée Carnavalet

Catalogue 157   B&W: Lauros-Giraudon; **Color:** Lauros-Giraudon; **Additional Credit:** Courtesy Musée Carnavalet

Catalogue 158   B&W: Photographic Service of the Réunion des Musées Nationaux; **Color:** Photographic Service of the Réunion des Musées Nationaux; **Additional Credit:** Courtesy Musée National du Château de Versailles and the Réunion des Musées Nationaux

Catalogue 159   B&W: Photographic Service of the Réunion des Musées Nationaux; **Color:** None; **Additional Credit:** Courtesy Musée National du Château de Versailles and the Réunion des Musées Nationaux

Catalogue 160   B&W: Michel Toumazet, Photographic Service of the Musée Carnavalet; **Color:** None; **Additional Credit:** Courtesy Musée Carnavalet

Catalogue 161   B&W: Photographic Service of Archives Nationales; **Color:** None; **Additional Credit:** Courtesy Archives Nationales

Catalogue 162   B&W: Photographic Service of Archives Nationales; **Color:** None; **Additional Credit:** Courtesy Archives Nationales

Catalogue 163   B&W: Photographic Service of Archives Nationales; **Color:** None; **Additional Credit:** Courtesy Archives Nationales

Catalogue 164   B&W: Photographic Service of Archives Nationales; **Color:** None; **Additional Credit:** Courtesy Archives Nationales

Catalogue 165   B&W: Photographic Service of Archives Nationales; **Color:** None; **Additional Credit:** Courtesy Archives Nationales

Catalogue 166   B&W: Photographic

Service of Archives Nationales; **Color:** None; **Additional Credit:** Courtesy Archives Nationales

Catalogue 167 **B&W:** Photographic Service of the Réunion des Musées Nationaux; **Color:** Photographic Service of the Réunion des Musées Nationaux; **Additional Credit:** Courtesy of the Mobilier National

Catalogue 168 **B&W:** Laurent Sully Jaulmes, Photographic Service of the Musée des Arts Décoratifs; **Color:** Dominque Bernard; **Additional Credit:** Courtesy Musée des Arts Décoratifs

Catalogue 169 **B&W:** Laurent Sully Jaulmes, Photographic Service of the Musée des Arts Décoratifs; **Color:** Dominque Bernard; **Additional Credit:** Courtesy Musée des Arts Décoratifs

Catalogue 170 **B&W:** Photo Ellebé; **Color:** None; **Additional Credit:** Courtesy Musée de la Céramique de la Ville de Rouen

Catalogue 171 **B&W:** Photo Ellebé; **Color:** None; **Additional Credit:** Courtesy Musée de la Céramique de la Ville de Rouen

Catalogue 172 **B&W:** Photo Ellebé; **Color:** None; **Additional Credit:** Courtesy Musée de la Céramique de la Ville de Rouen

Catalogue 173 **B&W:** Photo Ellebé; **Color:** None; **Additional Credit:** Courtesy Musée de la Céramique de la Ville de Rouen

Catalogue 174 **B&W:** Photograph Library, Metropolitan Museum of Art; **Color:** None; **Additional Credit:** Courtesy Metropolitan Museum of Art, Bequest of Catherine D. Wentworth, 1948

Catalogue 175 **B&W:** Photographic Service of the Réunion des Musées Nationaux; **Color:** None; **Additional Credit:** Courtesy Musée National de Céramique and the Réunion des Musées Nationaux

Catalogue 176 **B&W:** Photograph Library, Metropolitan Museum of Art; **Color:** None; **Additional Credit:** Courtesy Metropolitan Museum of Art, Bequest of Catherine D. Wentworth, 1948

Catalogue 177 **B&W:** Photograph Library, Metropolitan Museum of Art; **Color:** None; **Additional Credit:** Courtesy Metropolitan Museum of Art, Gift of James Jackson Jarves, 1881

Catalogue 178 **B&W:** Photographic Service of the Réunion des Musées Nationaux; **Color:** None; **Additional Credit:** Courtesy Musée National de Céramique and the Réunion des Musées Nationaux

Catalogue 179 **B&W:** Photographic Service of the Réunion des Musées Nationaux; **Color:** None; **Additional**

Credit: Courtesy Musée National de Céramique and the Réunion des Musées Nationaux

Catalogue 180 **B&W:** Photograph Library, Metropolitan Museum of Art; **Color:** Photograph Library, Metropolitan Museum of Art; **Additional Credit:** Courtesy Metropolitan Museum of Art, Gift of Reverend Alfred Duane Pell, 1902

Catalogue 181 *(Cup)* **B&W:** Photographic Service of the Réunion des Musées Nationaux; **Color:** None; **Additional Credit:** Courtesy Musée National de Céramique and the Réunion des Musées Nationaux

Catalogue 181 *(Saucer)* **B&W:** Photographic Service of the Réunion des Musées Nationaux; **Color:** None; **Additional Credit:** Courtesy Musée National de Céramique and the Réunion des Musées Nationaux

Catalogue 182 **B&W:** Photographic Service of the Réunion des Musées Nationaux; **Color:** None; **Additional Credit:** Courtesy Musée National de Céramique and the Réunion des Musées Nationaux

Catalogue 183 **B&W:** Photograph Library, Metropolitan Museum of Art; **Color:** None; **Additional Credit:** Courtesy Metropolitan Museum of Art, Bequest of Catherine D. Wentworth, 1948

Catalogue 184 **B&W:** Photograph Library, Metropolitan Museum of Art; **Color:** None; **Additional Credit:** Courtesy Metropolitan Museum of Art

Catalogue 185 **B&W:** Photo Ellebé; **Color:** None; **Additional Credit:** Courtesy Musée de la Céramique de la Ville de Rouen

Catalogue 186 **B&W:** Photo Ellebé; **Color:** None; **Additional Credit:** Courtesy Musée de la Céramique de la Ville de Rouen

Catalogue 187 **B&W:** Photo Ellebé; **Color:** None; **Additional Credit:** Courtesy Musée de la Céramique de la Ville de Rouen

Catalogue 188 **B&W:** Dominque Bernard; **Color:** None; **Additional Credit:** Courtesy Musée Bricard

Catalogue 189 **B&W:** Photograph Library, Metropolitan Museum of Art; **Color:** None; **Additional Credit:** Courtesy Museum of Art, Harris Brisbane Dick Fund, 1957

Catalogue 190 **B&W:** Dominique Bernard; **Color:** None; **Additional Credit:** Courtesy Musée Bricard

Catalogue 191 **B&W:** Photographic Service of the Bibliothèque Nationale; **Color:** None; **Additional Credit:** Courtesy Bibliothèque Nationale

Catalogue 192 **B&W:** Photographic Service of the Bibliothèque Nationale; **Color:** None; **Additional Credit:**

Courtesy Bibliothèque Nationale

Catalogue 193 **B&W:** Photographic Service of the Bibliothèque Nationale; **Color:** None; **Additional Credit:** Courtesy Bibliothèque Nationale

Catalogue 194 **B&W:** Photographic Service of the Bibliothèque Nationale; **Color:** None; **Additional Credit:** Courtesy Bibliothèque Nationale

Catalogue 195 **B&W:** Photographic Service of the Bibliothèque Nationale; **Color:** None; **Additional Credit:** Courtesy Bibliothèque Nationale

Catalogue 196 **B&W:** Photographic Service of the Bibliothèque Nationale; **Color:** None; **Additional Credit:** Courtesy Bibliothèque Nationale

Catalogue 197 **B&W:** Photographic Service of the Bibliothèque Nationale; **Color:** None; **Additional Credit:** Courtesy Bibliothèque Nationale

Catalogue 198 **B&W:** Photograph Library, Metropolitan Museum of Art; **Color:** None; **Additional Credit:** Courtesy Metropolitan Museum of Art, Gift of J. Pierpont Morgan, 1917

Catalogue 199 **B&W:** Photograph Library, Metropolitan Museum of Art; **Color:** None; **Additional Credit:** Courtesy Metropolitan Museum of Art, Gift of J. Pierpont Morgan, 1917

Catalogue 200 *(Jupiter)* **B&W:** Photographic Service of the Réunion des Musées Nationaux; **Color:** None; **Additional Credit:** Courtesy Musée du Louvre and the Réunion des Musées Nationaux

Catalogue 200 *(Juno)* **B&W:** Photographic Service of the Réunion des Musées Nationaux; **Color:** None; **Additional Credit:** Courtesy Musée du Louvre and the Réunion des Musées Nationaux

Catalogue 201 **B&W:** Georges Routhier, Studio Lourmel; **Color:** None

Catalogue 202 **B&W:** Geroges Routhier, Studio Lourmel; **Color:** None

Catalogue 203 **B&W:** Photographic Service of the Réunion des Musées Nationaux; **Color:** None; **Additional Credit:** Courtesy Musée du Louvre and the Réunion des Musées Nationaux

Catalogue 204 **B&W:** Photographic Service of the Réunion des Musées Nationaux; **Color:** None; **Additional Credit:** Courtesy Musée du Louvre and the Réunion des Musées Nationaux

Catalogue 205 **B&W:** Photographic Service of the Réunion des Musées Nationaux; **Color:** Photographic Service of the Réunion des Musées Nationaux; **Additional Credit:** Courtesy Musée du Louvre and the Réunion des Musées Nationaux

Catalogue 206 **B&W:** Photographic Service of the Réunion des Musées Nationaux; **Color:** Photographic Service of the Réunion des Musées Nationaux; **Additional Credit:** Courtesy Musée du Louvre and the Réunion des Musées Nationaux

Catalogue 207 **B&W:** Photographic Service of the Réunion des Musées Nationaux; **Color:** Photographic Service of the Réunion des Musées Nationaux; **Additional Credit:** Courtesy Musée National du Château de Versailles and the Réunion des Musées Nationaux

Catalogue 208 **B&W:** Photographic Service of the Réunion des Musées Nationaux; **Color:** Photographic Service of the Réunion des Musées Nationaux; **Additional Credit:** Courtesy Musée National du Château de Versailles and the Réunion des Musées Nationaux

Catalogue 209 **B&W:** Photographic Service of the Réunion des Musées Nationaux; **Color:** Photographic Service of the Réunion des Musées Nationaux; **Additional Credit:** Courtesy Musée National du Château de Versailles and the Réunion des Musées Nationaux

Catalogue 210 **B&W:** Photographic Service of Archives Nationales; **Color:** None; **Additional Credit:** Courtesy Archives Nationales

Catalogue 211 **B&W:** Studio M. Tscherniak; **Color:** Studio M. Tscherniak; **Additional Credit:** Courtesy Ministère des Relations Extérieures

Catalogue 212 **B&W:** Photographic Service of the Bibliothèque Nationale; **Color:** None; **Additional Credit:** Courtesy Bibliothèque Nationale

Catalogue 213 **B&W:** Maurice Chuzeville; **Color:** None; **Additional Credit:** Courtesy Musée du Louvre and the Réunion des Musées Nationaux

Catalogue 214 **B&W:** Photographic Service of the Bibliothèque Nationale; **Color:** None; **Additional Credit:** Courtesy Bibliothèque Nationale

Catalogue 215A **B&W:** Photographic Service of the Bibliothèque Nationale; **Color:** None; **Additional Credit:** Courtesy Bibliothèque Nationale

Catalogue 215B **B&W:** Photographic Service of the Bibliothèque Nationale; **Color:** None; **Additional Credit:** Courtesy Bibliothèque Nationale

Catalogue 216 **B&W:** Photographic Service of Archives Nationales; **Color:** None; **Additional Credit:** Courtesy Archives Nationales

Catalogue 217 **B&W:** Photographic Service of Archives Nationales; **Color:** None; **Additional Credit:** Courtesy Archives Nationales

Catalogue 218 **B&W:** Photographic Service of the Bibliothèque Nationale; **Color:** None; **Additional Credit:** Courtesy Bibliothèque Nationale

Catalogue 219 **B&W:** Photographic Service of the Bibliothèque Nationale;

Color: None; **Additional Credit:** Courtesy Bibliothèque Nationale

Catalogue 220 **B&W:** Charles de la Guerronière, Louisiana State Museum; **Color:** None; **Additional Credit:** Courtesy Louisiana State Museum

Catalogue 221 **B&W:** Photographic Service of the Musée de la Marine; **Color:** None; **Additional Credit:** Courtesy Musée de la Marine

Catalogue 222 **B&W:** Studio M. Tscherniak; **Color:** None; **Additional Credit:** Courtesy Ministère des Relations Extérieures

Catalogue 223 **B&W:** Studio M. Tscherniak; **Color:** Studio M. Tscherniak; **Additional Credit:** Courtesy Ministère des Relations Extérieures

Catalogue 224 **B&W:** Bernard Dupont, Graphic Photo; **Color:** Bernard Dupont, Graphic Photo; **Additional Credit:** Courtesy Count and Countess LeMoyne de Martigny

Catalogue 225 **B&W:** Photo J.M.; **Color:** None; **Additional Credit:** Courtesy Archives Nationales

Catalogue 226 **B&W:** Photographic Service of Archives Nationales; **Color:** None; **Additional Credit:** Courtesy Archives Nationales

Catalogue 227 **B&W:** None; **Color:** Dominique Bernard

Catalogue 228 **B&W:** Bernard Dupont, Graphic Photo; **Color:** Bernard Dupont, Graphic Photo; **Additional Credit:** Courtesy Count and Countesss LeMoyne de Martigny

Catalogue 229 **B&W:** Bernard Dupont, Graphic Photo; **Color:** Bernard Dupont, Graphic Photo

Catalogue 230 **B&W:** Bernard Dupont, Graphic Photo; **Color:** Bernard Dupont, Graphic Photo

Catalogue 231 **B&W:** Bernard Dupont, Graphic Photo; **Color:** Bernard Dupont, Graphic Photo

Catalogue 232 **B&W:** Photo J.M.; **Color:** Photo J.M.; **Additional Credit:** Courtesy Archives Nationales

Catalogue 233 **B&W:** Photographic Service of Archives Nationales; **Color:** Photo J.M.; **Additional Credit:** Courtesy Archives Nationales

Catalogue 234 **B&W:** Photographic Service of the Réunion des Musées Nationaux; **Color:** Photographic Service of the Réunion des Musées Nationaux; **Additional Credit:** Courtesy Musée National du Château de Versailles and the Réunion des Musées Nationaux

Catalogue 235 **B&W:** Photographic Service of the Bibliothèque Nationale; **Color:** None; **Additional Credit:** Courtesy Bibliothèque Nationale

Catalogue 236 **B&W:** Photo J.M.; **Color:** None; **Additional Credit:** Courtesy Archives Nationales

Catalogue 237 **B&W:** Photographic Service of the Réunion des Musées Nationaux; **Color:** Photographic Service of the Réunion des Musées Nationaux; **Additional Credit:** Courtesy Musée National du Château de Versailles and the Réunion des Musées Nationaux

Catalogue 238 **B&W:** Charles de la Guerronière, Louisiana State Museum; **Color:** None; **Additional Credit:** Courtesy Louisiana State Museum

Catalogue 239 **B&W:** Studio M. Tscherniak; **Color:** Studio M. Tscherniak; **Additional Credit:** Courtesy Ministère des Relations Extérieures

Catalogue 240 **B&W:** Studio M. Tscherniak; **Color:** None; **Additional Credit:** Courtesy Ministère des Relations Extérieures

Catalogue 241 **B&W:** Studio M. Tscherniak; **Color:** Studio M. Tscherniak; **Additional Credit:** Courtesy Ministère des Relations Extérieures

Catalogue 242 **B&W:** Photographic Service of the Réunion des Musées Nationaux; **Color:** Photographic Service of the Réunion des Musées Nationaux; **Additional Credit:** Courtesy Musée National du Château de Versailles and the Réunion des Musées Nationaux

Catalogue 243 **B&W:** Photographic Service of Archives Nationales; **Color:** None; **Additional Credit:** Courtesy Archives Nationales

Catalogue 244 **B&W:** Photographic Service of Archives Nationales; **Color:** None; **Additional Credit:** Courtesy Archives Nationales

Figure 1 **B&W:** Photographic Service, Bibliothèque Nationale; **Color:** None; **Additional Credit:** Courtesy Bibliothèque Nationale

Figure 2 **B&W:** Photographic Service, Bibliothèque Nationale; **Color:** None; **Additional Credit:** Courtesy Bibliothèque Nationale

Figure 3 **B&W:** Photographic Service, Bibliothèque Nationale; **Color:** None; **Additional Credit:** Courtesy Bibliothèque Nationale

Figure 4 **B&W:** Photographic Service, Bibliothèque Nationale; **Color:** None; **Additional Credit:** Courtesy Bibliothèque Nationale

Figure 5 **B&W:** Photographic Service, Bibliothèque Nationale; **Color:** None; **Additional Credit:** Courtesy Bibliothèque Nationale

Figure 6 **B&W:** Frank Davis Photography; **Color:** None; **Additional Credit:** Courtesy Robert Wyman Hartle

INDEX OF AUTHORS, ARTISTS, AND MAKERS

Ahmed III (Sultan of the Ottoman Empire)
Letter to Louis XV; Cat. 211
Albani
see Clement XI
Algardi, Alessandro
Jupiter; Cat. 201
(des) Alleurs, Pierre Puchot (Comte)
Coded Dispatch from Constantinople; Cat. 43
André, David
Sugar Caster; Cat. 174
Anguier, Michel
Jupiter; Cat. 201
Aram
see Lexinton
Arnould, Jean
The Magnificent Buildings of Versailles; Cat. 110
(d')Avaux, Jean-Antoine de Mesme (Comte)
Peace of Nymegen with Holland; Cat. 53.
Peace of Nymegen with Spain; Cat. 54

Bailly, Jacques I
Courses de Testes et de Bague Faittes par le Roy et par les Princes et Seigneurs de sa Cour en l'Année 1662; Cat. 149
Belle, Alexis-Simon (att. to)
Antoine Crozat, Marquis de Chatel; Cat. 242
Bérain, Jean (the elder)
Theater Scene; Cat. 164
Apollo; Cat. 5
(att. to) *Theater Scene;* Cat. 163
(studio of) *Scene of "Glory" or "Transfiguration";* Cat. 161
(studio of) *Theatre Perspective;* Cat. 166
Bernini, Gian Lorenzo (att. to or after)
Design of Fireworks Given by the Duc de Chaulnes; Cat. 50
Bernou, Claude (Abbé)
Map of North America . . .; Cat. 218
Beverningke, Jérome (of)
Peace of Nymegen with Holland; Cat. 53
Beaubrun, Henri and Charles (brothers) (att. to)
Anne Marie Louise d'Orléans, Duchesse de Montpensier; Cat. 136.
(att. to or after) *Louis XIV and his First Nurse;* Cat. 7
Marie-Thérèse d'Autriche, Queen of France and of Navarre; Cat. 26
Beauvais (Tapestry Works)
Apollo; Cat. 5
Bieberstein, Johann Augustus (Marshal of)
Peace of Utrecht with Prussia; Cat. 240
Bishop of Bristol, John
Peace of Utrecht with England; Cat. 239
Blondel, Jacques-François
Elevation of the Principal Facade of the Louvre on the Side of Saint-Germain-l'Auxerrois, Built Under the Reign of Louis XIV and the Ministry of Jean-Baptiste Colbert, on the Designs of Claude Perrault of the Royal Academy of Science; Cat. 94

Bocquet, Nicolas
The Terrestrial Globe Represented in Two Hemisphere Plans; Cat. 72
(de) Bonneuil, Nicolas-Auguste de Harlay (Sieur)
Peace of Ryswick with England; Cat. 222
Peace of Ryswick with the Empire; Cat. 223
Bourdon, Sébastien
Augustus Before the Tomb of Alexander; Cat. 18
René Descartes; Cat. 78
Boyer, Claude (Abbé)
Jephté; Cat. 85
Bristol
see Bishop of Bristol
Bullet, Pierre
Plan of Paris Taken by Order of the King; Cat. 89
Map of Paris Taken at the Order of the King; Cat. 90
Butterfield, Michael (att. to)
Instrument for Calibrating Sundials; Cat. 74
Buxbaum, Michael
Blunderbuss; Cat. 144

(de) Callières, François
Peace of Ryswick with England; Cat. 222
Peace of Ryswick with the Empire; Cat. 223
Castagnery
see Châteauneuf
(de) Champaigne, Philippe
Armand Jean du Plessis, Duke and Cardinal of Richelieu; Cat. 14
Jacquéline Marie, Mère Angélique Arnauld; Cat. 65
(manner of) *Jules, Cardinal Mazarin;* Cat. 19
(de) Châteauneuf, Pierre-Antoine de Castagnery (Marquis)
Coded Dispatch from Adrianople; Cat. 44
Chauveau, François
Courses de Testes et de Bague Faittes par le Roy et par les Princes et Seigneurs de sa Cour en l'Année 1662; Cat. 149
Chéron, Elizabeth-Sophie
Self Portrait; Cat. 88
Clément XI (Giovanni Francisco Albani)
Unigenitus; Cat. 64
Colbert, Jean-Baptiste
Memoir Addressed to Louis XIV; Cat. 39
Letter to the Marquis de Nointel; Cat. 40
Declaration of the King to Have the Experiments in the Royal Botanical Gardens Continued; Cat. 83
Draft of Statutes and Rules That the King Wishes and Orders to Be Observed in the Academy . . . That His Majesty Has Resolved to Establish in the City of Rome; Cat. 86
Colbert de Croissy
see Croissy
Colbert de Seignelay
see Seignelay
Colbert de Torcy
see Torcy
Cordova-Tello

see Tebes y Cordova-Tello
Coronelli, Vincenzo
Celestial Globe; Cat. 73.
America Settentrionale; Cat. 220
(de) Cotte, Robert (office of)
General Plan of the Château and Gardens of Versailles; Cat. 111
Section through the Vestibule of the Chapel and the Salon d'Hercule (of the Château of Versailles); Cat. 112.
Project for the Paving of the Chapel [of the Château of Versailles]; Cat. 119
Coustou, Nicolas
Hercules; Cat. 122
Coypel, Antoine
Louis XIV Crowned by Glory Between Abundance and Peace; Cat. 208.
(after) *Jean-Baptiste Poquelin, Called Molière;* Cat. 159
Coypel, Noël (the Elder)
Apollo Crowned by Minerva; Cat. 6
Coysevox, Antoine
Bust of Louis XIV; Cat. 98
Bust of Charles Le Brun; Cat. 103
(de) Crécy, Louis Verjus (Comte)
Peace of Ryswick with England; Cat. 222
Peace of Ryswick with the Empire; Cat. 223
Cristin, Jean-Baptiste
Peace of Nymegen with Spain; Cat. 54
(de) Croissy, Charles Colbert (Marquis)
Peace of Nymegen with Holland; Cat. 53
Peace of Nymegen with Spain; Cat. 54

D,I
see ID (monogram)
Dartford, Edward Villiers (First Earl of Jersey, Baron of Hoo, Viscount of)
Peace of Ryswick with England; Cat. 222
De Fer, Nicolas
Maps and General and Specific Descriptions . . .; Cat. 238
Delisle, Guillaume
Map of the Mississippi . . .; Cat. 235
(att. to) *Environs of the Mississippi;* Cat 236
Desportes, Alexandre-François
"Tane" Pointing Partridge; Cat. 146
Still Life of Partridge and Pheasant; Cat. 147
Pheasants; Cat. 148
Dolin, Nicolas
Chapelle Colbert de Villacerf; Cat. 69
(van) Donhoff, Otto Magnus
Peace of Utrecht with Prussia; Cat. 240
Doria
see Spinola-Doria

Errard, Gérard-Léonard
Chancellor Séguier; Cat. 41
(d')Estrade, Godefroy Louis (Comte)
Peace of Nymegen with Holland; Cat. 53
Peace of Nymegen with Spain; Cat. 54

Francisque
see Millet
Franquelin, Jean-Baptiste (after)
Map of Louisiana in North America; Cat. 219

(de la) Fuente, Pedro Ronquillo (Marquis)
Peace of Nymegen with Spain; Cat. 54

Gabriel, Jacques V. (office of)
Plan of the King's Apartment of the Château of Versailles; Cat. 115

Girardon, François
Left Foot of Louis XIV; Cat. 93
(att. to or studio of) *Jupiter and Juno*; Cat. 200

Gissey, Henri (att. to)
Costume for "War"; Cat. 156.
Costume for "A Fury"; Cat. 157

Gobelins (Tapestry Works)
Portière de Mars; Cat. 3
Château of Fontainebleau; Cat. 29
Visit of Louis XIV to the Gobelins; Cat. 167

Gobert, Jean (the Younger)
Equestrian Statue of Louis XIV; Cat. 4

Gobert Pierre (att. to)
Anne-Louise Bénédicte de Bourbon-Condé, Duchesse du Maine; Cat. 137
Marie-Adelaïde de Savoie, Duchesse de Bourgogne; Cat 138

Grand Vizir of the Ottoman Empire
see Koprili

Gribelin, Nicolas (att. to)
Watch; Cat. 76

Guérin, Gilles (after)
Louis XIV Adolescent, Trampling the Fronde; Cat. 21

Hardouin-Mansart, Jules
see Mansart, Jules Hardouin

Hardy, Jean
Religion Trampling Heresy; Cat. 66

Harlay
see Bonneuil

Heren, William (of)
Peace of Nymegen with Holland; Cat. 53

Hennepin, (Rev.) Louis (Antoine)
Description of Louisiana . . .; Cat. 215A
New Discovery of a Very Large Land . . .; Cat. 215B

Hérard
see Errard

Hoo, (Baron of)
see Dartford

Huguet, Jacques
Bracket Clock; Cat. 75

(d')Huxelles, Nicolas du Blé, (Marquis)
Peace of Utrecht with England; Cat. 239
Peace of Utrecht with Prussia; Cat. 240

ID (monogram)
Pair of Candlesticks; Cat. 183

IK (monogram)
Kitchen Grill; Cat. 187

IV (monogram)
Ewer; Cat. 176

(d')Iberville, Pierre Le Moyne (Sieur)
Ship's Journal on Board the "Badine"; Cat. 225
Ship's Journal on Board the "Renommée"; Cat. 226

Jersey (Earl of)
see Dartford

Jolliet, Louis
Map of the New Discoveries Which the Reverend Jesuit Fathers Made in 1672 . . .;

Cat. 214

K, I
see IK (monogram)

(von) Kaunitz, Andreas
Peace of Ryswick with the Empire; Cat. 223

Keller Brothers
Left Foot of Louis XIV; Cat. 93

Koprili, Amoudja Zadhk Hussein (Grand Vizir of the Ottoman Empire)
Letter to Louis XIV; Cat. 46

(de) La Fosse, Charles
The Triumph of Bacchus; Cat. 139

Langlois, Nicolas
The King Accompanied by His Court Visits the Hôtel of the Invalides and Its New Church; Cat. 99

(de) La Pointe, François
Topographic Journal of the King in Flanders During the Year 1680; Cat. 34

(de) Larmessin, Nicolas II
The Swearing of the Peace by the Two Kings of France and Spain and the Entry of the King and Queen into Their Good City of Paris, 26 August 1660; Cat. 23
The Royal and Magnificent Audience Given to the Very Illustrious Ambassadors of the Magnificent King of Siam; Cat. 47
The Royal Recompenses of Louis the Great; Cat. 55
The Pompous and Magnificent Entrance of Flavio, Cardinal Chigi, Lateran Legate in France; Cat. 63
The Royal Troupe of Italian Comedians; Cat. 160

(de) La Salle, René Robert Cavelier
Act of Possession of Louisiana at the Mouth of (the Mississippi River at) the Gulf of Mexico; Cat. 217

Law, John
Letter to Nicolas Desmarets; Cat. 244

Le Baillif
see Saint Jean

Le Bastier, Simon
Dish; Cat. 184

Le Blond (studio of)
Visit of Louis XIV to the Gobelins; Cat. 167

Le Brun, Charles
Portière de Mars; Cat. 3
Adoration of the Shepherds; Cat. 8
Château of Fontainebleau; Cat. 29
The Establishment of the Academy of Sciences and the Observatory; Cat. 70
Nicolas Fouquet; Cat. 101
Visit of Louis XIV to the Gobelins; Cat. 167
Jesus Carrying His Cross; Cat. 203

Le Clerc, Sebastien (the Elder)
Representation of the Machines That Served to Lift the Two Large Stones That Cover the Pediment of the Principal Entrance of the Louvre; Cat. 96
Representation of the Machines That Served to Lift the Two Large Stones That Cover the Pediment of the Principal Entrance of the Louvre; Cat. 97

Le Febure, Claude
Jean-Baptiste Colbert; Cat. 38
Charles Couperin and the Daughter of the Painter; Cat. 154

Le Febvre

see Le Febure

Le Hay
see Chéron

(von) Leilern, Johann Frederich (Baron)
Peace of Ryswick with the Empire; Cat. 223

Le Mesnager
see Saint Jean

Le Moyne, Pierre
see Iberville

Le Nègre, Pierre
The Magnificent Buildings of Versailles; Cat. 110

Le Pautre, Jean
The Basin of Latona; Cat. 123
Fireworks on the Grand Canal at Versailles; Cat. 152

Le Prestre
see Vauban

Lesueur, Charles
Map of the Mississippi . . .; Cat. 235

Le Vrac de Tournières, Robert
Louis Phélypeaux, Comte de Pontchartrain; Cat. 234

Lexinton, (Lord) Robert Sutton of Aram (Second Baron of)
Peace of Ryswick with England; Cat. 222

Lillieroot, Nils (Count of)
Peace of Ryswick with England; Cat. 222
Peace of Ryswick with the Empire; Cat. 223

(de) Lionne, Hugues
Letter on the Affairs of Europe; Cat. 31.
(att. to) *Fragment of a Letter*; Cat. 32

Louis XIV
Manner of Showing the Gardens of Versailles; Cat. 33
Edict According the Crown of France to the Royal Bastards; Cat. 133
Order of Payment to Cover the Gambling Debts of the Queen; Cat. 142
Last Words of King Louis XIV to Louis XV, His Great-Grandson; Cat. 212
Permission to the Sieur de La Salle to Discover the Western Part of New France; Cat. 216
Letters Patent for the Commerce of Louisiana in Favor of Sieur Crozat; Cat. 243

Mansart, Jules Hardouin
(office of) *Elevation of the Government Wing and Section Through the Royal Apartments and the Hall of Mirrors (of the Château of Versailles)*; Cat. 113
Project for the King's Bedroom: the Royal Alcove (at the Château of Versailles); Cat. 114
The Hall of Mirrors (of the Château of Versailles); Cat. 116
The Hall of Mirrors (of the Château of Versailles); Cat. 117
Drawing for Louis XIV's Mirrored Cabinet, Château of Versailles; Cat. 118

Maratta, Carlo
André Le Nôtre; Cat. 105

Marie-Thérèse d'Autriche
Note Requesting 200 Golden Louis to Pay a Gambling Debt; Cat. 143

Marot, Jean
Elevation of the Entrance of the Tuileries Side (of the Louvre), Design by Cavalier Bernini; Cat. 95

Marquette, Rev. Jacques, S.J.

Map of the New Discoveries which the Reverend Jesuit Fathers Made in 1672 . . .; Cat. 214

Marsy, Balthasar
The Basin of Latona; Cat. 123

Martin, Jean-Baptiste (the Elder)
View of the Château of Vaux-le-Vicomte Seen from the Garden Side; Cat. 102
(att to) *View of the Orangerie of Versailles*; Cat. 107

Martin, Pierre-Denis (the Younger)
View of the Church of the Royal Hôtel of the Invalides at the Time of the Visit of Louis XIV; Cat. 100
The Château de Marly; Cat. 207

Martin des Batailles
see Martin, Jean-Baptiste (the Elder)

Mehmed IV (Sultan of the Ottoman Empire)
Letter to Louis XIV; Cat. 45

Mellan, Claude
Courses de Testes et de Bague Faittes par le Roy et par les Princes et Seigneurs de sa Cour en l'Année 1662; Cat. 149

Mesmes
see Avaux

Meulen
see Van der Meulen

Meybom, F. L.
Watch; Cat. 77

Mignard, Pierre
The Magnificent Buildings of Versailles; Cat. 110
Françoise d'Aubigné, Marquise de Maintenon; Cat. 130
Philippe de France, Duc d'Anjou; Cat. 237
(att. to) *Philippe de France, Duc d'Orléans*; Cat. 134

Millet, Jean
View of the Observatory and Its Surroundings; Cat. 71

Nassau, William (of)
Peace of Nymegen with Holland; Cat. 53

Nevers (Faience Producers of)
Platter (Peace of the Pyrenees); Cat. 22
Urn (Theriaca); Cat. 84
Tile (Shop Sign for a Potter); Cat. 178
Bottle (for Vintner George Paille); Cat. 179
Pilgrim Bottle; Cat. 180

Nocret, Jean (the Elder)
Louise de La Baume Le Blanc, Duchesse de La Vallière; Cat. 127

Nolin, Jean Baptiste
The Terrestrial Globe Represented in Two Hemisphere Plans; Cat. 72
The Celestial Globe; Cat. 73

Pembroke, Herbert Thomas (Eighth Earl of)
Peace of Ryswick with England; Cat. 222

Perrault, Charles
Courses de Testes et de Bague Faittes par le Roy et par les Princes et Seigneurs de sa Cour en l'Année 1662; Cat. 149

Perrier, François
Orpheus Before Pluto and Proserpina; Cat. 206

(de) Poilly, Claude (att to)
Chalice and Paten; Cat. 229

Poussin, Nicolas

Saint John Baptisting; Cat. 204
Young Pyrrhus Saved; Cat. 205

Puchot
see Alleurs

Puget, Pierre
(after) *Milo of Crotona*; Cat. 202
(att. to workshop of) *"France" Personified as "Minerva"*; Cat. 221

(de) Richelieu, Armand Jean du Plessis (Cardinal)
Maxims of State or Political Testament; Cat. 15

Rigaud, Hyacinthe
Louis XIV, King of France and of Navarre; Cat. 209
(after) *Louis, Dauphin de France*; Cat. 131
(att. to or after) *Elizabeth-Charlotte de Bavière, Princess Palatine, Duchesse d'Orléans*; Cat. 135

Ronquillo
see Fuente

Rose, Toussaint
Order of Louis XIV to Gédéon de Metz to Pay 162,000 livres to Bearer; Cat. 36
Order of Louis XIV to Gédéon Berbier de Metz to Pay 12,000 livres to Boileau and to Racine; Cat. 37

Rouen (Faience Producers of)
Platter (radiant decor); Cat. 170
Plate (Blue and Red); Cat. 171
Ewer (Cameo Blue); Cat. 172
Sugar Caster; Cat. 173
Ewer (Nielloed-Ochre); Cat. 175

Rousselet, Gilles
Courses de Testes et de Bague Faittes par le Roy et par les Princes et Seigneurs de sa Cour en l'Année 1662; Cat. 149

Rousselet, Jean
Poetry and Music with the Bust of Louis XIV; Cat. 153

Saint Cloud (Ceramic Producers of)
Cup and Saucer; Cat. 181
Pharmaceutical Vase; Cat. 182

(de) Saint Jean, Nicolas Le Baillif (Comte)
Peace of Utrecht with England; Cat. 239
Peace of Utrecht with Prussia; Cat. 240

Santerre, Jean-Baptiste (after)
Jean Racine; Cat. 158

Sarrazin, Jacques (formerly att. to)
Louis XIV Enfant; Cat. 9

Savonnerie (Tapestry Works)
Louis XIII, Louis XIV Enfant, Anne d'Autriche and Monsieur; Cat. 16

(de) Seignelay, Jean-Baptiste Colbert (Marquis)
(supervisor) *The Great Book for Precious Stones*; Cat. 42

(de) Sève, Pierre
Visit of Louis XIV to the Gobelins; Cat. 167

Silvestre, Israël (the Elder)
The College of the Four Nations; Cat. 80
View of the Château of Versailles and Its Two Wings Seen from the Garden Side; Cat. 108
View of the Château of Versailles Seen from the Large Square; Cat. 109

Silvestre, Israël (the Younger)
The Fountain of Fame; Cat. 124
Courses de Testes et de Bague Faittes par le Roy et par les Princes et Seigneurs de sa Cour

en l'Année 1662; Cat. 149

Spinola-Doria, Pablo
Peace of Nymegen with Spain; Cat. 54

Stafford, Thomas (Count of)
Peace of Utrecht with England; Cat. 239

(von) Stratman, Henrich Johann (Count)
Peace of Ryswick with the Empire; Cat. 223

Sultan of the Ottoman Empire
see Ahmed III; see Mehmed IV

Sutton
see Lexinton

Tello
see Tebes y Cordova-Tello

(de) Tebes y Cordova-Tello, Gaspardo
Peace of Nymegen with Spain; Cat. 54

Testelin, Henri
The Establishment of the Academy of Science and the Observatory; Cat. 70

Thomas
see Pembroke

(de) Torcy, Jean-Baptiste Colbert (Marquis)
Letter to the Provost of Merchants and the Sheriffs of Paris; Cat. 67

Tournières
see Le Vrac

(de) Troy, François
Toussaint Rose, Secretary to the King; Cat. 30
Charles Mouton, Lute Player; Cat. 155

V, I
see IV (monogram)

Van der Meulen, Adam-François
The Château of Saint-Germain-en-Laye with Louis XIV and Turenne in the Foreground; Cat. 13
Crossing the Rhine; Cat. 51
View of the Château of Versailles from the Avenue de Paris; Cat. 106

Varin, Jean (att. to)
Louis XIV enfant; Cat. 9
Anne d'Autriche and Louis XIV/Church of the Val de Grâce; Cat. 10

(de) Vauban, Sébastien Le Prestre (Marquis)
Fortifications; Cat. 52

Verjus
see Crécy

Vignon, Philippe
Mademoiselle de Blois and Mademoiselle de Nantes; Cat. 129

Villiers
see Dartford

Vizir of the Ottoman Empire
see Koprili

Vouet, Simon
Louis XIII between "France" and "Navarre"; Cat. 11
Louis XIII, Louis XIV Enfant, Anne d'Autriche and Monsieur; Cat. 16

(de) Voulges
Proclamation of the Public Crier Announcing the Deaths of the Dauphin and the Dauphine; Cat. 132
Proclamation of the Public Crier Announcing the Burial Service of King Louis XIV; Cat. 210

(de) Vuez, Arnauld
Celestial Globe; Cat. 73

Williamson, Joseph
Peace of Ryswick with England; Cat. 222